INTERGOVERNMENTAL FISCAL TRANSFERS

Introduction to the Public Sector Governance and Accountability Series

Anwar Shah, Series Editor

A well-functioning public sector that delivers quality public services consistent with citizen preferences and that fosters private market-led growth while managing fiscal resources prudently is considered critical to the World Bank's mission of poverty alleviation and the achievement of the Millennium Development Goals. This important new series aims to advance those objectives by disseminating conceptual guidance and lessons from practices and by facilitating learning from each others' experiences on ideas and practices that promote *responsive* (by matching public services with citizens' preferences), *responsible* (through efficiency and equity in service provision without undue fiscal and social risk), and *accountable* (to citizens for all actions) public governance in developing countries.

This series represents a response to several independent evaluations in recent years that have argued that development practitioners and policy makers dealing with public sector reforms in developing countries and, indeed, anyone with a concern for effective public governance could benefit from a synthesis of newer perspectives on public sector reforms. This series distills current wisdom and presents tools of analysis for improving the efficiency, equity, and efficacy of the public sector. Leading public policy experts and practitioners have contributed to this series.

The first 13 volumes in this series, listed below, are concerned with public sector accountability for prudent fiscal management; efficiency, equity, and integrity in public service provision; safeguards for the protection of the poor, women, minorities, and other disadvantaged groups; ways of strengthening institutional arrangements for voice, choice, and exit; means of ensuring public financial accountability for integrity and results; methods of evaluating public sector programs, fiscal federalism, and local finances; international practices in local governance; and a framework for responsive and accountable governance.

Fiscal Management

Public Services Delivery

Public Expenditure Analysis

Local Governance in Industrial Countries

Local Governance in Developing Countries

Intergovernmental Fiscal Transfers: Principles and Practice

Participatory Budgeting

Budgeting and Budgetary Institutions

Local Budgeting and Financial Management

Tools for Public Sector Evaluations

Accountability for Performance

Macrofederalism and Local Finances

Citizen-Centered Governance

PUBLIC SECTOR
GOVERNANCE AND
ACCOUNTABILITY SERIES

INTERGOVERNMENTAL FISCAL TRANSFERS

PRINCIPLES AND PRACTICE

Edited by ROBIN BOADWAY and ANWAR SHAH

THE WORLD BANK
Washington, D.C.

ISBN-10: 0-8213-6492-8
ISBN-13: 978-0-8213-6492-5
eISBN-10: 0-8213-6493-6
eISBN-13: 978-0-8213-6493-2
DOI: 10.1596/978-0-8213-6492-5

Library of Congress Cataloging-in-Publication Data
Intergovernmental fiscal transfers: principles and practice / edited by Robin Boadway, Anwar Shah.
     p. cm. – (Public sector governance and accountability series)
  Includes bibliographical references and index.
  ISBN-13: 978-0-8213-6492-5
  ISBN-10: 0-8213-6492-8
     1. Intergovernmental fiscal relations. 2. Intergovernmental finance. 3. Revenue sharing. 4. Grants-in-aid. I. Boadway, Robin W., 1943- II. Shah, Anwar. III. Series.

HJ197.I58 2007
352.73–dc22

2005057765

Contents

Foreword xv

Preface xvii

Acknowledgments xix

Contributors xxi

Overview xxvii
Robin Boadway and Anwar Shah

CHAPTER

A Practitioner's Guide to Intergovernmental Fiscal Transfers 1
Anwar Shah
Instruments of Intergovernmental Finance 2
Achieving Results-Based Accountability through
  Performance-Oriented Transfers 9
Designing Fiscal Transfers: Dividing the Spoils or
  Creating a Framework for Accountable and
  Equitable Governance? 15
Institutional Arrangements for Fiscal Relations 44
Lessons from International Practices 48
References 51

Part I The Principles

2   Grants in a Federal Economy: A Conceptual Perspective   55
Robin Boadway
Three Views of the Role of Grants   57
Designing the System of Federal-Regional
    Fiscal Relations   65
Notes   74

3   Equity and Efficiency Aspects of Interagency Transfers in a Multigovernment Framework   75
Paul Bernd Spahn
The Case for Interjurisdictional Equity   76
Designing Equalization Schemes   78
The Case for Intragovernmental Efficiency   93
Designing Interagency Relations and Microtransfers   96
Summary   104
Notes   105
References   106

4   Achieving Economic Stabilization by Sharing Risk within Countries   107
Jürgen von Hagen
Principles of Regional Risk Sharing   109
Moral Hazard and the Political Economy of
    Regional Insurance   114
Empirical Evidence   117
The Macroeconomics of Regional Risk Sharing
    and Stabilization   123
Conclusions   125
Annex: A Model of Regional Stabilization and
    Risk Sharing   126
Notes   129
References   129

5

Grants and Soft Budget Constraints   133
Marianne Vigneault
The Soft Budget Constraint Problem Defined   136
Implications of Soft Budget Constraints   137
The Soft Budget Constraint Problem in Theory   138
The Soft Budget Constraint Problem in Practice:
    Country-Level Evidence   145
Lessons Learned   162
Concluding Comments   167
Notes   168
References   169

6

The Political Economy of Interregional Grants   173
Motohiro Sato
Political Motive and Political Competition   176
Fragmented Government and Rent Seeking   181
Intergovernmental Relations   185
The Commitment Problem   189
Institutional Reform   193
Notes   196
References   197

7

The Incentive Effects of Grants   203
Michael Smart
The Taxonomy of Grants   204
Vertical Transfers   205
Horizontal Transfers   211
Concluding Comments   220
Notes   221
References   221

8 **The Impact of Intergovernmental Fiscal Transfers: A Synthesis of the Conceptual and Empirical Literature**   225
Shama Gamkhar and Anwar Shah
Impact of Intergovernmental Transfers on Local Government
  Behavior: Theoretical Hypotheses   226
Empirical Approaches to Measuring the Impact of
  Intergovernmental Transfers on Local Fiscal Behavior   231
Concluding Remarks   252
Notes   254
References   255

Part II The Practice

9 **The Legal Architecture of Intergovernmental Transfers: A Comparative Examination**   259
Sujit Choudhry and Benjamin Perrin
Law and the Political Economy of Fiscal Federalism   260
Case Studies   262
Conclusions   284
Notes   289
References   290

10 **Institutional Arrangements for Intergovernmental Fiscal Transfers and a Framework for Evaluation**   293
Anwar Shah
Institutional Arrangements for Intergovernmental
  Transfers   294
Evaluating Institutional Arrangements for Equalizing Transfers
  Using a New Institutional Economics Framework   304
Comparing Alternate Institutional Arrangements Using a New
  Institutional Economics Framework   306
From Theory to Practice: How Accurate Are the Predictions of the
  New Institutional Economics?   310
Concluding Remarks   316
Notes   316
References   317

11

Resolving Fiscal Imbalances: Issues in Tax Sharing   319
M. Govinda Rao
Revenue Sharing as an Instrument of
    Intergovernmental Transfer   321
Sharing the Tax Base: Coordination, Efficiency,
    and Incentives   323
Revenue Sharing in Multilevel Fiscal Systems   328
Revenue-Sharing Formulas   333
Concluding Remarks   336
Notes   336
References   337

12

Macro Formulas for Equalization   339
Leonard S. Wilson
The Theory of Equalization   340
Macro Formulas   345
Macro Bases as Measures of Fiscal Capacity   346
Equalization in Canada, Australia, and South Africa   354
Conclusion   357
Notes   358
References   358

13

Fiscal Capacity Equalization in Horizontal Fiscal Equalization Programs   361
Bernard Dafflon
Local Fiscal Disparities   363
Conceptual Issues   366
Needs Equalization   368
Revenue Equalization   372
Designing Horizontal Equalization   380
Conclusion and Policy Proposals   390
Notes   391
References   393

14 **Compensating Local Governments for Differences in Expenditure Needs in a Horizontal Fiscal Equalization Program**   397
Andrew Reschovsky
Defining Expenditure Needs and Costs   400
Why Costs Differ   401
Approaches to Estimating Costs   404
Costing Methodologies in Selected Countries   410
Lessons for Developing Countries   419
Notes   421
References   422

15 **Financing Capital Expenditures through Grants**   425
Jeffrey Petchey and Garry MacDonald
Rationale for Capital Grants   426
Issues in the Design of Capital Grants   431
Real-World Experience with Capital Grants   432
A Capital Grant Simulation Model   435
Conclusion   445
Annex: Economic Rationales for Grants   446
Notes   449
References   450

16 **Grants to Large Cities and Metropolitan Areas**   453
Enid Slack
Characteristics of Large Cities and Metropolitan Areas
    and the Implications for Grant Design   454
Types of Transfers and Rationales for Their Use   459
Rationales for Intergovernmental Transfers   460
Grants to Large Cities and Metropolitan Areas   468
Concluding Comments   475
Notes   476
References   478

17

Grants to Small Urban Governments   483
Harry Kitchen
What Is a Small Urban Area?   483
What Are the Expenditure Responsibilities of
     Small Urban Areas?   485
How Should Expenditures Be Financed?   486
How Important Are Grants?   488
How Should Grants Be Designed?   498
Should Grants to Small Urban Areas Differ from
     Grants to Other Municipalities?   505
Summary   506
References   507

18

**Intergovernmental Transfers and Rural Local
Governments**   511
Melville L. McMillan
Country Profiles   511
Overview and Reflections   530
Conclusion   535
Notes   536
References   537

Index   539

BOXES
1.1   Well-Founded Negative Perceptions of Intergovernmental
        Finance   18
1.2   Financing Schools in the United States   21
1.3   South Africa's Equitable Share Formula for Central-Local
        Fiscal Transfers   45

FIGURES
1.1   Effect of Unconditional Nonmatching Grant   3
1.2   Effect of Conditional Nonmatching Grant   5

1.3   Effect of Open-Ended Matching Grant   6
1.4   Effect of Closed-Ended Matching Grant   8
1.5   Applying a Results-Based Chain to Education   11
10.1   Federal-Provincial Fiscal Arrangements in Canada   297
10.2   Structure of Federal-Provincial Fiscal Arrangements
       Committees in Canada   298
10.3   Fiscal Equalization in Australia, 1998/99–2002/03   312
10.4   Robin Hood at Work in Australia, 2004/05   315
11.1   Welfare Implications of Tax Assignment   322
11.2   Central Government Revenue in India from Shareable and
       Nonshareable Taxes, 1950–99   332
13.1   Stylized Representation of Revenue Equalization   373
15.1   Simulation 1: Backlogs, by South African Province   441
15.2   Simulation 1: Per Capita Capital Levels, by South African
       Province   441
15.3   Simulation 2: Backlogs, by South African Province   443
15.4   Simulation 2: Per Capita Capital Levels, by South African
       Province   443

TABLES

1.1   Taxonomy of Grants and Their Conceptual Impacts   10
1.2   Features of Traditional and Output-Based
       Conditional Grants   14
1.3   Measurement of Fiscal Needs, by Service Category   26
1.4   Weighting of Factors for Provincial-Local Expenditure
       Functions in Canada   28
1.5   Features of Fiscal Equalization Transfers in Selected
       Countries   34
1.6   Need Factors Used for Grant Financing of Health Care in
       Selected Countries   38
1.7   Principles and Better Practices in Grant Design   49
3.1   Interregional Equalization Instruments   80
4.1   Empirical Evidence on Regional Insurance in
       the United States   119
4.2   Empirical Evidence on Regional Insurance in
       Selected Countries   122
6.1   Consequences of Failure of Central Government to Meet
       Necessary Conditions   194

6.2 Stages of Decision Making in Formulating and Implementing Economic Policy 195

8.1 Empirical Results on the Impact of Intergovernmental Transfers, 1973–2005 238

10.1 Responsibility for Design of Intergovernmental Fiscal Transfers in Selected Countries 295

10.2 Transaction Costs and Potential Outcomes of Intergovernmental Forums and Independent Agencies (Grants Commissions) 309

10.3 Transaction Costs and Potential Outcomes of Intergovernmental Forums and Independent Agencies (Grants Commissions) in Selected Countries 311

10.4 Expenditure Need Factors for Secondary Education in Australia, 1995/96 314

13.1 Sources of Fiscal Disparities 365

15.1 Per Capita Capital Stock, by South African Province, 2002 437

16.1 Transfers to Selected National Capitals 474

17.1 Reliance on Grant Support in Selected Countries 489

18.1 Functional Division of Transfers to Rural Local Government in Karnataka, India, 2000/01 514

18.2 Local Government Spending in Latvia, 1999 518

18.3 Local Government Revenues in Latvia, 1999 519

18.4 Municipal Government Expenditure in Alberta, Canada, 2001 526

18.5 Municipal Government Revenue, Alberta, Canada, 2001 527

18.6 Sources of Property Tax Revenue, Alberta, Canada, 2001 528

18.7 Summary Information on Rural Local Governments in India, Latvia, and Canada (Alberta) 532

Foreword

In Western democracies, systems of checks and balances built into government structures have formed the core of good governance and have helped empower citizens for more than two hundred years. The incentives that motivate public servants and policy makers— the rewards and sanctions linked to results that help shape public sector performance—are rooted in a country's accountability frameworks. Sound public sector management and government spending help determine the course of economic development and social equity, especially for the poor and other disadvantaged groups, such as women and the elderly.

Many developing countries, however, continue to suffer from unsatisfactory and often dysfunctional governance systems that include rent seeking and malfeasance, inappropriate allocation of resources, inefficient revenue systems, and weak delivery of vital public services. Such poor governance leads to unwelcome outcomes for access to public services by the poor and other disadvantaged members of the society, such as women, children, and minorities. In dealing with these concerns, the development assistance community in general and the World Bank in particular are continuously striving to learn lessons from practices around the world to achieve a better understanding of what works and what does not work in improving public sector governance, especially with respect to combating corruption and making services work for poor people.

The Public Sector Governance and Accountability Series advances our knowledge by providing tools and lessons from practices in improving efficiency and equity of public services provision and strengthening institutions of accountability in governance. The series highlights frameworks to create incentive environments and pressures for good governance from within and beyond governments. It outlines institutional mechanisms to empower citizens to demand accountability for results from their governments. It provides practical guidance on managing for results and prudent fiscal management. It outlines approaches to dealing with corruption and malfeasance. It provides conceptual and practical guidance on alternative service delivery frameworks for extending the reach and access of public services. The series also covers safeguards for the protection of the poor, women, minorities, and other disadvantaged groups; ways of strengthening institutional arrangements for voice and exit; methods of evaluating public sector programs; frameworks for responsive and accountable governance; and fiscal federalism and local governance.

This series will be of interest to public officials, development practitioners, students of development, and those interested in public governance in developing countries.

Frannie A. Léautier
Vice President
World Bank Institute

Preface

Intergovernmental fiscal transfers are a dominant feature of subnational finance in most countries. They are used to ensure that revenues roughly match the expenditure needs of various levels of subnational governments. They are also used to advance national, regional, and local objectives, such as fairness and equity, and to create a common economic union. The structure of these transfers creates incentives for national, regional, and local governments that affect fiscal management, macroeconomic stability, distributional equity, allocational efficiency, and public service delivery.

This book reviews the conceptual and empirical literature to distill lessons for policy makers looking to design fiscal transfers in a manner that creates incentives for prudent fiscal management and effective service delivery. It covers new ground by providing practical guidance on designing output-based transfers that emphasize bottom-up, client-focused, and results-based government accountability and equalization transfers to ensure regional fiscal equity as well as the institutional arrangements for implementing such transfers.

This book advances the World Bank Institute agenda on knowledge sharing and learning from cross-country experiences with a view to supporting public governance better. It is intended to help policy makers make more-informed choices about strengthening public sector governance and improving social outcomes for their citizens.

Roumeen Islam
Manager, Poverty Reduction and Economic Management
World Bank Institute

Acknowledgments

This book brings together training modules on intergovernmental fiscal transfers prepared for the World Bank Institute learning programs over the past three years. These learning programs were financed by the governments of Canada, Italy, Japan, the Netherlands, the Republic of Korea, and Switzerland. The editors are grateful to the Canadian International Development Agency, the government of Italy, the Policy and Human Resources Development program of Japan, the Bank-Netherlands Partnership Program, the Korean Institute of Public Finance, and the Swiss Development Cooperation Agency for financial support for the development and publication of this book.

The volume has benefited from contributions to World Bank Institute learning events by senior policy makers from Argentina, Australia, Brazil, Canada, Chile, China, Germany, India, Indonesia, Kazakhstan, Kenya, the Kyrgyz Republic, Mexico, Pakistan, the Philippines, Poland, the Republic of Korea, the Russian Federation, South Africa, Switzerland, Tanzania, Thailand, Turkey, Uganda, and the United States.

The editors are grateful to the leading scholars who contributed chapters and to the reviewers, especially Sandra Roberts, who provided comments on all chapters. Sandra Gain, Mike Lombardo, Baoyun Qiao, Chunli Shen, Theresa Thompson, and Jan Werner helped during various stages of the preparation of this book. Maria Lourdes Penaflor Gosiengfiao provided administrative support for this project.

Contributors

ROBIN BOADWAY is the Sir Edward Peacock Professor of Economic Theory at Queen's University, Kingston, Ontario, Canada. He is a fellow of the Royal Society of Canada, a past president of the Canadian Economics Association, and a past chair of the economics department at Queen's University. He has been editor of the *Canadian Journal of Economics* and the *German Economic Review* and is currently editor of the *Journal of Public Economics* and editorial adviser for the *Canadian Tax Journal* and the *National Tax Journal*. He serves on the executive board of the International Seminar on Public Economics and is on the academic panel of the Fiscal Affairs Division of the International Monetary Fund.

SUJIT CHOUDHRY is associate professor of law and political science at the University of Toronto, Ontario, Canada, and a senior fellow at Massey College. He holds law degrees from the University of Oxford, where he was a Rhodes Scholar; the University of Toronto; and Harvard Law School. He served as a law clerk to Chief Justice Antonio Lamer of the Supreme Court of Canada, a consultant to the Royal Commission on the Future of Health Care in Canada (the Romanow Commission) and the National Advisory Committee on SARS and Public Health (the Naylor Committee), and a member of the academic advisory committee to the Province of Ontario's Democratic Renewal Secretariat and the Governing Toronto Advisory Panel, which reexamined the structure of municipal government in Toronto.

BERNARD DAFFLON is professor of public finance and public policy at the University of Fribourg, Switzerland. He provides expert advice on fiscal federalism, decentralization, and local public finance to the Council of Europe and the World Bank Institute. He also advises Swiss cantons and the federal government of Switzerland.

SHAMA GAMKHAR is associate professor of public affairs at the Lyndon B. Johnson School of Public Affairs at the University of Texas at Austin, United States. She is the author of *Federal Intergovernmental Grants and the States: Managing Devolution* and numerous scholarly articles in tax and public finance journals. She coauthored a report by the Transportation Research Board of The National Academies that reviews the long-term viability of the fuel tax for transportation finance in the United States.

HARRY KITCHEN is professor of economics at Trent University, Peterborough, Ontario, Canada. He has published widely on public finance, local and regional government organization, and service delivery. He has advised governments in both industrial and developing countries on a range of fiscal system reform and local governance issues.

GARRY MACDONALD is associate professor of economics at Curtin University, Perth, Australia. His research interests are in applied macroeconomics and econometrics. He has published widely in international academic journals.

MELVILLE L. MCMILLAN is professor of economics and a fellow of the Institute of Public Economics at the University of Alberta, Edmonton, Canada. His research interests are in public economics, particularly urban and local economics, fiscal federalism, and the demand for and supply of public goods and services. He has served on the editorial board of the *Canadian Tax Journal*.

BENJAMIN PERRIN is a member of the Institute of Comparative Law at McGill University, Montreal, Quebec, Canada, where he is completing graduate research as a Max Stern Fellow and Wainwright Scholar. He is assistant director of the Special Court for Sierra Leone legal clinic, which conducts legal research for judges of the Trial and Appeals Chamber in Freetown. He is also executive director of The Future Group, a nongovernmental organization that combats human trafficking. He has received the Governor General of Canada's Queen's Golden Jubilee Medal, a YMCA International Peace Medal, and the University of Calgary's Graduate of the Last Decade Award. After completing his graduate research, he will serve as a law clerk to Justice Marie Deschamps of the Supreme Court of Canada.

JEFFREY PETCHEY is professor of economics at the School of Economics and Finance, Curtin University, Perth, Australia. He has published on fiscal equalization, tax competition, the theory of voting, and the economic implications of various Australian constitutional arrangements. He has served as a consultant to the World Bank, the Financial and Fiscal Commission of South Africa, the Forum of Federations, AusAid, and various state governments in Australia.

M. GOVINDA RAO is director of the National Institute of Public Finance and Policy, in New Delhi, India, and a member of the Economic Advisory Council to the prime minister. His research interests include public finance and fiscal policy, fiscal federalism, and state and local finance. His recent publications include *Political Economy of Federalism in India*; *Sustainable Fiscal Policy for India: An International Perspective*, edited with Peter Heller; and *Poverty, Development and Fiscal Policy*, all published by Oxford University Press.

ANDREW RESCHOVSKY is professor of public affairs and applied economics at the University of Wisconsin-Madison, United States. He has written numerous articles on intergovernmental fiscal relations and tax policy. Since 1999 he has served as a technical adviser to the South Africa Financial and Fiscal Commission. He has also worked for the Office of Tax Analysis of the U.S. Department of the Treasury and as a technical adviser to the Organisation for Economic Co-operation and Development in Paris. He is currently organizing an international cooperative project designed to evaluate alternative strategies for dealing with fiscal problems facing large central cities.

MOTOHIRO SATO is associate professor of economics at the Graduate School of International Corporate Strategy and the Graduate School of Economics at Hitotsubashi University, Tokyo, Japan. His fields of research include fiscal federalism, tax policy, and social security. He is an associate editor of the *Journal of Public Economics* and a specialist member of the Government Tax Commission of Japan.

ANWAR SHAH is lead economist and team leader of the Public Sector Governance Program of the World Bank Institute, Washington, DC. He is also a fellow of the Institute for Public Economics, Edmonton, Alberta, Canada. While working for the government of Alberta, he was responsible for designing provincial fiscal transfers to local governments. While at the federal Ministry of Finance in Ottawa, he was responsible for designing and administering federal fiscal transfers to the provinces, with primary responsibility for the Canadian Fiscal Equalization Program. He has advised the governments of Argentina, Australia, Brazil, China, India, Indonesia, Mexico, Pakistan, Poland, South Africa, and Turkey on fiscal system reform issues, including the design of fiscal transfers.

ENID SLACK is the director of the Institute on Municipal Finance and Governance at the Munk Centre for International Studies at the University of Toronto, Ontario, Canada, where she is adjunct professor. She is president of her own consulting firm, which specializes in municipal, education, and intergovernmental finance. She advises governments and private companies on property taxes, intergovernmental transfers, and other local finance issues. She has coauthored four books and published numerous articles on urban public finance. Her most recent book is *International Handbook on Land and Property Taxation*, coedited with Richard Bird.

MICHAEL SMART is associate professor of economics at the University of Toronto, Ontario, Canada. He has written extensively on tax policy and fiscal federalism.

PAUL BERND SPAHN is professor emeritus of Goethe University, Frankfurt, Germany, and an adviser to the minister of finance and treasury in Bosnia and Herzegovina. He has served as vice president of the University of Frankfurt and as a consultant to numerous research institutes and international organizations, including the International Monetary Fund, the World Bank, the United Nations, the Council of Europe, and the European Commission. He has published widely in scholarly and policy-oriented journals and lectured and provided expert advice to governments in nearly 50 countries.

MARIANNE VIGNEAULT is professor of economics and former chair of the department of economics at Bishop's University, Sherbrooke, Quebec, Canada. She holds a BA from Bishop's University and an MA and PhD from Queen's University. Her research is in public economics, with emphasis on fiscal federalism and tax policies toward entrepreneurs, venture capitalists, and multinational corporations. She has worked as a consultant and researcher for the Canadian International Development Agency, the federal Department of Finance, and the Institute for the Economy in Transition in Moscow.

JÜRGEN VON HAGEN is professor of economics and director of the Center for European Integration Studies at the University of Bonn, Germany. He is a research fellow at the Centre for Economic Policy Research, a member of the Council of the German Economic Association and the Academic Advisory Council of the German Federal Ministry of Economics, a former member of the Council of the European Economic Association and the French National Economic Committee, and the first recipient of the Gossen Prize of the German Economics Association. He has been a consultant to the International Monetary Fund, the European Commission, the Federal Reserve Board, the Inter-American Development Bank, the World Bank, and numerous governments.

LEONARD S. WILSON is professor of economics at the University of Alberta, Edmonton, Canada. He has served as an economic adviser to the government of Kenya and the Malaysian Institute for Economic Research. His research focuses on public economics and the economics of developing countries.

Overview

ROBIN BOADWAY AND ANWAR SHAH

Apart from small city-states, every country has more than one level of government. In addition to the national government, these can include intermediate governments (states, provinces, cantons, *Länder*, prefectures, and so forth), municipal governments, and governing bodies that may take on relatively narrow responsibilities. In some cases, the structure of government is explicitly federal, in the sense that different levels of government have autonomous responsibilities typically enshrined in a constitution. In other cases, subnational levels of government are creatures of the national government and may be ultimately dependent on them for their authority. Regardless of the political or constitutional definition of the nation, subnational governments are almost never self-sufficient financially. Their revenue-raising responsibilities fall short of their expenditure responsibilities, forcing them to rely on financial transfers from the national government. This volume examines the role of intergovernmental transfers, in both theory and practice.

Practices governing intergovernmental transfers vary widely. The structures of multilevel government, the responsibilities exercised by each, and the relative importance of transfers differ widely across countries. To adopt the expression used by some of the contributors to this volume, "finance follows function" to varying degrees across nations. The way in which transfers are used by transferring governments to achieve their policy objectives, as opposed to simply closing the vertical fiscal gap, differs across nations as well.

Commonalities in Approaches to Intergovernmental Transfers

Despite these differences, certain common principles inform the role of transfers, and common practices are frequently found. Describing these commonalities helps provide some context for the overview of the volume that follows.

Patterns of Expenditure Decentralization

The assignment of expenditure functions across levels of government is broadly similar across nations. It is influenced by efficiency considerations in the delivery of public goods and services as well as benefits from allowing subnational governments discretion in choosing programs best suited to their constituent communities. Federal governments typically assume responsibility for national public goods (defense, foreign affairs, money and banking, national infrastructure) as well as some elements of social insurance (pensions, unemployment insurance). Intermediate governments (hereafter referred to as states) are often assigned the provision of important public services, such as health, education, and welfare, in addition to state public goods, such as roads and police protection. Local governments provide local public goods and services, including water and sanitation, local roads, and recreational facilities. These patterns of decentralization are found in nonfederal nations as well.

An important feature of this assignment of responsibilities is that higher levels of government have some interest in the manner in which expenditure programs are designed and delivered, for efficiency or equity reasons. On efficiency grounds, three sorts of arguments apply. First, program benefits may spill over to other communities. Second, decentralized decision making can lead to inefficiencies, because they distort cross-boundary transactions in products or factors, either intentionally or unintentionally. Third, fiscal competition among subnational governments may lead to inefficient choices of program spending. Equity issues particularly apply to state-level governments, which are responsible for providing public services such as health, education, and welfare, which fulfill redistributive roles that may be of national interest. Given this, most systems of intergovernmental transfers include design features intended to influence how subnational governments deliver these programs. More generally, the degree of discretion states have in designing these important social programs varies from federation to federation, as does the manner in which that discretion is constrained.

Revenue Decentralization

While on the expenditure side the proportion of government spending that is decentralized is reasonably similar across federations, the extent of revenue decentralization varies widely. Indeed, from a budgetary perspective, differences in fiscal decentralization are largely differences in revenue decentralization, or equivalently, differences in vertical fiscal gaps. The main distinction between centralized and decentralized fiscal federal systems is the extent to which state governments have discretionary access to broad-based taxes. In decentralized federations such as Canada, India, Switzerland, and the United States, state-level governments have full access to broad-based taxes such as income, sales, and payroll taxes. In more centralized federations, such as Australia and Germany, much less own-source tax revenue is raised, although in both cases, revenue-sharing applies to federal taxes.

A high degree of revenue decentralization does not mean there is no significant vertical fiscal gap. On the contrary, even in the most decentralized federations, intergovernmental transfers play an important role. More generally, the vertical fiscal gap is not something that is or can be determined by assignment. It is the outcome of more or less independent fiscal choices made by all levels of government. Whether one level can be considered dominant from this point of view is an important question that is addressed at various points in this volume. While one might at first think that the federal government plays a leadership role in determining the vertical fiscal gap by choosing its preferred level of transfers as well as how much tax room to occupy, it is certainly conceivable that the states can have some influence on the amount of money the federal government transfers to them.

Equalizing Transfers

Fiscal decentralization inevitably leaves states and municipalities with different financial abilities to provide public services to their citizens. Different jurisdictions will have different needs and costs of providing public services and different revenue-raising capacities with which to finance them. As a consequence, intergovernmental transfers usually have an equalizing element to them, with higher per capita transfers going to jurisdictions with lower fiscal capacities. The form and extent of equalization differ considerably across nations, and there may or may not be one general transfer that is dedicated to equalization. But where no single equalization transfer is made, equalizing elements are typically built into more-specific transfers, including shared-cost ones.

Federal Influence on State Decisions

Although federal constitutions may assign exclusive legislative powers to states, it is almost always the case that the use of these powers is subject to some influence by the federal government. That influence can take several forms, some more intrusive than others. Examples of highly intrusive federal influence include the ability to strike down state legislation and the ability to mandate state actions. Less intrusive forms of influence can be achieved through the use of intergovernmental transfers. Conditions can be imposed on transfers, and they can be subject to matching requirements. Moreover, the mere fact that the states are dependent on federal transfers can make them responsive to moral suasion by the federal government.

The ubiquitous possibility for the federal government to influence state fiscal decisions is a source of tension in virtually all federations to some extent. In addition, it can be a source of inefficiency in the operation of the intergovernmental relations system. An overly intrusive federal government can detract from some of the benefits of federal systems of government, especially those that arise from the ability of states to exercise discretion in their fiscal choices.

Caveats and Limitations

This volume is primarily about the economics of intergovernmental fiscal transfers. Before summarizing its contents, it is useful to state some caveats and limitations that apply to the role of economic analysis in evaluating and designing transfers.

Economic principles alone cannot suffice to determine the ideal system of intergovernmental transfers. Conflicting objectives are at stake, and different observers will trade off those objectives in different ways. For example, the need for transfers is directly related to the extent of decentralization. While decentralization contributes to the efficiency of the delivery of fiscal programs, it can also lead to violations of efficiency and equity in the national economy. The relative weight one gives these national objectives versus the benefits of decentralized decision making will influence one's view on the size of transfers (the vertical fiscal gap) and their design. Moreover, value judgments are inevitable in designing transfers, particularly the weight given to equity versus efficiency. Those who weigh efficiency relatively heavily will generally favor more decentralization and less oversight over program design at the subnational level, including through conditionality of transfers.

One's view of decentralization and the role of transfers will also be affected by an assessment of the workings of the market economy and the public sector. The trade-off between efficiency and equity and the efficiency consequences of decentralization will depend on how responsive private sector decisions are to government fiscal actions, an issue on which there is little reliable evidence. Moreover, an assessment of the effects of decentralization and the role of transfers depends on the extent to which governments are viewed as benevolent and responsive to the wishes of their constituents as opposed to being self-interested and self-serving. Broadly speaking, those who view governments as nonbenevolent typically favor more decentralized decision making as a means of putting a brake on these tendencies.

This discussion suggests that there is no "optimal" set of intergovernmental transfers that suits all circumstances. Instead, grants have to be tailored to each case depending on the objectives sought, the initial conditions, and resource constraints. Nevertheless, a review of international practices by Anwar Shah (chapter 1) provides important lessons on avoiding some common pitfalls and emulating some better practices. Practices to avoid include general revenue–sharing programs with multiple factors, which undermine accountability and do not advance fiscal efficiency or fiscal equity objectives; grants to finance subnational deficits, which create incentives for running higher deficits in the future; fiscal effort provisions in unconditional grant programs, which undermine efficiency and equity and support a leviathan view of government; input-based, process-based, or ad hoc conditional grant programs, which undermine local autonomy, flexibility, and fiscal efficiency and equity objectives; capital grants without assurance of funds for future upkeep, which have the potential to create white elephants; and negotiated or discretionary transfers, which may create dissention and disunity. Practices to strive for include selecting the simplest and most transparent design, as rough justice may be better than full justice in terms of enhancing accountability and gaining wider acceptability; focusing on a single objective in a grant program and ensuring that the design is consistent with that objective; including a sunset clause to ensure periodic review and renewal; equalizing fiscal capacity using an explicit standard that determines the pools as well as the allocations; equalizing fiscal need through specific-purpose transfers; providing results-oriented (output-based) national minimum standards grants; and establishing an intergovernmental forum to achieve consensus on the standard of equalization and objectives and design of all fiscal transfer programs.

The system that is suitable for a given country will depend on the circumstances of the country as well as on the consensus on redistributive objectives and solidarity within the nation. Nonetheless, some principles have evolved that establish a framework against which to evaluate existing and potential practices.

The Principles

The section of the volume on principles begins with a general overview of the role of intergovernmental transfers in federations and other multigovernment countries by Robin Boadway (chapter 2). Transfers are viewed as fulfilling three main purposes. One is simply to finance the difference between state expenditure and revenue-raising responsibilities (the fiscal gap). Although transfers themselves are passive, the federal government's role in determining the fiscal gap is by no means passive. A second purpose is to use equalizing transfers to compensate for differences in state fiscal capacities that arise from the decentralization of fiscal responsibilities. The capacity to raise revenues from own sources may differ across states, as may the expenditures required to provide given levels of services. A third purpose of transfers is to allow the federal government to exercise influence or oversight over the design of state programs.

More generally, intergovernmental transfers are a necessary complement to decentralization. They permit the benefits of decentralization to occur while at the same time undoing some of their potential adverse effects. The extent of transfers and their design thus depends very much on how one assesses the consequences of decentralization and how much oversight one wants to give the federal government over fiscal decisions made by the states. Boadway discusses the broad implications of these assessments for the principles of the design of the transfer system, emphasizing the key trade-off between the benefits of discretionary decision making by the states and the usefulness of federal oversight. The appropriate combination of decentralization and federal oversight is determined endogenously, with the federal government playing a large role. This limits the extent to which the principles of a good transfer system can be prescriptive.

Chapter 3, by Paul Bernd Spahn, calls into question the traditional fiscal federalism perspective of the role of transfers as the primary means of addressing relations among governments. Spahn recounts the equity and efficiency rationales for intergovernmental transfers and considers how they can best be achieved. He argues that public sector efficiency in particular could be enhanced if a "contractual" approach to federal-state fiscal relations were adopted wherever possible. Under such an approach, transfers from the federal to the state governments for, say, the delivery of services would be based on a contract mutually agreed to by the two sides and stipulating explicitly the terms of services, including any incentive payments. In other words, mechanisms such as those found in the private sector would be used in the public sector to reward performance and increase accountability. These mechanisms would replace the more hierarchical system whereby transfers are initiated by the federal government, which may also determine conditions or matching requirements to impose. Spahn suggests that these more traditional forms of transfer are appropriate in some circumstances, such as in financing public goods or accomplishing equalization. But where service delivery is involved, standard grants do not exploit all the opportunities to enhance cooperation, accountability, and cost-effectiveness.

The economic rationales usually offered for transfers are based on standard efficiency and equity arguments, adapted to a federal setting. However, transfer systems, particularly those that equalize fiscal capacities, also fulfill a risk-sharing or stabilization function. Chapter 4, by Jürgen von Hagen, studies this risk-sharing role. The issue arises when different states are subject to different economic shocks. To the extent that these shocks will be reflected in personal income shocks, households are exposed to risks they may not be able to insure against. This in turn exposes state governments to risks, since their tax revenues as well as some of their expenditure responsibilities (such as transfers to households) will respond. An intergovernmental transfer system that includes an equalization component will serve as a form of insurance to the state government and therefore indirectly to residents of the state. Of course, this presumes that states and households cannot self-insure against the risk of such shocks (and that the federal government can).

Equalizing transfers may also act as stabilization devices, especially if the shocks are lasting. There are two senses of stabilization. First, stabilization can refer to the manner in which the economy absorbs shocks by reallocating resources among activities. When an open economy is subject to an adverse shock, adjustment can occur in several ways: wages and prices may fall, the exchange rate may adjust, capital and labor may move away from the economy. In the case of a state in a federation, exchange rate adjustment is not possible, and wage and price adjustments may be sticky. The transfer system provides some relief, reducing the impact of the shock and facilitating transitional adjustment. Indeed, both the intergovernmental transfer system and the interpersonal tax-transfer system will have this effect.

Second, equalizing transfers can affect aggregate demand, as governments engage in fiscal policy in response to shocks. To the extent that these shocks are state specific, the transfer system will act as a built-in stabilizer.

Von Hagen summarizes these arguments and surveys the empirical evidence on the relative importance of intergovernmental transfers as risk-sharing and stabilization devices. Their effectiveness depends on the design of the transfer system and how responsive it is to shocks, in terms of both the timeliness and the magnitude of the response. Moreover, as with any insurance scheme, there may be adverse incentives. To the extent that states can undertake actions to affect the size of their own transfers, they may be induced to do so. This problem is analogous to the problem of adverse selection in insurance markets.

The possibility that states can influence the size of their transfers applies more generally than to just the risk-sharing function of intergovernmental transfers. It goes to the heart of the effectiveness of federal-state transfers as devices with which the federal government can achieve what it perceives as its national objectives. Intergovernmental transfers are traditionally viewed as policy instruments that the federal government uses to address the fiscal needs of the states or influence their program design. To use the terminology of game theory, the federal government moves first, announcing its transfer policy before states choose their fiscal policies, but it anticipates how the states will respond to federal transfer policies. However, even if the federal government announces its policy first, that policy will typically not be enacted until after state policies are in place. If the federal government cannot commit to undertaking the policies it has announced, it may choose to renege on them ex post. If the states recognize this lack of commitment, they may be able to exploit it by structuring their own policies in a way that induces the federal government to transfer more to them than they would have chosen to transfer if they could commit. This is the soft-budget constraint problem, surveyed in chapter 5 by Marianne Vigneault. In the extreme case, states may choose to run up their debt and be bailed out by the federal government. If the federal government could commit to a no bail-out policy ex ante, the states would not be inclined to run up their debt strategically, although it may not always be known whether state debts are a result of conscious choice or bad luck.

Vigneault surveys the empirical and theoretical literature on soft budget constraints, looking for lessons that can be learned from the experiences of various countries. She describes two quite different approaches to reducing the likelihood of soft budget constraints, a decentralized and a centralized version. In the decentralized version, states are given considerable discretion for fiscal decisions, including the ability to issue debt and raise their own revenues. The discipline against running up excessive debts is provided jointly by private capital markets, which finance the deficits, and state electorates, which hold politicians accountable. In the centralized version, the federal government imposes strict controls on the behavior of the states, restricting their ability to borrow, controlling their finances, and imposing conditions on their spending. Soft budget constraint problems tend to arise when intermediate circumstances apply, when states can borrow but have limited discretion over revenue-raising and political accountability is weak. What remedy is best for a given country depends on the institutional and other features of the country. In any case, even if bail-out problems can be avoided, it is unlikely that more limited forms of soft budget constraint can be. By their actions, states may still be able to influence the amount of transfers going in their direction.

The idea that transfers from the federal government to the states are malleable and subject to political influence is the subject of chapter 6, by Motohiro Sato, who provides a broad overview of the political economy of grants. While the normative theory emphasizes the role of grants in achieving efficient and equitable outcomes in a federation, the ideal set of grants may not be feasible for political reasons. The study of the political economy of grants is a special case of the political economy of economic policy making more generally, although some special issues arise in the case of grants. As in the broader literature, political influence on grants may take a top-down or a bottom-up approach. Both require that grants are discretionary rather than formula driven. Indeed, political economy reasons may drive the fact that grants have discretionary components. In the top-down approach, political parties use transfers to attract votes (the so-called "pork barrel" use of grants). Transfers tend to be allocated more to constituencies in which voters are less committed. In the bottom-up approach, grants are viewed as a response to lobbying of politicians and their parties by states and their interest groups. In this case, the allocation of grants is related to the ability of lobbyists representing local interests to organize.

Political economy arguments have an important bearing on the case for decentralization, what Sato refers to as the "constitutional stage." Decentralization can be seen as an antidote to bureaucratic power and rent seeking that reduces accountability and the efficient provision of public services. By bringing government closer to the people, the electorate can hold political decision makers more accountable. Competition among subnational jurisdictions can impose discipline on local politicians and their bureaucracies, and it can provide a yardstick against which the quality of local governance can be judged. Decentralization also reduces the size of rents and can therefore reduce the incentive for wasteful rent seeking. Of course, there may be some countervailing effects. Capture of government by local interests may be easier in a decentralized setting, unless local citizens are effective participants in local decisions. The political economy of grants, and more generally of decentralization, remains a lively area of study.

Chapter 7, by Michael Smart, is also concerned with political decision making, in particular the behavioral response of recipient governments to transfers received. Even in normative theories of federalism, decentralization and the grants that are used to facilitate decentralization can induce adverse incentive effects on state government. Equalization transfers, like other redistributive transfers, can influence the fiscal policies of recipient states. For example, transfers designed to equalize the revenue-raising capacity of governments often calculate the transfers by applying a standard state tax rate to actual state tax bases in order to determine how the ability to raise revenues varies across states. The revenue effects of policy actions that a state takes that reduce its tax bases will be offset by equalization transfers. Thus states will have an incentive to set tax rates that are too high or to discourage the development of tax bases where they have some ability to do so (in the development of resource properties, for example). To the extent that tax rates are too low to begin with, this incentive for states to raise their tax rates can be beneficial. Thus if tax competition effects are important, equalization transfers can neutralize them. However, the opposite is possible. State tax rates might be too high to begin with, either because of the kind of political economy arguments cited above or because of vertical fiscal externalities whereby the cost of increased state tax rates is partly borne by federal tax-payers because the common tax bases they use falls.

Grants can also have intentional incentive effects. This is most obviously the case for matching grants that reward states for increases in particular expenditures by federal cost-sharing. Indeed, the matching rates are often quite substantial (50-50), typically well beyond the magnitude of perceived spillovers. Conditional transfers that are not matching can also apparently affect stated spending significantly, even though from an economic point of view they are analogous to lump-sum income transfers. The fact of condi-tionality itself seems to be enough to induce states to spend grants on the programs for which they are intended, even in the absence of matching com-ponents. In fact, even if transfers are unconditional, they still seem to be treated by recipient governments differently from increases in income to their residents. This is the so-called "flypaper effect," whereby the expendi-tures of recipient governments respond more to increases in transfers than to increases in private incomes. Smart reviews the empirical evidence that fiscal choices by state governments respond both to transfers and to fiscal policies taken by other governments, both federal and state.

Shama Gamkhar and Anwar Shah take up similar themes in chapter 8. They put the flypaper effect into a much broader perspective as an example of a more general observation that the effect of grants is often different from what traditional theories of fiscal federalism—the so-called "first-generation theories"—would have predicted. They argue that the focus of intergovernmental grant theory has shifted from a preoccupation with flypaper effects and other incentive effects of grants designed to deal with interjurisdictional spillovers to second-generation theories that focus more on the efficiency and equity effects of decentralization and the role of transfers in accommodating that decentralization. Viewed from this perspective, issues concerning the interaction among governments, such as fiscal competition, soft budget constraints, and moral hazard responses to transfers, play a more prominent role. Gamkhar and Shah provide a detailed review of the empirical literature on the responsiveness of state and local fiscal policies to federal and state grants and attempt to reconcile seemingly contradictory predictions of theory with the results obtained in empirical studies.

The Practice

Part II of this volume addresses some of the issues that arise in putting the principles of intergovernmental transfers into practice. The fact that one level of government is making financial transfers to another suggests that some legal framework is needed for managing the transfers. Even if the transfers are unconditional and formula based, a legal basis must exist for determining the rules that enable the federal government to make (and change) such transfers, the manner in which formulas are determined, and the legal remedies to apply should disputes arise with respect to the amounts transferred. In the case of conditional or matching transfers, the need for legal sanction is even more pressing, especially if the conditions affect the manner in which states exercise their constitutionally sanctioned responsibilities. Sujit Choudhry and Benjamin Perrin review these legal issues in chapter 9, illustrating them with representative case studies of federations.

What emerges is an appreciation for the diversity of practices, reflecting the historical, political, and cultural characteristics of each federation. The legal basis for making transfers to the states varies depending on whether they are based on constitutional obligation, constitutional enabling authority, federal statute, or intergovernmental agreement. Most important, the manner in which the federal government exercises influence over state decisions varies from country to country, including the extent to which conditional grants (the spending power) are used as a federal policy instrument.

The existence of legally sanctioned institutions, such as arms-length advisory commissions, varies from federation to federation, as does the type of dispute settlement mechanism used to resolve conflicts over both the manner in which the federal government determines the transfer structure and conditions and the manner in which the states respond to the conditions. Despite that diversity, all federations struggle with one overriding issue: how to strike the appropriate balance between the autonomy of state decision making and the desire of the federal government to exercise influence, using conditional transfers among other instruments. Legal remedies are important in setting the rules of the game for intergovernmental fiscal relations and ensuring they are adhered to, but they are not sufficient. Legal approaches may not be flexible enough to deal with all issues. Accountability of governments to citizens must also rely on political and institutional processes.

The institutional framework used to facilitate intergovernmental fiscal relations is the subject of chapter 10, by Anwar Shah. Various countries use diverse arrangements to determine the size and allocation of intergovernmental fiscal transfers. A critical question not answered by the earlier literature is the relative efficacy of these arrangements in achieving a simple, fair, and transparent fiscal transfer system with potential to achieve a national consensus. To address this question, Shah develops a new institutional economics framework to evaluate alternate institutional arrangements. He applies the framework to a stylized view of these arrangements in selected countries. The framework is used to examine the transactions costs incurred by society as a whole to achieve defined grant design–related outcomes. This framework yields a comparative evaluation of two popular institutional models for intergovernmental transfers: intergovernmental forums and independent grants commissions. Intergovernmental forums are shown to produce simpler and fairer designs with lower transactions costs to society than independent grants commissions. Independent grants commissions are shown to be an inferior institutional choice in view of the perverse incentives regimes created by their underlying governance structures, which predispose them to recommending complex solutions with high agency costs.

The remaining chapters examine the design of actual systems of transfers, with each chapter focusing on a different element. In chapter 11, M. Govinda Rao considers the role of tax sharing as a means of getting revenues into the hands of states. There are two forms of tax sharing, which differ in the extent of discretion given to the states. Revenue-sharing systems stipulate a share of given revenue sources that are allocated to the states. These schemes can be based on constitutional dictate or legislated by the federal government. The allocation of shares among the states can be based on state financial needs or simply on population or the principle of derivation. Revenue sharing provides some predictability to the states, but it gives them no discretion over their own revenues. Moreover, the revenue source being shared may not be a buoyant one, and revenue sharing may discourage the federal government from using the shared base or administering it efficiently.

Some of these problems can be overcome by giving states the discretion to determine how much revenue to raise from a shared tax base while allowing them to take advantage of centralized tax administration. For example, states may simply piggyback onto federal taxes by imposing a state surtax on the federal base or on federal tax revenues collected by the state. These schemes preserve a harmonized tax system while affording the states the discretion to determine their own revenues. This presumably enhances accountability. But tax-base sharing of this sort is not sufficient for achieving all the objectives of fiscal transfers. In particular, since all state revenues accrue to the states in which they are raised, nothing is done to achieve equalization of fiscal capacities. The remaining chapters deal with various aspects of the design of transfers intended to address fiscal capacity differences across states.

Chapter 12, by Leonard Wilson, studies alternative ways of pursuing revenue equalization. Two main candidates have been proposed. The one used in many federations, the representative tax system approach, equalizes the ability to raise revenues based on the actual practices of states in the federation. The idea is to construct a representative tax system that reflects the bases chosen and the average tax rates applied across the federation. For each state the amount of revenue that would be raised per capita from this system is then calculated and used as the basis for making equalization entitlements. Because the representative tax system measures fiscal capacity based on the actual tax systems states use, it implicitly takes account of differences in the ability to raise revenues from different revenue sources. The system is a relatively complicated one, however, and relies on judgments for choosing representative tax bases when states adopt very different policies. Moreover, it relies on data that may not be available in all countries. Its complexities detract from its transparency for citizens and from its objectivity as a measure of fiscal capacity. In addition, for some revenue sources (such as property taxes), conceptually difficult issues are associated with applying this approach.

An alternative that seems to avoid some of these complexities is the so-called macro approach, whereby a single indicator, such as personal consumption of state output, is used to measure the potential fiscal capacity of states. While the representative tax system is simpler, it captures only imperfectly the ability of a state to raise revenues. Moreover, it does not avoid the adverse incentive effects of the representative tax system approach and does not address differences in needs across states. The macro approach may be better suited for federations, such as those in developing countries, whose public accounting systems make it difficult to apply the representative tax approach and are forced to rely on something simpler.

Chapter 13, by Bernard Dafflon, also considers the form of equalization that is best suited to meeting the equity and efficiency objectives of the system. He argues that a net, or self-financing, system whereby payments to states with below-average fiscal capacity are met by contributions of those with above-average capacity has some advantages. Such a system makes explicit the extent of redistribution that the equalization system achieved, so that the society's consensus for solidarity can be reflected in the scheme actually chosen. Dafflon argues strongly for a rules-based approach; in the case of revenue equalization, he suggests a representative tax–type system. He suggests that transparency can best be achieved by keeping equalization separate from other transfers and from having an autonomous body assess the system on a periodic basis and make recommendations for reform.

The objective of equalization is to reduce differences in the ability of state governments to provide public services, if not eliminate them altogether. These differences depend not only on the ability to raise revenues but also on the needs and costs of providing public services. Since much of state spending is on basic public services to citizens, such as education, health, and social services, needs for public services will depend on the demographic make-up of the population by age, skill, health status, and so on. Moreover, providing public services will be more costly in some locations than others. Labor costs, geographical factors, and population densities may all differ. In chapter 14 Andrew Reschovsky provides a detailed account of how an equalization system may be designed to take account of such differences in needs and costs. This is a difficult task, since expenditure programs are very diverse, with output difficult to measure, and many conditions determine costs and needs. Ideally, one would like measures of a state's fiscal need to be independent of actions the state might take. Reschovsky surveys various empirical techniques that might be used, from those based on detailed econometric techniques to those that require elements of considered judgment. Which method is suitable for any given country depends on the quality of the data available and the nature of the services provided at the state level.

An element of need that calls for special treatment, especially in developing countries, is capital and infrastructure spending, as Jeff Petchey and Garry MacDonald discuss in chapter 15. The public services provided by state governments require ample amounts of capital: schools are needed for education, hospitals and clinics for health, roads for transportation services, and so on. In developed federations, where these facilities have been built up in the past and states have access to capital markets to finance capital expansions, transfers to support capital costs can build in an amount for ongoing capital cost accruals. In contrast, many developing countries face backlogs and financing constraints, and it may be necessary to provide dedicated transfers based on existing needs for capital expenditures. Petchey and MacDonald examine the design of capital transfers and present a model for implementing that design that has been tested in South Africa.

The last three chapters address the special problems faced by local governments, which differ from states in the nature of their expenditure programs and in their access to adequate financing. Local governments also differ systematically in their size and geographic setting, as reflected in the distinctions among the three chapters. Enid Slack (chapter 16) focuses on larger cities and metropolitan areas, Harry Kitchen (chapter 17) on small cities, and Melville McMillan (chapter 18) on rural municipalities.

While larger cities have some unique expenditure requirements, such as social service spending, mass transit, and policing, they also have the ability to generate more revenue to the extent that they are called upon to exercise it. They have larger property tax bases and can use sales taxes or income taxes, sharing those bases with higher levels of government. User fees can also be an important source of revenue. In fact, as Slack points out, large cities typically rely to a significant extent on transfers from state governments, although they are responsible for raising marginal revenues from own sources. These transfers are often conditional, reflecting the facts that they may be required to deliver social services for the states and there may be spillovers of benefits from some expenditure programs. However, the pattern of transfers varies widely across countries, reflecting the diversity of circumstances facing cities and the nature of their expenditure and revenue responsibilities.

Smaller cities are also very diverse and face similar financing problems as large cities. Although their expenditure needs may be less than those of large cities, they also face more significant constraints on revenue raising, often relying heavily on property taxes. Some economies of service delivery are obtained by the existence of a higher tier of government encompassing several localities. Their need for transfers is affected by the extent to which they are called upon to deliver public services such as education and social services. As in the case of large cities, a substantial part of their transfers are conditional. This reflects the fact that cities exercise less discretion than states in designing and delivering their programs, which are typically the creatures of the states. As Kitchen points out, conditional transfers can also often be used to achieve state political objectives.

Rural governments face many unique problems. Since they are less densely populated than cities, it is more costly to deliver public services and to provide local public goods, such as roads, water, sanitation, and utilities. In addition, rural areas are usually poorer and have smaller revenue-raising capabilities, especially in countries that have been undergoing urbanization. They thus have a greater need for transfers, especially if they are required to deliver basic public services such as education and social services. The practice is very diverse and the literature very sparse, so McMillan proceeds by a series of illustrative case studies.

Most states have all three types of local governments. Since their fiscal capacities to deliver public goods and services differ considerably, efficiency and equity objectives call for a set of equalizing transfers, as the authors stress. Equalization will necessarily be rather complex and involve taking into account not only the diverse revenue-raising capabilities but also the special needs and costs faced by different cities. One way to simplify the process is to stratify the equalization system according to the type of municipality, in order to equalize fiscal capacity among large cities, among small cities, and among rural municipalities separately. The relative amounts of transfers that go to each group still needs to be determined, a choice that inevitably requires political judgment.

As this overview indicates, the design of an intergovernmental transfer system is an important topic for virtually all nations, federal or unitary, developed or developing. It is a challenging area because by its nature there is no single correct policy prescription. Conflicting objectives are involved, especially between the virtues of decentralized decision making and the achievement of national objectives; and political, institutional, and historical factors weigh into the discussion. The literature is evolving, and much more work needs to be done, including public education. It is hoped that this book will make a significant contribution.

1

A Practitioner's Guide to Intergovernmental Fiscal Transfers

ANWAR SHAH

Intergovernmental fiscal transfers finance about 60 percent of subnational expenditures in developing countries and transition economies and about a third of such expenditures in member countries of the Organisation for Economic Co-operation and Development (29 percent in the Nordic countries, 46 percent in non-Nordic Europe). Beyond the expenditures they finance, these transfers create incentives and accountability mechanisms that affect the fiscal management, efficiency, and equity of public service provision and government accountability to citizens.

This chapter reviews the principles and practices of intergovernmental finance, with a view to drawing some general lessons of relevance to policy makers and practitioners in developing countries and transition economies. It provides a taxonomy of grants, their possible impacts on local fiscal behavior, and the accountability of grant recipients to donor governments and citizens. The first section describes the instruments of intergovernmental finance. Section 2 discusses performance-oriented, or output-based, transfers, an important tool for results-based accountability. Section 3 describes the objectives and design of fiscal transfers in various countries around the world. It shows that in developing countries and transition economies, fiscal transfers focus largely on revenue-sharing transfers, with little attention paid to serving national objectives. It cites examples of simple but innovative grant designs that can satisfy grantors' objectives while preserving local autonomy and creating an enabling environment for responsive, responsible, equitable, and accountable public governance. Section 4 describes institutional arrangements for determining these transfers. The last section highlights some lessons of relevance to current policy debates in developing countries and transition economies. It lists practices to avoid as well as those to emulate in designing and implementing grant programs.

Instruments of Intergovernmental Finance

Intergovernmental transfers or grants can be broadly classified into two categories: general-purpose (unconditional) and specific-purpose (conditional or earmarked) transfers.

General-Purpose Transfers

General-purpose transfers are provided as general budget support, with no strings attached. These transfers are typically mandated by law, but occasionally they may be of an ad hoc or discretionary nature. Such transfers are intended to preserve local autonomy and enhance interjurisdictional equity. That is why Article 9 of the European Charter of Local Self-Government states that "as far as possible, grants to local authorities shall not be earmarked for the financing of specific projects. The provision of grants shall not remove the basic freedom of local authorities to exercise policy discretion within their own jurisdiction" (Barati and Szalai 2000, p. 21).

General-purpose transfers are termed block transfers when they are used to provide broad support in a general area of subnational expenditures (such as education) while allowing recipients discretion in allocating the funds among specific uses. Block grants are a vaguely defined concept. They fall in the gray area between general-purpose and specific-purpose transfers, as they provide budget support with no strings attached in a broad but specific area of subnational expenditures.

General-purpose transfers simply augment the recipient's resources. They have only an income effect, as indicated in figure 1.1 by the shift in the recipient's budget line (AB) upward and to the right by the amount of the grant (AC = BD), creating the new budget line CD. Since the grant can be spent on any combination of public goods or services or used to provide tax relief to residents, general nonmatching assistance does not affect relative

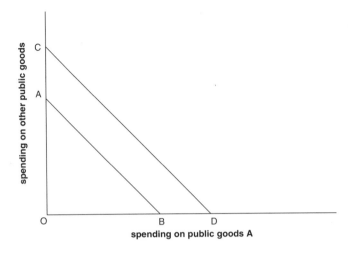

Source: Shah 1994b.

FIGURE 1.1 Effect of Unconditional Nonmatching Grant

prices (no substitution effect). It is also the least stimulative of local spending, typically increasing such spending by less than $0.50 for each additional
$1 of unconditional assistance. The remaining funds are made available as
tax relief to local residents to spend on private goods and services.

In theory, a $1 increase in local residents' income should have exactly the
same impact on local public spending as receipt of $1 of a general-purpose
transfer: both shift the budget line outward identically. In fact, all empirical
studies show that $1 received by the community in the form of a general-
purpose grant tends to increase local public spending by more than a $1
increase in residents' income—that is, the portion of grants retained for local
spending tends to exceed the effective tax rate imposed by local governments
on resident's incomes (Rosen 2005; Oates 1999; Gramlich 1977; chapter 8 of
this volume). Grant money tends to stick where it first lands, leaving a smaller
than expected fraction available for tax relief, a phenomenon referred to as
the "flypaper effect." The implication is that for political and bureaucratic reasons, grants to local governments tend to result in more local spending than
they would have had the same transfers been made directly to local residents
(McMillan, Shah, and Gillen 1980). An explanation for this impact is provided by the hypothesis that bureaucrats seek to maximize the size of their
budgets, because doing do gives them greater power and influence in the
community (Filimon, Romer, and Rosenthal 1982).

Formula-based general-purpose transfers are very common. The federal and state transfers to municipalities in Brazil are examples of grants of this kind. Evidence suggests that such transfers induce municipalities to underutilize their own tax bases (Shah 1991).

Specific-Purpose Transfers

Specific-purpose, or conditional, transfers are intended to provide incentives for governments to undertake specific programs or activities. These grants may be regular or mandatory in nature or discretionary or ad hoc.

Conditional transfers typically specify the type of expenditures that can be financed (input-based conditionality). These may be capital expenditures, operating expenditures, or both. Conditional transfers may also require attainment of certain results in service delivery (output-based conditionality). Input-based conditionality is often intrusive and unproductive, whereas output-based conditionality can advance grantors' objectives while preserving local autonomy.

Conditional transfers may incorporate matching provisions by requiring grant recipients to finance a specified percentage of expenditures using their own resources. Matching requirements can be either open ended, meaning that the grantor matches whatever level of resources the recipient provides, or closed ended, meaning that the grantor matches recipient funds only up to a prespecified limit.

Matching requirements encourage greater scrutiny and local ownership of grant-financed expenditures; closed-ended matching is helpful in ensuring that the grantor has some control over the costs of the transfer program. Matching requirements, however, represent a greater burden for a recipient jurisdiction with limited fiscal capacity. In view of this, it may be desirable to set matching rates in inverse proportion to the per capita fiscal capacity of the jurisdiction in order to allow poorer jurisdictions to participate in grant-financed programs.

Nonmatching Transfers

Conditional nonmatching transfers provide a given level of funds without local matching, as long the funds are spent for a particular purpose. Following the grant (AC), the budget line in figure 1.2 shifts from AB to ACD, where at least OE (= AC) of the assisted public good will be acquired.

Conditional nonmatching grants are best suited for subsidizing activities considered high priority by a higher-level government but low priority by local governments. This may be the case if a program generates a high

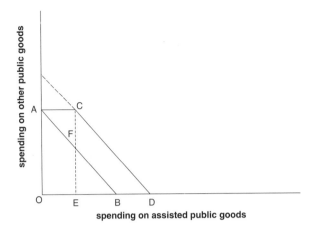

Source: Shah 1994b.

FIGURE 1.2   Effect of Conditional Nonmatching Grant

degree of spillovers up to a given level of provision (OE), after which the external benefits terminate abruptly.

For a given level of available assistance, grant recipients prefer unconditional nonmatching transfers, which provide them with maximum flexibility to pursue their own objectives. Because such grants augment resources without influencing spending patterns, they allow recipients to maximize their own welfare. Grantors, however, may be prepared to sacrifice some recipient satisfaction to ensure that the funds are directed toward expenditures on which they place a priority. This is particularly so when federal objectives are implemented by line agencies or departments rather than through a central agency, such as the Ministry of Finance, with a broader mandate. Federal departments do not want local governments to shift their program funds toward other areas. In this situation, conditional (selective) nonmatching (block) grants can ensure that the funds are spent in a department's area of interest (for example, health care) without distorting local priorities among alternative activities or inducing inefficient allocations in the targeted expenditure area.

Matching Transfers

Conditional matching grants, or cost-sharing programs, require that funds be spent for specific purposes and that the recipient match the funds to some degree. Figure 1.3 shows the effect on a local government budget of a

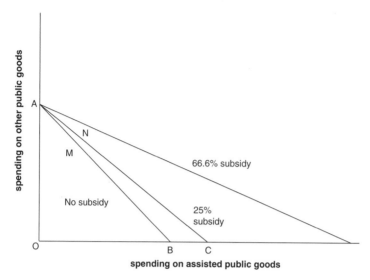

Source: Shah 1994b; McMillan, Shah, and Gillen 1980.

FIGURE 1.3 Effect of Open-Ended Matching Grant

25 percent subsidy program for transportation. AB indicates the no subsidy line—the combination of transportation and other public goods and services a city can acquire with a budget of OA = OB. A federal subsidy of 25 percent of transportation expenditures (that is, a grant of $1 for every $3 of local funds spent on transportation) shifts the budget line of attainable combinations to AC. At any level of other goods and services, the community can obtain one-third more transportation services. If the community chooses combination M before the grant, it will likely select a combination such as N afterward. At N more transportation is acquired.

The subsidy has two effects, an income effect and a substitution effect. The subsidy gives the community more resources, some of which go to acquiring more transportation services (the income effect). Since the subsidy reduces the relative price of transportation services, the community acquires more transportation services from a given budget (the substitution effect). Both effects stimulate higher spending on transportation.

Although the grant is for transportation, more other public goods and services may also be acquired, even though they become relatively more expensive, as a result of the substitution effect. If the income effect is sufficiently large, it will dominate and the grant will increase consumption of other goods and services. Most studies find that for grants of this kind, spending in the specified area increases by less than the amount of the grant, with the remainder going toward other public goods and services and tax relief (see chapter 8 of this volume). This is the so-called *fungibility effect* of grants. The fungibility of conditional grants depends on both the level of spending on the assisted public service and the relative priority of such spending. For example, if the recipient's own-financed expenditure on the assisted category exceeds the amount of the conditional grant, the conditionality of the grant may or may not have any impact on the recipient's spending behavior: all, some, or none of the grant funds could go to the assisted function. Shah (1985, 1988b, 1989) finds that while provincial assistance to cities in Alberta for public transit was partially diverted to finance other services, similar assistance for road transportation improvement was not.

Open-ended matching grants, in which no limit is placed on available assistance through matching provisions, are well suited for correcting inefficiencies in the provision of public goods arising from benefit spillovers, or externalities. Benefit spillovers occur when services provided and financed by a local government also benefit members of other local governments that do not contribute to their provision. Because the providing government bears all the costs but obtains only a portion of the benefits, it tends to underprovide the goods. If the affected communities cannot negotiate compensation, the situation can be corrected by a higher government subsidizing provision of the service, with the extent of the spillover determining the degree of subsidy or the matching ratio.

Matching grants can correct inefficiencies from spillovers, but they do not address uneven or inadequate fiscal capacities across state and local governments. Local governments with ample resources can afford to meet matching requirements and acquire a substantial amount of assistance. States with limited fiscal capacities may be unable to match federal funds and therefore fail to obtain as much assistance, even though their expenditure needs may be equal to or greater than those of wealthier states (Shah 1991). Other forms of assistance are needed to equalize fiscal capacities in such cases.

Grantors usually prefer closed-ended matching transfers, in which funds are provided to a certain limit, since such transfers permit them to retain control over their budgets. Figure 1.4 shows the effect of closed-ended matching grants on the local budget. AB is the original budget line. When $1 of assistance is available for every $3 of local funds spent up to a prespecified limit, the budget line becomes ACD. Initially, costs are shared on a one-third:two-thirds basis up to the level at which the subsidy limit of CG (= CE) is reached. Expenditures beyond OF receive no subsidy, so the slope of the budget line reverts back to 1:1 rather than 1:3 along the subsidized segment, AC.

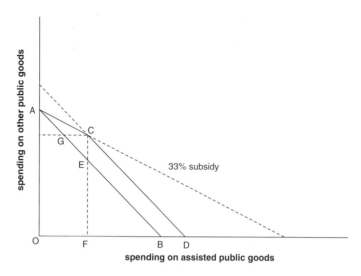

Source: Shah 1994b.

FIGURE 1.4 Effect of Closed-Ended Matching Grant

Empirical studies typically find that closed-ended grants stimulate expenditures on the subsidized activity more than open-ended grants (Gramlich 1977; Shah 1994b; chapter 8 of this volume). The estimated response to an additional $1.00 of this kind of grant is typically $1.50. Institutional factors may explain this surprisingly large response.

Why are conditional closed-ended matching grants common in industrial countries when they seem ill designed to solve problems and inefficiencies in the provision of public goods? The answer seems to be that correcting for inefficiencies is not the sole or perhaps even the primary objective. Instead, grants are employed to help local governments financially while promoting spending on activities given priority by the grantor. The conditional (selective) aspects of or conditions on the spending are expected to ensure that the funds are directed toward an activity the grantor views as desirable. This, however, may be false comfort in view of the potential for fungibility of funds. The local matching or cost-sharing component affords the grantor a degree of control, requires a degree of financial accountability by the recipient, and makes the cost known to the granting government.

Conditional closed-ended matching grants have advantages and disadvantages from the grantor's perspective. While such grants may result in a significant transfer of resources, they may distort output and cause inefficiencies, since the aid is often available only for a few activities, causing overspending on these functions while other functions are underfinanced. If capital outlays are subsidized while operating costs are not, grants may induce spending on capital-intensive alternatives.

Conditional open-ended matching grants are the most suitable vehicles to induce lower-level governments to increase spending on the assisted function (table 1.1). If the objective is simply to enhance the welfare of local residents, general-purpose nonmatching transfers are preferable, as they preserve local autonomy.

To ensure accountability for results, conditional nonmatching output-based transfers are preferable to other types of transfers. Output-based transfers respect local autonomy and budgetary flexibility while providing incentives and accountability mechanisms to improve service delivery performance. The design of such transfers is discussed in the next section.

Achieving Results-Based Accountability through Performance-Oriented Transfers

Economic rationales for output-based grants (used interchangeably with performance-oriented transfers in this chapter) stem from the emphasis on contract-based management under the new public management framework and strengthening demand for good governance by lowering the transaction costs for citizens in obtaining public services under the new institutional economics approach. The new public management framework seeks to strengthen accountability for results by changing the management paradigm in the public sector from permanent appointments to contractual appointment and continuation of employment subject to fulfillment of service delivery contracts. It seeks to create a competitive service delivery environment by making financing available on similar conditions to all providers, government and nongovernment.

The new institutional economics approach argues that dysfunctional governance in the public sector results from opportunistic behavior by public officials, as citizens are not empowered to hold public officials accountable for their noncompliance with their mandates or for corrupt acts or face high transaction costs in doing so. In this framework, citizens are treated as the principals and public officials the agents. The principals have bounded rationality—they act rationally based on the incomplete information they have. Acquiring and processing information about public sector operations is costly. Agents (public officials) are better informed than principals. Their self-interest motivates them to withhold information from the public domain, as releasing such information helps principals hold them accountable. This

TABLE 1.1 Taxonomy of Grants and Their Conceptual Impacts

Type of grant	Income effect			Price (substitution) effect			Total effect				Rank by objective function		
	a_1	A	U	a_1	A	U	a_1	A	U	$\partial A/\partial G$	Increases in expenditure	Accountability for results	Welfare
Conditional (input-based) matching													
Open-ended	↑	↑	↑	↑	↑	→	↑↑	↑↑	↑→	>1	1	3 (none)	3
Closed-ended													
Binding constraint	↑	↑	↑	↑	↑	→	↑↑	↑↑	↑→	≥1	2 or 3	3 (none)	4
Nonbinding constraint	↑	↑	↑	n.a.	n.a.	n.a.	↑	↑	↑	≤1	3	3 (none)	2
Conditional nonmatching	↑	↑	↑	n.a.	n.a.	n.a.	↑	↑	↑	≤1	3	3 (none)	2
Conditional nonmatching output-based	↑	↑	↑	n.a.	n.a.	n.a.	↑	↑	↑	≤1	3	1 (high)	1
General nonmatching	n.a.	↑	↑	n.a.	n.a.	n.a.	n.a	↑	↑	<1	3	3 (none)	1

Source: Adapted from Shah 1994b.

Note: a_1 = assisted subfunction; A = assisted function; U = unassisted function; G = grant; ↑ = positive impact; ↓ = negative impact; 1 = highest score; 4 = lowest score; n.a. = not applicable.

asymmetry of information allows agents to indulge in opportunistic behavior, which goes unchecked due to the high transaction costs faced by principals and the lack of or inadequacy of countervailing institutions to enforce accountable governance. Results-based accountability through output-based grants empowers citizens by increasing their information base and lowering their transaction costs in demanding action.

Output-based transfers link grant finance with service delivery performance. These transfers place conditions on the results to be achieved while providing full flexibility in the design of programs and associated spending levels to achieve those objectives. Such transfers help restore recipients' focus on the results-based chain (figure 1.5) and the alternate service delivery framework (competitive framework for public service delivery) to achieve those results. In order to achieve grant objectives, a public manager in the recipient government would examine the results-based chain to determine whether or not program activities are expected to yield the desired results. To do so, he or she needs to monitor program activities and inputs, including intermediate inputs (resources used to produce outputs), outputs (quantity and quality of public goods and services produced and access to such goods and services), outcomes (intermediate- to long-run consequences for consumers/taxpayers of public service provision or progress in achieving program objectives), impact (program goals or very long-term

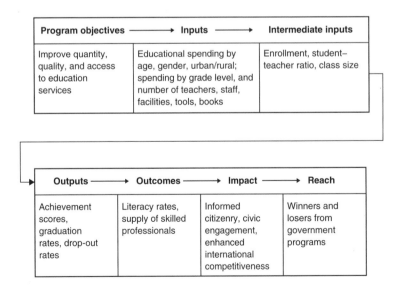

FIGURE 1.5 Applying a Results-Based Chain to Education

consequences of public service provision), and reach (people who benefit from or are hurt by a program). Such a managerial focus reinforces joint ownership and accountability of the principal and the agent in achieving shared goals by highlighting terms of mutual trust. Thus internal and external reporting shifts from the traditional focus on inputs to a focus on outputs, reach, and outcomes—in particular, outputs that lead to results. Flexibility in project definition and implementation is achieved by shifting emphasis from strict monitoring of inputs to monitoring performance results and their measurements. Tracking progress toward expected results is done through indicators, which are negotiated between the provider and the financing agency. This joint goal setting and reporting helps ensure client satisfaction on an ongoing basis while building partnership and ownership into projects (Shah 2005b).

Output-based grants must have conditions on outputs as opposed to outcomes, as outcomes are subject to influence by factors beyond the control of a public manager. Public managers should be held accountable only for factors under their control. Outcome-based conditions diffuse enforcement of accountability for results. Since the grant conditions are concerned with service delivery performance in terms of quality of output and access, the manager is free to choose the program and inputs to deliver results. To achieve those results, he or she faces positive incentives by grant conditions that encourage alternate service delivery mechanisms by contracting out, outsourcing, or simply encouraging competition among government and nongovernment providers. This can be done by establishing a level playing field through at par financing, by offering franchises through competitive bidding, or by providing rewards for performance through benchmarking or yardstick competition. Such an incentive environment is expected to yield a management paradigm that emphasizes results-based accountability to clients with the following common elements:

- Contracts or work program agreements based on prespecified outputs and performance targets and budgetary allocations
- Replacement of lifelong rotating employment with contractual appointments with task specialization
- Managerial flexibility but accountability for results
- Redefinition of public sector role as purchaser but not necessarily provider of public services
- Adoption of the subsidiarity principle—that is, public sector decisions made at the level of government closest to the people, unless a convincing case can be made not to do so

- Incentives for cost efficiency
- Incentives for transparency and competitive service provision
- Accountability to taxpayers.

Under such an accountable governance framework, grant-financed budget allocations support contracts and work program agreements, which are based on prespecified outputs and performance targets. The grant recipient's flexibility in input selection—including hiring and firing of personnel and implementation of programs—is fully respected, but there is strict accountability for achieving results. The incentive and accountability regime created by output-based transfers is expected to create responsive, responsible, and accountable governance without undermining local autonomy. In contrast, traditional conditional grants with input conditionality undermine local autonomy and budgetary flexibility while reinforcing a culture of opportunism and rent seeking (table 1.2).

Output-based grants create incentive regimes that promote a results-based accountability culture. Consider the case in which the national government aims to improve access to education by the poor and to enhance the quality of such education. A common approach is to provide grants to government schools through conditional grants. These grants specify the type of expenditures eligible for grant financing (books, computers, teacher aids, and so forth) as well as financial reporting and audit requirements. Such input conditionality undermines budgetary autonomy and flexibility without providing any assurance about the achievement of results. Moreover, in practice it is difficult to enforce, as there may be significant opportunities for fungibility of funds. Experience has shown that there is no one-to-one link between increases in public spending and improvements in service delivery performance (see Huther, Roberts, and Shah 1997).

Output-based design of such grants can help achieve accountability for results. Under this approach, the national government allocates funds to local governments based on the size of the school-age population. Local governments in turn pass these funds on to both government and nongovernment providers based on school enrollments. Nongovernment providers are eligible to receive grant funds if they admit students based on merit and provide a tuition subsidy to students whose parents cannot afford the tuition. All providers are expected to improve or at the minimum maintain baseline achievement scores on standardized tests, increase graduation rates, and reduce dropout rates. Failure to do so will invite public censure and in the extreme case cause grant funds to be discontinued. In the meantime, reputation risks associated with poor performance may reduce enrollments,

TABLE 1.2 Features of Traditional and Output-Based Conditional Grants

Feature	Traditional grant	Output-based grant
Grant objectives	Spending levels	Quality and access to public services
Grant design and administration	Complex	Simple and transparent
Eligibility	Recipient government departments/agencies	Recipient government provides funds to all government and nongovernment providers
Conditions	Expenditures on authorized functions and objects	Outputs-service delivery results
Allocation criteria	Program or project proposal approvals with expenditure details	Demographic data on potential clients
Compliance verification	Higher level inspections and audits	Client feedback and redress, comparison of baseline and postgrant data on quality and access
Penalties	Audit observations on financial compliance	Public censure, competitive pressures, voice and exit options for clients
Managerial flexibility	Little or none. No tolerance for risk and no accountability for failure	Absolute. Rewards for risks but penalties for persistent failure
Local government autonomy and budgetary flexibility	Little	Absolute
Transparency	Little	Absolute
Focus	Internal	External, competition, innovation, and benchmarking
Accountability	Hierarchical to higher-level government, controls on inputs and process with little or no concern for results	Results based, bottom-up, client driven

Source: Author.

thereby reducing the grant funds received. Schools have full autonomy in the use of grant funds and are able to retain unused funds.

This kind of grant financing would create an incentive environment for both government and nongovernment schools to compete and excel to retain students and establish reputations for quality education, as parental choice determines grant financing to each school. Such an environment is particularly important for government schools, where staff have lifelong appointments and financing is ensured regardless of performance. Budgetary flexibility and retention of savings would encourage innovation to deliver quality education.

Output-based grants thus preserve autonomy, encourage competition and innovation, and bring strict accountability for results to residents. This accountability regime is self-enforcing through consumer (parental choice in the current example) choice.

Designing Fiscal Transfers: Dividing the Spoils or Creating a Framework for Accountable and Equitable Governance?

The design of fiscal transfers is critical to ensuring the efficiency and equity of local service provision and the fiscal health of subnational governments (for a comprehensive treatment of the economic rationale of intergovernmental fiscal transfers, see Boadway and Shah forthcoming). A few simple guidelines can be helpful in designing these transfers:

1. *Clarity in grant objectives.* Grant objectives should be clearly and precisely specified to guide grant design.
2. *Autonomy.* Subnational governments should have complete independence and flexibility in setting priorities. They should not be constrained by the categorical structure of programs and uncertainty associated with decision making at the center. Tax-base sharing—allowing subnational governments to introduce their own tax rates on central bases, formula-based revenue sharing, or block grants—is consistent with this objective.
3. *Revenue adequacy.* Subnational governments should have adequate revenues to discharge designated responsibilities.
4. *Responsiveness.* The grant program should be flexible enough to accommodate unforeseen changes in the fiscal situation of the recipients.
5. *Equity (fairness).* Allocated funds should vary directly with fiscal need factors and inversely with the tax capacity of each jurisdiction.
6. *Predictability.* The grant mechanism should ensure predictability of subnational governments' shares by publishing five-year projections of funding availability. The grant formula should specify ceilings and floors for yearly fluctuations. Any major changes in the formula should be accompanied by hold harmless or grandfathering provisions.

7. *Transparency.* Both the formula and the allocations should be disseminated widely, in order to achieve as broad a consensus as possible on the objectives and operation of the program.

8. *Efficiency.* The grant design should be neutral with respect to subnational governments' choices of resource allocation to different sectors or types of activity.

9. *Simplicity.* Grant allocation should be based on objective factors over which individual units have little control. The formula should be easy to understand, in order not to reward grantsmanship.

10. *Incentive.* The design should provide incentives for sound fiscal management and discourage inefficient practices. Specific transfers to finance subnational government deficits should not be made.

11. *Reach.* All grant-financed programs create winners and losers. Consideration must be given to identifying beneficiaries and those who will be adversely affected to determine the overall usefulness and sustainability of the program.

12. *Safeguarding of grantor's objectives.* Grantor's objectives are best safeguarded by having grant conditions specify the results to be achieved (output-based grants) and by giving the recipient flexibility in the use of funds.

13. *Affordability.* The grant program must recognize donors' budget constraints. This suggests that matching programs should be closed-ended.

14. *Singular focus.* Each grant program should focus on a single objective.

15. *Accountability for results.* The grantor must be accountable for the design and operation of the program. The recipient must be accountable to the grantor and its citizens for financial integrity and results—that is, improvements in service delivery performance. Citizens' voice and exit options in grant design can help advance bottom-up accountability objectives.

Some of these criteria may be in conflict with others. Grantors may therefore have to assign priorities to various factors in comparing design alternatives (Shah 1994b; Canada 2006).

For enhancing government accountability to voters, it is desirable to match revenue means (the ability to raise revenues from own sources) as closely as possible with expenditure needs at all levels of government. However, higher-level governments must be allowed greater access to revenues than needed to fulfill their own direct service responsibilities, so that they are able to use their spending power through fiscal transfers to fulfill national and regional efficiency and equity objectives.

Six broad objectives for national fiscal transfers can be identified. Each of these objectives may apply to varying degrees in different countries; each calls for a specific design of fiscal transfers. Lack of attention in design to specific objectives leads to negative perceptions of these grants (box 1.1).

Bridging Vertical Fiscal Gaps

The terms *vertical fiscal gap* and *vertical fiscal imbalance* have been mistakenly used interchangeably in recent literature on fiscal decentralization. A vertical fiscal gap is defined as the revenue deficiency arising from a mismatch between revenue means and expenditure needs, typically of lower orders of government. A national government may have more revenues than warranted by its direct and indirect spending responsibilities; regional and local governments may have fewer revenues than their expenditure responsibilities.

A vertical fiscal imbalance occurs when the vertical fiscal gap is not adequately addressed by the reassignment of responsibilities or by fiscal transfers and other means. Boadway (2002b) argues that vertical fiscal imbalance incorporates an ideal or optimum view of expenditures by different orders of government and is therefore hard to measure.

Four causes give rise to vertical fiscal gaps: inappropriate assignment of responsibilities, centralization of taxing powers, pursuit of beggar-thy-neighbor tax policies (wasteful tax competition) by subnational governments, and lack of tax room at subnational levels due to heavier tax burdens imposed by the central government. To deal with the vertical fiscal gap, it is important to deal with its sources through a combination of policies such as the reassignment of responsibilities, tax decentralization or tax abatement by the center, and tax-base sharing (by allowing subnational governments to levy supplementary rates on a national tax base). Only as a last resort should revenue sharing, or unconditional formula-based transfers, all of which weaken accountability to local taxpayers, be considered to deal with this gap. Taxation by tax sharing, as practiced in China and India, is particularly undesirable, as it creates incentives for donors to exert less effort in collecting taxes that are shared than they would in collecting taxes that are fully retained. In industrial countries the fiscal gap is usually dealt with by tax decentralization or tax-base sharing. Canada and the Nordic countries have achieved harmonized personal and corporate income tax systems by allowing the central government to provide tax abatement and subnational governments to impose supplementary rates on the national tax base. In developing countries and transition economies, tax by both tax sharing and general revenue sharing are typically used to deal with the fiscal gap.

B O X 1 . 1   Well-Founded Negative Perceptions of Intergovernmental Finance

Perceptions of intergovernmental finance are generally negative. Many federal officials believe that giving money and power to subnational governments is like giving whiskey and car keys to teenagers. They believe that grant monies enable these governments to go on spending binges, leaving the national government to face the consequences of their reckless spending behavior. Past spending behavior of provincial and local officials also demonstrates that "grant money does not buy anything," that it is treated as a windfall gain and wastefully expended with little to show for in service delivery improvements. Citizens perceive the granting of intergovernmental fiscal transfers as the magical art of passing money from one government to another and seeing it vanish into thin air.

These perceptions are well grounded in reality in developing countries, where the primary focus of fiscal transfers is on dividing the spoils. In developing (and nondeveloping) countries, four types of transfers are common:

- *Passing-the-buck transfers.* These are general revenue–sharing programs that employ multiple factors that work at cross-purposes. Argentina, Brazil, India, the Philippines, and many other countries have such ongoing programs.
- *Asking-for-more-trouble grants.* These are grants that finance subnational deficits, in the process encouraging higher and higher deficits. China, Hungary, and India provide this type of grant.
- *Pork barrel transfers.* In the past politically opportunistic grants were common in Brazil and Pakistan. They are currently in vogue in India and Western countries, especially the United States.
- *Command-and-control transfers.* These are grants with conditions on inputs. They are used to micromanage and interfere in local decision making. They are widely practiced in most industrial and developing countries.

Cartoon by Peter Nicholson from *The Australian*, November 3, 1997. www.nicholsoncartoons.com.au

A number of countries, including China, India, Malaysia, Pakistan, South Africa, and Sri Lanka, have in the past provided deficit grants to fill fiscal gaps at subnational levels—with unwelcome results in terms of mushrooming of subnational deficits. These grants are still in vogue in China, Hungary, and South Africa.

Bridging the Fiscal Divide through Fiscal Equalization Transfers

Fiscal equalization transfers are advocated to deal with regional fiscal equity concerns. These transfers are justified on political and economic considerations.

Large regional fiscal disparities can be politically divisive and may even create threats of secession (Shankar and Shah 2003). This threat is quite real: since 1975 about 40 new countries have been created by the break-up of existing political unions. Fiscal equalization transfers could forestall such threats and create a sense of political participation, as demonstrated by the impact of such transfers on the separatist movement in Quebec, Canada.

Decentralized decision making results in differential net fiscal benefits (imputed benefits from public spending minus tax burden) for citizens depending on the fiscal capacities of their place of residence. This leads to both fiscal inequity and fiscal inefficiency in resource allocation. Fiscal inequity arises as citizens with identical incomes are treated differently depending on their place of residence. Fiscal inefficiency in resource allocation results from people in their relocation decisions comparing gross income (private income plus net public sector benefits minus cost of moving) at new locations; economic efficiency considerations warrant comparing only private income minus moving costs, without any regard to public sector benefits. A nation that values horizontal equity (the equal treatment of all citizens nationwide) and fiscal efficiency needs to correct the fiscal inequity and inefficiency that naturally arise in a decentralized government. Grants from the central government to state or local governments can eliminate these differences in net fiscal benefits if the transfers depend on the tax capacity of each state relative to others and on the relative need for and cost of providing public services. The more decentralized the tax system is, the greater the need for equalizing transfers.

The elimination of net fiscal benefits requires a comprehensive fiscal equalization program that equalizes fiscal capacity (the ability to raise revenues from own basis using national average tax rates) to a national average standard and provides compensation for differential expenditure needs and costs due to inherent cost disabilities rather than differences that reflect different policies. Some economists argue that if public sector tax burdens and service benefits are fully capitalized in property values, the case for fiscal equalization transfers is weaker, as residents in rich states pay more for private services and less for public services and vice versa in poorer states. According to this view, fiscal equalization is a matter of political taste. This view has gained currency at the federal level in the United States and explains why there is no federal fiscal equalization program there. In contrast, local fiscal equalization drives most state assistance to local governments in the United States, especially school finance (box 1.2).

Conceptually, full capitalization requires a small open area with costless mobility. Most federations and even states in large countries do not fulfill this condition. As a result, criticism of fiscal equalization using the capitalization argument may have only weak empirical support (Shah 1988a).

In principle, a properly designed fiscal equalization transfers program corrects distortions that may cause fiscally induced migration by equalizing net fiscal benefits across states. A reasonable estimate of the costs and benefits of providing public services in various states is essential to measure net fiscal benefits. Measures of differential revenue-raising abilities and the needs and costs of providing public services in different states must be developed. Equalization of net fiscal benefits could then be attempted by adopting a standard of equalization and establishing the means of financing the needed transfers.

Measuring Fiscal Capacity

Estimating fiscal capacity—the ability of governmental units to raise revenues from their own sources—is conceptually and empirically difficult. The two most common ways of doing so are with macroeconomic indicators and the representative tax system.

Various measures of income and output serve as indicators of the ability of residents of a state to bear tax burdens. Among the better known measures are the following:

- *State gross domestic product (GDP).* State GDP represents the total value of goods and services produced within a state. It is an imperfect guide to the ability of a state government to raise taxes, since a significant portion of income may accrue to nonresident owners of factors of production. For example, the Northern Territory has the highest per capita income in

BOX 1.2 Financing Schools in the United States

U.S. states have taken various approaches to school finance. The states of Hawaii, Idaho, and Washington fully finance primary and secondary education. In contrast, New Hampshire covers only 9 percent of school finance.

Delaware and North Carolina finance education through block grants that are indexed to population, GDP, and inflation growth rates. The grants are derived by calculating equal amounts per unit based on the number of students, teachers, classrooms, courses, classes, and other factors. The units can be standardized using various yardsticks, such as class size and teacher:pupil ratios. Various measures of students, including enrollment, average daily attendance, enrollment weighted by grades, types of programs, and number of students with special needs, are used.

Other states use equalization grants, including foundation grants, percentage equalization grants, and district power equalization grants.

Foundation grants vary inversely with the fiscal capacity of a school board. The grant allocation is based on an application of the representative tax system approach to fiscal capacity equalization per student across school districts. The following formula is used:

foundation grant = (maximum per student grant – own school district contribution per student based on mandated minimum tax rate applied to per student tax base) $\times$ enrollment

Forty-two states have adopted variants of this approach, with 22 states specifying the minimum mandated tax rate. Various measures are used to determine enrollment, including the number of students on the rolls on a specified date, average daily attendance, and average attendance over a period. Most states (36) use a scheme that weights enrollment by grade, program, and student disabilities.

Rhode Island uses a *percentage equalization* grant—a matching cum equalization grant for school spending based on the following formula:

grant per student = [1– matching rate $\times$ (per capita tax capacity in the district/ state average district tax capacity per capita)] $\times$ district spending per capita

District power equalization grants, used in Indiana and Washington, include incentives for increased tax effort in an equalizing grant. The formula used is:

grant = (per capita average fiscal capacity – per capita fiscal capacity of the district) $\times$ district tax rate

Source: Vaillancourt 1998.

Australia, but it is treated as the poorest jurisdiction in federal-state fiscal relations.

▪ *State factor income.* State factor income includes all income—capital and labor—earned in the state. It makes no distinction between income earned and income retained by residents.

▪ *State factor income accruing to residents only.* This measure represents a more useful measure, provided states are able to tax factor income.

▪ *State personal income.* The sum of all income received by residents of a state is a reasonable measure of the state's ability to bear tax burdens. It is an imperfect and partial measure of the ability to impose tax burdens, however, and therefore not a satisfactory measure of overall fiscal capacity.

▪ *Personal disposable income.* Personal disposable income equals personal income minus direct and indirect taxes plus transfers. This concept is subject to the same limitations affecting personal income.

In general, macro measures do not reflect the ability of subnational governments to raise revenues from own sources. Boadway argues against the use of macro indicators in an equalization formula on the grounds that a macro formula "ignores the fact that fiscal inefficiency and fiscal inequity are the products of the actual mix of taxes chosen by provincial governments" (Boadway 2002a, p. 12). This neglect runs the risk of violating the principles of equalization itself. A second major difficulty in the use of macro indicators is the availability of accurate and timely data at subnational levels. Such data become available only with significant lags, and the accuracy of such data may be questionable. Use of these data may therefore invite controversy (see Aubut and Vaillancourt 2001 for a Canadian illustration of this point). Despite these problems, both Brazil and India use macro indicators in their federal-state revenue-sharing programs.

The *representative tax system approach* measures the fiscal capacity of a state by the revenue that could be raised if the government employed all of the standard sources at the nationwide average intensity of use. Estimating equalization entitlements using the representative tax system requires information on the tax bases and tax revenues for each state. Fiscal capacity of the have-not states is brought up to the median, mean, or other norm. Using the mean of all states as a standard, the state equalization entitlement for a revenue source is determined by the formula:

$$E_x^i = (POP)_x \left\{ \left[(PCTB)_{na}^i \times t_{na}^i \right] - \left[(PCTB)_x^i \times t_{na}^i \right] \right\},$$

where E^i is the equalization entitlement of state x from revenue source i, POP is population, $PCTB^i$ is the per capita tax base of revenue source i, t^i is the national average tax rate of revenue source i, subscript na is the national average, and subscript x is state x. The equalization entitlement for a state from a particular revenue source can be negative, positive, or zero. The total of these values indicates whether a state receives a positive or negative entitlement from the interstate revenue-sharing pool. Since data on major tax bases and tax collections required to implement a representative tax system are usually published regularly by various levels of government, the representative tax system does not impose new data requirements and can be readily implemented in countries that have decentralized taxing responsibility to subnational levels, as most transition economies do. Of course, implementing such a system will not be feasible in countries with limited tax decentralization (very large vertical fiscal gaps) or poor tax administration.

Measuring Expenditure Needs

The case for fiscal equalization rests on eliminating different net fiscal benefits across states that give rise to fiscally induced migration. Such differential net fiscal benefits can arise as a result of decentralization of taxing authority and decentralized public expenditures. Differences in the demographic composition of the population across jurisdictions will result in differential needs for decentralized public services, such as education, health, and social welfare. Differences in age distribution affect the need for schools, hospitals, and recreational facilities. Differences in the incidence of poverty and disease may affect the need for education, training, health, social services, and transfer payments (table 1.3). Jurisdictions with higher need factors would have greater need for revenues to provide comparable levels of public services at comparable levels of taxation. These need differentials are likely to cause substantial variations across jurisdictions in the level and mix of public goods provided, resulting in different net fiscal benefits. A strong case for equalization can be established on grounds of efficiency and equity to compensate for need differentials that give rise to different net fiscal benefits.

The fiscal federalism literature treats differential costs as synonymous with differential needs, but some cost differences may arise from deliberate policy decisions by subnational governments rather than differences in need. Boadway (2004) argues that even for inherent cost disadvantages, such as differences between urban and rural areas, the equity advantage of more equal provision must be weighed against the efficiency costs. If it is more costly to deliver public services in rural areas than urban areas, it is inefficient for an equalization program to neutralize these cost differences. Even in unitary states, the level of public services in remote, rural, or mountainous areas is usually lower than in more densely populated urban areas. Under a decentralized fiscal system, a policy choice must be made about minimum standards, but there is no justification for providing the same level of services in remote and urban areas, as the Australian fiscal need equalization program does. Instead, as Boadway suggests, one could stratify locations in all regions by their costs and equalize across regions within comparable strata. Equalization grants should partially offset only inherent disabilities, disregarding cost differences that reflect deliberate policy decisions or differences in the efficiency with which resources are used.

In practice, expenditure need is more difficult to define and derive than fiscal capacity. The difficulties include defining an equalization standard; understanding differences in demographics, service areas, populations, local needs, and policies; and understanding strategic behavior of recipient states. Despite these formidable difficulties, numerous attempts have been made to measure expenditure need. The approaches can be broadly classified into three main categories: ad hoc determination of expenditure needs, the representative expenditure system using direct imputation methods, and the theory-based representative expenditure system.

Ad hoc determination of expenditure needs uses simple measures of expenditure needs in general-purpose transfers. The factors used and their relative weights are arbitrarily determined. Germany uses population size and population density adjustments, China uses the number of public employees, and India uses measures of backwardness.

The Canadian provinces use simple measures of expenditure need in their general-purpose transfers to municipalities. These include population size, population density, population growth factors, road length, number of dwelling units, location factors (such as northern location), urbanization factors (primary urban population and urban/rural class), and social assistance payments (see Shah 1994b). The most sophisticated of these approaches is the one taken by Saskatchewan, where the standard municipal expenditure of a class of municipalities is assumed to be a function of the total population of the class. Regression analysis is used to derive a graduated standard per capita expenditure table for municipal governments by population class.

An interesting example of the application of this approach is South Africa's use of it in its equitable share transfers to the provinces (South Africa 2006). The equitable share formula applicable for 2006–08 focuses almost entirely on need factors, with only a 1 percent weight given to negative needs (per capita GDP). The formula uses the following shares:

■ A basic share (14 percent weight) is derived from each province's share of the national population.

- An education share (51 percent) is based on the size of the school-age population (5–17) and the average number of learners (grades R–12) enrolled in public ordinary schools over the past three years.
- A health share (26 percent) is based on the proportion of the population with and without access to medical aid.
- An institutional component (5 percent) is divided equally among the provinces.
- A poverty component (3 percent) is based on incidence of poverty.
- An economic output component (1 percent) is based on data on GDP by region.

The *representative expenditure system using direct imputation methods* seeks to create a parallel system to the representative tax system on the expenditure side. This is done by dividing subnational expenditures into various functions, determining total expenditures by each jurisdiction for each function, identifying relative need/cost factors, assigning relative weights using direct imputation methods or regression analysis, and allocating total expenditures of all jurisdictions on each function across jurisdictions on the basis of their relative costs and needs for each function (see table 1.3 for a compilation of need factors used in grant formulas in industrial countries).

The advantage of this approach is that it obviates the need for the very elaborate calculations and assumptions to quantify the provision of services at some defined level. It does so by using the sum of actual total expenditures as the point of departure for measuring expenditure needs, thus reducing the problem to one of allocating total need among subnational governments on the basis of selected indicators of need, including proxies for need if desired. The disadvantage of this approach is that it does not necessarily exclude expenses incurred by any of the provinces that go beyond the concept of a "reasonable level of public service." However, the approach can be adjusted to exclude identifiable excesses from total expenditures (for example, gold standards for some services or relatively unaffordable benefits provided by some rich states) in respect of which needs are to be allocated.

A sophisticated variant of this methodology is used by the Commonwealth Grants Commission of Australia, which defines expenditure as the cost of supplying average performance levels for the existing mix of state-local programs. Relative expenditure needs are then determined empirically using direct imputation methods for 41 state-local expenditures. The following hypothetical example illustrates the treatment of welfare expenditures using a crude approach similar to that used by the Commonwealth Grants Commission for establishing expenditure needs under a representative expenditure system.

TABLE 1.3 Measurement of Fiscal Needs, by Service Category

Category	Fiscal need indicator	Per unit cost	Components of adjustment index
Education, primary and secondary	Population of school ages (e.g., ages 7–18)	National per capita public expenditure on primary and secondary education	Wage index = ratio of wage level in sector to national average; rental cost index = ratio of per square rental cost to national average; student disability index = ratio of percentage of students with physical disabilities to the national average; poor family index = the ratio of the percentage students from low-income families to national average
Health	Total population	National per capita public expenditure on health care	Health price index = ratio of health care cost to national average; infant mortality index = ratio of infant mortality rate to national average; inverse life expectancy index = ratio of national average life expectancy to life expectancy in region; inverse population density index = ratio of national average population density to density in region
Police and fire	Total population in region	National per capita public expenditure on police and fire protection	Wage index = ratio of wage level to national average; crime index = ratio of per capita crime rate to national average; fire index = ratio of per capita number of fires to national average; urbanization index = ratio of proportion of population in urban areas in region of municipality to national average
Social welfare	Total population in region	National per capita public expenditure on social welfare	Minimum wage index = ratio of minimum wage level to national average; poverty index = ratio of percentage of low-income population to national average; old age index = ratio of percentage of old population (e.g., age 60 or above) to national average; unemployment index = ratio of unemployment rate to national average; disability index = ratio of percentage of physically disabled people to national average
Transportation	Total length of roads in region	National per capita public expenditure on transportation	Wage index = ratio of wage level to national average; grade index = ratio of average road grade to national average; snow index = ratio of annual snowfall to national average; inverse population density index = ratio of national average population density to density in region
Other services	Total population in region	National per capita public expenditure on other services	Wage index = ratio of wage level to national average; real cost index = ratio of per square rental cost to national average; urbanization index of region = ratio of proportion of population in urban areas in region of municipality to national average

Source: Barati and Szalai 2000, p. 42.

Assume that there are 10 states in Grantland, that the unit costs of welfare are equal in all states, and that needs for welfare vary based on the percentage of the working-age population that is unemployed, the percentage of the population that is not of working age, and the percentage of families with a single parent. The independent grants commission assigns a 40 percent weight to the percentage of the working-age population that is unemployed, a 35 percent weight to the percentage of the population that is not of working age, and a 25 percent weight to the percentage of families with a single parent. Assume that expenditures by all states for welfare total $5 billion and that state A accounts for 4.8 percent of the 10-state total for the first factor, 3.0 percent of the total for the second factor, and 2.2 percent of the total for the third factor. State A's estimated need for a standard level of welfare expenditure would then equal:

$$\$5 \text{ billion} \times (0.048 \times 0.40) + (0.03 \times 0.35)$$
$$+ (0.022 \times 0.25) = \$176 \text{ million},$$

or 3.2 percent of all state expenditures.

Shah (1994a) provides an application of the approach using provincial-local expenditure functions for Canada that uses quantitative analysis in selecting and assigning weights to factors for various expenditure functions (table 1.4).

This approach is highly subjective and therefore potentially controversial. Recent experience in Australia vividly demonstrates the problems that arise if such an approach is followed in practice, as discussed in the following section. Some subjectivity and imprecision can be alleviated by using quantitative analysis in choosing factors and weights, as Shah suggests (1994a).

The *theory-based representative expenditure system* provides a way of improving upon the representative expenditure system. It uses a conceptual framework that embodies an appropriately defined concept of fiscal need and properly specified expenditure functions, estimated using objective quantitative analysis, as proposed by Shah (1996) for Canada. Under this refined approach, the equalization entitlement from expenditure category i equals the per capita potential expenditure of state A for category i based on own need factors if it had national average fiscal capacity minus per capita potential expenditure of state A on expenditure category i if it had national average need factors and national average fiscal capacity.

This approach is even more difficult to implement than the less refined approach, but it has the advantage of objectivity and it enables the analyst to derive measures based on actual observed behavior rather than ad hoc

TABLE 1.4 Weighting of Factors for Provincial-Local Expenditure Functions in Canada

Expenditure category	Need/cost factor	Relative weight
Transportation and communications	Snowfall (annual, in centimeters) (SNOW)	0.1020
	Highway construction price index (HCPI)	0.6580
	Paved roads and streets per square kilometer of area (RSPR)	0.0005
	Noncultivatable area as proportion of total area (NCAR)	0.2357
	Total	1.0000
	Index = $(0.10 \times ISNOW + 0.66 \times IHCPI + 0.0005 \times IRSPR + 0.24 \times INCAR) \times ISRP$	
Postsecondary education	Full-time enrollment in grade 13+(000)(PSS)	0.048
	Percentage of population speaking a minority language as mother tongue (ML)	0.190
	Provincial unemployment rate (UR)	0.018
	Education price index (EPI)	0.717
	Help wanted index (HWI)	0.010
	Foreign postsecondary students (FPS)	0.017
	Total	1.000
	Index = $(0.18 \times IPSS + 0.70 \times IML + 0.08 \times IUR + 0.04 \times IFPS) \times IHWI \times IEPI$	
Elementary and secondary education	Population under 18 (PO17)	0.014
	Population density (PD)	0.017
	Education price index (EPI)	0.969
	Total	1.000
	Index = $(0.02 \times IPD + 0.98 \times IEPI) \times IP017$	
Health	Alcoholism (hospitalizations for alcohol-related cases) (ALCO)	0.123
	Urban population (PU)	0.877
	Total	1.000
	Index = $(0.123 \times IALCO + 0.877 \times IPU)$	
Social services	Single-parent families (SPF)	1.000
Police protection	Criminal code offenses (CCO)	0.390
	Proportion of population in metropolitan areas (PMAR)	0.610
	Total	1.000
	Index = $(0.39 \times ICCO + 0.61 \times IPMAR)$	
General services	Private sector wages (industrial composite) (AMW)	0.7690
	Percentage of population having a minority language as mother tongue (ML)	0.0010
	Population density (PD)	0.0230
	Population (POPF)	0.0390
	Snowfall (annual, in centimeters) (SNOW)	0.1680
	Total	1.0000
	Index = $(0.001 \times ML + 0.175 \times ISNOW + 0.80 \times IAMW + 0.024 \times IPD) \times IPOPF$	

Source: Shah 1994a.
Note: Calculations based on regression coefficients. Variables prefixed by I indicate that a relative index of the variable is used.

value judgments. The relative weights assigned to various need factors and their impact on allocation of grant funds are determined by econometric analysis. Furthermore, this approach yields both the total pool and the allocation of fiscal need equalization grants among recipient units. This method requires specifying determinants for each service category, including relevant fiscal capacity and public service need variables. A properly specified regression equation yields quantitative estimates of the influence each factor has in determining spending levels of a category of public service. This information can be analyzed to determine what each state would actually have spent if it had national average fiscal capacity but actual need factors. This can then be compared with the standard expenditure for each service based on an evaluation of the same equation for determining what each state would have spent if it had had national average fiscal capacity and national average need factors. The sum of differences of these two expressions for all expenditure categories determines whether or not the state had above average (if sum is positive) or below average (if sum is negative) needs (see Shah 1996 for a Canadian application of this approach).

The formula for equalization entitlement based on expenditure classification i for state x could be stated as follows:

$$EE_x^i = (POP)_x \, [(PCSE)_x^i - (PCSE)_{na}^i],$$

where EE_x^i is the equalization entitlement for expenditure classification i for state x, POP_x is the population of state x, $PCSE_x^i$ is the per capita standardized expenditure by state x on expenditure classification i (or the estimated amount the state would have spent to meet actual needs if it had national average fiscal capacity), and $PCSE_{na}^i$ is the national average per capita standardized expenditure for classification i. This is the estimated expenditure for all states, based on national average values of fiscal capacity and need. The equalization entitlement for a particular expenditure classification could be positive, negative, or zero. The total of these entitlements in all expenditure categories is considered for equalization.

A comprehensive system of equalization determines the overall entitlement of a state by considering its separate entitlements from the representative tax system and the representative expenditure system. Only states with positive net entitlements are eligible for transfers of all or some fraction of the total amount, with the fraction determined by the central government based on the availability of funds.

PRACTICAL DIFFICULTIES IN EQUALIZING EXPENDI-
TURE NEEDS: AUSTRALIA'S EXPERIENCE. The Commonwealth Grants Commission of Australia found the theory-based
representative expenditure system approach difficult to implement. It opted
instead for an alternate representative expenditure system using direct
imputation methods that simply equalize what all states on average actually
spend. The Australian system seeks absolute comparability for all 41 state-
local services rather than just merit goods (some would question whether
this is worth pursuing).

Australia's approach raises several questions. Is equal access to all services
in remote areas desirable at any cost? If a rich state decides to buy limousines
for its officials or make higher welfare payments to its aboriginal population,
why should equalization payments to poorer states go up? Such an approach
diverts states' energies to demonstrate that they "need more to do less" or
"money does not buy much" as opposed to "doing more with less," as the
equalization grant formula rewards higher spending and discourages cost-
saving in delivering improved services. Such a system rewards some bad
behaviors, including excessive use of some services by specific groups, tax
expenditures by states to attract capital and labor, and state assumption of
contingent and noncontingent liabilities.

In addition to conceptual difficulties, the Australian program is plagued
with measurement problems. The determinants of expenditure needs for various expenditure categories are arrived at based on broad judgments. Arbitrary
procedures are used to derive factor weights and combine various factors into
functional forms. State disabilities stemming from various factors are multiplied. For highly correlated factors, disabilities are artificially magnified through
double counting and multiplication. The Australian experience highlights the
practical difficulties associated with implementing fiscal need compensation as
part of a comprehensive fiscal equalization approach (see Shah 2004).

CONCLUSIONS REGARDING THE PRACTICE OF FISCAL
NEED EQUALIZATION. Fiscal capacity equalization is relatively
straightforward to comprehend and feasible (with some difficulty) to implement once a (political) decision is made on the standard of equalization. Fiscal
need equalization is a complex and potentially controversial proposition,
because by its very nature it requires making subjective judgments and using
imprecise analytical methods. An analytical approach such as regression
analysis using historical data is inappropriate when underlying structures
are subject to change due to technology and other dynamic considerations.
Great care is needed to specify determinants of each service.

Australia's Commonwealth Grants Commission makes these calculations using broad judgments and sampling services. With the single exception of the Northern Territory, which has a large aboriginal population, there is little cross-state variations in the expenditure needs of the Australian states. A special grant for the Northern Territory would simplify the Australian program while achieving its equalization objectives.

Very few countries opt for a comprehensive program of fiscal equalization. In contrast, a few industrial countries use fiscal capacity equalization programs, both at the federal-state (Canada, Switzerland) and state-local levels (Canada, Denmark, Sweden, Switzerland). Fiscal need compensation is important, but for the sake of simplicity and objectivity, rather than implement a fiscal need equalization approach as part of the fiscal equalization program, it may be better instead to achieve fiscal needs compensation on a service-by-service basis through output-based national minimum standards grants. South Africa does not use output-based transfers, instead compensating for fiscal needs on a service-by-service basis in determining provincial entitlements for general-purpose grants from the central government to the provinces.

Frequently Raised Concerns in Designing Equalization Transfers

Concerns are often raised about defining the equalization standard, determining whether or not to include tax efforts provisions, ensuring stability, and forestalling strategic behaviors to qualify for higher level of transfers. Equalizing net fiscal benefits requires an explicit standard of equalization—the level to which each state is entitled to be raised to provide public sector net benefits per household that are comparable to other states. Simplicity dictates choosing either the mean or the median of the governmental units involved as the standard. The mean provides a good representation of the data as long as outliers are not present. If sample values have a wide range, the median, or the mean after eliminating outliers, provides a better representation of the sample. The mean is preferable to the median, however, for ease of computation.

An ideal fiscal equalization program is self-financing. Member governments are assessed positive and negative entitlements that total zero, with the federal government acting as a conduit (this system is used in Germany). If an interstate equalization pool creates administrative difficulties, the equalization program can be financed out of general federal revenues, as done in Canada, derived in part from the states receiving equalization.

There is general consensus in the academic literature that an equalization system should enable state governments to provide a standard package of public services if the government imposes a standard level of taxes on the bases at its disposal. State governments or their citizens should, however, be permitted to substitute lower rates of taxation for lower levels of services. In such cases, the equalization payments should be in the form of unconditional grants, which have only income effects. Service areas in which there is a good reason to set minimum national standards are better handled by output-based conditional grants and shared-cost programs. By raising a state's fiscal capacity, unconditional equalization grants enable poorer states to participate in shared-cost programs more easily.

Incorporating tax effort into the formula for determining equalization involves making the equalization entitlement a function of the ratio of actual tax collections in a state to the state's base. Potential nonrecipient states may wish to see such a factor incorporated into the program to prevent states with a positive fiscal deficiency in an area from collecting equalization payments even if they may not levy a tax in the area. Potential recipient states may wish to see tax effort incorporated because without it, extra tax effort on their part will be relatively unproductive compared with a wealthy state.

Several problems exist with incorporating tax effort into the program:

- The inclusion of tax effort will cause the program to depart from its unconditional nature. A state should be free to substitute grant funds for revenue from own sources.
- If a state raises taxes to provide a package of services that is more costly than the standard, it should not receive equalization for doing so; other states should not have to pay most of the cost if a state decides to paint its roads.
- Incorporating tax effort ties the federal government to the expenditure philosophies of the various states.
- Some states do not have tax bases in all areas.
- Incorporating tax effort may encourage the employment of strategy by a state.
- In view of the different abilities of the states to export taxes, the measurement of tax effort would be crude.
- Incorporating tax effort could result in an increase in taxes on the poor states.

In view of these considerations, including tax effort would not improve a program of equalization payments.

If equalization payments are based on relative measures of fiscal capacity, they should have a stabilizing effect on state revenues. The level of payments will move in the opposite direction of states' own revenue-raising capacity. Maximum stabilization of state-local revenues will occur when payments are based on all revenue sources, a national average standard of equalization is used, cyclical fluctuations in provincial economies are small, and the time lag in calculating the grants is relatively short. When any large component of the total base, such as natural resource revenues, is volatile, the destabilizing effects can be large. In this case, some sort of averaging formula should be used to ease difficulties associated with provincial budgeting in the face of uncertainty.

Strategy refers to action provincial/state governments can take to influence the level of payments they receive. A program that enables a state to employ strategy is undesirable, because in general the extra payments received may not have any relation to actual disparities. For example, a program employing tax effort could enable states to raise their entitlements by imposing heavy taxes in areas in which they have a tax base below the national average. This problem is less serious in practice than one might expect, since room for additional taxation from sources in which the potential have-not states are not well endowed is extremely limited.

Reflections on Comparative Practices of Fiscal Equalization Transfers

A small but growing number of industrial countries and transition economies have introduced fiscal equalization programs. These include Australia, Canada, China, Denmark, Germany, Indonesia, Latvia, Lithuania, Poland, the Russian Federation, Sweden, Switzerland, and Ukraine. All equalization programs are concerned with interjurisdictional equity or horizontal fiscal equity, not interpersonal (vertical) equity. Which level of government finances and administers an equalization program is determined either by the constitution (as in Canada, Germany, and Switzerland) or by the legislature (as in Australia) (table 1.5).

Paternal programs, in which higher-level governments finance equalization at lower levels are common (examples include Australia and Canada). Fraternal or Robin Hood–type (Robin Hood stole from the rich to give to the poor) programs, in which governments at the same level establish a common pool, to which rich jurisdictions contribute and poor jurisdictions draw, are rare (exceptions include Germany at the *Länder* level and Denmark at the local level). Robin Hood programs are preferred, as they represent an open political compromise balancing the interests of the union and the contributing jurisdictions, as done by the Solidarity Pact II in Germany. Such programs foster national unity, as poorer jurisdictions clearly see the contributions made for their well-being by residents of other jurisdictions. Paternal programs lack the discipline of fraternal programs, because unless enshrined in the constitution (as in Canada), they are guided largely by

TABLE 1.5 Features of Fiscal Equalization Transfers in Selected Countries

Feature	Australia	Canada	Germany	Switzerland
Objective	Build capacity to provide services at same standard with same revenue effort and same operational efficiency	Achieve reasonably comparable levels of public services at reasonably comparable levels of taxation across provinces	Equalize differences in financial capacity of states	Provide minimum acceptable levels of certain public services without much heavier tax burdens in some cantons than others
Legal status	Federal law	Constitution	Constitution	Constitution
Legislation	Federal parliament	Federal parliament	Federal parliament, initiated by the upper house (Bundesrat)	Federal parliament
Paternal or fraternal	Paternal	Paternal	Fraternal	Mixed
Total pool determination	Ad hoc	Formula	Formula	Ad hoc
Equalization standard determines pool and allocation	No	Yes	Yes	No
Allocation	Formula	Formula	Formula	Formula
Fiscal capacity equalization	Yes, representative tax system	Yes, representative tax system	Yes, actual revenues	Yes, major macro tax bases
Fiscal need equalization	Yes	No	No (only population size size and density)	Some
Program complexity	High	Low	Low	Medium
Political consensus	No (but not definite)	Yes (but not definite)	Yes (but not definite)	Yes
Who recommends	Independent agency	Intergovernmental committees	Solidarity Pact II	Federal government
Sunset clause	No	Yes, five years	No	No
Dispute resolution	Supreme Court	Supreme Court	Constitutional Court	Supreme Court

Source: Author.

national politics and the budgetary situation of the federal and state/provincial (for local equalization) governments.

Some countries combine both Robin Hood (fraternal) and paternal components in their grant programs. In Switzerland, effective 2007, the federal government will finance two-thirds of the program, with the remaining third financed by the rich cantons. The program has a fiscal capacity equalization component based on factor income, with 59 percent of the financing from the federal government and 41 percent from rich cantons. The cost equalization component is financed solely by the federal government. The German equalization program has a small supplementary component financed solely by the federal government. In Denmark equalization at the local level uses the Robin Hood approach for both fiscal capacity and fiscal need equalization for counties (using 85 percent of the national average standard) and large cities (90 percent of the national average standard for fiscal capacity and 60 percent of the national average standard for fiscal need); for smaller municipalities, it uses the paternal approach for fiscal capacity equalization (using 50 percent of the national average standard as the standard of equalization) and the Robin Hood approach for fiscal need equalization (using 35 percent of the national average as the standard of equalization).

Fiscal equalization programs also differ in terms of how the total pool of resources devoted to such programs is determined. In the Canadian and German programs, both the total pool and its allocation to provinces/states are formula driven. Under the Australian and Swiss programs, the total pool is arbitrarily determined by the federal government through an act of parliament—total proceeds of the general sales tax in Australia and an arbitrarily determined level of funding from the federal government and rich cantons in Switzerland.

The method of equalization also differs across programs. Australia, Canada, and Germany equalize per capita fiscal capacity using the representative tax system; Switzerland uses macro tax bases. It devotes 19 percent of equalization financing to cost equalization using eight factors: population size, area, population density, population older than 80, number of large cities, number of foreign adults resident for more than 10 years, unemployment, and number of people requesting social assistance from the canton. In Germany actual rather than potential revenues are used in these calculations, as both actual and potential revenues are the same due to the uniformity of state tax bases and tax rates through federal legislation. Germany makes simple expenditure need adjustments based on population size, density, and whether a city is a harbor. China uses potential revenues, although they equal actual revenues when there is uniformity of tax bases and tax rates, as mandated by central government legislation in China. The Canadian program does not include fiscal need compensation. Australia uses a comprehensive equalization program, equalizing fiscal capacity as well as need for all state expenditures. Introduction of expenditure needs compensation introduces complexity and controversy and dilutes political consensus. As a result, the Australian program is the most complex and controversial of all programs and has garnered the least political consensus.

Most equalization programs are introduced as permanent programs; an exception is Canada, where there is a sunset clause for quinquennial review and renewal by the national parliament. Such a clause is helpful in providing a regular periodic evaluation and fine-tuning of the system. Almost all programs in mature federations specify formal mechanisms for resolving disputes regarding the working of these transfer programs.

Overall, the experience of mature federations with fiscal equalization suggests that in the interest of simplicity, transparency, and accountability, it would be better for such programs to focus only on fiscal capacity equalization to an explicit standard that determines the total pool as well as the allocation among recipient units. Fiscal need compensation is best dealt with through specific-purpose transfers for merit goods, as is done in most industrial countries.

Most transition economies have equalization components in their grant programs to subnational governments. China, Latvia, Lithuania, Poland, Romania, the Russian Federation, and Ukraine have adopted transfer formulas that explicitly incorporate concerns about fiscal capacity, expenditure need equalization, or both. For local fiscal equalization, these countries nevertheless use one size fits all approaches to diverse forms of local government, creating equity concerns.

With the exception of Indonesia, developing countries have not implemented programs using explicit equalization standards, although equalization objectives are implicitly attempted in the general revenue-sharing mechanisms used in Argentina, Brazil, Colombia, India, Mexico, Nigeria, Pakistan, and South Africa. These mechanisms typically combine diverse and conflicting objectives into the same formula and fall significantly short on individual objectives. Because the formulas lack explicit equalization standards, they fail to address regional equity objectives satisfactorily. Even in the Indonesian program, the total pool is not determined by an explicit equalization standard. Instead, the equalization standard is implicitly determined by the ad hoc determination of total funds available for equalization purposes.

Setting National Minimum Standards

Setting national minimum standards in regional-local services may be important for two reasons. First, there is an advantage to the nation as a whole from such standards, which contribute to the free flow of goods, services, labor, and capital; reduce wasteful interjurisdictional expenditure competition; and improve the gains from trade from the internal common market. Second, these standards serve national equity objectives. Many public services provided at the subnational level, such as education, health, and social welfare, are redistributive in their intent, providing in-kind redistribution to residents. In a federal system, lower-level provision of such services—while desirable for efficiency, preference matching, and accountability—creates difficulty fulfilling federal equity objectives. Factor mobility and tax competition create strong incentives for lower-level governments to underprovide such services and to restrict access to those most in need, such as the poor and the old. Attempts to exclude those most in need are justified by their greater susceptibility to disease and potentially greater risks for cost curtailment. Such perverse incentives can be alleviated by conditional nonmatching grants, in which the conditions reflect national efficiency and equity concerns and there is a financial penalty associated with failure to comply with any of the conditions. Conditions are thus imposed not on the specific use of grant funds but on attainment of standards in quality, access, and level of services. Such output-based grants do not affect local government incentives for cost efficiency, but they do encourage compliance with nationally specified standards for access and level of services. Properly designed conditional nonmatching output-based transfers can create incentives for innovative and competitive approaches to improved service delivery. Input-based grants fail to create such an accountability environment.

With a few exceptions, noted below, both industrial and developing countries typically do not use output-based transfers for fiscal need compensation in sectoral grants. However, industrial countries typically keep the design of input-based conditional sectoral grants simple, using relatively simple demographic factors. In contrast, developing countries opt for complex formulas, using state of the art quantitative techniques (table 1.6).

A good illustration of a simple but effective output-based grant system is the Canadian Health Transfers program of the federal government. The program has enabled Canadian provinces to ensure universal access to high-quality health care to all residents regardless of their income or place of residence.

TABLE 1.6 Need Factors Used for Grant Financing of Health Care in Selected Countries

Country	Factors
Need-based top-up for health care in general grants	
Belgium	Age, gender, unemployment, disability
Finland (to local governments)	Age, disability, remoteness, local tax base
Germany	Age, gender
Netherlands	Age, gender, urbanization, income base
Switzerland	Age, gender, region, income
Need-based, specific-purpose transfers for core health services	
Denmark	Age, children of single parents
England	Age, gender, mortality, unemployment, elderly living alone
France	Age
Italy (two-thirds)	Age, gender, mortality
Northern Ireland	Age, gender, mortality, low birth weight
Norway (50 percent)	Age, gender, mortality, elderly living alone
Portugal (15 percent)	Burden of illness (diabetes, hypertension, AIDS, tuberculosis)
Scotland	Age, gender, mortality, rural costs
Spain	Cross-boundary flows
Sweden	Age, living alone, employment status, housing
Wales	Age, gender, mortality, rural costs
Health transfers using composite indexes based on principal component analysis	
Brazil	Infant mortality, 1–64 mortality, 65+ mortality, mortality rate by infectious and parasitic diseases, mortality rate for neoplasia, mortality rate for cardiovascular conditions, adolescent mother percentage, illiteracy percentage, percentage of homes without sanitation, percentage of homes without running water, percentage of homes without garbage collection.
South Africa	Percentage female; percentage children under 5; percentage living in rural area; percentage older than 25 without schooling; percentage unemployed; percentage living in traditional dwelling, shack or tent; percentage without piped water in house or on site; percentage without access to refuse disposal; percentage without access to phone; percentage without access to electricity; percentage living in household headed by a woman.

Source: World Bank 2006.

Under this program the federal government provides per capita transfers for health to the provinces, with the rate of growth of the transfers tied to the rate of growth of GDP. No conditions are imposed on spending, but strong conditions are imposed on access to health care. As part of the agreement to receive transfers from the federal government, the provinces undertake to abide by five access-related conditions:

1. *Universality:* All residents enjoy the same coverage.
2. *Portability:* Residents who move to another province retain health coverage in the province of origin for a transition period. Residents and nonresidents have equal access.
3. *Public insurance but public/private provision:* The province agrees to provide universal insurance to all. Both public and private providers are reimbursed from the public insurance system using the same schedule of payments, negotiated by the provincial medical association.
4. *Opting in and opting out:* Providers participating in the system cannot bill patients directly but are reimbursed by the province. All health care providers can opt out of the system, billing patients directly and not following the prescribed fee schedule. Patients of these providers are reimbursed according to a government schedule of payments by submitting claims.
5. *No extra billing:* Charges in excess of the prescribed schedule are not permitted by providers opting in the system.

Breaches in any of these conditions results in penalties. If any of the first four conditions is breached, grant funding can be terminated. If the last condition is breached, grant funds are reduced on a dollar for dollar basis.

Developing countries and transition economies rarely use conditional nonmatching output-based transfers to ensure national minimum standards in merit goods or fiscal need compensation. There are nevertheless a few shining examples of programs that marry equity with performance orientation in grant allocation. These include central government transfers to provincial and local governments for primary education and transportation in Indonesia (discontinued in 2001), per pupil grants to all schools and a 25 percent additional grant as a salary bonus for teachers in the best-performing schools in Chile (Gonzalez 2005), central grants to municipal governments to subsidize water and sewer use by the poor in Chile (Gomez-Lobo 2001), central per capita transfers for education in Colombia and South Africa, and federal per pupil grants to states for secondary education and to municipalities for primary education in Brazil (Gordon and Vegas 2004).

Indonesian education and road maintenance grants to districts before 2001 are examples of good grant design. The operating grant for schools in Indonesia used school-age population (7–12) as the criterion for distributing funds to district and town governments. These operating grants were supplemented by a matching capital grant for school construction (local government matching in the form of land for schools) to achieve minimum standards of access to primary schooling (having a primary school within walking distance of every community). The grants enabled Indonesia to achieve remarkable success in improving literacy and achieving minimum standards of access to primary education across the nation.

Before 2001 the Indonesian District/Town Road Improvement Grant used length of roads, condition, density (traffic use), and unit costs as criteria for distributing funds. This grant program helped monitor the health of the road network on a continuing basis and kept roads in good working conditions in most jurisdictions (Shah 1998).

In Chile and the state of Michigan in the United States, school grants finance vouchers for school-age children, giving parents choice in sending their children to public, private, or parochial schools. Grants to municipal governments in Chile for water and sewer access by the poor cover 25–85 percent (means tested) of a household's water and sewer bill for up to 15 cubic meters a month, with the client paying the rest (Gomez-Lobo 2001).

Brazil has two noteworthy national minimum standards grant programs for primary education and health care. Under the 14th amendment to the federal constitution, state and municipal governments must contribute 15 percent of their two principal revenue sources (state value-added tax and state share of the federal revenue-sharing transfers for states, and municipal services tax and the municipal share of the state revenue-sharing transfers for municipalities) to the special fund for primary education (FUNDEF). If the sum of the state and municipal required contributions divided by the number of primary school students is less than the national standard, the federal government makes up the difference. FUNDEF funds are distributed among state and municipal providers on the basis of school enrollments.

Fiscal transfers in support of Brazil's Unified Health System, which operationalizes the constitutional obligation of the universal right to free health services, are administered under a federal program called Annual Budget Ceilings. The program has two components. Under the first component, equal per capita financing from the federal government that passes through states to municipalities is provided to cover basic health benefits. The second component provides federal financing for hospital and ambulatory care. All registered health care providers—state, municipal, and private—are eligible for grant financing through their municipal government. Under this grant, funding for hospital admissions and high-cost ambulatory care is subject to a ceiling for each type of treatment (World Bank 2001).

Local governments in the Province of Alberta, Canada, use a novel approach to determine the allocation of taxpayers' contribution to school finance. Resident taxpayers designate the education component of their property tax bill to either public or parochial (religious, private) school boards. These declarations determine the total amount of property tax finance available to public and private providers. Schools receive grants on a per pupil basis, and parents retain the option to send their children to a school of their choosing regardless of the designation on their tax return. This approach encourages schools to compete for students and may explain the better performance of government schools in Alberta and several other provinces that use the approach. In the Province of Ontario, higher education financing assigns weights to enrollments in different programs, with medical and engineering education receiving higher weights than the humanities.

In conclusion, while output-based (performance-oriented) grants are best suited to grantor's objectives and are simpler to administer than traditional input-based conditional transfers, they are rarely practiced. The reasons have to do with the incentives faced by politicians and bureaucrats. Such grants empower clients while weakening the sphere for opportunism and pork barrel politics. The incentives they create strengthen the accountability of political and bureaucratic elites to citizens and weaken their ability to peddle influence and build bureaucratic empires. Their focus on value for money exposes corruption, inefficiency, and waste. Not surprisingly, this type of grant is blocked by potential losers.

Compensating for Benefit Spillovers

Compensating for benefit spillovers is the traditional argument for providing matching conditional grants. Regional and local governments will not have the proper incentives to provide the correct levels of services that yield spillover benefits to residents of other jurisdictions. A system of open-ended matching grants based on expenditures giving rise to spillovers will provide the incentive to increase expenditures. Because the extent of the spillover is usually difficult to measure, the matching rate will be somewhat arbitrary.

Although benefit-cost spillover is a serious factor in a number of countries, such transfers have not been implemented in developing countries other than South Africa. South Africa provides a closed-ended matching grant to teaching hospitals based on an estimate of benefit spillovers associated with enrollment of non-local students and use of hospital facilities by nonresidents.

Influencing Local Priorities

In a federation there is always some degree of conflict among priorities established by various levels of government. One way to induce lower-level governments to follow priorities established by the higher-level government is for the higher-level government to use its spending power by providing matching transfers. The higher-level government can provide open-ended matching transfers with a matching rate that varies inversely with the recipient's fiscal capacity. Use of ad hoc grants or open-ended matching transfers is inadvisable. Ad hoc grants are unlikely to result in behavioral responses that are consistent with the grantor's objectives. Open-ended grants may create budgetary difficulties for the grantor.

India, Malaysia, and Pakistan have conditional closed-ended matching programs. Pakistan got into serious difficulty in the late 1990s by offering open-ended matching transfers for provincial tax effort. The central government had to abandon this program midstream, after it proved unable to meet its obligations under the program.

Dealing with Infrastructure Deficiencies and Creating Macroeconomic Stability in Depressed Regions

Fiscal transfers can be used to serve central government objectives in regional stabilization. Capital grants are appropriate for this purpose, provided funds for future upkeep of facilities are available. Capital grants are also justified to deal with infrastructure deficiencies in poorer jurisdictions in order to strengthen the common economic union.

Capital grants are typically determined on a project by project basis. Indonesia took a planning view of such grants in setting a national minimum standard of access to primary school (within walking distance of the community served) for the nation as a whole. The central government provided for school construction, while local governments provided land for the schools.

South Africa has experimented with a formula-based capital grant to deal with infrastructure deficiencies. The Municipal Infrastructure Grant formula includes a vertical and horizontal division. The vertical division allocates resources to sectors or other priority areas; the horizontal division is determined based on a formula that takes account of poverty, backlogs, and municipal powers and functions. The formula includes five components:

1. Basic residential infrastructure, including new infrastructure and rehabilitation of existing infrastructure (75 percent weight). Proportional allocations are made for water supply and sanitation, electricity, roads, and "other" (street lighting and solid waste removal).
2. Public municipal service infrastructure, including construction of new infrastructure and rehabilitation of existing infrastructure (15 percent weight)
3. Social institutions and microenterprises infrastructure (5 percent weight)
4. Nodal municipalities (5 percent weight)
5. Final adjustment: A downward adjustment or top-up is made based on past performance of each municipality relative to grant conditions.

Experience with capital grants shows that they often create facilities that are not maintained by subnational governments, which either remain unconvinced of their utility or lack the means to provide regular upkeep.

Capital grants are pervasive in developing countries and transition economies. Most countries have complex processes for initiating and approving submissions for financing capital projects. These processes are highly susceptible to lobbying, political pressure, and grantsmanship, and they favor projects that give the central government greater visibility. Projects typically lack citizen and stakeholder participation, and they often fail due to lack of local ownership, interest, and oversight. In view of these difficulties, it may be best to limit the use of capital grants by requiring matching funds from recipients (varying inversely with the fiscal capacity of the recipient unit) and by encouraging private sector participation by providing political and policy risk guarantees. To facilitate private sector participation, public managers must exercise due diligence to ensure that the private sector does not take the public sector for a free ride or walk away from the project midstream.

Special Issues in Transfers from State/Province to Local Governments

General-purpose transfers to local governments require special considerations, as local governments vary in population, size, area served, and type of services offered. In view of this, it is advisable to classify local governments by population size, municipality type, and urban/rural character, creating separate formulas for each class of municipality. The higher-level government could adopt a representative tax system–based fiscal capacity equalization system and set minimum standards grants for each class and type of municipality. Where the application of a representative tax system is not feasible due to lack of significant tax decentralization or poor local tax administration, a more pragmatic but less scientific approach to general-purpose grants could be used. Some useful components in these grant formulas are an equal per municipality component, an equal per capita component, a service area component, and a fiscal capacity component. Grant funds should vary directly with the service area and inversely with fiscal capacity (see Shah 1994b on examples of state-local transfers from Australia, Brazil, and Canada). South Africa has applied a variant of this approach to central-local transfers (box 1.3).

Having a formal open, contestable, and deliberative process for municipal incorporation, amalgamation, and annexation should be a prerequisite for introducing an equal per municipality component in grant finance. The lack of such a process can create a perverse incentive for the break-up of existing jurisdictions to qualify for additional assistance, as demonstrated by the experience in Brazil (Shah 1991).

Institutional Arrangements for Fiscal Relations

Who should be responsible for designing the system of federal-state-local fiscal relations? There are various alternatives (see Shah 2005a for an evaluation framework and comparative reflections on alternate institutional arrangements). The most commonly used practice is for the federal/central government to design the system on its own. This option is often chosen on the grounds that the federal/central government is responsible for achieving the national objectives to be delivered through the fiscal arrangements. This is the norm in many countries, where one or more central government agencies assume exclusive responsibility for the design and allocation of fiscal transfers. A potential problem with this approach is the natural tendency of the federal/central government to be overly involved with state decision making and not to allow the full benefits of decentralization to occur. This biases the system toward a centralized outcome, even though the grants are intended to facilitate decentralized decision making. To some extent this problem can be overcome by imposing constitutional restrictions on the ability of the federal government to override state and local decisions. In China central government agencies

BOX 1.3 South Africa's Equitable Share Formula for Central-Local Fiscal Transfers

South Africa uses an equitable share formula to provide transfers from the central government to local governments. The size of the grant is determined as follows:

$$Grant = (BS + D + I - R) \pm C,$$

where BS is the basic services component, D is the development component, I is the institutional support component, R is the revenue-raising capacity correction, and C is a correction and stabilization factor.

Basic Services Component
The purpose of the basic services component is to enable municipalities to provide basic services (water, sanitation, electricity, refuse removal, and other basic services), including free basic services to households earning less than R800 (about $111) a month. (As of April 1, 2006, environmental health care services have been included as a basic service.) Since by its nature environmental health is delivered to everyone in a municipality, this subcomponent is calculated on all households, not only poor ones. For each subsidized basic service, there are two levels of support: a full subsidy for households that actually receive services from the municipality and a partial subsidy for unserviced households, currently set at one-third of the cost of the subsidy to serviced households. This component is calculated as follows:

BS = (water subsidy 1 $\times$ poor with water + water subsidy 2 $\times$ poor without water) + (sanitation subsidy 1 $\times$ poor with sanitation + sanitation subsidy 2 $\times$ poor without sanitation) + (refuse subsidy 1 $\times$ poor with refuse + refuse subsidy 2 $\times$ poor without refuse) + (electricity subsidy 1 $\times$ poor with electricity + electricity subsidy 2 $\times$ poor without electricity) + (environmental health care subsidy $\times$ total number of households).

Institutional Support Component
The institutional support component is particularly important for poor municipalities, which are often unable to raise sufficient revenue to fund the basic costs of administration and governance. Such funding gaps make it impossible for poor municipalities to provide basic services to all residents, clients, and businesses. This component supplements the funding of a municipality for administrative and governance costs. It does not fully fund all administration and governance costs of a municipality, which remain the primary responsibility of each municipality.

The institutional component includes two elements: administrative capacity and local electoral accountability. The grant is determined as follows:

I = base allocation + [admin support $\times$ population] + [council support $\times$ number of seats],

(Box continues on the following page.)

where the values used in the formula are I = R350,000 + [R1 $\times$ population] + [R36,000 $\times$ councillors].

The "base allocation" is the amount that goes to every municipal structure (except for a district management area). The second term of this formula recognizes that costs rise with population. The third term is a contribution to the cost of maintaining councillors for the legislative and oversight role. The number of "seats" that will be recognized for purposes of the formula is determined by the minister for provincial and local government.

The Development Component
The development component was set at zero when the current formula was introduced on April 1, 2005, pending an investigation of how best to capture the factor in the formula.

The Revenue-Raising Capacity Correction
The revenue-raising capacity correction raises additional resources to fund the cost of basic services and administrative infrastructure. The basic approach is to use the relationship between demonstrated revenue-raising capacity by municipalities that report information and objective municipal information from Statistics South Africa to proxy revenue-raising capacity for all municipalities. The revenue that should be available to a municipality is then "corrected" by imposing a "tax" rate of 5 percent. In the case of the Regional Service Councils levy replacement grant, the correction is based on the actual grant to each municipality.

Source: South Africa 2006.

assume sole responsibility without having any legislative checks (Shah and Shen 2006). In India the federal government is solely responsible for Planning Commission transfers and centrally sponsored schemes. These transfers have strong input conditionality with potential to undermine state and local autonomy. The 1988 Brazilian constitution provides strong safeguards against federal intrusion by enshrining the transfers' formula factors in the constitution. These safeguards represent an extreme step, as they undermine the flexibility of fiscal arrangements to respond to changing economic circumstances.

Alternatively, a separate body could be involved in the design and ongoing reform and enforcement of fiscal arrangements. This could be an impartial body or a body made up of both federal and state representatives. It could have true decision-making authority or be purely advisory. Whatever body is responsible, to be effective it needs to be able to coordinate decision making by the two levels of government. Three commonly practiced options are an independent grants commission, an intergovernmental forum, and an intergovernmental cum civil society forum.

Some countries set up a quasi-independent body, such as a grants commission, to design and reform the fiscal system. Such commissions can have a permanent presence, as they do in Australia or South Africa, or they can be brought into existence periodically to make recommendations for the next five years, as they do in India. India has also instituted independent grants commissions at the state level as advisory bodies for state-local fiscal transfers. These commissions have proven ineffective in some countries, largely because many of their recommendations have been ignored by the government and not implemented, as in South Africa. In other cases the government may have accepted and implemented the commission's recommendations but been ineffective in reforming the system due to self-imposed constraints, as in India. In some cases these commissions become too rigorous and academic in their approaches, contributing to the creation of an overly complex system of intergovernmental transfers. This has been the case with the Commonwealth Grants Commission in Australia.

A few countries use intergovernmental forums or executive federalism or federal-provincial committees to negotiate the terms of the system, as Canada and Germany do. In Germany this system is enhanced by having state governments represented in the Bundesrat, the upper house of the parliament. This system allows for explicit political input from the jurisdictions involved and attempts to develop a common consensus. Such forums usually opt for simplicity in design to make the system transparent and politically acceptable.

A variant of this approach is to use an intergovernmental cum legislative cum civil society committee with equal representation from all constituent units, chaired by the federal government to negotiate changes in existing federal-provincial fiscal arrangements. The Finance Commission in Pakistan is an example of this model. The commission is constituted and convened periodically to determine allocations for the next five years. Pakistan also uses province-level finance commissions to design and allocate provincial-local fiscal transfers. This approach has the advantage that all stakeholders—donors, recipients, civil society, and experts—are represented on the commission. Such an approach keeps the system simple and transparent. An important disadvantage of this approach is that due to the unanimity rule, such bodies may be permanently deadlocked, as has recently been witnessed at the federal level in Pakistan.

Lessons from International Practices

Review of international practices yields a set of practices to avoid and a set of practices to emulate. A number of important lessons also emerge (table 1.7).

Negative Lessons: Types of Transfers to Avoid

Policy makers should avoid designing the following types of intergovernmental grants:

1. Grants with vaguely specified objectives.
2. General revenue–sharing programs with multiple factors that work at cross purposes, undermine accountability, and do not advance fiscal efficiency or fiscal equity objectives. Tax decentralization or tax-base sharing offer better alternatives to a general revenue–sharing program, as they enhance accountability while preserving subnational autonomy.
3. Grants to finance subnational deficits, which create incentives for running higher deficits in the future.
4. Unconditional grants that include incentives for fiscal effort. Improving service delivery while lowering tax costs should be public sector objectives.
5. Input- (or process-) based or ad hoc conditional grant programs, which undermine local autonomy, flexibility, fiscal efficiency, and fiscal equity objectives.
6. Capital grants without assurance of funds for future upkeep, which have the potential to create white elephants.
7. Negotiated or discretionary grants in a federal system, which may create dissention and disunity.
8. One size fits all grants to local governments, which create huge inequities.
9. Grants that involve abrupt changes in the total pool and its allocation.

Positive Lessons: Principles to Adopt

Policy makers should strive to respect the following principles in designing and implementing intergovernmental transfers:

1. Keep it simple. In the design of fiscal transfers, rough justice may be better than full justice, if it achieves wider acceptability and sustainability.

TABLE 1.7 Principles and Better Practices in Grant Design

Grant objective	Grant design	Examples of better practices	Examples of practices to avoid
Bridge fiscal gap	Reassignment of responsibilities, tax abatement, tax-base sharing	Tax abatement and tax-base sharing (Canada)	Deficit grants, wage grants (China), tax by tax sharing (China, India)
Reduce regional fiscal disparities	General nonmatching fiscal capacity equalization transfers	Fiscal equalization with explicit standard that determines total pool as well as allocation (Canada, Denmark, and Germany)	General revenue sharing with multiple factors (Brazil and India); fiscal equalization with a fixed pool (Australia, China)
Compensate for benefit spillovers	Open-ended matching transfers with matching rate consistent with spill-out of benefits	Grant for teaching hospitals (South Africa)	Closed-ended matching grants
Set national minimum standards	Conditional nonmatching output-based block transfers with conditions on standards of service and access	Road maintenance and primary education grants (Indonesia before 2000) Education transfers (Brazil, Chile, Colombia) Health transfers (Brazil, Canada)	Conditional transfers with conditions on spending alone (most countries), pork barrel transfers (e.g., United States federal US$200 million transfer to Alaska in 2006 for "a bridge to nowhere"), ad hoc grants
Influence local priorities in areas of high national but low local priority	Conditional capital grants with matching rate that varies inversely with local fiscal capacity	Capital grant for school construction (Indonesia before 2000), highway construction matching grants to states (United States)	Capital grants with no matching and no future upkeep requirements
	Open-ended matching transfers (preferably with matching rate varying inversely with fiscal capacity)	Matching transfers for social assistance (Canada before 2004)	Ad hoc grants
Provide stabilization and overcome infrastructure deficiencies	Capital grants, provided maintenance possible	Capital grants with matching rates that vary inversely with local fiscal capacity	Stabilization grants with no future upkeep requirements

Source: Author.

2. Focus on a single objective in a grant program and make the design consistent with that objective. Setting multiple objectives in a single grant program runs the risk of failing to achieve any of them.

3. Introduce ceilings (linked to macro indicators) and floors to ensure stability and predictability in grant funds.

4. Introduce sunset clauses. It is desirable to have the grant program reviewed periodically—say, every five years—and renewed (if appropriate). In the intervening years, no changes to the program should be made, in order to provide certainty in budgetary programming for all governments.

5. Equalize per capita fiscal capacity to a specified standard in order to achieve fiscal equalization. Such a standard would determine the total pool and allocations among recipient units. Calculations required for fiscal capacity equalization using a representative tax system for major tax bases are doable for most countries. In contrast, expenditure need equalization requires difficult and complex analysis, inviting much controversy and debate; as desirable as it is, it may not therefore be worth doing. In view of this practical difficulty, it would be best to deal with fiscal need equalization through output-based sectoral grants that also enhance results-based accountability. A national consensus on the standard of equalization is critically important for the sustainability of any equalization program. The equalization program must not be looked at in isolation from the broader fiscal system, especially conditional transfers. The equalization program must have a sunset clause and provision for formal review and renewal. For local fiscal equalization, one size does not fit all.

6. In specific-purpose grant programs, impose conditionality on outputs or standards of access and quality of services rather than on inputs and processes. This allows grantors to achieve their objectives without undermining local choices on how best to deliver such services. Most countries need to establish national minimum standards of basic services across the nation in order to strengthen the internal common market and economic union.

7. Recognize population size class, area served, and the urban/rural nature of services in making grants to local governments. Establish separate formula allocations for each type of municipal or local government.

8. Establish hold harmless or grandfathering provisions that ensure that all recipient governments receive at least what they received as general-purpose transfers in the pre-reform period. Over time, as the economy grows, such a provision would not delay the phase-in of the full package of reforms.

9. Make sure that all stakeholders are heard and that an appropriate political compact on equalization principles and the standard of equalization is

struck. Politics must be internalized in these institutional arrangements. Arms-length institutions, such as independent grant commissions, are not helpful, as they do not allow for political input and therefore tend to opt for complex and nontransparent solutions.

Moving from a public sector governance culture of dividing the spoils to an environment that enables responsive, responsible, equitable, and accountable governance is critical. Doing so requires exploring all feasible tax decentralization options, instituting output-based operating and capital fiscal transfers, establishing a formal fiscal equalization program with an explicit standard of equalization, and ensuring responsible access to borrowing.

References

Aubut, Julie, and François Vaillancourt. 2001. "Using GDP in Equalization Calculations: Are There Meaningful Measurement Issues?" Working Paper, Institute of Intergovernmental Relations, Queen's University, Kingston, Ontario, Canada.

Barati, Izabella, and Akos Szalai, 2000. "Fiscal Decentralization in Hungary." Centre for Public Affairs Studies, Budapest University of Economic Sciences.

Boadway, Robin 2002a. "Revisiting Equalization Again: Representative Tax System vs. Macro Approaches." Working Paper, Institute of Intergovernmental Relations, Queen's University, Kingston, Ontario, Canada.

———. 2002b. "The Vertical Fiscal Gap: Conceptions and Misconceptions." Paper presented at the conference "Canadian Fiscal Arrangements: What Works, What Might Work Better," Winnipeg, Manitoba, May 16–17.

———. 2004. "The Theory and Practice of Equalization." *CESifo Economic Studies* 50 (1): 211–54.

Boadway, Robin, and Anwar Shah. Forthcoming. *Fiscal Federalism: Principles and Practices.* New York: Cambridge University Press.

Canada, Government of. 2006. *Achieving a National Purpose: Putting Equalization Back on Track.* Expert Panel Report on Equalization and Territorial Formula Financing, Department of Finance. Ottawa: Government of Canada.

Filimon, R., T. Romer, and H. Rosenthal. 1982. "Asymmetric Information and Agenda Control: The Bases of Monopoly Power and Public Spending." *Journal of Public Economics* 17 (1): 51–70.

Gomez-Lobo, Andres. 2001. "Making Water Affordable." In *Contracting for Public Services,* ed. Penelope Brook and Suzanne Smith, 23–29. Washington, DC: World Bank.

Gonzalez, Pablo. 2005. "The Financing of Education in Chile." Fund for the Study of Public Policies, University of Chile, Santiago.

Gordon, Nora, and Emiliana Vegas. 2004. "Education Finance Equalization, Spending, Teacher Quality and Student Outcomes: The Case of Brazil's FUNDEF." World Bank, Latin America and the Caribbean Region, Human Development Department, Education Sector, Washington, DC.

Gramlich, Edward. 1977. "Intergovernmental Grants: A Review of the Empirical Literature." In *The Political Economy of Fiscal Federalism,* ed. Wallace Oates, 219–39. Lexington, MA: Heath.

Huther, Jeff, Sandra Roberts, and Anwar Shah. 1997. *Public Expenditure Reform under Adjustment Lending: Lessons from World Bank Experiences*. Washington, DC: World Bank.

McMillan, Melville, Anwar Shah, and David Gillen. 1980. "The Impact of Provincial-Municipal Transportation Subsidies." Alberta Transportation, Edmonton, Alberta, Canada.

Oates, W.E. 2005. "Towards a Second Generation Theory of Fiscal Federalism." *International Tax and Public Finance* 12 (4): 349–73.

Oates, Wallace, E. 1999. "An Essay on Fiscal Federalism." *Journal of Economic Literature* 37 (September): 1120–49.

Rosen, Harvey S. 2005. *Public Finance*. 7th ed. Boston: McGraw-Hill/Irwin.

Shah, Anwar. 1985. "Provincial Transportation Grants to Alberta Cities: Structure, Evaluation, and a Proposal for an Alternate Design." In *Quantity and Quality in Economic Research*, ed. Roy Chamberlain Brown, vol. I, 59–108. New York: University Press of America.

———. 1988a. " Capitalization and the Theory of Local Public Finance: An Interpretive Essay." *Journal of Economic Surveys* 2 (3): 209–43.

———. 1988b. "An Empirical Analysis of Public Transit Subsidies in Canada." In *Quantity and Quality in Economic Research*, ed. Roy Chamberlain Brown, vol. II, 15–26. New York: University Press of America.

———. 1989. "A Linear Expenditure System Estimation of Local Response to Provincial Transportation Grants." *Kentucky Journal of Economics and Business* 2 (3): 150–68.

———. 1991. *The New Fiscal Federalism in Brazil*. Washington, DC: World Bank.

———. 1994a. "A Fiscal Need Approach to Equalization Transfers in a Decentralized Federation." World Bank Policy Research Working Paper 1289, Washington, DC.

———. 1994b. *The Reform of Intergovernmental Fiscal Relations in Developing and Emerging Market Economies*. Washington, DC: World Bank.

———. 1996. "A Fiscal Need Approach to Equalization." *Canadian Public Policy* 22 (2): 99–115.

———. 1998. "Indonesia and Pakistan: Fiscal Decentralization—An Elusive Goal?" In *Fiscal Decentralization in Developing Countries,* ed. Richard Bird and François Vaillancourt, 115–51. Cambridge: Cambridge University Press.

———. 2004. "The Australian Horizontal Fiscal Equalization Program in the International Context." PowerPoint presentation at the Heads of the Australian Treasuries (HOTS) Forum, Canberra, September 22, and the Commonwealth Grants Commission, Canberra, September 23.

———. 2005a. "A Framework for Evaluating Alternate Institutional Arrangements for Fiscal Equalization Transfers." World Bank Policy Research Working Paper 3785, Washington, DC.

———. 2005b. "On Getting the Giant to Kneel: Approaches to a Change in the Bureaucratic Culture." In *Fiscal Management*, ed. Anwar Shah, 211–27. Washington, DC: World Bank.

Shah, Anwar, and Chunli Shen. 2006. "Fine-Tuning the Intergovernmental Transfer System to Achieve a Harmonious Society and a Level Playing Field for Regional Development in China." Paper presented at the International Seminar in Public Finance, State Guest House, Beijing, June 26–28.

Shankar, Raja, and Anwar Shah. 2003. "Bridging the Economic Divide within Countries: A Scorecard on the Performance of Regional Policies in Reducing Regional Income Disparities." *World Development* 31 (8): 1421–41.

South Africa, Government of. 2006. *Budget 2006. National Budget Review.* Pretoria: Government Printing Service.

Vaillancourt, François. 1998. "Financing Formulas for Public Primary-Secondary Educations in the United States: Presentation and Evaluation." World Bank, Economic Development Institute, Washington, DC.

World Bank. 2001. *Brazil: Issues in Brazilian Fiscal Federalism.* Report 22523-BR, Brazil Country Management Unit, Washington, DC.

———. 2006. "Capitation Financing Options in the Health Sector: International Experience. Uzbekistan Programmatic Public Expenditure Review." Europe and Central Asia Region, Washington, DC.

PART One

The Principles

2

Grants in a Federal Economy: A Conceptual Perspective

ROBIN BOADWAY

G rants from national to subnational governments are an intrinsic feature of all federations. They also apply between subnational governments and local governments and are important in
unitary nations as well. Their magnitude and particular structural
features differ, however, due partly to country characteristics (history,
culture, politics, geography) and partly to the fact that the practice
of fiscal federalism inevitably involves a compromise between conflicting objectives. At the most general level, the conflict involves the
desire to decentralize fiscal decision making to subnational and
local governments while ensuring that national objectives are met.
Grants can be viewed as instruments for moderating that conflict—
that is, for facilitating the achievement of the advantages of decentralization while minimizing its adverse consequences for national
objectives.

In virtually all federations, fiscal decentralization involves
decentralizing to subnational governments the provision of important public services and some targeted transfers. Accountability
requires that at least some revenues used to finance these decentralized expenditures be raised by subnational governments. Both
expenditure and revenue decentralization can conflict with
national objectives for which the federal government bears special,
though not necessarily sole, responsibility. These objectives include
the standard economic objectives of efficiency and equity as they

apply in a federal context. Both decentralized expenditures and decentralized taxation can lead to violations of the efficiency of the internal economic union by interfering with the efficient allocation of products and factors of production across subnational boundaries. Decentralized decision making can also adversely affect the achievement of national equity objectives—including equality of economic outcomes, equality of opportunity, and economic security, versions of which are often found in a nation's constitution—as some of the most important policy instruments for achieving redistributive equity are precisely those public services and targeted transfers that are assigned to subnational governments.

Intergovernmental transfers serve as a potentially powerful instrument—in some cases, too powerful—for avoiding these adverse consequences. In the process of doing so, however, some of the advantages of decentralization, such as accountability and diversity, may be compromised. Inevitably some judgment is involved as to the most appropriate use of intergovernmental transfers.

The most apparent indicator of differences in the way in which federations resolve this conflict is in differences in the vertical fiscal gap, the excess of federal government revenues over the revenues needed for federal program spending. The amount of decentralization of expenditures is roughly similar across federations. What differs is the extent to which subnational governments are required to finance their spending from own-source revenues rather than transfers from higher levels of government. Differences in the extent of decentralization thus involve primarily revenue decentralization. Highly decentralized federations, such as Canada and Switzerland, have a much smaller vertical fiscal gap than centralized federations, such as Australia and Germany, although the ratios of subnational to total government spending are similar.

Although intergovernmental grants are smaller in decentralized than in centralized federations, the forms of grants used share some common features. Virtually all federations have a system of equalizing transfers in which the size of the transfer is related to some measure of the fiscal capacity of the recipient government (the main exception is the United States). In addition, in most federations, recipient governments must satisfy some condition to be eligible for grants. These conditions—the government's "spending power"—are the means by which the federal government can induce subnational governments to design public programs in ways that help meet national objectives.

Vigorous debates take place in federations regarding the extent and form of transfers. Three main classes of judgments affect one's view on these issues. The first involves one's views about the benevolence of governments—that is, whether one perceives governments as motivated to serve their citizens or as self-serving, interested in the aggrandizement of politicians or the bureaucracy. To the extent that governments are viewed as self-serving, one would emphasize the advantages of decentralization as a means of constraining the ability of decision makers to extract rents for themselves and increasing accountability.

The second judgment is a value judgment concerning the weight given to equity relative to efficiency. The more one emphasizes equity relative to efficiency, the more weight one will likely put on the use of the spending power of the federal government.

The third judgment involves an empirical judgment about how responsive the private sector is to the kinds of policies, especially redistributive ones, undertaken by governments. This is important because both federal and subnational governments are, to a large degree, institutions for redistribution. In most federations, a high proportion of federal government spending consists of transfers, which are explicitly redistributive in nature. Subnational spending is dominated by education, social welfare, and health programs, all of which serve redistributive purposes. Recognition of the fact that both levels of government play a redistributive role is important in discussing the role of transfers. It distinguishes the views set out here from classical views of fiscal federalism, in which the federal government has sole responsibility for redistribution and subnational governments are responsible for providing local public goods. In such a world, the role of transfers is primarily to internalize spillovers that may result from subnational spending; specific matching transfers are the chosen instruments. As the next section shows, this spillover managing role of transfers is of limited relevance in modern federations.

Three Views of the Role of Grants

Three different perspectives on the role of grants in federations can be distinguished. The first views grants as instruments for jointly balancing federal and subnational budgets—that is, closing a given vertical fiscal gap.[1] The second and third make the case for the usefulness of grants in their own right—that is, in determining the vertical fiscal gap. The three views are not mutually exclusive; the complete case for grants contains elements from all three perspectives.

The Passive Role of Grants: Closing the Fiscal Gap

Grants are needed whenever there is a vertical fiscal gap. This is the case regardless of whether there is an independent argument for grants as instruments of policy. According to this view, the case for decentralizing expenditures is stronger than the case for decentralizing revenue raising. Decentralizing expenditure is based on a number of arguments, which apply particularly to regional public goods, public services delivered to people, and targeted transfers. Regional governments are considered better informed about the needs and preferences of their residents than national governments. Decentralization encourages cost-effective delivery through fiscal competition and yardstick competition. It also encourages innovation and experimentation that can result in better ways of delivering services. Decentralization can reduce agency problems in controlling service agencies on the ground and reduce the number of layers of bureaucracy. Residents may also have more voice in the design of regional programs. They also have the option of moving to other regions. These arguments are apparently powerful enough in virtually all federations to result in substantial decentralization of spending to the regional level.

The case for decentralizing revenue raising derives mainly from the desire for regions to bear some responsibility for financing their expenditure from their own sources; decentralizing revenue raising is not efficiency enhancing per se. On the contrary, both centralized tax administration and a uniform national tax system improve efficiency. But, it is argued, regional government accountability is enhanced to the extent that governments are required to raise their own revenues to finance their expenditures programs.

This increase in accountability—and it is by no means clear how large it is—comes at a cost, however. Regional discretion to choose taxes can lead to inefficiency and inequity. Inefficient outcomes may occur because of tax competition or tax exporting, which creates incentives for regions to under- or overspend. Inefficiency can also occur if regional taxes distort cross-border transactions. From the point of view of taxpayers, compliance costs are higher where regions and the federal government have different tax systems. Inequity can occur if fiscal competition leads regions to change the progressivity of their fiscal policies in order to affect the composition of their population. More generally, as shown below, decentralization of revenue-raising responsibilities can cause both inefficiency and inequity, because it leaves different regions with different fiscal capacities for financing their public services.

Tax harmonization schemes can mitigate some of these effects of revenue decentralization. Accountability can be at least partly preserved by ensuring that regional governments have discretion over marginal changes in their revenues, so that they can determine the size of their budgets. Indeed, this may be the most important way of ensuring accountability.

Even where grants are implicitly determined by the difference between the decentralization of expenditure and revenue-raising responsibilities, there is no unambiguous size for the optimal fiscal gap. The most that can be said is that the case for decentralizing expenditures is stronger than the case for decentralizing revenue raising, so some fiscal gap is inevitable.

Active Role I: Equalization

Grants may be useful in their own right in a federation in which fiscal responsibilities have been decentralized to the regions. Decentralization of expenditure and revenue raising inevitably creates different fiscal capacities across regions, making it impossible for them to provide comparable levels of public services at comparable rates of taxation. To provide a given level of public services, different regions require different amounts of spending per capita, for two reasons. First, because the composition of the population differs across regions, the need for public services that are targeted to particular types of people (school-age children, the elderly, the ill, the disabled, the unemployed) differs. Second, the cost of providing a given level of public services differs, because wage costs, transportation costs, population densities, and other factors differ across regions. On the revenue-raising side, different tax bases per capita across regions generally require different tax rates to generate comparable levels of revenue per capita.

As a result of these differences, *net fiscal benefits*—the net benefits from government that accrue to otherwise identical households—differ across regions. A useful comparison can be made between federal systems and a unitary system, in which a common tax system is applied nationwide and comparable levels of public services are provided to comparable people throughout the country. In such a system, all households with the same income and needs do not necessarily have access to identical public services. If it is more costly to provide public services in rural than urban locations, the level of service in rural areas will be lower. However, otherwise identical individuals residing in locations with comparable costs will receive the same level of public services. In the absence of equalizing transfers, fiscal decentralization will make it impossible to replicate this outcome, so net fiscal benefits will systematically differ across regions with different fiscal capacities.

Differences in net fiscal benefits give rise to potential efficiency and equity problems. Inefficiency can arise because the net benefit from migration between two regions includes not only the differences in private earnings but also differences in net fiscal benefits. Thus if identical earnings could be obtained in two regions, households would prefer to reside in the region with the higher net fiscal benefits. To the extent that such fiscally induced migration occurs, there will be an inefficient allocation of labor across regions. If households of a given type choose to stay in their original location despite differences in net fiscal benefits, horizontal inequity will occur, at least from a national perspective; otherwise identical households will be treated differently by government depending on where they reside. Whether this deviation from horizontal equity is considered important involves a value judgment, one that goes to the heart of what it means to be a resident of a nation. To the extent that social citizenship applies nationwide, horizontal inequity across regions may be considered a bad thing. In a unitary nation, such horizontal inequity is automatically avoided, since policies do not discriminate across regions. In contrast, in a decentralized federation, the sense of national solidarity may not be as pronounced, and the primary community within which social citizenship applies may be the region. What follows assumes that residents have a national sense of social citizenship and that horizontal inequities and inefficiencies from fiscally induced migration are undesirable.

Differences in net fiscal benefits can come about not just because of interregional differences in fiscal capacities to provide public services. They can also reflect different regional choices in the mix of public services and taxes—because of regional differences in preferences, for example. Indeed, one of the defining features of federations is the ability of regional governments to make independent fiscal decisions. In this case, even if all regions had the ability to provide comparable levels of public services at comparable levels of taxation, differences in net fiscal benefits would still arise for particular types of residents. This kind of difference was emphasized in the classic Tiebout model, in which people migrated to find a region whose fiscal policies best suited their tastes. This ability of regions to provide different levels of public services can be regarded as a benefit of decentralization, as reflected in the Oates decentralization theorem. Presumably, one would not want to preclude differences in net fiscal benefits that result purely from differences in regional choices. In that sense, horizontal equity in its fullest sense conflicts with the principle of federalism and its emphasis on the benefit of decentralized decision making.

These considerations lead to discussion of the role of transfers. On the one hand, one wants to avoid fiscally induced migration and violations of horizontal equity arising because of differences in fiscal capacity across regions; to the extent that differences in net fiscal benefits contribute to such effects, these differences should be eliminated. On the other hand, one does not want to eliminate differences in net fiscal benefits that reflect differences in regional choices. The compromise found in typical federations is to implement a set of transfers that attempts to equalize the potential for regions to provide comparable levels of public services to its citizens at comparable tax rates, without compelling them to choose the same fiscal policies. In such circumstances, the potential for efficiency in labor allocation and horizontal equity is achieved, although its full realization may not be. If differences in net fiscal benefits are equalized on average across regions, fiscal efficiency and fiscal equity are said to be achieved.

In principle, fiscal efficiency and equity—the potential for all regions to be able to provide comparable levels of public services to their citizens at comparable tax rates—can be achieved by a purely redistributive set of interregional transfers. No vertical fiscal gap is required: payments to below-average regions come from levies imposed on above-average ones. This kind of system is referred to as a *net equalization system*. Such a system may not be feasible (or desirable, if grants are valued on other grounds). The federal government may not be able to "tax" regions of high fiscal capacity in order to finance transfers to the others. Even if this is the case, the objectives of fiscal efficiency and equity can still be achieved by a *gross equalization system*, in which the federal government raises sufficient revenues nationwide to be able to make transfers to all regions that implicitly equalize their potential for providing public services.

Under a gross system of equalization—the system federations commonly use—the total amount of equalization transfers, or the vertical fiscal gap, rises with the extent of decentralization. If the amount of expenditure decentralization is taken as given across federations, the more revenue decentralization there is, the greater the differences in per capita revenue–raising ability across regions and the greater equalization payments must be. If equalization were the sole determinant of the size of federal transfers, the region with the highest fiscal capacity would receive no transfers. Any attempt to increase revenue decentralization would be incompatible with full equalization. The vertical fiscal gap could be higher than that required for equalization purposes to the extent that transfers were seen as fulfilling other functions, such as those described below.

Active Role II: Achieving National Objectives

A system of gross equalization that is just sufficient to satisfy the equalization objective will provide varying amounts of transfers to regions, with the amount of the transfer declining with fiscal capacity, falling to zero for the region with the highest fiscal capacity. For equalization purposes, grants can be completely unconditional. However, for a variety of reasons, related to the effects that decentralized decision making has on national efficiency and equity objectives, the federal government may want to make grants to all regions and to impose conditions on them.

Maintaining National Standards of Public Services

Some of the public services assigned to regions are important for achieving equity objectives. A high proportion of regional expenditures consist of education, health, and welfare programs, all of which are important policy instruments for achieving redistributive equity. To the extent that the federal government has an interest in equity and regards the provision of these public services as contributing to national equity, it might want to ensure that program design satisfies minimal national standards. Given the desirability of allowing regions flexibility and discretion in the delivery of programs, a conflict of objectives exists. Ideally, a balance should be struck between the desire for regional autonomy and the design of public services meeting national standards. One way to achieve that balance is to define national standards in broad terms to include such features as portability of benefits, comprehensiveness of services, and universal coverage.

In principle, national standards could be fostered in a variety of ways, depending on the federation's constitution. The constitution may stipulate that the regions provide public services according to certain standards, with legal sanctions applying in the event of noncompliance. Instead of relying on the courts, federations may prefer legislative remedies. The federal government could mandate that regional governments design their programs with national standards in mind, presumably with funding accompanying the mandates. A more heavy-handed approach would be for the federal government to be able to disallow regional legislation that does not satisfy national standards.

A much more flexible way of proceeding, and one that is commonly used, would be for the federal government to use block conditional transfers to support regional funding of important public services. The conditions on block transfers could be defined in fairly general terms, with the federal government having some discretion in interpreting the conditions. While this method of inducing national standards is flexible and allows broad conditions to be imposed on regional programs, it has several potential pitfalls. There is a danger that the federal government will use its spending power too intrusively, imposing detailed conditions that will reduce the benefits of decentralized decision making. There is also a need for disputes to be settled in a way that is transparent, predictable, and fair. Presumably, the federal government would be the final arbiter, since its spending is at stake, but the process for settling disputes could be set out in a way that encourages cooperation between the federal and regional governments. For the federal government's spending power to be credible, some minimal amount of federal funding must be provided, although it is not possible to specify that amount. That funding should be predicable and transparent, thus presumably formula based.

Even in the absence of specific conditions, the mere existence of grants likely buys the federal government some influence, which it can use to persuade regions to design their programs with national objectives in mind. Moral suasion can be used as a covert way to achieve national standards, provided the level of grants is high enough and relations between the levels of government are amicable. A precondition for the federal government being able to influence regional program design is some minimal level of vertical fiscal gap beyond that required for equalization alone.

Achieving National Vertical Equity

The tax-transfer system is also important for achieving national redistributive objectives. The most important tax for this purpose is the direct personal tax system, including any refundable tax credits that are part of it. The ability to use the direct tax-transfer system as an effective instrument for redistribution requires that the federal government occupy a significant proportion of the direct tax room. Only in that case will it be able to have significant influence over the rate structure. Regions could co-occupy the income tax base, but to the extent that they have discretion, the incentives they face will be to compete down the progressivity of the rate structure. This requirement limits the extent to which revenue raising can be decentralized to the regions. The alternative to decentralizing income tax room is to allow the regions to levy sales taxes, but that is administratively difficult given that the ideal form of sales tax is a value added tax.

Harmonizing Policy

Quite apart from the desire to build some minimum common standards into public service design, it may be useful to harmonize regional fiscal policies in certain areas, in order to avoid unnecessary distortions in cross-border transactions and minimize compliance costs. Policy harmonization can be relevant in three areas. First, harmonization of regional tax systems can be done in a way that does not relieve regions of accountability for choosing how much own-source revenue to raise. For example, tax base harmonization accompanied by a single tax-collecting administration would reduce collection and compliance costs while allowing regions to choose their own tax rates. This would be particularly helpful if the taxes in question were co-occupied by the federal government. Such harmonization would not eliminate the incentive to use tax rates as strategic policy instruments to compete for mobile factors of production or to export tax liabilities, but it would reduce the complexity of the tax system and prevent more-egregious forms of fiscal competition, such as sector-specific tax benefits or subsidies. Tax harmonization arrangements are typically much easier to implement if the federal government plays a leadership role; the federal government is more effective playing such a role if it either occupies a large enough amount of the harmonized tax source or can use its spending power to persuade regions to harmonize their taxes.

Second, expenditures can be harmonized. It may be useful to harmonize education, health, and welfare policies to ensure that households can move from region to region without jeopardizing their benefits from social programs. Inducing mobility rights in regional social programs can be accomplished through spending power.

Third, harmonization of regulations on products and services that are mobile across borders is important to ensuring an efficient internal economic union. This includes harmonization of labor standards, regional procurement policies, environmental standards, product standards, and capital market rules, wherever these fall under the purview of regional jurisdiction.

Preventing Inefficiency in the Internal Economic Union

A concern in most multi-jurisdictional systems of government is ensuring that decentralized decision making does not lead to inefficiencies in the internal economic union. Such inefficiencies can occur when regions adopt fiscal policies that distort cross-border transactions, as a result of fiscal externalities or the discriminatory application of regional policies. Federations attempt to prevent distortions involving cross-border transactions in a variety of ways. In federations with constitutional proscriptions on regional measures that are distorting, the remedy can be judicial or federal disallowance. This remedy can deal only with what might be called negative integration, however—banning measures that distort the internal economic union. Equally relevant are positive measures, such as attempts to promote efficiency by harmonizing policies. These measures can be dealt with on an issue by issue basis, through the harmonization measures discussed above.

In some cases, broad agreements can be reached on internal trade analogous to international free trading and investment agreements. Achieving such agreements typically involves some federal leadership and possibly some requirement for the federal government to act as settler of disputes.

The ability of the federal government to play this role likely requires that the vertical fiscal gap be large enough that the federal government can use the power of moral suasion to induce regions to enter into what otherwise would be voluntary agreements.

Designing the System of Federal-Regional Fiscal Relations

Grants are part of a broader system of intergovernmental fiscal relations, which must be viewed as a whole. The federal system is very much conditioned by the politics, history, and institutions of the federation itself, as well as by rules set out in the constitution.

Constitutional Context

Several elements of constitutions affect the economic organization of the federation, including the respective powers and obligations of federal and regional governments. At the broadest level, constitutions may contain a set of overriding principles and obligations that apply to all levels of government. These can include a set of individual rights, such as freedom of speech, assembly, religion, and so forth, as well as economic and social rights, such as the right to basic necessities and private property rights. They may also include what may be thought of as objectives of distributive equity, such as equality of opportunity and the right to basic social services, such as education and health care. The constitution may state these rights as principles intended to guide government behavior, or it may impose obligations on governments to ensure these rights. Whether or not they can effectively be enforced in court, these rights impose political and moral obligations on government. Taken together, they may be thought of as conditions of social citizenship. They inform not only the design of government social and economic policies but also the manner in which the federal and regional governments interact in a federal system. As shown below, they are important for the design of the intergovernmental grant system as well as for other elements of federal-regional fiscal relations.

Constitutions may also contain broad requirements intended to foster efficiency in federations. These typically involve fostering the principles of an economic union, namely, the free flow of goods, services, labor, and capital across regional boundaries. The principles can be stated in general terms, or there can be specific proscriptions against measures that interfere with interregional transactions or discriminate in favor of a region's own residents. Regional governments may even be precluded from imposing taxes on nonresidents. These restrictions on regional policy are sometimes referred to as *measures of negative integration.*

The constitution can also encourage positive integration, in the form of harmonizing policies in order to reduce the costs of cross-border transactions. Typically, regions cannot be forced to undertake such policies, but the constitution may enable the federal government to institute incentives for regions to harmonize. The manner in which efficiency in the internal economic union is fostered and enforced and disputes are resolved—whether by the courts or by the federal government—varies from federation to federation.

While general constitutional principles set out broad principles that guide federal and regional policies, the division of powers of each level determines their detailed legislative responsibilities. This is the assignment issue of fiscal federalism. Legislative powers are necessarily assigned by function (defense, education, criminal justice) rather than by objective (redistribution, stabilization, allocation), as the classical literature emphasized. This is crucial, because a key feature of the division of powers is the fact that some of the responsibilities assigned to the regions are those that are important for achieving national objectives, such as redistributive equity or efficiency in the internal economic union. This implies that the federal government has some interest in the manner in which the regions exercise their legislative responsibilities, which has inevitable consequences for federal-regional fiscal relations.

The assignment of functions to the two levels of government can take several forms. Some functions may be assigned exclusively to one level. Others, such as taxation, may be shared, in the sense that both levels legislate on the function. Where functions are shared, one level may be paramount, in the sense that its legislation overrides that of the other. It may also be possible for one government to delegate its responsibility to the other. The assignment of responsibilities, or their delegation, may be asymmetric, in the sense that responsibilities of different regional governments may differ. The constitution must define which government is responsible for areas that have not been specifically assigned (residual power). It may also define public property rights, including ownership of public lands and natural resources (often a highly contentious and consequential area), the ability to borrow, and rules of public accountability. There may also be a catch-all function that gives governments broad responsibilities for acting in the interest of their residents.

The division of responsibilities is detailed and complex, but it is also flexible and open to interpretation. Naturally, the courts play an important role in adjudicating disputes over the legislative rights of both levels of government. Moreover, since the legislative responsibilities of regional governments typically have some consequences for national policy objectives, the federal government typically has an interest in influencing the policies and programs regions choose.

A variety of instruments is available for the federal government to exercise such oversight or influence. The courts can declare that regional government legislation is *ultra vires* (beyond powers). The federal government may disallow regional legislation, perhaps on very broad grounds. This is a fairly blunt instrument, which can have a significant impact on the types of policies implemented by the regions.

Perhaps as strong is the ability of the federal government to impose mandates on the regions, with or without funding, requiring them to legislate on items that the federal government deems of national interest. Not all federations allow the federal government such powers. In some, the federal government relies mainly on the power of the purse—its spending power—to provide incentives for regions to choose their policies in ways that conform to federally imposed standards. Spending power is a more flexible instrument than disallowance or mandates, and the conditions imposed can be fairly general. This is both a strength and a weakness: flexible federal conditions can be used to achieve national objectives in a way that allows for regional independence, but conditions can also be overly intrusive.

The power of the purse can also be used in more subtle ways, by reinforcing the use of moral suasion by the federal government, for example. Given that federal and regional governments are in close contact, moral suasion is a potentially important but often overlooked vehicle with which the federal government can influence regional policies. Among other things, it can be used as an argument for a vertical fiscal gap by those who emphasize the role of the federal government in achieving national objectives. Of course, explicit federal-regional agreements are also possible and have been used in most federations. Their success requires some means of dispute settlement and enforcement.

In the end, constitutions are quite flexible and allow for varying degrees of decentralization. Countries exhibit different degrees of fiscal decentralization, and fiscal decentralization in a given country can evolve significantly over time. Whatever the degree of decentralization, virtually all federations have a vertical fiscal gap that is filled by federal-regional transfers. They also have other elements of fiscal relations, such as formal harmonization measures.

Intergovernmental Fiscal Relations

Fiscal arrangements across jurisdictions at various levels can include several elements: interjurisdictional transfers (unconditional and conditional), tax harmonization measures, cooperative agreements among governments, and measures, such as mandates or directives, through which the higher-level government induces lower-level governments to incorporate elements of national importance into the design of their programs. The purpose of these elements is to facilitate effective decentralization by offsetting the inefficiencies and inequities outlined above that would otherwise occur.

Federal-Regional Equalization Grants

Virtually all federations have a vertical fiscal gap that is filled by the system of grants. Federal grants serve several purposes. They equalize the fiscal capacities of regional governments to provide comparable levels of public services, provide an incentive for them to design their programs in a way that reflects national norms of efficiency and equity, and encourage them to harmonize their policies.

Federal grants share some common features. The standard principle guiding the design of equalization grants is that all regions should have the potential to provide roughly comparable levels of public services at comparable tax rates. Providing comparable levels of service diminishes sizable differences in net fiscal benefits across regions, which in turn reduces fiscal inefficiency (fiscally induced migration) and fiscal inequity (unequal treatment of equals across regions). This principle can be only a rough guide, however, for a number of reasons. First, since regions adopt different fiscal policies, the interpretation of comparable public services and comparable tax rates is necessarily ambiguous. Second, if fiscal capacity differences are great, there may be limited consensus for full fiscal equity as an objective of national policy. That is, differences in the levels of public services across regions may be tolerated in diverse federations. Third, the institution of an effective equalization system will be constrained by measurement problems as well as adverse incentives that may result from equalization itself.

These principles can be put into practice in various ways, depending on the extent of decentralization, the statistical sophistication of the government, and the tolerance of voters. In practice, three kinds of elements may be included in the determination of equalization entitlements of regions. The first is the revenue-raising capacity of regional governments, an important element in federations that are fairly decentralized.

A standard approach to revenue equalization is the *representative tax system*, under which equalization entitlements of regions are based on the ability of a region to raise revenues using a standard regional tax system. For the case of revenue source i, the per capita equalization entitlement of region j, denoted, E_i^j, under full representative tax system treatment is

$$E_i^j = \bar{t}_i\left(\bar{B}_i - B_i^j\right),$$
(2.1)

where $\bar{t}_i$ is a standard tax rate for revenue source i (possibly the average rate used by the regions), B_i^j is region j's per capita tax base for revenue source i, and $\bar{B}_i$ is a standard per capita tax base for equalization purposes (possibly the national average per capita tax base). Per capita entitlements are calculated for each region and for each revenue source and aggregated to give total per capita equalization entitlements for all regions. Some of these are positive and some negative.

Under a full equalization system, national average tax rates and bases would be used, and full equalization entitlements, negative or positive, would be paid to all regions. In this case, aggregate entitlements would be zero, and the system would be a net equalization system.

In practice, it is difficult to extract negative equalization entitlements from regions with above-average revenue-raising capacity, so negative entitlements are enacted only if the vertical gap is large enough that negative entitlements can reduce grants that would otherwise have been received. Full equalization can be achieved by a system of equal per capita grants that are then revised by each region's equalization entitlements. To avoid negative payments, the size of the per capita grant must be at least as large as the largest negative entitlement.

Even where a representative tax system is used, it may not be fully applied. There may not be political consensus for full equalization if disparities are large. There may be incentive problems with some tax bases. Where regions can alter their policies to change the size of their tax bases, they will have an incentive to do so. Regions with natural resources, for example, may be reluctant to exploit them if doing so means sacrificing equalization grants. In addition, there may be measurement or conceptual problems with equalizing some revenue sources, such as user fees or property taxes. In these cases, partial equalization may be used.

Differences in revenue-raising capacity are not the only reasons why regional governments are unable to provide comparable levels of public services. Regions may also face differences in needs and costs of providing public services. Differences in needs arise because many public services are targeted at particular groups: health care for the ill, social welfare for the unemployed, education for the young, and disability benefits for the disabled. In a unitary nation, common levels of these services would be provided to people in similar circumstances in all regions. The problem is that the relative size of groups in need of these services differs across regions.

In principle, needs can be equalized using a representative expenditures approach. The per capita spending required to provide a standard set of services could be compared across regions and differences equalized. This approach would be consistent with achieving fiscal equity and fiscal efficiency across the federation, assuming that is an accepted objective. The issue of equalizing on a net versus gross basis would have to be confronted, just as it is with revenue-raising capacities. However, two factors make needs equalization potentially more complicated than revenue equalization. The first is that the concept of comparable levels of public services is inherently more complicated than comparable levels of revenue, because public services can vary in quality and complexity. Thus any attempt to establish a standard for needs with which to determine equalization entitlements is bound to be contentious.

The second complicating factor is that expenditures required to provide a common set of services can differ not just because of needs but also because of cost differences in different locations. Wages, property costs, and transportation costs may differ, because of different population densities and other factors. Even if differences in costs could be accurately measured, there is a conceptual problem in equalizing them, as even in unitary systems, the same level of public services is not provided throughout the country. Rural and urban areas have different levels of health care and roads because it costs more to provide such services in rural areas. Equalization systems typically do not try to fully equalize differences in costs. One way of dealing with the problem is to take as given differences in levels of public services in different geographic locations and to equalize the costs of providing those services for like areas across regions. This is the approach taken in Australia, where arguably the most comprehensive system of expenditure equalization exists. Public services are effectively disaggregated not just by type but also by geographic characteristics, and expenditure equalization is applied within all such categories.

Given these complications, the question may well be asked whether equalizing for differences in needs is worthwhile. It can be argued that the dispersion in needs across regions is much smaller than the dispersion of revenue-raising capacity, at least in federations in which revenue raising is highly decentralized. A country like Canada, which has a sophisticated system of revenue equalization, does not equalize expenditures at all. Indeed, even revenue equalization can be complicated. One option for avoiding complicated systems of revenue or needs equalization is to use a so-called macro formula, in which entitlements are based on some very rough indicator of fiscal capacity, such as per capita regional income or disposable income. Such measures are imperfect, because they are unlikely to reflect differences in the ability of regions to raise revenues, let alone their needs for them. Where national statistical systems are not reliable, however, federations may have to resort to such indicators.

A few other features of equalization grants should be noted. In principle, equation (2.1) could be used to determine the aggregate size of the equalization grant envelope. Federal governments may wish to control the total size of their grants to regions, however, in order to ensure some predictability in their own budget, for example. It is possible to adopt equation (2.1) to allow for a given total amount of equalization. One common way to do so is to adjust the grant going to each region in equal per capita amounts. This leaves absolute differences in equalization unchanged, so that the principles of fiscal equity and efficiency are maintained, at least for regions receiving equalization grants. (For federations that use gross systems, only recipient regions are affected by equal per capita changes in entitlements, so that fiscal inequity is not achieved between recipient and nonrecipient regions.) Where the equalization envelope is determined exogenously, it can be set in various ways. The federal government could do so with discretion annually or periodically. Alternatively, a formula, such as a fixed share of federal revenues, could be used to set the total amount of equalization. One potentially adverse consequence of such schemes is that they introduce uncertainty for regional budgets.

In addition to correcting for differences in fiscal capacity among regions, equalization serves an insurance function. In equation (2.1), changes in a region's revenues resulting from fluctuations in tax bases are automatically offset by equalization entitlements. To the extent that regions are unable to self-insure, this may be regarded as a useful role for equalization. However, the same equalization formula can be a source of instability. Fluctuations in the standard tax bases $\bar{B}_i$ can make equalization payments more volatile and compromise the insurance function. One way to guard against this is to use a multiyear moving average to determine standard tax bases.

Since the function of equalization payments is primarily to correct for differences in regional fiscal capacity that arise from decentralization, grants can be unconditional and determined by a formula such as equation (2.1). However, as noted earlier, grants serve two other main functions. They close the fiscal gap, so that differences in revenue-raising and expenditure responsibilities are reconciled. This function can be served while retaining the equalization function by adjusting grants by equal per capita amounts as appropriate. Of course, the ideal level of grants for this purpose is inherently ambiguous. Indeed, the optimal vertical gap is itself ill defined. In addition, since both levels of government have discretion over their spending and revenue raising, the vertical fiscal gap is a moving target. A fruitful way to look at the vertical gap is as an endogenous amount determined by the joint fiscal decisions of the federal and regional governments. To the extent that the federal government is a first mover, it determines the size of the vertical gap.[2]

Federal-Regional Conditional Grants

The choice of the vertical fiscal gap, assuming the federal government has some discretion over it, typically involves the third function of grants, which is to enable the federal government to influence the fiscal programs of regional governments. Regional tax and expenditure programs have consequences for national efficiency and equity. Regional tax policies as well as public services can distort the cross-border movements of goods and services, capital and labor. This can occur deliberately, as a result of beggar-thy-neighbor policies by regional governments, or it can occur simply because regional programs are not harmonized. Similarly, regional governments may design their programs in ways that create different standards of redistributive equity or that do not meet national objectives of equality of opportunity or social insurance. Of course, some tolerance of differences in regional preferences and needs for equity is part of the fabric of federalism. Nonetheless, there may be some consensus or constitutional requirement for broad national standards that still leave room for regional discretion.

One way that the federal government is able to encourage the regions to take these consequences into account is by using its spending power. This involves setting conditions on grants. The federal government's spending power can be used for two broad purposes, negative and positive integration. Conditions on grants may be used to prevent regions from engaging in policies that reduce the efficiency of the internal economic union or impinge on achievement of the national objective of equity. For example, grants may be contingent on regional programs being nondiscriminatory and applying to new migrants as well as long-time residents. For this purpose, fairly general conditions can be put on grants that are otherwise block grants. Failure to abide by the conditions can lead to withholding of a portion of the grants.

Grants can also be used to induce regions to introduce particular types of policies, such as health or welfare programs. In this case, grants can be more specific and include a financial inducement, such as a matching component.

Discussing the design of conditional grants, either block or specific, is beyond the scope of this chapter. A few general remarks can nonetheless be made. First, to be effective, especially in the case of block grants, the contribution of grants to regional expenditure programs to which the conditions are applied should be at least some minimal amount. Without such a minimum, the federal government will not have the political or moral authority to enforce the conditions. Of course, what constitutes the minimal required size of block grants is not well defined.

Second, there must be a transparent method of resolving disputes. Disputes will inevitably arise when the conditions on grants are of a general nature, which they must be when objectives of a general nature are at stake.

Third, there is a very fine line between federal government oversight and encouragement and regional accountability for regional programs. If the federal government is too intrusive and the regions too reliant on federal grants, regional accountability for designing and managing their own programs will suffer. The benefits of decentralization will be lost if regions lose the incentive to innovate and compete with other regions. Striking the right balance between federal oversight and regional discretion is perhaps the most difficult task arising from decentralization. Too often the tendency is for the federal government to be overly intrusive.

Fourth, a very important dimension of the federal granting and taxing power is its potential for subtly influencing regional policy choices. In contrast to the noncooperative modeling approach often adopted in the fiscal federalism literature, federal and regional governments within federations are in constant contact and negotiation. For better or worse, it is likely that a federal government that provides significant financial support to the regions will also have implicit leverage over the region's behavior, whether through moral suasion or outright jawboning. A potentially valuable outcome of this influence is that it can lead to policy harmonization by regional governments. It seems incontrovertible that tax harmonization across regions is more likely to occur and to be effective the larger the share of a given tax base is occupied by the federal government. This can be an important consideration in determining the extent and type of tax decentralization in a federation. Similarly, the larger the grants from the federal to the regional governments, the more likely is harmonization of regional expenditure programs, even in the absence of explicit conditions. More generally, the viability of federal-regional agreements in areas of overlapping interest is likely to be greatly enhanced by the federal power of the purse. But, as with everything else in a federal setting, a modicum of goodwill across levels of government must exist, and there must be some consensus about the importance of national equity and efficiency objectives.

Notes

1. To simplify the discussion, in what follows, only two levels of government—a federal one and a regional one—are assumed to exist.
2. It is not obvious that the federal government is always the first mover. Indeed, the so-called soft budget constraint problem arises precisely because the federal government cannot commit to a given level of grants but reacts in part to regional fiscal choices.

3

Equity and Efficiency Aspects of Interagency Transfers in a Multigovernment Framework

PAUL BERND SPAHN

W here public functions are shared across levels of government or among agencies at any one level of government, resources must be allocated to each authority in line with its assigned expenditure responsibilities. This is typically done through intergovernmental (or interagency) transfers. Such transfers usually seek to correct vertical and fiscal imbalances resulting from the assignment of own revenue and required outlays. The emphasis is thus on rebalancing and redistributing resources among government entities.

Where such rebalancing is done on the basis of formulas, it may create positive or negative incentive effects. For instance, a gap-filling transfer is likely to produce moral hazard and a waste of resources, which creates an incentive to relax fiscal discipline. Elements in the formula are often meant to induce positive incentive effects. Part of the transfer, for example, may be tied to the own-revenue raising ability of recipient authorities or linked to performance criteria for service delivery. Such linkages are expected to enhance efficiency, but it is often difficult to establish and monitor appropriate criteria, rendering the approach tentative and uncertain. Moreover, recipient agents may be able to manipulate the criteria to maximize grants while failing to achieve the desired objectives.

Purely redistributive transfers are best effected on the basis of standardized criteria that are not controllable by the grantee. This eliminates policy incentives, but it guarantees the neutrality of the grants system and avoids perverse incentive effects. Moreover, use of the transfers under such a system is unconditional. The fact that transfers are unconditional also underscores the autonomy of lower-tier governments to set their own spending priorities. In order to achieve neutrality—that is, the lack of interference with the behavior of the recipient government or public agency— the emphasis is on the pure income effect of the grant.

Intergovernmental and interagency transfers that affect the behavior of the recipient can also be justified. Such grants are typically linked to vertical and horizontal externalities or spillovers among different agencies. To internalize such spillovers, transfers are tailored so that they change relative prices (through cost sharing, for example). In addition to an income effect, such transfers produce a price or substitution effect.

This chapter argues that equalization transfers should be separated from transfers intended to affect policies of recipient public agencies. While this idea is often recognized in principle, it is almost never adhered to in practice. The grantor may attach conditions to the transfer, or the formula for grant allocation may include criteria that seek to influence the behavior of the grantee. Redistributive and allocation aspects of grants are combined, blurring equity and efficiency issues and sometimes producing perverse results.

The chapter also explores the relationship between redistributive and efficiency-enhancing aspects within a multigovernment framework. It is organized as follows: After making the case for interjurisdictional equity, the chapter discusses the design of equalization schemes. It then makes the case for intragovernmental efficiency and discusses the design of interagency relations and microtransfers. The last section summarizes the chapter's main conclusions.

The Case for Interjurisdictional Equity

One could argue that solidarity among regional governments is essential to establish social cohesion and assert the nation-state: the weaker social cohesion is, the greater the need for solidarity and equalization of transfers. Empirical evidence does not support this relationship, however. Germany, for example, has achieved a high degree of national homogeneity, but it uses an equalization system that could be considered excessive. Bosnia and Herzegovina has a long way to go to achieve national unity and social harmony, but it does not even address interregional equalization.[1]

Most federal countries use equalization schemes. But the case for interjurisdictional equity is shaky, based on value judgments about interregional fairness, solidarity, and national cohesion. Fairness and solidarity rarely go beyond satisficing existing political claims. Yet fairness and solidarity often fall short of satisficing, because majority regions or groups are not prepared to pay a price for pacifying minorities. Not paying this price could create political uproar and secessionist tendencies, which are often suppressed by military threat and intervention. This might be considered the cheaper option in the short run (although this is highly doubtful, as it ignores potential static and dynamic efficiency gains), but the policy is certainly painful and costly, and it is economically unsustainable over the longer term.

Australia's equalization scheme was introduced under the threat of Western Australia breaking away from the Commonwealth. Brazil's was shaped by mutual suspicion after decades of centralist military rule. Nigeria's tax-sharing system emerged as regional conflicts over oil loomed. The European Union's cohesion fund was created to facilitate the entry of less affluent southern countries. As a rule, equalization grants are minimal where interregional conflicts are contained (Switzerland, the United States) and tend to increase with widening regional tensions (Belgium). (Germany is an exception in this context.) Moreover, the smaller the region and the greater its nuisance potential, the greater its chance of receiving equalization payments. This is true not only for federations, where it could lead to asymmetric governance structures if nuisance potentials are unequally distributed (Canada, Spain) but also for international flows of official aid (Kosovo, the Palestinian Authority).

In addition to political expediency, equalization payments may also derive from constitutional principles and their rigid interpretation by the courts. The German equalization system was developed under a constitutional "uniformity of living conditions" clause. That clause has resulted in roughly equal per capita entitlement of public resources across the states. In addition, the federal government provides funds to states for specific purposes. Most, but not all, of these funds go to states in the former German Democratic Republic. The rigid interpretation of the constitution has led to "overequalization," a situation in which poorer states ex ante end up richer ex post than more affluent ones. But even the German scheme contains elements of political expediency, as the former German Democratic Republic has significant ability to mobilize decisive voters in elections to the federal parliament.

The political nature of equalization grants can be concealed in two ways. The system can remain opaque, with a number of negotiated hidden transfers that "bribe" political complacency, or the system can be enshrined in constitutional or legal codes that are branded in ethical terms propped up by politicians in populist oratory. But once equalization is codified in a transparent mode, objective criteria and solid statistical information determine intergovernmental transfers. Rendering equalization a technical issue by codifying it camouflages the political motivation behind it.

Designing Equalization Schemes

Codification of equalization schemes is essential for establishing arrangements that foster the stability and sustainability of public budgets within a multigovernment framework. Codification also enhances the transparency of budgetary relations and facilitates budget preparation and execution.

Most equalization schemes have evolved in response to ad hoc political necessities and claims. Once entrenched, the rules tend to be stubbornly defended, chiefly by governments that would lose out under a new scheme. The ad hoc nature of shocks to a transfer scheme, indifference by donor governments, and the militancy of beneficiaries render major revision of transfer arrangements almost impossible. An attempt is nevertheless made here to derive some principles that could guide the setting up of an equalization scheme if it were designed from scratch.

Two types of equalization schemes can be distinguished, interregional and interpersonal. A large body of literature exists on interregional equalization. Less attention has been given to interpersonal equalization.

Interregional Equalization within the Public Sector

Four approaches to interregional equalization—the generalized approach, the asymmetric approach, the eligibility approach, and the specific approach—are used, usually in combination. Under the generalized approach, all entities of a federation are treated identically. Often the constitution bans discrimination of individual entities in the federation (although discrimination might be implicit through the selection of distribution criteria). Examples of generalized equalization schemes are the Australian general-revenue grants, the *Fondos de Compensação* in Brazil, and the German *Finanzausgleich*. There is usually a single equalization fund and a single distribution formula for allocating funds among beneficiaries based on a uniform set of criteria. Other schemes may exist side by side with general equalization.

The asymmetric approach can take various forms, but it presumes that the entities of the federation possess different constitutional rights or status. This approach transfers funds from national to regional budgets by discrimination. Most subnational entities operate under the generalized scheme. Special arrangements can also exist between the national government and a small number of subnational governments. In Canada the more prosperous provinces neither contribute to nor benefit from the national equalization scheme. In Spain two prosperous regions possess full fiscal autonomy but are asked to make financial contributions in support of national policies.

Asymmetric equalization arrangements are often justified on economic grounds. For instance, a region may lack basic infrastructure, face specific costs, or have a reduced public revenue potential relative to the national average. These disadvantages are compensated for through asymmetrical grants. Intermunicipal equalization arrangements usually distinguish between metropolitan areas, urban areas (cities and townships), counties, villages, and rural areas. Some countries (Denmark, Sweden) attempt to cope with structural differences across municipalities using a common "umbrella" scheme (that is, by using common criteria for allocating grants irrespective of their character). Others (some German states) set up specialized funds for different categories of municipalities. Capital cities usually play a special role within municipal financing. In all these instances, asymmetries exist in intergovernmental financial relations.

The eligibility approach does not make an explicit attempt to equalize, although it does so implicitly. Under this approach, eligible regional governments and public agencies can apply to various centralized programs and funding schemes. The qualifying parameters and take-up rates determine the regional incidence of these grants. An example of this approach is the wide range of categorical grants offered by the federal government in the United States. Although such schemes may be geared toward fostering economically backward areas, their focus is predominantly on incentives and outputs rather than on redistribution across regions.

The specific approach is found in many countries, mainly with unitary governments, that pursue regional policy objectives (Chile, China, Peru). But it is also found in some federal countries with economically weak regions (Brazil, the Russian Federation). This approach is based on compensatory payments from the central government's budget; it is intimately linked to regional policy. Certain regions are declared economically weak on the basis of criteria such as unemployment, average income, or economic resources. This entitles them to benefit from a regional development program, as defined by the central government. The aim is to bring below-average regions up to national standards in order to mitigate internal migration and foster national cohesion. Australia started its equalization program with special grants directed to states whose delivery of regional public services was below standard. However, in the 1980s it introduced a comprehensive generalized system.

Interregional or interjurisdictional equalization puts the emphasis on the public sector only. An explicit formulation of equalization objectives is found in the terms of reference of the Australian Commonwealth Grants Commission (2005, p. 4): "State governments should receive funding . . . such that, if each made the same effort to raise revenue from its own sources and operated at the same level of efficiency, each would have the capacity to provide services at the same standard."

Germany's constitutional mandate for "uniformity of living conditions" across states is less precise, but it also emphasizes the provision of standard public services. In practice, however, it focuses on the ability to provide such services, for which per capita fiscal capacities act as a proxy.

Regional policy might also employ interregional equalization instruments that target delivery of public services, but its arsenal of policy instruments is much wider, addressing inadequacies of public and private infrastructure, deficiencies of private production, and general conditions of private life. Chile uses an array of regional policy instruments, which can be classified based on whether they are directed toward public agencies or private agents (table 3.1). This classification is more general, however, stretching well beyond the Chilean case.

Many of the instruments directed toward the private sector must be interpreted as regionalized government spending (tax expenditures). Such policy instruments exhibit many weaknesses, political and economic. They

TABLE 3.1 Interregional Equalization Instruments

Instruments directed toward public agencies	Instruments directed toward private agents
Wage bonuses for civil servants	Free trade zones and "light" regulation
Regional funds for public infrastructure	Exemptions from customs duties, indirect taxes
Municipal development funds	Exemptions from business income tax
Deconcentration of central public administration	
Regional focus of military spending	Exemptions from local real estate tax
	Wage subsidies
	Investment tax credit
	Investment funds and subsidies

Source: Author compilation.

are often ill defined, opaque, and unquantifiable; they escape budgetary control; they create loopholes through tax arbitrage; they bypass regional authorities, which could produce waste and overlaps; they provoke ruinous tax competition among lower-tier governments; they create significant inefficiencies for the economy as a whole; and they often fail to meet their objectives. Above all, the specific approach to equalization, including regional policy, is static in nature if the criteria for identifying deprived regions remain unchanged. It keeps regions in a "poverty trap," because "graduating" from underdevelopment is penalized by a loss of specific support.

A consistent and results-oriented regional policy needs performance indicators and benchmarks against which the success of regional policies can be measured. Such a policy would allow subsidized regions to become self-sufficient and self-sustained. Performance indicators should focus on reducing poverty and promoting growth and exports.

An antipoverty-focused regional policy must aim at helping poor regions and their residents move out of poverty. Subsidizing local consumption does not achieve this goal; instead, it creates economic and social dependencies, fosters rent-seeking behavior, discourages entrepreneurial behavior and risk taking, and keeps the local economy caught in a poverty trap forever.

Moving a region out of a poverty trap requires substantial public investments in local infrastructure and service delivery. It may also require the involvement of local citizens and interested groups to direct these resources toward their most effective use. This argues for channeling public resources through regional budgets rather than distributing them from the central budget. A prerequisite, however, is that regional authorities are capable of administering such policies. They must either act as accountable agents of the central government, which requires the implementation of appropriate principal-agent mechanisms, or, better, be democratically controlled by benefiting taxpayers/voters.

Several positive features of the European Union's regional policy are noteworthy:

■ Regions are formed on the basis of criteria that reflect the specifics of the regional economy. They are typically larger than municipalities and smaller than regional governments or provinces. They do not, therefore, correspond to the political turf of local officials and representatives.
■ Regions are classified according to an objective criterion of necessity (75 percent of average per capita income). Only regions that fall below this threshold qualify for support. This is a dynamic rather than a static

concept, because "poor" regions are allowed to mature over time, while new regions may qualify for support.

■ Regional policy focuses on supporting regional investment in infrastructure (and, to a minor extent, human capital formation). It works mainly through public budgets. Cofinancing regional projects requires regional authorities to match the grant and thereby express their own preferences in the light of their own budget restrictions. It also requires the regions to possess sufficient own revenue to match the funding supplied by the European Union.[2]

■ Support is mainly for projects; it thus ends once a project is completed.

The structural policies of the European Union combine the specific and the eligibility approaches. These policies render regional equalization more explicit than do the categorical grants used in the United States, but equalization still remains flexible, competitive, and output oriented.

Interpersonal Equalization across Jurisdictions

One argument against equalization across territorial jurisdictions is that poor people in an affluent region may be called on to support rich people in a poorer region. Although the argument is crude—because it is based on the naive assumption of proportional fiscal incidence by citizens—it touches on a sensitive political issue that concerns public budgeting generally. Even under a progressive income tax, more-affluent citizens may indeed draw larger net fiscal benefits from public budgets, because of their higher take-up rate of costly public services such as education, culture, and health. This problem explains a trend toward providing certain public services on a standard personalized basis (for example, vouchers for education, standard health packages, social assistance). It also explains the trend toward better targeting of the needy by personalizing welfare programs.

Where public services can be personalized or are provided through personalized funds, there is a case for interpersonal equalization, which may also have implicit regional equalization effects. As in the case of eligibility programs, such regional effects are not the primary objective, however. Some problems of interpersonal equalization are examined in the context of two personalized public programs found in many countries: public health insurance and social assistance to the poor.

Public Health Services and the Equalization of Risk Structures

The provision of public health services is always personalized, while its financing may or may not be (financing is personalized if it is based on individual contributions; it is not if paid for out of taxpayers' money). All health programs exhibit interpersonal redistribution effects, apart from the pooling of individual health risks through insurance. Risk insurance is not considered a redistributive device ex ante (disregarding moral hazard), although it will redistribute ex post. Individual risks do not make a case for equalization beyond risk compensation or insurance. Rather, the quest for interpersonal equalization is derived from legal provisions linking the public health scheme with intentional redistribution effects between large and small households, employed and unemployed people, young and elderly beneficiaries, and so forth.

Under a national public health scheme, financed through contributions or taxes, intended interpersonal redistribution would be a zero-sum game within a single specific health fund (that is, there would be full clearing). Adverse selection problems could be resolved by making membership in the health fund compulsory, as most public health schemes do. The aim is to prevent good risks from opting out of the national health scheme, leaving only the bad risks. Problems arise when several concurrent health funds operate on a regional, professional, or institutional basis.

Regional, professional, or institution-based health funds include members with different structures of health risks. If these funds were private funds, these differences would show up in different insurance premiums, which would lead to a segmentation of the insured into different risk classes. Where national health policy imposes a degree of interpersonal solidarity or fairness through mandatory insurance, some decentralized funds could end up with a bad risk structure, increasing spending on average, while other funds end up with a better risk structure.

This problem could be compounded by financing the system through contributions. In this case, a regional public insurance fund could find itself constrained from two sides: higher average spending through unfavorable risk structures and inappropriate financing through comparably lower contributions to the fund. Deficiencies in the ability to finance regional funds are typical in economically depressed areas with higher unemployment rates, rural areas with larger proportions of self-employed, regions with older populations, and so forth.

Do these structural differences make a case for interagency equalization? The answer varies from country to country. Many countries opt for a national scheme, which eliminates these problems. Others ignore the effect, treating decentralized public insurance agencies like private institutions—which they are not, because they are subject to legal constraints, including interpersonal redistribution—until they require bail outs. In Germany public health institutions engage in an interagency equalization process on the basis of a standard risk structure. Hence interpersonal equalization is effected on the basis of a standard risk structure or the ability to pay. Risk structure equalization in Germany (*Risikostrukturausgleich*) has benefited agencies organized along professional lines, where the activity is associated with specific health risks (for example, mining); it has also benefited states in the former German Democratic Republic.

Welfare and Unfunded Mandates

A case could be made for equalizing interjurisdictional differences in the structure of welfare recipients. Welfare functions are often delegated to subnational entities, notably municipal governments. Typically, there are large discrepancies across municipalities regarding the composition of the population and the percentage of welfare beneficiaries, which depends on the age composition of the population, the quality of the human capital, the state of the local economy, and employment opportunities, among other factors. As welfare payments are usually paid from public budgets, not personalized funds, such structural differences have to be equalized through general grants to achieve an equitable allocation of financial burdens on public agents in charge of welfare. Where specific factors are not taken into account—because the equalization system uses an equal per capita rule, for instance—regional inequities result from the assignment of unfunded mandates. Such mandates tend to have a disequalizing effect, because they have to be supported from own resources.

Benefits are often determined by national legislation to preserve a common "social space," in order to prevent the ruinous "shopping" of social benefits through migration of eligible individuals to jurisdictions whose welfare programs are more generous than average. Centralized legislation on welfare entitlements could exacerbate the problem of disequalization through unfunded mandates, however. Not only do national authorities determine how much subnational authorities spend from their own resources, they also "free ride" on subnational budgets, reaping the political benefits of overly generous social policies. Moral hazard may then affect the national government, which could destabilize the macro fiscal situation or disrupt the provision of welfare services. It is therefore argued that the agent responsible for policy setting should also cover the full costs of programs administered in a decentralized fashion (principle of connectivity).

This solution would create new types of inefficiency. The term *unfunded mandate* has meaning only if there is a principal-agent relationship between the policy-setting authority and a local executive agency. The principal (federal legislator) sets up a benefit program (eligibility criteria, payment schedule) and assigns the administration of the program to its agents (local governments) without providing the necessary funding. This is the case in Germany, where the social assistance program (*Sozialhilfe*) is purely federal and uniform throughout the country, but local governments have to pay out the benefits from their own budgets. The problem is not confined to Germany, however. Unfunded mandates are found in almost all countries where the national government is compelled to balance its budget, which it often does by decentralizing responsibilities without funding them. Prominent examples are Argentina, the Russian Federation, South Africa, and the United States.

Such unfunded mandates are based on typical incentive arguments from principal-agent theory. Local governments are in a more favorable position to administer programs, because they are "closer to the people" and can better "target" programs than a central administrator can. But full compensation of the costs of the program could encourage moral hazard by the local agency, which could interpret the federal rules up to the limits (and beyond) and run the program in a way that maximizes the local incidence of federal payments. Given a "funding guarantee" for the program, local governments would shift their own resources away from the funded program, spending them on other local programs that do not enjoy such guarantees. Hence a "funded program" risks becoming "unfunded" unless the federal government gives an unlimited "gap-filling" guarantee, which is difficult to reconcile with a hard budget constraint.

Given these problems, it makes sense to have local governments at least co-finance these decentralized programs, in accordance with principal-agent theory. Sufficient own resources of lower-tier governments and equalizing grants (provided on a "neutral" basis) are needed in order to enable local governments to fulfill their mandate. If these resources are not sufficient, the program could be run by the central government directly, with its own agencies, provided it can control these agencies throughout the territory. Principal-agency theory indicates, however, that the costs of a centralized system may well exceed those of a decentralized system.

The example of welfare payments in a federation raises a further question: should such benefits be centrally legislated at all? The answer rests on value judgments. However, from an economic point of view, the answer is no (unless the benefits are defined on the basis of questionable regional cost-of-living indices). It makes no sense to grant the same benefit to a person living in the capital city and to a person living in a remote rural village. A reasonable responsibility-sharing arrangement could be one in which the federal government legislates the program (that is, establishes eligibility criteria and provides "basic federal support" for the program, funded from the central budget) and local governments supplement this basic support according to "leverage ratios" that vary across regions. The leverage effect would reflect local preferences and budget restrictions and would have to be fully borne by local agents. A minimum leverage factor greater than one should be set by national legislation, indicating that local governments are expected to contribute to the program from own resources. This is one way of reconciling efficiency and equity within a personalized public support system that would strike a reasonable balance between centralized legislation and decentralized provision of service and remove unfunded mandates from the agenda. However, uniformity of public service provision links to much broader issues, connected to benchmark setting for any system of fiscal equalization. These issues are addressed below.

Designing Equalization Formulas

The foregoing discussion of interpersonal equalization may help elucidate the design of equalization formulas. Indeed, a substantial number of local public services are either personalized or have a higher incidence among certain groups of people. It is therefore convenient to elaborate the design of equalization formulas on a personal basis or by groups of public service users. However, as for all public agencies, for a substantial portion of government activities with public goods characteristics, personal incidence is not possible.

Personalized Local Public Services

If all spending of lower-tier governments could be personalized, as in the case of welfare payments, a case could be made for equalizing structural differences across beneficiaries in each region. The formula could benchmark, for instance, the situation for the nation as a whole and relate the local structure of welfare beneficiaries to the national one, in adjusting the formula for different types of households and benefit entitlements.

The grant could be calculated according to the following formula:

$$G_j = \left[\sum_h E_h \times \left(n_{jh} - \tilde{n}_h \times \frac{n}{\tilde{n}} \right) \right],$$

where E is the entitlement, n is local population, $\tilde{n}$ is national population, j is an index for the region, and h is an index for the household category.

This formula equalizes structural differences only. If the composition of local beneficiaries were the same as at the national level, no transfer would

be made. Regional governments with a higher percentage of eligible beneficiaries would obtain compensation through equalization grants; regional
governments with fewer beneficiaries would have to contribute to the fund.
The fund itself acts as a pure clearing device; it produces neither deficits nor
surpluses. This is true, however, only if the effective number of recipients is
the same as the number of entitled recipients.

This approach requires a number of qualifications, such as the following:

- Local governments have to make the average welfare payment from own
  resources; only structural differences are compensated by the formula. This
  may call for an addition to the grant formula to transfer resources to run
  the program effectively in a decentralized fashion. The additional element
  would consist of a lump-sum payment based on average per capita costs of
  the program at the national level, weighted by the local population. This
  introduces an element of vertical rebalancing within the formula that
  should be considered separately from a conceptual point of view.
- If the lump-sum payments finance the whole program (that is, there are
  no program-related vertical fiscal imbalances), it creates the type of moral
  hazard problem discussed above in the context of unfunded mandates.[3]
  To avoid such moral hazard, the lump-sum element should be scaled
  down to let local governments co-finance a portion of the program. This
  vertical rebalancing can be effected only by giving local governments
  access to independent own resources.
- The take-up rate for welfare payments is usually below 100 percent. In this
  case, the formula rewards local governments with a low take-up rate, creating an incentive to discourage entitled households from applying for benefits. If the effective number of welfare recipients is used for the formula,
  the incentive effects hinge exclusively on the proportion of co-financing.
- Payments from local budgets are often contingent, even if they are personalized. Where entitlements are contingent on a particular event—such as
  health or employment status—effective payments become unpredictable. If
  instead they are based on effective payments, the formula could be based on
  contingent claims. The formula could also be based on effective payments
  after the state of the events is revealed, but this would produce moral hazard if recipients can control the state of events, as they would attempt to
  manipulate events in order to maximize grants in the following period.
- Basing the formula on contingent claims in a standardized fashion rather
  than on effective (ex post) claims is arguably necessary to avoid negative
  incentive effects and moral hazard. If, for instance, unemployment
  benefits were largely compensated by an equalization formula, there

would be little incentive for regional governments to fight the causes of unemployment through appropriate economic and fiscal policies. Such a system would lock in economically depressed areas by rewarding passivity, resignation, and grant dependency while penalizing initiative and entrepreneurship.

▪ Some programs, such as education and health services, in which overhead costs are high, are provided to eligible groups of people. Although education could be personalized in principle (through vouchers, for example), it is typically produced by local governments themselves. The personal incidence remains unclear, as no cash payment is made to individuals. Equalization could still proceed along the lines of the proposed formula, by using average costs per student rather than the value of direct payments. Average costs of education would then be weighted by the number of school-age children to determine the size of the grant.

If average producer costs per person rather than direct payments are used for equalization, a new dimension of equalization will emerge: differences in the costs of producing a given output. Different universities often face vastly different costs of producing a graduate with a given type of degree. Should these differences be equalized? If they are, there is little incentive to contain costs. If they are not, government agencies that are compelled to operate in atypical, cost-intensive environments (for example, Australia's "flying doctors") would be unfairly penalized. In principle, exogenous cost differentials should be included in the formula while controllable cost differentials should be excluded. In practice, however, these differences are often difficult to identify or quantify.

Controllable cost differentials are often measured using standard capacity indicators. For instance, instead of equalizing the direct costs of a hospital, policy makers use the number of hospital beds as a proxy for standard costs or output. This "capacity equalization" creates yet another type of negative incentive. As this type of standard cost is easily manipulated by recipient public agencies, the institution is enticed to maximize the capacity indicator, in this case the number of beds, which may be unrelated to the number of patients treated.

Should the equalization formula consider differentials in taxing capacity? The answer is usually yes, because uncompensated differences in local taxing capacity would be reflected in the quantity and quality of local public services. Regional differences in public services could externalize regional inequities, lead to undesirable internal migration, and jeopardize national cohesion and political stability.

Taxing capacity has a general dimension, as it affects the total budget of the local entity, including the provision of nonpersonalized public goods, and a specific dimension, as it concerns the local population's ability to pay for specific personalized public services. The general dimension is dealt with in the next subsection; the specific dimension is addressed here.

Where the ability to pay for specific public services through user charges and fees is low in a region compared with some benchmark, should such differences be compensated for through local budgets or through subsidies to citizens? Both solutions are used in practice. From an economic point of view, the second option clearly deserves priority.

If the subsidy is channeled through local budgets, the average cost of the service is reduced, with a concomitant reduction in user charges. In this case, the objection that the poor of more affluent regions will support the rich in the poorer regions is likely to be correct, as the rich and the poor would benefit equally from subsidized prices. The problem is exacerbated if the rich use the subsidized local services more intensively than the poor. Of course, local governments could try to target the program through price discrimination, but this is often crude and may be subject to tax arbitrage. Moreover, subsidized prices will always lead to excessive demand for public services, which entails economic inefficiencies.

A personalized social welfare program is typically more effective in reaching the poor, who should be able to pay for the local service in full. The welfare benefit, for instance, could comprise a lump sum for basic electricity consumption, while the electricity bill would be based on effective consumption at the market price. Subsidizing the price of electricity instead would represent a generous gift to the rich, whose consumption is typically much higher than that of the poor. It would also produce inefficiency and encourage the waste of resources.

Local Public Goods

One of the characteristics of a public good is nonrivalry in consumption. Public goods are provided to a collectivity without regard to individual preferences or take-up. Street lighting, for example, is provided irrespective of whether a resident makes use of it or even wants it. A personalized approach to equalization would not therefore seem to make sense.

Equalization arrangements for financing public goods usually depart from the fiction of an "abstract user." Equalizing transfers are thus typically based on the number of people living in an area, whether or not they actually use the local public service.

Basing equalization transfers on the number of residents of a jurisdiction poses certain problems, however. Individuals undoubtedly benefit from infrastructure and public services in their municipality or region. But they may also benefit from services provided by other jurisdictions. Metropolitan areas, for example, tend to supply public services such as higher education and culture to surrounding areas. For larger jurisdictions, such regional spillovers may be negligible, because they are internalized; they could become more significant as the size of the jurisdiction shrinks, however. The German constitution explicitly defines the person as the abstract unit for equalizing public services, but the law on interstate equalization attaches a heavier weight to the population of city-states to compensate for some of these spillovers.

Attaching a heavier weight to the population of urban areas could also be motivated by large cost differentials among regional governments. Within a single economic space, these differentials usually reflect differences in the structure of local services. For instance, urban centers may operate theaters, museums, or costly mass transportation systems. It is common to consider such specific burdens on metropolitan public budgets as agglomeration costs, which require special attention and treatment. It is not easy to evaluate agglomeration costs, however, as doing so requires answering unanswerable questions such as "how many opera houses does Berlin need?" For this reason, weighting population figures must be considered a crude approach to taking differentials in the cost structure into account.

Another type of cost differentials is related to "bulky" fixed spending items, such as political administration. The general costs of administering a jurisdiction may vary little with population size, at least for some local entities. The relative burden of general administration is therefore typically higher for smaller units than for larger ones, which could reap significant benefits of scale. Equalization schemes take this into account by including a fixed-cost element in the distribution formula. (An example is the municipal equalization scheme in Brazil.) Doing so could create perverse results, however, as there is an incentive to maximize grants by dividing up existing jurisdictions. The Brazilian scheme has indeed fostered the proliferation of municipalities to some extent. But even where proliferation of government entities is not an issue, as in Germany, the question remains whether the equalization scheme should reward small jurisdictions for defending the status quo when there are economic and political reasons for merging jurisdictions.

Metropolitan centers often bear agglomeration costs. But they also often have greater taxing capacity. Whether this is the case depends on the assignment of taxes to lower-tier governments. It could well be that local tax potential is tapped or even fully absorbed by higher levels of governments rather than the local jurisdiction. This might even be dictated in the interest of equalization, because the metropolitan centers of many countries are home to the bulk of fiscal resources in a country, which has to be skimmed off by the national government in order to let other regions benefit. This is true, for instance, in Argentina, Mexico, and Peru. The assignment of tax with local incidence to the central government could also be a drain on potential sources of regional development, however, as in the case of the oil-rich Hanty-Mansiski Autonomous Region, which remains one of Russia's poorest regional governments.

Although the problems of interjurisdictional equalization are compounded for local public goods and institutions with high fixed costs, the general approach is similar to one based on personalized public services. The difference is that abstract units are used instead of effective (groups of) users, with some crude corrections to account for special factors such as agglomeration costs. The fact that equalization for specific programs (such as education) could be better targeted by using the number of eligible beneficiaries (students) rather than abstract users also explains why equalization may take various forms (general unconditional transfers, specific purpose transfers, and special transfers) (Spahn 2004). It also explains the fact that the grantor government often attaches conditions to grants, to ensure that the transfer is spent on the specific program supported.

Clauses on specific uses of grants are often inefficient, however. So-called specific-purpose transfers or grants, used in almost all countries, can be binding for the recipient government, in that they require that funds be spent on policies that may not be of high priority to residents. In this case, spending could represent a waste of public resources.[4] Alternatively, specific-purpose grants may be nonbinding, in that the recipient government would have spent a similar or even greater amount from its own budget anyway. Grants that include binding constraints could entail inefficiencies if forced spending is not accompanied by vertical spillovers. Grants that include nonbinding constraints are tantamount to general-revenue grants, because they free unconditional budget resources; they therefore entail a pure revenue effect and do not interfere with local priorities. Specific-purpose grants are only a crude approximation to efficiency-enhancing microtransfers, as discussed below. Moreover, the incentive effects are highly uncertain.

Despite these problems, specific-purpose transfers are extremely common in many countries, because of their potential to convey the policy priorities of the donor government to voters. Politicians are keen on the signaling function of such transfers to demonstrate their commitment to specific causes. Such grants allow them to claim to have spent money on certain policies, even though the recipient government would have spent the money on the policy anyway.

Australia, which uses both general and specific-purpose grants, provides an interesting illustration of the purely political function of specific-purpose transfers. General transfers are calculated partly on the basis of the relative fiscal capacity of recipient states. Specific-purpose transfers to state governments are for specific purposes, but most of them merely increase state governments' fiscal capacity. As a consequence, the Commonwealth of Australia "claws back" the relative effects of specific-purpose transfers through the system of general grants.[5] Although the revenue effect of specific-purpose grants is thus annihilated, Australian politicians nevertheless cherish retaining specific-purpose transfers, probably because of their high signaling potential.

Principles for Equalization Schemes

A number of principles govern the design of an equitable but efficient equalization system based on interagency grants:

- Equalization grants should be based on closed funding in order to maintain macroeconomic stability. The size of the fund not only imposes a hard budget constraint on grantee governments collectively, it also restricts the scope for redistribution.
- Equalization grants must try to avoid creating incentive effects, whether positive or negative. Equalization transfers should not penalize revenue efforts by regional governments by reducing grant entitlements. Doing so would induce recipient governments to reduce their own taxes, which relaxes budget constraints and reduces their accountability toward citizens.
- Equalization should be based on computable quantitative standards or benchmarks against which to measure the relative positions of all, or a part, of the jurisdictions participating in the scheme. Standards and benchmarks are almost everywhere defined in abstract per capita terms. Some countries attach weights to the population figures, or make appropriate corrections, to account for regional agglomeration or low-density effects.
- The equalization standards and the measures of fiscal need relative to the standard must not be open to manipulation by recipient governments. If they are, there will be a strong incentive to maximize grants through moral hazard.

Equalizing transfers are usually designed to bridge the gap between the relative fiscal position of recipient governments and those standards. Three different philosophies can be distinguished:

■ Where there are no significant differences between the level and the costing of service delivery across subnational governments, as assumed in Canada and Germany, it is sufficient to use revenue capacity as the single standard and to equalize only revenue capacity across jurisdictions. Some countries, such as Switzerland and South Africa, use regional GDP, which could be interpreted as a proxy for revenue capacity, instead.
■ For specific-purpose transfers, it is common to focus on expenditure needs—that is, on needs indicators translated into budget equivalents through the costing of a standard level of services. In some countries, such as the Russian Federation and South Africa, this philosophy also creeps into some equalization schemes for general-purpose transfers.
■ Both revenue capacity and expenditure needs can be used in a comprehensive approach to budget equalization. Australia represents the most prominent example of this approach.

Despite possible shortcomings, such as a high degree of complexity, the Australian system has become *the* model for an ideal equalization system. The basic approach is sound, complete, feasible, and reasonably transparent. The proliferation of criteria that render the Australian system so cumbersome result exclusively from political bargaining, not from an ill-designed system. It is true that the heavy information requirements and high level of technical expertise the Australian scheme requires for general-purpose transfers renders it difficult, if not impossible, to export to countries in which data are poor and administrative capacity weak. The scheme nevertheless remains the unique benchmark against which all equalization mechanisms have to be compared in terms of their vulnerability to manipulation and perverse incentives.

The Case for Intragovernmental Efficiency

Efficiency can be improved by internalizing spillover effects. Within the private sector, there is an incentive to exploit such externalities because doing so is usually profitable. Such rewards hinge on the unequivocal and clear assignment of property rights to independent decision-making agents. Under these conditions, the market provides incentives through contracting for enhancing efficiency in the presence of externalities.

Similarly, there may be scope for improving efficiency through public-private partnerships, that is, contractual arrangements to mobilize externalities accruing to governments and private firms alike. These arrangements are often looked at with suspicion, however. Such doubts may result from asymmetries in the assignment of property rights between public and private agents and from possible asymmetries in risk sharing, but there is no doubt as to the potential for efficiency-enhancing arrangements of such instruments.

The main hindrance for efficiency-enhancing reforms of the government sector is the organic view of the state and the corporatist interpretation of federalism (see Spahn 2006). This interpretation produces economic inefficiencies due to blurred cost accounting, especially where there is no accrual-based bookkeeping, as is typical for the public sector. It is true in particular for models of cooperative federalism, as in Austria and Germany. Not surprisingly, the current discussion on constitutional reform in Germany turns on issues such as "disentanglement" (*Entflechtung*) and "budget equivalence" (*Konnexität*). Discussion of disentanglement addresses issues of political accountability; discussion of budget equivalence aims to connect decision making and the financing of public services in order to enhance efficiency.

For a corporatist constitution, disentanglement poses a serious dilemma however: It appears to call for arrangements similar to those adopted in the United States, where policy, administration, and financing are all handled by the same level of government. Such an arrangement is impossible without surrendering the basic values of the corporatist state. But why should one seek to disentangle functions in the public sector given that the private sector of a modern economy thrives on a widening network of business contracts, outsourcing of functions, associations of enterprises, co-financing arrangements, and complex financial holdings?

Fortunately, disentanglement of functions is not necessary to establish accountability and transparency within government. All that is needed is to bring intergovernmental relations closer to those that govern business relations within the private sector. Where possible, contractual arrangements rather than legal or bureaucratic rules should govern intergovernmental relations. The financial flows corresponding to services rendered by public agencies within government will be referred to as *microtransfers*. They could become powerful instruments with which to enhance intragovernmental efficiency and an alternative to criteria-based specific-purpose grants.

Negotiated microtransfers among governments or public agencies exist to a certain extent, but they are usually regarded with even greater suspicion than public-private partnerships. Certainly, microtransfers can be abused for political favoritism, logrolling, and vote buying, which would expropriate the citizen-voter and discredit democratic processes. For a case to be made for contractual, efficiency-enhancing microtransfers within the government sector, between governments and public agencies, or between public and private agents, appropriate processes and control mechanisms must be designed that ensure transparency and fairness.

Another objection to interagency contracting within the public sector is of a legal nature. Some lawyers consider government to be an integral whole, which appears to exclude "self-contracting" within government or among public agencies. This view has its roots in the organic vision of the state and a corporatist interpretation of federalism. From an economic and administrative point of view, this "organic view" of government has to be rejected as obstructing possible efficiency gains. Contracting must take place not only among governments and public agencies but ideally within public administration as well. Intergovernment and interagency contracting would require a reorganization of the public sector in accordance with clear principal-agent relationships and well-determined delegated responsibilities.

Bringing intergovernmental relations closer to those that govern business relations within the private sector is easier said than done, because procedural arrangements in the public and the private sectors differ significantly. However, these differences can and must be overcome if coordination through interagency contracts and microtransfers is to become more flexible and responsive.

The network complexity of a modern private economy ensues from a host of contractual arrangements between organizations, firms, and individuals, in which service flows are directed by economic and financial incentives. An ideal contract pertains to specific services, involves a quid pro quo, assigns clear responsibilities, allocates and hedges risks, contains effective sanctions in the case of noncompliance, and is limited in time and hence flexible. Changing existing arrangements within the limits set by contracts typically offers rewards, which fosters commitment, entrepreneurship, and innovation.

By contrast, interaction within the public sector rests largely on legal and bureaucratic structures and processes. These processes are often rigid, ill defined, or inappropriate for addressing specific needs, and they may assign circular responsibilities that can be passed on indefinitely. Moreover, these processes typically fail the quid pro quo test, and they do not offer rewards for institutional or procedural developments. On the contrary: where they exist at all, penalties are imposed for not abiding by the rule, dampening personal initiatives and the willingness to experiment.

Government adoption of mechanisms similar to those used in the private sector would significantly enhance the transparency and efficiency of public administration within federal structures. Contractual arrangements among government entities and agencies could serve to define responsibilities in a clearer fashion, which would also foster political accountability. This is not to say that all intergovernmental relations should be "debureaucratized" in favor of contractual arrangements. Bureaucratic rule has many advantages, but it is often too rigid and insensitive to realize efficiency gains. Federal and intragovernmental relations that could be developed more flexibly on the basis of contracts rather than legal and bureaucratic arrangements need to be identified.

Intergovernmental and interagency contracting must be guided by clear objectives, and they must be based on output or performance indicators, not on inputs. Microtransfers ensuing from contracting must reflect interagency service flows. Such transfers should not only follow clear costing guidelines, they must also incorporate provisions to continue, or terminate, the flow of funds based on performance. This calls for appropriate monitoring, possibly including sanctions for public agents. Reforms must have consequences for the civil service. A clear delineation must be made between activities flowing from sovereign right and those relating to public service delivery, with activities flowing from sovereign right based on traditional forms of financing and activities relating to public service delivery based on microtransfers. Public service delivery could also be organized with the help of private agents based on market pricing, which will often form the benchmark for pricing microtransfers within the government sector.

Monitoring contractual arrangements requires proper accounting, including the transition from cash accounting to accrual accounting. Better accounting includes evaluating public assets and assessing appropriate charges for using public capital. Once built, for example, public buildings are typically considered "rent free." As a result, they are used in a suboptimal manner. Imposing a capital charge would improve the usage of real assets and provide the funds for a proper facility management. It would, of course, imply redressing all (sub) budgets of government institutions and public agencies in the initial period, after moving to such a system.

Designing Interagency Relations and Microtransfers

Intergovernmental contractual arrangements must be designed in a way to internalize interjurisdictional spillovers or externalities. If it is possible to determine the monetary equivalent of the external costs and benefits of policies across levels of government or within any level of government, a case can be made for coordinating interagency decisions through intergovernmental microtransfers based on contracts. Doing so would increase efficiency and foster political accountability. Flexible contracts also foster experimentation and hence innovation in the public sector. Contract federalism is therefore closely related to the concept of "laboratory federalism," which stresses the innovative power of decentralized intergovernmental relations.[6] Proponents of laboratory federalism have argued that with imperfect information, learning by doing and testing different options may enhance the quality of public policy. Experimentation is a particularly attractive feature of federal systems.[7]

Intragovernmental Efficiency and Macroeconomic Stability

New Zealand, a unitary country, pioneered the redesign of interagency relations within government during the early 1990s. Its reforms were guided by efficiency considerations, but the reforms also enhanced the conditions for macroeconomic stability through fiscal discipline: since its reforms New Zealand's public sector has consistently run operating surpluses.[8] It can even be argued that microeconomic incentive mechanisms, such as microtransfers based on contracts, are more powerful than bureaucratic rule in establishing fiscal discipline at the macro level.

Imposing fiscal discipline through microeconomic incentives and achieving macroeconomic stability has many positive features:

- Transparency becomes more important than a rigid interpretation of bureaucratic regulations.
- Procedural rules based on generic performance criteria set by parliament replace input-orientated budgeting.
- The executive branch is free to set budgets and make autonomous spending decisions, albeit with stringent monitoring provisions and supervision.
- Accountable public officials are separated from policies subject to democratic control, and dependable agents provide professional management and service delivery.
- Operating and capital budgets are clearly divided, accrual-based accounting and costing are introduced, and medium-term financial planning and monitoring instruments are used.
- Cross-subsidization within the public sector is eliminated, and interagency and intragovernmental transfer pricing (microtransfers), including

capital charges (interest, depreciation of public assets), is introduced for public infrastructure and equipment.

- Public service delivery is exposed to market forces, including the establishment of self-governing budget units, and functions are outsourced.
- Greater reliance is placed on market forces for public sector borrowing, modern debt management techniques and systematic risk-assessment and control are used, and public agencies are rated under a no bail-out presumption.

The Functional-Agency Approach to Public Administration

In order to establish an institutional framework for efficiency-enhancing microtransfers, it is essential to break down the public sector into quasi-autonomous functional agencies while maintaining a holistic vision of government and its responsibilities. This is an ambitious project. The institutional framework for government usually evolves along responsibility, not functional, lines. Responsibilities for a given portfolio are assigned to politicians (ministers) who are accountable to parliaments. The internal structure of the ministries is bureaucratic and hierarchical, and functions are carried out within departments under the control of the institution's head (minister, governor, mayor).

The bureaucratic structure of the public sector favors a budgeting process that emphasizes resource allocation, by parliament, to specific functions of the department and even to specific uses. The breakdown of budget items is often excessive, putting management processes in a financial straitjacket. The result is inefficiency and waste. Generally speaking, parliaments attempt to control the institution by allocating specific inputs for producing programmed outputs. These outputs are often ill defined and difficult to monitor, however. Legislators may be able to identify how much has been spent on a given program (say, higher education) and economic functions (say, wages) without being able to evaluate the outcome of the program. The corollary of this type of public budgeting is the system of specific-purpose grants within a multilevel government. As for budget allocations, the donor government attempts to tie the use of the grant to specific programs without necessarily being able to monitor their outcome.

The classical bureaucratic model of government exhibits a bias toward budget maximization, because politicians and bureaucrats do not form a true principal-agent relationship. Niskanen's (1971) seminal book on bureaucracy explores this relationship. From the standpoint of the demanding politician, the same supplier (the bureaucrat) delivers both policy advice and policy execution. The bureaucrat will almost always be able to convince politicians that certain measures and resources are indispensable to realize a given objective. If policy advice on public housing and the administration of public housing programs come from the same institution, for instance, it is reasonable to expect the budget for public housing to expand over time.[9]

A clear separation of policy and administrative responsibilities could remove such bias. What is more, bureaucratic organizations tend to develop functional units for their own portfolio rather than outsourcing such functions to other agencies. This creates duplication and overlap, especially for new functions, which requires regular organizational revisions to account for organizational change and development.

New Zealand's reforms have radically changed the way government works. Government is perceived as representing a holding structure of semi-autonomous departments led by managers on the basis of contractual arrangements. Managers possess a large degree of discretion under these contracts, yet they are responsible to politicians because they must meet performance criteria and results. Performance is preferably defined in terms of tangible outputs, and the budget is conditional on achieving these outputs, not on spending for specific uses. In other words, parliaments surrender control of inputs for control of outputs. This new approach requires appropriate contractual arrangements between accountable politicians and department managers as well as new instruments for monitoring the execution and implementation of the budget. It includes sanctions for nonperformance or bad performance, which could be a budget cut, the termination of the contract, or the dismissal of the manager. Autonomous or quasi-autonomous functional agencies are essential for defining contract-based microtransfers among such agencies and between agencies at different levels of government. Although this type of reorganization applies to both unitary and federal forms of government, it is particularly relevant in a multigovernment setting.

The reorganization of the public sector and the creation of functional agencies could proceed along the following lines. First, state functions (such as police and the judiciary) should be distinguished from public services that can be provided on a quid pro quo basis. State functions should retain their legal and bureaucratic structure and be financed in the conventional way. Only public services that can be provided in a market-like fashion should be financed with microtransfers. It makes sense to separate certain functions, such as production, financing, personnel, and procurement, within organizations and agencies and to assign clear management responsibilities for resolving potential functional conflicts.

Second, if possible, existing service units of bureaucratic organizations should form quasi-autonomous functional agencies that support various public organizations at the same time. This is likely to generate economies of scale. Different degrees of autonomy should be granted to these agencies: some should continue to remain part of the public sector in a narrow sense, others should be structured as autonomous (semi-) public corporations, yet others should be fully privatized. In order to establish competition among different types of service-delivering agencies and reduce public sector costs, the benchmark for pricing services should be market-like transactions. Public organizations should also be free to choose the service-providing agency (from within or from outside the public sector) on a competitive basis.

Third, public aspects of service delivery should be explicitly taken into account. This could be done in a number of different ways:

- Regulatory bodies could be created to compensate for potential market failures, such as quasi-monopoly power, captured markets, and asymmetric information. The regulatory body must ensure free entry into and exit out of markets by potential competitors. This is particularly important for privatized public services, such as telecommunication, energy, and transportation. Regulation may also be needed to protect consumers, enforce environmental control, establish a safe workplace, and so forth. It requires appropriate standard setting and monitoring.
- Subsidies could be transferred to service-delivering agencies to cope with broader public policy objectives. These grants would be detached from service-based microtransfers. They would allow service delivery based on market pricing to be distinguished from financial assistance to achieve public policy objectives. Higher education, for instance, could be subsidized from the state budget to account for spillovers to society as a whole. At the same time, students could be required to pay a fee for acquiring human capital that will yield private returns.
- When subsidizing agencies that provide public services, care must be taken to avoid distorting pricing. Compensating vertical spillovers through outright grants is nondistorting, as long as such spillovers accrue to society at large. Horizontal transfers to compensate for regional spillovers may also be nondistorting, provided they are calculated correctly. In Switzerland, for instance, some cantons without university institutions compensate neighboring cantons for accepting students from their region. Of course, such specific-purpose grants are only a surrogate for a personalized system of financial support (such as vouchers), which would be more transparent and better suited.

■ If the quality of services can be increased through performance-based subsidies to clients of the service-providing agency (for example, excellent university students), these subsidies should flow from the state budget directly to the agency. From these grants, the agency should form a fund to reward students based on performance, which the agency is in a better position to monitor than the government.

■ If subsidies are given to accommodate social objectives, a personalized scheme of financial support is needed to avoid economic distortions. Such a scheme would also allow better targeting of the needy. Direct subsidies to the service-providing agency could induce average cost pricing, which is both inefficient and inequitable.

Fourth, in decentralizing government and creating functional agencies, it is essential to establish an effective governance structure, with clear assignment of competencies and responsibilities, as well as effective processes to coordinate the various organizations and agencies. Financial incentives, such as microtransfers and basic funding through grants, are important coordination instruments, but they will not be adequate. What is needed is the gearing of budgeting processes toward outputs and the monitoring of budget execution.

Efficiency and equity can be reconciled by clearly separating support through specific-purpose grants and microtransfers based on the pricing of public services. Greater efficiency will neither jeopardize the welfare state nor put an end to solidarity with socially deprived people or poorer regions. Separating socially or otherwise motivated political transfers from efficiency-oriented microtransfers also allows better targeting of the needy, as it may reveal unjustified support to beneficiaries who profit from lack of transparency and the "churning" of unaccounted for inter- and intragovernmental resource flows.

Output-Oriented Budgeting

The characteristics of output-oriented budgeting can be illustrated by examining the budget process established in New Zealand. Unlike traditional government budgets, which include budget chapters and items, New Zealand's budget includes only general-purpose transfers ("votes") for specific policy areas. The government decides which outcomes a policy should have for society and the economy. On the basis of such decisions, it writes a strategy paper. In accordance with this strategy, ministers "purchase" outputs from their departments to realize the outcome. Production decisions are left entirely to the directors of the departments, who combine inputs (personnel, materials, services from other units) in a way that achieves the outputs at minimal costs. The substance of contractual arrangements, including price and other contractual arrangements, is subject to parliamentary approval. According to the logic of output-oriented budgeting, the budget cannot be separated from the content of contracts or from procedures to monitor their execution and evaluate their results. The budget law thus has a new character and quality.

A desired outcome could be the improvement of road safety, measured in terms of the number of accidents each year. The outputs or services purchased might be traffic controls, improved signaling, awareness campaigns, or enhanced road maintenance. To achieve the outputs, various combinations of inputs can be chosen, such as police and other personnel, motor vehicles, technical equipment, or press campaigns. On the basis of a given output, a single purchase agreement is reached between the minister and the department head. This agreement does not have the character of a private contract, in that it is nonactionable, but it could contain financial incentives and even sanctions.

According to the handbook of the Treasury of New Zealand (1995), the purchase agreement must contain the following elements:

- List of products to be purchased, their costs/prices, and terms of delivery
- Exact description of the product
- Total amount of contact and time profile of disbursements
- Responsible unit for reporting and methods to determine satisfactory service delivery
- Modalities for settling disputes.

Ministers need spending authorizations from parliament to purchase goods and services. Parliament makes these decisions based on the government's report on financial strategy and budget estimates for single "votes." These estimates elucidate the relationship between outputs and outcomes and analyze the achievements attained in the policy area during previous periods. The contractual commitments and quality standards for single departments are detailed in departmental forecast reports.

The treasury is continually developing criteria and processes to monitor output-oriented budgeting. It has formed departments dealing with quality management and consumer surveying. Experience shows that it is possible to connect product-oriented budgeting with contractual responsibilities and reporting requirements. The process of budget control in New

Zealand appears to be superior to that of most other countries, and it is continuously evolving and improving.

Costing and Pricing Microtransfers

In order to get incentives right through microtransfers, quasi-autonomous service agencies must be established within the public sector, and they must function like private firms, with which they often compete. Cost structures, including taxes and other public charges, of public service agencies and private firms need to be comparable, and similar accounting standards must be used. Most governments still use cash accounting, which conceals commitments and pending liabilities, and most deal inadequately with capital formation and capital costs. Once installed, capital is typically deemed to represent a free resource, except perhaps for maintenance costs, and even maintenance is often overlooked (and hence neglected) where the assignment of property rights falls short of efficiency considerations.

The use of efficiency-enhancing microtransfers requires governments to use accrual accounting for public sector operations. And it requires clear assignment of property rights for public assets. Real assets do not necessarily have to be reassigned, but the state should charge rents that correspond to the user costs of capital. This rental value of public buildings would include the opportunity costs of financing and depreciation. Contractual arrangements would include regular maintenance, which is often neglected under the "build-once-and-use-free-forever" approach typical of cash accounting. Of course, the introduction of a user charge must be financed from the state budget, a one-time leveraging of the agency's budget to pay for rents. This might look like simply inflating budgets, a pure recycling of resources through public budgets. In fact, it provides agencies with a realistic basis for costing, and it induces them to consider alternatives (such as renting another building for delivering its service).

Although it is conventional to grant public institutions immunity from taxes, doing so introduces a bias in the costing of services provided by public and private institutions. This bias can only partially be removed, and its effects may be ambiguous. However, the following guidelines should be considered:

■ No exemption of government agencies, including exemption of the municipality itself, appears to be appropriate for public user charges, fees, fines, or local taxes such as the property tax. Including these elements corresponds to eliminating implicit interagency flows of resources, as discussed above.

- Government agencies, like private enterprises, have to carry most indirect taxes. This is mandatory to avoid tax arbitrage in which individuals purchase goods or services for private use but claim to use them for public purposes. Some countries do exempt public agencies from taxes, which could entail serious misallocations. Such exemptions would have to be waived under the approach proposed here.

- Government agencies may face a disadvantage compared with private providers because they cannot make use of their input value added tax (VAT). This leads to cascading tax accumulation for services provided through public agencies. This is not true for intragovernmental and inter–public agency relations, which are free of VAT, but it does affect purchases of private goods and services by such institutions. To accommodate this effect, public service providers might be given the possibility to opt for VAT, especially if they provide substantial services to the private sector.

- Direct taxation of public agencies does not make sense, as they are usually nonprofit institutions as long as they operate within the public sector in a narrow sense. This nonprofit status does not apply to semi-public corporations or outsourced operations of service-delivering units. Direct taxation will thus be the decisive test for deciding whether an operation will be corporatized or privatized.

Unlike private suppliers, public service agencies are not expected to earn profits. This appears to give them a competitive edge over private institutions. Because public institutions operate in a less competitive environment, have less skilled managers, provide implicit or explicit job guarantees for civil servants, and experience higher job turnover, they usually have higher costs than private firms, which may erode this competitive edge and create a level playing field. The pricing of service delivery by public agencies via competition through markets together with appropriate cost accounting is likely to put pressure on public agencies. It may still give these agencies some rents that exceed the normal profits achieved by private competitors.

Summary

Intergovernmental and interagency transfers within the public sector aim to achieve different fiscal, vertical and horizontal equity, and efficiency objectives. In practice, these objectives often overlap, making intergovernmental financial relations nontransparent and difficult to analyze. Often it remains unclear whether given policy objectives have been achieved or not.

This chapter argues in favor of clearly separating different types of transfers according to their objectives. Fiscal and equalization objectives are best reached through unconditional general-revenue grants. Specific-purpose grants are popular, because they are expected to affect the recipient government's budget behavior. But they often fail to reach their goal, except where conditions attached to grants establish quality standards for public services. In any case, such grants are poor surrogates for personalized social assistance or microtransfers based on effective service delivery within contractual arrangements.

A thorough revision of intergovernmental financial arrangements and institutional reforms can achieve both equity and efficiency, if funding mechanisms are clearly separated. Government administrations need to be reorganized along functional lines by creating self-governing public service providers and agencies. These agencies must be able to monitor costing and pricing the way private service firms do. Budgeting and accounting procedures need to be revised so that costs are clearly assigned to service-delivering agencies, and output-oriented budget monitoring needs to be conducted.

Notes

1. This situation has recently changed. From the beginning of 2006, an equalization scheme was phased in both in the Federation of Bosnia and Herzegovina and the Republika Srpska—the two administrative entities.
2. This is a truism for the sovereign member countries of the European Union, which possess instruments to tap national tax bases. The prerequisite is not met, within the decentralization national framework. Lower tiers, in particular local governments, often possess little own revenue to meet cofinancing requirements. This problem has to be addressed through appropriate tax assignment.
3. Structural equalization transfers can be disregarded here, as they sum to zero.
4. In the presence of vertical externalities, this loss could be outweighed by national benefits.
5. Since the pool for general grants is closed, the volume of specific-purpose payments will have to be added to this pool to obtain the full budgetary impact. The expression "claw back" is therefore somewhat misleading.
6. See Oates (1999) for a survey of the literature on laboratory federalism.
7. The argument in favor of laboratory federalism is derived from von Hayek's critique of centralized economies. He argues that a central planning commission's ability to process information is weak compared with that of the market. Thus the ability of a nation to process information may increase as more than one level of government (or different governments at the same level) can test different options. Historians have argued that the European economies and nations of the Renaissance period constituted nothing but laboratories and that competition among those states spurred innovations and propelled them into leading positions in the world (see North 1981).

8. Government operating expenses as a percentage of GDP were reduced, and government debt fell from roughly 50 percent of GDP in the early 1990s to 28 percent of GDP in 2002/03. This draws, of course, from fiscal and other policy measures improving the prospects for economic growth. But it also results from a favorable institutional environment for public sector management and budget control through embedded microeconomic incentives.
9. At the very least, it is unreasonable to expect the bureaucracy to propose privatizing the program.

References

Commonwealth Grants Commission. 2005. *Report on State Revenue Sharing Relativities.* Canberra, Australia.

Niskanen, William A. 1971. *Bureaucracy and Representative Government.* Chicago: Aldine-Atherton.

Spahn, Paul Bernd. 2004. "Intergovernmental Transfers: The Funding Rule and Mechanisms." Working Paper 04-17, Georgia State University, Andrew Young School of Policy Studies, International Studies Program, Atlanta. http://isp-aysps.gsu.edu/papers/index.html.

———. 2006. "Contract Federalism." In *Handbook on Fiscal Federalism,* ed. Ehtisham Ahmad and Giorgio Brosio. Cheltenham, United Kingdom: Edward Elgar.

Treasury of New Zealand. 1995. *Purchase Agreement Guidelines with Best Practices for Output Performance Measures.* Wellington.

4

Achieving Economic Stabilization by Sharing Risk within Countries

JÜRGEN VON HAGEN

A fundamental feature of the modern state is that it provides risk-sharing mechanisms for its citizens. This chapter examines fiscal arrangements for risk sharing among different regions within a state.

Free trade and mobility of capital and labor within states create opportunities for citizens to share the risks emanating from region-specific shocks. But market-based risk-sharing mechanisms are often regarded as insufficient or imperfect, and internal migration can generate inefficient responses to regional shocks even if it is costless (Oates 1972; Boadway 2004).

State-provided regional risk sharing occurs when a nation's fiscal system redistributes income across regions in response to economic developments that affect these regions in different ways. Regional risk sharing may be simply a by-product of national welfare and tax systems that transfer income from rich to poor regions. In federal states, regional risk sharing is often provided by explicit mechanisms of fiscal equalization that provide for transfers between the constituent states of the federation. In Canada and Germany, for example, prominent examples of federations with horizontal equalization, tax revenues are shared by the constituent states of the federation. The Canadian equalization system aims at reducing differences in the standards of living across Canadian provinces by compensating poorer provinces for their less prosperous tax bases. According to Canadian legal tradition, equalization is an outflow of the principle of equality of all citizens before the law. The German equalization system, or *Länderfinanzausgleich*, has its constitutional justification in the principle that citizens should not be treated differently by the government simply because they live in different parts of the federation. In Australia, a prominent example of vertical fiscal equalization, the central government provides grants to constituent states based on their fiscal needs.[1]

Equalization has traditionally been regarded as a means of more equitably distributing tax revenues among states with different tax capacities or expenditure needs. It can also be regarded as a welfare-improving insurance mechanism against region-specific shocks (Boadway 2004; Bucovetsky 1998; Lockwood 1999). In unitary states and federations without explicit fiscal equalization—such as the United States, where an explicit equalization mechanism existed only between 1972 and 1981 (Dafflon and Vaillaincourt 2003)—regional risk sharing can result from budgetary transfers from the central government to regional or local governments. Like fiscal equalization, such mechanisms are generally based on equity considerations: they aim to protect regions against economic hardship. As Jacques Delors (1989, p. 89) put it in his plea for a risk sharing mechanism among the members of the European Monetary Union, such protection is part of the solidarity defining a society:

> In all federations the different combinations of federal budgetary mechanisms have powerful "shock-absorber" effects dampening the amplitude either of economic difficulties or of surges in prosperity of individual states. This is both the product of and the source of the sense of national solidarity which all relevant economic and monetary unions share.

Regional risk sharing stabilizes regionally divergent business cycles. Channeling income from prosperous regions to regions in distress can help attenuate asymmetries in the cyclical fluctuations of regions within a country, producing more even economic development across regions. This aspect of equalization has gained attention in the context of the European Monetary Union in the past 25 years (see, for example, the MacDougall Report/ European Commission 1977, Sachs and Sala-i-Martin 1991, Wyplosz 1991, Frenkel and Goldstein 1991, and Pisani-Ferry, Italianer, and Lescure 1993). But it applies more generally to countries whose regions are exposed to significant asymmetric shocks.

This chapter is organized as follows. It begins by introducing the basic principles of regional risk sharing. It then examines some moral hazard and political economy problems associated with regional risk sharing before reviewing the empirical evidence on regional risk sharing provided by fiscal mechanisms in the United States and other countries. The following section provides a macroeconomic perspective and discusses the connection between risk sharing and macroeconomic stabilization. The last section summarizes the chapter's conclusions.

Principles of Regional Risk Sharing

Economists have approached regional risk sharing from two perspectives. The traditional public finance literature considers risk sharing among consumers in different regions as a special case of consumption smoothing (see, for example, Asdrubali, Sørensen, and Yosha 1996; Atkeson and Bayoumi 1993; Athanasoulis and van Wincoop 1998; Boadway 2004; Bucovetsky 1998; and van Wincoop 1995). It seeks to determine the extent to which fiscal mechanisms can help consumers or subnational governments diversify region-specific income risk.

A second line of research starts from optimum currency area considerations. It regards intergovernmental transfer mechanisms as an alternative to flexible exchange rates and other market mechanisms for stabilizing regional output and employment. It seeks to determine the extent to which fiscal mechanisms can contribute to smoothing cyclical movements resulting from region-specific shocks to output demand and supply (see, for example, Fatas 1998, Goodhart and Smith 1993, Kenen 1969, Mundell 1961, Obstfeld and Peri 1998, von Hagen 1992, von Hagen and Hammond 1998, and Wyplosz 1991).

Consumption Smoothing

In a world of complete and frictionless markets, all risk sharing would be provided by capital markets.[2] Consumers would insure themselves against region-specific shocks by holding asset portfolios that pay systematically higher returns when their incomes from economic activities in their own region are low. As a result, consumption would be highly correlated across regions, and interregional consumption correlations would be stronger than interregional income correlations.[3]

When capital markets are incomplete, however, consumption smoothing can be achieved through fiscal transfers of income across regions.

Consider a country composed of $i = 1, \ldots, n$ regions.[4] The representative consumer in each region receives an income y_{it}, which is a random variable with expected value y_{oi} and a fixed variance.[5] For simplicity, assume that the consumer's utility, U_{it}, is linear quadratic in consumption, c_{it}, $U_{it} = c_{it} - \beta \mathrm{var}(c_{it})$, where β indicates the consumer's degree of risk aversion. Also assume that expected income is the same in all regions, $E(y_{it} = y_o)$ for all regions $i = 1, \ldots, n$, and that the variance of average income is normalized to 1. In the absence of any income redistribution across the n regions, the representative consumer's budget constraint in each region is $c_{it} = y_{it}$. Each consumer fully bears the income risk of his or her own region.

The central government can make consumers better off by using fiscal policy to pool income risk across regions. To do so, it imposes a tax on regional income and pays all consumers a transfer proportional to the average income in the country. Assume that central government taxation must be anonymous, in the sense that marginal tax rates on individual incomes are the same regardless of where individuals reside. If the tax rate on regional income is τ, the central government collects tax revenues of τy_i in each region and pays transfers of $g y_t$. Balancing the central government's budget requires that the sum of all taxes collected equals the sum of all transfers paid. This can be achieved by setting the tax rate equal to the transfer rate, $g = \tau$. The consumer's budget constraint is then $c_{it} = (1 - \tau)y_{it} + \tau y_t$. Alternatively, insurance can be provided by horizontal transfers across regions. In this case, each regional government pays τy_{it} into the equalization fund and receives a transfer of τy_t.

In this simple framework, the optimal tax and transfer mechanism aims at minimizing the variance of individual consumption. From the perspective of region i, the optimal regional risk-sharing arrangement would be obtained by choosing the tax rate τ^* that satisfies

$$\tau^{*i} = \frac{\sigma_i(\sigma_i - \rho_i)}{1 + \sigma_i(\sigma_i - 2\rho_i)}. \tag{4.1}$$

Here, ρ_i is the correlation between region i's and the country's average income. The relative riskiness of region i compared with the country average is given by $\sigma_i = (\mathrm{var}(y_{it})/\mathrm{var}(y_t))^{1/2}$.

This result provides several interesting insights. Region i's optimal tax rate depends on the correlation of its income with the country's average income and on the relative variance of its income. If all regional shocks are uncorrelated and identically distributed, the optimal tax and transfer rate is 1 ($\tau^{*i} = 1$ for all i) and optimal regional insurance amounts to the full equalization of all regional incomes ($c_{it} = y_t$ for all i). The same is true for all combinations of relative riskiness and correlation between regional and average income, for which $1 = \sigma_i \rho_i$. Generally, however, complete insurance is not optimal. Instead, the optimal degree of regional insurance depends on the risk profile of the regions. For relatively high-risk regions ($\sigma_i > 1$), the optimal tax rate increases with the correlation of its income with average income; the opposite is true for relatively low-risk regions. If the correlation between regional and average income is low, such that $\rho_i < 2\sigma_i/(1 + \sigma_i^2)$, the optimal tax rate increases as the relative riskiness of region i increases; otherwise the optimal tax rate falls with rising relative riskiness.

Equation (4.1) indicates that regions with different risk characteristics desire different tax rates and degrees of insurance. This implies that unless the risk profiles of all regions are identical, a single tax rate cannot be optimal for all regions. Nevertheless, the central government can make all regions agree on a higher tax rate by combining income-dependent transfers with fixed income-independent transfers implementing side payments between regions. In this case, the transfers become $g_{it} = \tau_{i0} + \tau y_t$. The consumer's budget constraint is $c_{it} = (1 - \tau)y_{it} + \tau y_t + \tau_{i0}$, and the government's budget balance requires that the fixed transfers sum to zero across all regions. The expected marginal utility from an increase in the marginal tax rate τ is $E(U_i') = 2\beta \text{var}(y)[(1 - \tau)\sigma_i^2 - (1 - 2\tau)\rho_i\sigma_i - \tau]$; the expected marginal utility from an increase in the fixed transfer is 1.

Consider the lowest tax rate and degree of insurance desired by any region, $\tau_{\min} = min_{i=1,\dots,n} (\tau^{i*})$. The optimality condition implies that the expected marginal utility $E(U_i'(\tau_{\min})) = 0$ for the region or regions desiring this lowest tax rate. In contrast, the expected marginal utility is positive at this tax rate for all other regions. This implies that the government can offer the region desiring the lowest tax rate a positive fixed transfer $\tau_i 0 > 0$ in return for accepting an increase in the marginal tax rate. This transfer can be financed by collecting fixed negative transfers from the regions that desire a larger degree of insurance. This will make residents in all regions better off. Thus the central government can compensate low-risk regions for agreeing to provide more insurance than they would otherwise desire (Persson and Tabellini 1996b). In such a scenario, high-risk regions pay a risk premium to low-risk regions for obtaining more than the minimal degree of insurance.

In federal states such as Australia, Canada, and Germany, fiscal equalization is based on transfers between the central government and subnational governments or transfers among subnational governments. A natural interpretation of such arrangements is that they aim to insure subnational government budgets against asymmetric shocks to their own tax revenues.[6]

It is straightforward to extend the arguments above to this case. To do so, reinterpret c_i as the public good provided by the government of region i in its own region, U_i as the utility citizens derive from the public good, and y_i as the regional government's own tax revenue.[7] In the case of horizontal fiscal equalization, τy_i is the amount of own revenues a regional government pays into the equalization fund, and g_i is the transfer it receives under the equalization scheme. In the case of vertical fiscal equalization, τy_i is the central government's share in the tax revenue collected in region i, and g_i is the transfer paid from the central to the regional government.

With this interpretation, a similar conclusion can be drawn: the optimal degree of insurance depends on the risk profile of the regional governments. Fixed transfers among regional governments or from the central government to the regional governments should be used to compensate regional governments that are farther away from their optimal insurance arrangement. One should thus expect regional insurance to combine permanent transfers with transfers that respond to regional revenue shocks.

Regional Stabilization

An alternative approach to regional risk sharing is based on the theory of optimum currency areas (Kenen 1969; Mundell 1961). It considers the scope for fiscal policy to cope with asymmetric shocks to regions sharing the same currency (Wyplosz 1991; Goodhart and Smith 1993; von Hagen and Hammond 1998). The macroeconomic perspective brings a broader range of alternative adjustment mechanisms into the picture. In addition to trade, capital flows, and migration, these include regional wage and price adjustments to regional shocks. Ingram (1959) first noted the potential usefulness of interregional fiscal transfers to achieve a greater degree of regional income and employment stability where market mechanisms do not provide sufficient regional stabilization.

The classic case under this approach was first presented by Mundell (1961). Consider a country consisting of two regions. Assume that an autonomous shift in aggregate demand reduces the demand for the products of one region and raises the demand for the products of the other. If each region had its own currency and the exchange rate were flexible, the decline in income in the first region would cause its currency to depreciate. Sticky prices imply that this would cause the relative price of its products to fall, both at home and in the other region. The result would be an increase in domestic and export demand that would partly offset the initial demand shock. Exchange rate adjustment thus helps stabilize the economies in both regions.

If the two regions share the same currency, other mechanisms for adjustment must play this role. While the required relative price adjustment could still work through output price and wage adjustments, in practice prices and wages do not seem sufficiently flexible.[8] This leaves factor movements, particularly movements of labor, as alternative market adjustment mechanisms.[9] As workers move from the first to the second region, full employment output adjusts to the shift in demand.

If labor markets do not provide sufficient adjustments, fiscal transfers between the two regions can do the job. Taxing the prospering region and giving the proceeds to the region in distress restores aggregate demand there and reduces aggregate demand in the taxed region. The same result can be obtained by increasing central government spending in the depressed region and reducing it in the prospering region.

Regarding fiscal transfers as a substitute for nominal exchange rate adjustments has an important implication. Researchers generally agree that nominal exchange rate flexibility accelerates economic adjustment to asymmetric shocks, but it is not a necessary condition for adjustment in the long run. Even if prices and wages are sticky and labor migration slow, regional markets sharing the same currency should eventually adjust to asymmetric shocks. This suggests that fiscal transfers offsetting temporary asymmetric shocks are more important to secure the viability of a monetary union than transfers tied to permanent shocks. The resulting limitation of regional risk sharing to temporary shocks seems much less natural under the consumption-smoothing approach, where insurance against both temporary and permanent shocks is considered.

Fiscal transfers that offset temporary asymmetric shocks between regions can be carried out in a fully discretionary, case by case manner. Mundell's analysis bears little relation to regional insurance per se, if insurance is understood as an ex ante guarantee that transfers be paid when asymmetric shocks occur. However, constitutional rules ensuring transfer payments between regions or the existence of a central budget providing for appropriate transfers can give assurance to all regions involved that payments will be executed should a region be hit by adverse shocks in the future. Such assurance may be important to make the promise of paying transfers to regions in distress credible.

Mutual Insurance versus Self-Insurance

In principle, regional governments can self-insure their regions against transitory shocks by borrowing and lending in international capital markets.

A depressed region's government could borrow and spend the proceeds on domestic output, while a prospering region's government could invest its higher tax revenues in international assets. Since the issue is insurance against transitory shocks, a region's borrowing and lending would be zero on average over sufficiently long time horizons. Thus no fiscal mechanism spanning across regions would be required.

Self-insurance of this kind requires that regions in distress have access to the capital market. In the presence of credit rationing, this may not be the case. Self-insurance then requires that a region's net position in the capital market never be negative, which demands the accumulation of a sufficiently large capital fund over time. The cost of this fund in terms of forgone consumption makes self-insurance less attractive than regional insurance. Regions, particularly if they are small, may also face higher borrowing rates than lending rates in the market. If they do, the average cost of self-insurance is positive even if the average level of borrowing is zero, and the cost is higher the larger the variance of the shocks insured. Capital market imperfections are thus important to justify the preference for regional insurance provided by fiscal mechanisms.

Bayoumi and Masson (1997, 1998) point to another advantage of regional insurance based on fiscal transfers between regions. Self-insurance implies that increased government spending during a recession is matched by a future tax liability. Rational, forward-looking consumers anticipate future tax payments and reduce consumption accordingly. In contrast, with regional insurance the transfers paid to a depressed region do not increase the expected future tax liabilities of taxpayers in that region if the expected value of future asymmetric shocks is zero and the insurance scheme is balanced across regions. Under these assumptions, regional insurance is a more effective tool for regional stabilization. Bayoumi and Masson report evidence from Canada suggesting that the demand effect of payments to provinces resulting from regional insurance is positive and significant, while debt-financed central government transfers to the provinces have no significant demand effects. This suggests that regional insurance is indeed more effective than fiscal policy at the national level.

Moral Hazard and the Political Economy of Regional Insurance

Moral Hazard Problems

Like all kinds of insurance, regional insurance is plagued by moral hazard problems. Three aspects of moral hazard deserve attention.

The first regards the incentive of regional governments participating in regional insurance to invest in risk-avoidance strategies. Persson and Tabellini (1996a) show that a government's incentive to raise local taxes and spend the proceeds on projects that make negative asymmetric shocks less likely in the home region is reduced by the prospect of transfers from other regions when such shocks hit. With decentralized policies geared at risk avoidance, local governments invest too little in such activities. The implication is that investment in risk-avoidance strategies by regional governments should not be left uncoordinated. A central government providing regional insurance will find it preferable to centralize policies aiming at risk avoidance or to subsidize investment in such strategies by regional governments in order to increase the level of their investment. Thus moral hazard creates an "incentive complementarity" (Persson and Tabellini 1996b), in the sense that making regional insurance a central government program raises the incentive to create central government programs related to regional risk.[10]

The second, related aspect arises if regional insurance targets regional government revenues. If transfer payments are tied to tax revenues collected by regional governments, they can be regarded as a "tax on tax revenue" (Baretti, Huber, and Lichtblau 2002), which reduces the regional governments' incentive to collect regional taxes. If the central government cannot observe tax effort in the regions, regional insurance will lead to a reduction in tax effort and, hence, tax revenues. Empirical evidence showing that fiscal equalization significantly affects regional tax policies in Germany (Baretti, Huber, and Lichtblau 2002; Büttner 2002), Canada (Snoddon 2003), and Australia (Dahlby and Warren 2003) suggests that regional governments do respond to such incentives and that regional insurance therefore has negative consequences for regional tax revenues.

The third aspect regards the effectiveness of market mechanisms for adjustment to transitory asymmetric shocks. Migué (1993) argues that, since taxes and transfers are generally distortive, redistributive policies reduce the incentive for individuals to adjust to regional shocks. Here it is important to go beyond Mundell's example and consider supply shocks. Individuals who receive transfers from the central government when their region fares poorly may see less reason to accept wage cuts, to move into other industries, or to move to other regions. The implication is that regional insurance provided by the central government can reduce the effectiveness of market mechanisms for adjustment.

Obstfeld and Peri (1998) discuss one important example of this—labor market adjustment to regional asymmetric shocks. They show that regional differences in unemployment rates are much more persistent in European countries than in the United States and that interregional migration contributes much less to the adjustment to asymmetric shocks in Europe than in the United States. Since cultural and language barriers, which may explain the slow labor market adjustment within Europe, do not exist within the United States but fiscal transfers paid in response to asymmetric shocks are much larger in Europe than in the United States, Obstfeld and Peri interpret this observation as showing that the generous welfare programs in Europe reduce the incentive for workers to move in response to economic shocks. European transfer programs thus reduce the effectiveness of labor market adjustment.

While the logic of the argument is compelling, interpreting the evidence is difficult, as the causality might be reversed. Countries in which markets adjust sluggishly for whatever reason would likely choose higher levels of regional insurance. Still, the theoretical arguments and the empirical evidence suggest that full regional insurance is unlikely to be desirable and that the choice of an efficient level of regional insurance is a complicated matter, particularly when regional insurance is a by-product of a central government budget or welfare system.

Political Economy Effects

Regional risk-sharing mechanisms are the product of political choices. The design and size of such programs are, therefore, likely to depend on the political processes by which they are chosen (Persson and Tabellini 1996a, 1996b). Consider the case in which regions of a country are exposed to uncorrelated regional income shocks, which give rise to risk pooling. Assume also that some regions are "riskier" than others, in the sense that the variance of their regional shocks is higher than in less risky regions. Efficient regional risk sharing under such circumstances requires that the "riskier" regions pay a risk premium to the less risky ones. To facilitate this, the insurance mechanism must combine state-dependent and state-independent transfer payments. But the existence of state-independent transfers implies a scope for permanent redistribution between regions and creates a source of conflict between residents of different regions.

Full insurance combined with the efficient risk premium can be obtained through transfers between regional governments if these transfers are the result of a Nash bargain (or unanimity vote) among representative agents from all region. In contrast, no voting equilibrium exists in which all regions decide separately on the same combination of fixed and income-dependent transfers. The reason why is that voters in each region will try to exploit the state-independent tax to extract permanent redistribution from other regions beyond the efficient risk premium. This implies that the efficient risk-sharing mechanism cannot be obtained by taking majority votes in all regions separately. With separate votes in all regions, a voting equilibrium can be reached only if the insurance mechanism is limited to income-dependent transfers, and this produces an undersupply of regional insurance. This implies that to provide efficient regional insurance, the mechanism should be determined at the constitutional design stage of a federation and reforms should be subject to ratification in each region.

If regional risk sharing is provided by a central government welfare program or unemployment insurance targeting individuals rather than regions and it is voted for in countrywide referenda, the efficient regional insurance can be obtained by a majority vote only if all regions have the same risk properties (Persson and Tabellini 1996a). With different degrees of riskiness, majority voting leads to inefficiencies, as voters try to achieve permanent redistribution in their favor. Furthermore, if voters are subject to risks other than regional income risk, such as industry-specific shocks, the countrywide referendum can facilitate the formation of coalitions across regional borders, allowing voters to exploit the mechanism designed for regional insurance to insure themselves against other types of risk. As regional risk sharing becomes intertwined with other purposes, such coalitions will vote to oversupply.

Empirical Evidence

Numerous empirical studies have provided evidence of regional insurance in the United States and other countries. Most of these studies focus on the fiscal transfer mechanisms involved. Regional insurance provided through capital markets is much harder to estimate, because of data problems.

Market-Based Insurance against Asymmetric Shocks in the United States

Atkeson and Bayoumi (1993) use state data from 1966 to 1986 to estimate the extent to which state incomes are insured against state-specific risks through U.S. capital markets. They regress changes in per capita incomes earned from capital located in a state on changes in per capita incomes earned from capital located in the rest of the country, state labor incomes, and state capital products. Their estimates suggest that state capital incomes are driven mainly by incomes earned from capital located in the rest of the country and that a decline in state labor incomes is offset by a small but significant increase in capital incomes. Thus asset markets provide little albeit significant regional insurance. The strong correlation between state consumption (proxied by retail sales) and state incomes also suggests that regional insurance is far from perfect.

Asdrubali, Sørensen, and Yosha (1996) estimate a model that is derived directly from accounting relations. It therefore involves no further assumptions about consumer choices, as Atkeson and Bayoumi's analysis does. Using data from 1964 to 1990, they estimate that capital markets smoothed 39 percent of cross-state fluctuations in gross state product and credit markets smoothed another 23 percent. These results give financial markets a much larger role in consumption smoothing than Atkeson and Bayoumi's results do. The more direct method of estimation lends more credibility to their results.

Athanasoulis and van Wincoop (1998) estimate the reduction of the standard deviation of state income due to financial markets at different time horizons. They find that financial markets smooth about 30 percent of shocks to gross state products at horizons of one to two years and 35 percent over up to 26 years.

Fiscal Insurance against Asymmetric Shocks in the United States

Many researchers have estimated the extent of regional insurance provided by the federal fiscal system in the United States (table 4.1). They estimate both the redistributive and insurance role of the transfers.

The MacDougall Report (European Commission 1977) examined regional insurance by asking by how much the U.S. federal fiscal system reduces income differences between U.S. states. Sachs and Sala-i-Martin (1991) ask the same question, considering the following regression:

$$\ln\left(\frac{tax_{it}}{tax_t}\right) = \alpha + \beta \ln\left(\frac{Y_{it}}{Y_t}\right) + trend + residual, \qquad (4.2)$$

where tax_{it} denotes the taxes paid by region i to the federal government in period t, tax_t is the national aggregate of tax_{it}, Y_{it} is personal income in region i in year t, and Y_t is the national aggregate of Y_t. Sachs and Sala-i-Martin run a similar regression with transfers as the dependent variable. They consider the nine U.S. census regions as geographical units.

Sachs and Sala-i-Martin interpret the coefficient β as a measure of the offsetting effect of the federal fiscal system to region-specific income shocks. They estimate the combined effect of taxes and transfers at $0.33–$0.40 per

T A B L E   4 . 1 Empirical Evidence on Regional Insurance
in the United States
(US cents)

Author	Purpose of transfer	
	Redistribution	Insurance
MacDougall Report (European Commission 1977)	28	
Sachs and Sala-i-Martin (1991)	33–40	
von Hagen (1993)	47	10
Atkeson and Bayoumi (1993)	—	7
Goodhart and Smith (1993)	15	13
Pisani-Ferry, Italianer, and Lescure (1993)	—	17
Gros and Jones (1994)	—	4–14
Bayoumi and Masson (1995)	7–22	7–30
Mélitz and Zumer (2002)	16	10–16
Asdrubali, Sørensen, and Yosha (1996)	—	13
Sørensen and Yosha (1997)	—	15
Fatas (1998)	—	11
Obstfeld and Peri (1998)	19	10
Athanasoulis and van Wincoop (1998)	20	10

Source: Author compilation.
Note: Entries indicate the estimated range of net federal transfers received by a region in response to a $1 differ-
ence in the level or change in state income or product compared with U.S. average income or product. Centered
entries refer to estimates that do not distinguish between redistribution and insurance. — = not available.

$1, concluding that the federal fiscal system provides very substantial insur-
ance against asymmetric regional shocks. This conclusion conforms with
that of the MacDougall Report, but it is problematic. As von Hagen (1992)
first noted, equation (4.2) shows the amount by which a region's tax liabilities and transfer benefits are reduced or increased relative to the national
average if its income is larger or smaller than the national average by a given
amount; it does not distinguish between permanent and transitory income
differences. Like the MacDougall Report, equation (4.2) lumps together two
very different elements of a federal fiscal system: permanent redistribution
to reduce secular income differences between regions and insurance against
asymmetric shocks. In order to get a better estimate of the insurance component, he considers the following regression:

Rather than estimating a trend, he allows the intercepts of his panel
regression to vary and

$$\Delta \ln(tax_{it}) = \alpha_{it} + \beta \Delta \ln(Y_{it}) + dummies + residual \qquad (4.3)$$

account for the U.S. business cycle. The dummies are for the oil-producing states. Von Hagen uses state gross products as the explanatory variable. The insurance effect obtained is substantially lower than the Sachs and Sala-i-Martin estimate (table 4.1), while the redistributive effect is about the same.

Subsequent papers have generally accepted the distinction between redistribution and insurance or regional stabilization and come up with estimates that are closer to von Hagen's (1992). Bayoumi and Masson (1995) estimate the insurance effect based on the following regression:

$$\Delta\left(\frac{Y_{it} - tax_{it} + transfer_{it}}{Y_t - tax_t + transfer_t}\right) = \alpha_i + \beta\Delta Y_{it} \ over Y_t + residual. \quad (4.4)$$

They estimate a relatively high insurance coefficient. This may be due to a second distinction between their regression and that of Sachs and Sala-i-Martin and von Hagen, however. As Fatas (1998) notes, an increase in the net transfers received by a state may be financed either by a reduction in the net transfers received by all others, which corresponds to regional insurance, or by an increase in the federal budget deficit, in which case the federal government implicitly borrows on behalf of that state. Neither Sachs and Sala-i-Martin (1991) nor Bayoumi and Masson (1995) distinguish between these two possibilities. In contrast, the time-varying intercepts in von Hagen's regression can be interpreted to do so implicitly.[11] Fatas (1998) shows that accounting for this distinction reduces the insurance effect implied by the Sachs and Sala-i-Martin estimate to about $0.10 per $1 change in relative income.

Mélitz and Zumer (2002) compare estimates based on state income with estimates based on gross state products as the measure of regional economic activity. They find that the insurance effect associated with gross state product estimates tends to be lower than the effect associated with state income estimates. They argue that since state income is closely related to private consumption, estimates based on state income are more informative with regard to regional insurance of individual consumption. Conceptually, however, this raises the difficulty that state incomes include incomes earned from economic activities outside the state—that is, it is exposed to shocks originating in other regions. Gross state product is closely related to macroeconomic activity in a state. Therefore, estimates based on gross state product are more informative with regard to regional stabilization.

Athanasoulis and van Wincoop (1998) estimate the stabilizing role of the federal fiscal system at time horizons of different lengths. They find that the federal fiscal system reduces the standard deviation of changes in state incomes by about 10 percent at one to two years and by 15 percent on average over all horizons.

Pisani-Ferry, Italianer, and Lescure (1993) use a very different methodology. They use a macroeconomic simulation model augmented by a model of budgetary flows within a country based on government accounting relations to assess the tax and transfer effects of asymmetric regional shocks. Their estimate for the United States is similar to most of the results published since 1991.

In sum, the empirical studies of the 1990s confirm that the federal fiscal system in the United States provides significant regional insurance. Although there is disagreement about the magnitude of the effect, the evidence suggests that it is much smaller than the redistributive effect of the federal fiscal system.

Regional Insurance in Other Countries

Several studies have presented estimates for countries other than the United States (table 4.2). Canada is of particular interest, because it has an explicit, constitutionally grounded mechanism for horizontal transfers among the provinces.

The MacDougall Report estimates that the Canadian federal system reduces income differences between provinces by $0.32 per $1. Bayoumi and Masson (1995) estimate the insurance effect at $0.14 per $1 (less than their estimate for the United States) and the redistributive effect at $0.39 per $1. Other studies confirm the magnitude of the regional insurance in Canada but provide different estimates of the redistributive effect.

One difficulty with the Canadian equalization system is that it is designed to bring relatively poor provinces up to a standard defined by the average per capita revenues of British Columbia, Manitoba, Ontario, Quebec, and Saskatchewan (Courchene 1999). Under the rules of the system, Alberta, British Columbia, and Ontario receive no equalization payments, the remaining provinces that are included in the standard receive a partial offset for a revenue shortfall, and provinces that are not included in the standard receive a full offset for a decline in revenues. At the same time, a poor province receives a transfer when revenues in the provinces included in the standard increase, even if the province's economy performs as well as the average Canadian province. This shows the emphasis on redistribution rather than regional insurance and implies that regressions like equation (4.4) are likely to misrepresent the working of the system.

Results for France, Germany, Italy, and the United Kingdom show surprisingly wide variation across countries. Mélitz and Zumer (2002) and Goodhart and Smith (1993) obtain similar estimates for the United Kingdom, where regional insurance seems somewhat greater than in Canada and the

TABLE 4.2 Empirical Evidence on Regional Insurance
in Selected Countries
(national currency units/100)

	Purpose of transfer	
Country/author	Redistribution	Insurance
Canada		
MacDougall (European Commission 1977)	32	—
Bayoumi and Masson (1995)	39	14
Goodhart and Smith (1993)	—	12–19
Mélitz and Zumer (2002)	16–30	10–14
Obstfeld and Peri	53	13
France		
MacDougall (European Commission 1977)	54	—
Pisani-Ferry, Italianer, and Lescure (1993)	—	37.4
Mélitz and Zumer (2002)	38	16–17
Germany		
MacDougall (European Commission 1977)	29	—
Pisani-Ferry, Italianer, and Lescure (1993)	—	34–42
Büttner (2002)	—	6.5–21.1
Makipaa and von Hagen (2005)	55–62	0–18
Italy		
MacDougall (European Commission 1977)	—	47
Obstfeld and Peri (1998)	8	3
United Kingdom		
Goodhart and Smith (1993)	—	21
Mélitz and Zumer (2002)	26	26

Source: Author compilation.
Note: Entries indicate the estimated range of net federal transfers received by a region in response to a $1 difference in the level or change in state income or product compared with U.S. average income or product. — = not available.

United States. Mélitz and Zumer find that regional insurance is substantially greater in France than in Canada or the United States. Using a different methodology, Pisani-Ferry, Italianer, and Lescure (1993) find a similar result. While this might suggest that insurance is generally greater in unitary states than in federations, Obstfeld and Peri (1998) estimate that regional insurance is negligible in Italy. Pisani-Ferry, Italianer, and Lescure (1993) find that regional insurance in Germany is as large as in France. Estimates by Büttner (2002) and Makipaa and von Hagen (2005), based on the same methodology as the other studies, indicate a much lower degree of regional insurance. Makipaa and von Hagen find that the insurance function of Germany's fiscal federalism vanished after unification in 1990, while its redistributive effect remains very large.

In sum, the empirical evidence shows that regional insurance is a significant part of the fiscal systems in federal and unitary states. But the size of the insurance varies greatly across countries.

The Macroeconomics of Regional Risk Sharing and Stabilization

The discussion so far takes the desirability of regional risk sharing for the stabilization of regional economies for granted and assumes that there is no conflict between regional risk sharing and stabilization of a nation's aggregate economy. This section examines the macroeconomics of regional risk sharing. It assumes that regional risk sharing is a rules-based approach that aims to reduce income differences across regions through interregional taxes and transfers.

The annex develops a model of regional macroeconomic stabilization for a country consisting of two regions. The two regions produce outputs that are imperfect substitutes in demand; they share the same currency and an integrated capital market. Both are affected by demand and supply (wage and productivity) shocks. The model has a new Keynesian flavor: prices and wages are assumed to be sticky, which allows aggregate demand to have short-run real effects. The two regions are assumed to have heterogeneous economic structures, in the sense that the aggregate demand effect of government spending and the real interest rate elasticities of aggregate demand are different in the two regions. This structural heterogeneity is of key importance for the analysis that follows. Empirically, it is validated by the fact that structural parameters can vary substantially across countries in structural multicountry models and by the observation that monetary policy shocks affect different regions in different ways in existing monetary unions.[12] Regional fiscal policy is represented by regional government spending. In principle, it is able to offset the effects of relative demand and supply shocks in this economy.

Regional Risk Sharing and Regional Stabilization

Consider a transfer mechanism between two regions that aims at reducing income differentials between them:

$$g = -g^* = -\frac{\alpha}{2}(y - y^*). \tag{4.5}$$

The region with larger output reduces government spending in its own region and pays a transfer to the region with lower output, allowing that region to increase government spending. The parameter α indicates the degree of insurance: the larger it is, the more closely regional incomes are tied to the average national income.

How does such a mechanism affect output and prices in the home region in the presence of purely asymmetric shocks? Equations (4A.5) and (4A.6) provide the basis for an answer.

Consider first the case of a relative demand shock that shifts demand from the home region to the foreign region. Home output falls, and so does the regional output price. In the absence of fiscal transfers, this relative price shift is equivalent to a real exchange rate depreciation and helps the home region recover from the initial shock. The larger the relative price elasticity of demand, the greater the effect. If this price elasticity is taken as a measure of economic integration, asymmetric shocks matter less when regions are highly integrated.

If the effect of fiscal impulses on output is the same in both regions, the transfer from the foreign to the home region unambiguously stabilizes both output and prices in the home region. However, if the output effect of a fiscal impulse is larger in the foreign region than in the home region, the transfer scheme can be counterproductive, in the sense that it weakens the economy's self-stabilizing capacity. The reason is that the transfer paid by the foreign region reduces demand there by more than the initial shift in autonomous demand increased it, lowering the foreign region's private import demand for domestic output. In this case, home output would be more stable in the absence of a fiscal transfer mechanism.

Consider next the case of a negative relative wage or productivity shock. As before, the fiscal transfer mechanism stabilizes home output unless the impact of government spending on foreign aggregate demand is too large. However, the transfer scheme amplifies the response of the home output price. The reason why is straightforward. The transfer increases demand for the home product in a situation in which output is down and prices are already rising due to the supply shock. The desirability of a fiscal stabilization mechanism thus depends on the relative size of the price effect and the relative weight of regional price stability in the utility function of the residents of the region. Clearly, when output is inelastic to price changes, the transfer mechanism only raises inflation in the home region and is entirely undesirable.[13]

To summarize, the stabilization properties of a fiscal transfer system depend critically on the relative magnitudes of the supply and demand elasticities in the donor and recipient regions. Unless these magnitudes are known with sufficient certainty, there is a risk that a transfer mechanism may be destabilizing.

Regional Risk Sharing and National Stabilization

What are the implications of the regional stabilization mechanism for aggregate output and price level fluctuations? Equation (4A.7) shows that regional asymmetries in the response of aggregate demand to a fiscal impulse imply that the fiscal transfer mechanism translates purely relative fluctuations into aggregate ones. The reason is that the transfer reduces (increases) demand in one region by less than it increases (reduces) demand in the other, raising national aggregate demand as a result. In the presence of such asymmetries, the transfer scheme can create a conflict between stabilization policy at the national level and stabilization of regional economies. A central bank firmly committed to price stability would be enticed to raise interest rates, for example, if the regional stabilization scheme caused aggregate demand to rise following a relative demand or supply shock between the two regions The monetary restriction would exacerbate the recession in the region affected by a negative shock. Thus in the presence of asymmetric regional responses to fiscal stimuli, the regional transfer mechanism can intensify conflicts between the national monetary and fiscal authorities.

These results were derived assuming equal interest rate elasticities of aggregate demand in the two regions. Relaxing that restriction turns attention to the aggregate shock in the two regions, including asymmetric responses to the common monetary policy. As the income differential now depends on the size of the aggregate shock (equation 4A.8), the transfer mechanism triggers income flows between the regions in response to aggregate shocks. If a monetary contraction affects output demand in the home region more than elsewhere, for example, it will cause a deeper recession at home. As a result, the region will receive transfers from the other region. The regional stabilization mechanism can increase or reduce the effect of an aggregate shock on aggregate income, depending on the relative size of the regional responses to a fiscal impulse (see annex). Thus in the presence of asymmetries in the regional propagation mechanisms of aggregate shocks and fiscal policy, regional risk sharing can reduce or improve the effectiveness of monetary policy.

Conclusions

Regional risk sharing through a nation's tax and transfer system is a fundamental aspect of the fiscal system of developed economies. It can generally be justified by the desire to smooth consumption over time and to stabilize regional output and employment in the absence of exchange rate flexibility between regions. Moral hazard problems and political economy considerations, however, suggest that full risk sharing of asymmetric shocks is not optimal.

Empirical evidence shows that regional risk sharing through the fiscal system is significant in many countries, although the degree of variation in the size of the regional insurance provided by the tax and transfer system varies. In the United States, as in most countries for which empirical evidence exists, actual risk sharing seems to be modest. The empirical literature shows that the distinction between redistribution and insurance or stabilization is crucial in the proper estimation. Surprisingly, perhaps, there is no clear evidence that regional risk sharing is greater in unitary than in federal states. The research gives no basis for explaining why countries chose the degree of regional risk sharing they have or for judging whether the observed degree of risk sharing is close to the optimal one.

An important aspect of tax- and transfer-based regional risk sharing is that payments cannot be implemented to offset regional shocks directly, since shocks are not directly observed. Implementation of regional risk sharing must rely on rules tying payments to income differentials. Such transfers, however, can increase the variability of regional output and prices and interfere with the stabilization of the national economy. Interference between regional and national stabilization may be one reason why more regional risk sharing is not observed through the fiscal system in large federations such as Canada and the United States.

Annex: A Model of Regional Stabilization and Risk Sharing

Consider a country consisting of two regions, the home region and the foreign region. Let y be output, p the output price, r the nominal interest rate common to both regions, m the country's money supply, and g the fiscal impulse. (An asterisk superscript denotes variables of the foreign region.) All variables denote relative deviations from steady state. Output demand in the two regions is

$$y^d = a - c(r - \pi^e) + d(p^* - p) + g ,$$

$$y^{d*} = a^* - c^*(r - \pi^e) - d(p^* - p) + f^* g^*.$$

(4A.1)

The expected national rate of inflation is denoted by π^e, a and a^* are shocks to the levels of demand, and $p^* - p$ is the relative price of home output, that is, the home region's real exchange rate. With $c^* \neq c$ and $f^* \neq 1$, some asymmetry is allowed in the propagation mechanisms of the two regions. Output supply is characterized by price-setting functions

$$p = w + \theta + \gamma y, \quad p^* = w^* + \theta^* + \gamma y^*, \tag{4A.2}$$

where w is a nominal wage shock and θ is a productivity shock. Money market equilibrium is given by the condition:

$$m + \frac{1}{2}(p + p^*) = y + y^* - \frac{1}{2}br. \tag{4A.3}$$

For now, assume that $c^* = c$ and that all current shocks are transitory. For the analysis to follow, it is convenient to define E as the aggregate shock common to both regions and D as the asymmetric shock, which affects the two regions with opposite sign.[14] Using these definitions, inflation expectations are $\pi^e = -E - 0.5\gamma(y + y^*)$. Taking this into account yields the equilibrium solutions

$$y = \frac{1}{\Delta}[a + g + (2 + \gamma)bc(g - f^* g^*) + \phi(f^* - 1)g^* + E + D], \tag{4A.4}$$

$$y^* = \frac{1}{\Delta}[a^* + f^* g^* - (2 + \gamma)bc(g - f^* g^*) + \phi(f^* - 1)g^* + E - D],$$

where $\Delta > 0$.

Consider now the transfer mechanism defined in equation (4A.5). Calculating the equilibrium solutions yields

$$y = \frac{2 - \dfrac{\alpha(1 - f^*)}{\Gamma}}{2(1 + 2\phi) + \alpha(1 + f^*)}\left[a + \frac{1 + (2 + \gamma)bc + 2\phi}{(1 + 2\phi)\Gamma}D\right], \tag{4A.5}$$

where $\Gamma = 1 + 2(2 + \gamma bc)$. The equilibrium solution for the home region's output price level is

$$p = \frac{1 - \dfrac{\alpha(1 - f^*)}{\Gamma}}{2(1 + 2\phi) + \alpha(1 + f^*)}\gamma a$$

$$+ \left[1 - \frac{2 - \dfrac{\alpha(1 - f^*)}{\Gamma}}{2(1 + 2\phi) + \alpha(1 + f^*)}\frac{1 + bc(2 + \gamma) + 2\phi}{(1 + 2\phi)\Gamma}2\gamma\right](w + \theta). \tag{4A.6}$$

Consider first the case of a relative demand shock, $a < 0$. With $0 < f* \leq 1$, the fiscal transfer mechanism unambiguously stabilizes both output and prices in the home region. However, if $f* > 1$ and becomes too large, the fiscal transfer scheme increases the volatility of home output in response to demand shocks.[15]

Consider next the case of a negative relative supply shock to the home region, $w > 0$ or $\theta > 0$. Output is stabilized unless $f*$ is too large. The mechanism increases the response of the output price of the home region, however.

Aggregate, national output and prices are the following:

$$y + y* = \frac{\alpha}{\Delta}(f* - 1)(y - y*), \quad \frac{1}{2}(p + p*) = \frac{\alpha\gamma}{4\Delta}(f* - 1)(y - y*). \quad (4A.7)$$

Equation (4A.7) shows that with $f* \neq 1$, the sum of the two regional outputs depends on the difference between the two if $\alpha > 0$. That is, the fiscal transfer mechanism transforms purely relative fluctuations into aggregate fluctuations.

To study the implications of asymmetric interest elasticities of aggregate demand and simplify the analysis, set all asymmetric shocks to zero, that is, $a = a*$, $w = w*$, and $\theta = \theta*$, implying that $D = 0$. Furthermore, let $d = 0$. Assuming $f* = 1$, this yields

$$y - y* = -\frac{\left(b - \frac{1}{2}\right) \quad (c - c*)E}{\Delta' + \alpha[1 + b(2 + \gamma)(c + c*)]}, \quad (4A.8)$$

$$\Delta' = 1 + (c + c*)[0.5\gamma + b(2 + \gamma)] + 2bcc*(2 + \gamma)$$

for the income differential. Thus aggregate shocks, including monetary policy shocks, affect income in the two regions in different ways. With asymmetric effects of fiscal policy in the two regions, the transfer scheme can reduce or amplify the impact of aggregate shocks on the two region's combined incomes, which, in this case is:

$$y + y* = \frac{-\left(b - \frac{1}{2}\right)c*}{\Delta'}\left\{1 + \zeta + c\gamma - \frac{\alpha}{2}[1 - f* + \gamma(1 - \zeta f*)]\right.$$

$$\left. \times \frac{1 - \zeta}{\Delta' + \alpha[1 + c*(1 + \zeta)(2 + \gamma)]}\right\}E, \quad (4A.9)$$

where $Z = c/c*$.

Notes

1. For reviews of existing equalization mechanisms, see Spahn (1993) and Spahn and Shah (1995).
2. Asdrubali, Sørensen, and Yosha (1996) distinguish between capital markets and credit markets. While this distinction is useful in their analysis for statistical reasons, the term *capital markets* is used here in the more general sense of financial markets. As Obstfeld and Peri (1998) show, free trade in the goods and services produced by the regions can also provide complete insurance against regional income shocks.
3. There is an obvious analogy here with models of international risk sharing tested in the context of tests of international capital mobility (see, for example, Backus, Kehoe, and Kydland 1992).
4. See Fatas (1998) for a similar exposition.
5. For simplicity, the discussion abstracts from private sector saving. Alternatively, one might assume that y_{it} contains asset incomes and is defined net of saving.
6. See for example, Konrad and Seitz (2001) and Lockwood (1999). Lockwood also considers regional insurance against shocks to the spending needs or cost of providing public goods.
7. See Lockwood (1999) for an analysis of regional insurance when regional public goods create fiscal externalities between regions.
8. Hochreiter and Winckler (1995) present empirical evidence suggesting that real wage flexibility increased under the "hard" peg of the Austrian schilling to the Deutsche mark. Nevertheless, the role of price and wage flexibility in adjusting to regional shocks seems very limited in practice, as Obstfeld and Peri (1998) show for the United States, Canada, and European countries.
9. The importance of labor mobility for the operation of a common currency was first stressed by Mundell (1961).
10. Courchene (1993) points to the example of Quebec, which maintained a higher minimum wage than other Canadian provinces in the 1970s and was able to shift the cost of higher unemployment in bad times on to the federal budget.
11. Fatas (1998) notes that a necessary condition for regional insurance is that the correlation between shocks at the state level and shocks at the national level be less than 1. Empirically, he finds that the average correlation coefficient between state and aggregate U.S. annual real income growth rates is 0.72.
12. For empirical evidence on these issues, see von Hagen and Waller (1999).
13. See Hervé and Holzmann (1998), who discuss this case in the context of the classical transfer problem of international economics.
14. The aggregate shock is $E = \varphi(a + a^* + g + g^* - \kappa(1 + 2\varphi)(w + w^* + \theta + \theta^* - 2m)$ and the differential shock $D = (2 + \gamma)bc(a - a^*) + [1 + 2\varphi + (2 + \gamma)bc](w^* - w + \theta^* - \theta)$, where $\varphi = (d + 0.5c)\gamma$ and $\kappa = c(b - 0.5)$.
15. This is the case if $f^* > (1 + \varphi + bc[2 + \gamma])/(\varphi - bc(2 + \gamma)) > 1$.

References

Asdrubali, Pierfederica, Bent Sørensen, and Oved Yosha. 1996. "Channels of Interstate Risk Sharing: United States 1963–1990." *Quarterly Journal of Economics* 111 (4): 1081–110.

Athanasoulis, Stefano, and Eric van Wincoop. 1998. "Risk-Sharing within the United States: What Have Financial Markets and Fiscal Federalism Accomplished?" Research Paper 9808, Federal Reserve Bank of New York.

Atkeson, Andrew, and Tamim Bayoumi. 1993. "Do Private Capital Markets Insure Regional Risk? Evidence for the U.S. and Europe." *Open Economies Review* 4 (3): 303–24.

Backus, David K., Patrick J. Kehoe, and Finn E. Kydland. 1992. "International Real Business Cycles." *Journal of Political Economy* 100 (4): 745–75.

Baretti, C., Bernd Huber, and Karl Lichtblau. 2002. "A Tax on Tax Revenue: The Incentive Effects of Equalizing Transfers. Evidence from Germany." *International Tax and Public Finance* 9 (6): 631–49.

Bayoumi, Tamim, and Paul R. Masson. 1995. "Fiscal Flows in the United States and Canada: Lessons for Monetary Union in Europe." *European Economic Review* 39 (2): 253–74.

———. 1997. "The Efficiency of National and Regional Stabilization Policies." In *Business Cycles and Macroeconomic Stability*, eds. Jean-Olivier Hairault, Pierre-Yves Hénin, and Franck Portier, 149–70. Boston: Kluwer Academic Publishers.

———. 1998. "Liability-Creating versus Non-Liability-Creating Fiscal Stabilization Policies: Ricaridan Equivalence, Fiscal Stabilization, and EMU." *Economic Journal* 108 (449): 1026–45.

Boadway, Robin. 2004. "The Theory and Practice of Equalization." *CESifo Economic Studies* 50 (1): 211–54.

Bucovetsky, Sam. 1998. "Federalism, Equalization, and Risk Aversion." *Journal of Public Economics* 67 (3): 301–28.

Büttner, Thiess. 2002. "Fiscal Federalism and Interstate Risk Sharing: Empirical Evidence from Germany." *Economics Letters* 74 (2): 195–202.

Courchene, Tom. 1993. "Reflections on Canadian Federalism: Are There Implications for European Economic and Monetary Union?" In *The Economics of Community Public Finance*, European Economy Reports and Studies 5, 123–66. Brussels: European Commission.

———. 1999. "Subnational Budgetary and Stabilization Policies in Canada and Australia." In *Budgetary Institutions and Budgetary Performance*, ed. James Poterba and Jürgen von Hagen, 301–48. Chicago: University of Chicago Press for the National Bureau of Economic Research.

Dafflon, Bernard, and Francois Vaillancourt. 2003. "Problems of Equalization in Federal (Decentralized) Systems." In *Federalism in a Changing World: Learning from Each Other*, ed. R. Blindenbacher and A. Koller, 479–505. Montreal: McGill-Queens University Press.

Dahlby, Bev, and Neil Warren. 2003. "The Fiscal Incentive Effects of the Australian Fiscal Equalization System." *Economic Record* 79 (247): 434–49.

Delors, Jacques. 1989. *Report on Economic and Monetary Union in the European Community*, ed. Committee for the Study of Economic and Monetary Union. Luxembourg: Office for Official Publications of the European Community.

European Commission. 1977. Report of the Study Group on the Role of Public Finances in European Integration (MacDougall Report). Brussels: European Commission.

Fatas, Antonio. 1998. "Does EMU Need a Fiscal Federation?" *Economic Policy* 26: 163–202.

Frenkel, Jacob, and Morris Goldstein. 1991. "Monetary Policy in an Emerging European Economic and Monetary Union." IMF Staff Papers 38: 356–73, International Monetary Fund, Washington, DC.

Goodhart, Charles E.A., and Stephen Smith. 1993. "Stabilization." In *The Economics of Community Public Finance*, European Economy Reports and Studies 5, 417–55. Brussels: European Commission.

Gros, Daniel, and Eric Jones. 1994. "Fiscal Stabilizers in the US Monetary Union: Measurement Errors and the Role of National Fiscal Policy." CEPS Working Document 83, Centre for Economic Policy Studies, Brussels.

Hervé, Yves, and Robert Holzmann. 1998. *Fiscal Transfers and Economic Convergence in the EU: An Analysis of Absorption Problems and an Evaluation of the Literature.* Baden-Baden, Germany: Nomos.

Hochreiter, Eduart, and Georg Winckler. 1995. "The Advantages of Tying Austria's Hands: The Success of a Hard-Currency Strategy." *European Journal of Political Economy* 11 (1): 83–111.

Ingram, J.C. 1959. "State and Regional Payments Mechanisms." *Quarterly Journal of Economics* 73 (4): 619–32.

Kenen, Peter B. 1969. "The Theory of Optimum Currency Areas: An Eclectic View." In *Monetary Problems of the World Economy*, ed. Robert Mundell and Alexander Swoboda. Chicago: University of Chicago Press.

Konrad, Kai, and Helmut Seitz. 2001. "Fiscal Federalism and Risk Sharing in Germany: The Role of Size Differences." Discussion Paper FS IV 01–20, Wissenschaftszentrum für Sozialforschung, Berlin.

Lockwood, Ben. 1999. "Inter-Regional Insurance." *Journal of Public Economics* 72 (1): 1–37.

Makipaa, Arttu, and Jürgen von Hagen. 2005. "Regional Insurance and Redistribution in Germany." Center for European Integration Studies, University of Bonn.

Mélitz, Jacques, and Silvia Vori. 1993. "National Insurance against Unevenly Distributed Shocks in a European Monetary Union." *Recherches Économiques de Louvain* 59 (1): 81–104.

Mélitz, Jacques, and Frédéric Zumer. 2002. "Regional Redistribution and Stabilization by the Centre in Canada, France, the U.K. and the U.S.: A Reassessment and New Tests." *Journal of Public Economics* 86 (2): 263–84.

Migué, Jean-Luc. 1993. "Federalism and Free Trade." Hobart Paper, Institute of Economic Affairs, London.

Mundell, Robert. 1961. "A Theory of Optimal Currency Areas." *American Economic Review* 51 (4): 657–65.

Oates, Wallace E. 1972. *Fiscal Federalism.* New York: Harcourt Brace Jovanovich.

Obstfeld, Maurice, and Giovanni Peri. 1998. "Regional Non-Adjustment and Fiscal Policy." *Economic Policy* 26: 205–69.

Persson, Torsten, and Guido Tabellini. 1996a. "Federal Fiscal Constitutions: Risk Sharing and Moral Hazard." *Econometrica* 64 (3): 623–46.

———. 1996b. "Federal Fiscal Constitutions: Risk Sharing and Redistribution." *Journal of Political Economy* 104 (5): 979–1009.

Pisani-Ferry, Jean, Alexander Italianer, and Roland Lescure. 1993. "Stabilization Properties of Budgetary Systems: A Simulation Analysis." In *The Economics of Community Public Finance*, 417–55. European Economy Reports and Studies 5. Brussels: European Commission.

Sachs, Jeffrey, and Xavier Sala-i-Martin, 1991. "Fiscal Federalism and Optimum Currency Areas: Evidence for Europe from the United States." In *Establishing a Central Bank: Issues in Europe and Lessons from the U.S.*, ed. Matthew Canzoneri, Vittorio Grilli, and Paul Masson. Cambridge: Cambridge University Press.

Snoddon, Tracy. 2003. "On Equalization and Incentives: An Empirical Assessment." Working Paper 2003-06 EC, Wilfrid Laurier University, Waterloo, Canada.

Sørensen, Bent E., and Oved Yosha. 1997. "Federal Insurance of U.S. States: An Empirical Investigation." In *Globalization: Public Economics Policy Perspectives*, ed. Assaf Razin and Efraim Sadka. Cambridge: Cambridge University Press.

Spahn, Paul B. 1993. "The Design of Federal Fiscal Constitutions in Theory and Practice." *European Economy Reports and Studies* 5: 63–100.

Spahn, Paul B., and Anwar A. Shah. 1995. "Intergovernmental Fiscal Relations in Australia." In *Macroeconomic Management and Fiscal Decentralization*, ed. Jayanta Roy. Washington, DC: World Bank

van Wincoop, Eric. 1995. "Regional Risk-sharing." *European Economic Review* 39 (8): 1545–68.

von Hagen, Jürgen. 1992. "Fiscal Arrangements in a Monetary Union: Some Evidence from the U.S." In *Fiscal Policy, Taxes, and the Financial System in an Increasingly Integrated Europe*, ed. Don Fair and Christian de Boissieux, 337–60. Deventer, the Netherlands: Kluwer Academic Publishers.

———. 1993. "Monetary Union and Fiscal Union: A Perspective from Fiscal Federalism." In *Policy Issues in the Operation of Currency Unions*, ed. Paul R. Masson and Mark P. Taylor, 264–98. Cambridge: Cambridge University Press.

von Hagen, Jürgen, and George W. Hammond. 1998. "Regional Insurance against Asymmetric Shocks: An Empirical Study for the European Community." *The Manchester School* 66 (3): 331–53.

von Hagen, Jürgen, and Chris J. Waller. 1999. *Regional Aspects of Monetary Union in Europe*. Boston: Kluwer Academic Publishers.

Wyplosz, Charles. 1991. "Monetary Union and Fiscal Policy Discipline." *European Economy* Special Edition 1: 165–84.

Grants and Soft Budget Constraints

MARIANNE VIGNEAULT

In most countries, intergovernmental transfers constitute an important element in the relationship between central and lower levels of government. A large literature deals with the optimality of this relationship. Arguments in support of a more decentralized form of governance point to the achievement of greater efficiency when the provision of goods and services is carried out by the level of government that is closest to the people. The well-known Tiebout (1956) hypothesis argues that such an arrangement enhances efficiency because competition among jurisdictions for mobile people ensures that local governments offer residents their preferred mix of taxation and public expenditure. Brennan and Buchanan (1980) argue that decentralization of revenue-raising authority also provides an element of competition that constrains governments seeking to exploit their taxation powers. Decentralizing expenditure provision and revenue-raising authority also improves accountability, by ensuring that the level of government responsible for providing goods and services is also responsible for financing them. All of these arguments have been invoked recently in defense of the trend toward greater decentralization in many countries.

Proponents of a more centralized form of governance argue that many countries, especially developing countries and transition economies, exhibit features that fail to satisfy the assumptions under which the Tiebout hypothesis is likely to hold (Prud'homme 1995).

In many countries, large disparities in income, not voter preferences, across regions are the primary reason for regional differences. Furthermore, local politicians often fail to take constituents' preferences into account, either because electoral systems are inefficient or because elected officials have no incentive to do so. Maximum efficiency in a decentralized system also requires that lower-level governments internalize all the social benefits and costs of their policy choices.

One danger of decentralization is that regional governments acting on behalf of their own constituents fail to take into account the effects of their decisions on people outside their jurisdictions. Many regional public goods and services have benefits or costs that cross regional boundaries. These spillovers (or externalities) can take many forms. Highways, for example, can benefit people residing outside the local boundary. Education can benefit people in other jurisdictions, either directly (if residents of one state attend a state university in another, for example) or indirectly (if residents of one jurisdiction migrate to another, bringing the skills learned with them). Externalities are also created when people move across jurisdictions to take advantage of generous health or welfare programs. The existence of spillovers provides a rationale for central government intervention in the provision of local public goods and services.

Spillovers also arise on the revenue side. Competition for mobile tax bases results in too little tax revenue being raised locally—and, as a result, too little provision of public goods. Similarly, an attempt by a local government to redistribute income from the rich to the poor induces poorer people to immigrate to its jurisdiction and wealthier people to emigrate to lower-tax jurisdictions. Thus an argument on the basis of equity can be made that assigns redistributive tax policies to the central government (Musgrave 1959). Scale economies in tax collection also provide an efficiency argument for assigning greater taxation powers to the central government.

These are the traditional efficiency and equity rationales for an asymmetry in expenditure and revenue-raising responsibilities that gives rise to vertical fiscal imbalances that are addressed by intergovernmental transfers. The idea is that both the central and regional governments have an interest in providing goods and services to the nation's people. The objective is therefore to design a transfer scheme that provides regional governments with the needed revenues and the correct incentives for efficient and equitable spending, taxing, and borrowing.

An implicit assumption in traditional theories of public finance is that regional governments take the grant structure as given when making their spending decisions (Wildasin 2004). Recent inspection of the incentives created by intergovernmental transfers has revealed a new challenge facing decentralizing countries around the world. Regional governments may engage in opportunistic behavior in an effort to extract greater resources from the central government. The incentive to do so resides in the regional governments' failure to internalize the full costs of transfers on national tax-payers and in the recognition that the central government maintains a strong interest in the affairs of the regions (Rodden, Eskelund, and Litvack 2003a). Additional resources or outright bailouts have the effect of softening regional government budget constraints, creating inefficiencies that may result in severe costs for the nation as a whole. In addressing this soft budget constraint problem, the challenge is to design intergovernmental transfer systems that reduce the incentives for fiscally irresponsible behavior on the part of lower-level governments and reduce the incentives for the central government to provide additional resources to regional governments that violate their budget constraints.

This chapter provides an overview of the soft budget constraint problem in intergovernmental relations, in both theory and practice, and discusses the ways in which intergovernmental transfer systems can exacerbate or reduce the soft budget constraint problem. An important lesson is that the soft budget constraint problem arises under a variety of circumstances, which are a function of a nation's fiscal, political, and financial institutions. Indeed, the conditions under which hard budget constraints are likely to arise are relatively rare and appear to fall into two categories (Rodden 2001). In the first, the central government has sufficient constitutional authority and sufficient motivation to place effective restraints on the spending and borrowing autonomy of regional governments. This is not the case in many federations with politically weak central governments and regional governments with the political power to resist attempts at limiting their autonomy. In the second, regional governments face few restrictions in their spending and borrowing powers, and voters and creditors serve to discipline irresponsible governments. Such market mechanisms for instilling fiscal discipline can operate effectively only if a nation has a strong and independent legal system and well-functioning capital markets, and voters are willing and able to hold regional governments accountable for their actions. These conditions are unlikely to hold in many countries; if any of them is not present, soft budget constraint problems can result.

Particularly troublesome institutional features are a large vertical fiscal imbalance combined with regional government borrowing autonomy (Rodden 2001). Vertical fiscal imbalances that are addressed by intergovernmental transfers sever the link between regional government taxing and spending and directly involve the central government in the fiscal outcomes of the regions, compromising regional government accountability in the eyes of voters and creditors. Vertical fiscal imbalances addressed by intergovernmental transfers thus provide incentives for regional governments to overspend and, if they are able to, overborrow from private capital markets. Additional features of a nation's fiscal institutions that exacerbate soft budget constraint problems are discretionary transfers, equalization programs, and overlapping responsibilities of the central and regional levels of government.

This chapter is organized as follows. It begins by formally describing the soft budget constraint problem, before examining the implications of soft budget constraints for the health of the nation's economy. It then summarizes the theoretical literature before discussing several real world experiences with soft budget constraints. The chapter closes by summarizing the lessons learned from the theoretical and empirical literature.

The Soft Budget Constraint Problem Defined

Kornai (1979, 1986) was the first to observe and document the soft budget constraint problem in relation to state-owned enterprises in transition economies. He observed that even when state-owned enterprises were vested with the responsibility to maximize profits, those that incurred losses were provided additional resources that prevented them from failing. The government's action in bailing out these failing enterprises "softened" their budget constraints, as these loss-making enterprises came to expect additional resources. This affected their motivation to maximize profits and to select the levels and types of investment that would maximize the chances of the firm's survival.

Since these initial observations, the soft budget constraint problem has been identified as a leading cause of numerous inefficient outcomes in the private and public sectors. Indeed, concern with the problem has become widespread, and efforts to eliminate or mitigate it have become a primary preoccupation of academics and practitioners. The problem is not confined to developing countries and transition economies, although it may be more severe in these countries because their fiscal, financial, and political institutions are still evolving.

The extension of the soft budget constraint theory to intergovernmental relations has occurred more recently in light of the increasing emphasis on fiscal decentralization in many countries. This problem arises from the ability of regional governments to manipulate the size of transfers received from the central government. According to Inman (2003) and Kornai, Maskin, and Roland (2003), the ability of regional governments to manipulate transfers arises from the inability of central governments to commit to a transfer scheme announced before regional governments make their spending and borrowing decisions. The interaction between the central and regional levels of government is typically modeled in a sequential fashion. In the first stage, the central government announces a set of intergovernmental transfers selected to maximize social welfare before the spending, borrowing, and taxing decisions of the regional government are made—that is, they are optimal ex ante. In the second stage, if the regional government faces a hard budget constraint, it takes this level of transfers as given when enacting its policies. If, instead, the regional government opts for excessive expenditure or borrowing levels or insufficient taxation levels, then in the third stage, the central government must decide whether it will provide additional resources to cover the resulting deficit. If it has an incentive to do so and the regional government is aware of this incentive, the regional government will come to expect additional resources, affecting its decisions in stage 2. The budget constraint is said to be "soft," in that policy makers are not constrained to finance their expenditures from a fixed budget.

Two conditions are necessary for soft budget constraints. The first is that the central government must find it optimal to grant additional resources or even provide a bailout to the regional government in stage 3. It will do so only if the costs of denying additional resources exceed the costs of providing them—that is, if the granting of additional funds is optimal ex post. The second necessary condition is that, given that the central government has an incentive to provide additional resources in stage 3 and the regional government is aware of this incentive, the regional government finds it optimal to behave strategically and selects an excessive level of expenditure in stage 2. The literature on the soft budget constraint problem in intergovernmental relations seeks to identify the circumstances under which these two conditions hold.

Implications of Soft Budget Constraints

When regional budget constraints are softened by the expectation of additional resources from the central government, the marginal benefit of public expenditure or borrowing exceeds the marginal cost. Spending and borrowing levels are inefficient, because regional governments fail to take into account the effects of their decisions on national taxpayers, present and future. Regional government behavior thus imparts a negative externality on national taxpayers that is referred to as the "common pool problem" (see Goodspeed 2002, Pisauro 2001, and von Hagen and Dahlberg 2004). An important consequence of soft budget constraints is therefore inefficiently high expenditure levels, borrowing levels, or both. Evidence of this has been documented in the empirical literature. In particular, a positive correlation has been found between the dependence of regional governments on transfers and the size of government (see Winer 1983, Stein 1999, Rodden 2001, and Rodden 2003c). The soft budget constraint problem may become so severe that regional governments' buildup of unsustainable deficits ultimately induces a bailout by the central government.

Another regrettable consequence of soft budget constraints arises from the implicit insurance provided by the central government against the risk of fiscal crisis (Pisauro 2001). The prospect of increased funding makes the regional government less inclined to efficiently manage the risk associated with fiscal outcomes. The composition of public expenditures will therefore be biased in favor of riskier projects. Another danger results when regional policy makers have an incentive to divert scare resources toward expenditures on political perks and pork barrel projects, with the full knowledge that the central government will provide additional resources when the regional government finds itself unable to adequately provide essential services such as basic education and medical care.

At the macroeconomic level, the excessive expenditure levels and large transfers associated with soft budget constraints and bailouts may interfere with the central government's stabilization efforts. Furthermore, their contribution to aggregate demand may put upward pressure on prices and thus interfere with the central government's effective use of monetary policy to stabilize inflationary pressures. Inflationary pressures in some developing countries may also be exacerbated if the central government finances bailouts by printing money.

The Soft Budget Constraint Problem in Theory

The theoretical literature on the soft budget constraint problem focuses on the circumstances under which the central government is unable to commit to a system of intergovernmental transfers announced before regional governments make their spending and borrowing decisions, the implications of the central government's inability to commit to a system of transfers, and the circumstances under which regional governments engage in opportunistic behavior, given their knowledge of the central government's commitment problem. The circumstances under which the last condition arises are straightforward and result from the common pool problem. When the central government grants additional resources to the regional government, lack of fiscal discipline results, because the regional government internalizes only part of the cost of its expenditure and borrowing decisions. One result of the common pool problem is that the regional governments' incentives for engaging in opportunistic behavior are stronger for smaller regions than for larger ones, because their share of the tax cost of transfers is relatively small. All theoretical models incorporate the common pool problem in some form. They differ in the underlying causes of the central government's commitment problem or its implications for efficient behavior.

The "Too-Big-to-Fail" Theory

Wildasin (2004) maintains that the soft budget constraint problem is more severe for larger jurisdictions, because they are seen as "too big to fail" in the eyes of the central government. To model this formally, he argues that the central government's bailout incentive results from regional government provision of regional public goods that benefit people residing in other regions. People from all regions may, for example, benefit from regional government provision of basic education or a vaccination program. The central government provides a matching grant to induce the regional government to provide the level of the regional public good that incorporates these external benefits in addition to those that accrue to the region's own residents. In the event that the regional government underprovides the public good, the central government may have an incentive to provide an additional grant over and above the matching grant, in order to ensure the provision of the socially efficient level of the public good.

In Wildasin's model the central government pays for the additional grant by reducing its own provision of a national public good. Therefore, in deciding whether to select a suboptimal level of public good provision that would induce a bailout, the regional government compares the level of regional welfare attained with a bailout with the level attained without one. With a bailout, the regional government faces a reduced cost of providing the public good (the common pool problem), but its people receive suboptimal levels of both the regional and national public goods. Similarly, in deciding whether to provide additional grants to the government of region A, the central government weighs the benefits accruing to people residing in other regions from increased provision of region A's public good against the costs of reducing provision of the national public good. The benefits of a bailout thus increase in step with the externalities generated from region A's public good. For this reason, larger regions are more likely to receive bailouts than smaller regions.

The too-big-to-fail hypothesis helps explain bailouts of regional governments whose buildup of debts threatens the financial security of the nation as a whole. Such bailouts have been frequent in Argentina and Brazil since the 1980s. The bailouts of New York City, and Medellín, Colombia, may also be viewed as evidence of the too-big-to-fail hypothesis.

Numerous bailouts have been granted to small jurisdictions. Thus, the too-big-to-fail hypothesis is but one of many possible explanations for the central government's lack of commitment ability.

Political Economy Models of the Soft Budget Constraint

Aizenman (1998) examines the soft budget constraint problem in a model in which voters dislike public debt. In his model the central government has limited control over the spending behavior of regional governments. In each budget period, the regional government receives a fiscal allocation from the central government that is financed by shared tax revenues and a burgeoning deficit. The central government finances excessive spending by regional governments by increasing its own debt. Regional governments face conflicting incentives when determining their spending levels. First, the common pool problem arises when the regional government obtains the full benefit from excessive spending while shifting part of the burden onto future national taxpayers. The second incentive derives from the voting public's dislike for public debt. Specifically, voters are able to remove both the regional and central governments from office if debt levels are too high. The first incentive tends to induce excessive spending, whereas the second tends to countermand it. When the second incentive dominates, the macroeconomic equilibrium is a cooperative one and debt levels remain low. A limited cooperative outcome occurs when the central government is able to adjust the fiscal allocation to the highest level that induces cooperation. A noncooperative outcome occurs when the central government is unable to constrain the spending behavior of regional governments. Aizenman shows that adverse shocks can result in regime switches from cooperative to noncooperative outcomes. More specifically, an adverse shock encourages opportunistic behavior, because the benefits from additional spending increase when regional incomes are reduced in the wake of such a mishap. Soft budget constraints should accordingly be more common during economic downturns.

Goodspeed (2002) examines the soft budget constraint problem that arises when the central government seeks to maximize its chance of reelection, which in turn depends on maximizing the welfare of people in all regions. He models both the incentives of the central government to provide a bailout to regional governments and the implications of bailouts for regional governments' borrowing behavior. As a result of the central government's reelection objective, when regional governments borrow to finance their current expenditures, the central government responds by increasing grants in order to offset the consequent reduction in private consumption required to pay off regional government debt. The central government's reelection objective also decreases the incentive to increase grants in smaller regions where it already receives strong support, because favoring these regions has little effect on the chances that the central government will be reelected. Confirmation of this hypothesis can be found in the recent experience of Argentina and Germany, where bailouts were granted to regions whose governments did not belong to the same party as the central government.

Goodspeed's model also demonstrates how the soft budget constraint prompts regional governments to take the central government's incentives into account when making their borrowing decisions. Goodspeed identifies two effects of the central government's bailout response on regional government borrowing. The first is a common property effect, whereby the central government responds to an increase in region A's borrowing by increasing grants to all regions. All regions therefore experience an increase in taxes, which results in a tax cost to region A that discourages excessive borrowing. The second effect reflects the reduction in borrowing costs when the central government increases the grant to region A. This effect encourages excessive borrowing. Goodspeed shows that when the second effect dominates the first, regional governments face soft budget constraints and excessive borrowing results. The opposite results when the first effect dominates the second and regional governments therefore face hard budget constraints. An interesting special case implicit in Goodspeed's analysis arises when the central government increases grants to all regions by the same amount as the increase in region A's borrowing. The resulting tax cost is such that region A's incentive to increase borrowing is eliminated, and it therefore selects a more efficient level of borrowing.

Varying Degrees of Decentralization

Garcia-Milà, Goodspeed, and McGuire (2002) examine the incentives for regional government spending and borrowing under three different forms of fiscal decentralization in a federation: the federal government devolves spending authority to the regional government but maintains taxing authority at the federal level and does not adjust the level of transfers in response to changes in regional government spending, the federal government devolves both spending and taxing authority to the regional government, and the federal government increases grants to cover excessive spending and borrowing by the regional government. In their model each level of government seeks to maximize the welfare of its people; the central government takes into account the welfare of people in all regions, whereas regional governments take into account only the welfare of people residing in their jurisdictions. The first two forms of fiscal decentralization result in hard budget constraints at the regional level. In the first form of fiscal decentralization, a vertical fiscal imbalance exists in the federation, but the central government remains committed to an announced transfer. The regional government thus does not expect the central government to provide additional transfers in response to excessive spending or borrowing at the regional level. The regional government therefore faces a hard budget constraint and selects the efficient level of borrowing. In the second form of fiscal decentralization, regional governments are given the means to finance their spending and borrowing decisions. They thus internalize the full benefits and costs of spending and borrowing. In the third form of fiscal decentralization, a vertical fiscal imbalance is maintained and the regional government expects the federal government to provide additional transfers in response to excessive spending and borrowing at the regional level. This expectation results in soft budget constraints at the regional level.

The authors show that the effect of soft budget constraints on borrowing and spending depends on the federal government's grant structure. One effect results from the common pool problem, whereby the regional government reaps the full benefits of spending and borrowing but bears only part of the cost because that cost is shared by all people in the federation. This effect is likely to be larger the smaller the region. An additional effect arises if the federal government's grant is based on aggregate borrowing, which may be the result of collective political pressure on the federal government to respond to regional needs. Thus when one region borrows or spends excessively, the federal government responds by increasing grants to all regions. Therefore, the larger the region, the larger its share of the federal government's grant and the more incentive it has to overspend and overborrow.

Credibility and Reputation Effects

Inman (2003) provides an analytical framework for assessing the circumstances that are likely to result in soft budget constraints, a framework applicable to all countries. He argues that the central government bears two types of costs from denying a bailout to a regional government. The first is the financial cost of not providing a bailout, which arises when regional governments' financial crises create spillovers that affect the entire economy. The second is the distributional cost of not providing a bailout, which arises when regional taxpayers and creditors are favored over national taxpayers. When one or both of these costs is sufficiently large, the central government faces a commitment problem and soft budget constraints are likely to result.

It is questionable whether regional governments are fully aware of the size of these costs, especially the distributional cost. If regional governments face uncertainty as to the true commitment ability of the central government and if the regional and central governments repeatedly interact, then even a central government with weak commitment ability can adopt a no-bailout policy early on to fool regional governments into believing it is tough on regional fiscal indiscipline. But for this strategy to be successful in hardening budget constraints, the central government must be able to rely on enough time for the benefits of fiscal discipline to outweigh the costs of denying a bailout.

Rules versus Discretion

Sanguinetti and Tommasi (2004) explore the tradeoff between risk sharing and fiscal discipline in a model in which regional incomes are subject to asymmetric shocks. The tradeoff arises because the central government has an incentive to redistribute resources across regions after the realization of the shocks to regional incomes but doing so necessitates the basing of transfers on regional government spending and borrowing decisions. Commitment to a transfer scheme can therefore eliminate inefficiencies arising from soft budget constraints. However, commitment necessarily entails forgoing the discretionary ability to respond to shocks to regional incomes. Optimum risk sharing is thus compromised. The federal government may therefore face a tradeoff between the benefits of risk sharing and the benefits of hard budget constraints. Sanguinetti and Tommasi explore scenarios in which commitment to a set of transfer rules, and the resulting fiscal discipline this engenders, may be inferior to those under noncommitment and soft budget constraints.

Vertical Fiscal Imbalance and Soft Budget Constraints

Boadway and Tremblay (2006) analyze vertical fiscal imbalance in a federation experiencing shocks to regional production. Under asymmetric shocks, the region experiencing a negative shock receives a transfer from the central government. Boadway and Tremblay define the concept of vertical fiscal imbalance as the deviation from the optimal gap between regional expenditures and revenues. This optimal fiscal gap is the level of transfers that would exist if the regional and central governments coordinated their actions in a way that internalizes all costs and benefits of taxing and spending. Deviations from the optimal fiscal gap occur because regional governments create externalities when their actions are not coordinated.

Boadway and Tremblay analyze two forms of externality. One arises when both levels of government levy distortionary taxes on the same tax base, in this case production. The distortion arises when an increase in either the central or regional governments' tax rate reduces the tax base. Consequently, a regional government, acting on behalf of its own residents, fails to take into account the full cost of an increase in its tax rate, because part of this cost falls on the central government in the form of a reduction in the base. When the federal government is able to commit to a level of transfers that is chosen before the spending decisions of the regional governments, only this type of externality arises. The result is that the transfer to the region experiencing a negative shock is lower than under the optimal fiscal gap.

The second form of externality is the common pool problem, which occurs when the central government is unable to commit to a transfer policy. Aware of this commitment problem, regional governments ignore their budget constraints when making their spending and taxing decisions, anticipating that the central government will finance their expenditures. As a result, regional tax rates are too low (zero in this case) and spending too high.

Directions for Future Research

Theoretical analyses of the soft budget constraint problem are relatively recent and tend to focus on a particular aspect of the central government's commitment problem. The problem is exceedingly complex. Its causes are rooted in the interplay among the fiscal, financial, and political institutions that gives rise to the expectation on the part of regional governments that the central government will come to their rescue in times of difficulty. Theoretical models necessarily provide a simplified picture of the complex interactions between the central and regional governments.

The task for researchers is to build on the progress that has been made so far in the theoretical literature. One area that seems particularly worthy of investigation is a more thorough examination of the tradeoffs involved in devising an intergovernmental transfer system that provides the correct incentives for efficient and equitable spending, taxation, and borrowing. In particular, efforts to lessen or eliminate the soft budget constraint problem have to be assessed in light of their effects on regional spillovers, tax competition, and regional disparities. For example, tradeoffs certainly exist in which efforts to mitigate the soft budget constraint problem may widen regional disparities. Different transfer systems have different implications for equity and efficiency. A thorough assessment of any intergovernmental transfer system also has to consider the nation's entire institutional structure— fiscal, financial, and political—and how it is expected to evolve. The task for researchers is therefore a difficult but very important one.

The Soft Budget Constraint Problem in Practice: Country-Level Evidence

Countries have dealt with the fiscal indiscipline of lower-level governments in various ways. The evidence of fiscal indiscipline reported here is drawn from case study analyses. Other, much less numerous, analyses involve the empirical measurement of the soft budget constraint problem.

The relative scarcity of empirical studies reflects the difficulty of measuring soft budget constraints. Soft budget constraints arise from regional governments' expectations of additional resources in the event of financial difficulty. Expectations are notoriously difficult to measure, and this difficulty is compounded by the fact that regional government expectations of additional resources can arise from a number of different circumstances that are influenced by a country's social, economic, and political environment. Analyses of the data must therefore be able to detect fiscal indiscipline as opposed to fiscal difficulties that result from factors beyond the regional governments' control.

A selection of analyses is reviewed here in order to highlight the key features of intergovernmental transfer systems that are likely to give rise to soft budget constraints. The case studies and empirical analyses selected describe a variety of experiences that identify the features of the intergovernmental fiscal relationship that have contributed to or helped mitigate the soft budget constraint problem. As these studies show, numerous features of intergovernmental fiscal systems can give rise to soft budget constraints, and many of these features are common to developed countries, developing countries, and transition economies, as well as to both unitary and federal systems.

Rodden's (2001) cross-national analysis of the soft budget constraint problem in 43 transition economies, developing countries, and members of the Organisation for Economic Co-operation and Development is an ideal starting point for a discussion of the international evidence on the soft budget constraint problem in intergovernmental relations, because it seeks to identify the factors that account for the large variation in fiscal outcomes of regional governments across countries. His analysis focuses on the roles of vertical fiscal imbalance, borrowing autonomy, and federal institutions as determinants of regional government fiscal indiscipline, highlighted in the country case studies that follow. Fiscal indiscipline is measured as excessive and persistent regional government debt. The rationale for this measure is that the soft budget constraint problem gives rise to expectations of additional resources, leading to excessive borrowing. He then tests various hypotheses to determine the factors that are most important in affecting regional government debt levels.

Rodden's findings can be summarized as follows:

- Large vertical fiscal imbalances alone have no effect on regional fiscal performance.
- The negative relationship between regional fiscal performance and vertical fiscal imbalance is strongest when regional governments depend on general-purpose and equalization transfers.
- Countries with high levels of vertical fiscal imbalance tend to restrict borrowing by regional governments.
- The average regional government deficit is smaller in countries that restrict borrowing by regional governments.
- The average regional government deficit is much higher in countries with high levels of vertical fiscal imbalance and in countries in which regional governments have borrowing autonomy.
- Federalism alone is not associated with fiscal indiscipline.
- Regional governments in federations tend to have a higher degree of borrowing autonomy.
- A relationship exists between federalism and fiscal indiscipline, but it is evident only in countries with high levels of vertical fiscal imbalance.

Rodden's analysis highlights the importance of the combination of vertical fiscal imbalances and borrowing autonomy for the soft budget constraint problem. The problem also appears to be most severe when vertical fiscal imbalances are addressed with general-purpose and equalization transfers.

Two fiscal arrangements appear to result in hard budget constraints, one with high levels of vertical fiscal imbalance combined with borrowing restrictions, the other with low levels of vertical fiscal imbalance combined with borrowing autonomy. The first arrangement relies on hierarchical controls to enforce hard budget constraints, the second relies on market discipline (voter and creditor) to ensure that regional governments are held accountable for their actions and thus face hard budget constraints. Many countries' intergovernmental fiscal and financial arrangements fall between these two extremes and are thus more likely to give rise to fiscal indiscipline by regional governments.

The rest of this section reviews country case studies and empirical analyses. These case studies confirm Rodden's findings and provide a deeper understanding of the many factors that contribute to or help mitigate the soft budget constraint problem.

Germany

Germany has three levels of government: federal (*Bund*), state (*Länd*), and local (*Gemenden*).[1] The intergovernmental fiscal system in Germany exhibits a high degree of vertical fiscal imbalance. In particular, subnational governments in Germany have very little discretionary power in raising own-source revenues. State governments have few exclusive state taxes, and their revenues are derived mainly from shared taxes with the federal government that are subject to rates and bases determined by the federal government. Similarly, local governments rely to a large extent on shared taxes with the federal and state governments. Although local governments have some discretion for establishing tax rates on real property and trade, other tax sources are subject to either federal or state legislation. In addition, subnational governments are responsible for providing most public goods and services and for implementing federal expenditure policies that are subject to uniform federal laws.

These laws are meant to ensure "equivalent living conditions" for all German people, as mandated in the Constitution. An important component of the equivalent living conditions provision is the equalization system. This system involves three stages, with the second and third stages providing horizontal redistribution of revenues across states and federal supplementary grants to the poorest states.

In contrast to their limited powers of taxation and centrally dictated requirements for the uniform provision of public goods and services, state governments in Germany face very few restrictions on borrowing. Local governments are also able to borrow to finance expenditures. The central government has no power to restrict or review the borrowing activities of the states. The states, however, have introduced their own restrictions, which prevent them from borrowing more than the amount required for investment purposes. These "golden rule" provisions are detailed in the state constitutions. In practice, the states are often able to sidestep these restrictions due to the ambiguous definition of "investment purposes." Some states simply ignore these restrictions.

Buettner (2003) provides an empirical analysis of the soft budget constraint problem at the municipal government level in Germany. He analyzes the role of intergovernmental transfers in restoring fiscal balance in 1,102 German municipalities in the Baden-Württemberg *Länd* between 1974 and 2000. The analysis examines the adjustment of municipalities' revenues and expenditures—own-source revenues, grants, equalization transfers, debt service, and expenditures—to changes in municipal governments' budgets. Buettner finds that the response of expenditures in restoring fiscal balance is the largest among the five budget items. In particular, an increase in the deficit elicits a decrease in expenditures that is close to nine times larger than intergovernmental grants. Indeed, for an increase in the deficit, the response of grants, including equalization, in restoring fiscal balance, is quite small, indicating that excessive borrowing arising from the soft budget constraint problem may not be too severe for municipalities in Baden-Württemberg. This finding may be influenced by the fact that Baden-Württemberg is a rich *Länd* and therefore faces little disincentives from the third stage of the equalization system, which awards supplementary transfers to only the poorest *Länder*. However, Buettner finds that the equalization system can create a disincentive for revenue raising that can contribute to the soft budget constraint problem. His results show that an innovation in a municipality's own revenues results in subsequent increases in its net contributions to the equalization system. Thus the equalization system prevents municipal governments from reaping the full benefits of their taxing efforts.

Buettner also investigates how city size affects the response of intergovernmental grants in restoring budget balance. He finds that medium-size and large cities tend to rely more on adjustments in intergovernmental grants than do small cities. This finding may confirm Wildasin's (2004) hypothesis that the larger the municipality, the larger the externalities associated with public good provision and thus the more severe the soft budget constraint problem. It may also confirm Goodspeed's (2002) hypothesis that the central government favors municipalities that have greater impact on the central government's chances of reelection.

Rodden (2000) also investigates the soft budget constraint problem in the German federation. Unlike Buettner, he finds evidence of the existence of a soft budget constraint problem in creating incentives for excessive borrowing. His investigation of the role of intergovernmental transfers in affecting fiscal discipline differs from Buettner's in three important respects.[2] First, Rodden examines fiscal outcomes in all of the "old" *Länder*, that is, those of the old Federal Republic of Germany. Buettner's analysis focuses on municipalities within a single *Länd*—Baden-Württemberg, one of the richest in Germany. Second, Rodden conducts a long-run investigation to test the hypothesis that the common pool problem manifests itself in the perception that part of the cost of current deficits will be borne by future national taxpayers. Buettner's analysis, in contrast, investigates how transfers may be used to restore short-run fiscal balance. The two analyses differ, moreover, in their evaluation of the variation in the importance of the equalization system as a source of distortion across the *Länder*. Most of the distorting incentives arising from the equalization system are the result of the supplementary transfers awarded to the *Länder* with the poorest fiscal performance, which is not representative of municipalities in Baden-Württemberg.

An important feature of Rodden's analysis is that intergovernmental transfers reduce fiscal deficits at the *Länd* level in the short run but increase them in the long run. The short-run result confirms Buettner's findings for municipalities in Baden-Württemberg. Rodden interprets the long-run result as evidence that *Länd* governments require sustained increases in transfers to create the expectation of additional transfers in the presence of fiscal deficits. He also finds that deficits tend to be higher in smaller *Länder*. This is further evidence of the common pool problem, whereby the perceived cost of additional spending is smaller for small jurisdictions, because they bear a small proportion of the total tax cost of additional transfers. Larger jurisdictions, in contrast, bear a larger proportion of the tax cost of transfers and thus internalize more of the social cost of additional spending. Rodden also finds that the common pool problem is eased if the *Länder* and central governments are controlled by the same parties.

The institutional structure in Germany exhibits several features conducive to soft budget constraints. The most important features are the heavy reliance of subnational governments on federal transfers, the limited flexibility of subnational governments in adjusting revenues and expenditures in response to fiscal difficulties, the minimal restrictions on borrowing by subnational governments, and the equalization system, which provides incentives for fiscal indiscipline by the poorest *Länder*. The first two features can give rise to the common pool problem across state and local governments; combined with the third feature, they can result in excessive spending and borrowing. The first two features also reduce the accountability of subnational governments in the eyes of voters and creditors. State and local governments can therefore justifiably expect that the federal government will come to their assistance in the event of any fiscal difficulty.[3] This expectation is heightened in the poorest states by the equalization system, whose purpose is to ensure equivalent living conditions across the federation. Indeed, two German states—Bremen and Saarland—recently used the equivalent living conditions provision in the Constitution to successfully argue that the federal government is compelled to offer additional financial assistance to help cope with their excessive debt loads.

Italy

The reliance of regional governments in Italy on central government transfers and the restrictions faced by regional governments in respect to their taxing and spending autonomy have been even more pronounced than in Germany.[4] Furthermore, there is a large degree of overlap of responsibilities among the different levels of government with regard to the provision and financing of important public services, such as education and health care. These responsibilities, and intergovernmental fiscal relations in general, have undergone significant upheaval in the past three decades. In the early 1970s, in response to economic crises and social unrest, the central government reduced the fiscal autonomy of subnational governments. At the same time, a system of grants was put in place to equalize regional governments' abilities to provide public goods and services. The allocation of grants was based on a confusing array of objectives, and individuals still expected the central and regional governments to share responsibility for providing many public goods and services.

The reduction in regional fiscal autonomy as a result of the reform of intergovernmental fiscal institutions was so severe that by the end of the 1970s regional governments were dependent on central transfers for almost 97 percent of their financing. As in Germany, the central government in Italy established very specific guidelines on how grant monies were to be spent, in an attempt to equalize the provision of public goods across regions. These guidelines were especially constraining in the health care sector. The combination of the common pool problem and a lack of accountability contributed to increases in spending that were so rapid that regional governments routinely exceeded their budgets and began financing their deficits through borrowing from commercial banks. This rapid increase in spending was compounded by political instability that weakened the central government's ability and motivation to reign in fiscal excesses at the regional level. The result of the changes introduced in the 1970s was a rapid increase in local government expenditures, especially in the health care sector. Excessive spending by regional governments resulted in excessive borrowing, with the resulting deficits ultimately financed by the central government. A continuous system of bailouts was thus created. These bailouts were largely discretionary and tended to reward the most irresponsible governments. What transpired was not surprising given that regional governments internalized very little of the costs of public spending and viewed the central government as ultimately responsible for any financial difficulties that arose.

Severe financial crises in the early 1990s provided an environment conducive to massive reforms of the intergovernmental fiscal institutions that had given rise to fiscal indiscipline in the 1970s and 1980s. Intergovernmental transfers were reduced considerably, and the revenue autonomy of local governments was increased. In addition, new electoral laws were put in place to make local governments more accountable to their citizens.

The reforms introduced in the 1990s went some way toward hardening local government budget constraints, but the soft budget constraint problem in Italy has not been eliminated. Accountability of regional governments in Italy still suffers from the overlapping responsibilities with the central government. Furthermore, many transfers are still allocated on a discretionary basis, which results in wasteful lobbying and the practice of granting transfers on the basis of political ties to the central government. The soft budget constraint problem in the health sector continues to be a concern because of the importance of health care in the central government's priorities.

Several important features of the fiscal and political institutions in Italy have given rise to fiscal indiscipline at the regional government level. Some of these features mirror those in Germany. The important features are the heavy reliance of regional governments on federal transfers, the limited flexibility regional governments have in adjusting revenues and expenditures in response to fiscal difficulties, the overlapping responsibilities of the various levels of government, the use of discretionary transfers to bail out regional governments, and political instability. The first two features generate the common pool problem and reduce accountability of regional governments in the eyes of voters and creditors. The third feature reduces the accountability of regional governments. The fourth feature exacerbates the soft budget constraint problem, because discretionary transfers are easily manipulated by regional governments. The fifth feature reduces the resolve of the central government to reign in fiscal indiscipline, because the benefits of doing so accrue in the future, in the form of improved fiscal discipline, but the future is not weighted very highly in an unstable political environment.

Sweden

In contrast to the institutional setting in Germany and Italy, regional governments in Sweden have considerable autonomy in choosing the level, quality, and measures of financing regional public expenditures, as long as they satisfy the minimum requirements set by the central government.[5] The financing of public goods and services at the local level is done mainly through tax revenues obtained from a proportional income tax. The base of this tax is set by national law, but local governments are free to set their own tax rates. Central government grants are also an important revenue source, constituting about 25 percent of revenues. Local governments are free to use most grant revenues as they see fit. They also face very few borrowing restrictions, domestically or internationally.

An important feature of the Swedish intergovernmental structure is the equalization system, with its objective of allowing regional governments to provide similar levels and standards of public goods and services. Another important feature is the constitutional provision that municipalities cannot legally default, which has been interpreted as an obligation on the part of the central government to assist regional governments in financial difficulty. Combined with local government borrowing autonomy, these two features are likely to have contributed to fiscal indiscipline during the 1970s and 1990s. During these periods, many municipalities found themselves in financial difficulty due to rising debt levels, especially those of the municipal housing companies. The central government felt obliged to come to their assistance by implementing a special financial relief program. This program was largely discretionary and tended to reward municipalities that had incurred the most debt, providing incentives for fiscal inefficiency by regional governments. Indeed, Pettersson-Lidbom and Dahlberg (2003) show that this program affected the borrowing and spending behavior of municipal governments and resulted in the creation of expectations of bailouts. In total, 1,697 bailouts were granted to municipalities during this period.

Dahlberg and Pettersson-Lidbom's analysis is a first attempt at identifying the expectation of bailouts as a determinant of fiscal indiscipline. They find that municipalities that received transfers exhibited a greater buildup of debt than those that did not receive transfers. In addition, the fact that a municipality received a bailout in the past was a good predictor of whether it would receive a bailout in the present or future. The incidence of current bailouts increased with the average number of bailouts received in the past by other municipalities. This persistence in bailout episodes suggests that municipalities may have engaged in strategic behavior during this period.

The most important features of the intergovernmental fiscal system that have exacerbated the soft budget constraint problem in Sweden are the equalization system, regional government borrowing autonomy, a constitutional provision forbidding local government defaults, and the use of discretionary transfers. The first two features contribute to the expectation on the part of regional governments that the central government will come to their rescue in the event of financial difficulty. The third feature provides the means by which regional governments can exceed their budgets. The fourth feature provides incentives for fiscal indiscipline, because discretionary transfers are easily manipulated.

Argentina

The intergovernmental fiscal relationship in Argentina exhibits a high degree of vertical fiscal imbalance.[6] Provincial governments are responsible for providing many public goods and services, but they are precluded from accessing the major tax bases. For this reason, intergovernmental transfers finance a large proportion of provincial expenditures. Provincial governments have also enjoyed considerable freedom in accessing domestic and foreign capital markets. Large vertical fiscal imbalances at the provincial level combined with borrowing autonomy have given rise to problems of fiscal indiscipline that have contributed to severe financial crises in the recent past. During these crises, the risk of the collapse of the provincial banking sector prompted the central government to begin providing financial assistance to the most irresponsible provinces on a discretionary basis. The result was a decline in fiscal discipline.

The severe crises of the 1990s provided the impetus for much needed reforms of the macroeconomy and provincial financial institutions. A program of privatizing provincial banks was begun, and the central government began allocating grants to the most indebted provinces, based on conditions that included deficit reduction targets, the freezing of public employment levels, and borrowing restrictions. One interesting reform that has had a perverse effect on fiscal indiscipline is the provision that allows banks to deduct debt service payments from shared revenues. While this provision increases the province's borrowing costs and thus helps harden budget constraints, it has had the perverse effect of increasing the banks' desired lending to provincial governments. As a result, provincial debt has increased. The reforms have helped harden provincial budget constraints, but Argentina is still vulnerable to the soft budget constraint problem and to financial crises, as witnessed in 2002.

Jones, Sanguinetti, and Tommasi (1999, 2000) analyze the common pool problem as a determinant of fiscal outcomes of Argentine provinces. Argentina's experience with soft budget constraints in the 1980s and its attempts to harden budget constraints in the 1990s offer an interesting example of the evolutionary process of intergovernmental reform. The authors demonstrate that the fiscal behavior of provincial governments has been affected by the common pool problem. In particular, they find that the provinces that are more heavily dependent on transfers have tended to have higher per capita spending. Provinces whose governors belong to the same political party as the president tend to have lower per capita spending, because, they argue, there is better coordination and internalization of externalities when the two levels of government belong to the same party. If the two governments are controlled by different parties, the provincial government has less incentive to take into account the effects of its decisions on central government finances and more of an incentive to behave irresponsibly and place the blame for any financial difficulties on the central government.

Jones, Sanguinetti, and Tommasi (2000) construct an index to measure constitutional restrictions on provincial and municipal governments that relate to borrowing autonomy and auditing of lower-level government budgets. They find that provinces with a higher "fiscal institutionalization" index tend to have lower per capita spending.

The key factors that have been identified as conducive to soft budget constraints are large vertical fiscal imbalances at the provincial level of government, a low degree of autonomy in adjusting provincial own-source revenues and expenditures, the use of discretionary transfers, provincial government borrowing autonomy, and different political affiliations of the central and provincial governments. The first three features contribute to the common pool problem and provide incentives for fiscal indiscipline of regional governments. Combined with borrowing autonomy, these features are especially potent causes of the soft budget constraint problem. The fifth feature provides an interesting example of how the power of the central government in enforcing fiscal discipline can be compromised by regional governments from opposition parties. Argentina's attempts at reforming its intergovernmental fiscal and financial institutions also illustrate how central governments can use severe crises to generate support for reforms that restrict provincial government autonomy.

Brazil

Brazil experienced severe macroeconomic crises in the 1980s and 1990s that resulted in numerous bailouts to state governments.[7] The federal government's weakness in denying bailouts and the state governments' expectations of bailouts are the result of Brazil's inadequate and often ad hoc approach to decentralization. Among developing countries, Brazil exhibits a relatively high degree of decentralization. State and local governments receive a high proportion of their revenues through shared taxes with the federal government. State revenue autonomy and accountability are compromised, however, by restrictions on the ability of the states to alter tax bases and rates and to exploit new tax bases. Brazil's constitution specifies that the most important expenditure responsibilities, such as education, health, and welfare, are to be provided by state governments, according to national standards dictated by the federal government. In practice, there is a considerable overlap of responsibilities in the provision of public goods and services. The federal government's involvement in public good provision provides an incentive for state governments to lobby the federal government for additional funds. Transfers obtained this way are allocated on an ad hoc basis and thus confuse the issue of which level of government is ultimately accountable for efficient spending practices.

Difficulties with fiscal indiscipline during the 1980s and 1990s were compounded by the ability of state governments to borrow on domestic or foreign financial markets. Brazil's constitution provides the federal government with the ability to regulate state borrowing, but it has been largely unsuccessful in preventing excessive deficits. Hierarchical restrictions, such as those on borrowing from state commercial banks, have been implemented, but they have easily been evaded. Moreover, the federal government's involvement in state borrowing activities fueled expectations that the federal government implicitly backed state debt. These expectations were confirmed when the federal government agreed to assume state debt when the states defaulted. The state governments thus won their gamble that the federal government would not risk a deepening financial crisis by not coming to their rescue. Thus despite the existence of constitutional controls on state borrowing, borrowing by state governments has been relatively easy, as credit markets, which perceive that the federal government guarantees state debt, have been willing to lend.

The weakness in the federal government's hierarchical control of state fiscal discipline during the 1980s and 1990s was largely a result of political institutions that prevented the federal government from effectively implementing the powers allocated to it in the Constitution. State governments have strong representation in the federal legislature, which have allowed them to influence many federal decisions regarding state finances. Indeed, relations between the federal and state governments have been characterized by lobbying, negotiations, and appeasement of state governors. Effective reforms to reduce fiscal indiscipline are very difficult in this environment.

Ukraine

Ukraine's transition to a market-oriented economy has been characterized by fiscal inefficiency at all levels of government.[8] Although there have been no episodes of dramatic bailouts of lower-level governments, incentives for soft budget constraints are found throughout Ukraine's fiscal, political, and financial institutions. Lower-level governments in Ukraine have access to few own-source revenues. They are mandated by the central government and the Constitution to provide essential goods and services, although existing legislation provides little clarity regarding the assignment of these expenditure responsibilities. The resulting gap between expenditures and revenues is not adequately addressed by transfers from higher-level governments. Intergovernmental transfers are negotiated at the start of each budget year on an ad hoc basis, but the pool of revenues from which transfers are derived is often overestimated, which results in a shortfall between budgeted and actual allocations of transfers. This results in a buildup of arrears and the widespread use of promissory notes, called *veksels*, to settle transactions. The negotiations that determine the level of intergovernmental transfers take place in a competitive rather than a cooperative atmosphere. Lower-level governments are also provided very little incentive to increase own-source revenues, because doing so results in a reduction in transfers from the central government.

Financial institutions in Ukraine are still in the development phase while the economy transforms itself into a more market-oriented economy. The relative immaturity of the financial system is manifested by a severe lack of legislative oversight. No legislation guides borrowing procedures or dictates the procedures to be followed by creditors and regional governments in the event of bankruptcy. Lower-level governments often borrow from higher-level governments, who charge zero interest and provide funds only as a means of financing deficits. The allocation of credit in this manner rewards irresponsible governments and bears no relation to the quality of programs implemented by the borrowing government or to its creditworthiness.

Political institutions in Ukraine are also developing and are in the process of adapting to democratic practices. But the political system is unstable and lacks transparency. Voters therefore lack the information and incentives necessary to hold elected officials accountable for their policy choices.

Many features of the fiscal, financial, and political institutions in Ukraine can give rise to soft budget constraint problems. These features include the high degree of vertical fiscal imbalance at the subnational levels of government, severe disincentives to raise own-source revenues, limited autonomy in adjusting expenditures, unclear assignment of responsibilities, insufficient intergovernmental transfers to close the vertical fiscal gap, an inefficient bargaining system over transfers, immature financial institutions, and immature and unstable political institutions. The common pool problem and problems of accountability are severe in Ukraine. Neither voters nor creditors have any incentive to hold regional governments accountable for fiscal outcomes, and regional governments face strong incentives to act in their own interest, to the detriment of the overall efficiency of the economy. Procedures for addressing vertical fiscal imbalances are so inadequate that they compound the soft budget constraint problem through the buildup of arrears, whereby deficits are passed on from one level of government to the other and then ultimately to firms and workers. The lack of mature political and financial institutions means that the central government lacks the power or motivation to undertake reforms of the fiscal, political, and financial institutions in ways that would improve fiscal discipline at the regional government level.

Hungary

In contrast to the experience of Ukraine, reforms to the fiscal, financial, and political institutions in Hungary during its transition to a free market system have been largely successful in instilling market discipline by regional governments.[9] The most important reforms in this regard are those made to Hungary's democratic processes, its budget management system, and its laws and regulations regarding regional government borrowing. The Hungarian experience provides an example of a fiscal arrangement that results in hard budget constraints by combining high levels of vertical fiscal imbalance and borrowing restrictions.

The Hungarian intergovernmental fiscal system is very centralized, with the central government dominating revenue raising and directing a large proportion of expenditure undertaken at the regional government level. This arrangement is primarily the result of the large number of very small local governments, which effectively limits their power in relation to the central government. The consequences of this arrangement are that local governments have very little expenditure and revenue-raising autonomy, and a large proportion of regional government revenues are derived from central government transfers.

The intergovernmental transfer system in Hungary is exceedingly complex. The most important transfers are the normative grants, which provide funds on the basis of formulas for about 50 expenditure areas. The normative grants are allocated based on regional government estimates of expenditure needs, but if an auditing of the funded program reveals that the regional government overestimated the program cost, it must pay back the difference with interest. Regional governments can also apply for investment funds under a variety of different programs. This transfer system provides incentives for excessive applications for funding that result in large administrative costs, poor coordination of grants, and inefficient allocation of funds. Regional governments with excessive deficits can also apply for deficit grants. Although conditions that attempt to reduce fiscal irresponsibility are attached to these grants, they nonetheless provide disincentives for raising own-source revenues and for efficient spending.

Despite the regional governments' limited fiscal autonomy, political mechanisms at the regional level are evolving in ways that increasingly allow voters to hold elected officials accountable for their policy choices. The political system also exhibits a degree of openness and stability that is lacking in many other transition economies. In particular, there is a high degree of competition among political parties, which increases the political power of the citizenry. Furthermore, the transition from one party in power to another is carried out within a stable environment.

Reforms have been made to Hungary's financial sector. During the early phases of Hungary's transition to a free-market economy, regional governments faced few borrowing restrictions. In response to burgeoning regional government deficits, both the regional governments and private creditors began lobbying the central government for debt bailouts. In response to these demands, the central government used its powerful status to implement laws and regulations that have been successful in hardening budget constraints. These laws and regulations limit new debt and debt payments to own-source revenues, providing an important incentive for regional governments to improve own-source revenues. A bankruptcy law, enforced by independent courts, provides clear administrative procedures for both creditors and regional governments to follow in the event of bankruptcy. The law also specifies a no-bailout clause and states that regional governments risk losing their autonomy in managing local affairs in the event of bankruptcy.

Key features of Hungary's fiscal, financial, and political institutions that affect regional governments' incentives for efficient spending and borrowing include large vertical fiscal imbalances at the provincial level of government, limited autonomy in adjusting provincial own-source revenues and expenditures, a complex system of intergovernmental transfers, the use of formulas in allocating normative grants, a dominant central government, a relatively stable and open political system, restrictions on regional government borrowing, and a strong legal system that includes a no-bailout clause and bankruptcy standards. The first three features can give rise to soft budget constraint problems. The remaining features have helped Hungary contain incentives for fiscal indiscipline. Perhaps the most important feature in this regard is the power of the central government in effecting reforms and contributing to a stable and open political system. This was essential in effecting the reforms to the legal system and to the implementation of hierarchical restrictions on regional governments' ability to spend and borrow.

Australia

Australia's experience provides an informative example of the role played by hierarchical controls in hardening budget constraints.[10] The Australian federation is highly centralized. The central government controls all major tax sources, and it uses its financial superiority to impose restrictions on state government spending through specific-purpose grants in areas of state jurisdiction. State governments also receive unconditional transfers in order to equalize disparities in their ability to provide comparable levels and quality of public goods and services at comparable levels of taxation. These equalization transfers are allocated on the basis of formulas that address differences across states in potential fiscal capacity.

The central government in Australia has used its fiscal dominance to invoke hierarchical controls on state borrowing. The Loan Council controls the total amount of borrowing by all levels of government as well as the allocation of loans across states. The central government dominates Loan Council decisions because of its unequal voting rights and its ability to use its financial superiority to threaten states into abiding by Loan Council dictates. For most of the Loan Council's history, it has been very successful in constraining the buildup of state debt. The one exception was the late 1970s and early 1980s, when restrictions were relaxed and states responded by increasing substantially their borrowing domestically and internationally.

The fact that regional governments are highly dependent on central government grants and have very little discretion over spending and revenue raising has the potential to heighten soft budget constraint problems in Australia. However, the dominance of the central government has allowed it to invoke hierarchical controls that have been effective in hardening state budget constraints. Thus a powerful central government can constrain inefficient regional government behavior. Equalization transfers in Australia are allocated on the basis of formulas that address differences in fiscal capacity. These formulas are largely independent of the states' policy choices and are thus unlikely to contribute much to soft budget constraint problems.

Although hierarchical controls have been successful in constraining excessive borrowing in Australia, they have come at a cost. Before 1990 the central government borrowed on behalf of the states. This arrangement allowed the states to borrow at favorable interest rates that reflected the central government's creditworthiness, not necessarily their own. A consequence of this arrangement was that the efficient allocation of credit across states was compromised, because states were shielded from market scrutiny. Global borrowing limits and loan allocations across states tended to reflect macroeconomic targets and were thus unrelated to the needs of individual states. The Loan Council's interference with the allocative function of private capital markets has thus compromised efficiency at the same time that it has enhanced it by hardening budget constraints.

The United States

The United States experience provides an example of an alternative fiscal arrangement that is conducive to hard budget constraints: reliance on market forces to discipline regional governments.[11] Necessary conditions for market forces to be effective are that voters hold state and local governments accountable for their policy choices and are able to punish irresponsible governments at the polls, which is largely the case in the United States. In addition, well-functioning capital markets in the United States serve to punish irresponsible governments with higher borrowing costs. In many states and for many local governments, the disciplining role of private capital markets is assisted by enforceable bankruptcy standards, balanced-budget rules, and constitutional regulations prohibiting bailouts.

Many of the institutional features in place in the United States are the product of a long history of reacting to state and local government defaults. The vast majority of defaulting governments were not rescued by the central or state government. Each fiscal crisis presented an opportunity for the defaulting government or the higher-level government to make improvements to its institutions in order to deter irresponsible behavior by future governments.

Although the United States has been very successful in minimizing bailout episodes in times of severe fiscal crisis, features of its intergovernmental fiscal system are conducive to soft budget constraints. One feature is the presence of vertical fiscal imbalances at the state and local government levels, despite the fact that lower-level governments have access to a wide variety of tax sources. Another feature that compounds soft budget constraint problems is the reliance of lower-level governments on conditional transfers to address vertical fiscal imbalances. Conditional transfers help ensure that state and local government provision of many goods and services meets minimum national standards, but they compromise accountability and create expectations that the central government will come to a regional government's assistance if it is unable to meet national standards. Regional interests are strongly represented in the national legislature. These features give rise to the common pool problem and have fueled the growth in demand for national financing of state and local services.

Canada

There are many parallels between the experience with soft budget constraints of Canada and the United States.[12] Like the United States, Canada is very successful at controlling bailout expectations of provincial and local governments. The provinces face very few taxing, spending, or borrowing restrictions, and they exercise their rights in these areas to such an extent that the size of the provincial government sector rivals that of the central government. Like the United States, Canada has a mature banking system and competitive bond markets that discipline fiscal excess with higher borrowing costs. Canada's fiscal and budgetary institutions have also evolved in response to reforms initiated in times of financial crisis. Democratic institutions provide voters with the means to punish irresponsible governments. Thus at the provincial level, market forces work well in enforcing hard budget constraints.

The provincial-local intergovernmental system is in striking contrast to the federal-provincial system. While the federal-provincial system reflects an extremely decentralized system that relies on market mechanisms to enforce hard budget constraints, the provincial-local system is characterized by strict hierarchical controls. Provincial governments tightly control local revenue raising, spending, and borrowing. Large vertical fiscal imbalances also exist between the provincial and local levels of government, which result in extreme dependence on intergovernmental transfers to finance most local public goods and services. These formal constraints are the result of provincial governments' experiences with local crises. The changes brought about as a result of these crises have produced an effective hierarchical management of municipal fiscal affairs.

Lessons Learned

The soft budget constraint literature concludes that there is no single underlying cause of the central government's incentive to provide additional resources to regional governments that violate their budget constraints. The soft budget constraint problem has its roots in the fiscal, financial, and political institutions through which the central and regional governments interact, institutions that differ considerably across countries. Thus a method that works best for hardening budget constraints in one country may not be effective or even possible in another. For practitioners and policy makers, the task of hardening budget constraints can represent a challenging problem.

The Role of Vertical Fiscal Imbalances

Vertical fiscal imbalances are the norm in intergovernmental fiscal relations and are addressed through intergovernmental transfers from higher levels of government to lower levels. Vertical fiscal imbalances sever the link between the benefits of regional spending and its cost, giving rise to a common pool problem that ultimately results in inefficiently high levels of spending and borrowing. Vertical fiscal imbalances involve the central government in regional fiscal outcomes, which compromises the regional government's accountability in the eyes of voters and creditors. These imbalances also limit the flexibility of regional governments in their ability to raise additional revenues in times of crisis. Regional governments may therefore feel justified when calling on the central government to provide additional resources, because only it has the ability to do so (Rodden, Eskelund, and Litvack 2003a).

Pisauro (2001) and Rodden (2001) warn, however, that closing the vertical fiscal gap by providing regional governments with sufficient revenues to finance their expenditures may not result in fiscal discipline. When regional governments have access to a large number of tax bases but have little autonomy to set tax rates or create new bases, they are unable to adjust own-source revenues in response to financial crises. This has been the case in Brazil and Germany. As a result, voters and creditors may not hold regional governments accountable for financial crises if the regional governments have limited flexibility in securing additional revenues from own sources. Thus unless the central government is completely devoid of any concern for regional fiscal outcomes, regional governments may come to expect additional resources from the central government even with vertical fiscal balance. The temptation to grant additional resources may be irresistible if denying them results in the closing of hospitals and schools or the failure of national financial institutions (Pisauro 2001; Rodden 2001; Rodden, Eskelund, and Litvack 2003a).

The Role of Market Mechanisms

Closing the fiscal gap can mitigate the soft budget constraint problem if regional governments have the ability to solve financial crises on their own. Full taxing, spending, and borrowing autonomy makes regional governments fully accountable to voters and creditors for fiscal outcomes, breaking the expectation of central government involvement in the regions' fiscal affairs. Competition for voter support and the discipline of capital markets can then serve to enforce hard budget constraints (Qian and Weingast 1997; Inman 2003; Rodden, Eskelund, and Litvack 2003b). These market mechanisms for hardening budget constraints have been successful in the Canadian provinces and the United States. However, the successful employment of market discipline requires a number of essential institutional features that are lacking in many countries.

One of the most important preconditions for instilling market discipline is a strong and stable central government that refuses to succumb to the pressures of regional governments in granting additional resources (Inman 2003). In many developing countries and transition economies, and in some developed economies, the central government does not have the strength or stability to resist these pressures. In many countries, regional interests are well represented in the upper chamber or parliament, which can severely limit the central government's ability to modify fiscal institutions in ways that could harden budget constraints. Furthermore, weak and potentially short-lived governments fail to weigh the benefits of denying bailouts very heavily in their decision making, as the benefits accrue in the future, in the form of improved fiscal discipline.

Other necessary institutional features for the successful employment of market mechanisms are those that ensure that voters and creditors are able to punish irresponsible governments. For this to take place, voters must be well informed and able to express their discontent in a democratic fashion

(Rodden 2001; Inman 2003; Rodden, Eskelund, and Litvack 2003b). Private capital markets must also be well developed and efficient for creditors to punish irresponsible regional governments with higher borrowing costs. In many countries, there is also the expectation that the central government implicitly or explicitly backs the regional governments' debt. This has been the case in Argentina, Brazil, Germany, Sweden, and Ukraine, for example. In such cases, regional government borrowing costs tend to reflect the creditworthiness of the central government, which compromises the efficient allocation of credit.

If any of the institutional features outlined above are lacking, soft budget constraints are likely to be a problem. This is one reason why very few countries have devolved full expenditure, revenue, and borrowing autonomy to regional governments. Others are the arguments laid out in the introduction for the involvement of the central government in regional government affairs. Full decentralization can result in inequities and inefficiencies beyond the soft budget constraint problem, and it can limit the central government's ability to stabilize the macroeconomy. These dangers of decentralization are also likely to be more pronounced in developing countries and transition economies (Prud'homme 1995). A strong case can therefore be made on equity, efficiency, and stability grounds for the central government to remain heavily involved in the affairs of regional governments. The optimal relationship would be for the central government to maintain dominance in revenue raising and regional governments to maintain dominance in the provision of regional public goods and services, with intergovernmental transfers used to address the vertical fiscal imbalance that results from this arrangement. Such transfers can take varied forms. As a result, the type of transfer and its purpose can have different implications for efficiency and equity.

The Role of Equalization Schemes

There is considerable variation across countries in the ability of regional governments to provide comparable levels of public goods and services at comparable levels of taxation. Because regions differ in their abilities to provide goods and services, people in similar circumstances are treated differently across regions. Poor regions must levy higher tax rates than rich regions in order to provide the same level and quality of services.

There can also be considerable variation in the need for and the costs of certain types of expenditures across regions. For example, some regions may have a larger proportion of elderly or poor people.

Equalization systems attempt to address differences across regional governments in revenue-raising capacity, needs, and costs. The way in which these three sources of differences are addressed in the equalization formula can have significant implications for regional government fiscal incentives. It is generally recognized that equalization systems that pool revenues or are based at least in some part on tax effort exacerbate the common pool problem and provide poor incentives for efficient revenue-raising activity (Bird and Smart 2002). For equalization systems to have minimal adverse incentives, the criteria for allocating transfers must be based on fiscal parameters that are not easily manipulated by regional governments. For example, equalization systems that address differences in potential fiscal capacity are preferable to those that are based on actual revenues.

Equalization transfers can also exacerbate the soft budget constraint problem when they create the expectation that the central government will grant additional resources in times of difficulty. The central government may feel obligated to come to a region's assistance when horizontal fiscal balance is compromised, especially if it is mandated to do so in its constitution. Two German *Länder*—Bremen and Saarland—and the Swedish municipal governments received bailouts in this way.

The Role of Discretionary Transfers

Rodden (2001) warns that intergovernmental transfers that are allocated on a discretionary basis exacerbate the soft budget constraint problem, because they are necessarily based on the regional governments' spending, borrowing, and taxing decisions. Indeed, the soft budget constraint problem would not arise if transfers were completely nondiscretionary. Discretionary transfers also provide incentives for regional governments to petition the central government to use its discretionary powers in their favor. Such behavior has been an important factor in the poor fiscal discipline of regional governments in Argentina and Brazil. In order to avoid these problems, transfers should be allocated according to clear and transparent rules, such as the number of school children or elderly people residing in a particular jurisdiction (Bird and Smart 2002; Rodden, Eskelund, and Litvack 2003b).

Compounding the dangers of discretionary transfers is the informational asymmetry regarding the causes of a region's financial distress. Regional governments have obvious incentives to place the blame for their financial difficulties on factors beyond their control. The central government may therefore be unable to determine the underlying factors that resulted in a fiscal crisis. That is, the central government is unable to determine whether the region's predicament is the result of an adverse shock or the regional government's opportunistic behavior. Alesina and Perotti

(1999) report that part of the complexity of regional government budgets may be an effort to deflect the blame for poor fiscal performance in the eyes of the central government and the region's residents. To this end, regional governments may overestimate the expected growth of the economy, the effects of government policies, and the revenue effects of small changes in tax policy and announce a multiyear budget in which most of the difficult adjustments occur in the future. The confusion created by deliberate complexity in the budgeting process makes it difficult for voters to hold regional governments accountable for financial difficulties experienced at the end of the fiscal year. Necessary instruments for reducing these informational asymmetries are the regular and effective monitoring and auditing of regional governments' budgets in order to detect fiscal indiscipline and prevent it from reaching crisis levels (Inman 2003).

The Role of Overlapping Responsibilities

Accountability is compromised when both the central and regional governments are responsible for funding key public goods and services or regional governments are mandated to provide these goods and services according to standards dictated by the central government. The involvement of the central government in this regard is meant to address the efficient provision of goods and services that generate positive spillovers to people throughout the country. Examples include such sensitive areas as health, education, and policing.

Overlapping responsibilities, however, make it difficult for voters to discern which level of government is ultimately responsible for providing public goods and services and thus make it difficult for regional governments to adjust to fiscal crises on their own. Overlapping responsibilities also create the expectation that the central government considers these goods and services to be essential and will therefore feel obligated to prevent the regional government from defaulting on its responsibilities in times of crisis. This is an example of Wildasin's (2004) "too-big-to-fail" hypothesis and the "too sensitive to fail" hypothesis proposed by von Hagen and others (2000). The recent history of Italy's health care sector is a prime example of the adverse incentives generated when both levels of government are heavily involved in the provision of a key public service.

The Role of Hierarchical Mechanisms

In his multinational analysis of the soft budget constraint problem, Rodden (2001) finds that very large vertical fiscal imbalances combined with strong hierarchical controls of regional government spending and borrowing can mitigate the soft budget constraint problem. Fiscal discipline in the local government sectors in Canada and Hungary has substantially improved with strong hierarchical oversight. Without these controls, soft budget constraint problems would undoubtedly arise, because with very high vertical fiscal imbalance, a local government is justified in turning to the central government for assistance, since only it has the flexibility to adjust spending and taxing levels in times of crisis.

Rodden, Eskelund, and Litvack (2003b) warn that while hierarchical mechanisms may be very effective in hardening budget constraints, they come at the cost of constraining market mechanisms in efficiently allocating credit. Furthermore, regional governments have obvious incentives to circumvent hierarchical controls, even when they are enshrined in the constitution. The Brazilian provinces, for example, have been very successful in accessing private capital markets, despite the central government's constitutional ability to regulate borrowing. Rodden, Eskelund, and Litvack (2003b) and Inman (2003) emphasize the importance of institutional features in preventing regional governments from circumventing hierarchical controls on borrowing and spending. These include no-bailout clauses, bankruptcy standards that require repayment of debts and are enforced by independent parties, balanced-budget rules for current account spending, and regular monitoring and auditing of regional government budgets.

Concluding Comments

The review of the theoretical, empirical, and case study literature indicates that expectations of additional resources on the part of regional governments and incentives to grant them on the part of the central government can arise under various circumstances. Some features of intergovernmental fiscal institutions are more conducive to hard budget constraints than others, but their ultimate impact on fiscal discipline depends on the country's financial and political institutions.

The main findings of the literature can be summarized as follows:

- Full revenue, spending, and borrowing autonomy can harden budget constraints only if voters and creditors hold regional governments accountable for their actions and are able to punish irresponsible governments.
- Large vertical fiscal imbalances combined with strong hierarchical controls can harden budget constraints only if institutional features are put

in place that prevent regional governments from circumventing these controls.

■ Discretionary transfers should be avoided and transfers allocated on the basis of clear and transparent rules.

■ Each level of government should be assigned exclusive expenditure and revenue authority.

This summary highlights the importance of the interaction among fiscal, financial, and political institutions in hardening budget constraints. Some of the mechanisms by which budget constraints can be hardened are unavailable in many countries, because of the particular fiscal, financial, and political institutions currently in place. Rodden, Eskelund, and Litvack (2003b) point out that as these institutions evolve over time, many countries can expect that some mechanisms for hardening budget constraints that are unavailable today may become so tomorrow. They also note that periods of financial crises and bailout episodes can provide the impetus for needed reforms, as has been the case in most of the countries surveyed in this chapter.

On a more cautious note, the issue of fiscal efficiency encompasses more than hard budget constraints. The soft budget constraint problem is but one potential source of fiscal inefficiency that results from the interactions among governments within a country and that are addressed by intergovernmental transfers. Horizontal disparities also provide a rationale for intergovernmental transfers. It is therefore possible that some of the mechanisms by which the soft budget constraint problem can be mitigated may serve to aggravate inefficiencies and disparities in some other way. The challenge for researchers and practitioners is to weigh these tradeoffs in crafting the optimal design of intergovernmental fiscal institutions.

Notes

1. For case study analyses of the soft budget constraint problem in Germany, see Seitz (1999), von Hagen and others (2000), and Rodden (2003a).
2. Other important and interesting differences between the two analyses are not discussed here, because of their focus on factors other than intergovernmental transfers in affecting fiscal indiscipline.
3. Evidence of the extent of federal government involvement in the affairs of state governments is that all states have the same credit rating as the federal government, and thus face the same interest rates, despite wide variation in debt levels. Private credit markets are therefore not effectively disciplining state governments in Germany.
4. For case study analyses of the soft budget constraint problem in Italy, see von Hagen and others (2000) and Bordignon (2000).

5. For case study analyses of the soft budget constraint problem in Sweden, see von Hagen and others (2000) and von Hagen and Dahlberg (2004).
6. For case study analyses of the soft budget constraint problem in Argentina, see Nicolini and others (2000) and Webb (2003).
7. For case study analyses of the soft budget constraint problem in Brazil, see Bevilaqua (2000) and Rodden (2003b).
8. For a case study analysis of the soft budget constraint problem in Ukraine, see O'Connell and Wetzel (2003).
9. For a case study analysis of the soft budget constraint problem in Hungary, see Wetzel and Papp (2003).
10. For case study analyses of the soft budget constraint problem in Australia, see von Hagen and others (2000) and Grewal (2000).
11. For a case study analysis of the soft budget constraint problem in the United States, see Inman (2003).
12. For a case study analysis of the soft budget constraint problem in Canada, see Bird and Tassonyi (2003).

References

Aizenman, Joshua. 1998. "Fiscal Discipline in a Union." In *The Political Economy of Reform*, ed. F. Sturzenegger and M. Tommasi, 185–208. Cambridge, MA: MIT Press.

Alesina, Alberta, and Roberto Perotti. 1999. "Budget Deficits and Budget Institutions." In *Fiscal Institutions and Fiscal Performance*, ed. James Poterba and Jurgen von Hagen, 13–36. Chicago: University of Chicago Press.

Bevilaqua, A. 2000. "State Government Bailouts in Brazil." Working Paper 421, Catholic University of Rio de Janeiro, Department of Economics.

Bird, Richard, and Michael Smart. 2002. "Intergovernmental Fiscal Transfers: Lessons for Developing Countries." *World Development* 30 (6): 899–912.

Bird, Richard, and Almos Tassonyi. 2003. "Constraining Fiscal Behavior in Canada: Different Approaches, Similar Results?" In *Fiscal Decentralization and the Challenge of Hard Budget Constraints*, ed. Jonathan Rodden, Gunnar Eskelund, and Jennie Litvack, 85–132. Cambridge, MA: MIT Press.

Boadway, Robin, and Jean-François Tremblay. 2006. "A Theory of Fiscal Imbalance." *Finanzarchiv* 62 (1): 1–27.

Bordignon, Massimo. 2000. "Problems of Soft Budget Constraints in Intergovernmental Relationships: The Case of Italy." Research Network Working Paper R-398, Inter-American Development Bank, Washington, DC.

Brennan, Geoffrey, and James Buchanan. 1980. *The Power of Tax: Analytical Foundations of a Fiscal Constitution.* Cambridge: Cambridge University Press.

Buettner, Thiess. 2003. "Municipal Fiscal Adjustment in Germany." Center for European Economic Research (ZEW) and Mannheim University, Mannheim, Germany.

Careaga, Maite, and Barry Weingast. 2000. "The Fiscal Pact with the Devil: A Positive Approach to Fiscal Federalism, Revenue Sharing, and Good Governance." Working Paper, Stanford University, Department of Political Science, Stanford, CA.

Garcia-Milà, Teresa, Timothy J. Goodspeed, and Therese J. McGuire. 2002. "Fiscal Decentralization Policies and Sub-National Government Debt in Evolving Federations." Universitat Pompeu Fabra Working Paper 549, Barcelona, Spain.

Goodspeed, Timothy J. 2002. "Bailouts in a Federation." *International Tax and Public Finance* 9 (4): 409–21.

Grewal, Bhajan S. 2000. "Australian Loan Council: Arrangements and Experience with Bailouts." Research Networking Working Paper R-397, Inter-American Development Bank, Washington, DC.

Inman, Robert. 2003. "Transfers and Bailouts: Enforcing Local Fiscal Discipline with Lessons from U. S. Federalism." In *Fiscal Decentralization and the Challenge of Hard Budget Constraints*, ed. Jonathan Rodden, Gunnar Eskelund, and Jennie Litvack, 35–83. Cambridge, MA: MIT Press.

Jones, M., P. Sanguinetti, and M. Tommasi. 1999. "Politics, Institutions, and Public-Sector Spending in the Argentine Provinces." In *Fiscal Institutions and Fiscal Performance*, ed. J. Poterba and J. von Hagen, 135–50. Chicago: University of Chicago Press.

———. 2000. "Politics, Institutions, and Fiscal Performance in a Federal System: An Analysis of the Argentine Provinces." *Journal of Development Economics* 61 (2): 305–33.

Kornai, Janos. 1979. "Resource-Constrained Versus Demand-Constrained Systems." *Econometrica* 47 (4): 801–19.

———. 1986. "The Soft Budget Constraint." *Kyklos* 39 (1): 3–30.

Kornai, Janos, Eric Maskin, and Gerard Roland. 2003. "Understanding the Soft Budget Constraint." *Journal of Economic Literature* 41 (4): 1095–1136.

Musgrave, Richard. 1959. *The Theory of Public Finance: A Study in Public Economy*. New York: McGraw-Hill.

Nicolini, J.P., J. Sanguinetti, P. Sanguinetti, and M. Tommasi. 2000. "Decentralization, Fiscal Discipline in Subcentral Governments, and the Bailout Problem: The Argentine Case." Working Paper, Inter-American Development Bank, Washington, DC.

O'Connell, Sean, and Deborah Wetzel. 2003. "Systemic Soft Budget Constraints in Ukraine." In *Fiscal Decentralization and the Challenge of Hard Budget Constraints*, ed. Jonathan Rodden, Gunnar Eskelund, and Jennie Litvack, 353–91. Cambridge, MA: MIT Press.

Pettersson-Lidbom, Per, and Matz Dahlberg. 2003. "An Empirical Approach for Estimating Soft Budget Constraints." Working Paper 2003:28, Uppsala University, Department of Economics, Uppsala, Sweden.

Pisauro, Giuseppe. 2001. "Intergovernmental Relations and Fiscal Discipline: Between Commons and Soft Budget Constraints." IMF Working Paper 01/65, International Monetary Fund, Washington, DC.

Prud'homme, R. 1995. "The Dangers of Decentralization." *World Bank Research Observer* 10 (2): 201–20.

Qian, Yingyi, and Barry R. Weingast. 1997. "Federalism as a Commitment to Preserving Market Incentives." *Journal of Economic Perspectives* 11 (4): 83–92.

Rodden, Jonathan. 2000. "Breaking the Golden Rule: Fiscal Behavior with Rational Bailout Expectations in the German States." MIT, Department of Political Science, Cambridge, MA.

———. 2001. "The Dilemma of Fiscal Federalism: Grants and Fiscal Performance around the World." MIT, Department of Political Science, Cambridge, MA.

———. 2003a. "Soft Budget Constraints and German Federalism." In *Fiscal Decentralization and the Challenge of Hard Budget Constraints*, ed. Jonathan Rodden, Gunnar Eskelund, and Jennie Litvack, 161–86. Cambridge, MA: MIT Press.

———. 2003b. "Federalism and Bailouts in Brazil." In *Fiscal Decentralization and the Challenge of Hard Budget Constraints*, ed. Jonathan Rodden, Gunnar Eskelund, and Jennie Litvack, 213–48.Cambridge, MA: MIT Press.

———. 2003c. "Reviving Leviathan: Fiscal Federalism and the Growth of Government." *International Organization* 57 (4): 695–729.

Rodden, Jonathan, Gunnar Eskelund, and Jennie Litvack. 2003a. "Introduction and Overview." In *Fiscal Decentralization and the Challenge of Hard Budget Constraints*, ed. Jonathan Rodden, Gunnar Eskelund, and Jennie Litvack, 1–31. Cambridge, MA: MIT Press.

———. 2003b. "Lessons and Conclusions." In *Fiscal Decentralization and the Challenge of Hard Budget Constraints*, ed. Jonathan Rodden, Gunnar Eskelund, and Jennie Litvack, 431–65. Cambridge, MA: MIT Press.

Sanguinetti, P., and M. Tommasi. 2004. "Intergovernmental Transfers and Fiscal Behavior Insurance versus Aggregate Discipline." *Journal of International Economics* 62 (1): 149–70.

Seitz, Helmut. 1999. "Subnational Government Bailouts in Germany." Working Paper, Center for European Integration Studies (ZEI), Bonn.

Stein, Ernesto. 1999. "Fiscal Decentralization and Government Size in Latin America." *Journal of Applied Economics* 2 (2): 357–91.

Tiebout, Charles. 1956. "A Pure Theory of Local Expenditures." *Journal of Political Economy* 64 (5): 416–24.

von Hagen, Jürgen, and Matz Dahlberg. 2004. "Swedish Local Government: Is There A Bailout Problem?" In *Fiscal Federalism in Unitary States*, ed. Per Molander, 47–76. Norwell, MA: Kluwer Academic Publishers.

von Hagen, Jürgen, Massimo Bordignon, Matz Dahlberg, Bhajan S. Grewal, Per Pettersson, and Helmut Seitz. 2000. "Subnational Government Bailouts in OECD Countries: Four Case Studies." Research Network Working Paper R-399, Inter-American Development Bank, Washington, DC.

Webb, Steven. 2003. "Argentina: Hardening the Provincial Budget Constraint." In *Fiscal Decentralization and the Challenge of Hard Budget Constraints*, ed. Jonathan Rodden, Gunnar Eskelund, and Jennie Litvack, 189–211. Cambridge, MA: MIT Press.

Wetzel, Deborah, and Anita Papp. 2003. "Strengthening Hard Budget Constraints in Hungary." In *Fiscal Decentralization and the Challenge of Hard Budget Constraints*, ed. Jonathan Rodden, Gunnar Eskelund, and Jennie Litvack, 353–91. Cambridge, MA: MIT Press.

Wildasin, David E. 2004. "The Institutions of Federalism: Toward an Analytical Framework." *National Tax Journal* 57 (2): Part 1: 247–72.

Winer, Stanley. 1983. "Some Evidence on the Effectiveness of the Separation of Spending and Taxing Decisions." *Journal of Political Economy* 91 (1): 126–40.

6

The Political Economy of Interregional Grants

MOTOHIRO SATO

Conflicting views have been expressed on intergovernmental transfers. Normative public economics addresses decentralization failures, such as fiscal externalities and inequity. In this view, interregional transfers serve as a means to deal with decentralization failure while preserving the benefits of decentralization (Boadway and Hobson 1993). These transfers can also be used to ensure national minimum standards of key public services, such as education and health, with the central authority exercising "spending power." The basic task in transfer design is therefore to "get prices right," ensuring that local governments are fully accountable for their decisions at the margin (Bird and Smart 2002). The presumption is that governments act in the interests of their constituencies.

The public choice school of thought perceives governments as self-interested or Leviathan-like entities, which act against the interests of their citizens. It regards intergovernmental competition as a way to contain the monopolistic power of governments to exploit their citizens. In this view, decentralization is a way to promote competition so that taxes and fees decline, just as competing private firms reduce the prices of goods. Given the nonbenevolent nature of governments, interregional transfers are not necessarily welfare enhancing. Serving as a collusion device among government units rather than a coordination device, they can give rise to excessive expansion of the public sector.

The normative theory of intergovernmental transfers ignores political issues, focusing instead on the economic rationale for their use. It is conceivable, and often observed in practice, however, that governments direct more central funds to politically powerful regions in the hope of securing their votes. Central bureaucrats and line ministries may be motivated to maximize their budgets. The central authority may abuse its spending power, excessively intruding into local matters and undermining local autonomy. Special interest groups or local governments may engage in lobbying activities to manipulate grant allocations in their favor. Interregional grants are then used to fund public projects whose benefits are geographically concentrated but whose costs are borne by the nation as a whole.

With a hierarchical fiscal tie, the central government may eventually be obligated to rescue indebted regions, undermining the fiscal accountability of local governments. Such bailouts may not be required by the constitution but instead reflect political pressure. Local residents may be reluctant to monitor and discipline their local governments when they perceive that local spending is not coming out of their own pockets but paid by someone else.

Of course, policy making of any sort is ultimately a political matter. According to Inman (1988), the normative theory of intergovernmental grants does not provide a satisfactory explanation of the practice of transfer programs in the United States that do little to internalize spillovers or to grant fiscal support to low-income or resource-poor regions. A political economy model does a much better job. This is not to say that economic analysis of transfers is irrelevant. The economic consequences of politically motivated but poorly designed transfers could be detrimental to the economy. The challenge is to avoid inflicting collateral damage in the course of achieving political objectives (Bird and Smart 2002).

This chapter overviews political economy models of grants, examining both intergovernmental and interregional transfers that may be directly provided to residents by the center. The chapter is not purely positive; normative inferences of emerging politico-economic equilibrium are examined as well.

An important distinction should be made between the normative and positive aspects of interregional transfers. Normative considerations examine how transfers should be provided to enhance efficiency and equity, abstracting from political economy considerations. Positive considerations describe how transfers emerge as the political economy consequence of decisions and interactions among stakeholders. The two are not necessarily coincident. Some argue that political feasibility should be taken into account by normative studies if the policy recommendations are to be approved and implemented through the political process. This chapter does not examine the role of public choice considerations in the normative public economics, a subject that has been discussed elsewhere (Boadway 2002). Instead, it examines the political economy of interregional transfers, taking a positive view and assessing the resulting equilibrium from the conventional normative perspectives. It then considers the "rules of the game," or the institutional structure, that bind decisions of relevant stakeholders.

At this point, it is worth noting that for the normative prescription to hold in practice, several conditions must be met:

■ The central government must be benevolent in pursuing social welfare. Its benevolence may result from the presumption that there is an institutional arrangement, such as a well-functioning democracy, that functions as a disciplinary device to ensure that the government acts in the interest of its citizens.

■ The central government must act as a single decision maker. It must be capable of coordinating central polices governing taxes, public goods, and intergovernmental and interpersonal redistribution in order to meet a single objective.

■ The central government must possess hierarchical control over lower-level governments and exclusive control over central policy instruments. In some countries, the central government must consult with lower-level governments regarding policies that affect them. In addition, if a region does not have confidence in the center, it may secede from the nation. The possibility of secession constrains the central government in designing interregional grants.

■ The central government must be able to commit to its policies.[1]

This chapter examines the consequences that result when any of these conditions is not met.

The chapter is organized as follows. The next section examines self-interested governments and political competition. It begins by addressing the "flypaper effect," which has been associated with self-interested motives of local governments, before turning to the selfish motives of the center. The second section examines pork barrel politics and rent seeking due to the fragmented nature of the central government. The third section illustrates transfers, addressing intergovernmental bargaining and the threat of a nation breaking up. The fourth section examines soft budget and holdup problems associated with commitment problems. The last section examines institutional reform to cope with the politics of transfers.

Political Motive and Political Competition

This section considers the motives of the central and local governments. First, it shows how local politics lead to anomalies in intergovernmental transfers, a phenomenon known as the "flypaper effect." Second, it considers how interregional transfers can reflect purely tactical moves by vote-maximizing governments rather than ideological or equity concerns.

The Flypaper Effect

If regional voters possess full sovereignty with single-peaked preferences, making the median voter pivotal, that voter's share of lump-sum grants is a fungible asset that can be used for public or private purposes and can thus be included in his total income. The response to an increase in grants would thus be similar to the response to an increase in private income (Bradford and Oates 1971). Deviation from this prediction may reflect the fact that local policy decisions are not based on the median voter's preference but instead reflect the selfish motives of local governments pursuing their own interest.

Fiscal decentralization is believed to discipline otherwise self-interested local politicians into acting in the interest of citizens, fostering interregional competition.[2] Decentralization can spur "voting with one's feet" and "yardstick competition" (performance comparison), which can motivate otherwise self-interested local politicians to act in the interest of their constituents. Competition does not alter politicians' objectives (say, reelection or the maximization of their political rents); it means that serving citizens' needs become the means to achieve such ends. It induces politicians to behave in a benevolent manner, even though it is not in their nature to do so. For competition to have a disciplinary effect, however, citizens must be cost conscious about local public spending. Fiscal accountability (at the margin) is thus essential if fiscal decentralization is to be successful.

Intergovernmental transfers can introduce a wedge between benefits and costs, however. As Bird and Smart (2002) note, people tend to be more careful about spending money they have to earn. When local governments spend what local residents view as other people's money, citizens are unlikely to put much pressure on politicians to use funds efficiently. They mistakenly perceive the grants as free lunches, even though they are financed by national taxes that they pay. Indeed, empirical studies of intergovernmental transfers reveal that lump-sum grants lead to disproportionately large increases in local spending compared with the effect of increases in private income.

Filimon, Romer, and Rosenthal (1982) consider the case in which the flypaper effect arises due to voters' ignorance and local bureaucrats' maximization of their budgets. In their model, local voters are not aware of the existence or exact amounts of intergovernmental grants and vote according to their own perception of tax price. This leaves local bureaucrats free to direct "hidden resources" to expand the local budget without being recognized by regional voters. The budget-maximizing spending authority with inside information and ability to hide it benefits from the fact that such information is hidden.

Informational advantage enables better-informed local bureaucrats to exercise control over the agenda. Romer and Rosenthal (1980) provide an analytical framework of the institutional structure of local decision that features the agenda-setting power of bureaucrats. They consider the case of local policy decisions on a single public service, such as education. Under the agenda-setter model, regional voters' choice is limited to either approving or rejecting a proposal made by their agent. If they reject the proposal, the level of public service provision reverts to an exogenously determined level. This increases bureaucrats' scope to manipulate the agenda in a way that maximizes their budgets. If grants are not fungible for regional voters, local expenditure in equilibrium is excessive from the median voter or principal's standpoint; when a reversion/default policy involves a high level of public spending, intergovernmental grants generate the flypaper effect.

Grants can distort local public choices, undermining the disciplinary functions of local autonomy, which in turn gives rise to overexpansion of local spending. There is no consensus on the cause of this flypaper effect, however. Wyckoff (1991) reviews the literature and concludes that the observed anomaly may be due to misspecification in empirical studies. He rejects the hypothesis of fiscal illusion in his own empirical work (see also Bailey and Connolly 1998). Hines and Thaler (1995) note that flypaper effects may arise due to irrational behavior or the perception that voters are loss averse or do not treat funds as fungible. Under a more complicated and plausible political economy model, such as political competition, Roemer and Silvestre (2002) note that the anomaly of the flypaper effect can disappear.

Political Competition

The tactical nature of intergovernmental grants can be modeled in two ways, bottom up (demand driven) and top down (supply driven). The bottom-up approach addresses the universal norm in the legislature that allows pork barrel politics as well as lobbying activities by regional interest groups. It is discussed in the next section. This section examines the top-down approach.

Dixit and Londregan (1998a) develop an empirically testable model of a federal country in which competing political parties attempt to buy votes in an election campaign by transferring funds to groups of voters or regions. Each party acts as a single decision maker in choosing a platform, which involves a bundle of public policies, including promised transfers. Dixit and Londregan implicitly assume that strong leadership and internal discipline exist within a party. They also assume that parties can credibly commit to delivering their platform.

Political competition occurs in central and local elections and is captured by probabilistic voting behavior. Conflicts of interest among voters is due to the fact that they are concerned with their own consumption, which is affected by transfer policies, as well as by what they take as different ideological positions on political matters, such as environment protection and national defense. Differences in ideological positions generate randomness in their voting behavior. Voting is assumed to be prospective, that is, it responds to political platforms during the campaign rather than on politicians' past performance (retrospective voting). In addition, the model assumes that political parties cannot observe the policy preferences or ideological positions of individuals but must rely on membership in groups, observable from such indicators as income, residence, and occupation.

The central government undertakes interregional and interpersonal lump-sum transfers, whereas local governments redistribute income within their jurisdictions. The center is assumed to act as a first mover, which takes into account the way local governments react to central redistribution policy in designing their own.

Suppose that political parties are fully apolitical, in that their sole concern is being elected (ideological concerns can be incorporated without altering the essence of the argument) (Dixit and Londregan 1998b). The use of interregional transfers is thus a purely tactical move used to attract votes. Dixit and Londregan (1998a) show that the politicoeconomic equilibrium is symmetric, in which competing political parties announce the same policy platform during the campaign.

At both the central and local levels, a group that has less attachment to ideology and thus includes more swing voters gains more transfers. Low-income people are favored as well. Moreover, within their jurisdictions, local governments can invalidate the interpersonal distribution of income desired by the center by using their own distributive policy instruments. Consequently, the center can affect only the distribution of resources across regions. If matching grants are added to the central policy instruments, the central government can make use of them to influence the local governments' incentives for redistribution in its favor.[3]

Johansson (2003) tests the hypothesis of Dixit and Londregan (1998a) in the context of Swedish grant allocations. She measures the importance of swing voters in two ways. First, she measures the difference between the vote shares of the conservative and socialist parties, referred to as a "closeness proxy." Second, she estimates voters' preferences and their distribution through factor analysis, using survey data from Swedish election studies, which in turn are applied to calculate the densities at the cut-off points. Johansson finds that the closeness proxy is not statistically significant but that the size of the swing voter block, measured by the estimated densities, has a positive and significant impact on grants, implying that tactics could matter.

This swing voter theory may be compared with machine politics, in which a political party favors its core support group in distributive politics (Dixit and Londregan 1996). Machine politics arise when political parties differ in their abilities to target redistributive benefits to different groups. Such a difference exists because each party has its core groups of voters preferences, whose preferences it knows well as a result of a well-developed support network. "This greater understanding translates into greater efficiency in the allocation of particularistic benefits" (Dixit and Londregan (1996, p. 1134). This implies that more transfers are directed to the government's core support groups at the expense of "outsiders" and that political competitors adopt different policies.

A region whose government is affiliated with the central government party may be regarded as such a core support group. It will credibly convey information on local needs and preferences for transfers to the center and deliver more votes for the central government's party. Grossman (1994) refers to regional politicians' ability to deliver votes for their central counterparts as *political capital* and measures it by the party affiliation of regional legislators. A U.S. state possesses a large stock of political capital when the majority in its legislature is the same as the majority in the U.S. House of Representatives. Grossman (1994) finds this proxy to be positive and significant.

Dixit and Londregan (1998a) assume that the national assembly seats are assigned to regions in proportion to their population and then establish that group size—that is, regional population—is irrelevant in determining per capita allocation of transfers because a large group is vote rich but costly to allocate the government budget. The result may change, however, if regional representation in the national assembly is biased—for instance, favoring smaller regions. Porto and Sanguinetti (2001) examine how federal grants are allocated across provinces in Argentina. They measure the political representation of a province by the per capita number of central legislators elected within it. They show that overrepresented provinces receive more grants.

Efficiency Issue

In the studies by Dixit and Londregan (1998a, b), the selfish motivation of the central government does not necessarily undermine efficiency: resource allocation is efficient (at least in the second-best sense), albeit not necessarily equitable. Along this line, McGuire and Olson (1996) claim that self-interested governments may have an interest in lowering taxes, removing inefficient regulations, and supplying public goods in order to expand production, which governments can tax to fulfill their own long-run interests of confiscating citizens' wealth—a political version of the "invisible hand."

Two different views have been posited regarding the efficiency implications of tactical transfers (Boadway and Keen 2000). The Virginia view is that redistribution tends to be inefficient. Rent-seeking activities waste valuable resources and disrupt economic activities. The Chicago view is that because there are incentives to use efficient instruments, a redistribution policy that appears at first glance to be inefficient could actually be a second-best solution. Along these lines, Hettich and Winer (1988) examine the choices between distorting taxes in the context of probabilistic voting and political competition. They conclude that in the political economy equilibrium, the tax structure is Pareto efficient, in the second-best sense.

Wittman (1995) goes farther, suggesting that democracy is efficient, at least in theory. This efficiency argument hinges on the idea of political entrepreneurship. Suppose that the status quo of central public policies is inefficient. By definition, there is an alternative set of policies that is feasible and Pareto improving. Given that competing political parties want to be elected, at least one would offer such a policy, since enhancing the well-being of the voters should garner it more votes. If existing parties or incumbent politicians prefer the status quo for some reason, a new party or politician will enter the political market with better policies. Thus, inefficient policies cannot be sustained when political competition works.

Political entrepreneurship assumes away the transaction costs associated with commitment and entry. Regarding commitment, Dixit and

Londregan (1995) consider government support for a declining industry. The efficient way to redistribute income toward such an industry is to provide lump-sum compensation for workers and reallocate them to higher-income or more productive sectors. However, this alters the political influence of the industry, since reassigning workers to new and different interest groups prevents them from acting collectively. If the government fails to commit to the lump-sum compensation and redesigns tactical transfers of income in line with the ex post distribution of political influence, the ex ante promised compensation will not be forthcoming. In anticipation of such reneging on the agreement, the declining industry would not accept lump-sum compensation that is efficient but would instead favor a subsidy to keep it afloat and keep workers in the sector. The economy is therefore locked into an inefficient policy that distorts labor allocation. The same story should apply to interregional grants replacing the declining industry by a declining region with population reallocation being efficiency-enhancing.

Fragmented Government and Rent Seeking

The discussion so far has assumed that the central government acts as a single decision maker. This implies that policies are coordinated and relevant externalities internalized. In practice, the central government does not behave in such a manner; many stakeholders are involved in policy making. This section examines the demand-driven, bottom-up nature of intergovernmental transfers. It analyzes pork barrel or distributive politics in the central legislature and rent-seeking activities by local governments or their representatives that lead to the tragedy of the commons and thus inefficiency.[4]

The Common Pool Problem

In most democratic countries, the legislative body and the administrative body are separated, and legal institutions are politically independent. Legislators may represent the interests of their constituent jurisdictions and of particular social classes rather than the nation as a whole, engaging in pork barrel or distributive politics. This is especially so when strong leadership and hierarchical discipline within a political party are absent. Every central politician asks for excessive interregional transfers to his or her own region, and such demands can be accepted.

Inman and Rubinfeld (1996) claim that pork barrel politics arises due to the decentralized nature of the legislature and the fact that the central government is weak. Individual legislators demand projects that benefit a particular geographic area or an identifiable group of constituents; the costs of these projects are funded by the center. These projects may be executed by the local government that receives the transfers or directly by the center. Cost sharing creates a fiscal wedge between social marginal costs and locally borne marginal costs. The result is that projects are overexpanded, because individual legislators undervalue their prices and impose a large fiscal burden on the nation as a whole. The tragedy of the commons (also known as the common pool problem) occurs, as public expenditures (and thus transfers) become excessive and regions impose fiscal burdens on one another. Consequently, the political economy equilibrium is not efficient. Velasco (2000) extends this problem to the dynamic context and establishes that the consequence of pork barrel politics is excessive accumulation of debt over time.

Pork barrel politics is associated with the informal norm that legislators vote to avoid the political instability that stems from multidimensional voting. The result is a structure-induced equilibrium in which reciprocity, called "universalism" or the "norm of deference" ("you scratch my back, I'll scratch yours"), is established. Each legislator agrees to support the preferred allocations of all other legislators, knowing that deviation from the norm of mutual support may induce others to deviate (Inman and Fitts 1990).[5] The consequence is that "elected legislators demand more of a locally beneficial project when the costs of that project are shared with nonlocal taxpayers" (DelRossi and Inman 1999).

Election rules may also be important. Where a plurality rule holds and there is a single seat in an election district, politicians are more inclined to serve local interests and thus engage in pork barrel politics (Sorensen 2003). This does not mean, however, that proportional representation can better restrain the pork barrel politics. It often leads to coalition governments, containing different parties with different political priorities, which could exacerbate the common pool problem. Indeed, Kontopoulos and Perotti (1999) provide empirical evidence to show that public spending increases with the number of coalition parties. Given that coalition governments have more veto players, they become more prone to fiscal deficits, with the dynamic common pool problem locked into status quo policies. Thus stabilization efforts may be delayed. Hallerberg and von Hagen (1999) also link the common pool problem to the form of government.

DelRossi and Inman (1999) test the common pool problem following passage of the Water Resource Development Act of 1986 in the United States, which increased local cost sharing. They find that the price elasticities of legislators' demand for distributive public goods, such as flood control and large navigation projects, are relatively high and conclude that "one solution to the common pool resource problem is to have the legislators' constituents pay a greater share of the marginal costs of these local goods" (271).

The propensity to overspend can be constrained by enhancing the leadership of political parties and thus replacing the norm of deference by a more centralized, more unified decision by making structure less susceptible to local interests or by limiting the number of states in the federalist hierarchy (Inman and Rubinfeld 1996). Strong presidents or party leaders are accountable for the overall fiscal and economic performance of the country. Inman and Fitts (1990) explore the roles of political parties in controlling the behavior of individual representatives. Strong parties interested in the collective benefits of all members will act to internalize the fiscal consequences of each legislator's demand. A president who uses his veto power can also contain distributive politics. The president's political influence is strengthened by nationwide support from the electorate. Inman and Fitts (1990) present empirical evidence to support these hypotheses.

Jones, Sanguinetti, and Tommasi (2000) consider the common pool problem in the context of intergovernmental relations in Argentina, where provincial governors instead of the central legislators act as stakeholders. They find that spending is relatively low in provinces in which the governor belongs to the same party as the president—perhaps because the president can prevent opportunistic behavior by governors of the same party by exerting party discipline. Rodden and Eskeland (2003) note that partisan ties linking the president, the legislature, and provincial governments may have helped make reforms possible in Argentina.

Rent Seeking

Central legislators play an active role in pork barrel politics. Local governments may also undertake rent-seeking or lobbying activities in order to obtain more transfers. They forge contacts with the central ministries in charge of interregional grants. Their lobbying may target politicians elected from their regions. For their part, politicians engage in pork barrel politics. Thus rent seeking and pork barrel politics are tied together. Small lobbying groups (or regions) may be more successful than larger ones, because the cost of transfers to them is so widely spread so that it is not noticeable (Becker 1983).[6]

One form of lobbying by local governments takes the form of information transmission to national politicians and ministries to update their perceptions of the economic benefits of grant-financed local services and of the political effect of grants on their chances of reelection. Local governments are better informed about local matters that concern them. They are, of course, motivated to manipulate such information in their favor by overstating benefits or underestimating costs, a tendency that is foreseen by the center (Austin-Smith 1997). Without hard evidence, information may not be credible and thus not very informative (Sorensen 2003). If local governments can somehow ensure the credibility of their information, the center can effectively target transfers to maximize political support to it, making such localities "core support groups." Recall the discussion of Dixit and Londregan (1996).

Local governments can also lobby by giving financial and logistic support to local party organizations during national election campaigns, providing more support to candidates considered to more actively promote local interests. Local governments can also ensure that local media and voters are aware of centrally financed projects and their benefits to local economies, avoiding discussion of the costs of the projects borne by the nation as a whole (Brock and Ownings 2003). In Grossman's (1994) terminology, lobbying governments utilize their "political capital."

The devolution of policy functions and responsibilities to local governments may give them the standing of principals in relation to the central authority. Their rent-seeking activities can therefore be modeled as a common agency problem. The central government acts as a common agent to local governments or to special interest groups representing them, which independently make (pecuniary or nonpecuniary) contributions to obtain favorable policies (Person and Tabellini 2000). The contributions are intended to help ensure that central politicians adopt local government objectives as their own. In determining central policies, including transfers, regulations, and public projects affecting local governments, the center maximizes a weighted sum of utilities, placing a higher weight on governments that lobby. Dixit, Grossman, and Helpman (1997) formulate a general common agency problem and establish that the emerging equilibrium is efficient, as only efficient policy instruments are sustainable. Resources are redistributed from unorganized groups to organized ones or from regions with less political influence to those with greater access to the center. This is in line with the Chicago School. Dixit, Grossman, and Helpman (1997) note, however, that with the use of efficient policy instruments, lobbyists' payoff could be lower in equilibrium than it is in the absence of rent seeking, as the game of lobbying for transfers turns into a prisoners' dilemma for local governments in which only central government politicians and bureaucrats are winners.[7]

These efficiency arguments rely on the presumption that pecuniary compensation or contribution to the central government is feasible and credible and that the government is capable of coordinating all policies at its disposal. In addition, the common agency model is static. As Murphy, Shleifer, and Vishny (1993) note, however, in a dynamic setting, rent seeking could be detrimental to economic growth if more individuals and groups devote their efforts to it. Local governments could instead have spent time and resources on entrepreneurship activity to enhance regional economic growth. Rent seeking is a zero-sum game, whereas growth-promoting activities are positive-sum games, increasing the size of the entire economy. Lobbying to gain more transfers from the center may prevail, however, if it is regarded as more profitable from the regional perspective.

What does the empirical evidence show? Sorensen (2003) studies Norway, where local governments rely heavily on central grants and have little tax autonomy. He shows that grant allocation is motivated by a desire for political power by both local and national politicians. Local politicians aiming to maximize grants seek to influence grant decisions, while national politicians make tactical use of grants to maximize votes in the national election. The rent-seeking activities of municipality governments are measured by the number of lobbying contacts between regional council representatives and central government bodies, including members of parliament and central government ministries. Lobbying contacts with central ministries are then shown to increase grants to rent-seeking municipalities.

Brock and Ownings (2003) show that both geographical and political distance affect local governments' rent-seeking costs in the United States. Geographical distance is measured by the distance between a local jurisdiction and the state capital. Brock and Owings postulate that distance is important because of the face to face nature of lobbying activities. They also construct an index that measures political closeness between the county and state legislatures. A county is politically closer to the state government if it is affiliated with the same party as the governor or the majority in the state parliament. Using data from California counties, Brock and Owings confirm their hypothesis that the amount of per capital intergovernmental transfer is negatively correlated with the physical distance and positively related to political closeness. This result is consistent with that of Grossman (1994) but at odds with Jones, Sanguinetti, and Tommasi (2000), who claim that partisan ties reduce transfers.

Intergovernmental Relations

The literature on fiscal federalism presumes that the central government can design transfers unilaterally.[8] Transfers may be determined through intergovernmental bargaining, however, in which grant-receiving governments have a voice. A government may use transfers to hold the nation together in the face of a separation movement, for example. This section addresses such an intergovernmental relationship. Finally, for fiscal decentralization to be growth enhancing, the center must be strong enough to prevent market disturbing activities at the local level and direct local governments' incentive to preserve markets. Transfers may be used for this purpose.

Fiscal Federalism versus Federal Finance

Bird (1994, 1999) distinguished between "federalism" and "federal states" with respect to intergovernmental relations. "Federalism" applies to unitary nations, such as Japan and the United Kingdom, where the central authority prevails politically. "Federal states" is a more relevant description of traditional federal nations, such as Canada and the United States. In a federal state, important federal policies, such as intergovernmental transfers and central regulations on local public services, including health and education, are subject to political bargaining and compromise by different levels of government. Watts (1996) defines Canadian federalism as "executive federalism." Inman and Rubinfeld (1997) refer to U.S. federalism as "cooperative federalism." They note that "the principle of cooperative federalism requires all central government policies to be unanimously approved by the elected representatives from each of the lower tier governments" (p. 48). The situation resembles pork barrel politics, but cooperative federalism addresses intergovernmental bargaining rather than fragmented/noncooperative decision making by the legislature. Pork barrel politics could be the consequence of "democratic (majority rule) federalism" without strong leadership or party discipline (Inman and Rubinfeld 1997, p. 5). Under cooperative federalism, bargaining may take place and agreement reached within a central legislative body or through intergovernmental agreement, along with Coasian-like compensation to negatively affected regions. Transfers are used as coordination devices or compensation to ensure cooperation rather than as incentive schemes for local governments. This is likely the case for a heterogeneous federation such as Canada, in which the unity of the country cannot be taken for granted.

Using Transfers to Hold a Nation Together

There have been an increasing number of works on political integration and separation. For an extensive survey of the literature, see Alesina, Perotti, and

Spolaore (1995). In this literature, the costs of integration are associated mainly with the loss of autonomy (Alesina and Spolaore 1997; Bolton and Roland 1997). The policy of the central government may not match regional preferences, since the national median voter differs from the median voter that would have been decisive had the two regions remained sovereign.

Different regional preferences for unification may necessitate "asymmetric federalism," in which different treatments apply to different regions based on their political power and desire for separation. Regions with different fiscal capacities and needs will receive different transfers under a given formula even in a unitary nation, but asymmetric federalism calls for different rules, different revenue-sharing rates, and different grant formulas in different regions. This is especially so when a country is heterogeneous in terms of culture, religion, and language.

The asymmetric nature of (de facto) federalism has been observed in practice. In Indonesia, for instance, the central government provides special treatment of tax revenue sharing with Aceh, in an attempt to accommodate the independence movement there. This kind of use of transfers comes with an economic cost, however, as it exacerbates fiscal imbalances, with poor but politically less powerful regions left without adequate funds.

A minority region may be afraid that its political rights and economic benefits are undermined within a united nation, or they may not feel solidarity with other parts of the country. Economic interests, such as natural resources within their jurisdiction, may fuel eagerness for independence in order to monopolize such interests. In such a case, intergovernmental transfers are used as political side payment—glue for national unity—to ensure that a region is better off remaining within a united nation than separating from it. Bolton and Roland (1997) show how the threat of secession constrains tax transfer policy. More transfers are directed to discontent regions in which there is a political movement for separation. Leite-Monteiro and Sato (2003) note that a federal regime in which policies are decided by interregional negotiation and transfers are given as side payments sustains the unity of a nation better than a centralized regime when the economy becomes more globalized.

Local governments need not simply receive adequate transfers to discharge their expenditure functions, they must also be confident of receiving them. Lack of security or accountability endangers political support for the transfer system and eventually the unity of the nation. Indeed, revenue-led decentralization observed in countries such as Indonesia may be due to lack of confidence in intergovernmental transfers, with local governments aiming to ensure their financial resources by capturing buoyant tax bases within their own jurisdictions.

Political Centralization and Market-Preserving Federalism

From the normative standpoint, fiscal decentralization does not undermine the role of the central authority. More sophisticated central involvement is needed to control and discipline local governments. Fragmented policy decisions within the central government causing pork barrel politics and rent seeking weaken such control.

Some studies suggest that the partisan link between the center and the regions restrains pork barrel politics (Jones, Sanguinetti, and Tommasi 2000). Others suggest that it facilitates local governments' access to central funds (Brock and Ownings 2003; Grossman 1994). The result is likely to depend on the level of centralization within the party and its political leadership. Enikolopov and Zhuravskaya (2003) provide empirical evidence from developing countries and transition economies that the growth and quality of government depend on the presence of strong central parties, which enhance the positive effects of the partisan linkage. Their results confirm Riker's (1964) work, which emphasizes the role of political parties in keeping the federalist order intact (Shleifer and Treisman 2000). Local politicians respect this order to advance their national careers through political parties. A federation without such incentives for local politicians, known as a "peripheralized federation," would fall apart.

In comparing Chinese and Russian federalism in the 1990s, Blanchard and Shleifer (2000) note that along with fiscal decentralization, political centralization under the Communist Party enabled the central authority in China to retain the power to remove or penalize inefficient local governments. This power serves as a "stick"; regional autonomy and locally retained tax revenues serve as a "carrot." Transfers are used as a tactical device to control local governments. After the collapse of communism, the national political party disappeared in Russia, leaving the federal government with little de facto authority over regional governments. As a result of political decentralization, local governments pursue their own interests, at the expense of the national welfare. Protectionist actions in favor of regional monopolists and stakeholders are an example. The comparison reveals that there must be a strong central government that centralizes policy decisions and can discipline local governments when needed.

These results are consistent with the market-preserving view of federalism. There has been increasing awareness that subnational governments play an important role in initiating or hindering regional economic development. A decentralized fiscal system in which local governments both compete and experiment with different development strategies can contribute to the economic development of a nation (Qian and Weingast 1997; Weingast 1995). For decentralization to be growth promoting, the central government must preserve or enforce a common market, preventing anticompetitive actions at the local level. The market-preserving federalism view also focuses on the balance of power among government units, which prevents them from preying on economic activities or markets. The central role in preserving a common market in order to secure free mobility of economic units such as labor and capital must be enhanced. In addition, each local government should face a hard budget, suffering the consequences of any losses due to overspending (Motinola, Qian, and Weingast 1996). A decentralized fiscal system must also be sufficiently institutionalized so that the central authority cannot frequently change the rules of the game.

In market-preserving federalism, tax revenue sharing works as an incentive device. Tax revenue–sharing arrangements between governments are observed in both developed and developing countries. They may contain equalization components, however. Shared revenue can be allocated on a population basis rather than on a derivation basis, for example, turning revenue sharing into an equalization program or general purpose grant.

"True" revenue sharing occurs when revenue allotment follows the derivation principle that transferred revenues accrue to revenue-raising jurisdictions. In this case, regional efforts to enhance revenues are directed to more productive uses, such as provision of infrastructure. Increasing shared revenues yields sufficient financial sources for growing regions to finance their spending on infrastructure, which further accelerates economic development.[9]

The Commitment Problem

The commitment problem arises when the central government is motivated and able to reoptimize its own policies ex post, after the state of the economy is revealed. Even if the government is benevolent, the commitment problem may exist.

The Soft Budget Problem

The term *soft budget constraint* describes the situation in which "an entity, say, local- level governments, can manipulate its access to funds in an undesirable way" (Rodden, Eskeland, and Litvack 2003, 7). In a seminal work, Kornai (1986) describes the financial relationship between the state and state enterprises in a socialist economy. Dewatripont and Maskin (1995) illustrate the soft budget problem as a sequential game in credit markets between lenders and borrowers. They associate it with the incentive problem that exists as a result of the lack of commitment of lenders not to bail out borrowers ex post, even though not bailing them out is desirable for the lender ex ante.

In the context of intergovernmental relations, the soft budget problem arises from close fiscal ties between different levels of government. The central government may be motivated to bail out fiscally troubled local governments that have overborrowed, overspent, or inefficiently managed their affairs (through excessive employment or risk taking, for example). Assistance may take the form of an emergency fund or a change in the allocation formula of grants. Ex post rescue can be justified based on equity grounds or by macroeconomic concerns about the negative consequences of a local government's insolvency. The central government may, for example, view the undersupply of important local public services due to financial constraints as inequitable, or the default of a local government could endanger the national banking system. Political concerns about national security or reelection may also motivate bailouts.

Whatever the motivation, bailouts are undertaken ex post, after local governments engage in fiscal mismanagement, if the central authority fails to commit not to do so. Such actions may be socially optimal ex post, given that local governments engage in fiscal mismanagement and their fiscal status is revealed. The ex post optimum does not account for the ex ante incentives of bailed-out governments, however. Anticipating such ex post rescue, local governments choose to be inefficient ex ante, that is, to overspend, overborrow, and take on risky projects. The problem is exacerbated if ex ante monitoring and regulations on local borrowing and spending are absent. Therefore, fiscal rescue that may be desirable ex post gives rise to ex ante moral hazard at the local level. The problem arises because the government is allowed to exert ex post discretion in its policy making or because there is no external device to prevent its discretion.

Wildasin (1999) and Goodspeed (2002) present structured models of the soft budget problem, formulated in the context of a sequential game in which the local government moves first and the central government sets its transfer policy after the local fiscal status is revealed. In Wildasin (1999) the ex post motive for bailout is the presence of interregional spillovers of locally provided services, which the center aims to internalize. The central government adds conditional grants to a region that underprovides these services. A large jurisdiction that generates more spillovers is more likely to be bailed out than a smaller one ("too big to fail"). In anticipation of such ex post rescue, local governments underspend.

Goodspeed (2002) describes the ex post tactical use of transfers by a central government seeking reelection. More bailout may occur in regions ruled by opposition parties than those with partisan ties to the center. Although the contexts are different, this resembles the hypothesis of Jones, Sanguinetti, and Tommasi (2000). The soft budget is similar to pork barrel politics, in that reduced local cost sharing leads to excessive expenditure decisions (Inman 2003). The two issues differ, however since in the soft budget problem, the ex post cost-sharing arrangement is determined as the consequence of the ex post optimization of the center (that is, lack of commitment), whereas the common pool problem is due to fragmented decision making within the central government.

Several studies provide empirical evidence of soft budgets. Dillinger, Perry, and Webb (2003) find that rapid decentralization combined with the separation of taxing and expenditure decisions in Latin America has put stress on the central budget and ultimately macroeconomic stability, as the central government rescues indebted local governments ex post.

Von Hagen and Dahlberg (2002) illustrate the practice of bailing out local governments in Sweden after the housing company crisis of 1992. They report that the municipalities that applied for financial relief from the center had accumulated debt considerably faster than those that did not apply, after controlling for external factors, such as changes in population and tax base. This implies that financial relief was not merely a form of risk sharing but was intended to rescue the municipalities ex post. Baretti, Huber, and Lichtbalau (2002) study the revenue-pooling arrangement of regionally collected taxes in Germany known as horizontal equalization. They show that the system discourages the states from raising shared taxes, lowering rates of tax collection.

Three points are worth making. First, the soft budget problem includes both supply- and demand-driven aspects of grants. Ex post, transfers may be initiated unilaterally by the central authority and thus regarded as supply driven. Ex ante, however, local governments act in a strategic way to manipulate the ex post allocation of transfers in their favor, which represents demand-driven aspects.

Second, the discussion has focused on ex post vertical fiscal ties between higher and lower levels of governments. But nonresidents of bailed-out regions must bear the fiscal burden of bailouts, through increases in national taxes or reductions in national public services. If the ex post rescue is financed by borrowing by the central government, the burden will be carried over to future generations. Interregional or intergenerational externalities are thus created.[10]

Third, the soft budget literature supposes that the ex post decision of bailing out indebted or overspending regions may be occasional and explicit, involving policy changes from the ex ante announcement. But it is also conceivable that ex post rescues are frequent and embedded in the manipulation of grant formulas in ways that reflect the ex post optimum; the formula of intergovernmental transfers could be determined to rationalize the intended allocation (Bird 1994). More-generous transfers can be made to compensate overspending regions in the name of internalizing spillovers or accounting for region-specific fiscal needs.

To mitigate the problem, authority should be granted to those accountable for the overall fiscal and economic performance of the country (Rodden, Eskeland, and Litvack 2003). Argentina's experience shows that fiscal reform that seeks to harden budgets is facilitated by partisan ties linking the president, the legislature, and provincial governors. With weak and fragmented political parties and presidents, the states can easily seek bailouts and stand in the way of intergovernmental fiscal reform, as is the case in Brazil (Rodden 2003).

The Holdup Problem

The paternalistic attitude of the central authority can give rise to ex post bailouts of fiscally troubled regions. Alternatively, the central authority can exploit local governments, decreasing intergovernmental transfers or lowering local tax-sharing rates in shared revenues. This "holdup problem" is the flip side of the soft budget problem coin.

Ex ante delegation of revenue responsibility may be regarded as desirable, since it improves regional incentives for developing assigned tax bases, mobilizing resources for efficient use. The central authority may not be able to commit itself to preserve a decentralized fiscal system, however. The local efforts of economic development and tax collection being sunk, the central government may unilaterally change the rules ex post, reducing intergovernmental transfers or shared revenues. Regional incentives for development are diluted if future confiscation is anticipated. Repeated interactions between governments would not solve this problem, unless the central authority is sufficiently farsighted. Indeed, all stakeholders tend to act in a myopic way unless future benefits from honoring the ex ante consensus are large.

Shleifer and Treisman (2000) address the ad hoc nature of federal transfers in the Russian Federation in the 1990s. They find that better tax collection and mobilization in a region was followed by a smaller transfer allocation to the region. Although equalization grants, known as "funds for financial support of the regions," are formula based to ensure that regions with lower revenue in a "base year" receive larger transfers, the "base year" is often moved forward. Zhuravskaya (2000) provides evidence from the Russian Federation that indicates that increasing own revenue at the municipal level is largely offset by subsequent decreases in shared revenue and transfers from upper-level governments. This high drawback rate must have hindered local efforts to mobilize tax bases (Martinez-Vazquez and Boex 2001).

Before the 1994 tax reform, China had in place a fiscal contracting system in which remittance of revenue raised in a region and sent to the center was bilaterally negotiated. Contracts were occasionally renegotiated and thus failed to ensure stable prospects for future revenues at the provincial level (Ma 1997). In addition, the central government relied on nonstandard instruments to increase its own share of revenue by borrowing from lower-level governments, offloading expenditure obligation on an ad hoc basis, and taking over ownership of public enterprises previously owned by lower-level governments in order to tax them (Ma 1997).

The holdup problem not only creates negative incentive effects ex ante, it also generates distrust among local governments in the central authority. This lack of confidence or sense of assurance makes intergovernmental cooperation increasingly difficult. One way to build trust would be to create a separate authority or grants commission. In Australia and India, after consulting with central and local government officials, the grants commission regularly conducts a review and drafts a proposal for revamping the intergovernmental transfer formula based on updated information. Accountability and transparency can be ensured with the public grant formula and information/data upon which the formula is based being disclosed to the public. For interregional transfers to promote confidence in grant-receiving regions, it is critical that the participating governments agree on the process to be used to determine the relative fiscal needs and capacities of each region and are ensured that they are treated fairly.

Institutional Reform

Interregional transfers can be used tactically or in a discretionary manner rather than to achieve an economic goal. Selfish motives of governments do not per se imply inefficiency, since their interest could be aligned with that of society if political institutions and intergovernmental competition are properly designed. It is the absence of strong political leadership and the lack of commitment to hard budgets that have perverse effects on efficiency and the macroeconomy, leading to overspending and increases in fiscal deficits. Intergovernmental bargaining along with transfers as side payments can secure the unity of a nation and coordinate policy, but it can come at the expense of fiscal equity, as more transfers are directed to more-outspoken regions rather than to regions in greatest need.

When the conditions discussed at the beginning of this chapter are not met, the consequences can be grave (table 6.1).

The public choice literature describes a hierarchical structure of collective decisions in which the rules of the game are established in the constitutional phase, which is followed by an individual policy-making stage that determines the outcome of the game (Dixit 1996). Four stages of decision making are involved in formulating and implementing economic policy (table 6.2).

During the constitutional stage, institutions are designed in a way that shapes the allocation of functions between the public and market sectors as well as among different levels of governments. The constitution, for instance, outlines the types of interregional transfers (general purpose transfers, specific purpose transfers, tax revenue sharing) as well as their funding. In the second stage, politicians at the central- and local-government levels choose policies—say, amounts and allocation of interregional transfers—according to an allocation of authority assigned to them decided in the previous stage. A political economy equilibrium emerges that may feature pork barrel politics, rent seeking, soft budgets, or other problems. The third

TABLE 6.1 Consequences of Failure of Central Government to Meet Necessary Conditions

Problem	Consequence
Central government is not benevolent.	Transfers are used tactically as part of political competition.
Central government does not act as single decision maker.	Politicians engage in pork barrel politics and rent seeking.
Central government does not act as principal to local government agents.	Transfers are the outcome of intergovernmental bargaining or used to hold together nations.
Central government cannot commit to its policies.	Local governments ignore hard budget constraints, central government "holds up" local governments.

Source: Author.

TABLE 6.2 Stages of Decision Making in Formulating and
Implementing Economic Policy

Stage	Description
1. Constitutional	Rules governing government decision making in subsequent stages are set out.
2. Legislative	Policies are enacted in the legislatures through collective decision making. There can be more than one level of legislature at this stage.
3. Implementation	Policies enacted in the legislative stage are implemented by the bureaucracy at the relevant level of government.
4. Market response	Private sector agents make their decisions given the policies that have been set, and a market outcome results.

Source: Boadway 2002.

stage involves the implementation of public policies by bureaucrats, whose interests differ from those of their principals. This gives rise to the principal-agent problem within government. In the last stage, private agents (consumers, firms) make their own decisions, leading to market equilibrium.

In the second stage, policy makers are not assumed to act in a benevolent manner but to seek their own interests; policy-making decisions (stage 2) as well as responses to them by agents in the subsequent stages (stages 3 and 4) within a given institution are viewed descriptively. The design of an institution at stage 1 is evaluated from a normative standpoint: one institution is judged better than another when it is likely to yield a more desirable equilibrium.

Different constitutional rules clearly make a difference. Inman (2003) identifies several conditions that must be met to harden local budgets and enforce local fiscal discipline. They include an efficient central government redistribution policy to mitigate ex post demand for transfers, clear and enforceable accounting standards, and an informed and sophisticated municipal bond market that is expected to exert market discipline. The balanced-budget rule works if it is properly designed and enforced: the rule must require that the budget be balanced at the end, not just the beginning, of the fiscal year and that it be enforced by a politically independent party. Poterba (1994) provides evidence from the United States that the fiscal deficits of states with these rules and supporting institutions are significantly lower than those without such rules. In Argentina during the 1990s, privatization of province-owned banks together with the convertibility law of 1991 limited the ability of provincial governments to shift the burden of their debts onto the central authority: the convertibility law imposed hard budgets on the central authorities, which in turn hardened the budgets of local authorities. Deducting debt service from revenue-sharing transfers—that is, the use of transfers as collateral—also restrained federal government discretion of bailouts (Webb 2003).

Of course, a reform that is economically sound in terms of efficiency and equity may not necessarily overcome political obstacles. As Dixit (1996) notes, institutional reform is not quite done behind a veil of ignorance; all stakeholders are aware of their gains and losses. The equilibrium nature of institutions may thus be understood by an evolutionary view that accounts for interaction between the design of institutions and the resulting equilibrium. Stakeholders who lose from a reform are often better organized politically, while those who benefit are widely dispersed, uncertain, not visible, or unorganized. Reform of intergovernmental transfers at the constitutional stage must then be accompanied by tactics that overcome political opposition from stakeholders within and outside the central government. According to Haggard (2000) and Williamson and Haggard (1993), for a policy reform to succeed, certain political conditions, including a solid political base, a fragmented and demoralized opposition, social consensus, and a visionary leader, are necessary.

Politics is a part of contemporary life; it determines policy making of many kinds. The consequences of politically motivated policies, including interregional transfers, are particularly critical in developing countries and transition economies, where market economies and democracy are not yet mature. Whether these transfers enhance or retard economic development and political accountability depends on how they are designed and implemented. Politics matter, but so does the institutional arrangement that shapes the rules of the game.

Notes

1. In addition, the central government must be rational and possess adequate knowledge and information. Throughout this chapter, the center is assumed to be rational, although its rationality may be contentious.
2. In this chapter, competition is considered to be an efficiency-enhancing disciplinary device, not a beggar-thy-neighbor mechanism.
3. In Dixit and Londregan (1998a), voters who are concerned about both own consumption and ideology may prefer to have divided government, with the center and state being governed by different political parties.
4. Pork barrel politics also differs from political competition with respect to voters' behavior. Political competition assumes that voting is prospective, while pork barrel politics assumes that voting is retrospective.

5. Alternatively, legislative decision making may be a "minimum winning coalition." As Inman and Fitts (1990) point out, however, such a coalition could be politically unstable, and each legislator faces uncertainty as to whether or not he or she will be in the winning coalition. In this case, the informal norm of universalism may be favored.

6. The notion that a minority can exploit the majority dates back to Olson (1965), who notes that it is easier for small groups to overcome free rider problems. The transaction costs associated with rent seeking by these groups are therefore lower.

7. The organized groups may prefer to endorse a rule restricting the government to inefficient policy instruments to avoid the prisoners' dilemma (Dixit, Grossman, and Helpman 1997).

8. In the rent-seeking model, the central government is the "common agent" of local governments, but the authority to allocate transfers, for which local governments lobby is exclusive to the central government.

9. Some observers cite the de facto federalist nature of China's fiscal system, in which town and village enterprises owned by municipal-level governments have been an engine of economic growth, as a successful case of market-preserving federalism (see Qian and Roland 1996). Others take a critical view of fiscal decentralization in China (Ma 1997; Young 2000).

10. The decentralized leadership model addresses the horizontal externalities associated with ex post interregional transfers optimized by the central government. It claims that when local governments supply a pure public good that generates interregional spillovers, ex post transfers lead to a Pareto-efficient outcome (Caplan, Cornes, and Silva 2000). In their context, the soft budget that induces overspending exactly offsets the motive of free riding on a purely public good provision leading to under provision.

References

Alesina, A., R. Perotti, and E. Spolaore. 1995. "Together or Separately? Issues of the Costs and Benefits of Political and Fiscal Unions. *European Economic Review* 39 (3–4): 751–58.

Alesina, A., and E. Spolaore. 1997. "On the Number and Size of Nations." *Quarterly Journal of Economics* 112 (4): 1027–56.

Austin-Smith, D. 1997. "Interest Groups: Money, Information and Influence." *Perspectives on Public Choice*, ed. D.C. Muller, 296–321. Cambridge: Cambridge University Press.

Bailey, S.J., and S. Connolly. 1998. "The Flypaper Effect: Identifying Areas for Further Research." *Public Choice* 95 (3–4): 335–61.

Baretti, C., B. Huber, and K. Lichtbalau. 2002. "A Tax on Tax Revenue: The Incentive Effects of Equalizing Transfers. Evidence from Germany." *International Tax and Public Finance* 9 (6): 631–49.

Becker, G.S. 1983. "A Theory of Competition among Pressure Groups for Political Influence." *Quarterly Journal of Economics* 98 (3): 371–400.

Bird, R.M. 1994. "A Comparative Perspective on Federal Finance." In *The Future of Fiscal Federalism*, ed. K.G. Bating, D.M. Brown, and T.J. Couchene, 293–322. Queen's University, School of Policy Studies, Kingston, Ontario.

———. 1999. "Threading the Fiscal Labyrinth: Some Issues in Fiscal Decentralization." In *Tax Policy in the Real World*, ed. J. Slemrod, 141–61. Cambridge: Cambridge University Press.

Bird, R.M., and M. Smart. 2002. "Intergovernmental Fiscal Transfers: International Lessons for Developing Countries." *World Development* 30 (6): 899–912.

Blanchard, O., and A. Shleifer. 2000. "Federalism with and without Political Centralization: China versus Russia." NBER Working Paper 7616, National Bureau of Economic Research, Cambridge, MA.

Boadway, R. 2002. "The Role of Public Choice Considerations in Normative Public Economics." In *Political Economy and Public Finance: The Role of Political Economy in the Theory and Practice of Public Economics*, ed. S.L. Winer and H. Shibata, 47–68. Cheltenham, United Kingdom: Edward Elgar.

Boadway, R., and P. Hobson. 1993. *Intergovernmental Fiscal Relations in Canada.* Canadian Tax Foundation, Toronto.

Boadway, R., and M. Keen. 2000. "Redistribution." In *Handbook of Income Distribution,* vol. 1, ed. A.B. Atkinson and F. Bourguignon, 677–789. Amsterdam: Elsevier Science.

Bolton, P., and G. Roland. 1997. "The Breakup of Nations." *Quarterly Journal of Economics* 112 (4): 1057–89.

Bradford, D.F., and W.E. Oates. 1971. "Toward a Predictive Theory of Intergovernmental Grants." *American Economic Review* 61 (2): 440–48.

Brock, R., and S. Ownings. 2003. "The Political Economy of Intergovernmental Grants." *Regional Science and Urban Economics* 33 (2): 139–56.

Caplan, A., R. Cornes, and E. Silva. 2000. "Pure Public Goods and Income Redistribution in a Federation with Decentralized Leadership and Imperfect Labor Mobility." *Journal of Public Economics* 77 (2): 265–84.

DelRossi, A.F., and R.P. Inman. 1999. "Changing the Price of Pork: The Impact of Local Cost Sharing on Legislators' Demands for Distributive Public Goods." *Journal of Public Economics* 71 (2): 247–73.

Dewatripont, M., and E. Maskin. 1995. "Credit and Efficiency in Centralized and Decentralized Economics." *Review of Economic Studies* 62 (4): 541–55.

Dillinger, W., G. Perry, and S. Webb. 2003. "Is Fiscal Stability Compatible with Decentralization? The Case of Latin America." In *Public Finance in Developing and Transitional Countries: Essays in Honor of Richard Bird*, ed. J. Martinez-Vazquez and J. Alm, 232–60. Cheltenham, United Kingdom: Edward Elgar.

Dixit, A.K. 1996. *The Making of Economic Policy: A Transaction Cost Politics Perspectives.* Cambridge, MA: MIT Press.

Dixit, A.K., G.M. Grossman, and E. Helpman. 1997. "Common Agency and Coordination: General Theory and Application to Government Policy Making." *Journal of Political Economy* 105 (4): 752–69.

Dixit, A.K., and L. Londregan. 1995. "Redistributive Politics and Economic Efficiency." *American Political Science Review* 89 (4): 856–66.

———. 1996. "The Determinant of Success of Special Interests in Redistributive Politics." *Journal of Politics* 58 (4): 1132–55.

———. 1998a. "Fiscal Federalism and Redistributive Politics." *Journal of Public Economics* 68 (2): 153–80.

———. 1998b. "Ideology, Tactics, and Efficiency in Redistributive Politics." *Quarterly Journal of Economics* 113 (2): 497–529

Enikolopov, R., and E. Zhuravskaya. 2003. "Decentralization and Political Institutions." CEPR Discussion Paper 3857, Centre for Economic Policy Research, London.

Filimon, R., T. Romer, and H. Rosenthal. 1982. "Asymmetric Information and Agenda Control: The Bases of Monopoly Power in Public Spending." *Journal of Public Economics* 17 (1): 51–70.

Goodspeed, Timothy J. 2002. "Bailouts in a Federation." *International Tax and Public Finance* 9 (4): 409–21.

Grossman, P.J. 1994. "A Political Economy of Intergovernmental Grants." *Public Choice* 78 (3–4): 295–303.

Haggard, S. 2000. "Interests, Institutions, and Policy Reform." In *Economic Policy Reform: The Second Stage*, ed. A. Kruger, 21–57. Chicago: University of Chicago Press.

Hallerberg, M., and J. von Hagen. 1999. "Electoral Institutions, Cabinet Negotiations and Budget Deficits in the European Union." In *Fiscal Institutions and Fiscal Performance*, ed. J. Poterba and J. von Hagen, 209–32. Chicago: University of Chicago Press.

Hettich, W., and S.L. Winer. 1988. "Economic and Political Foundations of Tax Structure." *American Economic Review* 78 (4): 701–12.

Hines, J.R., and R.H. Thaler. 1995. "Anomalies: Flypaper Effect." *Journal of Economic Perspectives* 9 (4): 217–26.

Inman, R. 1988. "Federal Assistance and Local Services in the United States: The Evolution of a New Federalist Order." In *Fiscal Federalism*, ed. H. Rosen, 33–74. Chicago: University of Chicago Press.

———. 2003. "Transfers and Bailouts: Enforcing Local Fiscal Discipline with Lessons from U.S. Federalism." In *Fiscal Decentralization and the Challenge of Hard Budget Constraints*, ed. J.A. Rodden, G.S. Eskeland, and J. Litvack, 35–83. Cambridge, MA: MIT Press.

Inman, R.P., and M.A. Fitts. 1990. " Political Institution and Fiscal Policy: Evidence from the U.S. Historical Record." *Journal of Law, Economics and Organization* 6: 79–132.

Inman, R.P., and D.L. Rubinfeld. 1996. "Designing Tax Policy in Federalist Economies: An Overview." *Journal of Public Economics* 60 (3): 307–34.

———. 1997. "Rethinking Federalism." *Journal of Economic Perspectives* 11 (4): 43–64.

Johansson, E. 2003. "Intergovernmental Grants as a Tactical Instrument: Empirical Evidence from Swedish Municipalities." *Journal of Public Economics* 87 (5–6): 883–915.

Jones, M., P. Sanguinetti, and M. Tommasi. 2000. "Politics, Institutions and Fiscal Performance in a Federal System: An Analysis of the Argentina Province." *Journal of Development Economics* 61 (2): 305–33.

Kontopoulos, Y., and R. Perotti. 1999. "Government Fragmentation and Fiscal Policy Outcomes: Evidence from the OECD Countries." In *Fiscal Institutions and Fiscal Performance*, ed. J. Poterba and J. von Hagen, 81–102. Chicago: University of Chicago Press.

Kornai, J. 1986. "The Soft Budget Constraint." *Kyklos* 39 (1): 3–30.

Leite-Monteiro, M., and M. Sato. 2003. "Economic Integration and Fiscal Devolution." *Journal of Public Economics* 87 (11): 2507–25.

Ma, J. 1997. *Intergovernmental Relations in Economic Management in China*. New York: MacMillan Press.

Martinez-Vazquez, J., and J. Boex. 2001. *Russia's Transition to a New Federalism*. WBI Learning Resources Series. Washington, DC: World Bank Institute.

McGuire, M.C., and M. Olson. 1996. "The Economics of Autocracy and Majority Rule: The Invisible Hand and the Use of Force." *Journal of Economic Literature* 34 (1): 72–96.

Montinola, G., Y. Qian, and B.R. Weingast. 1996. "Federalism, Chinese Style: The Political Basis for Economic Success." *World Politics* 48 (1): 50–81.

Murphy, K.M., A. Shleifer, and R.W. Vishny. 1993. "Why Is Rent Seeking So Costly to Growth?" *American Economic Review* 83 (2): 409–14.

Olson, M. 1965. *The Logic of Collective Action: Public Goods and the Theory of Groups.* Cambridge, MA: Harvard University Press.

Person, T., and G. Tabellini. 2000. *Political Economics: Explaining Economic Policy.* Cambridge, MA: MIT Press.

Porto, A., and P. Sanguinetti. 2001. "Political Determinants of Intergovernmental Grants: Evidence from Argentina." *Economics and Politics* 13 (3): 237–56.

Poterba, J. 1994. " State Response to Fiscal Crises: The Effects of Budgetary Institutions and Politics." *Journal of Political Economy* 102 (4): 799–821.

Qian, Y. 2000, "The Process of China's Market Transition, 1978–1998: The Evolutionary, Historical, and Comparative Perspectives." *Journal of Institutional and Theoretical Economics* 156 (1): 151–71.

Qian, Y., and G. Roland. 1996. "The Soft Budget Constraint in China." *Japan and the World Economy* 8 (2): 207–23.

Qian, Y., and B.R. Weingast. 1997. "Federalism as a Commitment to Preserving Market Incentives." *Journal of Economic Perspectives* 11 (4): 83–92.

Riker, W. 1964. *Federalism: Origins, Operations, Significance.* Boston: Little, Brown.

Rodden, J.A. 2003. "Federalism and Bailouts in Brazil." In *Fiscal Decentralization and the Challenge of Hard Budget Constraints*, ed. J.A. Rodden, G.S. Eskeland, and J. Litvack, 213–48. Cambridge, MA: MIT Press.

Rodden, J.A., and G. S. Eskeland. 2003. "Lessons and Conclusion." In *Fiscal Decentralization and the Challenge of Hard Budget Constraints*, ed. J.A. Rodden, G.S. Eskeland, and J. Litvack, 431–65. Cambridge, MA: MIT Press.

Rodden, J.A., G.S. Eskeland, and J. Litvack, eds. 2003. *Fiscal Decentralization and the Challenge of Hard Budget Constraints.* Cambridge, MA: MIT Press.

Roemer, J.E., and J. Silvestre. 2002. "The Flypaper Effect Is Not an Anomaly." *Journal of Public Economic Theory* 4 (1): 1–17.

Romer, T., and H. Rosenthal. 1980. "An Institutional Theory of the Effect of Intergovernmental Grants." *National Tax Journal* 33 (4): 451–58.

Shleifer, A., and D. Treisman. 2000. *Without a Map: Political Tactics and Economic Reform.* Cambridge, MA: MIT Press.

Sorensen, R.J. 2003. "The Political Economy of Intergovernmental Grants: The Norwegian Case." *European Journal of Political Research* 42 (2): 163–95.

Velasco, A. 2000. "Debts and Deficits with Fragmented Fiscal Policymaking." *Journal of Public Economics* 76 (1): 105–25.

von Hagan, J., and M. Dahlberg. 2002. "Swedish Local Government: Is There a Bailout Problem?" Prepared for the Project on Fiscal Federalism in Sweden, Center for Business and Policy Studies (SNS), Stockholm, Sweden.

Watts, R. 1996. "Comparing Federal Systems in the 1990s." Queen's University, Institute of Intergovernmental Relations, Kingston, Ontario.

Webb, S.B. 2003. "Argentina: Hardening the Provincial Budget Constraint." In *Fiscal Decentralization and the Challenge of Hard Budget Constraints,* ed. J.A. Rodden, G.S. Eskeland, and J. Litvack, 189–211. Cambridge: Cambridge, MA: MIT Press.

Weingast, B.R. 1995. "The Economic Role of Political Institutions: Market Preserving Federalism and Economic Development." *Journal of Law and Economic Organization* 11 (1): 1–31.

Wildasin, D.E. 1999. "Externalities and Bail-Outs: Hard and Soft Budget Constraints in Intergovernmental Fiscal Relations." Policy Research Working Paper 1843, World Bank, Washington, DC.

Williamson, J., and S. Haggard. 1993. "The Political Conditions for Economic Reform." In *The Political Economy of Policy Reform*, ed. J. Williamson, 527–96. Washington, DC: Institute for International Economics.

Winer, S.L., and H. Shibata, eds. 2002. *Political Economy and Public Finance: The Role of Political Economy in the Theory and Practice of Public Economics.* Cheltenham, United Kingdom: Edward Elgar.

Wittman, D.A. 1995. *The Myth of Democratic Failure: Why Political Institutions Are Efficient.* Chicago: University of Chicago Press.

Wyckoff, P.G. 1991. "The Elusive Flypaper Effect." *Journal of Urban Economics* 30 (3): 310–28.

Young, A. 2000. "The Razor's Edge: Distortions and Incremental Reform in the People's Republic of China." *Quarterly Journal of Economics* 115 (4): 1091–1135.

Zhuravskaya, E. 2000. "Incentives to Provide Local Public Goods: Fiscal Federalism Russian Style." *Journal of Public Economics* 76 (3): 337–68.

7

The Incentive Effects of Grants

MICHAEL SMART

Intergovernmental fiscal transfers have long been a dominant feature of public finance in many countries, for good or for ill. The appropriate level of transfers across governments is often determined by appealing to notions of fairness and equity. When evaluating the structure of transfer programs, however, it is essential to pay close attention to the incentives they create for central and local governments and, indirectly, residents of different regions. Whether the results of transfers are positive or negative depends on the incentives—intended or not—that are built into transfer systems.

This chapter reviews the central issues that arise in designing intergovernmental transfers and surveys the approaches adopted in a number of countries. While it examines some principles that emerge from analyzing the experience with transfers in developed countries, the focus is on developing countries, where the inherent difficulties of operating a multilayered system of government are often compounded by more-basic problems at all levels of government in gaining access to revenues and maintaining accountability.

The focus of the chapter is on the effects of transfers on policy outcomes, in particular allocative efficiency. Since circumstances and objectives differ from country to country, no simple, uniform pattern of transfers is universally appropriate. Experience around the world reinforces the common sense argument that, for services to be efficiently provided, those receiving transfers need a clear mandate, adequate resources, and sufficient flexibility to make decisions. They must also be held accountable for results. To satisfy these conditions, transfers must be properly designed.

The basic task in transfer design is thus to get prices "right" in the public sector, in the sense of making local governments fully accountable, at least at the margin of decision making, to both residents and, where appropriate, higher levels of government. Transfers that are properly designed can achieve this goal even if they finance 90 percent of local expenditures. Poorly designed transfers will not, even if they finance only 10 percent of expenditures.

The chapter is organized as follows. The first section provides a simple taxonomy of "vertical" and "horizontal" grants and introduces the perspective used in the subsequent analysis. The following two sections examine vertical and horizontal grants, focusing on the principles that should govern transfer design and the actual practice of transfers, especially in developing countries.[1] The last section summarizes what the literature concludes about good federal fiscal arrangements.

The Taxonomy of Grants

Decentralization of spending powers to lower-level governments is a widespread phenomenon, one that appears to have become more common in recent years. The argument for decentralizing decision making is familiar to economists and is most closely associated with the work of Tiebout (1956) and Oates (1972). Decentralization has often been held to increase the responsiveness of policy to the preferences of citizens and to increase accountability in government. A unitary central government tends to provide uniform public programs nationwide; local governments are believed to respond better to the preferences and needs of their residents. Moreover, informational advantages and greater political accountability may permit local governments to provide public services and even targeted redistribution at a lower cost than central governments.

Most economists believe that the benefits of decentralization do not extend to the same degree to the revenue side of the government budget. The potential for tax competition among local governments, for tax exportation to local nonresidents, and a variety of other fiscal externalities reinforce the commonly held notion that revenue-raising authority should be more centralized in a federation than expenditure authority. The result is typically a vertical fiscal gap between revenue and expenditure on own account at the central and local levels, which must be closed through transfers.

Even when tax powers are decentralized, revenues are apt to be unequally distributed across local governments, creating problems of both efficiency and equity in government policy (Boadway and Flatters 1982). In the absence of horizontal equalizing transfers, governments would be unable to provide public services at the tax rates that would otherwise prevail in a centralized setting. Thus equalization can be seen as an instrument for facilitating effective decentralization by enabling its benefits to be achieved while avoiding its adverse effects.

In this fairly conventional perspective, intergovernmental grants are a mere residuum, determined to balance government budgets at every level after the appropriate assignment of tax and spending authority has been determined. But such a view is too simplistic. Just as some grant systems are more equal than others, some are more "incentive compatible" than others. The focus of this chapter is therefore on determining how fiscal constitutions may achieve appropriate redistribution of net fiscal resources, either vertically or horizontally, while maintaining appropriate incentives for revenue and expenditure decisions at all levels of government.

Vertical Transfers

When local governments are expected to play a major role in delivering social services, they inevitably depend in large part on central fiscal transfers to do so. The design of such transfers takes two quite different approaches. To the extent that the primary objective is to ensure that all regions have adequate resources to provide such services at acceptable minimum standards, simple lump-sum transfers, with no conditionality other than the usual requirements for financial auditing, seems indicated. This "federalist" approach assumes that the funds flow to responsible local political bodies, that there is sufficient accountability, and that it is neither necessary nor desirable for the central government to attempt to interfere with local expenditure choices. When the central government explicitly employs local governments as agents in executing national policies—as it does in providing primary education, for example—it may make sense to make transfers conditional on the funds actually being spent on education or on the achievement of a certain standard of educational performance.

Matching versus Block Grants

Some type of vertical grant (usually from the center to regions) will typically be required in a country with multitier government. Should such grants be block (lump sum) in structure or have a matching (cost-sharing) component? What conditions can appropriately be imposed on the ultimate use of the funds?

In some circumstances, matching grants may be consistent with "getting prices" right in a decentralized public sector. The case for a matching component is usually made on one of two grounds. The prevalence of fiscal spillovers among governments in a federation means that matching may be required as a "Pigouvian" subsidy to efficient behavior by governments. (The notion is that as a portion of the benefits to such expenditures will flow to residents of other jurisdictions, a matching grant is required to cause local government decision makers to "internalize" the spillover.) This is particularly true of expenditure programs that are locally administered but that have positive spillovers for residents of other jurisdictions in the country (Oates 1999), as is the case, for example, with spending on roads, telecommunications, and possibly public education. On the revenue side of the budget, local decisions to raise taxes create positive spillovers for nonresidents, to the extent that tax bases are mobile across jurisdictions of the federation (as discussed in the next section). It has been suggested (by Wildasin 1991, for example) that matching grants might be designed to internalize the resulting fiscal externality. A more compelling case for matching grants can probably be made on the basis of informational and political considerations (Bucovetsky, Marchand, and Pestieau 1998). A federal government with at least a mild preference for redistribution should seek to allocate more of its resources to regions whose residents most value public services. While a block grant from the center might in principle be regionally differentiated, informational and political constraints make it difficult to do so. A matching grant requires local residents to share in the costs of increased spending from the center. Correctly designed, it can induce revelation of local preferences for public spending in an efficient manner.

Incrementality

In principle, the incentive effects of a block categorical grant to local governments are simple to analyze. Theory suggests that receipt of $1 in grants earmarked, say, for public education should have an effect of total education spending no different from an increase of $1 in the total private income of the jurisdiction's residents. The reason is that a block grant is lump sum in nature and local decision makers are free to reallocate other tax and spending decisions to offset the effects of the grant (as long as the total spent on the earmarked category exceeds the federal grants received). Except for income effects, which should be fairly small, incremental federal grants should merely "crowd out" local spending from other revenue sources and should therefore be neutral with respect to local decisions.

In contrast to this view, a large body of empirical literature has demonstrated that intergovernmental transfers are disproportionately spent on public services, rather than tax cuts, and indeed on the category of public spending for which the grant was nominally earmarked. This empirical regularity has become known as the "flypaper effect": money sticks where it hits. Hines and Thaler (1995) survey 10 studies of U.S. grants in which a marginal dollar of categorical grants is estimated to induce an increase in public spending of $0.64 on average.

A number of ingenious explanations have been proposed to reconcile the theory to this apparent empirical fact. A number of authors have proposed alternative theories in which an increase in federal grants induces a change in political equilibrium and therefore different local spending decisions than would a corresponding increase in local private incomes (Filimon, Romer, and Rosenthal 1982; Roemer and Silvestre 2002). Some researchers question whether the empirical regularity of the flypaper effect constitutes a true causative effect of grants on local spending. Moffitt (1984) notes that many grants have implicit or hidden matching components that induce price as well as income effects on local behavior. Accounting for actual price subsidies in one U.S. federal grant, he finds that the flypaper effect disappears. Chernick (1995) notes that estimating the behavioral response to federal grants can be problematic in general. A common approach in the literature is to use cross-section or time-series variation in the level of grants for identification. The resulting estimates, however, may partly capture "permanent" differences across jurisdictions in spending propensities or changes in underlying economic environments in the case of across-the-board transfer reforms. Occasionally, however, reforms yield a natural experiment from which to gauge their behavioral impacts. Baker, Payne, and Smart (1999) examine a reform that converted a matching grant to a block grant for some provinces in Canada but not others. They find robust evidence that assisted spending was lower under the block grant than the matching grant.

Even when grants are truly specified in lump-sum terms, the actual level of transfers is typically the product of negotiation between federal and local authorities. Consequently, when a jurisdiction's demand for public services in a particular category rise, grants from the center will tend to rise as well; grants and spending will be positively correlated even in the absence of causal effect running from the former to the latter. Accounting for such endogeneity in the allocation of U.S. federal highway grants, Knight (2002) finds that the flypaper effect disappears.

Much of the evidence for and against a flypaper effect comes from high-income, federal countries, where subnational governments often have considerable fiscal resources of their own, as well as long traditions of independent decision making that may stand in sharp opposition to federal objectives. In many developing countries, in contrast, subnational authorities are far more dependent on federal transfers and have less autonomy in decision making. In this context, a flypaper effect of transfers would be less anomalous, as local authorities are apt not to have sufficient leeway to undo the effects of grants from the center (Bird 1993). One example of this is the current system of revenue sharing among municipalities in Colombia, which imposes tight conditions on the way in which grants are spent by local authorities. Chaparro, Smart, and Zapata (2005) exploit a reform in the grant program that reallocated funds among municipalities to estimate the extent to which such conditions are binding. They find that on average in most communities, additional funds were allocated to spending areas in almost exactly the proportions specified by federal legislation. For large urban municipalities, however, there was much more evidence of reallocation across programs.[2] This is unsurprising, since it is only the large urban governments in Colombia (as elsewhere) that have sufficient own fiscal resources to undo the effects of federal grants and for which money is truly fungible.

These considerations notwithstanding, local decisions may in some circumstances undo the effects of federal grants and stymie the intent of federal policy makers. It is this consideration that explains the tight conditions that are often attached to incremental grants: if the earmarked spending category is sufficiently narrowly defined, the conditions may actually bind on the ultimate spending decisions of the local government and marginal grants may be truly incremental. Conditionality of this sort is often criticized by public finance economists. Permitting local governments more discretion might allow spending to be targeted better to meet local needs. Furthermore, it is sometimes contended that greater local control can have knock-on benefits in the political sphere, as greater involvement of local interest groups in spending decisions may enhance accountability.

Vertical Grants in Practice: Cross-Country Evidence

The Philippine model seems close to the federalist approach. Most funds transferred to local governments come from internal revenue allocation. Part of these transfers is allocated equally to each province, part is transferred based on population and area. The poorest region (Bicol) receives slightly higher than average transfers, while the Cordillera Administrative

Region receives almost twice the average regional transfer per capita. On the whole, there is not much apparent relation between per capita transfers and levels of regional poverty in the Philippines (Bird and Rodriguez 1999).

General-purpose transfers represented only 23 percent of all transfers in Indonesia in 1990–91 (Shah and Qureshi 1994). Transfers per capita were lower than the average provincial transfer for Jakarta (as for metropolitan Manila in the Philippines). On the whole, however, per capita transfers appear to be more closely related to poverty levels in Indonesia. The two poorest provinces, both in Timor, received much higher per capita transfer levels, presumably reflecting in part the political situation in that region. The frontier province of Irian Jaya received more than three times the average provincial per capita transfer.

Frontier regions also receive strong attention from central governments in Argentina and Chile. In sharp contrast to Indonesia, however, only 14 percent of transfers to provinces were conditional in Argentina in 1992. As in Indonesia, the relationship between transfers and poverty was broadly positive, with poorer provinces receiving more support from the central government, though the very poorest provinces did not receive the largest transfers (Porto and Sanguinetti 1993). Per capita transfers to the poorest provinces (Chaco, Formosa, and Santiago del Estero), in which about 40 percent of the population is under the poverty line, were only slightly higher than the average per capita transfer to all provinces, while some relatively wealthier provinces, such as Catamarca, received almost twice the average per capita transfer.

Experience in Australia and Canada suggests that considerable reliable disaggregated data are required before the detailed norm approach makes sense. In the absence of such data, simpler approaches—based, for example, on population and a simple categorization of localities (by size, type, perhaps region)—seem more likely to prove useful in measuring general expenditure needs.

A number of developing countries distribute transfers by a formula intended both to equalize public expenditures in localities with differing needs and capacities and to stimulate local fiscal efforts. Severe data problems often constrain the parameters employed in such formulas, however. Simpler approaches—such as those used in Colombia and Morocco—based on such generally available (and moderately reliable) factors as population and a simple "categorization" of localities have sometimes proved helpful as guides to general expenditure needs.

There appear to be few good examples of matching grants in developing countries. One reason why may be that even important interjurisdictional spillovers may largely be inframarginal—in the sense that what matters to spillovers is some base levels of expenditures—and the appropriate subsidy (matching) rate is, of course, that which applies at the margin. Another reason may be that in practice redistributional concerns, not efficiency concerns, determine matching rates in many countries. Poor localities receive more assistance because they are poor, not because a higher matching rate is required to induce them to produce the socially optimal amount of the service in question.

Perhaps the most basic problem with the matching approach, however, is that it is very demanding in terms of information. Ideally, its application requires a clear specification of the level of service to be provided. Often, for example, in education grants, many different types and levels of education service (language training, music, special education, and so forth) are specified. In addition, fairly accurate and up to date estimates of the costs of providing each level of service are needed. Moreover, local governments need to have a fair degree of tax autonomy if they are to be able to respond appropriately to the incentives. In addition, standard tax rates need to be carefully specified, estimates of local fiscal capacity must be made, and, ideally, some idea of the probable effect of income differentials on local responses to differential matching rates (the price of the aided service) is needed (see Feldstein 1975). As a rule, even the abundant information available in developed countries is insufficient to determine the precise matching rate appropriate for particular expenditure programs, let alone how those rates should be varied in accordance with the very different characteristics of different local governments. Whatever their theoretical merits, in practice in many countries conditional transfers seem to have become so detailed and onerous that they hamper effective local government.

Matching grants exist in some developing countries, and matching rates are occasionally differentiated based on characteristics of the recipient regions. In Zambia, for example, local governments receive a transfer equal to the difference between the estimated cost of providing a specified level of local services and the expected revenues to be raised locally by applying a standard set of local tax rates. A similar matching grant exists in the Republic of Korea. Similar systems, with varying degrees of refinement, have been proposed in many other countries (such as Hungary) and to a limited extent already exist for some services in others (such as Colombia). The basic problem with this approach is that it requires a great deal of information.

Transfers intended to finance particular types of service (such as road maintenance or education) are often linked to particular measures of need, such as length of roads or number of students. At one extreme, this approach leads to the sort of norms found in Vietnam and a number of other transition economies (such as Hungary) and gives rise to patterns (such as allocating funds on the basis of installed capacity) that may reflect past political decisions rather than need. More-careful determination of expenditure needs may play a role with respect to conditional grants—for basic education, for example—but it seems less likely to prove useful with respect to grants intended to finance general local expenditures.

Horizontal Transfers

Horizontal fiscal balance—or equalization, as it is usually called—is controversial, both because different countries have very different preferences in this respect and because it is a concept with many different interpretations. For example, if horizontal fiscal balance is interpreted in the same gap-filling sense as vertical fiscal balance, the implication is that sufficient transfers are needed to equalize revenues (including transfers) and the actual expenditures of each local government.

The horizontal balance perspective implies that transfer policies should be designed to achieve interregional redistribution, which is quite different from the conventional objective of interpersonal redistribution. The principal objective of equalization is to eliminate differences in net fiscal benefits accruing to residents of different regions of a federation rather than reducing differences in individual incomes within or across regions. In a sense, the objective is one of horizontal rather than vertical equity and should be pursued regardless of society's attitude to vertical redistribution among people of different incomes. Indeed, the objective of eliminating net fiscal benefits is a matter not merely of horizontal equity but also of allocative efficiency, since regional differences in net fiscal benefits can lead to a misallocation of productive resources in the federation (Boadway and Flatters 1982; Boadway 2003).

Equalizing the actual outlays of local governments in per capita terms (raising all to the level of the richest local government) in effect ignores differences in local preferences, one of the main rationales for decentralizing in the first place. It also ignores local differences in needs, costs, and own revenue-raising capacity. Equalizing actual outlays would discourage both local revenue-raising effort and local expenditure restraint, since under this system those with the highest expenditures and the lowest taxes receive the largest transfers.

A grant system can thus create poor incentives for local governments to raise their own revenues. This effect is most obvious in a revenue-pooling system, such as that used in Germany, the Russian Federation, and other countries, in which a given share of locally collected taxes is distributed among all local governments. In such a system, local governments receive only a fraction of the revenue collected in their own jurisdictions, with the rest distributed to other governments, usually through an equalization formula of some sort.

To understand this and the subsequent analysis, consider a federation with N jurisdictions, each with equal population and each levying a tax rate t_i on a local tax base X_i. In a system of equal per capita revenue pooling, each government's equalized fiscal resources are

$$G_i = \frac{1}{N} \sum_j t_j X_j.$$

Since the cost of local taxation is higher than the benefit to the local treasury, the marginal cost of public funds appears artificially high to the local government. This disincentive effect is so clear that such revenue-pooling arrangements seem never to be used when local governments can influence the tax rate levied on shared bases. But problems can arise even when tax rates are set by the central government if the revenues are actually collected by local governments. Baretti, Huber, and Lichtblau (2001), for example, argue that this incentive has led to observably lower rates of tax collection by state governments in Germany. Similar problems led to the centralization of value added tax (VAT) collection in Mexico, where the central VAT was originally supposed to be collected by state governments. Such disincentives have also been prominent in transition economies (such as China before 1994 and the Russian Federation) in which central revenues are collected by tax administrations that are significantly influenced by local governments (Bird, Ebel, and Wallich 1995).

To avoid such problems, most countries that have formal equalization transfers avoid revenue pooling and aim to equalize the capacity of local governments to provide a certain level of public services or the actual performance of this level of service by local governments. The performance criterion, which adjusts the transfer received in accordance with the perceived need for the aided service (and which may also allow for cost differentials), is generally more attractive to central governments, because the level of service funded is then in effect determined centrally and transfers can be made conditional on the provision of that level of service. Unfortunately, unless adequate adjustment is made for differential fiscal capacity, the government that tries least receives the most.

In contrast, under capacity equalization the aim is to provide each local government with sufficient funds (own-source revenues plus transfers) to deliver a centrally predetermined level of services. (Differentials in the cost of providing services may or may not be taken into account.) An equalization grant is a particular system of federal revenue sharing that is already employed in a number of countries.[3] In its idealized form, an equalization system sets the (per capita) transfer to each government equal to the difference between its tax capacity and the average capacity of all regions, multiplied by some standard tax rate, usually equal to the average of all regions' tax rates. Tax capacity is measured by the observed per capita tax base of each jurisdiction. Thus the program aims to equalize differences in tax revenue but implements transfers through an indirect formula, based on differences in observed tax bases.

In the canonical system, each government receives a per capita transfer, in addition to its own-source revenues $t_i X_i$, equal to

$$T_i = \bar{t}(\bar{X} - X_i),$$

where $\bar{X}$ is the target fiscal capacity chosen by the transfer authorities and is the effective tax rate at which deficiencies in capacity relative to the target are compensated. When the equalization formula is calculated on the basis of the "representative tax system," the target tax rate is the actual average of tax rates levied by jurisdictions, and the standard fiscal capacity is the average of actual measured tax bases. When all governments choose the same tax rate, the formula guarantees equal per capita net revenues.

Transfers are based on a measure of each jurisdiction's potential revenue-raising capacity (such as assessed values for property taxes or measured tax bases for other taxes) and not on actual revenues. If revenue capacity is measured accurately—often not an easy task—such transfers will create no disincentive for local governments to raise revenues, because at the margin the local government still bears full fiscal responsibility for expenditure and taxing decisions, essentially because transfers are lump sum (inframarginal) in nature.

If all governments choose the target tax rate, capacity differences are fully equalized and all jurisdictions have the same (per capita) fiscal resources. Of course, if local governments can directly or indirectly manipulate the proxies for capacity used in the transfer formula, capacity equalization may induce undesirable incentive effects. Indeed, Smart (1998) has argued that capacity equalization may drive local tax rates higher than is desirable from a national point of view. Measured tax bases will generally decrease as tax rates rise—for instance, as higher taxes are capitalized in property values and economic activity moves to other jurisdictions (or more lightly taxed transactions). Consequently, local governments that raise their tax rate above the target will see their tax bases depressed and their transfers rise. Under capacity equalization, the local government's equalized fiscal resources are

$$G_i = \bar{t}\bar{X} + (t_i - \bar{t})X_i(t_i).$$

The effect of the grant is then most clearly seen by considering a revenue-maximizing local government that sets t_i optimally such that $dG_i/dt_i = 0$, or

$$t_i^* = \bar{t} - \frac{X_i}{dX_i/dt_i},$$

so that $t_i > \bar{t}$ for any distortionary tax. (Smart 1998 extends the argument to welfare-maximizing governments and to multiple tax bases.) The problem is that a government raising its tax rate marginally above the target rate experiences an increase in transfers that exactly compensates for the marginal deadweight loss (or own-source revenue loss) of the tax. Put another way, when the local tax is just at the target level, the marginal excess burden of higher taxation perceived by the local government is zero because of the transfer effect, although it is strictly positive for the country as a whole.[4]

Of course, federal transfer policies that induce higher levels of tax effort by local governments need not always be welfare decreasing for the country if equilibrium local tax rates are lower than the rates that would be chosen by a welfare-maximizing central planner for the country. Köthenbürger (2002) and Bucovetsky and Smart (2006) consider an environment in which competition among local governments for a mobile tax base tends to drive local tax rates lower than a unitary decision maker would choose: a tax cut by a single region causes an inflow of the tax base to the region, which mitigates the revenue loss of the tax cut, at the expense of government revenues in other regions. This fiscal externality creates an inefficiency in the supply of public goods to the nation. By changing the fiscal consequences of a tax cut in the way just described, a representative tax system capacity equalization grant can have a remarkable effect in limiting this type of harmful tax competition. In the presence of equalization, the increase in the local tax base caused by a tax cut also reduces the deviating government's entitlement under the grant formula. This offsets the impact of the tax cut on own-source revenue and so tends to increase equilibrium tax rates of all regions. It turns out that the equalization effect exactly offsets the fiscal externality, making regional governments willing to implement the tax policies that would be chosen by a unitary central government.

To understand the mechanism, consider a simple example that captures the logic of the argument in Köthenbürger (2002). A federation consists of two identical jurisdictions and a single tax base that is in fixed supply to the country as a whole but perfectly mobile between jurisdictions. Denote the tax rates of the two jurisdictions t_1 and t_2, and let the corresponding tax bases be $x(t_1 - t_1)$ and $1 - x(t_1 - t_2)$, where $x(0) = 1/2$ because of symmetry. From a unitary perspective, a tax on the national base is lump sum in nature (without deadweight loss), and the rate should be raised to the level at which the marginal social benefit of revenue equals the value of forgone private consumption. Consider, however, the decentralized tax problem from the perspective of the government of jurisdiction 1, which is paid an equalization transfer $\bar{t}$ $(1/2 - x[t_1 - t_2])$, in addition to its own-source revenues $t_1 x(t_1 - t_2)$. The marginal net revenue from a local tax increase is therefore

$$\frac{\partial G_1}{\partial t_1} = x(t_1 - t_2) + (t - \bar{t})x'(t_1 - t_2) + \frac{1}{2}(1/2 - x(t_1 - t_2))$$

in a symmetric tax-setting equilibrium, $t_1 = t_2 = \bar{t}$, and the last two terms in this expression drop out, implying that local governments behave as if the local tax base were inelastic with respect to tax rates. In other words, an equalization formula based on the representative tax system decentralizes the unitary optimum in this case.

An emerging empirical literature provides some evidence of the tax-raising effects of capacity equalization. Boadway and Hayashi (2001) report that provinces in Canada that receive equalization are more inclined than others to raise business tax rates when the national average rate goes up, as the theory predicts. Esteller and Sole (2002) find a similar effect for personal tax rates in Canada. Dahlby and Warren (2003) report that equalization grants induce higher levels of taxation by state governments in Australia. Buettner (2006) finds similar results for the municipal business taxes that are equalized in many German states.

Of course, many federal grant systems other than equalization could be designed to achieve the optimum; all that must be done is to set the slope of the transfer formula to correct regional governments' incentives and to set the intercept to equalize spending appropriately. Thus, for example, Wildasin (1991) proposes a system of linear matching grants for local tax rates, and Figuieres, Hindriks, and Myles (2004) propose a transfer system that pools a fraction of local revenues and shares it equally among all governments. What is noteworthy about the result presented here is that a simple equalization formula decentralizes the optimum in a rich set of environments, regardless of the degree of regional mobility of capital or the differences in the tax capacities and populations of regions. The simplicity of the formula is an attractive feature of equalization, especially when differences among regions are large and variable over time, which seems to be precisely when such grants are most often observed in practice.

Equalization in Practice

Explicit representative tax system capacity equalization grants are common in industrial countries but rare in developing countries. Instead, central government authorities in developing countries have adopted a variety of ad hoc systems to address differences in local fiscal resources while attempting to preserve appropriate incentives for local fiscal effort.

Any good transfer system should distribute funds on the basis of a formula. Discretionary or negotiated transfers are always undesirable. The essential ingredients of most formulas for general transfer programs (as opposed to matching grants, which are specifically intended to finance narrowly defined projects and activities) are needs, capacity, and effort. Often needs may be roughly but adequately proxied by some combination of population and the type or category of local government. (Of course, a transfer formula that incorporates observable measures of need may induce further incentive problems, as discussed below.) A more difficult, but conceptually critical, problem is including some measure of the capacity of local governments to raise resources and their efforts in doing so.

Fiscal Capacity

A possible aim of such a transfer system might be to provide each local government with sufficient funds (own-source revenues plus transfers) to deliver a centrally predetermined level of services. Differentials in needs and in the cost of providing services may be taken into account as desired. Caution is necessary in this respect, however, since it is all too easy to turn a simple, transparent formula into an obscure and manipulable one by introducing too many refinements. Argentina, for example, had a transfer formula from 1973 to 1988 of which 65 percent was based on population, 10 percent on the inverse of population density, and 25 percent on an index of a "developmental gap," which in turn was based on measures of the quality of housing, the number of vehicles per inhabitant, and the level of education. Relatively few developing countries include explicit measures of the potential tax capacity of recipient jurisdictions in their formulas. Many countries, however, use transfers to return some or all of certain taxes to where they are collected, a policy that benefits most those localities in which more taxes are collected. In Spain 30 percent of personal income taxes are allocated based on local tax collections. This approach may perhaps make the inclusion of a more redistributive component in transfers more acceptable to the rich regions. For example, other Spanish transfers are distributed mainly on the basis of population and are much more equalizing. Such tax-sharing arrangements generally have undesirable incentive effects. In contrast, Denmark and Sweden, like Canada and Australia, explicitly allocate local transfers on the assumption that an average "national" local tax rate is applied, thus creating an incentive to levy at least average taxes, since localities that levy above-average local taxes are not penalized while those that levy below-average taxes are not rewarded. Chile goes farther, actually "taxing" richer localities to some extent by reducing their transfers and raising those granted to poorer localities. The Republic of Korea assumes that a standard tax rate is applied by cities and lowers the transfer if the actual rate is lower. Of course, such approaches make sense only if local governments have the ability to vary local tax rates, at least within limits. The absence of much local autonomy with respect to local taxes combined with data difficulties probably explains the small number of transfer programs incorporating explicit capacity measures in developing countries.

Fiscal Effort

In some countries, attempts are made to incorporate explicit measures of "fiscal effort" into distributive formulas. Brazil allocates some transfers in accordance with per capita income levels in the different states. Nigeria includes a measure of tax effort—which in turn requires some concept of capacity to measure effort—in the basic distributional formula to states. Colombia includes such an element in one of its transfer programs.

In general, it is not advisable to include explicit measures of fiscal effort in such formulas, for a number of reasons. Conceptually, while it is not easy to define fiscal effort, it is probably most meaningfully understood as the ratio of actual taxes collected to potential taxes, estimated on the basis of some standard measure of fiscal capacity and some standard (for example, national average) tax rate. Even when so defined, the general absence of reliable empirical estimates of fiscal capacity renders the concept largely nonoperational. The measurement of fiscal effort is complex. If, for instance, tax bases are sensitive to tax rates, the usual measures overestimate capacity in low tax rate areas (and hence underestimate the effort needed to increase tax rates), because the base will decline if the rate is increased. Moreover, given the limited flexibility, most local governments in developing countries have to alter their revenues through their own actions. In any case, it is unclear to what extent it is meaningful to interpret the behavior of revenues as reflecting their effort. In addition, placing too much weight on fiscal effort in allocating grants often unduly penalizes poorer areas, where, by definition, a given percentage increase in effort (as usually measured) is more difficult to achieve. The problem giving rise to the need for equalization in the first place is that the fiscal capacity (tax base) of poor areas is too low, not that their tax rates are too low. Imposing an additional penalty on poor localities in a transfer program that, given the shortage of resources in developing countries, will almost inevitably fall short of fully equalizing fiscal capacity seems hard to justify.

Experience in some countries suggests that introducing an effort correction (conventionally defined as actual collections over potential collections) into fiscal transfers may end up giving still more to poorer areas—that is, increasing the redistributive effect of transfers. This result comes about because poorer areas may levy higher taxes than their richer neighbors, in part, perhaps, because of the incentive for excessive taxation discussed above. In Canada, for example, the highest tax rates on both income and sales are found in the poorest provinces (those with the lowest fiscal capacity). Combined with the fact that properly designed equalization transfers in any case embody a strong implicit incentive for transfer recipients to levy taxes at least at average levels, such arguments suggest that it is neither necessary nor desirable to include explicit effort factors in transfer formulas, even if such factors could be calculated in some reliable way. Nonetheless, it is important to take fiscal effort into account in a more general sense in designing transfers. The reason is not because of some technical worry about the substitutability of transfers for local resources but rather because it seems essential to require local residents to pay in some meaningful sense for what they get if those who make local expenditure decisions are to be held accountable through local political institutions for their actions. As long as local governments are spending what they and their constituents view as other people's money, they are unlikely to be under much local pressure to spend this money efficiently.

Experience everywhere suggests that people are more careful spending money they have to earn (taxes they have to pay themselves), because they are aware of both the pain of taxation and the pleasure of expenditure and because they feel more ownership of the activity. Local resource mobilization is thus an essential component of any successful decentralization exercise. Unless increased transfers are matched by a local contribution—however small that contribution may be in the poorest communities—the full efficiency benefits of decentralization are unlikely to be realized. People do not, it seems, take ownership of what is given to them in the same way as they do of goods and services they have to pay for themselves, at least in part; without local ownership, expenditure efficiency seems unlikely to be enhanced by decentralization.

What this argument implies is that transfers are unlikely to have good incentive effects on local revenue mobilization unless at least two conditions are satisfied. First, transfers should be designed so that the amount received is neither larger when local fiscal effort is weaker nor smaller when it is stronger. Second, local governments must have both the freedom and the responsibility to impose some significant taxes of their own (perhaps as surcharges on national taxes).

Grants and Migration Incentives

The focus of this chapter has been on the impact of intergovernmental transfers on the incentives of decision makers in recipient governments. But federal authorities must also be aware that transfers have indirect implications for incentives facing individual residents of subnational jurisdictions, as taxpayers and consumers of government-provided goods and services. The literature on subnational government policy and incentives for internal migration has been extremely influential for thinking about grants, but it is too voluminous to be dealt with here; the reader is referred to other chapters of this volume. The key idea, associated with Boadway and Flatters (1982), is that mobile residents will base their location decisions on the net fiscal benefits available in each jurisdiction of the federation, as well as on pre-fisc economic considerations. To the extent that net fiscal benefits differ across jurisdictions, labor, human capital, and perhaps firms will not be allocated across the country in a way that maximizes production efficiency. On this basis, there is a prima facie case for horizontal transfers to equalize (some) local differences in tax and spending capacity. Indeed, despite the explicitly redistributive nature of horizontal equalization, such transfers may in some circumstances induce a Pareto improvement, benefiting residents of all jurisdictions, over the fully decentralized equilibrium without transfers.

When such efficiency gains are available through intergovernmental transfers, however, it has been argued that they should arise through voluntary arrangements among subnational governments, without the need for intervention by central authorities. The argument appears to be akin to the Coasian one for decentralized bargaining alone to solve externalities in the private sector, but in fact it is different from Coase's insight and perhaps more convincing. Building on the insights of Boadway (1982), Myers (1990) considers a model of a federation in which homogeneous workers are perfectly mobile across regions, but source-based taxes may be unequally distributed.

For a game in which each local government simultaneously chooses tax rates, spending, and transfers to other governments to maximize local welfare, Myers shows the existence of a Nash equilibrium in which each government voluntarily gives to others an amount sufficient to achieve the optimal allocation of labor and the maximum level of per capita utility in the nation.

While the result is remarkable, it is probably not the basis for a convincing case for dismantling federal fiscal arrangements in the real world. Subsequent research has shown that the result is quite dependent on specific assumptions about the objective function of local governments, the degree of interregional mobility, and the nature of heterogeneity among taxpayers (Boadway 2003). In any case, grants from the center should fully crowd out voluntary horizontal transfers, just as vertical categorical grants should fully crowd out local own-account spending. Thus even if a central transfer authority does no good, it should do no harm. Regardless of the prescriptive implications of Myers' result, however, it is a useful basis for insights into the way federal fiscal arrangements are actually negotiated and allocated among national and subnational governments.

Concluding Comments

What does the literature have to say about the design of good federal fiscal arrangements?

1. As a rule, there is a role for both general-purpose and special-purpose matching grants (for example, for infrastructure).
2. From the points of view of both the grantor and recipient governments, it is generally advisable that the total pool of resources to be distributed in general-purpose transfers be set in a stable but flexible way (for example, as a percentage of central taxes, adjustable every few years).
3. In principle, a general-purpose grant should take into account both need and capacity, but it should do so in as simple, reliable, and transparent a fashion as possible.
4. If the general-purpose grant is properly designed, and local governments have some discretion in tax policy, there is no need to include specific incentive features to encourage additional tax effort.
5. As a rule no conditions should be imposed (through earmarking or mandates, for example) on how such general-purpose grants are spent. Special-purpose grants should usually have a matching component, which probably should vary with both the type of expenditure and the fiscal capacity of the recipient.

6. All local governments should be required to manage financial matters in accordance with standard procedures, to maintain adequate and current accounts, and to be audited regularly and publicly. Similarly, although central governments should not preapprove or direct in detail local government budgets and activities, they should maintain up to date and complete information on local finances and make such information publicly available. In the world of intergovernmental fiscal relations, better information is not a luxury but an essential component of a well-functioning system.

Countries that can do all these things correctly will have good systems of intergovernmental fiscal transfers. Those that do not will not.

Notes

1. This section draws heavily on Bird and Smart (2002).
2. In all municipalities, however, there was evidence that a substantial portion of marginal grants were returned to residents in the form of lower tax effort; in this sense, the flypaper effect was absent.
3. These include Canada, Denmark, Sweden, Switzerland, and a large number of developing countries. The equalization formula is the basis of local school district financing in a number of U.S. states (Card and Payne 2002).
4. Dahlby and Wilson (1994) examine the optimal design of equalizing transfers when subnational governments may impose distortionary taxes on many tax bases. They show how transfer formulas should be adjusted in order to equalize the marginal excess burden of taxation of each tax base and each jurisdiction.

References

Baker, Michael, Abigail Payne, and Michael Smart. 1999. "An Empirical Study of Matching Grants: The 'Cap on Cap.'" *Journal of Public Economics* 72: 269–88.

Baretti, Christian, Bernd Huber, and Karl Lichtblau. 2001. "A Tax on Tax Revenue: The Incentive Effects of Equalizing Transfers: Evidence from Germany." *International Tax and Public Finance* 9: 631–49.

Bird, Richard M. 1993. "Threading the Fiscal Labyrinth: Some Issues in Fiscal Decentralization." *National Tax Journal* 46: 207–27.

Bird, Richard M., and Edgardo Rodriguez. 1999. "Decentralization and Poverty Alleviation." *Public Administration and Development* 19: 199–219.

Bird, Richard M., and Michael Smart. 2002. "Intergovernmental Fiscal Transfers: International Lessons for Developing Countries." *World Development* 30: 899–912.

Bird, Richard M., and François Vaillancourt. 1998. *Fiscal Decentralization in Developing Countries.* Cambridge: Cambridge University Press.

Bird, Richard M., Robert D. Ebel, and Christine I. Wallich. 1995. *Decentralization of the Socialist State.* Washington, DC: World Bank.

Boadway, Robin W. 1982. "On the Method of Taxation and the Provision of Local Public Goods: Comment." *American Economic Review* 72: 846–51.

———. 2003. "The Theory and Practice of Equalization." *CESifo Economic Studies* 50: 211–54

Boadway, Robin W., and Frank R. Flatters. 1982. "Efficiency and Equalization Payments in a Federal System of Government: A Synthesis and Extension of Recent Results." *Canadian Journal of Economics* 15: 613–33.

Boadway, Robin W., and Masayoshi Hayashi. 2001. "An Empirical Analysis of Intergovernmental Tax Interaction: The Case of Business Income Taxes in Canada." *Canadian Journal of Economics* 34: 481–503.

Bucovetsky, Sam, and Michael Smart. 2006. "The Efficiency Consequences of Local Revenue Equalization: Tax Competition and Tax Distortions." *Journal of Public Economic Theory* 8: 119–144.

Bucovetsky, Sam, Maurice Marchand, and Pierre Pestieau. 1998. "Tax Competition and Revelation of Preferences for Public Expenditure." *Journal of Public Economics* 44: 367–90.

Buettner, Thiess. 2006. "The Incentive Effect of Fiscal Equalization Transfers on Tax Policy." *Journal of Public Economics* 90: 477–499.

Card, David, and Abigail Payne. 2002. "School Finance Reform: The Distribution of School Spending and the Distribution of Student Test Scores." *Journal of Public Economics* 83: 49–82.

Chaparro, Juan, Michael Smart, and Juan Gonzalo Zapata. 2005. "Municipal Taxation and Transfers in Colombia." In *Fiscal Reform in Colombia: Problems and Prospects*, ed. J. Poterba, R. Bird, and J. Slemrod, 287–317. Cambridge, MA: MIT Press.

Chernick, Howard. 1995. "Fiscal Effects of Block Grants for the Needy: A Review of the Evidence." In *Proceedings of the National Tax Association Annual Conference on Taxation*, 24–33.

Dahlby, Bev, and Neil Warren. 2003. "Fiscal Incentive Effects of the Australian Equalization System." *Economic Record* 79: 434–45.

Dahlby, Bev, and L.S. Wilson. 1994. "Fiscal Capacity, Tax Effort, and Optimal Equalization Grants." *Canadian Journal of Economics* 27: 657–72.

Esteller, Alex, and Albert Sole. 2002. "Tax Setting in a Federal System: The Case of Personal Income Taxation in Canada." *International Tax and Public Finance* 9: 235–57.

Feldstein, Martin S. 1975. "Wealth Neutrality and Local Choice in Public Education." *American Economic Review* 65: 75–89.

Figuieres, C., J. Hindriks, and G.D. Myles. 2004. "Revenue Sharing versus Expenditure Sharing in a Federal System." *International Tax and Public Finance* 11: 155–74.

Filimon, R., T. Romer, and H. Rosenthal. 1982. "Asymmetric Information and Agenda Control." *Journal of Public Economics* 17: 51–70.

Hines, James, and Richard Thaler. 1995. "The Flypaper Effect." *Journal of Economic Perspectives* 9: 217–26.

Knight, Brian. 2002. "Endogenous Federal Grants and Crowd-Out of State Government Spending: Theory and Evidence from the Federal Highway Aid Program." *American Economic Review* 92: 71–92.

Köthenbürger, Marko. 2002. "Tax Competition and Fiscal Equalization." *International Tax and Public Finance* 9: 391–408.

Moffitt, Robert. 1984. "The Effects of Grants-in-Aid on State and Local Expenditures: The Case of AFDC." *Journal of Public Economics* 23: 279–306.

Myers, Gordon. 1990. "Optimality, Free Mobility, and the Regional Authority in a Federation." *Journal of Public Economics* 43: 107–21.

Oates, Wallace E. 1972. *Fiscal Federalism*. New York: Harcourt, Brace, Jovanovich.

———. 1999. "An Essay on Fiscal Federalism." *Journal of Economic Literature* 37: 1120–49.

Porto, A., and P. Sanguinetti. 1993. *Descentralizacion fiscal: El caso argentino*. Serie Politica Fiscal 45, CEPAL (Economic Commission for Latin America), Santiago, Chile.

Roemer, John E., and Joaquim Silvestre. 2002. "The Flypaper Effect Is Not an Anomaly." *Journal of Public Economic Theory* 4, 1–17.

Shah, Anwar, and Zia Qureshi. 1994. "Intergovernmental Fiscal Relations in Indonesia." Working Paper 239, World Bank, Washington, DC.

Smart, Michael. 1998. "Taxation and Deadweight Loss in a System of Intergovernmental Transfers." *Canadian Journal of Economics* 31: 189–206.

Tiebout, Charles. 1956. "A Pure Theory of Local Expenditure." *Journal of Political Economy* 44: 416–24.

Wildasin, David E. 1991. "Income Redistribution in a Common Labor Market." *American Economic Review* 81: 757–74.

The Impact of Intergovernmental Fiscal Transfers: A Synthesis of the Conceptual and Empirical Literature

SHAMA GAMKHAR AND ANWAR SHAH

Intergovernmental fiscal transfers are frequently used to achieve diverse objectives, including dealing with vertical fiscal gaps, addressing horizontal fiscal inequities, providing compensation for benefit spillouts, and influencing subnational policies in taxing, spending, and regional and local economic stabilization. This chapter surveys the conceptual and empirical literature that attempts to measure the impact of these transfers on recipients' fiscal behavior.

The chapter is organized as follows. The first section reviews the conceptual literature on the impact of grants, paying special attention to the debate on the "flypaper effect" of general-purpose transfers. The second section provides a brief overview of the recent empirical literature on this subject. It reviews the conceptual and methodological issues in measuring the impact of intergovernmental grants, traces the evolution of refinements in the empirical literature for measuring the impact of intergovernmental grants on subnational fiscal behavior, and tests the explanatory power of alternative theoretical explanations of the flypaper effect. The last section provides concluding remarks.

Impact of Intergovernmental Transfers on Local Government Behavior: Theoretical Hypotheses

At the theoretical level, in a setting of perfect information and political competition, the allocative and distributive effects of lump-sum grants to a locality should not be different from the effects of distributing the lump-sum funds directly to local residents. This is known as the "veil hypothesis" (Bradford and Oates 1971). In the case of specific-purpose matching grants, the response of local expenditure should be the same as the effect of a marginal tax price reduction equivalent to the subsidy provided by the matching grant. For a public good with income elasticity greater than one, the theory predicts that the expenditure stimulation impact of open-ended matching grants will be greater than that of general-purpose (nonmatching lump-sum) grants.

A large body of empirical work has produced results that are at variance with these predictions. Several studies show that the stimulus to local public expenditure from lump-sum or general-purpose nonmatching grants far exceeds the effect of equal increases in private income (Gramlich 1977; Hines and Thaler 1995; Bailey and Connolly 1998). The marginal effect of private income on local government spending is estimated at $0.10 (Borcherding and Deacon 1972), while the estimated marginal effect of unconditional grants is about $0.50 (Hines and Thaler 1995). The empirically observed response of local expenditure to lump-sum grants is known as the flypaper effect, the notion that "money sticks where it hits" (Arthur Okun). The flypaper effect was a dominant concern in the earlier literature on grants, the so-called first generation theories. More recently, in second-generation theories, the efficiency and equity implications of these grants have come to command greater attention.

The Impact of Grants: First-Generation Theories

The theoretical explanations of the flypaper effect in the first-generation theories (Oates 2005) range from traditional neoclassical ones to those based on perspectives from the public choice literature (self-interested politicians, imperfect competition in the political system, and fiscal illusion on the part of citizens about the workings of the public sector). These explanations can be divided into groups, based on the assumptions made: models that assume that voters/residents face fiscal illusion, self-interested politicians, and an absence of political competition (fiscal illusion hypothesis); models that assume no fiscal illusion among voters/residents but view politicians as self-interested and assume that there is imperfect competition in the political system (budget-maximizing, monopolistic government hypothesis); and models that assume harmony of interests between politicians and voters, political competition, and no fiscal illusion (efficient government hypothesis).

Fiscal Illusion Hypothesis

The explanations by Oates (1979); Courant, Gramlich, and Rubinfeld (1979); and Filimon, Romer, and Rosenthal (1982) are based on the premise that residents of a jurisdiction act under fiscal illusion about the impact of an intergovernmental grant on the local public sector and that local officials want to expand the public budget. Oates and Courant, Gramlich, and Rubinfeld argue that budget-maximizing local government officials use these grants to lower the tax liability or average tax price of the public good, thereby inducing residents to vote for larger budgets.

Budget-Maximizing, Monopolistic Local Government Hypothesis (No Fiscal Illusion)

The allocation of resources for the provision of public services in models of this hypothesis is a function of the variables determining the bargaining strength of coalitions and groups of voters and the reversion level of public service included in the local constitutions. The bargaining strength of a coalition is derived from its relative size and from the constitutional rules and other institutions of the political system.[1]

The politically dominant group sets the agenda and must obtain a majority vote in favor of its proposed budget. Voters choose between the proposed budget and the reversion level stated in the local legislation. They favor a budget proposed by the agenda setter as long as the proposed budget leaves them at least as well off as the reversion level (Romer and Rosenthal 1979). The lower the reversion level of public services, the greater will be the level of expenditure that a high-spending politically dominant group can support (Filimon, Romer, and Rosenthal 1982). Filimon, Romer, and Rosenthal argue that in jurisdictions with a constitutionally determined minimum expenditure level (reversion level), lump-sum grants augment this minimum expenditure, but local public officials interested in maximizing their budget conceal the true information about the grant from voters and use their agenda-setting powers (discussed below) to induce a flypaper effect.

Craig and Inman (1982, 1986) postulate that voters form coalitions on the basis of income (the appropriate dimension along which coalitions are formed could vary from state to state), with the politically dominant group setting the agenda and proposing a budget to attract a majority winning coalition. In their version of the budget-maximizing model, the flypaper effect occurs when a high-spending coalition, like a high-income group, is politically dominant at the local level.

Efficient Government Hypothesis

Jonathan Hamilton (1986) argues that local tax-financed expenditures have an excess burden, due to the use of distorting taxes, whereas grant funds are relatively free of such costs, making the effective resource cost of grant-financed public expenditure lower than tax-financed expenditure. Therefore, a voter-responsive local government will select a higher socially optimal level of expenditure when the expenditure is grant financed (explaining the flypaper effect) than when local public expenditures are financed by local taxes only. He assumes, however, that the deadweight loss from taxation by the higher-level of government used to finance intergovernmental grants is less than the deadweight loss from local taxation.

Where the local tax is a property tax and there are effective local zoning restrictions, Bruce Hamilton (1975) shows that a local property tax becomes a benefit tax. In this case, the basic argument of the efficient government hypothesis is considerably weakened.

Impact of Intergovernmental Grants in Decentralized Systems: Second-Generation Theories

In more-recent research—referred to as second-generation theories (Oates 2005)—the primary focus has moved away from explaining the flypaper effect toward a broader concern with the equity and efficiency effects of intergovernmental grants in decentralized federal systems. Three themes dominate this research (Oates 2005): the tradeoff between accountability and fiscal interdependencies in situations of interjurisdictional competition, the soft budget constraint (the problem of decentralized governments "raiding the fiscal common" in a federation and weakening the fiscal restrictions placed on them by a balanced-budget constraint), and the moral hazard problem created by the fact that the federal government insures state and local government budgets against negative economic shocks. The role of federal intergovernmental grants in dealing with these issues is examined using principal-agent and game theory models.

The second-generation literature finds that the effect of intergovern-mental grants depends on the structure of the subnational fiscal system (the nature of tax competition, tax assignment, and types of functions performed by subnational governments, for example) and that the institutional arrangements for implementing intergovernmental programs (the enforce-ment capacity of government and fiscal rules such as balanced-budget requirements, for example) are important. These issues are discussed in detail below.

Fiscal Competition

Fiscal competition in a decentralized system enhances the accountability of governments to their citizens, but it also creates negative externalities that affect the level and pattern of economic activity (Oates 2005). The negative effects of competition arise because jurisdictions compete for relatively mobile capital resources, with potential for a "race to the bottom" in local tax rates and public expenditure (Cai and Treisman 2004). Federal govern-ment intervention in this case is desirable—it could collect taxes from the mobile tax bases and allocate corrective matching grants to jurisdictions that are losers from such competition. However, where the enforcement of federal tax and other regulation on the private sector are administered by subnational jurisdictions, the jurisdiction has strong incentives to protect business interests and lower the cost of doing business in the jurisdiction by weakly enforcing federal regulations (Cai and Treisman 2004). This is likely to "corrode" the federal government's ability to use a tax transfer policy to correct the externalities created by the competition.

In addition, when state income rises, a system of equalizing transfers typically imposes a penalty on the state, if the transfers are reduced when tax revenues rise (Baretti, Huber, and Lichtblau 2002). This creates a perverse incentive for the grant recipient jurisdiction, since the jurisdiction avoids this penalty by slackening the enforcement of federal tax regulations. Again, this weakens the federal government's ability to use transfers to counter any externalities created by interjurisdictional competition (a case in point is the German federal system). In the papers by Cai and Treisman (2004) and Baretti, Huber, and Lichtblau (2002), the central enforcement capacity is endogenous in subfederal decision making, pointing to the importance of an independent mechanism of federal enforcement or monitoring of state enforcement of federal tax regulation.

One of the negative externalities of expenditure competition between jurisdictions is that it worsens redistributive outcomes in these jurisdictions (Figuieres, Hindriks, and Myles 2004). This literature also raises the question of the appropriate form of intervention by the federal government in such situations. Figuieres, Hindriks, and Myles show that if jurisdictions compete for tax base, selecting an expenditure-sharing arrangement (matching grants) to balance the budgets of the competing jurisdictions worsens redistribution outcomes; instead, a revenue-sharing program is needed. Revenue sharing on net encourages regions to raise their taxes, because it transfers part of the cost of taxation and redistribution to other jurisdictions. Figuieres, Hindriks, and Myles recommend expenditure sharing for correcting the externalities created by competition on public expenditure among jurisdictions.

Soft Budget Constraint

Decentralization of the allocation function in public service provision enhances the efficiency of this function in the public sector (Oates 1972), but lower-level jurisdictions often have insufficient revenue capacity to meet all their expenditure needs, creating a vertical fiscal gap. In such situations, federal governments use intergovernmental transfers (referred to as equalizing transfers) to close the fiscal gap.

Unless they are designed appropriately, transfers create soft budget constraints (Kornai 1979) and the expectation that the federal government will "bail out" the failing subnational government. If the costs to the federal government are significant enough to warrant a federal bailout, what is the best intergovernmental mechanism to provide revenue support to a local government without creating the perverse expectations of a bailout? Oates (2005) examines various arguments favoring a bailout, as well as various ways in which the local government budget constraints could be "hardened" to prevent fiscal crises. Ihori and Itaya (2004) explore some of these options in the context of fiscal reconstruction as experienced in Japan during the early 1990s. They suggest that limits on public spending on certain functions are usually the first step in fiscal reconstruction. Transferring tax bases from federal to local governments, the authors argue, can reduce the size of the intergovernmental transfers from the federal government, but it does not alleviate the fiscal crisis. Such transfers turn out to be a zero-sum game, because a reduction in federal grants is generally accompanied by a reduction in tax revenue raised by the federal government, offsetting the local gains in revenue. Raising both local and national taxes can reduce public debt, but, if effective in raising revenues, this measure could increase the size of government, diverting resources away from private sector activity (crowding out). The authors recommend a revenue-sharing system in which taxes are generated locally and distributed back in uniform amounts to the local governments. This, they argue, is a way to stop the rent-seeking and free-riding behavior of subnational governments that creates soft budget constraints.

Federal Insurance and the Moral Hazard Problem

Intergovernmental transfers among states can serve as a form of insurance against stochastic negative shocks to the subnational economy. These transfers are typically designed as equalizing transfers: a decrease in the output of a state increases the net transfer payments received by the state. However, equalizing transfers distort states' own fiscal decision making by causing a moral hazard problem: the federal insurance against stochastic shocks may discourage states from making provisions for contingencies in their own budgets, such as maintaining "rainy day" funds (Oates 2005). In addition, Bucovetsky (1997) shows that federal fiscal equalization through intergovernmental transfers could raise state marginal tax rates on the rich, causing too much redistribution, because the state or region does not bear the full cost of the loss in tax base that ensues from taxing the rich, since it is subsidized by the federal government when state income decreases. This federal subsidy is, however, exactly what is needed to counter the externality created by interjurisdictional competition (causing too little redistribution) discussed earlier. Insurance transfers and the interjurisdictional competition thus have opposite effects on redistribution that might cancel each other out during periods of recession, when interjursidictional competition is also likely to be more severe.

Empirical Approaches to Measuring the Impact of Intergovernmental Transfers on Local Fiscal Behavior

A typical empirical model estimating the spending impact of various types of grants on local expenditure postulates the level of local government expenditure as a function of determinants of the demand for public goods (local government expenditure serves as a proxy for such demand). In a typical case, the set of determinants include grants, private income, tax price, and other relevant independent variables. The size of the coefficient of the grant variable (expected to be positive) measures the responsiveness of local expenditures to the intergovernmental grant. Comparison of this coefficient with the income coefficient is used to draw inferences, such as the flypaper effect.

A number of studies adopt the median voter model of public good demand; in these cases the private income and tax price variables are defined for the median voter. The median voter is typically considered to be the household with the median value of income. However, where the median voter is not relevant or is not easy to identify, the average income and mean values of the tax price variable are considered.

Another formulation examines the effects of grants on local own-source revenue along with other determinants of such revenue. In this case the relationship between own-source revenue and the grant variable is expected to be negative.

Econometric Issues

The own-source revenue and expenditure equations described above are basically two sides of the budget identity, given a balanced-budget constraint. The two variables are therefore simultaneously determined; estimation procedures should account for this simultaneity. Two additional critical econometric issues arise in estimating the public expenditure model used for measuring the expenditure impact of grants—the endogeneity of the grant variables and the econometric problems created by piecewise linear budget constraints, in the case of specific-purpose closed-ended grants.

In the case of matching grants, where the level of grants from a federal or state government is determined simultaneously with the level of local expenditure, the grant is clearly endogenous. This simultaneity in the determination of the grant and local expenditure biases the coefficient of the grant variable upward. Researchers who correct for this by adopting two-stage least squares estimation methods come up with lower estimated coefficients of the grant variable (Gramlich 1977).

Knight (2002) shows that (in the case of U.S. highway programs) state representation in federal budgetary decisions makes federal grant decisions a function of state preferences for public goods. Therefore, even nonmatching intergovernmental grants are likely to be endogenous in the grant recipient's expenditure equation. This would also be true for local grants received from state and federal governments. Another case of endogeneity of the grant variable is in situations where the grants fund only part of the project costs and the levels of project aid received by a jurisdiction are a function of the extent of local sharing of the cost of the project but the project selection itself is unaffected by the cost sharing (Chernick 1979).

Closed-ended matching grants create piecewise linear budget constraints. Moffitt (1984) shows that in this case the local government has essentially a two-part decision to make in response to a change in grant funding: it must choose a particular segment on the new piecewise budget constraint and select a particular location on the chosen segment of the budget constraint. A standard expenditure function alone will predict only the local government behavior on a chosen segment of the budget constraint. The choice of the segment itself needs to be modeled separately. Moffitt demonstrates that the demand function created by piecewise linear budget constraints are nonlinear in the parameters and in the error terms. Therefore, in the case of closed-ended matching grants or other types of nonlinear intergovernmental grant formulas, standard estimation techniques, such as ordinary or two-stage least squares, do not provide reliable estimates of the impact of these grants. A nonlinear maximum likelihood estimation technique is needed to obtain reliable estimates of the coefficients of the grant recipient government's expenditure equation (Moffitt 1984).

Model Specification Issues

Several explanations for the flypaper effect are based on a misspecification of the expenditure function due to either omitted variables (in the estimated equation) or adoption of an incorrect functional form for the public goods demand equation.

Omitted Demand Determinants

Bruce Hamilton (1983) argues that an understatement of the propensity to spend on public goods out of private income accounts for a substantial part of the observed flypaper effect. His basic premise is that public services are produced with both purchased and nonpurchased inputs. Nonpurchased inputs include various socioeconomic characteristics of the community, such as private income, educational level, employment, family stability, and so forth. Some of these characteristics are highly correlated with private income. If the estimated public expenditure function excludes socioeconomic characteristics as explanatory variables, private income serves as a proxy for these omitted variables and as a direct determinant of expenditure. If the correlation between income as a proxy variable for nonpurchased inputs and expenditure is negative while the correlation between local income and local public expenditure is positive (keeping the public service output constant), the income elasticity of demand is biased downward. While intergovernmental grants can be converted into private income by the expediency of a tax cut, they do not serve as a proxy for socioeconomic characteristics in the expenditure function. Thus the relationship between grants and expenditure remains essentially unaltered by the misspecification.

Correlated Demand Determinants

Gordon (2004) argues that poverty is an important determinant of various revenue streams for public school districts in the United States (federal aid, state aid, and school district own-source revenues, mostly from ad valorem property taxes). It is difficult to separate out the effect, for example, of federal aid on school district expenditure from the effects of other determinants, such as state aid and poverty. Gordon (2004) uses an instrumental variable for predicting federal education (Title 1) grants, thereby correcting for both the specification problem (described above) and the econometric problem (endogeneity of the grant variable). Grossman (1989) finds that the income variable in the public demand equation is highly correlated with the matching rate for welfare grants in the United States (the match is based on relative state income): the simple correlation based on data for 1973–77 is 0.93. Consequently, Grossman drops the matching rate variable and instead includes the level of federal welfare grants and the private income variable in the regression equation. This correlation of income and the federal matching rate in the equation explaining welfare spending is particularly problematic after 1965. Subsequent research on the welfare program also raises this issue (Chernick 2000; Baicker 2005). Baicker also uses an instrumental variable strategy to overcome this problem (discussed below).

Omitted Grant Conditions

Gramlich (1977) refers to maintenance of effort restrictions influencing the responsiveness of local public expenditure to lump-sum intergovernmental grants. Typically, these restrictions come along with potential penalties, but the conditions for compliance are so broadly stated that the restrictions are often not binding on the grant recipient. Jacobsen and McGuire (1996) observe a statistically significant effect of maintenance of effort restrictions on the expenditure response of states to block grants for alcohol and drug abuse programs in the United States. In contrast, Gamkhar and Sim (2001) find that maintenance of effort restrictions are essentially ineffective in influencing state spending of grant money. A similar result is observed by Gordon (2004), who finds that maintenance of effort restrictions in federal Title 1 education grants for local school systems and state governments are nonbinding, except as moral suasion.

Endogeneity of Grant Conditions

The initial design of a conditional grant may differ from its effective form, a notion referred to as the fungibility hypothesis. McGuire (1973), Shah (1985, 1988, 1989), and Zampelli (1986) consider the nominal conditions regarding price and income changes made in the local public sector by intergovernmental grants as inappropriate in analyzing the impact of grants, due to the variation in implementing these conditions by the state/local government. They therefore model the postgrant price and income-changing components of the public expenditure equation as unknown parameters of the fiscal system and estimate them empirically to gauge the impact of these components on local public fiscal behavior.

McGuire (1973), Shah (1989), and a few other studies use the Stone-Geary utility function, which yields an expenditure equation that is amenable to linear estimation techniques; the function systematically accommodates local need and effort variables as determinants of local expenditure. Zampelli (1986) uses a constant elasticity of substitution function. Becker (1996) shows that the estimation of the flypaper effect is sensitive to the functional form of the expenditure equation.

Short-Run versus Long-Run Determinants

Gramlich (1977) and Gramlich and Galper (1973) point out that there is likely to be a discrepancy between the short-run and long-run impact of grants on local expenditure. A survey of local governments in the United States, conducted to assess the impact of new schemes of nonmatching grants in the 1970s, shows that local governments initially invested a large portion of these grants in capital projects, because of the fear that these grants were only temporary. Gramlich and Galper (1973) find that the impact of nonmatching grants on local expenditure was small in the short run relative to the long run. Gamkhar (2000) finds that U.S. federal highway grants allocated in the previous two years can affect current state and local highway spending, primarily because of the provisions of the grant program that allow funds allocated for a particular year to be carried forward to future years. The combined coefficients for the impact of highway grants on state and local highway spending considering the lags are larger than the impact of current year grants on current year spending. Gordon (2004) finds that state and local revenue per pupil in public school education is unaffected by U.S. federal education (Title 1) grants in the initial year (no displacement effect), "but local governments substantially and significantly crowd out changes in Title 1 within a three-year period." Here "crowd out" implies that the community reduces its self-financed spending while utilizing the grant—a displacement effect.

Asymmetric Response

Goldfeld and Brainard (1973) point out that some discretionary expenditure may be predetermined or difficult to cut (for example, education expenditures). As a result, there may be a ratchet effect in expenditure changes—that is, it may be easier to increase rather than decrease certain discretionary expenditures. They suggest that this feature of discretionary expenditure needs to be incorporated in the model to make it more realistic. In light of the efforts to decentralize and reduce the size of government, researchers have questioned whether the effects of increases and decreases in intergovernmental grants on subnational expenditure would be symmetric (see, for example, Gramlich 1987, Stine 1994, and Gamkhar and Oates 1996).

Various model specification strategies have been used to test the symmetry hypothesis; these strategies are discussed in some depth by Gamkhar and Olson (2001). In one specification, in addition to the regular grant variable, a new variable, defined as a change in the value of the grant when the grant is decreasing, is added to test for asymmetry. If the coefficient on this "asymmetry" variable is not statistically significant or zero, there is symmetry. In this case, if the response to an increase in grants results in a flypaper effect, a decrease in grants has a "reverse flypaper effect." Alternatively, if the coefficient (on the asymmetry variable) is statistically significant, the coefficient could be positive or negative. A positive coefficient suggests a retrenchment effect when there is a decrease in grants; the cutback in local spending in response to cutbacks in grants is larger than suggested by the symmetric response. If the coefficient is negative, this suggests a replacement effect—that is, the cutback in local spending in response to cutbacks in grants is smaller than suggested by the symmetric response.

Empirical Evidence

A mix of studies—on Canada, Germany, Italy, Sweden, the United States, and other countries—was selected for this review, covering the period from 1973 to 2005. Most studies are based on pooled cross-section and time series data and measure the impact of federal grants to states/provinces or local governments. This is not a comprehensive survey of the empirical literature on intergovernmental grants but rather a discussion of selected papers on the central themes in the literature.

General-Purpose Nonmatching Grants

A wide range of estimates of the effects of general-purpose nonmatching grants on grant recipient's expenditure emerge from these studies (table 8.1). The effects of grants on grant recipient spending range from no effect/statistically insignificant effects (full displacement) to a $0.60 effect of a $1 increase in grants (flypaper effect). As expected, the effect of an increase in income on local public expenditure is much lower ($0.03–$0.10). There is, however, a concern about the reliability of these estimates, for the reasons described below.

Most of the estimates of the effects of general-purpose nonmatching grants listed in table 8.1 do not account for the endogeneity of the grant variables in their estimation procedure. These estimates may therefore not be consistent and could be upward biased, given the rationale provided by Knight (2002) regarding the endogeneity of the nonmatching aid. Many of the studies on the impact of U.S. grants do not single out the pure general-purpose nonmatching grants. Instead, the grant variable used in the grant recipient's expenditure equation is a combination of all types of programs minus the open-ended matching aid (Assistance to Families with Dependent Children [AFDC] and Medicaid). Most U.S. federal matching grant programs are closed-ended matching grants. For these grants, the studies implicitly assume that the grant recipient is already spending more than the grantor-determined upper limit in any particular fiscal year, so that the grant variable is modeled as a nonmatching grant. Most of the grant programs in the United States are specific-purpose grants; the main general-purpose grant revenue-sharing program has been discontinued and not replaced.

The studies of the effects of general-purpose nonmatching grants focus on a variety of relevant fiscal issues. A commonly neglected issue in estimating the effects of intergovernmental grants is the distinction between the long-term and short-term effects of grants. Gramlich and Galper (1973) introduce the dynamic adjustment of state and local spending to changes in grants. They estimate the long-term impact of all state exogenous resources,[2] including federal lump-sum transfers on state and local spending, at $0.43 (the corresponding impact of private income is $0.10). This effect is substantially larger than the short-term effect, which is not statistically significant.

Including political and institutional variables in the grant recipient's expenditure equation and disaggregating grant recipient's spending categories suggests that the flypaper effect comes from various sources (Craig and Inman 1986). A $1 increase in federal lump-sum grants leads to a $0.09 (not statistically significant) increase in state revenue; the private income impact

TABLE 8.1 Empirical Results on the Impact of Intergovernmental Transfers, 1973–2005

Study/type of grant	Area, sample, period: dependent variable	Impact on recipient government's expenditure		Government expenditure elasticities		Type of model and estimation technique
		Marginal impact of private income (dollars)	Marginal impact of intergovernmental grant (dollars)	Private income	Price/grant	
General-purpose nonmatching grants (revenue-sharing or equalizing transfers)						
Bergstrom, Dahlberg, and Mork (2004) Central government general	Sweden, 245 municipalities, 1988–95: municipal employment	0.17	Before 1993: 0.63 After 1993: 0.33	Short run: 0.369 Long run: 0.620	Short run before 1993: 0.06 Short run after 1993: 0.03 Long run before 1993: 0.10 Long run after 1993: 0.04	Dynamic median voter employment model, pooled time series and cross-section; first difference form; generalized method of moments with heteroskedasticity correction
Baretti, Huber, and Lichtblau (2002) Federal equalization	Federal Republic of Germany, 10 western states (except Berlin), 1970–98: combined state income and corporate tax revenues as percentage of state GDP	Marginal tax rate: −.007	-1.3×10^{-5}**	n.a.	n.a.	Representative government model; pooled time series and cross-section; Hausman and Taylor (1981) estimator with lagged dependent variable
Gamkhar and Oates (1996) Federal nonwelfare grants	United States, state government, 1952–90: combined state and local government expenditure	0.14	0.47	n.a.	n.a.	Standard demand model; time series; ordinary least squares–autoregressive 1
		0.27	0.60	n.a.	n.a.	Standard demand model; time series; two-stage least squares–autoregressive 1

Study	Program				Methodology
Grossman (1989) Federal nonwelfare grants	United States, state government, 1973–77: state own-source (direct) expenditure	0.03	1.14	n.a.	Vote-maximizing grantor government; pooled time series and cross-section; fixed effects; ordinary least squares
Craig and Inman (1986) Federal general revenue sharing	United States, state government, 1966–80:				Representative voter utility maximization model augmented with political institutions; pooled time series and cross-section; ordinary least squares
	State revenue	0.03*	0.09**	0.32	
	State education expenditure	n.a.	0.08**	0.13	
	State welfare expenditure	n.a.	0.09*	0.45	
	State other expenditure	n.a.	1.21	0.26	
Gramlich (1977)	Survey based on various studies	0.05, 0.10	0.25, 1.0	n.a.	Various models (estimates from reduced-form equations)
Gramlich and Galper (1973) Federal lump sum	United States, state and local government, 1954–72: state and local government current expenditure	0.1	0.43	n.a.	Standard demand analysis framework; quarterly time-series data; ordinary least squares with distributed lags
	United States, large urban government, 1962–70: local government expenditure	0.05	0.25	n.a.	Standard demand analysis framework; pooled time series and cross-section; ordinary least squares

Specific-purpose nonmatching grants

Study	Program				Methodology
Gordon (2004) Federal education	United States, state government, 1992–95: local school district education instructional spending	n.a.	Short run: 1.41 Long run: 0.12**	n.a.	Pooled time series and cross-section; two-stage least squares

(*continued*)

239

TABLE 8.1 Empirical Results on the Impact of Intergovernmental Transfers, 1973–2005 (*continued*)

Study/type of grant	Area, sample, period: dependent variable	Impact on recipient government's expenditure		Government expenditure elasticities		Type of model and estimation technique
		Marginal impact of private income (dollars)	Marginal impact of intergovernmental grant (dollars)	Private income	Price/grant	
Levaggi and Zanola (2003) Federal health	Italy, 18 regional governments, 1989–93: state government health expenditures	0.01	0.84	0.14	0.70	Pooled time series and cross-section; fixed effects; ordinary least squares Utility maximizing median voter model
Fisher and Papke (2000) State education (operations)	United States, state and local government time series, 1995–96: school district expenditure	n.a.	State aid: 0.3, 0.7 Federal aid: 0.2, 0.9	0.40, 0.65	−0.15, −0.50	Various models and estimation techniques
Duncombe and Yinger (1998) State education (operations)	United States, 631 New York state school districts, 1991: education outcome index	0.10	0.33	0.89	0.31/3.4	Cross-section; two-stage least squares
Craig and Inman (1986) Federal education Federal welfare (lump sum) Other federal	United States, state government, 1966–80: State aid for education K-12 State welfare expenditure Other state expenditure	0.003** 0.008* 0.019	0.43 0.08 1.19	0.13 0.45 0.26	n.a. n.a. n.a.	Representative voter utility maximization model augmented with political institutions; pooled time series and cross-section; ordinary least squares

Study	Coverage					Comments
Filimon, Romer, and Rosenthal (1982) State education	United States, Oregon state school districts, 1971: total education expenditure per student	n.a.	n.a.	0.48	−0.23	Median voter model; cross-section; full information maximum likelihood
				0.82	−0.36	Grant illusion model; cross-section; full information maximum likelihood
				0.82	−0.37	Agenda control-grant illusion model; cross-section; full information maximum likelihood
Specific-purpose open-ended matching grants						
Baicker (2005) Federal Aid to Families with Dependent Children (AFDC)	United States, state government, 1948–63: Total AFDC spending per capita	n.a.	n.a.	1.33	Price of additional benefits: −0.31; price of additional recipients: 0.05**	State-fixed effects; decomposes total per capita AFDC spending into benefits per recipient and recipients per capita; uses simulated price and contribution as instruments for actual values
	AFDC benefits per recipient	n.a.	n.a.	0.29	Price of additional benefits: −0.38; price of additional recipients: 0.33	
	Recipients per capita	n.a.	n.a.	1.04	Price of additional benefits: 0.07***; price of additional recipients: −0.28	
Ribar and Wilhelm (1999) Federal AFDC	United States, state government, 1969–92: state AFDC benefits per recipient	n.a.	n.a.	0.11, 0.82	−0.14, 0.02	Pooled time series and cross-section; two-stage least squares with fixed effects

(continued)

TABLE 8.1 Empirical Results on the Impact of Intergovernmental Transfers, 1973–2005 (*continued*)

Study/type of grant	Area, sample, period: dependent variable	Impact on recipient government's expenditure		Government expenditure elasticities		Type of model and estimation technique
		Marginal impact of private income (dollars)	Marginal impact of intergovernmental grant (dollars)	Private income	Price/grant	
Baker, Payne, and Smart (1999) Federal welfare: Canada Assistance Plan	Canada, 10 provincial governments, 1980/81–1994/95:					Time series and cross-section variation
	Growth rate of provincial welfare expenditure	n.a.	−0.094	n.a.	n.a.	
	Growth rate of welfare beneficiaries in provinces	n.a.	−0.074	n.a.	n.a.	
	Statutory welfare rate in capped and uncapped provinces	n.a.	0.004**	n.a.	n.a.	
Gamkhar and Oates (1996) Federal welfare	United States, state and local government, 1952–91: state and local welfare expenditure	n.a. n.a.	1.51 1.21*	n.a. n.a.	n.a. n.a.	Ordinary least squares Two-stage least squares
Ribar and Wilhelm (1996) Federal AFDC	United States, state government, 1988–91: state AFDC benefits per recipient	n.a.	n.a.	−0.14, 0.46	−0.08, 0.20	Pooled time series and cross-section; two-stage least squares with fixed effects
Shroder (1995) Federal AFDC	United States, state government, 1982–88: state-guaranteed AFDC and Food Stamp benefits to three-person household	n.a.	n.a.	−0.17, 0.39	Ratio of recipients to total population: −0.11, 0.12 State share of welfare pending: 0.04, 0.58	Pooled time series and cross-section with fixed effects and cross-section; three-stage least squares; simultaneous regressions of benefit and recipiency ratio

Study	Description					Method
Moffitt (1990) Federal AFDC	United States, state government, 1960–84: state AFDC guaranteed benefit	n.a.	n.a.	0.98	0, −0.17	Ordinary least squares
Grossman (1989) Federal welfare	United States, state government, 1973–77: state own-source expenditure	0.03	1.51	n.a.	n.a.	Vote maximizing grantor government; pooled time series and cross-section; fixed effects; ordinary least squares
Craig and Inman (1986) Federal welfare	United States, state government, 1966–80: state welfare spending	0.008**	n.a.	0.45	−0.17	Representative voter utility maximization model augmented with political institutions; pooled time series and cross-section; ordinary least squares
Specific-purpose closed-ended matching grants						
Gamkhar (2003) Federal highway expenditure	United States, state and local government, 1976–90: state and local government spending on highways	0.01	0.37	n.a.	n.a.	Standard demand model; pooled time series and cross-section; two-stage least squares
Knight (2002) Federal highway expenditure	United States, state government, 1980–2000: state spending on highways (excluding federal grants)	n.a.	−1.12	n.a.	n.a.	Pooled time series and cross-section; limited information maximum likelihood
		0.01	−0.88	n.a.	n.a.	Pooled time series and cross-section; two-stage least squares
Gamkhar (2000) Federal highway obligation	United States, state and local government, 1976–90: state and local government spending on highways	0.01	Symmetry: 0.76 Asymmetry: 0.87 increase; 0.81 decrease	n.a.	n.a.	Standard demand model; pooled time series and cross-section; lagged dependent variables; autoregressive 1

243

TABLE 8.1 Empirical Results on the Impact of Intergovernmental Transfers, 1973–2005 (*continued*)

Study/type of grant	Area, sample, period: dependent variable	Impact on recipient government's expenditure		Government expenditure elasticities		Type of model and estimation technique
		Marginal impact of private income (dollars)	Marginal impact of intergovernmental grant (dollars)	Private income	Price/grant	
Shah (1989) Provincial transportation Provincial nontransportation	Canada, Alberta local governments, 1966–78: disaggregated local government spending on transportation and nontransportation activities	0.06 0.94	3.17 (−0.11)	n.a. n.a.	0.85 (−0.83)	Pooled time series and cross-section: linear expenditure system Fungibility model: linear expenditure system with Stone-Geary utility function; considers income and price effects of grants and tests whether grants strategy rewards effort or compensates need
Zampelli (1986) Social services Urban support Direct general government	United States, 18 large cities, 1974–78: disaggregated city spending on social services, urban support, and direct general government	n.a. n.a. n.a.	n.a. n.a. 0.18**	0.31 0.48 0.84	−0.32 −0.42 −0.64	Fungibility model: constant elasticity of substitution utility function; pooled time series and cross-section; first-difference specification; full information maximum likelihood
McGuire (1978) Education Noneducation Combined	United States, local governments, 1964–71: disaggregated local government spending on education and noneducation activities	0.02 0.07 0.09	0.98 0.82 0.82, 0.98	n.a. n.a. n.a.	n.a. −0.02 −0.27	Pooled time series and cross-section Fungibility model: Stone-Geary utility function

Note: All estimates are statistically significant at the 5 percent level unless marked by an asterisk.
*Statistically significant at the 10 percent level.
**Not statistically significant.

on state government revenue is $0.03. A $1 increase in general-purpose non-matching grants increases state welfare expenditure by $0.09. It has a statistically insignificant effect on state education expenditure and increases other state expenditure by $1.21 (a large flypaper effect).

Grossman (1989) estimates the effect of state grants to local governments on state own-source expenditure (–$0.17, or an elasticity of –0.08 at the mean). The results, reported in table 8.1, are the estimated effects of federal general-purpose nonmatching grants on state own-source (direct) expenditure of $1.14.

Gamkhar and Oates (1996) estimate the effects of increases and decreases in federal grants to state and local governments in the United States, considering federal nonwelfare grants and using a two-step least squares estimation technique. They find a grant effect of $0.60—much higher than the effect of private income of $0.27 (all grant types other than open-ended matching grants are treated as nonwelfare grants). They find no asymmetry in the response to increases and decreases in these grants.

Baretti, Huber, and Lichtblau (2002) estimate the effects of equalizing transfers from federal to state governments in Germany (not statistically significant) and the accompanying (statistically significant) effect of an implicit tax on state revenues (–$0.007). The effect of the implicit tax on state revenues suggests a strong displacement effect of the equalizing transfer program in richer versus poorer jurisdictions.

Bergstrom, Dahlberg, and Mork (2004) examine federal grants to municipalities in Sweden and the effects on municipal employment of converting from specific-purpose to general-purpose nonmatching grants in 1993. They examine whether there is a differential in the effect on municipal employment of grants relative to private income. The estimated effect of grants ($0.63 before 1993, $0.33 after 1993) and private income ($0.17) suggest that the conversion from specific- to general-purpose grants has reduced the effects of general-purpose nonmatching grants on municipal employment generation in the local economy, but it is still larger than the marginal effect of private income. However, the stimulus to municipal employment by an increase in grants, measured by the elasticities, is relatively small, both before (0.06) and after (0.03) the reforms.

Specific-Purpose Nonmatching Grants

Specific-purpose nonmatching grants are subdivided by function (education, welfare, and health). Most public education grants in the United States originate at the state level and go directly to local school districts or municipalities.

These grants are of two types: lump-sum foundation grants and matching grants based on a guaranteed tax base formula (also referred to as power-equalizing grants). A survey of responses to education grants (Fisher and Papke 2000) finds that local education expenditure responses to state education block grants range from $0.30 to $0.70 per grant dollar, suggesting that grant-induced increases in spending are about three to seven times the spending induced by increases in private income ($0.10) (see table 8.1). This finding is corroborated in New York school districts during 1991 (Duncombe and Yinger 1998) and in Oregon school districts in 1971 (Filimon, Romer, and Rosenthal 1982). The Oregon study shows that if there is fiscal illusion about the grant variable among residents, it tends to increase the income and price elasticity of the jurisdiction's response.

Federal education grants in the United States, mostly distributed as specific-purpose nonmatching grants, represent a smaller proportion of a school district's revenue. However, these grants are more important in poorer districts, since federal education grants are targeted toward lower-income households. In education, estimates of the impact of federal grants on local spending range from $0.20 to $0.90 (Fisher and Papke 2000). The mean value of these impacts suggests that, due to the flypaper effect, the bulk of federal grant money for public education is still being used for tax reduction or noneducation public services at the local level. Similar results are observed in more-recent studies of the effects of federal nonmatching grants for education, described below.

Despite the effort across states in the United States to both equalize and provide adequate resources for public school education, actual spending could still be unequal and inadequate if grants have a large displacement effect (substitution of school district's own-source revenues by grants), as observed in the earlier estimates of education grants on local spending. Grantors would like to see grant money create new spending on the grant-funded item. To encourage new spending, grantors add maintenance of effort restrictions as well as incentives to stimulate spending in education aid programs. The success of the conditions on the grants in achieving the grantor's objectives depends on whether the conditions are binding on the grant recipient and on the stringency of enforcement of the conditions. Craig and Inman (1982) find that resources displaced in education by the receipt of education grants are transferred to other public service needs, such as welfare and other local services, as well as tax reduction. Their estimates suggest a $0.43 marginal impact of lump-sum federal education aid to states, with the remaining portion of $1.00 of federal aid going to welfare ($0.09), other expenditure ($0.09), and tax reduction ($0.39).[3] Gordon (2004) finds that federal education grants for income-disadvantaged students (Title 1) initially increase total school district revenue and instructional spending (grant coefficient of $1.41) but that the initial effects are completely displaced by the third year (the grant coefficient is not statistically significant).[4] The fungibility of resources causes a decline in local revenue (in the third year) and other changes in the intergovernmental grant structure at the state level.[5] Gordon points out that despite the insignificant changes in instructional spending as a result of the grant, federal mandates regarding maintenance of effort restrictions are followed to the letter by the jurisdictions receiving federal grants, essentially because the federal maintenance of effort restrictions is relatively broadly defined and consequently not binding at the local level.

Soft budget constraints that allowed regions to spend more than their revenues without any credible punishment from the federal government are being restricted in a number of countries with stricter financial policy requirements and, in a number of cases, reductions in the amount of the federal grants. Levaggi and Zanola (2003) estimate the response of regional health care expenditures in Italy to different sources of funding (in particular nonmatching health care grants). They test whether there is asymmetry in the response to increases and decreases in these grants and examine whether the soft budget constraint is affecting the expenditure response of the grant recipient. They find that in the presence of a soft budget constraint, the estimated marginal effect is $0.84 for grants and $0.01 for private income—a large flypaper effect. These effects are higher than the effects of grants in a specification without a soft budget constraint. Levaggi and Zanola (2003) find that the asymmetry in response to grants results in a strong retrenchment-type asymmetry when grants are decreased—referred to as a "super flypaper effect"—when the soft budget constraint is ignored. A "super flypaper effect" is observed when a decrease in grants causes the grant recipient's expenditure to decrease by more than the decrease in grants.[6] However, controlling for the soft budget constraint, Levaggi and Zanola observe a milder form of retrenchment: grant recipient's expenditure decreases by more than the symmetric effect but by less than the decrease in the grants.

Specific-Purpose Open-Ended Matching Grants

The estimated effects of specific-purpose open-ended matching grants are reported in table 8.1. The focus is on welfare grants in the United States and Canada. In the United States, Aid to Families with Dependent Children (AFDC) was primarily an open-ended matching grant that was converted to a block grant (Temporary Assistance for Needy Families [TANF]) in

1996. In Canada the welfare program, Canada Assistance Plan (CAP), was converted from an open-ended matching grant to a block grant in 1990. The key policy issue in both the U.S. and Canadian welfare programs is whether the changes in these programs limiting the federal aid contributions and the conversion of matching open-ended grants for welfare to block grants will lower the level of welfare benefits and adversely affect redistribution at the state (provincial) level.

Several papers address this issue (Moffitt 1990; Shroder 1995; Chernick 1998, 2000; Ribar and Wilhelm 1996, 1999; Baicker 2005; Baker, Payne, and Smart 1999). In all of them, increases in welfare spending are attributable to an increase in recipients or an increase in benefit levels. The price of welfare for the state is determined by the federal share in state spending s and the recipiency ratio (the ratio of recipients (R) to taxpayer population (N), or R/N); the price is measured by $(1 - s) \times R/N$. States are also sensitive to the benefit levels provided by their neighbors and often use nonincome restrictions on recipients to adjust to price changes (Baicker 2005).

The complexity of the cash assistance program in the United States before 1996 creates some tricky identification problems in estimation. The problems arise due to endogenous variables in the spending equation and linkages (incentives and eligibility) between AFDC and other welfare programs, such as Food Stamps (an in-kind counterpart of AFDC).[7] These programmatic factors make it difficult to estimate reliable price and income elasticity measures for the AFDC program.

AFDC—a matching grant program (matching ranged from 50 to 80 percent across states)—was converted to a nationwide block grant program in 1996 (matching rate of zero). The shift caused as much as a 120 percent increase in state costs of running the cash assistance program (Baicker 2005).[8] Researchers have attempted to predict the effect of this conversion on the program's key outcomes—benefit levels per recipient and recipients per capita—using the price and income elasticity estimates from the AFDC program. Together these two outcomes account for total spending per capita on AFDC. The range of elasticity estimates reported in table 8.1 is wide, each based on different assumptions about the exogeneity of key variables in the estimated equation and the price and eligibility linkages across programs as well as within the AFDC program.

Craig and Inman (1986) consider state welfare spending levels but not the federal matching rate as endogenous. For 1966–80 they estimate the state welfare spending income elasticity at 0.45 and the price elasticity at –0.17. Shroder (1995) considers a later period (1982–88) and assumes that the proportion of welfare recipients in the population is a function of the benefits per recipient and vice versa. He estimates a simultaneous equation model for these two components of AFDC spending. He finds a lower income elasticity of benefits per recipient (−0.17, −0.39) than do Craig and Inman and a positive price elasticity of benefits per recipient with respect to the state matching share (0.02, −0.58). The positive price elasticity is also observed in other studies of AFDC benefit levels, which attribute it to the positive correlation between state income and its federal matching rate for welfare programs. The price elasticity of benefits per recipient with respect to the proportion of welfare recipients in the population is also positive in some of the panel data estimates reported by Shroder (−0.11, 0.12).

One of Moffitt's contributions to this literature is his estimation strategy for measuring income and price elasticity with respect to benefit levels per recipient. He proposes an estimation technique that accounts for the nonlinear budget constraints created by the AFDC program's matching rate policy (Moffitt 1984). Unlike in his 1990 paper, where he considers cross-sectional data for 1960, here he simplifies the matching rate variable by considering the value of the 1960 matching rate as the rate applicable at the mean value of benefits.[9] Using data from 1960, he comes up with an income elasticity of 0.98 and a price elasticity of −0.17.[10]

Ribar and Wilhelm compile two data sets—one for 1969–92 (Ribar and Wilhelm 1999) and one for 1988–91 (Ribar and Wilhelm 1996)—and replicate several specifications (from the literature) of the AFDC expenditure equation. They correct for the endogeneity of the price $[(1 - s) \times R/N]$ variable and measure the elasticities of this variable with respect to benefit levels per recipient, finding income elasticities of 0.11, 0.82 and price elasticities of −0.14, 0.02.[11] Their results indicate that welfare benefits are less responsive to economic factors than the studies by Moffitt and other researchers had shown. For example, Moffitt finds the income elasticity to be close to 1, whereas Ribar and Wilhelm find that it is considerably less than 1. Craig and Inman (1986) and Shroder (1995) come up with higher estimates, but their estimates are also lower than Moffitt's in absolute terms.

Baicker (2005) decomposes the price and income elasticities with respect to benefit per recipient and recipients per capita by estimating two separate equations. She estimates the cross-price elasticity between benefits and recipients, correcting for the endogeneity of the federal matching rate variable using simulated state AFDC shares and federal contributions—a strategy that overcomes some of the problems of endogeneity and weak instruments used in earlier studies. Baicker finds that the price elasticity with respect to benefits is −0.38 and the price elasticity with respect to the number of recipients is −0.28. While the price elasticities from separate equations for benefits and number of recipients are slightly higher in absolute terms than the estimates obtained from previous studies, she finds that the cross-price elasticities between the level of benefits and the number of recipients are also positive and statistically significant. The price elasticity estimates reported in previous studies do not account for the cross-price elasticities between benefits and recipients and are therefore misleading (Baicker 2005). For total AFDC spending, the income and price elasticities of benefits are 1.33 and −0.31; the elasticity of total spending with respect to recipients is not statistically significant. The conversion from open-ended matching AFDC grants to TANF block grants effectively raised the price of both benefits and recipients by about 120 percent. Based on the estimated elasticities, Baicker predicts a 40 percent decrease in welfare cash assistance expenditure.[12]

The Canadian experience with conversion of federal welfare grants from open-ended matching grants to a closed-ended block grant is useful because the conversion was undertaken in just 3 of Canada's 10 provinces. Baker, Payne, and Smart (1999) studies the three provinces that were affected by the conversion, using the unaffected provinces as a control group for other changes in the environment that coincided with the imposition of the cap. They predict that over the medium term, the "cap on CAP" policy in Canada will reduce the growth rate of welfare expenditure by 8–9 percent below the (predicted) levels had the program not been capped. They find that the downward adjustments in total welfare spending by the affected provinces to meet the caps were made by reducing the growth in beneficiaries, changing the eligibility requirements, monitoring, providing supplementary benefits, and changing the classification of beneficiaries, not by adjusting benefit rates.

Specific-Purpose Closed-Ended Matching Grants

The key features of specific-purpose closed-ended matching grants are the conditions these grants impose with respect to the programs on which the money has to be spent, the matching rate, and the upper limit on the grants. The conditions attached to the grants create a piecewise linear budget constraint that requires a special two-step estimation technique (Moffitt 1984). In the United States, own spending on the program by the grant recipient is greater than the upper limit on the grant in most cases (Bezdek and Jones 1988). Therefore, the grant has a marginal effect similar to a nonmatching grant (Gamkhar 2000, 2003; Knight 2002).

Other researchers contend that the price and income effects of closed-ended matching grants are endogenously determined. They have developed and implemented empirical tests for this phenomenon, referred to as the fungibility hypothesis. The studies taking this approach treat the price and income changes caused by specific-purpose closed-ended matching grants as unknown parameters (McGuire 1973; Shah 1989; Zampelli 1986).

Budgetary institutions affect the timing of the disbursement of federal grants and the effects that these grants have on grant recipient spending. In the case of the U.S. federal highway aid program, the conventionally used measure of federal grants (actual spending by the federal government on the aid program) is a reimbursement of state and local spending on highway projects that qualify for federal aid. Federal aid obligations precede the state and local expenditures and are therefore more-appropriate measures of federal highway aid. Additionally, budgetary institutions permit states to carry forward their highway aid obligations to future years until they are fully expended.

Budgetary flexibility in timing the use of grant money is also available in other federal aid programs, such as the U.S. federal alcohol, drug abuse, and mental health grants, where a two-year carryover of grant funds is permitted (Gamkhar and Sim 2001). In a model explaining contemporaneous state and local highway spending that considers the above-mentioned budgetary features of the highway aid program in the estimated model, Gamkhar (2000) finds that the combined effect of current and two-period lags of federal aid obligations on state and local highway spending during the fiscal years 1976/77 to 1989/90 was $0.76 and the effect of private income was $0.01—a large flypaper effect. Gamkhar (2000) also allows for asymmetric effects of increases and decreases in grants, finding that the response to increases in highway grants was $0.87 and the response to decreases $0.81. These estimates indicate replacement asymmetry.

Knight (2002) considers a symmetric response model but corrects for the potential endogeneity of federal highway expenditures (essentially reimbursements of state and local spending). He finds that the impact of $1 of federal highway expenditures on state highway spending (including grant funded spending) varies from $0.33 to $0.12. Gamkhar (2003) estimates a similar expenditure equation, considering the effects of contemporaneous federal highway expenditures (correcting for endogeneity of federal expenditures) on current period state and local government expenditure. She estimates the effect of $1 of federal highway grants at $0.37, considerably higher than Knight's estimate.[13]

Considering grant conditions as endogenous and fungible, McGuire (1973) explains local government response to federal grants in the United States, finding strong evidence of fungibility. About 64–69 percent of

U.S. education grants and 76 percent of noneducation grants are fungible. McGuire also observes a positive trend in fungibility over the 1964–71 period, confirming that bureaucracies are becoming increasingly proficient at circumventing nominal restrictions on grant use. Applying a similar model to explain city governments' response to provincial transportation assistance in Alberta, Canada, Shah (1989) finds no statistically significant evidence of fungibility. Zampelli (1986) finds that the fungibility parameter on U.S. state aid is statistically insignificant. McGuire (1973), Shah (1989), and Zampelli (1986) examine the impact of aid from different levels of government. McGuire's study considers federal aid to local governments, Shah and Zampelli consider provincial/state aid to localities. The results of these studies could be interpreted to suggest that fungibility varies directly with the degree of separation between the grantor and the recipient. Federal assistance to local governments is more fungible than state assistance as the federal government has less ability to monitor local fiscal behavior.

These studies produce very different findings on the flypaper effect. McGuire's results support the phenomenon, Zampelli's do not. In Shah's study, the phenomenon has no relevance, since the upper limits on matching grants cannot be reached due to their closed-ended nature. Shah finds that $1 of closed-ended matching grants induces about $3 in local self-financed expenditure in the case of transportation. His results show that while both categories of grants (transportation and nontransportation) have positive effects on local self-financed expenditure on transportation, they have a negative effect on self-financed nontransportation expenditure; the combined effect of grants on total expenditure is not statistically significant.

Concluding Remarks

This chapter synthesizes the conceptual and empirical literature to explain the divergence between actual results and theoretical predictions. It shows that the actual results obtained depend on the specific design of the grant and implementation mechanisms; the nature of political and fiscal institutions that guide public spending including fiscal rules; and the nature of political and fiscal competition within and across jurisdictions, horizontally and vertically. Policy makers will therefore be well advised to reflect on these issues in designing grant programs to achieve specific objectives.

Economic theory suggests that the taxonomy of grants can be used to predict the impact of grants on recipient's fiscal behavior. General-purpose nonmatching grants are considered to have the least stimulative impact on local spending, as these grants do not modify relative prices of local public goods but simply augment local budgets. Because these grants preserve local autonomy and spending flexibility, they are expected to maximize local welfare while stimulating local expenditures less than the grant funds, since part of the grant funds will be used to provide tax relief to residents. Specific-purpose nonmatching grants do not modify the relative prices of local public services but limit local budgetary flexibility if the recipient government was spending less than the amount of the grant on the assisted service. The stimulative impact of such a grant is predicted to be less than the grant funds received. Specific-purpose open-ended matching grants are predicted to increase recipient's assisted expenditures more than the grant funds, because they increase both local budgets and the relative prices of assisted versus nonassisted services. Closed-ended matching grants have similar impacts only if the closed-end constraint was binding.

The empirical work on the impact of grants does not always substantiate the predictions of the theory. Several studies suggest that the portion of general-purpose grants retained for greater local spending tends to exceed local government's own revenues relative to residents' income. Grant money tends to stick where it lands. Thus even general-purpose transfers can stimulate local expenditures more than predicted by the theory.

First-generation theories of intergovernmental grants distinguished between the objectives of different forms of grants: nonmatching grants were recommended for relieving fiscal capacity constraints of subnational jurisdictions, while matching grants were recommended for correcting externalities in the provision of public services at the subnational level. Second-generation theories have shown that these transfers could exacerbate tax competition across jurisdictions and create moral hazards for the federal government, as lower-level governments start to assume soft budget constraints because of expectations of federal bailouts. Second-generation theories recommend tying federal transfers to tax efforts by lower-level governments and encouraging these governments to adopt fiscal policies that are sensitive to contingencies (such as rainy day funds). Alternatively, when faced with interjurisdictional expenditure competition, expenditure sharing could be achieved through matching grants. These issues are particularly relevant in newly decentralizing or newly formed federal systems.

A somewhat neglected aspect of intergovernmental grants in this literature is the management and administration of programs and their role in determining the effects of grants on spending. The issue is briefly mentioned in the context of the role of subnational governments in enforcing federal tax regulation and the need for different levels of government to monitor one another. When a federal tax is collected by the subnational government, the subnational government under pressure from interjurisdictional competition has a perverse incentive to slacken the enforcement of federal tax regulations, particularly when dealing with business tax bases. The effectiveness of federal oversight of tax enforcement is critical not only for the federal government's fiscal health but also for the sustainability of the federal intervention.

Estimation of the effects of grants on grant recipient's spending behavior has been riddled with problems. These include the endogeneity of the grant variable in the expenditure equation; the complexity of grant mechanisms, such as closed-ended matching grants, which create nonlinear budget constraints that make linear estimation techniques inappropriate; omitted variables, particularly the variables and model specifications that take into account the intricate grantor conditions on grant programs and the omitted nonpurchased inputs in the demand for public goods (these are not directly observed in government budgets, but their omission from the estimated equations can bias the grant effects); and questions about the symmetry of the response of grant recipient's spending to increases and decreases in grants.

The solutions to these problems have led to the use of more-sophisticated estimation techniques than the simple ordinary least squares estimates used early on. Most grant programs have conditions that are based on the socioeconomic circumstances of the residents of the grant-receiving jurisdiction. The disentangling of the public expenditure effects of these socioeconomic factors from the grant variable is critical to assessing the effects of the grant. Recent research on grants has creatively used the instrumental variable method along with the endogeneity of the grant variable to correct this problem. When grant conditions create nonlinear budget constraints or become endogenous to the grantor's behavior, nonlinear estimation techniques are recommended.

Notes

1. These include the agenda-setting powers of legislative committees, jurisdiction and budgetary bargaining rules on how local money can be allocated, and the size of voting blocks within the legislature or community.
2. Gramlich and Galper (1973) define state exogenous resources as including federal lump-sum transfers, interest and principal on outstanding debt, and matching expenditures on categorical closed-ended grants.

3. An additional $1.21 from federal welfare grants to states would generate $0.34 more in welfare spending, $0.54 less in state education expenditures, $0.63 less in state taxes, and $0.78 more in other state services (Fisher and Papke 2000).

4. Gordon (2004) suggests that the additional spending on instructional uses does hurt support services (−0.43), with a statistically significant drop in such services observed the year after the grant is received.

5. Gordon (2004) observes that in the third year after the initial Title 1 grant, state aid for public education switched from formula-based to categorical grants. She argues that this was done to help districts that lose out in federal aid allocations and to penalize school districts that benefit disproportionately in federal aid allocations.

6. Gamkhar and Oates (1996) coin this term for describing the extreme retrenchment phenomenon observed by Stine (1994) in response to cutbacks in federal grants to local governments in Pennsylvania.

7. Once the eligibility conditions for AFDC were met, individuals qualified for Medicaid (health care) and other welfare benefits. AFDC (cash assistance) and Food Stamps (in-kind welfare program) were linked because any increase in cash assistance (by the state) resulted in a drop in Food Stamp receipts (from the federal government) (Chernick 1998).

8. States faced an average marginal price of about $0.40 on the dollar in 1995. TANF raised the cost of spending increases to $1, keeping the size of the federal grant unchanged. This represented a 120 percent increase in the price of AFDC spending (Baicker 2005).

9. Moffitt (1990) examines the effects of the linkages between the AFDC, Food Stamp, and Medicaid programs. His findings confirm that state AFDC benefits have declined and that states have substituted Food Stamps and Medicaid benefits for AFDC in the total benefit package.

10. Moffitt (1990) also provides estimates of income and price elasticities for 1984. For the most part, these estimates are similar to the 1960 estimates reported in table 8.1.

11. Baicker (2005) raises some concerns about the instruments used because of their likely correlation with AFDC benefits.

12. Baicker's (2005) results also suggest that states reacted to changes in the marginal price of recipients by controlling eligibility by imposing discriminatory recipiency requirements and that they responded to changes induced by their neighbor's spending.

13. The federal grant variables in both papers are endogenous, because federal expenditure on highways is a reimbursement of state and local expenditure on highways (Gamkhar 2000, 2003) and state preferences for highway expenditure are reflected in the federal allocations of highway grants due to the state's representation in the U.S. Congress (Knight 2002). Both sets of estimates correct for endogeneity, albeit for different reasons.

References

Baicker, Katherine. 2005. "Extensive or Intensive Generosity? The Price and Income Effects of Federal Grants." *Review of Economics and Statistics* 87 (2): 371–84.

Bailey, Stephen J., and Stephen Connolly. 1998. "The Flypaper Effect: Identifying Areas for Further Research." *Public Choice* 95 (3–4): 335–61.

Baker, Michael, A. Abigail Payne, and Michael Smart. 1999. "An Empirical Study of Matching Grants: The 'Cap on CAP.'" *Journal of Public Economics* 72 (2): 269–88.

Baretti, Christian, Bernd Huber, and Karl Lichtblau. 2002. "A Tax on Tax Revenue: The Incentive Effects of Equalizing Transfers: Evidence From Germany." *International Tax and Public Finance* 9 (6): 631–49

Becker, Elisabeth. 1996. "The Illusion of Fiscal Illusion: Unsticking the Flypaper Effect." *Public Choice* 86 (1/2): 85–102.

Bergstrom, Pal, Matz Dahlberg, and Eva Mork. 2004. "The Effects of Grants and Wages on Municipal Labour." *Labour Economics* 11 (3): 315–34.

Bezdek, Roger, H., and Jonathan D. Jones. 1988. "Federal Categorical Grants-in-Aid and State and Local Government Expenditures." *Public Finance* 43 (1): 39–55.

Borcherding, Thomas E., and Robert T. Deacon. 1972. "The Demand for Services of Non-federal Governments." *American Economic Review* 62 (5): 891–901.

Bradford, D., and W. Oates. 1971. "The Analysis of Revenue Sharing in a New Approach to Collective Fiscal Decisions." *Quarterly Journal of Economics* 85 (3): 416–39.

Bucovetsky, S. 1997. "Insurance and Incentive Effects of Transfers among Regions: Equity and Efficiency." *International Tax and Public Finance* 4: 463–82.

Cai, Hongbin, and Daniel Treisman. 2004. "State Corroding Federalism." *Journal of Public Economics* 88 (3–4): 819–43.

Chernick, Howard. 1979. "An Economic Model of the Distribution of Project Grants." In *Fiscal Federalism and Grants in Aid*, ed. P. Mieszkowski and W. Oakland, 81–103. Washington, DC: Urban Institute.

———. 1998. "Fiscal Effects of Block Grants for the Needy: An Interpretation of the Evidence." *International Journal and Public Finance* 5 (2): 205–33.

———. 2000. "Federal Grants and Social Welfare Spending: Do State Responses Matter?" *National Tax Journal* 53 (1): 143–52.

Courant, P.N., E.M. Gramlich, and D.L. Rubinfeld. 1979. "The Stimulative Effects of Inter-Governmental Grants, or Why Money Sticks Where It Hits." In *Fiscal Federalism and Grants in Aid*, ed. P. Mieszkowski and W. Oakland, 5–21. Washington, DC: Urban Institute.

Craig, S., and R.P. Inman. 1982. "Federal Aid and Public Education: An Empirical Look at the New Fiscal Federalism." *Review of Economics and Statistics* 64 (4): 541–52.

———. 1986. "Education Welfare and the New Federalism: State Budgeting in a Federalist Public Economy." In *Studies in State and Local Public Finance*, ed. H. Rosen, 187–221. Chicago: University of Chicago Press.

Duncombe, William, and John Yinger. 1998. "School Finance Reform: Aid Formulas and Equity Objectives." *National Tax Journal* 51 (2): 239–62.

Figuieres, Charles, Jean Hindriks, and Gareth D. Myles. 2004. "Revenue Sharing versus Expenditure Sharing in a Federal System." *International Tax and Public Finance* 11 (2): 155–174.

Filimon, R., T. Romer, and H. Rosenthal. 1982. "Asymmetric Information and Agenda Control: The Bases of Monopoly Power and Public Spending." *Journal of Public Economics* 17 (1): 51–70.

Fisher, Ronald C., and Leslie E. Papke. 2000. "Local Government Responses to Education Grants." *National Tax Journal* 53 (1):155–74.

Gamkhar, Shama. 2000. "Is the Response of State and Local Highway Spending Symmetric to Increases and Decreases in Federal Highway Grants?" *Public Finance Review* 28 (1): 3–25.

————. 2003. "Federal Budget and Trust Fund Institutions: Do They Matter in Measuring the Impact of Federal Highway Grants?" *Public Budgeting and Finance* 23 (1): 1–21.

Gamkhar, Shama, and Wallace Oates. 1996. "Asymmetries in the Response to Increases and Decreases in Intergovernmental Grants: Some Empirical Findings." *National Tax Journal* 49 (4): 501–12.

Gamkhar, Shama, and Jerome Olson. 2001. "Asymmetric Responses in Economic Models." *Journal of Policy Modeling* 23 (5): 553–68.

Gamkhar, Shama, and ShaoChee Sim. 2001. "The Impact of Federal Alcohol and Drug Abuse Block Grants on State and Local Government Substance Abuse Program Expenditure: The Role of Federal Oversight." *Journal of Health Politics, Policy and Law* 26 (6): 45–71.

Goldfeld, Stephen, and William Brainard. 1973. "Comments and Discussion on 'State and Local Fiscal Behavior and Federal Grant Policy.'" *Brookings Papers on Economic Activity* 1: 59–65.

Gordon, Nora. 2004. "Do Federal Grants Boost School Spending? Evidence from Title I." *Journal of Public Economics* 88 (9–10): 1771–92.

Gramlich, E.M. 1977. "Intergovernmental Grants: A Review of the Empirical Literature." In *The Political Economy of Fiscal Federalism*, ed. W.E. Oates, 219–39. Lexington, MA: D.C. Heath.

————. 1987. "Federalism and Federal Deficit Reduction." *National Tax Journal* 40 (3): 299–313.

Gramlich, E.M., and H. Galper. 1973. "State and Local Fiscal Behavior and Federal Grant Policy." *Brookings Papers on Economic Activity* 1: 15–65.

Grossman, Philip J. 1989. "Intergovernmental Grants and Grantor Government Own-Purpose Expenditures." *National Tax Journal* 42 (4): 487–94.

Hamilton, Bruce. 1975. "Zoning and Property Taxation in a System for Local Governments." *Urban Studies* 12 (2): 205–11.

————. 1983. "The Fly-Paper Effect and Other Anomalies." *Journal of Public Economics* 22 (3): 347–61.

Hamilton, Jonathan. 1986. "The Fly-Paper Effect and the Deadweight Loss from Taxation." *Journal of Urban Economics* 19 (2): 148–55.

Hausman, J.A., and W.E Taylor. 1981 "Panel Data and Unobservable Individual Effects." *Econometrica* 49 (6): 1377–98.

Hines, James R., Jr., and Richard H. Thaler. 1995. "The Flypaper Effect." *Journal of Economic Perspectives* 9 (4): 217–26.

Ihori, Toshihiro, and Jun-Ichi Itaya. 2004. "Fiscal Reconstruction and Local Government Financing." *International Tax and Public Finance* 11 (1): 55–67.

Jacobsen, Karen, and Thomas G. McGuire. 1996. "Federal Block Grants and State Spending: The Alcohol, Drug Abuse and Mental Health Block Grant and State Agency Behavior." *Journal of Health Politics, Policy and Law* 21 (4): 753–70.

Knight, Brian. 2002. "Endogenous Federal Grants and Crowd-Out of State Government Spending: Theory and Evidence from Federal Highway Aid Program." *American Economic Review* 92 (1): 71–92.

Kornai, J. 1979. "Resource Constrained versus Demand Constrained Systems." *Econometrica* 47 (4): 801–19.

Levaggi, Rosella, and Roberto Zanola. 2003. "Flypaper Effect and Sluggishness: Evidence from Regional Health Expenditure in Italy." *International Tax and Public Finance* 10 (5): 535–47.

McGuire, Martin C. 1973. "Notes on Grants-in-Aid and Economic Interactions among Governments." *Canadian Journal of Economics* 6 (2): 207–21.

———. 1975. "An Econometric Model of Federal Grants and Local Fiscal Response." In *Financing the New Federalism*, ed. W.E. Oates, 115–38. Washington, DC: Resources for the Future.

———. 1978. "A Method for Estimating the Effect of a Subsidy on the Receiver's Resource Constraint with an Application to U.S. Local Governments 1964–1971." *Journal of Public Economics* 10 (1): 25–44.

Moffitt, R. 1984. "The Effects of Grants in Aid on State and Local Public Expenditure: The Case of AFDC." *Journal of Public Economics* 23(3): 279–305.

———. 1990. "Has State Redistribution Policy Grown More Conservative?" *National Tax Journal* 43 (2): 123–42.

Oates, W.E. 1972. *Fiscal Federalism*. New York: Harcourt Brace Jovanovich.

———. 1979. "Lump-Sum Grants Have Price Effects." In *Fiscal Federalism and Grants in Aid*, ed. P. Mieszkowski and W. Oakland, 23–30. Washington, DC: Urban Institute.

———. 2005. "Towards a Second-Generation Theory of Fiscal Federalism." *International Tax and Public Finance* 12 (4): 349–73.

Ribar, David C., and Mark O. Wilhelm. 1996. "Welfare Generosity: The Importance of Administrative Efficiency, Community Values, and Genuine Benevolence." *Applied Economics* 28 (8): 1045–54.

———. 1999. "The Demand for Welfare Generosity." *Review of Economics and Statistics* 81 (1): 96–108.

Romer, T.R., and H. Rosenthal. 1979. "Bureaucrats vs. Voters: On the Political Economy of Resource Allocation by Direct Democracy." *Quarterly Journal of Economics* 93 (4): 563–87.

———. 1980. "An Institutional Theory for the Effect of Intergovernmental Grants." *National Tax Journal* 33 (4): 451–58.

Shah, Anwar. 1985. "Provincial Transportation Grants to Alberta Cities: Structure, Evaluation, and a Proposal for an Alternate Design." In *Quantity and Quality in Economic Research*, vol. I. ed. Roy Chamberlain Brown, 59–108. New York: University Press of America.

———. 1988. "An Empirical Analysis of Public Transit Subsidies in Canada." In *Quantity and Quality in Economic Research*, vol. II, ed. Roy Chamberlain Brown, 15–26. New York: University Press of America.

———. 1989. "A Linear Expenditure System Estimation of Local Response to Provincial Transportation Grants." *Kentucky Journal of Economics and Business* 2 (3): 150–68.

Shroder, M. 1995. "Games the States Don't Play: Welfare Benefits and the Theory of Fiscal Federalism." *Review of Economics and Statistics* 77 (1): 183–91.

Stine, William F. 1994. "Is Local Government Revenue Response to Federal Aid Symmetrical? Evidence from Pennsylvania County Governments in an Era of Retrenchment." *National Tax Journal* 47 (4) : 799–816.

Zampelli, Ernest M. 1986. "Resource Fungibility, the Flypaper Effect, and the Expenditure Impact of Grants-in-Aid." *Review of Economics and Statistics* 68 (1): 33–40.

PART Two

The Practice

9

The Legal Architecture of Intergovernmental Transfers: A Comparative Examination

SUJIT CHOUDHRY AND BENJAMIN PERRIN

An enormous body of literature exists on intergovernmental transfers between central governments and federal subunits. This work focuses almost exclusively on the economic justifications for such transfers, their design, and the challenges they pose to democratic accountability, transparency, and the autonomy of federal subunits. The legal dimension of intergovernmental transfers has received comparatively little scholarly attention. This oversight may be deliberate, as it has been argued that "in the end intergovernmental transfers are the *instruments*, not the *determinants* of public policy" (Bird and Tarasov 2002, p. 23, emphasis in original).

Legal frameworks cannot be entirely neutral. Systems of intergovernmental transfers are constituted and governed by domestic constitutional law, intergovernmental agreements, and legislation. One cannot fully appreciate how these systems operate without studying the legal instruments through which intergovernmental transfers are provided as well as their interpretation and enforcement by the courts. Each legal framework involves crucial design choices that determine which level of government makes the rules governing intergovernmental transfers, who may modify those rules and under what conditions, and who resolves inter-governmental conflicts when they arise. Every design choice reflects policy preferences in favor of centralization versus decentralization, political decision making versus adjudication, fiscal autonomy versus fiscal restraint, and acceptance of economic disparity versus insistence on fiscal solidarity. Policy preferences are thus embedded in the legal structure of every intergovernmental transfer system.

This chapter examines the legal architecture of intergovernmental transfers through a series of case studies. The first section draws on the Canadian experience. It briefly reviews the political economy of intergovernmental transfers in federations. While both equity and efficiency concerns argue in favor of intergovernmental transfers, the Canadian experience illustrates how these transfers may pose challenges to democratic accountability, transparency, and the autonomy of federal subunits. A series of general design features are examined in order to assess and compare the legal arrangements of this aspect of fiscal federalism. The second section uses these design features to explore case studies of Belgium, Germany, India, and South Africa. The last section draws some tentative conclusions from the case studies about the impact of legal design on the legitimacy, effectiveness, and stability of systems of intergovernmental transfers.

Law and the Political Economy of Fiscal Federalism

The political economy of fiscal federalism illustrates the importance of the legal design of intergovernmental transfers. The principal economic argument for decentralized decision making (including federalism) is that it produces a better fit between citizens' preferences and public policies than would be the case in a unitary state, for two reasons (Tiebout 1956). First, the existence of federal arrangements allows a territorially concentrated minority to become a local majority, allowing it to vote for policies that would not win majorities at the national level. Second, through migration citizens presumably sort themselves into provincial populations that are much more homogeneous than the national population as a whole.

By contrast, unitary states are less sensitive to different preferences for publicly provided goods and services, which are averaged out by the national majority. Though these preferences may vary over time, unitary states are more likely to provide a single package, which citizens cannot opt out of (except through emigration). But as Boadway (2001) argues, intergovernmental fiscal transfers are necessary to ensure that the benefits of decentralization do not come at the expense of overarching objectives such as efficiency and equity.[1] Intergovernmental transfers help offset inefficient fiscally induced migration driven by differences in fiscal capacity across federal subunits. From the vantage point of equity, intergovernmental transfers guard against redistributive races to the bottom and promote horizontal equity by providing federal subunits of varying fiscal capacities with the ability to provide comparable levels of public services at comparable levels of taxation. Indeed, in Canada the importance of promoting horizontal equity is signaled by its inclusion in the constitution as a principle to which the federal government is committed, through the mechanism of equalization payments.

These standard arguments in favor of intergovernmental transfers have been widely discussed in academic and policy circles for more than 50 years. It is therefore of interest that they have generated a host of normative criticisms, which have been framed as a combination of arguments from federalism and democratic accountability (Petter 1989). To a considerable extent, these criticisms have been driven by the use of conditional grants by the federal government to ensure provincial compliance with national standards for health care and (earlier) social assistance (although there is some dispute as to whether these national standards are sufficiently detailed to qualify as conditions).

In Canada these debates over intergovernmental transfers have often involved legal arguments. Some political actors have challenged the constitutionality of transfers and conditional payments. Others have advanced a vast array of policy proposals regarding the legal architecture of transfer payments—that the rules governing transfer payments be constitutionally entrenched, that they require provincial consent to establish new federal transfer programs, that provinces be given the right to opt out of conditional programs with full compensation, that federal-provincial agreements be constitutionally entrenched, that the courts enforce such arrangements, and so on. The lesson from the Canadian experience is that law has infused the fiscal federalism discourse and has been a principal mechanism for addressing concerns about the design of intergovernmental transfer payments.

The Canadian experience suggests that the following general design features can be used to assess and compare the legal aspects of fiscal transfers in a federation:

1. *Legal basis of intergovernmental transfer system.* Does the central government have a legal duty to make intergovernmental transfers to subunits? To what extent is the system based on a combination of constitutional law, federal statutes (super-majority and simple majority), regulations,

ministerial decisions, and intergovernmental agreements? Does the central government have the legal power to directly make transfers to provinces to subsidize public expenditures in areas of provincial jurisdiction (that is, is there federal spending power)?

2. *Procedures for establishing and modifying intergovernmental transfers.* Does the central government have the power to unilaterally establish, modify, and terminate the terms of intergovernmental transfers (for example, level, conditions), or is subunit involvement legally required? If subunit involvement is legally required, what is the nature of participation—notice, consultation, or consent? May individual subunits and the central government enter into intergovernmental agreements for transfers?

3. *Conditional and unconditional transfers.* May the central government attach conditions to fiscal transfers, or must grants be unconditional? If grants may be conditional, are there any legal limits on the specificity of these conditions? If grants may be conditional, what are the legal consequences, if any, for subunits that violate these conditions? Do subunits have the right to opt out of conditional intergovernmental transfers? If so, do they have the right to compensation if certain conditions are met?

4. *Dispute resolution and adjudication.* How are disputes concerning intergovernmental fiscal transfers addressed? May intergovernmental transfers be judicially enforced, or are they nonjusticiable? To what extent does dispute resolution rely on constitutional principles (that is, federal loyalty), ad hoc political negotiations, mediation/conciliation, administrative proceedings, or constitutional adjudication? How have these mechanisms worked in practice?

Together these design features constitute the legal framework of fiscal federalism. Given that intergovernmental fiscal transfers play an important role in realizing the theoretical benefits of a federal system of government, they warrant particular attention.

Case Studies

These design features are used to explore case studies of Belgium, Germany, India, and South Africa. The cases include countries in which the scope of legislative authority matches the scope of executive authority (India) and those in which subunits administer federally enacted and designed policies (Germany). It includes developed countries (Belgium, Germany) and developing ones (India, South Africa); new (Germany, India) and very new

(Belgium, South Africa) federations; and federations from both the common law (India, South Africa) and civil law (Belgium, Germany) traditions.

Systems of Government in the Case Study Countries

Before describing and analyzing the legal architecture of intergovernmental transfers in the countries selected, it is necessary to identify the different levels of government involved and the powers attributed to them.

Belgium

Belgium embarked on its federal project in 1970. In 1993 its Constitution was substantially overhauled to create an innovative federal system of government, with two overlapping types of subunits: regions, which are geographically defined (Flemish, Walloon, and Brussels), and communities, which are based on language (Flemish, French, and German).[2]

Articles 127–130 of the Belgian Constitution grant jurisdiction to communities in the fields of cultural affairs, education, health, language policy, intercommunity cooperation, and international cooperation. Many of these areas, such as health, are the subject of shared jurisdiction with the federal government. The regions, however, are not explicitly granted legislative authority over certain areas of responsibility. Instead, these are defined in special legislation that requires a two-thirds majority vote by both the federal Chamber of Representatives and the Senate. The regions have assumed jurisdiction in areas such as economic policy, employment, transportation, public works, trade, agriculture, and energy. Since 1993 the federal government has formally enjoyed residual jurisdiction until its powers are more clearly delimited. The intergovernmental agreements discussed in detail below suggest that "the federal government is more decentralized at present and its fields of jurisdiction are diminishing for the benefit of the regions, not the communities" (Van der Stichele and Verdonck 2002, p. 40).

Germany

Federalism was not a new phenomenon in Germany after World War II, but it was solidified in the Basic Law of 1949.[3] It remained the structure of government after reunification with East Germany in 1990. The two main levels of government are the federal government (the *Bund*) and the (16) states (*Länder*).

The federal division of powers in Germany is set out in the Basic Law. The *Länder* exercise residual powers and are responsible for implementing and administering many federal laws. They also share jurisdiction with the *Bund* in several areas. In practice, the *Bund* "has widely eroded the legislative power of the states [*Länder*] and enacts the overwhelming majority of legislation today" (Larsen 1999, pp. 433–44). Germany does not have watertight compartments in its division of powers (Heun 1995).

An important institution in German fiscal federalism is the Council of State Governments (the *Bundesrat*), the upper house of the federal government. Specifically designed to represent the interests of the *Länder,* the *Bundesrat* is made up of members appointed (and recalled) by the *Land* governments. Each *Land* has a minimum of three and a maximum of six votes (depending on the size of its population), which must be voted as a block in the *Bundesrat;* the members of the *Bundesrat* do not act in their personal capacities but are agents of their *Land* government. While the *Bundesrat* is not as powerful as the *Bundestag,* the elected lower house, it does have "a suspensive veto over legislation generally and an absolute veto over all legislation affecting the vital interests of the *Länder*" (Kommers 1997, p. 97). It is well accepted that any law affecting the revenue of the *Länder* falls within the scope of an absolute veto and therefore requires the consent of the *Bundesrat.*

India

India has a system of government that is "basically federal, but with striking unitary features" (Vithal and Sastry 2001, p. 14). It comprises the union, 28 states, 7 union territories, and local governments. India's constitution defines the exclusive and concurrent powers of the states and the union. The union retains residual powers and may make any law imposing a tax not mentioned in the lists annexed to the Constitution. The exclusive powers of the union include defense, foreign affairs, banking, insurance, railways, currency, stock exchanges, and enumerated taxes. The exclusive powers of the states include health, unemployment, agriculture, and enumerated taxes. Concurrent areas of power include criminal law and procedure, forests, economic and social planning, competition law, and electricity, to name a few. The states determine the revenue that will be devolved to local governments through state finance commissions.

South Africa

The Constitution of South Africa, 1996 does not explicitly identify its system of government as federal.[4] Instead, it describes a government "constituted as national, provincial and local spheres of government which are distinctive, interdependent and interrelated" (Constitution of the Republic of South Africa). Schedule 4 of the Constitution sets out concurrent areas of responsibility of the national and provincial governments; Schedule 5 enumerates exclusive areas of provincial responsibility. The nine provinces are responsible for health, education, welfare, and roads. Nevertheless, the Constitutional Court of South Africa has ruled that the provinces enjoy limited autonomy and that they "are the recipients of power and not the source of power" (Constitutional Court of South Africa 1996, para. 14). Local governments, which have undergone consolidation, are responsible for urban infrastructure, including water, sanitation, traffic, and garbage collection. Municipal governments have the right to administer matters listed in Part B of Schedules 4 and 5.

Legal Basis of Intergovernmental Transfer System

The legal architecture of an intergovernmental transfer system may consist of constitutional law, federal statutes, regulations, ministerial decisions, and intergovernmental agreements. Every country relies on these legal instruments to varying degrees and in different ways. A given legal instrument may be mandatory (imposing a duty to transfer an "equitable share" of national revenue, as in South Africa, for example) or enabling (allowing grants to be made for "any public purpose," as in India, for example).

The extent to which each type of legal instrument is relied on has important implications for the legitimacy, transparency, political acceptance, justiciability, certainty, and flexibility of an intergovernmental transfer system. Designing an intergovernmental transfer system that will meet these short- and long-term objectives is a complex task, as each legal instrument offers its own advantages and disadvantages. A constitutional clause may help ensure legitimacy and certainty, for example, but it may be inflexible and lack political acceptance in the future. A unilateral ministerial decision may be flexible and politically expedient, but it may lack transparency and certainty.

Since no single legal instrument can optimize each of the objectives of an intergovernmental transfer system, most countries adopt a complex, interlocking set of legal instruments to suit the current and prospective needs of society. In addition to being economically and legally complex, these laws evolve over time, making them difficult to rationalize from a comparative perspective. Therefore, in considering the legal architecture of the intergovernmental transfer systems under review, emphasis is placed on their enduring and general qualities.

Belgium

The development of Belgium's intergovernmental fiscal transfer system is based on a series of political negotiations that have been codified in "special" federal legislation. This legislation requires a two-thirds majority in the federal legislature and a majority among each of the two linguistic groups in the federal parliament. The legislation is the culmination of negotiations and renegotiations among political actors. The first set of such laws came into existence in August 1980, when the regions received fiscal transfers based on three criteria of equal weight: population, personal income tax revenues, and territorial surface area. The communities were financed based on an approximate percentage of the population that was French and Flemish (Gérard 2001, pp. 12–13).

As new fields of jurisdiction were transferred to the regions and communities, special legislation was passed to provide appropriate levels of intergovernmental transfers. The Regionalization Law (August 8, 1988) established a federal transfer of 28 percent of income tax revenues to the regions. The Special Financing Act (1989) provided for a value added (VAT) and personal income tax transfer to the communities. Communities had complete financial autonomy in terms of the use of transferred funds, but they were unable to affect either the amounts or sources of these transfers (Van der Stichele and Verdonck 2002, p. 5).

This act was originally designed to function during a transitional phase between 1989 and 1999. However, after only four years, the French community faced serious difficulties in financing education. As a result, the Saint-Michel Agreement of 1993 was adopted, by a special law of July 16, 1993 (amending the Special Financing Act). Complementing this agreement, the Saint-Quentin Agreement of 1993 authorized the transfer of certain fields of its jurisdiction to the Commission Communautaire Française (in the Brussels region) and the Walloon region, without making sufficient transfers to cover the previous budgets of these areas of responsibility. This action was implemented through Decree II of the French-speaking community of July 19, 1993.[5] As the transitional phase came to a close, political negotiations encountered difficulties. It was not until May 23, 2000, that a new act was adopted, based on the Saint-Éloi Agreement of 1999, altering the allocation of the value added transfer between the communities.

A more permanent solution to the chronic community underfunding was the subject of the Saint-Polycarpe (or Lambermont) Agreement of January 2001, embodied in two pieces of special legislation passed July 13, 2001. The first regarded the refinancing of the communities and the broadening of the tax jurisdiction of the regions. The second concerned the transfer of various fields of jurisdiction to the regions and communities.

In contrast to the French- and Flemish-speaking communities, the German-speaking community relies largely on structural grants not connected to any tax base (OECD 2002). In practice, the transfers, which are unique to this community, are based on the number of German-speaking students (Van der Stichele and Verdonck 2002, p. 15).

The Belgian Constitution is vague regarding the existence of a federal spending power, but it has been "progressively gaining ground" (Commission sur le Déséquilibre Fiscal 2002). Generally speaking, "spending power" does not find a constitutional basis in Belgium, and federated entities may "in principle be freely assigned to their expenditures" (Van der Stichele and Verdonck 2002, p. 29). Braun (2003, p. 55) has gone as far as to state that "one can contend that in the Belgian system there is no unilateral action on the part of the federal government in fiscal policy making because the federal government is composed of regional actors."

The legal basis for intergovernmental transfers in Belgium relies less on constitutional law and more on ad hoc political negotiations that are then codified in special legislation at the national level. As practice has confirmed, this design feature has privileged flexibility over certainty.

Germany

The federal Constitutional Court of Germany has ruled that the fiscal provisions of the Basic Law are the cornerstone of German federalism (Macdonald 1996). These provisions are interlocked with several pieces of legislation. In 1949 and again in 1990, Germany was faced with vast regional disparity, which meant that "balanced regional development and uniformity of living conditions throughout the nation became attractive features for policy making and institution building" (Spahn 2001, p. 2).[6] While intergovernmental fiscal transfers have always been important in German federalism, they surged after major reforms in 1969 and again with reunification.

Chapter X of Germany's Basic Law sets out the complex intergovernmental transfer system. The *Bund* provides the *Länder* with funding when they implement and administer federal law, based on the principle of fair compensation, which promotes vertical fiscal balance. The *Bundestag*, which is composed of *Länder* appointees, maintains oversight over most federal laws dealing with intergovernmental finance in Germany.

Revenues from various taxes are allocated to the *Bund*, the *Länder*, or jointly. In determining the allocation of joint taxes (income taxes, corporation taxes, and VAT, which account for about 75 percent of tax revenue

[Larsen 1999]), the Basic Law provides that the *Bund* and *Länder* share revenues from income taxes and corporate taxes equally. Income tax allocated to the *Länder* is distributed among them based on the residence of the taxpayer (not the *Land* in which the taxpayer works). Corporate taxes are distributed based on a formula that deals with firms with operations in more than one *Länder*. The distribution of the VAT is more complex and involves indirect equalization.

The horizontal fiscal equalization system in Germany is made up of three constitutionally mandated elements, all of which require federal legislation to implement: VAT sharing, *Länder* financial adjustment, and federal auxiliary assignments. The Basic Law mandates a federal statute, requiring the approval of the *Bundesrat*, to determine how the VAT is to be divided between the *Bund* and *Länder* and among the *Länder*. This is guided by Article 106(3)(2) of the Basic Law, which requires that federal legislation comply with the principle that uniformity of living conditions in the federal territory be ensured.[7]

At least three-quarters of the VAT revenues transferred from the *Bund* to the *Länder* are distributed among the *Länder* based on their per capita share of national VAT revenues (Larsen 1999). The remaining quarter is distributed to *Länder* in which the per capita revenue from *Land* taxes, income taxes, and corporate taxes is below the national average of all the *Länder* combined. The federal Constitutional Court has criticized the distribution of the VAT in this fashion, since equalization can be achieved in a better and simpler manner through other mechanisms, discussed below (Larsen 1999).

Since the premise of German fiscal federalism is vertical balance, a system of direct horizontal transfers is required for any effective equalization scheme. The constitutional basis for direct equalization is set out in the Basic Law, which requires "that a reasonable equalization between financially strong and financially weak *Länder* is achieved." The *Bundesrat* must consent to the equalization formula.

This wording is given effect in the equalization law. The formula for the law is extremely complex. It includes four distinct processes: assessing the financial capacity of each *Land,* determining the demographics of each *Land*, applying an equalization index, and collecting contributions from *Länder* with surpluses and making contributions to *Länder* with deficits (Wilkins 2001).

This system has given rise to several constitutional showdowns between the *Bund* and certain *Länder* before the federal Constitutional Court. These cases demonstrate the significance of the constitutionalization of principles and mechanisms of intergovernmental fiscal transfers when combined with a strong adjudicative body.

In the Finance Equalization Case I (1952), the federal Constitutional Court ruled that horizontal financial adjustments from an economically stronger *Land* in favor of a poorer *Land* was consistent with the Basic Law but that this would not be the case "if it would weaken the [financial] capacity of the contributing states or lead to a financial leveling of the states" (cited in Kommers 1997, p. 91). The Court relied on Article 109 of the Basic Law, which states that the *Länder* are "autonomous and independent of each other with regard to their respective budgets," but it tempered its judgment based on the language of solidarity, holding that "the states have duties as well as rights. . . . [Strong states are] to assist, within limits, the financially poorer states"(cited in Kommers 1997, p. 91).

In the Finance Equalization Case II (1986), the Court invalidated various parts of the equalization law for "excessive leveling" and for miscalculating the economic strength of the *Länder* (Currie 1994). In particular, it found that the law violated Article 107(2) of the Basic Law, which requires that financial equalization be "reasonable." By way of a remedy, the Court instructed the legislature to change the basis for allocating tax revenues among the *Länder* by 1998 (Kommers 1997).

In 1999 Bavaria, Baden-Württemberg, and Hesse challenged the equalization law before the federal Constitutional Court. They argued that horizontal equalization transfers had become excessive and that better incentives for economic performance were needed. The Court recognized the need for a "degree of competition among the individual states as secured by the federal principle [that is also] innovation-fostering" (Spahn 2001, p. 15). It not only required revision of the existing equalization law, it also mandated that it be based on a new law on general standards. This law would have quasi-constitutional status and "define in an abstract and general way the objectives of adjustments as well as the factors underlying an adjustment in vertical and horizontal equalization on the basis of the regulations laid down in the constitution" (Beierl 2001, p. 8). It appears that the new law restricts transfers to neutral assessments and excludes pork barreling.

The 1999 federal Constitutional Court ruling on the equalization law found that equalization of the *Länder* at 95 percent of the national average is sufficient to conform to the Basic Law. The new equalization legislation, which decreases contributions by some *Länder,* provides for corresponding increases in supplementary grants by the *Bund*.

Supplementary grants from the *Bund* in favor of certain *Länder* are a third aspect of equalization transfers in Germany (vertical asymmetric transfers). Article 107(2) of the Basic Law permits these intergovernmental transfers to be made through a federal statute. Based on this nonmandatory language, it is not surprising that these supplementary grants were insignificant in the early years of German federalism. Only after reunification have they come to play an important role in the intergovernmental transfer regime. Solidarity Pact I and Solidarity Pact II, discussed below in the section on conditional and unconditional transfers, are the most notable forms of supplementary grants.

The federal Constitutional Court has upheld the asymmetric nature of supplementary grants. However, based on the doctrine of federal equal treatment, similarly situated *Länder* are entitled to receive the same supplementary grants according to their financial need.

Applying this doctrine in the Finance Equalization Case III (1992), the federal Constitutional Court rejected the claim of Hamburg that it was entitled to receive a grant given to Bremen and Saarland, on the grounds that Hamburg was not as heavily indebted as they were. The Court found that "Bremen had been the victim of constitutional discrimination because the city[-state] had received no transfer payments for several years and later received less financial aid than Saarland, even though Bremen had substantially higher debts than Saarland. Finally, the court ruled that the federal government's vertical payments to Bremen and Saarland had been too low in view of the serious budgetary problems of both states" (Kommers 1997, p. 91). The remedy was for the *Bund* and other *Länder* to provide additional financial assistance to both Bremen and Saarland.

The federal Constitutional Court has also held that there is a direct relationship between the level of equalization achieved through the equalization law and supplementary grants. According to the Court, "the lower the financial equalization law sets the equalization level for the horizontal equalization, the more the providing of general supplemental grants becomes a virtual duty of the Federation" (Larsen 1999, p. 459).

Germany does not have unrestrained spending power, because the *Länder* have a direct voice in authorizing federal spending in their areas of jurisdiction through the *Bundesrat*. This rule was applied by the federal Constitutional Court in 1976, when it invalidated a federal program that directly gave funds to local governments for, inter alia, the construction of waste disposal facilities, on the grounds that it infringed *Länder* autonomy because the *Länder* had not given their formal agreement to the program and the *Bundesrat* had not approved it.

The legal basis for intergovernmental transfers in Germany is archetypically constitutional in nature. The shortcomings of such heavy reliance on constitutional provisions, such as inflexibility, have been felt, but these provisions have simply been the subject of more-frequent amendment than other constitutional articles.

India

India's system of intergovernmental transfers is a "complicated mix of constitutional assignments, institutional precedents, discretion and negotiation" (Rao and Singh 2000, p. 2).[8] The Constitution "recognizes that the assignment of tax powers creates vertical imbalances and provides principles for the sharing of resources between the center and states" (Purfield 2004, p. 27). An additional underlying consideration of the framers was that horizontal imbalances would need to be addressed "for an even and equitable development of all regions of the country" (Vithal and Sastry 2001, p. 24). To accomplish these goals, the Constitution includes mandatory and enabling provisions for intergovernmental transfers.

India's intergovernmental transfer system is best understood when deconstructed into the three main federal institutions that constitute it: the Finance Commission (central tax revenue distribution and grants), the Planning Commission (grants and loans for development), and various central ministries (shared cost programs). The notion of a neutral and expert advisory commission to deal with intergovernmental transfers was based on the early success of the Commonwealth Grants Commission, created in 1933 for Australia. In 1949 the Constitution of India established a finance commission to make recommendations to the president, which are placed before Parliament, on the distribution of net tax revenues to be divided between the union and the states as well as on the allocation among the states; to establish principles to govern the grants-in-aid to states from the consolidated fund; to set up measures to augment the needs of local governments, as recommended by state finance commissions; and to handle other matters of finance referred by the president. These recommendations are usually accepted by the central government.[9]

The Constitution of India requires the president to appoint a finance commission every five years, or earlier as necessary.[10] The Finance Commission (Miscellaneous Provisions) Act, 1951 specifies the qualifications and manner of selection of members of the Finance Commission as well as their powers. Section 3 of the act requires the chairman to have "experience in public affairs"; the other four members of the Finance Commission must meet more-specific criteria. The presence of a judicial member on the Finance Commission is "supposed to give it an independent, semi-judicial status" (Rao and Singh 2000, p. 90). This is buttressed by Section 8(1) of the act, under which the Finance Commission is given all the powers of a civil court. Individual members of a given Finance Commission are able to append a "Minute of Dissent or Minute expressing an individual member's thoughts on the subject under review" (Vithal and Sastry 2001, p. 91).

The 80th Amendment to the Constitution (2000) fundamentally altered the union tax revenues subject to distribution among the states. Before this amendment, only specific taxes were subject to intergovernmental transfer. The new distribution of tax revenues is believed to provide greater certainty and stability of state revenue and increased flexibility in tax reform. Article 270 of the Constitution provides that all taxes and duties of the union (with a few minor exceptions) shall be distributed between the union and the states based on a percentage recommended by the Finance Commission and prescribed by the president.[11] Each Finance Commission will review the percentage of net union tax revenue (tax proceeds less the cost of collection) to be distributed to the states and between them. From 1996 to 2000, 29 percent of gross union tax revenue proceeds were transferred to the states.

Under Article 275 of the Constitution, the Finance Commission also makes recommendations for grants-in-aid to be made from the union to specific states that are "in need of assistance." These grants can be adopted only on the recommendation of the Finance Commission (Vithal and Sastry 2001). These are typically gap-filling transfers based on projected shortfalls between a state's revenues (after the above transfers are made) and its non–development plan expenditures.[12]

The Planning Commission is a political body, established by an executive order of the central government in March 1950. It has a smaller but increasingly important role in recommending a combination of grants and loans from central ministry programs to states for their development plans. Transfers made on the recommendation of the Planning Commission are nonstatutory transfers.

The constitutional basis of Planning Commission transfers is said to be Article 282 of the Constitution, which provides that "the Union or a state may make any grants for any public purpose." Grants under this article are controversial for two reasons. First, they circumvent the oversight of the Finance Commission. Second, they were originally intended for emergencies such as natural disasters or famine but have been used much more broadly (Sury 1999). As a result, some Indian constitutional experts question the legitimacy and constitutionality of these grants (Rao and Singh 2000).

The Planning Commission provides some indirect equalization. With some modifications, the prevailing approach has been the "Gadgil formula," under which the ratio of grants to loans provided to a state depends on whether it is classified as being in financial need. The formula was created by consensus of the National Development Council, an informal intergovernmental body established in 1952 that is chaired by the prime minister and includes members of the Planning Commission, central government cabinet ministers, and state chief ministers.

Central government ministries in India make fiscal transfers that states are required to match (to various degrees, depending on the project) to implement policies of the center. These programs are recommended by the Planning Commission. Since the programs usually concern powers vested in the states, they can be seen as a manifestation of a spending power. Patil (1995) suggests that in some state areas of responsibility, spending by the center may even outstrip state spending. States have also complained of heightened spending by the center in concurrent areas of responsibility.

A mélange of legal instruments serve as the legal basis for intergovernmental transfers in India. This has resulted in some uncertainty and concerns over the legitimacy of some transfers, including Planning Commission grants, which have been without a strong basis in constitutional law or statute.

South Africa

With the end of apartheid, South Africa faced the "special challenge of redressing enormous disparities—both political and economic—among jurisdictions that had long been subject to strict racial segregation and very different types and levels of public services and revenues" (Smoke 2001, p. 15). As a result, intergovernmental transfers took on an important role in this period. One of the founding constitutional principles applied by the Constitutional Court in certifying the 1996 Constitution was whether it made "adequate provision for fiscal and financial allocations to the provincial and local levels of government from revenue collected nationally" (Certification Case, Constitutional Court of South Africa, para. 45(k)).

Chapter 13 of the Constitution deals with intergovernmental fiscal transfers. Section 227(1)(a) enshrines the principle that provincial and local governments are "entitled to an equitable share of revenue raised nationally to enable it to provide basic services and perform the functions allocated to it." This fiscal transfer is to take place "promptly and without deduction." Section 214(1) mandates that an act of Parliament must provide for the system of intergovernmental transfers, including:

■ The equitable division of revenue raised nationally by the national, provincial, and local spheres of government.

- The determination of each province's equitable share of the provincial share of that revenue.
- Any other allocations to provinces, local governments, or municipalities from the national government's share of that revenue and any conditions on which those allocations may be made.

The Constitutional Court has stated that there are both "substantive and procedural safeguards in determining the actual amount of the equitable share" (Certification Case, Constitutional Court of South Africa). Procedurally, provincial and organized local governments must be consulted and the recommendations of the Financial and Fiscal Commission considered before this "equitable share" law may be adopted. The Constitution requires that the following factors be taken into account:

- The national interest.
- Any provision that must be made in respect of the national debt or other national obligations.
- The needs and interests of the national government, determined by objective criteria.
- The need to ensure that the provinces and municipalities are able to provide basic services and perform the functions allocated to them.
- The fiscal capacity and efficiency of the provinces and municipalities.
- Developmental and other needs of provinces, local governments, and municipalities.
- Economic disparities within and among the provinces.
- The obligations of the provinces and municipalities in terms of national legislation.
- The desirability of stable and predictable allocations of revenue shares.
- The need for flexibility in responding to emergencies or other temporary needs.
- Other factors based on similar objective criteria.

Since 1998 the framework legislation giving effect to these constitutional provisions has been the Intergovernmental Fiscal Relations Act, 1997. Section 10 of this act states that a division of revenue bill must be adopted annually to specify the "equitable share" transfer to be made. The Financial and Fiscal Commission makes recommendations to Parliament on each such bill.

The Division of Revenue Act, 2004 provides a typical example of the straightforward nature of these annual statutory allocations. Schedule 1 identifies the monetary amount of revenue that is divided among the three levels of government for the year. Schedule 2 divides the provincial share among the nine provinces; Schedule 3 does the same for municipal governments. Schedule 4 provides for general nationally assigned functional transfers to the provinces. Schedule 5 identifies specific conditional grants, and Schedule 6 identifies recurrent conditional grants.

The Financial and Fiscal Commission is a permanent expert commission that plays a major advisory role in South Africa's intergovernmental fiscal transfer system, with primarily "consultative and investigative powers but not lawmaking or enforcement powers" (Motala and Ramaphosa 2002, p. 97). Sections 220–222 of the Constitution created the Financial and Fiscal Commission, tasked with making independent and impartial recommendations pertaining to fiscal matters. The Financial and Fiscal Commission Act, 1997 provides a more thorough elaboration of the functions and procedures of the commission. A constitutional amendment and the Financial and Fiscal Commission Amendment Act, 2003 reduced the membership of the commission from 22 to 9 members, effective January 2004.

Before 1998 South Africa's national government made direct expenditures on health, social services, and roads—all areas of provincial responsibility. Since 1998 a new system of largely unconditional transfer has become the rule, diminishing federal spending power (Bahl 2001).

Given the relatively recent adoption of South Africa's Constitution and passage of the Intergovernmental Fiscal Relations Act, it remains to be seen whether the legal basis for intergovernmental transfers will serve South Africa well in the long run. But the relatively straightforward architecture of constitutional provisions that mandate an annual statute, based on input from an expert commission, holds much promise.

Procedures for Establishing and Modifying Intergovernmental Transfers

Two main approaches to establishing and modifying intergovernmental fiscal transfers prevail in the countries examined here. The first, and more straightforward approach, is negotiation between the federal government and subunits in which final agreement is subject to subunit consent (most often in the upper house of the federal government). This approach is used in developed countries, such as Belgium and Germany. The second, and more complex approach, is consultation of the subunits combined with the involvement of a specialized, independent commission that makes recommendations on the operation of the intergovernmental transfer system. This approach is used in developing countries, such as India and South Africa.

Belgium

Belgium's intergovernmental transfer system relies on special legislation that includes the requirement that the French and Flemish communities consent. Since this effectively gives these communities veto power, negotiation and consensus building is a necessary part of any initiative to create or modify the intergovernmental transfer system. The existing order can be overturned rapidly to reflect political or economic exigencies. The Saint-Polycarpe (or Lambermont) Agreement of January 2001, for example, enhanced the fiscal autonomy of the regions and assisted communities by increasing federal transfers after the French community's education program faced financial difficulties.

Another player in Belgium's fiscal landscape is the Conseil Supérier des Finances, which is made up of 12 members, with an equal number of French- and Flemish-speaking members and equal representation from federal and subunit governments. The Conseil Supérier des Finances makes annual recommendations on the financial requirements of the federal and subunit governments. Its recommendations have strong moral force and to date have been largely followed.

Germany

An intergovernmental committee and the *Bundesrat* establish and modify Germany's intergovernmental transfer system, within the confines of the relevant constitutional provisions. Simply put, "all federal financial legislation that allocates revenue that accrues to the states requires *Bundesrat* consent" (Larsen 1999, p. 433). Therefore, the intergovernmental transfer system can be modified only with the consent of the *Länder*. These negotiations include incentives for the *Länder* to "team up" against the *Bund*, casting aside political party affiliations in the interest of obtaining the best share for the *Länder* possible. The *Bund* may use asymmetric supplementary grants to try to break this coalition (Beierl 2001).

The *Länder* have legal standing to challenge intergovernmental fiscal transfer legislation before the federal Constitutional Court, which has played an activist role in setting the legislative agenda. The Court has held that the Basic Law creates entitlements for financially distressed *Länder* to claim financial assistance from the *Bund*. In one case, the Court agreed that Bremen and Saarland were entitled to financial assistance but did not prescribe a specific remedy, instead suggesting options, including additional transfer payments to the poor *Länder* or even a redrawing of the territory to create economically sustainable subunits. The *Bund* opted to make DM3.4 billion in additional transfers to the two *Länder* through an amendment to the equalization law.

India

The central government maintains wide discretion in creating and modifying India's system of intergovernmental transfers. While the recommendation of the Finance Commission must be sought on such changes, the Commission does not include members nominated by the states and its recommendations are not binding. With respect to Planning Commission transfers, the states play an influential consultative role, through the National Development Council, an intergovernmental body chaired by the prime minister that includes members of the Planning Council, center cabinet ministers, and state chief ministers.

South Africa

South Africa's Constitution allows the "equitable share" intergovernmental transfer to be "calculated based on cabinet judgments" (Bahl 2001, p. 28). But it requires that provincial and organized local governments be consulted. In practice, this involves a "complex bargaining process between distinct layers of government to determine the total amount of centrally provided unconditional transfers" (Brosio 2000, p. 25). Fiscal transfers to local governments in South Africa are generally based on annual decisions of the central government, although some involve multiyear commitments.

Unlike in India, provincial nominees are appointed to the Financial and Fiscal Commission in South Africa. However, despite the ability of the provinces and local governments to nominate certain members, the Constitutional Court has cautioned that "the Commission is hardly a vehicle for the exercise of power by individual provinces" (Certification Case, Constitutional Court of South Africa).

The provinces have a formal consultative role in intergovernmental fiscal transfers in South Africa through the Budget Council, an intergovernmental political body with a general consultative mandate concerning fiscal and financial matters. A representative of the Financial and Fiscal Commission attends the Budget Council's meetings, which take place at least twice a year. The Local Government Budget Forum is a similar body for municipal government issues. It is through these bodies that consultation of the provinces and local government is achieved each year before passage of the division of revenue bill.

The nature of provincial consultation has been clarified by the Constitutional Court based on the fact that the "equitable share" of a South African province is a "direct charge" from the National Revenue Fund. The Court has considered the importance of this terminology and concluded that it does not contemplate a money bill but "necessitates additional and direct consultation with provincial interests rather than a mere indirect engagement through the second House."[13] The Constitution of the Republic of South Africa Second Amendment Act, 2001 made it explicit that a money bill does not include equitable share transfers under Section 214 of the Constitution, affirming the consultative role of the provinces in modifying the system of intergovernmental transfers.

Conditional and Unconditional Transfers

Most intergovernmental transfer systems include a mix of conditional and unconditional transfers. The legal basis for these transfers and the consequences of violating the conditions may be clear and explicit or ambiguous. In most countries, conditional grants are controversial but continue to be relied on.

Conditional transfers are rare in Belgium's system of intergovernmental transfers and have been criticized as having a weak constitutional basis. In Germany unconditional grants are generally the rule, with the notable exception of some supplementary grants and shared-cost programs. The trend in India has been toward increased use of conditional transfers to the states in a vast array of centrally designed programs, including shared-cost programs. South Africa relies on unconditional and conditional fiscal transfers, both of which have an explicit constitutional basis.

Belgium

Conditional transfers are an exception to the norm in Belgium that federated entities maintain fiscal discretion to manage their own resources. Conditional transfers have been made, however, for measures for developing the international role of Brussels and for regional programs to help the unemployed find work. A nominal conditional transfer to communities also exists for employment programs and programs for foreign students. Conditional transfers have been characterized as being "on the borderline of the Constitution" in Belgium (Commission sur le Déséquilibre Fiscal 2002, p. 41).

Germany

Federal authorities in Germany must essentially convince a majority of the *Länder* in the *Bundesrat* in order to make conditional transfers, and such transfers have been criticized by the federal Constitutional Court. This has meant that intergovernmental transfers are generally unconditional, notwithstanding important exceptions that involve supplementary grants and shared-cost programs (see Bird and Tarasov 2002). In a 1975 case, the federal Constitutional Court held that providing grants for urban renewal "creates the risk that the *Länder* may become dependent upon the Federation and thus endangers their constitutionally guaranteed autonomy . . . [Therefore federal grants] remain the exception, and they must be so structured as not to become the means of influencing decisions of the constituent states in fulfilling their own responsibilities" (cited in Currie 1994, p. 58). On the facts of the case, the transfer was allowed, since it preserved the autonomy of the *Länder* by allowing them to determine where and how to spend the funds and was expected to significantly enhance economic growth.

The conditionality of supplementary grants is more complex. Generally speaking, "because they are meant to cover general financial need, the supplementary grants may not be in the form of grants tied to particular projects or tasks" (Larsen 1999, n. 51). An exception appears to relate to the previous system of supplementary grants to the new *Länder*. Solidarity Pact I consisted of an unconditional fiscal transfer (two-thirds) and a conditional fiscal transfer (one-third) for specific investments under the Investment Promotion Law Recovery East. Under Solidarity Pact II the grant is no longer conditional in any way, but annual reports to the intergovernmental Financial Planning Council are required on the use of funds.

India

Both the Finance Commission and the Planning Commission make general-purpose transfers to the states to use at their discretion. However, since the First Finance Commission, conditional grants have been considered permissible under Article 275 of the Constitution, and these grants have recently grown in importance in Indian fiscal federalism.[14] In some cases, "poorer states are unable to provide counterpart funds and are unable to receive even the allocations made to them" (Rao n.d., p. 19).

Historically, conditional grants-in-aid that were recommended by the Finance Commission were not scrutinized to determine whether their conditions were satisfied. Since the Seventh Finance Commission, however, the terms of reference have often sought recommendations on "the manner in which such expenditure could be monitored" (Vithal and Sastry 2001, p. 156).

Planning Commission grants may be awarded based on certain conditions, but the Constitution "does not provide principles governing such grants" (Patil 1995, p. 59). The Planning Commission also monitors specific earmarked grants for central sponsored schemes. These central ministry programs may include conditions related to staffing, infrastructure, and implementation, with quarterly disbursements to promote compliance.

South Africa

The Constitution of South Africa expressly authorizes the provincial and local government to "receive other allocations from national government revenue, either conditionally or unconditionally." Until 1998 fiscal transfers to local governments in South Africa were a combination of general and conditional transfers. It was widely held that this meant that "each province was thus then at the mercy of the central government" (Brosio 2000, p. 27). A major policy shift took place in 1998 to a formula-based system of largely unconditional intergovernmental transfers, known as the equitable shares program (Bahl 2001).[15] The total transfer is itself unconditional.

There has been a "differential capacity and willingness of provinces to supplement conditional grant funding with their unconditional equitable share funds" (Submissions to Parliament 2004/05). This and other reasons have led the Financial and Fiscal Commission to recommend "a negotiated relationship between transferring and recipient authorities in respect of conditional grants and a restraint on the use of conditional grants" (Submissions to Parliament 2004/05).

The legal framework for conditional grants in South Africa is further defined in the Division of Revenue Act. The act "assigns the role of compliance monitoring to transferring national departments, but the monitoring capacity of some of the departments is weak" (Financial and Fiscal Commission 2004). Where a province or municipal government does not comply with the conditions of a fiscal transfer, the transferring entity (national or provincial spheres) may delay, in full or in part, the payment of the allocations, after consulting with the national treasury and relevant provincial treasuries. If there is a "serious and persistent material breach" of the conditions, the transfer may be withheld by a decision of the national treasury (Financial and Fiscal Commission 2004).

Dispute Resolution and Adjudication

Disputes over intergovernmental fiscal transfers are resolved through a combination of mechanisms and proceedings, including constitutional principles, ad hoc political negotiations, mediation/conciliation at intergovernmental forums, administrative proceedings, and litigation, including constitutional adjudication. While most countries examined in this chapter initially rely on political negotiations between the governments in disputes, a range of possibilities exist.

In Belgium the federal loyalty principle places emphasis on political negotiations or mediation/conciliation. A recent trend has been for certain disputes over intergovernmental fiscal transfers to escalate to administrative proceedings before the Cour d'Arbitrage and ultimately the Conseil d'État.

While the existence of a federal loyalty principle in Germany's constitution has encouraged mediation, constitutional litigation has played a significant role in disputes over the intergovernmental transfer system. The federal Constitutional Court has developed important jurisprudence in this field that has been the basis for successful challenges to the equalization law.

The dispute resolution process governing India's intergovernmental fiscal transfers is not discussed in any detail in the literature reviewed. This is likely due to the high degree of federal discretion involved in the system of grants and the lack of a substantial provincial role in their creation or modification.

In South Africa the constitutional principle of cooperation places a strong emphasis on extrajudicial dispute resolution to resolve conflicts over intergovernmental fiscal transfers, including resort to mediation. Disputes over conditional grants are determined initially by a unilateral decision of the transferring entity and more permanently by a decision of the national treasury. While the Constitutional Court has not been very active in adjudicating specific disputes over intergovernmental transfers, it has made important pronouncements that provide a basis for such claims.

Constitutional Principles

The constitutions of several of the countries examined enshrine principles related to the emergence of conflict between levels of government. These principles serve as a starting point in these countries when disputes concerning intergovernmental transfers arise.

Belgium and Germany recognize the federal loyalty principle, or doctrine of federal comity (*Bundesrüe*). This doctrine essentially mandates the mutual respect and cooperation of subunits and the federal government such that they "act in such a way as to avoid all conflict of interest among themselves, the objective being to ensure that the various institutions function as a balanced whole" (OECD 1997, p. 27). In Germany the federal Constitutional Court has held that the *Bundesrüe* is an important constitutional principle with respect to fiscal equalization.

Section 41 of the Constitution of South Africa enshrines a similar principle of cooperation in intergovernmental relations, mandating an act of Parliament to "establish or provide for structures and institutions to promote and facilitate intergovernmental relations ... and provide for appropriate mechanisms and procedures to facilitate settlement of intergovernmental disputes." The South African Division of Revenue Act, 2004 has as one of its purposes "to ensure that legal proceedings between organs of state [sic] in the three spheres of government are avoided as far as is possible."

Ad Hoc Political Negotiations

In most countries ad hoc political negotiations are the first avenue for resolving a dispute over intergovernmental fiscal transfers. Belgium's system has been described as based on compulsory negotiation, which includes the dispute resolution role of the Senate and fiscal coordination through the Conseil Supérier des Finances (Braun 2003). Despite the existence of these formal mechanisms of conflict resolution, "most coordination or conflict resolution takes place within or between political parties" (Braun 2003, p. 43).

In South Africa, Section 31(1) of the Division of Revenue Act, 2004 provides that litigation is the absolute last resort in resolving any intergovernmental fiscal dispute between state organs, after negotiated settlement and the procedures in the Intergovernmental Fiscal Relations Act have been exhausted. In theory, these procedures could include referral of the dispute to the Budget Council, a statutory intergovernmental body with consultative powers. Individuals responsible for prematurely resorting to litigation risk liability for costs.

In Germany the Conference of the Finance Ministers of the *Länder*, composed of the *Land* ministers of finance, negotiates common positions of the *Länder* governments on fiscal matters with the *Bund*. Party affiliations, however, play an important role in this process.

Mediation/Conciliation

Mediation/conciliation is an important step that is taken when ad hoc political negotiations fail to reach a compromise. Belgium's Coordination Committee is an intergovernmental political body to which the federated entities or federal government may refer a dispute to be resolved on the basis of consensus. In Germany conflicts surrounding intergovernmental fiscal transfers often involve the Mediation Committee of the *Bundesrat*, considered part of a "compulsory negotiation system." In South Africa the Mediation Committee deals with bills related to the functions of the Financial and Fiscal Commission as well as bills affecting the finances of provincial governments. Where mediation fails to resolve a dispute, the National Assembly may still pass the bill if it can muster a two-thirds majority.

Administrative Proceedings

In Belgium the Cour d'Arbitrage "is empowered to settle jurisdictional disputes between the federal government, the Communities and the Regions stemming from legislative measures" (Commission sur le Déséquilibre Fiscal 2001, p. 33). However, it is not considered to be part of the judiciary. The chair of the Court alternates each year between a native French speaker and a native Flemish speaker. The Cour d'Arbitrage has been asked to intervene to enforce the legislative provisions of the intergovernmental transfer system in Belgium.

The Conseil d'État has administrative jurisdiction to review legislation to ensure that authorities do not exceed their powers. It held that it was by no means clear that the Cour d'Arbitrage would be able to apply a purported jurisdictional limit on regional taxation autonomy included in the Sainte-Thérése agreement.

In South Africa the Division of Revenue Act calls for an administrative process when a conflict arises over the conditions of a conditional fiscal transfer. The first stage is a unilateral decision of the transferring entity (national or provincial government), after consulting with the national treasury and relevant provincial treasuries. The second stage involves a decision of the national treasury.

Judicial Review and Adjudication

Constitutional adjudication of disputes over intergovernmental fiscal transfers is most developed in Germany, where multiple cases on the matter have been decided since 1952. The federal Constitutional Court has jurisdiction to interpret the Basic Law and to adjudicate disputes between the *Bund* and the *Länder* and among the *Länder*. Half of the judges of the Court are elected by the *Bundesrat* and half are elected by the *Bundestag*. Wealthier *Länder* have launched several constitutional challenges to the equalization law, based in large part on the constitutional prohibition against leveling, which was developed by the Court. Based on this doctrine, "financial equalization may not reduce the wealthier states' per capita tax income level all the way down to that of the poorer states" (Larsen 1999, p. 446).

The Constitutional Court of South Africa has not been as involved in adjudicating disputes as the federal Constitutional Court in Germany. However, in the Certification of the Constitution of the Republic of South Africa, 1996, it made important pronouncements in describing the constitutional principles related to the system of intergovernmental transfers that may provide a basis for future constitutional litigation.

Conclusions

Of the range of factors involved in making an intergovernmental transfer system work, its legal architecture is but one. Political, economic, social, geographic, and other influences contribute substantially to the success or failure of aspects of each of the regimes described in this chapter.

This chapter focused on the practical benefits and shortcomings of these systems that are connected to their legal frameworks. From this assessment, some preliminary lessons can be drawn.

Belgium

Federal transfers are a vital aspect of fiscal federalism in Belgium. An eight-country study by Bird and Tarasov (2002) finds that Belgium has had a consistently high vertical fiscal imbalance, demonstrating the importance of intergovernmental transfers in financing regional expenditures.

The ability of special legislation to accommodate innovative economic design concepts for intergovernmental transfers demonstrates its main strength: its flexibility. Despite the difficulties faced during periods of political renegotiation, the use of special legislation rather than regular legislation or fully entrenched constitutional rules appears to have provided the best compromise in Belgium's unique form of federalism. During the negotiations over the so-called "permanent phase" of the intergovernmental transfer system in Belgium, "tension between the federal government and the communities overall was palpable. No entity wanted to renegotiate the matter each year. However, the establishment of a fixed criterion risked proving unfavorable to one level of government or the other" (Van der Stichele and Verdonck 2002, p. 14). Special legislation has demonstrated itself flexible enough to accommodate midterm entrenchment of a political compromise in a way that annual arrangements and long-term constitutional provisions do not.

In contrast, the political renegotiation process in Belgium has been criticized as favoring the subunits at the expense of the federal government and taxpayers generally. The creation of political agreements, followed by special legislation, has been the subject of judicial scrutiny in Belgium, to the extent that these agreements present difficulties in adjudication.

Germany

Germany has had a consistently low vertical fiscal imbalance, indicating that intergovernmental transfers are less important in financing regional expenditures there than in some other countries (Bird and Tarasov 2002). Even *Länder* that criticize the intergovernmental transfer system in Germany, such as Bavaria, recognize the benefits of having constitutional authorization and principles for these transfers. With respect to vertical transfers, this prevents transfers from becoming "subject to the free interplay of political forces" (Beierl 2001, p. 3). The federal Constitutional Court has interpreted the constitutional provisions in a way that has "shaped the political process within certain parameters" (Heun 1995, p. 182).

While it has faced challenges and tensions, the legal architecture of Germany's system of intergovernmental transfers has proven to be a remarkably versatile and stable vehicle through which the social consensus of the country has manifested itself. Its constitutional framework, with principles governing fiscal transfers; implementing laws, which require subunit consent; and a neutral process for adjudicating disputes represent a powerful combination.

Shah (2004, p. 11) applauds Germany's fiscal capacity equalization scheme to address regional fiscal disparities as an example of better practice. In contrast, Spahn (2001, p. 11) argues that the intergovernmental transfer system in Germany "has clearly been pushed beyond limits," particularly with respect to postunification interregional equalization. He illustrates the enormity of these equalization transfers by noting that they amount to "more than twice the official development aid of all industrialized countries to all developing countries in the world" (Spahn 2001, p. 13). Germany's equalization transfers have been criticized for "discouraging entrepreneurial spirit, and by inducing moral hazard" (Spahn 2001, p. 13); limiting the flexibility and responsiveness of the *Länder*; and reducing accountability of politicians.

Not surprisingly, the power of the *Bundestag* (made up of representatives appointed by the *Länder*) to approve the federal statute that governs vertical fiscal transfers (such as the VAT) has led to progressive increases in the percentage allotted to the *Länder* at the expense of the *Bund*; a similar phenomenon occurred in Belgium. The complexity and lack of transparency in Germany's intergovernmental fiscal transfer regime are also problems in and of themselves.

India

Serious concerns have been raised about the effectiveness of the intergovernmental transfer system in India, and studies have linked some of these problems to the way in which its legal architecture has evolved. The involvement of several agencies in the intergovernmental transfer system has been criticized as inefficient and wasteful.

In a leading study of Indian fiscal federalism, Rao and Singh (2000, p. 2) find "some evidence to support the hypothesis that states with greater political and economic influence or importance receive higher per capita transfers." This has been facilitated by a reduction in the percentage of fiscal transfers determined based on objective factors in favor of increased discretion. Khemani (2003) confirms that political bodies without constitutional authority, such as the Planning Commission, have a tendency to award funds based on political considerations (such as party affiliation of the state government and the number of seats from a given state in the central government's ruling party or coalition). With respect to central ministry grants, Khemani (2003, p. 5) finds that "national politicians indeed pursue disaggregated targeting of individual districts to serve particular political objectives." Constitutional rules that determine intergovernmental transfers, it is concluded, do indeed make a difference.

Indian fiscal federalism has also been criticized on the grounds that the multiple central government agencies that are involved lack coordination. Rao (n.d.) recommends that the Finance Commission focus on fiscal transfers while the Planning Commission focuses on loans for infrastructure projects. The criticism of the central ministry schemes, of which there are now more than 250, is that they are highly susceptible to political manipulation. Not surprisingly, an investigative report commissioned by the National Development Committee recommended that these grants be scaled down. Shah (2004, p. 6) has gone so far as to label these as "pork barrel transfers or political bribes." He also criticizes India's transfers to address regional fiscal disparities as a practice to avoid, given that it involves general revenue sharing based on multiple factors. At the municipal level, the result has been that "as state governments themselves are faced with several resource constraints, the local bodies are unable to deliver the required standards of public services" (Rao n.d., p. 6).[16]

States also appear to have suffered from federal control over intergovernmental fiscal transfers—the opposite of the pattern seen in Germany and Belgium. The result is that the average state deficit in India increased from 3 percent of GDP in the 1980s to 4.4 percent in the 1990s. The relationship between state fiscal transfers and indebtedness is particularly troubling. On the one hand, fiscal transfers increase borrowing capacity. On the other hand, borrowing increases dependence on the fiscal transfers. Rao (n.d.) concludes that the state indebtedness that has resulted from this situation is unsustainable for both those states that receive extra assistance from the Planning Commission and those that do not. Khemani (2002) casts some doubt on this conclusion.

Purfield (2004, p. 4) concludes that the financial decline of Indian states is the result of the institutions of fiscal federalism, which promote "transfer dependence, common-revenue pools, moral hazard, and soft budget constraints." State responsibilities are not met by their revenue-generating capacity, so that transfers account for some 40 percent of state revenues. Purfield also claims that the Tenth and Eleventh Finance Commissions actually increased the financial disparity between states.

Conflict between the Finance Commission and the Planning Commission has also arisen. Rao and Singh (2000) charge this has led to numerous problems, including a decrease in equalization, poor coordination, and incentives for states to offer different projections to the two commissions. The five-year tenure of the Finance Commission has also been criticized as denying the body the institutional memory necessary to fulfill its functions.

South Africa

South Africa has one of the highest fiscal imbalances in the world, at least with respect to provinces. Provincial governments are highly dependent on their unconditional equitable share transfers, with such funds constituting 87 percent of provincial budgets on average between 1999 and 2004. The opposite is true in municipalities, transfers to which have been growing faster than the national equitable share. Provincial deficits are projected to reemerge as a result of higher social security costs in the coming years.

Shah (2004) has criticized South Africa's transfers to address regional fiscal disparities, because they involve general revenue sharing based on multiple factors. Smoke (2001) also argues the need to improve the transfer system, given the vertical fiscal imbalance and prevalence of conditional transfers. Since the provinces do not have any independent sources of revenue, they must rely entirely on central grants (Brosio 2000).

Common Findings

Some lessons can be drawn from this analysis. First, some important conclusions can be drawn about the general legal framework of intergovernmental fiscal transfers. The transfers should be objectively and transparently determined, usually based on a recognized formula that is not the subject of ongoing political negotiations. These arrangements should be established by the central government, an expert commission, or an intergovernmental committee (World Bank 2001).

Second, the menu of procedures available for adopting and modifying intergovernmental fiscal transfers involves tradeoffs. While some theorists argue for nonnegotiable rules, in practice rules are almost always negotiable. Every country resolves the tension between flexibility (for economic or political reasons) and certainty (for planning public policy agendas) differently, and the equilibrium between these two goals has shifted over time. The traditional view of intergovernmental finance, prevailing in the 1970s, suggested that virtually everything to do with intergovernmental fiscal transfers should be decided unilaterally by the federal government. This view still prevails in developing countries such as India and South Africa. The emerging model is one in which "jurisdictional boundaries and the assignment of functions and finances have to be taken as determined at some earlier (constitutional) stage and not open to further discussion in normal circumstances" (Bird and Smart 2001, p. 12).

Third, conditional transfers remain a prevalent but troubling aspect of intergovernmental fiscal finance. Indeed, "both theory and experience suggest strongly that it is important to state expenditure responsibilities as clearly as possible in order to enhance accountability and reduce unproductive overlap, duplication of authority, and legal challenges" (World Bank 2001, p. 267).

Fourth, the limits of law in optimizing an intergovernmental fiscal transfer system are greatest when problems arise and dispute resolution or adjudication is required. This is so because a well-considered legal framework is a necessary condition for any effective intergovernmental transfer system, but it is not in itself a sufficient safeguard. As Smoke (2001, p. 3) notes, "no matter what a constitution or enabling law says, central agencies rarely have a desire to decentralize services, thereby losing prestige and resources."

This chapter began by observing that it has been argued that "in the end intergovernmental transfers are the *instruments*, not the *determinants* of public policy" (Bird and Tarasov 2002, p. 23, emphasis in original). The findings presented here demonstrate that legal frameworks are not simply empty vessels to be filled. Each legal framework has its own internal biases, based on who makes the intergovernmental transfer rules, who modifies them and under what conditions, and who resolves conflicts when they arise. Each of these "neutral" decisions carries intrinsic biases in favor of centralization versus decentralization, political decision making versus more objective assessment, fiscal autonomy versus fiscal prudence, and acceptance of economic disparity versus insistence on fiscal solidarity. These preferences are embedded in every intergovernmental transfer system and should be deliberately considered at the moment their legal frameworks are conceived and reformed.

Notes

1. The seminal work is Oates (1972).
2. In Flanders the Flemish region and community have become essentially the same unit, through a series of close cooperative agreements.
3. For a discussion of the earlier roots of German federalism and fiscal federalism, see May (1969) and Bird (1986).
4. For a discussion of the constitutional debates surrounding this issue, see Haysom (2001).
5. See Decree II of the French-speaking community of July 19, 1993, regarding the transfer of certain fields of jurisdiction from the French-speaking community to the Walloon region and the Commission Communautaire Française (Van der Stichele and Verdonck 2002).
6. Citizens of the former German Democratic Republic represented about 20 percent of Germany's population in 1990 but contributed less than 6 percent of value added (Spahn 2001).
7. Legislation provides that "the tax receipts of financially weak states are raised to up to 92 percent of the average tax receipts of all states per inhabitant" (Beierl 2001, p. 6). See also Spahn (2001).
8. For an overview of intergovernmental finance in India before independence, see Vithal and Sastry (2001).
9. For a discussion of the early Finance Commissions, see Vithal and Sastry (2001), Rao (1992), and May (1969).
10. Several Finance Commissions have considered whether there should be a permanent Finance Commission, but the idea has been rejected on the grounds that a freshly constituted set of members can be expected to be unbiased and treated differently from full-time government employees (Vithal and Sastry 2001).
11. Parliament may increase any union custom or duty by a surcharge whose proceeds go entirely to the union. It is too early to tell whether this will allow the union to circumvent the general spirit of Article 270, which presumes that union taxes are shared.
12. For a discussion of the controversy of the gap-filling approach, see Sury (1999).
13. All bills from the National Assembly are considered by the National Council of Provinces, which is composed of 10 delegates from each province. If a bill does not affect the provinces, the National Assembly may pass it regardless of the concerns of the National Council of Provinces. If a bill does affect the provinces and the National Council of Provinces rejects it, the matter is referred to a mediation committee, made up of an equal number of National Assembly and National Council of Provinces members. If the committee cannot resolve the issue, the National Assembly may still pass the bill if it has at least a two-thirds majority.
14. Conditional transfers accounted for about 15 percent of state expenditures in the 1990s, up from just 7 percent in the 1980s (Rao and Singh 2000).
15. The provincial equitable sharing formula includes seven weighted components: education (41 percent), health care (19 percent), social development/welfare (18 percent), economic activity (7 percent), "basic" (7 percent), institutional (5 percent), and capital "backlogs" (3 percent) (Financial and Fiscal Commission 2004).

16. In the 1980s total state revenue grew 15.3 percent and total transfers 15.8 percent, while expenditures grew 15.5 percent. In the 1990s fiscal imbalance emerged, as total state revenue grew 12.8 percent and total transfers just 11.5 percent, while total expenditures grew 14.3 percent (Rao n.d.).

References

Bahl, Roy. 2001. "Equitable Vertical Sharing and Decentralizing Government Finance in South Africa." Working Paper 01–6, Georgia State University, Andrew Young School of Policy Studies, International Studies Program, Atlanta.

Beierl, Otto. 2001. "Reforming Intergovernmental Fiscal Relations in Germany: The Bavarian Point of View." Commission sur le Déséquilibre Fiscal, Quebec, Canada. http://www.desequilibrefiscal.gouv.qc.ca.

Bird, Richard M. 1986. *Federal Finance in Comparative Perspective: Financing Canadian Federation.* Toronto: Canadian Tax Foundation.

Bird, Richard M., and Michael Smart. 2001. "Intergovernmental Fiscal Transfers: Some Lessons from International Experience." World Bank, Washington, DC.

Bird, Richard, and Andrey V. Tarasov. 2002. "Closing the Gap: Fiscal Imbalances and Intergovernmental Transfers in Developed Federations." Working Paper 02-02, Georgia State University, Andrew Young School of Policy Studies, International Studies Program, Atlanta.

Boadway, Robin. 2001. "The Imperative of Fiscal Sharing Transfers." *International Social Science Journal* 53: 103–10.

Braun, Dietmar. 2003. *Fiscal Policies in Federal States.* Aldershot, United Kingdom: Ashgate.

Brosio, Giorgio. 2000. "Decentralization in Africa." International Monetary Fund, Washington, DC.

Commission sur le Déséquilibre Fiscal. 2001. *Intergovernmental Fiscal Arrangements: Background Paper for the International Symposium on Fiscal Imbalance.* Quebec, Canada. http://www.desequilibrefiscal.gouv.qc.ca.

———. 2002. *The Federal Spending Power.* Quebec: Bibliothéque Nationale du Québec. http://www.desequilibrefiscal.gouv.qc.ca.

Constitutional Court of South Africa. 1996. *Certification of the Constitution of the Republic of South Africa, 1996,* Case CCT 23/96, 6 September 1996. http://www.constitution-alcourt.org.za/site/home/htm.

Currie, David P. 1994. *The Constitution of the Federal Republic of Germany.* Chicago: University of Chicago Press.

Financial and Fiscal Commission. 2004. *Submission for the Division of Revenue 2005/6: Proposals from the Financial and Fiscal Commission Review of the Intergovernmental Fiscal Relations System.* Midrand, South Africa.

Gérard, Marcel. 2001. "Fiscal Federalism in Belgium." Paper presented at the "Conference on Fiscal Imbalance," Quebec, Canada, September 13–14. http://www.desequilibrefiscal.gouv.qc.ca.

Haysom, Nicholas. 2001. "Federal Features of the Final Constitution." In *The Post-Apartheid Constitutions: Perspectives on South Africa's Basic Law,* ed. Penelope Andrews and Stephen Ellmann. Johannesburg: Witwatersrand University Press.

Heun, Werner. 1995. "The Evolution of Federalism." In *Studies in German Constitutionalism: The German Contributions to the Fourth World Congress of the International Association of Constitutional Law,* ed. Christian Starck, 175–76. Baden-Baden: Nomos Verlagsgesellschaft.

Khemani, Stuti. 2002. "Federal Politics and Budget Deficits: Evidence from the States of India." Policy Research Working Paper 2915, World Bank, Washington, DC. http://econ.worldbank.org/files/20840_wps2915.pdf.

————. 2003. "Partisan Politics and Intergovernmental Transfers in India." Policy Research Working Paper 3016, World Bank, Washington, DC. http://econ.worldbank.org/files/25492_wps3016.pdf.

Kommers, Donald P. 1997. *The Constitutional Jurisprudence of the Federal Republic of Germany.* 2nd. ed. Durham: Duke University Press.

Larsen, Clifford. 1999. "States Federal, Financial, Sovereign and Social: A Critical Inquiry into an Alternative to American Financial Federalism." *American Journal of Comparative Law* 47 (429): 433–34.

Macdonald, R. St. J. 1996. "Solidarity in the Practice and Discourse of Public International Law." *Pace International Law Review* 8259 (259): 294.

May, R.J. 1969. *Federalism and Fiscal Adjustment.* Oxford: Clarendon Press.

Motala, Ziyad, and Cyril Ramaphosa. 2002. *Constitutional Law: Analysis and Cases.* Oxford: Oxford University Press.

Oates, Wallace. 1972. *Fiscal Federalism.* New York: Harcourt Brace Jovanovich.

OECD (Organisation for Economic Co-operation and Development). 1997. "Belgium." In *Managing Across Levels of Government.* Paris: OECD.

————. 2002. *Fiscal Decentralization in EU Applicant States and Selected EU Member States.* Paris: OECD.

Patil, S.H. 1995. *Central Grants and State Autonomy.* New Delhi: Atlantic Publishers and Distributors.

Petter, Andrew. 1989. "Federalism and the Myth of the Federal Spending Power." *Canadian Bar Review* 68 (3): 448–79.

Purfield, Catriona. 2004. "The Decentralization Dilemma in India." IMF Working Paper WP/04/32, International Monetary Fund, Washington, DC.

Rao, Ananda. 1992. *Finance Commissions in India.* New Delhi: Deep and Deep Publications.

Rao, M. Govinda, and Nirvikar Singh. 2000. "The Political Economy of Center-State Fiscal Transfers in India." World Bank Institute, Public Finance, Decentralization and Poverty Reduction Program, Washington, DC.

Rao, M. Govinda. n.d. "Dynamics of Indian Federalism." World Bank Institute, Public Finance, Decentralization and Poverty Reduction Program, Washington, DC.

Shah, Anwar. 2004. "Lessons from International Practices of Intergovernmental Fiscal Transfers." World Bank, Washington, DC.

Smoke, Paul. 2001. "Fiscal Decentralization in East and Southern Africa: A Selective Review of Experience and Thoughts on Making Progress." World Bank Institute, Public Finance, Decentralization and Poverty Reduction Program, Washington, DC.

Spahn, Paul Bernd. 2001. "Maintaining Fiscal Equilibrium in a Federation: Germany." Commission sur le Déséquilibre Fiscal, Quebec, Canada. http://www.desequilibrefiscal.gouv.qc.ca.

Sury, M.M.1999. "Federal Fiscal Relations: Constitutional Provisions." In *Federal India: Emerging Economic Issues,* ed. V.S. Jafa, 138–41. New Delhi: Indian Tax Institute.

Tiebout, C. 1956. "A Pure Theory of Local Expenditures." *Journal of Political Economy* 64 (5): 416–24.

Van der Stichele, Géraldine, and Magali Verdonck. 2002. "The Lambermont Agreement: Why and How?" Commission sur le Déséquilibre Fiscal, Quebec, Canada. http://www.desequilibrefiscal.gouv.qc.ca.

Vithal, R., and M.L. Sastry. 2001. *Fiscal Federalism in India.* New Delhi: Oxford University Press.

Wilkins, Roger. 2001. "Germany: An Overview of Fiscal Arrangements." Forum of Federations, Ottawa, Canada. http://www.forumfed.org.

World Bank. 2001. "Intergovernmental Fiscal Relations." Washington, DC.

10

Institutional Arrangements for Intergovernmental Fiscal Transfers and a Framework for Evaluation

ANWAR SHAH

Intergovernmental fiscal transfers are important features of subnational finance in unitary and federal countries alike. Institutional arrangements for policy and administration of these transfers vary across countries, with wide variations in the form and membership of the relevant decision-making bodies.

These arrangements have not yet received the attention that is due given their importance in creating a credible and stable fiscal transfers regime. Only a handful of recent papers (Searle 2004; Boex and Martinez-Vazquez 2004) has documented these arrangements and commented on alternate regimes. No work has yet evaluated the relative merits of different institutional arrangements.

The success of these arrangements depends on a multitude of factors, including not only the incentive regime associated with governance structures but also the interactions between those structures with other formal and informal institutions in the country. This chapter presents a simple framework for understanding these incentives and interactions. It examines their impacts on transaction costs for society as a whole and the achievement of societal objectives. These concepts are applied to the specific case of institutional arrangements for fiscal equalization transfers, and the predictions based on the theory are compared with observed experiences in major federal countries. The results show that the framework presented has significant power for predicting potential impacts.

The chapter is organized as follows. The first section briefly discusses the goals of intergovernmental fiscal relations and describes various institutional arrangements adopted by countries to further these goals. The second section presents a simple framework for comparing and evaluating institutional arrangements. The third section compares and evaluates two commonly used models, intergovernmental forums and independent grants commissions.

Institutional Arrangements for Intergovernmental Transfers

Institutional arrangements for fiscal transfers are typically structured to fulfill a number of objectives. Program objectives seek to design a program that is consistent with general revenue-sharing or equalization objectives. The design should be simple, so that it is easily understood and can forge broad consensus and garner wide ownership and support. It should use uncontestable data and transfer funds in a way that respects local autonomy while creating an incentive environment that is compatible with accountability for results. These program objectives require a process of consultation with recipient governments that is open and transparent, is conducive to consensus building, and entails relatively low transaction cost for all parties concerned. The process should also aim to ensure wide public acceptance of the implemented programs.

While these objectives are commonly shared, specific institutional arrangements to fulfill those objectives vary widely across countries. Four stylized groupings of these arrangements are examined.[1]

Central/National Government Agency

The central/national government agency model is the most commonly used model in both industrial and developing countries (table 10.1). A central agency—typically either the president or prime minister's office or the Ministry of Finance, the Ministry of Home Affairs, or the Ministry of Local Government or Planning (or a planning commission)—assumes sole or shared responsibilities for policy making and implementation of fiscal transfers, including equalization transfers.

TABLE 10.1 Responsibility for Design of Intergovernmental Fiscal
Transfers in Selected Countries

Model	Responsibility
Central/national government agency model	**Office of the President** Kyrgyz Republic Tanzania (regional administration and local government unit) **Ministry of Finance** China Italy (policy only) Kazakhstan Netherlands (shared with the Ministry of Home Affairs) Poland Switzerland Ukraine **Ministry of Home Affairs** Italy (distribution of funds only) Netherlands (with Ministry of Finance) Philippines (Ministry of Interior and Local Government) Republic of Korea (Ministry of Government Administration and Home Affairs) **Ministry of Local Government** Ghana (Ministry of Local Government and Rural Development) Zambia **Planning Commission** India (for plan and capital grants) **Ministry of Public Administration** Japan (Ministry of Finance is consulted)
National legislature model	Brazil: Senate
Intergovernmental forum model	Canada: Fiscal Arrangements Committee Germany: Financial Planning Council Indonesia: Regional Autonomy Advisory Board Nigeria: Revenue Mobilization, Allocation and Fiscal Commission Pakistan: National Finance Commission
Independent agency (grants commission) model	Australia: Commonwealth Grants Commission India: Finance Commissions South Africa: Fiscal and Financial Commission Uganda: Local Government Finance Commission

Source: Author.

National Legislature

In all countries except China, the national legislature must enact legislation to provide a legal basis for transfers from the central government to state and local governments. In Brazil the 1988 constitution specifies the pool and the broad criteria for revenue-sharing transfers and the Senate serves as the primary decision-making body for establishing the formula and monitoring compliance. Senate regulations spell out the specific distribution criteria for state and municipal participation funds (Shah 1991).

Intergovernmental Forum

Intergovernmental forums facilitate consultations among different levels of government, strike a balance among competing interests, and mediate conflicts. Such institutional arrangements are common in federal countries. In some countries, such as Australia and South Africa, where an independent agency has been assigned a strong role in intergovernmental fiscal relations, intergovernmental forums review and decide on independent agency recommendations. Canada, Germany, Indonesia, Nigeria, and Pakistan rely solely on intergovernmental forums for decisions on fiscal transfers. The 1994 constitutional amendments in Argentina provided for the establishment of a Federal Fiscal Commission, made up of representatives from the federal provincial (including the city of Buenos Aires) governments to oversee the tax-sharing/co-participation arrangements. This commission has not yet been established (Hernandez forthcoming).

Canada: The Fiscal Arrangements Committee

In Canada primary legal responsibility for the design of fiscal transfers to provinces and territories rests with the federal government (the Ministry of Finance); final approval rests with the national parliament. The federal government of Canada nevertheless places strong emphasis on intergovernmental consultation and shared decision making on intergovernmental fiscal transfers (figure 10.1). Federal-provincial fiscal arrangements committees play a pivotal role in providing substance to such dialogues (figure 10.2). The Federal-Provincial Relations Division in the Ministry of Finance provides a secretariat for these committees, which are made up of federal and provincial finance or treasury officials concerned with fiscal transfers. They meet periodically but exchange information and comments on a continuing basis on all technical aspects of fiscal arrangements.

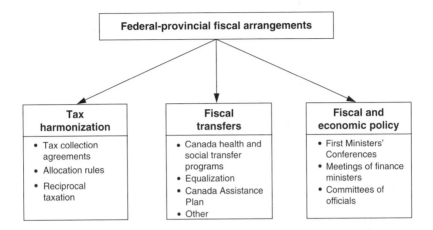

Source: Author.

FIGURE 10.1 Federal-Provincial Fiscal Arrangements in Canada

Their recommendations are sent to the Continuing Committee of Officials on Fiscal and Economic Matters, made up of federal and provincial deputy ministers of finance (or treasurers). This committee, chaired by the federal deputy minister of finance, usually meets on a quarterly basis. The final recommendations of the committee for further action are forwarded to regular (typically semiannual) meetings of federal and provincial ministers of finance, provincial treasurers, or both, chaired by the federal minister of finance. Final decisions reached at these meetings and unresolved issues are communicated to the First Ministers Conferences (attended by the prime minister of Canada and the premiers of the provinces), which are held biannually. These committees monitor and review the fiscal equalization program on a continuing basis, conducting an intensive review every five years to suggest revisions for the enactment of new national legislation for the next five-year period. A newer dimension to these consultations was introduced by the 2003 establishment of the Council of the Federation. The council, made up of provincial premiers and the leaders of the three northern territories, aims to develop a common position on national and interprovincial issues, including federal-provincial-territorial fiscal arrangements (Hueglin forthcoming).

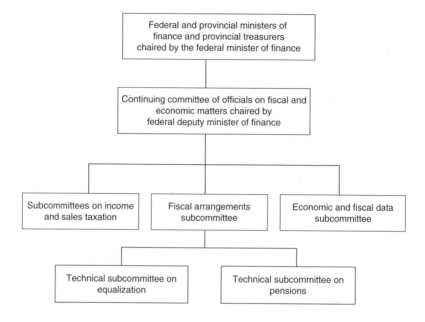

Source: Author.

FIGURE 10.2 Structure of Federal-Provincial Fiscal Arrangements Committees in Canada

Germany: The Financial Planning Council

The German federal system emphasizes sharing of responsibilities and joint decision making embodied in uniform federal legislation applicable to all *länder* (states). The upper house of the parliament, the Bundesrat, with representation from *länder* governments, serves to strengthen a common approach. In fiscal relations, major decisions on the fraternal equalization transfers program are reached through a solidarity pact at a forum of federal and state presidents. Substantive inputs for reaching this pact come from the Financial Planning Council (*Finanzplanungsrat*), which establishes guidelines and recommendations for policy action on the financing of budgets in the short and medium term. The council aims to reach agreement on fiscal policy coordination among federal and state governments. This council is made up of federal ministers of finance and economics, the state ministers responsible for finance, and four representatives of the municipalities (appointed by the Bundesrat based on nominations by municipal associations). The council, chaired by the federal minister of finance, is required to meet at least twice a year.

Indonesia: The Regional Autonomy Advisory Board

Indonesia's Regional Autonomy Advisory Board serves as an important intergovernmental forum in support of Law 22/1999 (on regional governance) and Law 25/1999 (on the fiscal balance between the central government and the regions). The board advises the president on all aspects of local government organization and finance issues. The board is chaired by the minister of home affairs, with the minister of finance serving as the deputy chair. Other members of this board include the secretary of state; the minister of administrative reform; the minister of defense; the chairman of the National Development Planning Board (BAPENNAS); two representatives from the provinces, two representatives from the districts, and two representatives from the towns; and one representative from the association of provinces, one representative from the association of districts, and one representative from the association of towns (Searle 2004). Technical work on fiscal matters, including fiscal equalization grants, is conducted by the Directorate General for Center-Region Fiscal Balance of the Ministry of Finance. Work on planning grants is carried out by the National Planning Board. The Regional Autonomy Advisory Board reviews the recommendations of the Ministry of Finance and the National Planning Board and makes final decisions. Responsibility for monitoring and implementation lies with the Ministry of Home Affairs.

Nigeria: The Revenue Mobilization, Allocation and Fiscal Commission

Nigeria's 1999 constitution mandated the creation of the Revenue Mobilization, Allocation and Fiscal Commission to administer fiscal transfers across levels of government and to provide advice on mobilizing revenue at the state and local levels. The commission is chaired by the federal minister of finance and includes finance commissioners or accountants general from each state. Its meets every month to review financial flows (Boex and Martinez-Vazquez 2004). Its recommendations are forwarded to the Council of the State, which is chaired by the president and includes state governors and the leadership of the National Assembly.

Pakistan: The National Finance Commission

Pakistan's constitution mandates the establishment every five years of a limited duration National Finance Commission. The commission is empowered to make recommendations to the president on the pool of revenues to be distributed as well as the allocation criteria. The commission also advises on the exercise of borrowing powers by all levels of government. Chaired by the federal minister of finance, the commission includes provincial ministers of finance and other civil society members (legislators, academics, experts, distinguished citizens) appointed by the president after consultation with provincial governors. The federal ministry of finance serves as a secretariat for the commission. The commission makes its decision by consensus. If it fails to reach consensus on the formula for allocating transfers, as has been the case in recent years, the formula that was operative in the previous five years continues to operate until a new consensus is forged.

Independent Agencies (Grants Commission)

Independent agencies are sometimes created, usually by the central government, to report either to the executive or legislature on a permanent or periodic basis. Australia pioneered this model, which has since been adopted in several other countries, including India, South Africa, and Uganda.

Australia: The Commonwealth Grants Commission

The Commonwealth Grants Commission was created in 1933 in response to dissatisfaction by states, especially a secession threat by Western Australia, over bilateral negotiations with the federal government on applications for special grants. In its 1936 report, the commission articulated that its assessment of the states' funding needs were to be based on their capacity to raise revenue and any abnormal expenditure influences they faced. It stated that "special grants are justified when a state, through financial stress from any cause, is unable efficiently to discharge its functions as a member of the federation, and should be determined by the amount of help found necessary to make it possible for that state by reasonable effort to function at a standard not appreciably below that of other states" (Commonwealth Grants Commission 1995a, p. 42).

The commission's mandate was vastly expanded in 1973, when it assumed responsibility for calculating the per capita relativities (adjustment factor applied to national average per capita figure to achieve per capita figure for the state) for allocating federal general revenue-sharing assistance to all states, the Northern Territory, and the Territory of Cocos (Keeling) Islands; financing works and services in the capital; determining state entitlements for local government; and determining state grants to local governments. In 1975 state commissions relieved the Commonwealth Grants Commission of its role in determining state grants to local governments. The determination of state entitlements for local governments was terminated by the Local Government Financial Assistance Act of 1986. The special grant program for selected states under Section 9 of the constitution was terminated in 1981.

It was replaced by a program of assistance for all states and calculation of state relativities for general revenue grants that includes tax sharing, health, and special grants on a five-year basis with annual updates.

The commission consists of a chair and a maximum of five members, appointed by the federal government in consultation with the states. It has a permanent secretariat of about 60 staff members. The day-to-day business of the commission is handled by a secretary and two assistant secretaries responsible for expenditure analysis and revenue, budgets, and research divisions.

The commission is constituted as an advisory body and empowered to conduct its business only within the purview of the terms of references provided by the federal minister of finance and administration. It does not have the power to initiate and pursue inquiries on its own authority. In recent years, the main references have sought the commission's advice on per capita relativities for distributing among the states and territories the pool of general revenue assistance made available by the Commonwealth. For this purpose, in 2004 the commission applied a specific principle of fiscal equalization, which states that "state governments should receive funding from the pool of goods and services tax revenue and health care grants such that, if each made the same effort to raise revenue from its own sources and operated at the same level of efficiency, each would have the capacity to provide services at the same standard" (Commonwealth Grants Commission 2004, p. x).

Another important matter on which the commission has reported in recent years is the interstate distribution of general-purpose grants for local government. Although the references are provided by the minister for finance and administration, their content is usually decided in negotiations between the Commonwealth and the states, conducted largely through their treasuries. A formal mechanism for this purpose is the Heads of the Australian Treasuries Forum, which meets periodically. The resulting commission reports are provided formally to the Commonwealth Government and made available to the states immediately thereafter. The relativities recommended in the reports are considered at the annual treasurers' conference. The commission's relativities are almost always accepted by the treasurers' conference, as preliminary relativities are publicly defended by the commission in open adversarial proceedings in all states before their formal presentation. Only in 1981 (when the commission was asked to recalculate the relativities and present a new report) and 1982 did the Commonwealth Government choose not to accept the commission's recommendation. Instead, the Premiers' Council, under the leadership of Prime Minister J.M. Fraser (Commonwealth Treasurer, J.M. Howard) chose to modify the Commission relativities (Commonwealth Grants Commission 1995a).

India: The Finance Commissions

The Finance Commissions of India, which include a chair and four members, are constituted by the president every five years to meet the constitutional requirement to redress the fiscal gaps in the revenues and expenditures of the union (federal) and state governments arising out of a mismatch of revenue means and expenditure needs at various levels. They are mandated to make recommendations to the president regarding:

- The distribution between the union and the states of net proceeds of taxes that are, to be, or may be divided between them and the allocation between the states of the respective shares of such proceeds.
- The principles that should govern the grants-in-aid of the revenues of the states out of the consolidated fund of India.
- The measures needed to augment the consolidated fund of a state to supplement the resources of the *panchayats* (rural councils) in the state on the basis of the recommendations made by the Finance Commission of the state.
- The measures needed to augment the consolidated fund of a state to supplement the resources of the municipalities in the state on the basis of the recommendations made by the Finance Commission of the state.
- Any other matter referred to the commission by the president in the interests of sound finance that can be achieved through revenue sharing and special grants to needy states. The commission is also required to recommend allocation among states of their share of federal taxes.

The first Finance Commission was established in 1951 by an act of parliament. Since then these commissions have been reconstituted every five years, with new terms of reference for the next five-year period. According to the 1951 act, the chair of the commission must have experience in public affairs. Members must be, have been, or be qualified to be appointed as judges of a high court; have special knowledge of the finances and accounts of the government; have had wide experience in financial matters and administration; or have special knowledge of economics. The commission members are usually a mix of politicians, retired civil servants, and experts in fiscal federalism. Each commission creates a temporary secretariat managed by a secretary appointed by the federal government, usually from the Planning Commission. The commission is disbanded upon submission of a report consistent with its terms of reference. The commission does not have the mandate to initiate an inquiry outside its terms of references. The commission's recommendations are not binding on the government, but under Article 281 of the constitution, they must be presented to both houses of the parliament, along with the government response's to each recommendation.

South Africa: The Fiscal and Financial Commission

South Africa's Fiscal and Financial Commission was established in 1993. The commission was to have 18 members: 9 members appointed by the president and 1 member designated by each of the 9 provincial cabinets. The interim constitution gave a broad mandate to the commission in providing advice on financial and fiscal requirements of the national provincial and local governments.

The constitution of 1996 expanded the commission membership to 22 by adding two representatives from the organized local government structure and two additional presidential appointments. Such a large membership was subsequently seen as unwieldy, and an amendment to the constitution in 2001 reduced the commission membership to the current strength of nine, to be appointed by the president in consultation with the cabinet and executive councils of the nine provinces. The nine members include a chair and a deputy chair, three members recommended by provincial premiers, two members recommended by local governments, and two other members.

The 1996 constitution narrowed the commission's mandate to provide advice on the equitable allocation of central revenue sharing to provincial and local governments, provincial taxation, municipal fiscal powers and function, subnational borrowing, and central government guarantees. The role of the commission was further clarified by central legislation. The Borrowing Powers of Provincial Governments Act of 1966 authorizes the minister of finance to seek the commission's advice on provincial borrowing and debt management issues. The Provincial Tax Regulation Process Act of 2001 empowers the commission to provide comments on tax proposals by the provinces.

The Intergovernmental Fiscal Relations Act of 1997 clarified the institutional arrangements and the processes for the commission's advice to executive and legislative organs. The commission was given an observer status at the Budget Council, a forum of the ministers of finance of the central government and the provinces. The act requires the commission to provide advice on equitable shares at least 10 months before the commencement of the fiscal year; the Division of Revenue Bill must include comments by the national government on the commission's recommendation. The constitutional-legal foundation for the commission's playing the role of an influential adviser on intergovernmental fiscal relations is strong. This role was carefully crafted to ensure that "it can bark but not bite" (Wehner 2003, p. 5).

Uganda: The Local Government Finance Commission

The Local Government Finance Commission of Uganda is mandated under the 1995 constitution to serve as an advisory body to the national government (the minister of local government) on all matters relating to the transfer of resources to local governments and to advise local governments on the appropriate levels of local revenues. It is expected to recommend both the total pool of transfers as well as allocations to local governments in the form of equalization and conditional grants. It monitors compliance of local governments with the legal requirements associated with their taxing and spending decisions and is empowered to mediate financial disputes among local governments.

The commission consists of seven commissioners appointed by the president. They include three commissioners nominated by the district councils through the Uganda Local Authorities Association, one commissioner nominated by the urban councils through the Urban Authorities Association of Uganda, and three commissioners nominated by the minister of local government in consultation with the minister of finance, planning, and economic development. The president designates two of the commissioners as chair and deputy chair. These commissioners work full time. The other commissioners serve on a part-time basis. A permanent secretariat headed by a secretary with 31 staff conducts the day-to-day business of the commission (Uganda, Republic of 2004).

Evaluating Institutional Arrangements for Equalizing Transfers Using a New Institutional Economics Framework

The literature provides no framework for comparing the diverse institutional arrangements for decision making on transfers across levels of government. This section attempts to fill that void by borrowing ideas and concepts from the relatively new discipline of new institutional economics (North 1990). Under this framework, both principals and their agents act rationally in their own self-interest, and access to information is costly and not uniformly available to all. In such circumstances, the agent may not secure the interests of their principals, and the principals may not be able to restrain opportunistic behaviors of their agents, due to the "bounded rationality" of principals and the high transaction costs associated in overcoming this handicap.

In the context of institutional arrangements for a fiscal equalization program, the problem manifests itself as follows. First, there needs to be a national compact on equalization principles and standards so that the mandate given by the principals (citizens) is clear. This compact can take the form of a constitutional provision, legislative enactment, or an informal but universally shared consensus on the goals of fiscal equalization. This compact will have to be administered by various public agents (such as executive and legislative organs, typically at the national level). Such administration may mean that it may be in the self-interest of some agents not to respect the compact. For example, the national executive or legislative leadership may come from a region with little enthusiasm for interstate equity. Alternatively, the current regime may be committed to equalization but unable to tie the hands of future regimes, thereby threatening the durability of the compact. Enshrining equalization principles in the constitution is often motivated by these considerations. Constitutional enshrinement limits but does not overcome the commitment problem, as current coalitions can be replaced by coalitions of opposing interests and policy preferences in the future.[2]

Institutional arrangements for administering the compact also entail a number of transaction costs for principals and their agents. For principals various types of arrangements impose differential participation and monitoring costs. There are also costs associated with legislative and executive decision making. These costs are the time and effort needed to strike a legislative compromise or an executive decision. They are higher when the stakes for individual parties are high, when there are strong conflicts of interest, and when there is some uncertainty as to the future revenue streams available to donor and recipient governments—a frequently recurring situation in negotiations on fiscal transfers. All institutional arrangements entail costs incurred by principals to induce compliance by their administrative agents with the compact, so-called agency costs. Agency costs arise because the administrative agents who are to implement the compact on behalf of the principals may not share the objectives pursued by the principals. They may make decisions that serve the narrow self-interest of bureaucratic power or enrich themselves. Because of high transaction costs, civil society or the legislature may not be able to exercise effective oversight over these decisions. In view of the difficulty of monitoring and taking corrective action ex post, legislatures typically try to influence the appointment of executives to ensure that they share the same goals and do not undermine enacted legislation. In addition, they rely much more on civil society monitoring, responding to "fire alarms" raised by unhappy constituents (Horn 1997). Their response to such alarms may be constrained if the executive agency is given a significant degree of autonomy.[3] There are also risks and uncertainty costs associated with unstable regimes. They arise because the potential benefits and costs of a given compact may not be fully known at the time a deal is struck and because any deal may be undone by a new coalition and constellation of interests.

The analytical framework described above argues for instituting administrative arrangements and governance structures that facilitate greater access to information by citizens, interested sectors of civil society (including the media and academics), and legislators. These structures would help citizens hold to account the agents (governments) involved in equalization decision making. They would minimize agency costs, uncertainty costs, and transaction costs associated with participation, monitoring, and decision making. And they would create an incentive structure that encourages both legislative and administrative agents to comply with their compact with the principals.

This is a complex task because of the interdependencies associated with various actions. As Horn (1997) notes, attempts to reduce agency loss between citizens and legislatures by restraining the influence of legislatures on the executive may potentially increase agency losses between legislatures and government executives. There are further difficulties in ensuring the durability of legislation, which can be undermined through lack of effective enforcement even if the legislation remains unchanged.

Comparing Alternate Institutional Arrangements Using a New Institutional Economics Framework

Intergovernmental forums and independent agencies are compared here using the new institutional economics framework. These two options are not exclusive choices, and both arrangements can coexist. When they do, the incremental value added provided by the independent agency must be rigorously examined.

Intergovernmental Forum

An intergovernmental forum provides a framework for institutionalized but restricted political bargaining.[4] Bargaining is restricted, as the constitution and the legal framework usually define the limits to such bargaining. There is, however, strong peer pressure to strike a bargain. Thus intergovernmental forums are usually successful in defining an explicit political compact acceptable to all parties. As such a political compact cannot be easily reached when complex criteria are put on the table, this institutional model places a high premium on simplicity and "rough justice," as opposed to complex but precise justice. Conflicting interests are represented at these forums. Unless the discussions of the forum are conducted in camera, political grandstanding may prevent political compromises. The durability of such compromises is usually ensured, as all parties stand to loose from a deal that unravels. Blame shifting is also not possible, as the members of the forum assume full responsibility for their decisions. The forum further enables participating governments representing competing interests and varying commitments on equalization to reach a broader consensus.

Independent Agency (Grants Commission)

An independent agency is usually established to seek an independent, professional, transparent, and rigorous view of the complex task of developing recommendations on the determination of the pool, the allocation criteria, and the distribution of funds among recipient governments. The presumption is that if such a decision is divorced from politics, the criteria and associated distribution better serves the broader interests of the nation as well as its constituent units.

These theoretical advantages are rarely achieved in practice, for two reasons. First, decisions on the standard of equalization (such as the minimum level of per capita fiscal capacity to which all jurisdictions are entitled to be raised) cannot and should not be divorced from politics. Second, such an institutional arrangement creates a number of agency problems, as discussed below.

Mission Creep

To secure its long-term existence and enlarge its spheres of influence, an independent agency faces continuous imperatives to justify its existence and continuously seek broader mandates to enlarge the scope of its activities. Such "mission creep" goes unchecked, as politicians do not want to be seen curtailing the search of such agencies for the holy grail—the ultimate formula for the equitable distribution of federal funds.

Incentives for Complexity

An independent agency faces powerful incentives to seek ever more complex solutions to simple questions, because complexity and associated expertise fuel demand in the external market for professionals serving these agencies. The greater the complexity of formulae and associated calculations, the greater the premium placed by the market on professionals possessing those skills. Interested parties' submissions makes it politically imperative to accommodate ever growing complexity. Outside academic experts typically clamor for further complexity to achieve more-precise justice. There is no escape from this circle, as part-time or term employment of members of the commission limits the oversight provided by them. It takes some time for term members to grasp the complexity of the allocation rules; by the time they can form their own judgment on their relative merits, it is usually time for them to leave. In any case, the staff would be resistant to any simplification, and recipient governments that benefit from the complexity and associated inequities of the system would likely block any reforms. Independent think tanks and researchers may call for greater complexity to bring practice into conformity with the theory. Constraining influences to keep the system simple and easily comprehensible are thus stunted by the very existence of an independent agency.

"Fire Alarm" Oversight

Citizen oversight of independent agencies becomes infeasible for several reasons. First, the more complex the distribution criteria, the more difficult it is for individual citizens and civil society groups to make informed comments. The fact that different groups advance their own agendas increases the broad discretion granted to such agencies in the interest of an apolitical, scientific approach. Even "fire alarm" oversight sought by legislatures becomes too costly and impractical, as unhappy constituents make conflicting demands on their representatives.

Tentative Conclusions

Assessment of the relative merits of each institutional arrangement must be guided by an analysis of the incentive regime created by each, the associated agency costs, and each arrangements' success in achieving simple, equitable, and durable outcomes. The new institutional economics framework predicts that overall transaction costs will be higher and potential outcomes less desirable under an independent agency model than under an intergovernmental forum, because the independence and autonomy offered to grant commissions weaken citizen oversight (table 10.2). The drive for optimal (ideal) systems invites complexity and undermines transparency and accountability. As a result, participation and monitoring costs as well as agency costs rise.

In contrast, intergovernmental forums look for simple and feasible alternatives. They seek to strike a political bargain and to reduce transaction costs for the nation as a whole. The higher transaction costs associated with independent grants commissions are not expected to secure better outcomes. Moreover, the grants commission processes do not necessarily encourage the consensus building that is achieved by forging a political compact on the equalization standard. In the absence of such a political compact, both the pool and allocation among constituent units are determined independently of the equalization standard. Stability of allocation criteria is also not ensured by a grants

TABLE 10.2 Transaction Costs and Potential Outcomes of Intergovernmental Forums and Independent Agencies (Grants Commissions)

Item	Intergovernmental forum	Independent agency
Transaction costs		
Participation and monitoring costs	Low to medium	Low to high
Legislative and executive decision-making costs	High	High
Agency costs	Low	High
Uncertainty costs	Low	Medium
Potential outcomes		
Political compact on equalization standard	Yes	No
Durability of political compact	Yes	n.a.
Pool determined by equalization standard	Yes for some, no for others	No
Allocation determined by equalization standard	Yes	No
Stability of allocation criteria	Yes	Maybe

Source: Author.
Note: n.a. = not applicable.

commission, as the desire for perfection may lead to frequent changes in the methodology. In summary, the independent grant commission is a poor substitute for an intergovernmental forum. Its usefulness as a complementary institution forum is also limited, in view of high agency costs and its predisposition toward optimal as opposed to feasible reforms.

These conclusions run counter to the predominant view in the fiscal federalism literature that independent grant commissions personify best practices. Indeed, international development agencies and consultants often recommend establishing such commissions in developing countries and transition economies (Searle 2004; Boex and Martinez-Vazquez 2004). From a new institutional economics perspective, the popularity of such commissions is not surprising. Independent agencies find strong support among academic scholars, think tanks, and politicians by playing to the enlightened self-interest of these groups. These agencies cater to elites, especially academic elites, as they give them a forum for disseminating their research. The agencies support the consulting industry by seeking their advice and analysis. They serve as convenient tools for national and regional politicians, as they are seen as providing fair, balanced, and professionally rigorous analysis. For any unpopular distribution criteria, politicians have the ability to distance themselves from the analysis and shift blame onto the agency. Furthermore, the presence of such agencies allows them to avoid making hard decisions by simply accepting the agency's view as a "take it or leave it" proposition. Given these incentives, it is no wonder that a growing chorus of professionals and politicians advocates the independent agency approach to vital decisions on equalization transfers.

From Theory to Practice: How Accurate Are the Predictions of the New Institutional Economics?

This section examines the experiences of Canada and Germany with intergovernmental forums and of Australia and India with independent grant commissions in order to compare the two approaches (table 10.3). It abstracts from the complexity in Australia that the independent grants commission complements the intergovernmental forum, the Heads of the Australian Treasuries' Forum. This should not bias the analysis, as the recent history of the Commonwealth Grants Commission demonstrates that it has enjoyed significant independence and autonomy, and its recommendations have almost always been accepted by the federal cabinet.

Transaction Costs

The institutional arrangements in the four countries are associated with different levels of citizen participation and different monitoring costs, agency costs, and uncertainty costs. Intergovernmental forums typically lead to lower transaction costs for the principals (citizens), primarily due to greater transparency, simplicity, and media and civil society scrutiny. Agency costs are highest under the Australian program, due to greater autonomy and incentives for complexity and mission creep by the Commonwealth Grants Commission staff. The periodic grants commission in India has medium agency costs, as it is constrained by its limited duration tenure. Legislative and executive decision-making costs are very similar across case study countries. Intergovernmental forums appear to offer a less costly way for principals to induce compliance from their agents.

Outcomes

Program outcomes are judged for the clarity of the mandate by the principals, the durability of political consensus, and the simplicity and equity of the equalization transfer programs. Equalization programs in Canada and Germany are enshrined in their constitutions. The Australian program is mandated by federal law. The Indian program is concerned primarily with the equitable distribution of the federal revenue-sharing pool and has no explicit equalization objective.

TABLE 10.3 Transaction Costs and Potential Outcomes of Intergovernmental Forums and Independent Agencies (Grants Commissions) in Selected Countries

Item	Intergovernmental forum		Independent agency	
	Canada	Germany	Australia	India
Transaction costs				
Citizen participation and monitoring costs	Low	Medium	High	High
Legislative costs	Low	Low	Low	Low
Executive decision-making costs	Medium	Medium	Medium	Medium
Agency costs	Low	Low	High	Medium
Uncertainty costs	Low	Low	Medium	Medium
Potential Outcomes				
Political consensus on equalization	Yes, constitution	Yes, constitution	Yes, federal law	No
Durability of consensus	Yes	Yes	Yes	No
Political compact on equalization standard	Yes, constitution	Yes, solidarity pact	No	No
Type of equalization program	Paternal	Fraternal	Paternal	Paternal
Pool determined by equalization standard	Yes	Yes	No	No
Allocation determined by equalization standard	Yes	Yes	No, but formula	No
Fiscal capacity equalization	Yes, representative tax system	Yes, actual revenues	Yes, representative tax system	No
Fiscal need equalization	No	No	Yes	Yes, some
Stability of allocation criteria	Yes	Yes	No	No
Sunset clause	Yes	No	No	No
Dispute resolution	Supreme Court	Constitutional Court	Supreme Court	Supreme Court
Program equity	Yes	Yes	Maybe	Maybe
Program complexity	Low	Low	High	High

Source: Author.

There is a reasonable degree of political consensus on the principles of equalization in Australia, Canada, and Germany. No such consensus has yet emerged in India. What distinguishes the Canadian and German programs from those in Australia and India are the clarity of the equalization standard and the simplicity of implementing it. The Canadian and German programs have a number of shortcomings, but they are simpler and more transparent than the Australian and Indian programs. The equalization standards in both the Australian and Indian programs are determined by an arbitrarily set total pool of resources. In addition, the Australian program is highly complex.

Australia uses a comprehensive program that attempts to equalize fiscal capacity as well as fiscal needs. Massive amounts of data are analyzed to calculate revenue disability for 18 tax bases and expenditure disabilities for 41 programs, with countless relevant determinants . The procedures used to determine expenditure needs are highly subjective and overly complex, making the Australian program a black box even for a serious student. The fiscal capacity of Australian states varies significantly. On the expenditure need side, if the Northern Territory is excluded as an outlier, the variation across the remaining states is minor (figure 10.3). The program could thus

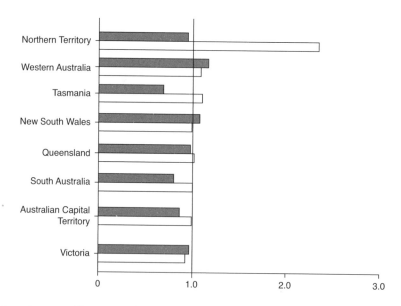

Source: Commonwealth Grants Commission 2004.
Note: Shaded bars show states' average relative revenue-raising capacities over the same period. Unshaded bars show states' average relative costs of providing services over the 1998/99–2002/03 period.

FIGURE 10.3   Fiscal Equalization in Australia, 1998/99–2002/03

be simplified by focusing on fiscal capacity equalization and providing fiscal need compensation through sectoral transfers or by providing a special grant to the Northern Territory.

The program thrust is on absolute comparability of services across states and territories. It attempts to make access to all services in remote areas equal to that in urban areas. Its method of expenditure equalization is based on actual nationwide state expenditures. Therefore, if a rich state decides to send a man to Mars, to buy limousines for its officials, or to pay higher welfare payments to its aboriginal population, equalization payments to have-not states automatically go up. The methodology is flawed, as it assumes that the costs of public services are independent of the management paradigm and that the use of public services is not influenced by incentives. The methodology rewards bad behaviors and imprudent fiscal management. For example, excessive use of services by specific groups and higher use of tax expenditures and assumption of contingent and noncontingent liabilities by states lead to higher equalization payments.

The focus on actual expenditures diverts states' energies to proving that "they need more to do less" as opposed to "doing more with less." The overall approach to expenditure needs is highly dependent on data and subjective judgment, and constant refinements to deal with concerns by individual states lead to complexity and nontransparency. For highly correlated factors, disabilities are artificially magnified by double counting and multiplication. For government secondary education, for example, category disability is lower than a simple or weighted average of individual disability factors for rich states and higher for poor states (table 10.4). Under such a program, use of judgment on factors and weights is inevitable, but such judgments invite controversy and compromise the credibility of the whole program. The results are often disappointing. As the commission acknowledges, "given the number of conceptual and empirical difficulties . . . and numerous judgments . . . different relativities (and grant outcomes) could be just as valid as those presented [here]" (Commonwealth Grants Commission 2000, p. 2).

Because the program lacks an explicit equalization standard, it is overly generous for the Northern Territory, Tasmania, and South Australia and punitive for Victoria and New South Wales (figure 10.4). The program is not equitable, and grant allocations vary directly with most macro fiscal capacity indicators (see Shah 2004 for a detailed critique of the Australian program and suggestions for simplification).

The Indian formula is less complex, but it uses arbitrary factors and weights. Curiously enough, all recent commissions have insisted on using 1971

TABLE 10.4 Expenditure Need Factors for Secondary Education in Australia, 1995/96

Disability factor	New South Wales	Victoria	Queensland	Western Australia	South Australia	Tasmania	Australian Capital Territory	Northern Territory
Dispersion	0.9973	0.9921	1.0093	1.0106	0.9972	0.9952	0.9885	1.0710
Grade cost	1.0014	1.0028	0.9966	0.9950	0.9992	0.9998	1.0016	0.9979
Input cost	1.0120	0.9950	0.9860	1.0030	0.9910	0.9900	1.0080	1.0340
Relevant population	0.9749	0.8874	1.0983	1.1639	0.9679	1.1422	0.9750	1.2226
Administrative scale	0.9946	0.9946	0.9946	1.0065	1.0105	1.0304	1.0463	1.1139
Service delivery scale	0.9922	0.9906	1.0031	1.0153	1.0166	1.0380	0.9714	1.1141
Vandalism and security	1.0023	1.0023	0.9973	0.9973	0.9973	0.9923	0.9923	0.9923
Cross-border	0.9965	1.0001	1.0001	1.0001	1.0001	1.0001	1.0660	1.0001
Category disability	0.9692	0.8658	1.0815	1.1941	0.9772	1.1917	1.0440	1.6605

Source: Commonwealth Grants Commission 1995b.

a. Variations from equal per capita distribution ($1,900) of GST

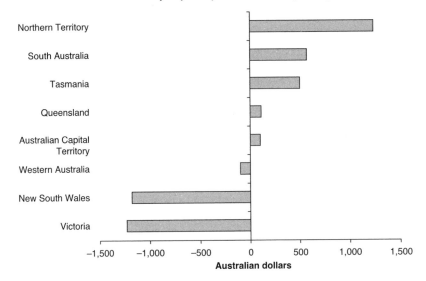

b. Distribution of per capita subsidy (tax) compared with point of collection of GST revenues

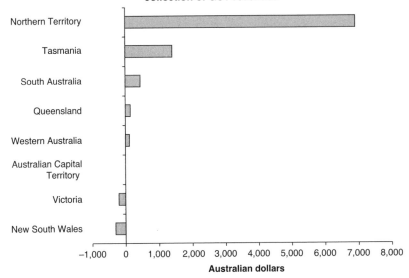

Source: Author's calculations based on Commonwealth Grants Commission of Australia 2004.
Note: GST = goods and services tax.

FIGURE 10.4 Robin Hood at Work in Australia, 2004/05

state population figures to calculate grant shares. The rationale presented—that India adopted a population control policy in that year—is not defensible, as state populations have experienced major changes due to migration.

The role of the Fiscal and Financial Commission of South Africa is constitutionally strong, but in practice this commission is weaker and less relevant in ensuring regional fiscal equity than the others. Neither the national treasury nor the provinces have paid much attention to the commission's recommendations (Murray forthcoming; Wehner 2003).

Concluding Remarks

The simple new institutional framework has significant power for predicting potential impacts. It shows that the case for independent grants commissions to enhance the transparency, equity, and accountability of the intergovernmental finance system is vastly exaggerated and has little or no empirical support. Practice confirms that such commissions contribute to ever more complex and inequitable systems that raise transaction costs and erode the stability and durability of political compact.

Notes

The author is grateful to Robin Boadway, Roy Bahl, Richard Bird, Jamie Boex, Fred Gorbet, Jorge Martinez, David Peloquin, and Bob Searle for comments on an earlier version of the paper prepared for Martinez-Vazquez and Searle (forthcoming).

1. Subnational government forums may exist to form a common position on national transfers, but there is no example in which such forums are the decision-making bodies on higher-level transfers.

2. The cast of "agents of the citizenry" is potentially much broader than just the executive and legislative organs of the central government. Through intergovernmental competition, especially among states/provinces, these agents can help ensure transparent self-regulation of any equalization governance regime through a system of checks and balances that minimizes the risk of "capture" and the resulting domination of a narrow set of more or less private interests in the governance regime.

3. In a personal communication to the author, Peloquin argued that it is not immediately clear who the "unhappy constituents" may be in the equalization context: presumably, provincial/state governments are most likely to first raise "fire alarms," fueling secondary alarms on the part of local civil society actors and the local citizenry (as recent Canadian experience demonstrates only too well). Since provinces/states would be the main clients and intervenors of any autonomous grants agency, it is not clear that such an agency could in any sense be indifferent to them, given the credible threat of "going public" and appreciably raising the political and electoral stakes when they suspect their interests are not being given fair consideration.

4. These restrictions should not reduce political bargaining to a zero-sum game, as the benefits of a federal bargain would be significantly curtailed under such a scenario.

References

Boadway, Robin, and Anwar Shah. Forthcoming. *Fiscal Federalism: Principles and Practices.* New York and London: Cambridge University Press.

Boex, James, and Jorge Martinez-Vazquez. 2004. "Developing the Institutional Framework for Intergovernmental Fiscal Relations in Decentralizing LDCs." Georgia State University, Andrew Young School of Policy Studies, Atlanta.

Commonwealth Grants Commission of Australia. 1995a. *Equality in Diversity: History of the Commonwealth Grants Commission.* 2nd ed. Canberra: Australian Government Printing Service.

———. 1995b. *Report on the State Revenue Sharing Relativities, 1995/96.* Canberra: Australian Government Printing Service.

———. 2000. "Simplicity." Discussion Paper CGC 2000/07, Canberra.

———. 2004. *Report on State Revenue Sharing Relativities.* Canberra: Australian Government Printing Service.

Government of India. 2003. *Fifty Years of Fiscal Federalism.* 12th Finance Commission of India. New Delhi: Government of India.

Hernandez, Antonio. Forthcoming. "Republic of Argentina." In *Legislative, Executive and Judicial Powers in Federal Countries*, ed. Katy Le Roy and Cheryl Saunders. Montreal and Kingston: McGill-Queen's University Press.

Horn, Murray J. 1997. *The Political Economy of Public Administration.* New York: Cambridge University Press.

Hueglin, Thomas. Forthcoming. "Canada." In *Legislative, Executive and Judicial Powers in Federal Countries*, ed. Katy Le Roy and Cheryl Saunders. Montreal and Kingston: McGill-Queen's University Press.

Martinez-Vazquez, Jorge, and Bob Searle, eds. Forthcoming. *Fiscal Equalization: Challenges in the Design of Intergovernmental Transfers.* Berlin: Springer-Verlag.

Murray, Christina. Forthcoming. "Republic of South Africa." In *Legislative, Executive and Judicial Powers in Federal Countries*, ed. Katy Le Roy and Cheryl Saunders. Montreal and Kingston: McGill-Queen's University Press.

North, Douglas. 1990. *Institutions, Institutional Change and Economic Performance.* Cambridge: Cambridge University Press.

Peloquin, David. 2005. "Backgrounder on Equalization and TFF Governance Issues." Department of Finance, Ottawa.

Searle, Bob. 2004. "Institutional Aspects of the Balancing Fund." Ministry of Finance, Jakarta, Indonesia.

Shah, Anwar. 1991. *The New Fiscal Federalism in Brazil.* World Bank Discussion Paper 124, Washington, DC.

———. 2004. "The Australian Horizontal Fiscal Equalization Program in the International Context." Presentation at the Heads of the Australian Treasuries' Forum, September 22 and the Commonwealth Grants Commission, Canberra, September 23.

Uganda, Republic of. 2004. *Local Government Finance Commission, Corporate Strategy 2004–2008.* Kampala, Uganda.

Wehner, Joachim. 2003. "The Institutional Politics of Revenue Sharing in South Africa." *Regional and Federal Studies* 13 (1): 1–30.

11

Resolving Fiscal Imbalances: Issues in Tax Sharing

M. GOVINDA RAO

The literature on fiscal federalism notes that multilevel fiscal systems are able to cater to diverse preferences while reaping the benefits of economies of scale. Fiscal federalism is therefore considered an optimal institutional framework for providing public services, because it combines the advantages of closeness to people—and hence sensitivity to their preferences—with economies of scale and scope.

The superiority of fiscal federalism in efficiently providing public services is captured by the decentralization theorem, which states that "in the absence of cost savings from the centralized provision of a good and of interjurisdictional externalities, the level of welfare will always be at least as high (and typically higher) if Pareto-efficient levels of consumption are provided in each jurisdiction than [if] *any single, uniform* level of consumption is maintained across all jurisdictions" (Oates 1972, p. 54; emphasis added). In this formulation, the loss of efficiency is attributable to the uniform provision of public services rather than to centralization per se, but informational and political constraints limit the ability of the centralized system to meet diverse preferences. A decentralized system is superior in providing public services, because it faces fewer such constraints (Oates 1999).

Critical to achieving optimality is the assignment system. An important rule in implementing fiscal decentralization is that functions should follow finance (Shah 1991, 1994). However, although subnational governments have a comparative advantage in implementing expenditure programs, they have a comparative disadvantage in raising revenues from certain taxes, particularly broad-based taxes (that is, those in which the tax base is spread across the country) and taxes with mobile tax bases. This disadvantage arises because of the high level of evasion and avoidance of taxes when such taxes are levied by subnational governments. In addition, mobile tax bases encourage the creation of tax havens and may lead to distortions in resource allocation (Breton 1995; Musgrave 1983). Subnational governments should therefore levy only residence-based (as opposed to resource-based) taxes and user charges. Higher-level (central) governments should levy nonbenefit taxes, particularly those needed for redistributive purposes. To the extent that subcentral governments need to levy nonbenefit taxes, they should use tax bases that are relatively immobile across jurisdictions. Central governments also have distinct advantages over subnational governments in their ability to borrow and to create resources through seignorage.

How should the assignment of taxes and expenditure functions across different levels of government be sequenced? The literature suggests that the assignment of spending responsibility should precede the assignment of taxing powers, because it should be determined by the requirements of different spending agencies (as well as the principles of tax assignment) (Shah 1994). Having a perfect correspondence between revenue and expenditure powers at subnational levels would be ideal, since it would require that the consumers of public services fully pay for the services they consume. However, an assignment system based on comparative advantage will necessarily result in subnational governments having greater expenditure responsibilities than their taxation powers would permit. In those situations, mechanisms should be instituted to resolve such vertical fiscal imbalances. Differences between the capacities of subnational units to raise revenues could violate horizontal equity among individuals residing in different jurisdictions.

Various instruments can be used to resolve these vertical and horizontal fiscal imbalances within a country. These instruments and their design vary in terms of the degree of fiscal autonomy, involve different incentive systems, and have different equity implications. The instruments include (general-purpose) revenue-sharing arrangements and specific-purpose transfers (with or without matching requirements from subnational governments).

This chapter examines the design of alternative forms of revenue-sharing systems, their effect on incentives, and experiences of revenue sharing in some important multilevel fiscal systems. In the next section, theoretical issues of intergovernmental transfers and the roles of revenue assignment and sharing in offsetting fiscal disabilities are discussed. The following two sections analyze the effects of revenue-sharing systems on equity and incentives. These analyses, based on international experience with revenue sharing, help identify the objectives of revenue-sharing systems and their appropriate design to fulfill those objectives. The last section summarizes the chapter's main conclusions.

Revenue Sharing as an Instrument of Intergovernmental Transfer

Finances should follow functions. The problem is that although assigning functions to subnational governments is relatively easy, finding adequate and potentially nondistorting tax handles to finance those functions is difficult. The predominant responsibility of the central government for redistribution and stabilization requires that broad and mobile tax bases be assigned to it. Furthermore, assignment of such tax bases to local governments can result in a "race to the bottom" to attract investments and trade, potentially creating significant tax disharmony between different units of subnational governments. The noncooperative game in setting taxes can often result in the introduction of taxes that impede the movement of products and violate the principle of a common market.[1]

As the proportion of expenditures financed by the assignment of tax handles increases, greater fiscal autonomy and linkage between revenue-spending decisions will improve accountability and incentives and thus enhance welfare (figure 11.1). Ideally, from the viewpoint of accountability, each government unit should be able to raise the revenues it needs to finance its expenditures from its own sources. That situation would ensure linkage between costs and benefits within the jurisdiction, an important precondition for stable intergovernmental competition (Breton 1987, 1995). Thus as fiscal autonomy increases, greater efficiency and accountability will create welfare gains. At some point, however, as a larger proportion of expenditures is financed from the jurisdiction's own taxes, tax disharmony and inefficiency will result, because subnational taxation will cause a welfare loss to the community. (This situation is denoted by the curve AA.) Assignment of

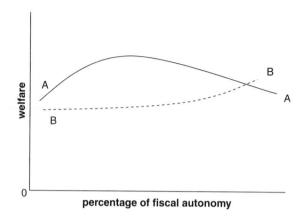

Source: Author.

FIGURE 11.1 Welfare Implications of Tax Assignment

taxes will be optimal at the point at which the marginal welfare gain from fiscal autonomy is equal to the marginal welfare loss from tax disharmony.

In the preceding discussion, tax powers were assumed to be assigned exclusively to the central or subnational governments. However, it is possible to minimize the adverse effects of tax disharmony through an arrangement in which central and subnational governments jointly tax, in the spirit of cooperative federalism. Of course, even with such arrangements, noncooperative games may take place between the central and subnational governments or among subnational units. These games can result in perverse incentives and inequities unless a regulatory system is put in place with clearly specified rules and a mechanism to effectively monitor intergovernmental competition.

Revenue sharing is an arrangement in which the revenue from a given tax base accrues to both the central and subnational governments. It ensures subnational governments a specified source of revenues to carry out their functions while attempting to provide greater harmony in levying taxes. In other words, revenue sharing is an attempt to enhance net welfare gains by ensuring greater fiscal autonomy on the one hand and by minimizing the welfare loss from tax disharmony on the other.

Revenue-sharing arrangements can be of two types: those in which multiple levels of government share the tax base and those in which revenue is collected by one level but shared by different levels. In the first type of system, the higher-level government determines the tax base, and the lower levels levy rates supplementary to those levied by the higher-level government or piggyback their tax rates on the tax base determined by the higher-level government. If the different levels of government do not cooperate, this type of system can lead to inefficiency from uncoordinated and disharmonized taxation. If, for example, the tax is on consumption and the tax base is shared on the basis of origin, substantial interjurisdictional tax spillovers can result that have significant efficiency and equity implications.

In the second type of system, important issues must be considered about the proportion of central revenues to be shared between central and subnational governments and the formula for sharing among subnational governments. The system can include only the central and regional (state or provincial) governments, or it can include local governments as well. The system of revenue sharing can be specified in the constitution, determined by a constitutional commission that is appointed periodically, or decided on the basis of agreements between the central and subnational governments. Sharing can be based on origin of revenues, in which case the objective of tax sharing is merely to offset vertical imbalance, or it can be based on population and thus distributionally neutral. It can be used to offset fiscal disabilities by equalizing fiscal capacity or need, or it can be designed to achieve regional development or improve tax effort. In general, the central government collects revenue and shares it with subnational governments. However, in some cases the tax is levied by the central government and collected and appropriated by the regional governments. There have also been arrangements, such as the one that prevailed in China before recentralization reform in 1994, in which the central government levied the tax, the regional governments collected it, and both levels shared the proceeds. Each arrangement entails different incentive systems.

Sharing the Tax Base: Coordination, Efficiency, and Incentives

The following analysis applies to revenue-sharing systems in which the various levels of government share the same tax base.

Concurrency, Competition, and Efficiency

Tax-base sharing results when multiple levels of government are assigned concurrent powers to levy taxes. This concurrent taxing power can happen by design (that is, as part of the constitutional scheme of assignment itself) or by default because those who draft the constitution define tax bases for legal purposes without considering their economic interdependence.

To ensure clarity and prevent the spillover of taxes, it is desirable to follow the principle of separation in assigning tax powers to different levels of government. However, even when the principle is followed in a legal sense, effective separation is not always possible. Of course, tax bases of all taxes are related to one another in some sense, because, ultimately, all taxes are paid out of incomes—past, present, or future. But the extent of concurrency is much larger in the case of some taxes than others.

Tax-base sharing has some important advantages, even when it causes inefficiency and interregional inequity. First, giving greater tax powers to subnational jurisdictions helps link revenue-expenditure decisions at the margin. Second, when adequate tax handles are provided and a system of intergovernmental transfers is instituted, the system helps enforce hard budget constraint at subnational levels. Third, tax-base sharing provides maneuverability and certainty in revenues by transferring ownership of those taxes to subnational governments, helping them plan their provision of public services.

Sharing the Tax Base of Direct Taxes

Most transition economies prefer harmonized and unified tax systems over the fiscal autonomy of subnational governments. They have therefore centralized taxing powers. Although some type of subnational governmental structure existed in these economies under central planning, subnational units had no fiscal or legislative responsibility (Bird, Ebel, and Wallich 1995). This was the case even in socialist countries that were formally called federations, such as the Soviet Union.

Although some functions have been decentralized, fiscal imbalance is resolved mainly through the intergovernmental transfer system, including tax sharing. In many transition economies, the major challenge is replacing public enterprise revenues with tax revenues. Given the culture of centralization, instituting a centralized tax system and avoiding subnational tax disharmony are relatively easy. No transition economy has assigned broad-based taxes to local governments. In recent years, however, local governments have been permitted to piggyback their own levies or impose surcharges on central taxes such as personal income tax (Bird, Ebel, and Wallich 1995).

The most important cases of tax-base sharing are in advanced market economies, such as Canada, Switzerland, and the United States, where corporate taxes are levied concurrently at both the central and subnational levels. This system results in administrative complexity and the misallocation of resources. Because different regions can levy taxes at different rates, subnational tax competition results. Such competition can influence investment location decisions and thus distort resource allocations (Boadway 1992). Furthermore, apportioning the profits of major corporations, which may have operations in various areas within the country, is difficult. The United States adopted a complex formula, using sales, asset values, and employment figures to determine what each state can legitimately tax. Unless the profit allocation is properly done, the system can lead to significant tax exportation by subnational units.

An important candidate for sharing the base between central and subnational units is the personal income tax. Although the literature assigns this broad-based and mobile tax base to the central government for stabilization and redistribution reasons, subnational governments in Canada, the Scandinavian countries, and the United States are allowed to levy personal income tax concurrently. Piggybacking local rates on the uniform tax base determined by the central government makes such local taxation administratively feasible. However, subnational differences in tax rates can cause significant mobility of individuals and businesses and can distort resource allocation. In developing countries and transition economies, however, interjurisdictional mobility is relatively low. Piggybacking local rates on the centrally determined tax base is therefore often recommended (Bird, Ebel, and Wallich 1995).

In India separation of taxing powers between the central government and the states has created a coordination problem in the case of direct taxes. The central government has the power to levy taxes only on nonagricultural income and wealth; the power to tax agricultural income and wealth is assigned to the states. For political reasons, however, the states have found taxing agricultural income and wealth impossible. As a result, tax evaders declare their nonagricultural income to be agricultural income. Not surprisingly, farmhouses near major urban agglomerations are an attractive investment opportunity.[2]

Sharing the Consumption Tax Base

In most multilevel fiscal systems, taxes on the consumption of goods and services are levied at the central level, with revenues either entirely appropriated by the central government or shared with subnational governments.[3] Important exceptions are Canada, Brazil, and India.

Canada

In Canada both federal and provincial governments can levy all direct taxes, and the courts have interpreted sales tax to be a direct tax. The federal government levies a value added tax (VAT) (called the goods and services tax [GST]) on both goods and services, and the provinces levy retail sales taxes. Considerable attempts at harmonization have been made in order to minimize overlapping. New Brunswick, Newfoundland and Labrador, and Nova Scotia levy a harmonized sales tax (HST). In these provinces, a joint federal-provincial VAT of 15 percent is levied, which includes a 7 percent GST for the federal government and an 8 percent HST for the provinces. The revenue is shared among the three provinces based on their consumption patterns. British Columbia, Manitoba, Ontario, and Saskatchewan levy their retail sales tax on the tax base determined for the GST. Quebec levies and collects both the federal and provincial tax, passing on the federal tax to the federal government. Alberta does not levy sales tax at all. Canada thus has several models of a dual VAT, but the system is well harmonized. In the case of provinces that levy HST, complete harmonization exists. In other provinces, harmonization exists to the extent that the tax base is identical to the GST base and the combined tax rates of the federal and provincial taxes do not exceed 15 percent.

Brazil

Brazil also levies VAT at both the central and state levels. The federal government levies the IPI (*imposto sobre productos industrializados*, or tax on industrial products), a value added tax on the manufacturing sector. The IPI is a complicated tax, with rates ranging from 4 to 333 percent. States levy a VAT up to the retail level. This tax, the ICMS (*imposto sobre operações relatives à circulação de mercadorias e serviços*, or merchandise circulation tax), is levied at five rates: 7, 8.8, 12, 18, and 25 percent. In addition, a separate central tax of 9–11 percent is levied on the interstate sale of goods. This tax is generally levied at lower rates in poorer states.

Because it is so complicated, Brazil's system has a very high compliance cost. Considerable interstate tax competition creates adverse effects on efficiency and interregional equity. The system has also been abused by taxpayers through tax tourism and invoice sightseeing (Bird and Gendron 2001).[4]

India

India's Constitution adopts the principle of separation in assigning tax powers, which implies that taxes assigned to the central government are not assigned to the states and vice versa. In a legal sense, exclusivity exists. Concurrency is not avoided, however, because the separation of taxes in a legal sense does not prevent economic interdependency of tax bases. For example, the central government has the right to levy excise duties on manufactured products, while the states have the power to levy taxes on the sale and purchase of goods. In effect, such excise duties were nothing but a manufacturers' sales tax, which has gradually been converted into a central VAT at the manufacturing stage. The states, meanwhile, have been levying the sales tax. Until recently, most states levied the sales tax at the point of manufacture (on the value of excise duty paid) or on imports from one state to another. The states also levy a tax on the interstate sale of goods (central sales tax), subject to the ceiling rate set by the central government (4 percent). In April 2005, 21 of the 28 states agreed to switch to a retail-stage VAT. However, the tax credit mechanism for this VAT will apply only to intrastate sales and purchases, and the tax on interstate sales levied by the exporting state will continue. A proposal has been made to phase out the central sales tax in 2007. When that reform is complete, the state-level VAT will become a destination-based tax extending up to the retail stage. To facilitate this reform, the central government has instituted an information system on interstate transactions in goods.

Thus considerable overlap exists in the consumption tax system in India. Even when the reform is complete, a dual VAT will exist: one up to the manufacturing stage, levied by the central government, and another destination-based VAT up to the retail stage, levied by the states. Although these taxes will work in parallel, central VAT paid is not deductible in the state VAT system and vice versa. By no means will the system be simple. But in the prevailing environment—in which states emphasize autonomy—the dual system seems to be the best option. The Task Force on Fiscal Responsibility and Budget Management Act (Government of India 2004) recently recommended that a unified goods and services tax be adopted. However, with states vigilantly guarding their autonomy, tax unification is unlikely to be an acceptable solution in the foreseeable future.

The lesson from the Indian experience is that institutional realities are important; for reforms to be politically acceptable, they may have to be less than perfect. Thus, even though the dual system results in some overlap and inefficiency, significant interstate tax exportation is likely because of its origin-based nature, and administrative and compliance costs will be significantly higher than for a unified GST. A broad consensus has emerged around this solution, making it at least possible to implement politically.

Conclusions on Tax-Base Sharing

Tax-base sharing could be an important instrument to resolve horizontal imbalances. It provides tax handles to the subnational governments; if the tax base is harmonized with the central levy, it can minimize disharmony from subnational tax systems; and it allows subnational governments fiscal autonomy while correcting horizontal imbalance.

Tax-base sharing without adequate safeguards can provide scope for subnational governments to indulge in unhealthy tax competition, however—a "race to the bottom." States can provide liberal fiscal and financial incentives to attract capital into their jurisdictions. Such policies segment factor and commodity markets, distort the pattern of resource allocation, rob federations of common market advantages, cause significant interstate tax exportation, create noncorrespondence between taxes and public services, and redistribute resources in favor of more-powerful jurisdictions, which is necessarily inequitable. In countries in which significant sharing of tax bases exists, it is important, therefore, that the central government monitor and regulate intergovernmental competition in the interest of efficiency in resource allocation and equity.

Revenue Sharing in Multilevel Fiscal Systems

The following analysis applies to revenue-sharing systems in which revenue is collected by one level of government but shared by different levels.

Sharing Systems in Different Countries

In contrast to tax-base sharing systems, in a system in which different levels of government share the revenue collected, the level of government that receives revenue is not politically responsible for raising it. The system ensures that the subnational governments receive a stable and buoyant source of revenue while avoiding the disharmony and distortions arising from tax competition among subnational jurisdictions. The central government normally raises the revenue and shares it with subnational governments according to a predetermined formula. The revenue-sharing arrangement may be mandated in the constitution or adopted as a convention.

Revenue sharing is a feature in a number of federations, both developed and developing. Among developed countries, the system is most prominent in Germany, where tax sharing is mandated by the constitution. All broad-based taxes, such as individual income tax, corporate income tax, and

VAT, are shared. The revenue from individual income tax is shared by the federal government (42.5 percent), states (*Länder*) (42.5 percent), and municipalities (15 percent). Corporate income tax and capital yields taxes are shared equally by the federal government and the *Länder*. The VAT is distributed between the federal government and the *Länder* on the basis of legislation approved by the *Bundesrat* (the national legislature representing the *Länder*). Municipalities are required to remit 15 percent of their business tax revenues to the federal government and *Länder* (Fisher 1997).

Australia assigns the entire revenue received from the goods and services tax to the states on the basis of an equalization or "relativities" formula. States' equalization payments are reduced by an amount proportional to the share of the goods and services tax they receive. In effect, this arrangement simply ensures a source of equalization payments (Madden 2002).

In Austria both the states and municipalities receive revenues from the VAT levied and collected by the central government. The states receive 18.6 percent of VAT collections, while municipalities receive 12.4 percent.

Among developing countries, tax sharing is most prominent in India. Until the amendment of the constitution in 2000 (80th amendment), the central government was required to share the proceeds of the personal income tax (Article 270), and it could opt to share revenues from union excise duties (Article 272). The level of sharing of the two taxes and the criteria for their distribution were determined on the recommendation of the Finance Commission, which was appointed every five years by the president. The proportion of revenue from the two taxes that was shared and the criteria used for their distribution were different. The 2000 constitutional amendment abolished article 272 and altered article 270 to include revenue from all central taxes in the shareable pool.

In several transition economies, local governments are given a share of taxes collected by the central government. Such sharing is common in all of the former Soviet republics as well as in Hungary, Poland, the Russian Federation, and Ukraine, where some or all of personal income tax is shared. Part of the reason for this sharing can be found in the growing revenue requirements associated with fiscal decentralization. In the Russian Federation, the central government now shares all of its personal income tax, a portion of VAT, and a portion of corporate income tax with the oblasts. In Romania local governments have a claim on both profit and dividend taxes levied by the central government on locally owned enterprises (Bird, Ebel, and Wallich 1995). An important trend in these economies is the tendency to reduce deficits when fiscal pressure at the central level increases. Thus Hungary reduced the share of personal income tax to local governments from 100 percent in 1991 to 30 percent in 1994. Bulgaria reduced the share of personal income tax to the local governments from 100 percent to 70 percent (Bird, Ebel, and Wallich 1995). Sharing on the basis of origin is disequalizing, and it can also result in significant tax spillovers when source-based taxes (such as profits tax or corporate income tax, cascading-type sales tax, and even VAT, which is origin rather than destination based) exist.

Another important feature in transition economies is that tax sharing is generally done on a derivation basis, in part because of the subnational governments' strong notion of source entitlement and primary claim on tax revenues generated within their jurisdictions (Bird, Ebel, and Wallich 1995). The problem arises when local governments collect revenues and are required to pass them on to the central government after retaining their shares according to the contracted or predetermined ratios, as in China before the 1994 reforms and in Vietnam (Rao 2002; Rao, Bird, and Litvack 1998).

Systems of revenue sharing can vary widely, depending on the scope of shareable taxes and the methods and criteria adopted for sharing. In some countries, revenues from specified taxes are shared between central and subnational governments. In most cases, shared taxes tend to be the more efficient ones, and they tend to create incentives for national governments to make more use of inefficient taxes, such as import duties or social security (as occurred in Argentina in recent years) (Tommasi 2002).

The scope of shared taxes and their division between the central and local governments can be defined by the constitution, determined by an independent body, or decided by the central government (as it is in many transition economies). The ratios and shares allocated to individual subnational governmental units can be determined annually or at regular intervals of three to five years. Allowing the central government to determine the ratios every year provides it leeway in calibrating stabilization policy. Not surprisingly, in such systems deficits can easily be passed down to subnational governments, leaving them with considerable uncertainty about how to provide their public services. Allocating shares at predetermined intervals of several years provides stability and certainty to subnational governments and helps them plan their activities.

Most transition economies distribute shareable taxes to subnational governments on the basis of origin or source. Others countries, such as Mexico and Pakistan, distribute the bulk of shared taxes on the basis of population and origin. Brazil and India distribute revenues on the basis of a formula that incorporates objectives that often conflict (Shah 1994).

Sharing Revenue from Specific Taxes or Aggregate Central Revenues

The incentive structure depends on whether revenues from specific taxes or aggregate tax revenues are shared. Because of fiscal pressure on the central government, sharing of specific taxes causes the central government to focus its revenue efforts on the nonshareable sources. This structure can result in distorted tax systems, reduce the revenue productivity of the tax system, and affect tax equity.

The classic case of disincentives arising from selective tax sharing was seen in India before the 2000 constitutional amendment abolished the compulsory sharing of personal income tax and optional sharing of union excise duties. The successive finance commissions that were responsible for determining both the allocation and the proportion shared by the states increased the states' share until the late 1990s, which saw the transfer of 87.5 percent of the net proceeds of personal income tax and 47.5 percent of the revenue from union excise duties. In addition to increasing the states' share, the Finance Commission gave greater weight to a backwardness factor in an effort to make the transfer system more progressive. Because the distribution of taxes among the states was based on population and other general economic indicators, it could not be targeted to fiscally disabled states. Therefore, to prevent more resources from going to relatively better-off states, the weight of the backwardness factor had to be increased over the years.

These mechanisms created perverse incentives. When some central taxes are shared and others are not, the central government has the incentive to raise more revenue from taxes that are not shared with the states. Although the central government's proportion of revenue from shareable taxes declined from 70 percent in 1970/71 to 52 percent in 1990/91, stabilizing at that level thereafter, its revenue from nonshareable taxes increased correspondingly over the years (figure 11.2). Among the taxes not shared was the customs duty, which increased steadily when the government began to use it as a revenue instrument (Rao 1998). Only after the sharp reduction in import duties following the structural adjustment program did the increase in revenue from unshared taxes slow. The phenomenon continued until 1995/96, after which the two ratios shown in figure 11.2 stabilized at about 50 percent. Later, in 2000, reforms in the tax-sharing system replaced the sharing of selective taxes with the sharing of revenues from the total tax revenue of the central government.

The wrong incentives implicit in the tax-sharing scheme that prevailed in India before 2000 were the subject of serious debate. Burgess and Stern (1993)

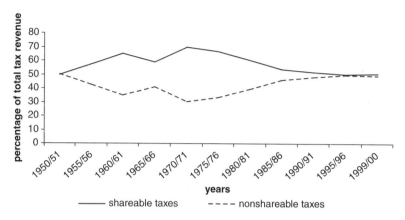

FIGURE 11.2 Central Government Revenue in India from Shareable and Nonshareable Taxes, 1950–99

Source: Government of India, various years.

and Joshi and Little (1996) attribute the slow growth of tax revenue from the two shared taxes and the sharp increase in the revenue from customs duties to the tax-sharing phenomenon. According to Joshi and Little (1996, 93–94):

> such a division of revenue produces a crazy set of incentives for levying different taxes . . . . There is no doubt that the stagnation of personal direct taxation and the burgeoning of customs revenue owe much to the fact that centre until recently retained only 12.5 percent of the former and 100 percent of the latter. There is also no doubt that this cockeyed growth of the tax system has harmed the whole economy.

On many occasions the central government preferred to change administered prices of public monopolies rather than increase excise duties in order to avoid sharing revenues from excise duties. This policy further distorted prices. Eventually, on the basis of the recommendation of the 10th Finance Commission, the Constitution was amended and general tax sharing replaced the sharing of individual taxes.

Disincentives from Tax Sharing in Decentralized Tax Administrations

Decentralized collection of central taxes can also create disincentives. In China's fiscal contract system, introduced in 1988, the central government determined tax bases and rates, but local tax administrations collected the taxes, retained their share, and remitted the remainder to the central government. This system provided independent revenues to local governments but created incentives for them to avoid remitting taxes through a variety of means (Ma 1995; Wong 1997). The differential sharing mechanism enhanced the powers of more-affluent provinces and reduced the central government's share of revenues.

The adverse consequences of this system were many. First, the central government lost its ability to undertake regional redistribution. Second, the declining share of central revenues and overlapping expenditure assignments enabled the central government to push down expenditure responsibilities to lower levels. Third, the system created significant inequities in the sharing of resources among local governments. Richer localities were better able to use the extrabudgetary resources to provide public services. Fourth, because an increasing proportion of spending was done outside the budget—extrabudgetary funds were estimated to represent about 8–10 percent of China's GDP in 1995 (World Bank 2000)—the system reduced accountability.

Not surprisingly, the ratio of revenues to GNP fell, from 35 percent in 1978 to 12 percent in 1996. The expenditure share of the central government declined from about 51 percent in 1979 to 27 percent in 1994 (Wong 2000; World Bank 2000).

The recentralizing reforms introduced in 1994 were intended to arrest the fiscal decline, reestablish the role of central government, make the budgeting system comprehensive, eliminate distortions in the tax system, and revamp intergovernmental fiscal arrangements. These important measures included the introduction of a VAT, the distribution of 75 percent of VAT revenues to the central and 25 percent to local governments, the reassignment of taxes between central and local governments to provide tax handles to each, and the establishment of separate tax administrations for central and local governments.

Revenue-Sharing Formulas

In most transition economies, tax sharing is done on the basis of some indicators of origin or accrual (Bird, Ebel, and Wallich 1995). In such systems, the objective of tax sharing is merely to offset vertical fiscal imbalances. Central tax powers use tax sharing to provide subnational governments ensured sources of revenue within the framework of harmonized taxes. This sharing may be required because subnational capacity to administer taxes is lacking, or it may be a deliberate attempt to minimize disharmony in the tax system arising from the subnational levy of taxes.

Some countries have a tax-rental arrangement in which the central government collects the provincial tax and distributes the proceeds on the basis of origin. An important example of the tax-rental arrangement was the leasing of the power to levy income tax by the states to the commonwealth government in Australia during World War II. The arrangement continued even after the war. The states received an income tax entitlement grant that was eventually merged with the general grants given to offset fiscal disabilities on the basis of the estimate of revenue capacity and expenditure need by the Commonwealth Grants Commission (Mathews and Grewal 1997).

The revenue-sharing systems in India and Pakistan evolved from a common system developed before partition under the Government of India Act, 1939. In both countries, the constitution provides for tax sharing and finance commissions determine the shares provincial governments receive. In Pakistan the constitution of 1973 mandates sharing of the major taxes collected by the central government. The excise duty and royalty on gas, the surcharge on gas, the royalty on crude oil, and profits from hydroelectricity are shared among the provinces on the basis of origin. Revenue from income taxes, sales tax, export duties on cotton, and excise duties on sugar and tobacco are shared by the federal (62.5 percent) and provincial (37.5 percent) governments. Revenues are distributed among the provinces based on population. The scheme of tax sharing is determined by the National Finance Commission, which has a checkered history (Shah 1998).

In India tax sharing is used extensively, not only to offset vertical fiscal imbalance but also to deal with horizontal imbalances. The distribution and allocation of tax revenues is determined by the Finance Commission, which, over the years, has included a variety of factors capturing backwardness, cost disability, and need—with varying weights assigned to them—in the distribution formula. The most recent (12th) Finance Commission recommended that the states receive 30.5 percent of the tax revenue collected by the central government between 2005 and 2010. The shares that individual states receive depends on five factors: population (25 percent weight), distance from the state with the highest per capita GDP (50 percent),[5] area (10 percent), tax effort (7.5 percent), and fiscal discipline (7.5 percent). These factors represent revenue and cost disabilities as well as expenditure needs.

Revenue-sharing systems are intended to provide independent revenue sources to subnational governments by minimizing tax disharmony and distortions. When the revenue share is distributed entirely on the basis of accrual, the system is meant merely to offset vertical fiscal imbalance. Such a system ensures fiscal autonomy to the extent that it provides an independent revenue source, retains its buoyancy over time if the ratio that is shared is not reduced, and minimizes distortions by avoiding tax competition. In some countries, such as Pakistan, the bulk of revenue sharing is based on population (Shah 1998). Population is a basic "need" factor that the system takes into account, and it helps ensure per capita equality. Other cost and revenue disabilities are not considered under this design.

The Indian system takes into account a number of need and performance factors in the tax devolution formula. This design has led to several problems. First, in trying to contain the overall level of transfers, the finance commissions have, over the years, increased the complexity of the formula by including capacity and need variables. The Eighth and Ninth Finance Commissions took into account the inverse of per capita state GDP and the distance from the state with the highest per capita GDP. Second, the choice of variables and the weights assigned reflect the judgments of the commission and are not based on any objective considerations.[6] Third, weighing multiple variables has often caused the effects of one variable to offset the effects of another. The measures of tax effort, for example, were positively related to per capita state GDP. Earlier commissions took both accrual and backwardness into account in distributing income tax. Inclusion of various backwardness variables in the devolution factor by successive commissions created an incentive for the states to minimize their own interventions to reduce backwardness. Fourth, to provide an incentive for states to adopt an active family planning agenda, the commissions were directed to use 1971 population data wherever population was used in the devolution formula. This factor penalized states with high population growth attributable to migration from other states.

Including capacity and need variables as criteria for tax devolution makes the tax-sharing scheme work as a substitute for block grants. Like grants, such tax sharing tries to offset fiscal disabilities and attempts to resolve both horizontal and vertical fiscal imbalances. Some important differences exist, however.

First, as long as it is possible to measure the disability, unconditional grants to offset revenue and cost disabilities can be targeted to the provinces with the disability. In contrast, tax devolution based on general indicators is received by all provinces, according to the values of the variables they reflect.

Second, the share in taxes increases over time, depending on their buoyancy with respect to incomes and prices. In contrast, unless they are explicitly linked to price changes or a growth rate is explicitly factored in, grants are not responsive to changes in prices and incomes. This could be important when the intergovernmental transfer formula is decided once every five years. Not surprisingly, in their depositions before the finance commissions, the states in India have argued for a larger volume of transfers through tax devolution than through grants.

Third, grants can be designed to affect aggregate fiscal performance in states. In contrast, tax devolution affects only the economic variables chosen for distribution. If any of the variables is within the control of the states, this factor could result in the moral hazard.

Concluding Remarks

Tax sharing is an important instrument of intergovernmental transfer to harmonize the tax system and ensure the stability and autonomy of subnational fiscal policy. The simplest form of tax sharing is to piggyback on central taxes, such as individual income tax, or allow the subnational government to levy a surcharge on central taxes. This method should be used only for destination-based taxes. If origin-based taxes, such as corporate income tax, are shared, complex formulas must be used to distribute revenues, because distribution on the basis of collection could result in significant spillover of taxes across subnational jurisdictions.

Some countries use tax sharing as a substitute for unconditional grants. Doing so provides a stable and certain source of revenue to subnational governments, and it has built-in buoyancy. However, when taxes are shared not merely to offset vertical fiscal imbalance but also as a substitute for equalizing grants, formulas have to be used that include revenue and cost disabilities. In such cases, it is important to ensure that the formula is simple and transparent and has the right incentives. Tax devolution with an equalizing formula is less targeted than unconditional grants designed to offset revenue and cost disabilities.

Wide differences are apparent in tax-sharing systems around the world. Tax-sharing systems adopted in particular countries tend to depart from the ideal because of the historical, institutional, and political factors that helped create these systems. Even when the perverse incentives created by prevailing systems are recognized, systems are difficult to change. Nevertheless, identifying a system's shortcomings and attempting to build consensus to change the system can help reduce disincentives and distortions.

Notes

1. In India, for example, the strategic reduction in tax rates for commodities with high price elasticity of demand has led some states to levy an entry tax (see Rao and Singh 2005). For similar noncooperative games in Argentina, see Tommasi (2002).

2. In its preliminary report, the Task Force on Direct Taxes (Government of India 2002) recommended that the central government conclude an agreement with the state governments to rent the tax on agricultural income. Such an agreement would

allow it to levy tax on the income that taxpayers declared as agricultural in their tax returns. The revenue collected would then be distributed among the states on the basis of origin. This recommendation created so much opposition that it was not included in the final report.

3. In the United States, the power to levy sales tax lies with the states.

4. Tax tourism refers to diversion of trade through cross-border shopping. Invoice sightseeing refers to creation of fake invoices to claim false credit.

5. This factor is determined by the formula $(Y_h - Y_i)P_i/\Sigma(Y_h - Y_i)P_i$, where Y_i represents per capita domestic product of the ith state, Y_h represents per capita domestic product of the highest-income state, and P_i represents the population of the ith state.

6. There was considerable debate on the inclusion of a poverty ratio as one of the factors in the First Report of the Ninth Finance Commission. For details, see Rao and Singh (2005).

References

Bird, Richard M., and Pierre-Pascal Gendron. 2001. "VATs in Federal Countries: International Experience and Emerging Possibilities." *Bulletin for International Fiscal Documentation* 55 (7): 293–309.

Bird, Richard M., Robert D. Ebel, and Christine Wallich. 1995. *Decentralization of the Socialist State: Intergovernmental Finance in Transitional Economies*. Washington, DC: World Bank.

Boadway, Robin. 1992. *The Constitutional Division of Powers: An Economic Perspective*. Ottawa: Economic Council of Canada.

Breton, Albert. 1987. "Towards a Theory of Competitive Federalism." *European Journal of Political Economy* 3 (1–2): 263–329.

———. 1995. *Competitive Governments*. Cambridge: Cambridge University Press.

Burgess, R., and N. Stern. 1993. "Tax Reform in India." Working Paper 45, London School of Economics, Development Economics Research Programme.

Fisher, Ronald. 1997. *Intergovernmental Fiscal Relations*. Norwell, MA: Kluwer Academic Publishers.

Government of India. 2002. "Report of the Task Force on Direct Taxes." Ministry of Finance, New Delhi.

———. 2004. "Report of the Task Force on Implementation of Fiscal Responsibility and Budget Management Act, 2003." Ministry of Finance, Delhi.

———. Various years. "Public Finance Statistics." Ministry of Finance, New Delhi.

Joshi, V., and I.M.D. Little. 1996. *India's Economic Reforms, 1991–2001*. Oxford: Oxford University Press.

Ma, Jun. 1995. "The Reform of Intergovernmental Fiscal Relations in China." *Asian Economic Journal* 9 (3): 205–31.

Madden, John. 2002. "Australian Fiscal Federalism, Global Integration, and Economic Reforms." Paper presented at the conference "Federalism in the Global Environment," Stanford University, Center for Research in Economic Development and Policy Reform, Palo Alto, CA, June 6–7.

Mathews, Russel, and Bhajan S. Grewal. 1997. *The Public Sector in Jeopardy: Australian Fiscal Federalism from Whitlam to Keating*. Victoria University, Centre for Strategic Economic Studies, Melbourne.

Musgrave, R. 1983. "Who Should Tax, Where and What?" In *X Assignment in Federal Countries*, ed. Charles McLure, 2–29. Canberra: Australian National University Press.

Oates, Wallace E. 1972. *Fiscal Federalism*. New York: Harcourt-Brace.

———. 1999. "An Essay on Fiscal Federalism." *Journal of Economic Literature* 37 (3): 1120–49.

Rao, M. Govinda. 1998. "Reforms in Tax Devolution and Evolving a Coordinated Tax System." *Economic and Political Weekly* 33 (29–30): 1971–96.

———. 2002. "Challenges of Fiscal Decentralization in Developing and Transitional Economies: An Asian Perspective." In *Public Finance in Developing and Transitional Countries*, ed. Jim Alm and Jorge Martinez, 35–62. Cheltenham, United Kingdom: Edward Elgar.

Rao, M. Govinda, and Nirvikar Singh. 2005. *Political Economy of Federalism in India*. New Delhi: Oxford University Press.

Rao, M. Govinda, Richard Bird, and Jennie Litvack. 1998. "Fiscal Decentralization and Poverty Alleviation in a Transitional Economy." *Asian Economic Journal* 12 (4): 353–78.

Shah, Anwar. 1991. "Perspectives on the Design of Intergovernmental Fiscal Relations." Working Paper WPS 726, World Bank, Washington, DC.

———. 1994. "The Reform of Intergovernmental Fiscal Relations in Developing and Emerging Market Economies." Policy and Research Series 23, World Bank, Washington, DC.

———. 1998 "Indonesia and Pakistan: Fiscal Decentralisation: An Elusive Goal?" In *Fiscal Decentralization in Developing Countries*, ed. Richard Bird and François Vaillancourt, 115–51. Cambridge: Cambridge University Press.

Tommasi, Mariano. 2002. "Federalism in Argentina and the Reforms of the 1990s." Paper presented at the conference "Federalism in the Global Environment," Stanford University, Center for Research in Economic Development and Policy Reform, Palo Alto, CA, June 6–7.

Wong, Christine. 1997. "Overview of Issues in Local Public Finance in the PRC." In *Financing Local Government in the People's Republic of China*, ed. Christine Wong. Hong Kong: Oxford University Press.

———. 2000. "Central-Local Relations Revisited: The 1994 Tax Sharing Reform and Public Expenditure Management in China." Paper presented at the conference "Central-Periphery Relations in China: Integration, Disintegration or Reshaping of an Empire?" Chinese University of Hong Kong, March 24–25.

World Bank. 2000. *China: Managing Public Expenditures for Better Results*. Report 20342–CHA. Washington, DC.

12

Macro Formulas for Equalization

LEONARD S. WILSON

Equalization systems are typically designed to make aggregate treatment by government equal across subnational jurisdictions. This is typically done, at least in part, by equalizing potential government revenue—by somehow transferring revenues across jurisdictions so that they can afford similar levels of expenditure at similar tax rates. The amounts necessary to transfer are typically calculated on the basis of tax rates and representative tax bases.

It has been suggested that rather than using the representative tax base to calculate transfers, some more "macro" measure, such as provincial per capita GNP, could, or should, be used. This chapter explores the arguments for and against this alternative approach and discusses what the best basis to use in calculating equalization transfers might be. It examines whether the representative tax system (RTS) or macro bases better satisfies the theoretical justifications for equalization systems and whether, even if the RTS is theoretically better, a macro system could approximate the system in a simpler and less costly manner.

The chapter is organized as follows. The first section lays out the theory of equalization and presents an equalization formula. The second section makes the case for and against macro formulas. The third section looks at real-world examples from

Canada, Australia, and South Africa. The last section summarizes the chapter's main conclusions.

The Theory of Equalization

Boadway, Roberts, and Shah (1994) clearly distinguish between the rationales for other types of intergovernmental transfers and those for equalization payments. These distinctions are important for the discussion here, because the rationale for transfers has implications for what base is best for determining the size of the transfers. Much of the work in this field relates to countries, particularly Australia and Canada, that have complex and complete systems of both lower-level government taxation and equalization payments.

Boadway (2002) examines the Canadian case, directly addressing the issue of what base might be best to use in calculating equalization. He supports the RTS system but suggests that in more-complicated federal systems, where lower levels of government have more-complete taxation powers, the RTS might more easily be approximated by some macro measure.

In a unitary state, residents are treated equitably by the state, with like residents paying the same taxes and receiving the same levels of public goods and services. This may not be the case in a federation, where subfederal levels of government (hereafter referred to as provinces) are likely to differ in their abilities to provide such goods and services. A system of equalization transfers is necessary to ensure that like people are treated in a similar fashion by the government.

The most frequently used example of this, and an important real world cause of discrepancies, is the case in which provinces have access to resource revenues but these resources are not spread evenly across provinces. In this case, public goods are provided at lower tax rates in some provinces than in others, and like residents in different provinces are not treated alike.

The idea that like should be treated alike within a federation or nation is the principle of horizontal equity. Whether the satisfaction of this principle will be viewed as important involves, to some extent, the concept of the nation. Residents may feel that horizontal equity is necessary across provinces for fairness to prevail.

There is a second important argument for the equalization of net fiscal benefits: the notion that equalization will improve efficiency. If equalization is not maintained, factors of production (labor and capital) will have an incentive to move to provinces with the largest net fiscal benefits. Since these net fiscal benefits will not be related to productivity differences, factors may be misallocated. Labor, for example, may migrate to a province that provides larger net fiscal benefits, even though it may have a lower marginal product there and thus receive a lower wage than it would elsewhere.[1] In this case, labor would not be distributed where its productivity is greatest.

Net fiscal benefits differ across jurisdictions for three main sets of reasons. First, "source-based" tax revenues, such as resource rents, differ across jurisdictions.

Second, net fiscal benefits, which result from redistribution funded through residence-based taxation, differ. For example, when benefits are distributed on a per capita basis but taxes are raised through proportional taxation of income, net fiscal benefits are greater in provinces with larger proportions of high-income taxpayers. Progressive taxation amplifies this effect; any system in which benefits are related to income diminishes it. In contrast, if all benefits are funded through benefit taxation, for example, there is no need to equalize transfers, as there are no net fiscal benefits. This issue is important in determining which sources of government revenue should be equalized. On the basis of this theory, fees charged for government-provided services (such as fares for public transportation) should not be included in the base used for equalization.

Third, demographic differences across provinces account for differences in net fiscal benefits. Just as labor may migrate to jurisdictions with a larger proportion of high-income people, if taxes are proportional or progressive, it may also migrate out of jurisdictions with large proportions of older people needing more of some government service.

The design of equalization systems is entwined with the allocation of tax and expenditure responsibilities across levels of government. The problem of unequal net fiscal benefits could most simply be solved by having those with greater net fiscal benefits transfer funds to those with fewer funds. This requires, however, that the "have" provinces agree to these transfers.

Other possibilities exist. A greater share of tax responsibilities could be assigned to higher levels of government and a greater share of expenditure responsibilities to lower levels. If this is done, transfers from higher to lower levels of government will be necessary, and all provinces may be recipients. The size of these transfers can vary so that those with the highest net fiscal benefits receive the smallest transfers and equalization is attained by actions of the central government.

Transfers other than Equalization Transfers

It is worth briefly discussing other types of intergovernmental transfers to be clear about what equalization is meant—and not meant—to do. Two other types of transfers are particularly important for this purpose. First, in many—indeed, perhaps all—federations, there is an imbalance between the allocation of expenditure responsibilities and the allocation of tax sources across the levels of the federation, a vertical fiscal imbalance, or "fiscal gap." There is a presumption that it is more likely to be optimal to assign expenditure responsibilities than taxation powers to lower levels of government (see Boadway, Roberts, and Shah 1994). Many government expenditures are for local public or quasi-private goods or services with local catchment areas. Local provision allows governments to provide different levels of service in different areas and to respond to differences in taste. Local provision also increases efficiency, because the providers are closer to the recipients of the services and thus more responsive to their wishes. Interjurisdictional competition may also lead to more efficiency.

In contrast, it may make sense for taxation be to be handled by higher levels of government. There are advantages to tax harmonization, for example, that can be most easily handled by assigning taxes to the national government. Tax competition between provincial governments may result in distortion away from the optimal mix of taxes. For this reason, in many countries, the tax powers assigned to lower levels of government are very limited.

The desirability of devolving spending power to local areas but assigning taxation powers to the central government means that there is an imbalance between revenue-raising capability and expenditure responsibilities—a fiscal gap—between levels of government that will require transfers. These transfers can be thought of as separate from equalization, in that transfers are necessary even if all provinces have identical net fiscal benefits. At the same time, these transfers are entwined with the process of equalization, in that they can be used to implement it. Transfers to redress vertical fiscal imbalances can be varied across provinces in order to equalize net fiscal benefits. This is the case in Australia, where all states receive transfers, the size of which depends on the state's fiscal capacity (as well as on needs). The existence of a large vertical imbalance, in other words, may make equalization easier to implement.

Equalization is not meant to deal with vertical equity, the transfer from rich to poor individuals (see Boadway 2002). It is meant to ensure horizontal equity—the principle that like individuals are treated equally by the government wherever they live. This can mean that funds must be transferred from governments of provinces with low average incomes to those of provinces with high average incomes. If, for example, a low average income province has high government-owned resource rents, and thus its residents have high net fiscal benefits, it may be necessary to transfer funds from this province to other provinces, even though the recipient provinces may have higher average incomes. This will entail low-income taxpayers in the province with high net fiscal benefits paying taxes so that transfers can be made that will benefit high-income taxpayers in the recipient province. This counterintuitive result has been cited as an argument against equalization.

Normally, of course, in absence of resource rents, this will not happen. Net fiscal benefits will arise from income redistribution within a province if expenditure is roughly on a per capita basis and taxation is proportional or progressive. Under these circumstances, net fiscal benefits will depend on average income and the degree of progressivity of tax and expenditure policies. Higher-income provinces can be expected to provide higher net fiscal benefits for individuals of given ability. Normally, then, equalization to solve problems of horizontal equity will also entail some redistribution from rich to poor. Solving problems of vertical equity, however, should not be thought of as the purpose of equalization systems. Vertical equity should be solved by other types of transfer programs, usually transfers to individuals.

Although not usually discussed in these terms, equalization and the need to transfer to correct for the fiscal gap may nearly coincide in cases where lower levels of government have very few tax powers. In the extreme case, where lower levels have no tax powers, in the absence of considering needs, all provinces would offer the same—that is, no—net fiscal benefits, and equalization would not be necessary. All transfers would go to covering the fiscal gap, and they would need to be made in such a way as to preserve the equity of net fiscal benefits across provinces. For example, if per capita benefits of provincial public expenditure were equal, then transfers to provinces based on population would ensure equal net fiscal benefits.

An Equalization Formula

An important feature of federations is that lower levels of government are left free to make their own tax and expenditure choices. This is important because it allows residents to sort themselves by tastes. It also allows for experimentation in ways of taxing and providing services and thus may make for more-efficient provision of public goods. The equalization scheme must thus be designed so as not to penalize these sorts of differences. That is, a province that chooses low taxes and a low level of public good provision should not be penalized.

To insure that lower levels of government are not penalized for their tax and expenditure choices, equalization schemes are often based on potential rather than actual tax revenues. The Canadian system, for example, determines equalization transfers on the basis of the size of tax bases rather than on actual revenues. Designing transfers in this way also ensures that provincial governments make optimal decisions at the margin—that is, that they equate the marginal benefits of an expenditure to the total marginal costs. This may not be the case, for example, if transfers are in the form of matching grants.

These considerations strongly suggest the use of an equalization formula that is based on potential tax revenues relative to some measure of average potential. In Canada entitlements of province i are calculated as

$$\sum_{j=1}^{37} E_{ij} = \sum_{j=1}^{37} t_j \left(\frac{B_{Rj}}{P_R} - \frac{B_{ij}}{P_i} \right) P_i, \tag{12.1}$$

where j is the revenue source, E_{ij} is entitlement under revenue source j in province i, B_{Rj} is the national base for revenue source j, P_R is the national population, B_{ij} is province i's base for revenue source j, P_i is the population of province i, and t_j is the national average tax rate for revenue source j, or

$$t_j = \frac{\sum_{i=1}^{10} TR_{ij}}{\sum_{i=1}^{10} B_{ij}}, \tag{12.2}$$

where TR_{ij} is actual revenues from revenue source j in province i (see Boadway and Hobson 1993).

In the Canadian case, if ΣE_{ij} is greater than 0, province i will receive equalization of this amount from the federal government. If ΣE_{ij} is less than 0, however, the province will not "pay in" to the scheme. This would not be desirable in an ideal system, as it means that net fiscal benefits are not fully equalized across all provinces.

Thirty-seven revenue sources are incorporated in the calculation (that is, $j = 1, ..., 37$). The bases for these sources are defined by the federal government, after consultation with the provinces; they are standardized across provinces. In this sense, the bases are "notional," in that individual provinces may define a given base differently. Different provinces, for example, may exempt different commodities from sales taxes. Thus "revenues generated by the application of a national average rate to a province's notional base will typically differ from those generated by the application of the same rate to its actual base" (Boadway and Hobson 1993, p. 41).

The Canadian system broadly takes into account the issues raised above. The entitlements of individual provinces are based not on their actual tax revenues but rather on what they would raise if they applied the average tax rates to their bases. The entitlements, in other words, are based on potential rather than actual revenues, leaving the provinces free to choose their levels of expenditure and taxation without being penalized. "Rich" provinces (those with high net fiscal benefits) do not transfer directly to those with low net fiscal benefits. Instead, the federal government transfers to recipient provinces.

The Canadian system has some obvious failings, of course. The failure to "equalize down" provinces with higher than average net fiscal benefits is one. Another is that the Canadian system does not take differences in needs into account, something theory suggests is important in eliminating net fiscal benefits. Different provinces may, for example, have different demographic mixes—more elderly people or school-age children—resulting in greater expenditure needs for the same level of service provision. In this case, even if government revenues per capita were equal, like would still not be treated as like. The Australian equalization system, discussed below, takes needs into account in a comprehensive way. In many countries lower-level government tax revenues are small, so that most potential differences in net fiscal benefits result from needs differences.

Macro Formulas

The discussion above suggests that equalization transfers should be calculated on the basis of available tax bases. Criticisms have been made of this approach and alternatives suggested. In particular, more macro measures, such as personal income, provincial GDP or GNP, or GNP per capita, have been proposed. The arguments for alternative approaches have been of three types. First are arguments that a more macro approach is superior in theory or in terms of some broad criteria that should be used in assessing transfer systems. Second are arguments that a macro approach, while perhaps not better in theory, would be simpler or more transparent to apply. Data needs may be less, and there may be a strong correlation between the macro measure and the more theoretically correct RTS base. Finally, there are arguments about the failings of the RTS approach. In some cases, the application of the approach provides incentives for provincial governments to withhold development, in order to change a base, or set what would otherwise be suboptimal tax rates. It has also been argued that the RTS approach leads to instability in revenues for lower levels of government. In both these cases, it has been argued that a macro alternative would be better.

Proposals for specific macro measures vary, depending partly on the perceived problem with the RTS approach. In general, the proposals are variants of measures of the aggregate resources available to residents of a province. Measuring this exactly needs to be traded off against simplicity, as the complexity of the RTS approach is one of the criticisms leveled against it. Barro (2002) suggests that a correct measure would be provincial GNP modified to take into account taxes paid to, and subsidies received from, the federal government and the ability of the province to raise tax revenue from nonresidents by exporting taxes. Others, such as Smart (2002) and Boothe and Hermanutz (1999), propose simpler measures, such as provincial GDP.

Proposals for how the macro formula should work also vary, although all are variants of the RTS formula (equation 12.1). The closest formula to the RTS formula would treat each province as having only one overall base (see Courchene 1984). Thus province i's equalization entitlement would be

$$E_i = t \left(\frac{B_R}{P_R} - \frac{B_i}{P_i} \right) P_i, \tag{12.3}$$

where E_i is the entitlement in province i, B_R is the national macro base, P_R is the national population, B_i is province i's macro base, P_i is the population of province i, and t is the national average tax rate over all sources, or

$$t = \frac{\sum_{i=1}^{10} TR_i}{\sum_{i=1}^{10} B_i}, \tag{12.4}$$

where TR_i is actual tax revenue in province i.

This formula still allows for some tax-back effect: a province with a lower than average per capita base can raise equalization entitlements by raising its tax rates. In order to eliminate this effect, some proponents of the macro approach have proposed using a fixed "equalization rate" to replace t in equation (12.3). Smart (2002), for example, chooses a rate for Canada based on its ability to simulate actual past transfers under the RTS.

Macro Bases as Measures of Fiscal Capacity

Barro (1986, 2002) proposes using GNP, or a modification of GNP, as the base on which to calculate transfers. He argues that the best measure of provincial fiscal capacity is the overall resources available to the people of the province—that is, provincial GNP or provincial GNP modified to take into account transfers to and from the federal government and the possibility of gaining access to further resources by exporting taxes. Barro argues that whether to spend these overall resources on private or public consumption is a political decision and that only the overall level should thus be considered.

This seems likely to be a good argument only in cases in which provincial governments have easy access to these resources and access does not differ across provinces. There seem to be two broad problems with this approach. First, even if provinces have broad tax powers and the same per capita GNP, there may be differences in the make-up of GDP and thus in the "excess burden" of raising tax revenue. Dahlby and Wilson (1994) stress that the elasticities of the bases available are important. Provinces in which GDP is made up of a greater portion of bases that are inelastic with respect to tax rates will have an easier time and will impose less excess burden in raising taxes than will other provinces. In some federations, for example, provincial governments have access to a share of state-owned oil and gas revenues. If these resources are not distributed evenly—as is the case in Canada and Malaysia—provinces will differ in the ease with which they can raise revenues, and net fiscal benefits will differ across provinces.

Second, this argument seems likely to hold only where provincial governments have access to a complete range of taxes. In Canada and the United States, countries on which Barro bases his arguments, this is the case. In many other countries, however, the tax powers of lower levels of government are constrained, in many cases severely. In Malaysia, for example, states have access only to resource revenues and some license and other fees (Ariff 1991; Wilson 1996). Fewer tax sources will mean that provinces will be more likely to differ in the net fiscal benefits they provide even if more broadly defined measures of income are equal.

Usher (1995, 2002) stresses two other, related arguments. First is the point that under some circumstances, the RTS approach requires the transfer of revenues from poor provinces, as measured by GNP per capita, to rich ones. This could be the case if the poor province had easier access to tax revenue, say, because the provincial government owns some natural resource base. Using GNP per capita as the base for calculating equalization would ensure that this could not happen. In Malaysia, for example, the two states on the island of Borneo, Sabah and Sarawak, have the largest share of petroleum resource rents, one of the few revenue sources allocated to the states. In both states, however, average income is well below the Malaysian average. Equalization of state government revenues in this case would require transfers from the poor, at least as measured by average income, to the rich.

Usher views the difference between the way collectively and privately owned resource revenues are treated as fundamentally wrong. If, for example, petroleum resources are owned by provincial governments, all revenues from their sale become provincial government revenues and need to be equalized under the RTS. If, however, these resources are privately owned, the revenue from their sale becomes someone's income, and only that portion collected through the provincial tax system becomes part of provincial government revenue and needs to be equalized. This same problem might arise from the profits of state-owned, as opposed to private, corporations. A macro formula, using per capita GNP as the base, would correct for this problem, if it is a problem, as resource revenues or corporate profits would appear the same regardless of how they are owned.

It is difficult to know what to make of these arguments. Equalization seeks to improve horizontal equity, to ensure that like are treated as like. Thus even if on average province A is made up of poor people, if these people have access to large net fiscal benefits relative to those of the same income in province B, where on average there are more rich people, transfers need to be made from the government of A to the government of B. The problems of vertical equity should be left to some other set of policies, perhaps transfers directly to individuals rather than to their provincial governments. Similarly, government revenues, which contribute to differences in net fiscal benefits, need to be equalized regardless of whether there are other inequities in the way they are treated.

This set of comments can be judged only in the overall context of what one defines as the purpose of equalization. Here the purpose is defined quite narrowly as improving horizontal equity. At times, this goal can conflict with other social goals, such as vertical equity. When this is the case, other policy tools will also be necessary.

Incentive Problems

A second set of arguments for replacing the RTS approach with a broader macro approach is that, under some circumstances, the RTS provides incentives for individual provinces to behave suboptimally. In some cases, the provinces can affect the equalization payments they receive (or pay) by altering their tax rates ("rate tax-back") or the size of their base

("base tax-back"). This is not surprising given that equalization is broadly meant to bring provincial revenues per capita to similar levels.

Rate Tax-Back

The problem of rate tax-back is recognized in the Canadian case (equation 12.1), in that the tax rate determining a province's entitlement from a particular base, j, is the national average rate, t_j, rather than the province's own tax rate on the base. In some systems, such as the German one, this is not the case; equalization is based directly on own-source revenues, making the problem potentially more severe (Baretti, Huber, and Lichtblau 2000).

Even in the Canadian case, however, there will be situations in which a province can affect its equalization entitlements by changing its tax rates. This will be the case when the base is concentrated in a single province. In this case, the national average tax rate becomes that of the province, since it is the only province taxing the base, and revenues from increasing the rate will be offset by decreases in equalization receipts. This is an extreme case, but the problem will exist as long as individual provinces have disproportionate shares of some bases. This creates an incentive for provinces to change their tax mix away from that which would be most efficient in the absence of these effects.

How important this is will depend on how unevenly distributed bases are. Most often the problems arise from resource revenues. In both Canada and Malaysia, for example, off-shore oil revenues are concentrated in only a few provinces or states. The likelihood that bases will be unevenly distributed depends on how bases are defined. If they are defined broadly (say, as all resource revenues) rather than separately (as off-shore petroleum revenues, gold mining revenues, and so forth), this uneven distribution will be less likely to occur and the ability of individual provinces to take advantage of the rate tax-back effect will be diminished. The more broadly the bases are defined, however, the more obscured are distinctions in provincial revenue-raising capacity. Different mixes of resource bases may imply very different burdens in raising the same tax revenues; lumping them together hides these differences.

The rate tax-back problem suggests that bases should be defined more broadly. The extreme version is to use a measure such as provincial GNP as a whole (that is, a macro formula). A criticism of using a macro formula exactly parallels the problem of broadening the definitions of the bases used. The broader the bases, the less clear are differences in revenue-raising capacity from different bases across provinces.

Base Tax-Back

Provinces can also affect their equalization receipts (or payments) by altering their tax bases. This can be done directly, by encouraging or refusing permission for economic activity, or indirectly, through tax changes. In equation (12.1), an increase in the provincial base B_{ij} will directly cause provincial tax receipts to rise, but it will result in some, or all, of this revenue being "taxed back" through a decline in equalization (if the province is a recipient). If the province levies the average tax rate on a base, an increase in the base will result in complete tax-back; if the provincial tax rate is less than the average, the tax-back will exceed 100 percent. This problem is exacerbated if the increase in economic activity imposes costs on the provincial government. Unlike the case of rate tax-back, however, this problem will not be solved by moving to a macro formula. Since any equalization formula seeks to compensate for deficiencies in the tax base, an increase in the base will result in a decline in the payment received.

In summary then, a macro formula, or any formula in which the bases are more aggregate in nature, will reduce incentives for provinces to distort their tax mixes in order to affect the equalization they will receive. This will be more of a problem where provinces have very different mixes of bases, such that a single province can have an affect on the national average tax rate. The problem will also be more severe if equalization is based not on some average rate but on actual tax revenues. In this case, if provinces can set their own rates, the incentives would be for them not to tax at all.

Definition, Complexity, and Transparency

One of the main criticisms of the RTS approach in Canada has been its complexity and hence lack of transparency. This has been a major motivation for suggesting the use of some macro measure as the base, although some of the measures suggested as alternatives are themselves quite complicated.

In Canada, where provinces have wide taxation powers, 37 provincial revenue sources are included in the calculations. For many of these sources, provinces differ in the exact definition used in tax collection. Provinces may, for example, exempt different items, such as children's clothing, from sales taxation. Taxes may be per unit or based on value. This means that bases, for the purpose of calculating equalization, must be standardized across provinces through negotiation. The resulting "notional" bases may not correspond to any base actually used, and revenues assumed in a province may not correspond to actual revenues. The inclusion of property taxation, where the base is market value, has presented particular problems, as not everyone agrees that high property prices represent an increase in fiscal capacity.

The theory discussed above suggests that benefit taxes—taxes that would not lead to net fiscal benefits—should not be included. Fees for services provided by local governments or provinces should not be included in equalization, even though they can make up a significant portion of local revenues. Excluding these fees presents definitional difficulties. Provinces may differ in how they fund certain activities—through fees or general taxation—and fees may not exactly cover costs (there may be some profits on the service, yielding net fiscal benefits). This makes decisions about what to include as revenues to be equalized difficult. It could also make using a simple measure of fiscal capacity, such as total provincial government revenues, inaccurate.

These difficulties make the system appear complex, especially in systems like the Canadian one, in which provinces have many tax sources. They also make the system appear to lack transparency, as what is included appears to be the result of negotiations of politicians and civil servants rather than the results of some well thought-out formula.

Advocates of a macro formula argue that a measure such as per capita GNP would be more easily understood by, and might seem fairer to, the public than the RTS. Finding the appropriate macro formula also presents some difficulties, however.

One problem stems from the fact that different advocates of macro formulas have different justifications for their support for this approach. Some see the motivation for a system of equalization transfers as different from that suggested here. Others see the purpose of equalization as horizontal equity but think that using some macro base might be a simpler way to achieve it.

Barro (2002) advocates using overall resource capacities as the measure of the fiscal capacity of the provinces. The justification for doing so seems to be that overall resource capacity represents what is available to the residents of a province for public or private consumption and it is this that should be used to calculate equalization entitlements. Equalization itself would be based on the province's macro base per capita relative to the national base per capita and the overall tax rate, as described in equations (12.3) and (12.4).

Accepting Barro's proposals leads to a definition of the base as the overall resources available for public or private consumption in the province. No standard measure, such as personal income, GDP, or GNP, is quite complete for measuring this base. What is needed is a measure of "total resident income, comprehensively measured" less taxes paid to the central government plus central government financial aid to the province and "subordinate" local governments plus "taxes and other public revenues collected from nonresident households and businesses" or "exported taxes" (Barro 2002, p. 3). Total resident income could be thought of as the provincial equivalent of a national GNP measure. It is the "exported taxes" that "most complicate capacity measurement"(Barro, 2002, p. 3). These include taxes paid by cross-border shoppers and tourists, taxes collected from nonresidents working in the province, and taxes on capital and businesses owned by residents elsewhere. In summary, a simple measure of macro capacity as Barro wishes is not available.

Other researchers are less idealistic about the correct measure for the equalization base than Barro is. They view a macro base as a simpler approach unencumbered by some of the problems of the RTS (such as the rate and base tax-back). For them, simplicity is a goal in itself, and the best base is one that best approximates the current equalization results. Boothe and Hermanutz (1999), for example, look at three possibilities—provincial GDP, personal income by province, and an adjusted personal income in which modifications are made for farm inventories, provincial transfers to individuals, and federal taxes paid—settling on the last. Smart (2002) uses GDP at market prices. Usher (2002) argues strongly in favor of using a measure of overall resource availability similar to that proposed by Barro as the base. Among the issues he examines are whether there should be some imputation for leisure, whether needs should be taken into account,[2] whether transfers from the federal government and depreciation should be included, how to incorporate tax revenues collected from outside the jurisdiction, and whether some adjustment for price levels should be made. These issues make the use of a macro measure more complicated than its proponents might wish.

Measuring the Base

One of the advantages of the RTS is that it is based on tax revenues, for which provincial or state governments will have reasonably good accounts, even in countries that lack good national accounts. Macro measures, in contrast, require provincial or state account data that may not be collected. In developing countries, therefore, macro measure may not be easier to use than the RTS, because the data are not available and would be costly to obtain.

Usher (2002) notes that even in countries with sophisticated accounts, the measurement of bases is not always straightforward. This means that the

RTS approach is not as different from the macro approach as theory might have it. In the Canadian system, for example, about 45 percent of equalization payments are directly based on personal income taxation. Personal income is also used as the base for several other tax sources, because the true base is hard to measure. Measures of personal and industrial property tax; medical insurance premiums (charged by some, but not all, provinces); and revenues from games of chance are all based on personal income. Together, sources of income account for another 20 percent of overall transfers. The bases for other large provincial tax revenue sources are highly correlated with personal income. Usher argues that a move to a macro base such as personal income would not represent as great a change as critics would have it.

Stability of Transfers

The stability of transfers under alternative definitions of the base has been studied in the Canadian case. In general, annual tax revenues seem to be more stable than personal income or GDP (see Smart 2002). Boothe and Hermanutz (1999) propose using a five-year moving average of their adjusted personal income base. They find that when this measure is used in their formula for calculating equalization, payments are more stable than under the RTS approach.

Neumann (2002) raises the issue of the instability in measurement of both the RTS and macro variables. There is significant revision for several years after initial publication of national income accounts data in most counties, and these revisions have implications for transfers. On the basis of limited analysis, Neumann believes that this revision problem would be more severe for macro variables than for the RTS variables, with implications for the revision of transfers.

An Alternative "Nonmacro" Base

The discussion of macro bases has been in the context of countries with well-developed lower-level government tax systems. These provincial tax systems are seen as leading to differences in net fiscal benefits across like individuals in different provinces. The question is whether some macroeconomic variable other than the RTS might be a better basis for equalization to eliminate these differences.

In many countries the lower-level government tax base is very limited. Provincial governments may be constitutionally assigned few tax sources, resulting in large fiscal gaps and transfers from the central government to all provinces. In the extreme case, all lower-level government revenue may be from this source. In this case, differences in net fiscal benefits across jurisdictions will depend on differences in needs, and the best determinants of transfers may be neither the RTS approach nor the type of macro variables discussed but rather some variable, such as a demographic one, that measures lower-level government need. If, for example, lower-level government expenditures are such that benefits are distributed on a per capita basis, federal to provincial transfers should be based on population. Other determinants of needs, such as age distribution, which affect education and health care requirements, may be important. In many countries, then, federal to provincial transfers go to all provinces and are based on variables such as the size and age distribution of the population. If provinces have little or no own-source revenue, these "nonmacro" bases may be best for determining transfers to ensure equal net fiscal benefits across jurisdictions.

In some cases, the needs approach may suggest a macro variable of the type discussed here as a measure of need. A component of need in South Africa, discussed below, is based on a macro variable. State governments in Malaysia argue that federal-state transfers should take economic activity into account, as it imposes expenditure requirements on state governments (Wilson 1996). New factories, for example, require new roads, water, and sewerage facilities, all state expenditure responsibilities. States in Malaysia have limited tax bases, thus revenues are unresponsive to these changes in economic activity. These arguments suggest that a component of need might be directly related to economic activity and that some measure of this might thus be useful in determining equalization payments.

Equalization in Canada, Australia, and South Africa

Equalization programs in Canada, Australia, and South Africa provide examples for discussion of the use of macro formulas in determining equalization.

Canada

Most research on using macroeconomic variables to determine equalization has been on Canada, although even there the RTS is still used to define the base. There are several reasons for this interest. First, Canada has a highly developed equalization system. The provinces have extensive tax powers, they differ significantly in the make-up of their tax bases, some provinces have large resource revenues, and average incomes differ significantly across provinces. These factors have led to a long concern with equalization, going back to the 1930s, resulting in a comprehensive RTS–based set of arrangements.

The comprehensiveness of these arrangements has meant that most of the potential problems with the RTS approach have actually occurred. There are examples of both rate and base tax-back policies on the part of provincial governments. The possibility exists of provinces with below-average incomes having to pay into the system. Large revenues to provincial governments from nonrenewable resources have been difficult to deal with. The gross nature of the system, in which the federal government pays equalization to the "have-not" provinces rather than having the "have" provinces contribute directly to the "have-nots," has at times stretched the federal government's revenues, particularly when resource prices have been high. The system is complex, with 37 bases, some of which are difficult to define or measure. The result is a system that is difficult for many people to understand. There has also often been confusion over the purpose of the scheme, with some seeing it as a method of correcting for vertical inequality, transferring to low average-income provinces so that their provincial governments can in turn make transfers to individuals. All this has led to serious interest in an alternative base.

Problems with the RTS notwithstanding, it has been retained in Canada for the reasons discussed above. The logic of equalization points strongly to using differences in tax capacity as the base, especially as measurement of alternative macro bases is difficult.

Australia

The Australian system differs from the Canadian system in several ways (see Courchene 1995). First, and most important, is the existence of the Commonwealth Grants Commission. This Commission acts as an arbiter between the states and the federal government and handles much of the administration and allocation of federal-state grants. The Australian system includes "needs" and "costs" differences in the formula, both determined by the Commission.

Second, relative to their expenditure responsibilities, states in Australia have smaller tax bases than do Canadian provinces. This results in all states facing fiscal gaps with the federal government and thus in the federal government transferring funds to all states. Full equalization occurs without any need to have richer states transfer directly to poorer states.

Third, the entitlements under these transfers are based not just on potential revenues, as calculated using the RTS, but also on some measurement of needs or expenditures required to supply similar levels of services. States may differ in the cost of supplying a particular service because of demand differences or costs of provision (per capita) differences. The cost of providing education may vary, for example, because of different proportions of school-age children or because costs per pupil differ (because the population is more spread out, for example). The methodology the Commonwealth Grants Commission uses to determine these differentials in expenditure needs involves examining relevant data, making field visits, and holding public hearings (Shah 1996). "Socio-demographic composition, population density, urbanization and physical environment figure prominently in assessing differential costs" (Shah 1996, p. 103).

Fourth, the entitlements calculated on the bases of the RTS and needs requirements determine not the actual amount of transfers, as in the Canadian system, but the "relativities." The federal government sets an overall transfer amount, and these relativities are used to allocate the amount among the states.

Like the Canadian system, the Australian system uses the RTS approach to calculate equalization entitlements, at least on the revenue side. Variables other than state tax rates and bases do enter the formula, however, in calculating needs. These calculations reflect costs and demand factors for each of 40 expenditure components. Such factors as economies of scale, dispersion costs, and demand differences resulting from demographic composition are taken into account (see Courchene 1995). The Australian system, therefore, broadens the information used in calculating equalization entitlements beyond the data used under the RTS, but it does not use macro variables of the type proposed in Canada, such as provincial GDP.

South Africa

South Africa's equalization system, the Provincial Equitable Sharing System, depends completely on needs, as provincial own-source revenues are small. Less than 3 percent of provincial expenditure is financed from own-source revenues.[3] As with other needs-based approaches, transfers are determined by a variety of demographic and other variables. One component of these needs is calculated on the basis of a standard macro variable: the share of national remuneration of employees earned by employees within the province. Changing this measure to provincial GDP has been proposed.

The South African system is based on seven needs components, each weighted according to the component's importance in the past. The seven components are education (41 percent), health (19 percent), welfare (18 percent), a basic component (7 percent), an economic activity component

(7 percent), an institutional component (5 percent), and a backlog component (3 percent). The needs requirements for each province for each component are calculated and summed to arrive at the provincial share of the grant. The provinces are then free to allocate their revenues, including these transfers, as they choose.

The education component of the grant is based on the number of children in school and the number of school-age children in the province. The health component is based on the number of people with and without private medical insurance. The welfare or social development component is based on the number of people receiving transfers and the number of people in the province who are in the bottom 40 percent of the national income distribution. The economic activity component is determined by the province's share in total remuneration of employees. This share of the transfer reflects the notion that the need to create and maintain physical and social infrastructure depends on the level of overall economic activity. The basic component is determined by the province's share of the national population. The institutional component is a lump sum, shared equally across all provinces. The backlog component is based on surveys of needs in the health and education sector as well as on the degree of ruralness.

The Financial and Fiscal Commission (FFC), a constitutional organization similar to Australia's Commonwealth Grants Commission, has criticized the approach to the economic activity component on several grounds (South Africa 2004). First, since the program was designed, better data have become available. South Africa now has measures of GDP by province, which the FFC argues would be a better measure. Second, infrastructure requirements depend on more than just economic activity: factors such as the vintage and type of infrastructure are important. Rates of growth in economic activity, rather than levels, might be a better measure of need. Finally, the FFC notes that this component of the grant is regressive, as provinces with high levels of economic activity receive the greatest share of transfers.

Conclusion

The desirability of substituting a macro base for an RTS approach depends, at least partly, on the perceived purpose of equalization. The standard idea is that equalization serves to ensure horizontal equity, that like individuals are treated alike by the government regardless of where they live within a country. This is a different goal from achieving vertical inequality across individuals. Even in Canada, where these issues have received a great deal of attention, there seems to be confusion over the goal of equalization.

The desirability of moving to a macro base also depends on the range of the tax base available to the lower level of government. If provinces have very limited tax powers, a macro base is less likely to approximate their fiscal capacity than if they have greater powers. In many countries, then, moving to a macro base seems unattractive.

The concentration of interest in the Canadian case has meant that there has been little discussion in the literature of the possibility that a macro variable might work well as a base in cases where needs are an important determinate of equalization. It seems likely that, depending on lower-level government expenditure responsibilities, the type of macro variable discussed here would be useful in calculating at least part of the required equalization transfers. The South African case provides an example of this.

For many countries, perhaps the most important consideration will be the availability of data. The management and collection of taxes will ensure that lower-level governments have data on taxes and bases. In contrast, macro data, such as national accounts data, may not be available on a regional basis. This may make using the RTS approach more practical. If the definition of macro variables is broadened and needs are included as a basis for calculating equalization, many other variables, in particular geographic and demographic variables, will be important, as they have been in Australia and South Africa.

Most important, however, there is a straightforward link between the use of the RTS approach and the purpose of equalization. If policy makers want to ensure that fiscal capacities are equalized across lower levels of government, tax powers and tax bases seem the obvious basis on which to do so.

Notes

1. This argument, of course, depends on the free migration of labor and capital across provinces.
2. This is also an issue in equalization systems based on the RTS approach (see Shah 1996).
3. See South Africa (2004) for a detailed description of the South African system.

References

Ariff, M. 1991. "Case Study: Malaysia." In "Fiscal Decentralization and the Mobilization and Use of National Resources for Development: Issues, Experience and Policies in the ESAP Region." New York: UN Economic and Social Commission for Asia and the Pacific.

Baretti, C., B. Huber, and K. Lichtblau. 2000. "A Tax on Tax Revenue: The Incentive Effects of Equalizing Transfers: Evidence from Germany." CESisfo Working Paper 333, Center for Economic Studies & Info Institute for Economic Research, Munich.

Barro, Stephen M. 1986. "State Fiscal Capacity Measures: A Theoretical Critique." In *Measuring Fiscal Capacity,* ed. H. Clyde Reeves. Boston, MA: Oelgeschlager, Gunn & Hain.

———. 2002. "Macroeconomic versus RTS Measures of Fiscal Capacity: Theoretical Foundations and Implications for Canada." Queen's University, Institute for Intergovernmental Relations, Kingston, Ontario.

Boadway, Robin. 2002. "Revisiting Equalization Again: RTS vs. Macro Approaches." Queen's University, Institute for Intergovernmental Relations, Kingston, Ontario.

Boadway, Robin, and P. Hobson. 1993. "Intergovernmental Fiscal Relations in Canada." Toronto: Canadian Tax Foundation.

Boadway, Robin, S. Roberts, and A. Shah. 1994. "The Reform of Fiscal Systems in Developing and Emerging Market Economies: A Federalism Perspective." Policy Research Working Paper Series 1259, World Bank, Washington, DC.

Boothe, Paul, and D. Hermanutz. 1999. "Simply Sharing: An Equalization Scheme for Canada." Commentary 128, C.D. Howe Institute, Ottawa.

Courchene, T.J. 1984. "Equalization Payments: Past, Present and Future." Economic Council, Toronto.

———. 1995. "Fiscal Federalism and the Management of Economic Space: An Australian-Canadian Comparison." Australian National University, Federalism Research Centre, Canberra.

Dahlby, Bev, and L.S. Wilson. 1994. "Fiscal Capacity, Tax Effort, and Optimal Equalization Grants." *Canadian Journal of Economics* 27 (3): 657–72.

Neumann, Ron. 2002. "Equalization in Canada: Reform of the Representative Tax System or Move to a Macro Approach? Further Reflections in Consideration of Recent Developments." Queen's University, Institute for Intergovernmental Relations, Kingston, Ontario.

Shah, A. 1996. "A Fiscal Need Approach to Equalization." *Canadian Public Policy* 22 (2): 99–115.

Smart, Michael. 2002. "Redistribution, Risk, and Incentives in Equalization: A Comparison of RTS and Macro Approaches." Queen's University, Institute for Intergovernmental Relations, Kingston, Ontario.

South Africa. 2004. "Financial and Fiscal Commission, Submission for the Division of Revenue 2005/06." Midrand.

Usher, Dan. 1995. "The Uneasy Case for Equalization Payments." Fraser Institute, Vancouver.

———. 2002. "The Case for Switching to a Macro Formula." Queen's University, Institute for Intergovernmental Relations, Kingston, Ontario.

Wilson, L.S. 1996. "Federal-State Fiscal Relations in Malaysia." International and Development Studies Working Papers, Queen's University, John Deutsch Institute for the Study of Economic Policy, Kingston, Ontario.

13

Fiscal Capacity Equalization in Horizontal Fiscal Equalization Programs

BERNARD DAFFLON

Fiscal equalization refers to attempts within a federal system of government to reduce fiscal disparities across jurisdictions. Equalization is vertical when the policy is conducted by the central government and financed out of the central budget. Equalization is horizontal when it is done by subnational government units at the same level, through monetary transfers from units with high capacity to units with low capacity, however *capacity* is defined. *Fiscal disparities* refers to the variation across subnational jurisdictions in their ability to raise revenue to meet the public expenditure needs of their residents.

Because a balance between the assignment of responsibilities and the assignment of revenue sources at decentralized levels is not guaranteed over time and because expenditure needs and tax revenues do not follow the same pace in every jurisdiction, fiscal equalization is becoming increasingly important and controversial. Several questions have been subject to debate. Is horizontal fiscal equalization a necessary feature of fiscal federalism? What are the reasons for introducing some form of equalizing policy—would it not be simpler to reassign functions and revenues? Why should equalization flow from "rich" to "poor" jurisdictions rather than from rich to poor households? Why should equalization be horizontal and not solely vertical? If equalization is necessary or unavoidable, how are fiscal disparities measured across jurisdictions?

The European Charter of Local Self-Government (Council of Europe 1985) can serve as a starting point for addressing these questions. It states that local governments should have full discretion over the execution of their responsibilities and that the supervision of local governments should be limited.[1] At the same time, the resources available to local governments should match their responsibilities and be sufficient to enable them to keep pace with changes in the costs of their functions. Because it could be difficult over time to maintain a good balance between evolving responsibilities and own revenues, any fiscal imbalance raises the case for financial equalization transfers. Thus Article 9 Paragraph 5 of the charter states, "the protection of financially weaker local authorities calls for the institution of financial equalization procedures or equivalent measures which are designed to correct the effects of the unequal distribution of potential sources of finance and of the financial burden they must support. Such procedures or measures shall not diminish the discretion local authorities may exercise within their own sphere of responsibility."

This directive for local public policy is important because not only Western European countries with a long tradition of federalism or decentralization but also most Eastern European transition economies refer to the charter for their local finance. Paragraph 5 is expressed in general terms and is oriented toward the equalization of resources; the key expressions are the "unequal distribution of potential sources of finance" and the "financial burden." There is no explicit reference to needs or costs or to vertical versus horizontal equalization.

Starting from this statement, this chapter tries to understand why the system is revenue oriented and how the distinction between horizontal and vertical equalizing transfers affects the issue. The next section deals with the current state of the art in tracking the possible causes of fiscal disparities at the local level. Identifying these causes is important because they serve to separate the equalization of revenue sources from the equalization of needs and, accordingly, horizontal equalization measures from vertical ones.

The second section examines efficiency and equity, two principles often used to argue in favor of fiscal equalization. The delineation between vertical and horizontal equalization is predominantly a political preoccupation.[2]

With central public budgets facing tight finances or deficits, the political debate on what kind of equalization should be made—horizontal or vertical—and the debate about the necessity of horizontal equalization as a substitute for vertical equalization is fierce. The underlying argument is that revenue equalization may be horizontal as well as vertical, whereas needs or cost equalization can be vertical only, an issue examined in the third section of the chapter.

For practitioners, the theory of fiscal equalization is elusive. Since technical equalizing formulas are embedded in many ad hoc systems, generalization and policy guidance are difficult. The fourth section of the chapter attempts to overcome this difficulty, using a graphical tool that allows most specific revenue equalization schemes to be represented and compared.

The fifth section of the chapter examines actual experiences. It describes the design of equalization schemes and the incidence of horizontal equalization. The last section of the chapter provides a set of policy proposals.

Local Fiscal Disparities

The need for equalization must be examined in the context of the fiscal design of federalism and decentralization. As a rule, the allocation of revenue sources among government tiers should follow the assignment of functions. This usually occurs through gradual constitutional changes. However, two difficulties are linked to this process. First, even if the initial balance between functions and resources is achieved at every government tier, the balance may not be obtained for each government unit within each tier. Even the best vertical allocation will not prevent some subnational or local governments from having high tax bases and low expenditure needs and others having low tax bases and high expenditure needs. Second, decentralized functions undergo some modifications over time, following changes in the preferences for local service provision or the technology of public goods production. There is ample evidence that local own resources do not follow the same path. The initial balance between functions and revenues can be destroyed if one government tier is allocated a tax, such as the income tax, that increases from one year to another at a higher rate than GNP and another government tier receives taxes, such as the property tax, that tend to stagnate.

Because a unit-by-unit adjustment of functions and resources is not foreseen in most federal or decentralized countries (most constitutions provide equal rights and competencies to all subnational government units, regardless of size or capacity) and the periodical reallocation of functions and revenues has proved a perilous if not impossible political exercise, financial transfers have been used to correct fiscal imbalances. If transfers are unavoidable, should equalization be introduced alongside it? Can equalization be justified on efficiency or equity grounds?

The attempt to categorize the origins of differences between local governments opens the way to justify or reject fiscal equalization policies. The objective is to distinguish between differences that result from local choices in the fiscal expenditures–taxes mix from those differences that are due to low tax base–high needs situations that are outside the control of local government, referred to here as "disparities." Fiscal disparities arise because "the capacity to raise revenue to finance publicly provided services relative to the amount needed to provide a standard package of public services varies across jurisdictions" (Ladd 1999a, p. 123). In this definition, resources are balanced against a "standard package" of local public services. This is a bit more specific than Article 9 of the European Charter, which considers responsibilities assigned by the national constitution and laws and the resulting financial burden on local governments. Following the Charter, three possible origins of fiscal disparities can be identified: the capacity to raise (tax) revenues, expenditure needs, and the net residual, expressed as needs minus capacity.

Both the definition of the "standard package" and the origins of fiscal disparities remain too vague to allow the policy-relevant frontier line to be drawn between "differences" that result from local choices and "disparities" that have exogenous causes. The literature is not very clear on this distinction; only a few contributions to the political economy of equalization tackle this issue (table 13.1). It distinguishes four possible origins of fiscal disparities (classes A–D) and two origins of differences in the fiscal position of decentralized government units (classes E and F). Categories A and F relate to the revenue side. Category A concerns the potential tax bases at the disposal of local governments (something that can be approximated by a representative tax system [RTS]); category F corresponds to the tax arrangements that are possible at the local level given the flexibility of the legal system of taxation. Categories B–E refer to local expenditure functions. Categories B–D group the conditions of provision of local public services; only class E deals with local preferences for public service provision.

The logic behind this classification is twofold. Items that are within the scope of decision and the fiscal management of subnational governments should not be taken into consideration for equalization, as they belong to the subnational governments' sphere of autonomy and responsibility. Items that are outside the scope of local decision should be compensated, at least partly, if they result in significant differences in the fiscal positions of different governmental units. Class A concerns resource equalization: taxable resources depend greatly on the geographic position of government units (proximity of urban areas or economic centers, location at the periphery); on the kind of economic activities or clusters; and

TABLE 13.1 Sources of Fiscal Disparities

Category	Source	Reference
A	Differential access to resources due to differences in communal property, natural resources, or income/wealth of residents	Oakland (1994)
	Differences in taxable resources of local jurisdictions	Dafflon (1995)
	Differences in tax bases of local jurisdictions	Gilbert (1996)
	Differences in per capita taxable resources	King (1997)
	Differences in economic position and opportunity	Dafflon and Vaillancourt (2003)
B	Differences in scope of compulsory public goods local jurisdictions must provide for exogenous reasons	Gilbert (1996)
	Differences in per capita needs	King (1997)
C	Differences in costs due to different input-output relationships	Break (1980, cited in Shah 1996)
	Differential costs of providing public services due to differences in input costs or the fact that some populations are more costly to serve than others	Oakland (1994)
	Differences in unit costs of public goods that local jurisdictions have to provide	Dafflon (1995); King (1997); Dafflon and Vaillancourt (2003)
D	Differences in costs due to nature of service areas and composition of population	Break (1980)
	Differences in economies of scale in service provision	Dafflon (1995); Dafflon and Vaillancourt (2003)
E	Need to distinguish between need/cost differentials due to differential tastes/inherent cost disabilities and differences due to policy decisions	Break (1980)
	Local preferences for nonmandated public services or quantity or quality of mandated services that exceeds minimum standard level	Dafflon (1995); Gilbert (1996); Dafflon and Vaillancourt (2003)
F	Strategic behavior on the part of the (Canadian) provinces with respect to federal transfer payments	Break (1980)
	Local preferences for (nonbenefit) taxes and user charges (benefit taxes, including the choice, if any, among different forms of taxes)	Inman and Rubinfeld (1996)

Source: Author compilation.

on telecommunication networks. Within an open market economy, local governments cannot influence these characteristics, thus they must be treated as exogenous variables.

Classes B–D refer to the provision of local public goods and services at standard levels fixed by higher government tiers—the so-called mandated functions and decentralized merit goods. Class D needs some refinement: local governments can cooperate (or amalgamate) in order to benefit from economies of scale whenever possible. The decision to do so is a local choice. If cooperation is refused, in order to retain local autonomy or because preferences are heterogeneous, local governments should support the fiscal consequences of their decision and not count on equalization to make up for the differences in costs. Small is beautiful, but it has its price. Differences under classes E and F result from local preferences and hence need not be reduced by any kind of equalization or transfer payments.

Conceptual Issues

When examining the impact of public policies, economists distinguish between efficiency and equity issues. Efficiency issues relate to the change in the behavior of economic agents induced by a given public policy (taxation, subsidies). Such a change can be a source of increased or decreased welfare for the society. Equity issues relate to who wins and who loses, who pays for and who benefits from a given public policy.

Efficiency

Two efficiency arguments are frequently raised with respect to equalization. The first is related to the mobility of people, the second to the behavior of recipient governments.

Mobility

The mobility argument has swung between two views: the notion that equalization induces inefficient immobility of labor and the notion that the absence of equalization induces inefficient mobility of labor. Courchene (1970) forcefully makes the first argument. He argues that in Canada, a combination of explicit and implicit equalization through regionally differentiated unemployment insurance parameters (different number of weeks worked required for eligibility and a variable pay-out period) reduced the level of out-migration from the Atlantic Provinces below what was optimal for the country. The migration took place in the context of regional disparities that were not the result of large differences in natural resource endowments.

Boadway and Flatters (1982) argue that equalization is efficiency enhancing. In a model in which one region is rich in natural resources and the state government collects a substantial share of the natural resource rents (the difference between production costs and world market price), the only way residents of other regions of the country can access the revenues from these resources is by moving to that region, in order to benefit from lower personal taxation, higher public spending, or both. Consequently, the amount of labor migrating to the resource-rich region will be too large, with some workers willing to accept lower wages than they could earn elsewhere (that is, be paid less than their marginal productivity in the poor region), since their overall returns to migration (wage income and lower taxes plus better public services) make it worthwhile to migrate. Put differently, low provision of local public services, high taxation, and poverty will bring about out-migration, but it can also polarize the difference between residents and newcomers in the regions of immigration, exacerbating social imbalances. Put more simply, it can cause congestion costs in the destination region. In this case, financial transfers from the center or from rich to poor regions may alleviate the pressure and allow for better provision of public services or lower taxes in the poor region with a large emigration potential. This view is strongly supported by regional economists who advocate central aid to peripheral regions not in the sole interest of equity but for allocative reasons when the price of equalization is lower than the congestion and social costs in the jurisdictions of destination.

Behavior

The existence of an equalization scheme based on an RTS means that a reduction in the per capita tax base of a beneficiary commune can be partly or fully compensated for by an increase in equalization grants. Some economists, such as Smart (1998), argue that some jurisdictions make no effort to foster economic activities, because passive behavior that reduces some tax bases is compensated through equalization.

Equalization and tax competition often occur simultaneously in a federation. This occurs when communes have the right to set their own tax coefficients for a significant part of their revenues. Rich communes are sufficiently richer than poor ones that they can finance their own public services and their contribution to the equalization scheme, if any, while still setting lower tax rates than poor communes. Poor communes offer a level of public services similar to rich ones, financing those services through own revenues and equalization grants. In such cases, tax competition may lead to increasing disparities between poor and rich communes in terms of their tax bases. This type of outcome appears more likely when equalization is not very generous in terms of the difference in spending potential it offsets (that is, there are no explicit intercommunal transfers).

Large fiscal disparities are not always tolerated by the electorate at large. For this reason, richer communes may prefer to engage in more-generous equalization schemes rather than allow the centralization of service delivery and taxation at the intermediate level as a response to communal disparities.

Equity

The debate on equity in the context of equalization often revolves around the distinction between people and place prosperity. Opponents of equalization argue that if individuals in a commune are poor and thus unable to finance public services similar to those offered in rich communes, they, and not their communes, should be the recipients of grants or the beneficiaries of measures, such as job search grants or skill-enhancing training, that allow them to prosper outside the poor commune. Individual aid, they argue, is more appropriate than intergovernmental transfers.

For proponents of equalization, the equity argument is simple and straightforward: large differences in the fiscal burden among local governments are unacceptable if their causes are beyond the control of local authorities. There are ceilings in the tax burden and lower limits to the provision of local public services that should not be exceeded. To avoid exceeding these limits, compensation should be paid. It is up to the beneficiary jurisdiction to decide how to allocate the transfer received—by providing additional services, by improving the quality of existing ones, or by lowering taxes.

Needs Equalization

An active debate is under way over horizontal fiscal equalization. The literature on the design of equalization transfers distinguishes between revenue equalization and expenditure, or needs, equalization. The combination of both is often referred to as need-capacity gap equalization. The distinction between differences in needs, costs, and expenditures, or the need-capacity gap, is far from evident and presents a great deal of conceptual and technical difficulties.[3] Moreover, these categories do not inform whether transfers for the purpose of equalization should be horizontal or vertical (Ahmad and Craig 1997). In fact, in most of the case studies presented in Shah (1996),

Ahmad (1997), and Färber and Otter (2003), equalization of the expenditure needs of subnational governments or local governments is vertical. At first sight, only Australia and Denmark seem to be exceptions, as both have engaged in horizontal equalization (see below).

Consider first the concept of needs or expenditure equalization. In Switzerland the federal equalization policy among the 26 cantons is vertical and partly indirect. It is vertical because it is paid entirely from the federal budget to the cantons; it is indirect because it applies a system that differentiates the rates of grants-in-aid for specific cantonal functions according to a mixed index of capacity and needs indicators. Needs are approximated by two criteria: the larger the proportion of mountainous areas in each canton and the lower the population density, the more "needy" the canton (Dafflon 2004).

In unitary countries, indicators of expenditure needs are often used to allocate general funds to local governments when own resources and taxes are not sufficient to serve as an indicator for the grant design. In the United Kingdom, for example, the standard spending assessment is a major instrument of local government finance, but it is a vertical scheme only (Else 2003; Flowerdew, Francis, and Lucas 1994). Denmark uses a scheme of horizontal expenditure needs equalization based on the difference between the average per capita spending and the effective spending of local governments (Lotz 1997). But needs are defined by the center; needs criteria have no direct, numerical relation to the actual expenses of municipalities, and grants for equalizing expenditure needs are block grants (Mau Pedersen 2003).[4]

Opinions differ as to whether cost equalization is adequate. Canada has been reluctant to take this issue into account, since policy makers there believe that cost differences are more arbitrarily measured than fiscal capacity differences (Shah 1996; Dafflon and Vaillancourt 2003). Petchey (1995) shows that in the presence of specific locational rents, compensation for cost differences prevents inefficiency due to migration. He does not mention the explicit design of the transfer, though he implicitly recommends a vertically organized equalization system to attain the described effect. Boadway (1998) argues that for the purpose of equalization, only needs should be taken into account. Cost equalization always comes with a loss of efficiency, since prices of publicly provided goods are distorted (Boadway 2004). In this case, equalization would eliminate the incentive to adapt the production of public goods to the variation in costs.

The needs-capacity gap refers to the net residual between revenue capacity and expenditure needs of subnational governments. For Ladd (1994), the result can serve as an approximation for transfers from the central government to subnational units (or from the intermediate tier to local governments). In her opinion, these transfers are vertical. The Canadian equivalent is the so-called "fiscal need principle," enshrined in the federal Constitution Act 1982 (Section 36.2), which commits the federal authorities to ensure reasonably comparable levels of public services within a chosen locality at a cost in line with what would be paid elsewhere (Clark 1969; Shah 1996). Bahl, Martinez-Vazquez, and Sjoquist (1992) call it a "resource-requirements" gap; Tannenwald (1999) refers to "fiscal comfort." But on no account do they suggest horizontal equalization payments.

Australia provides perhaps the most prominent example of a needs-capacity gap assessment. Grants Commission recommendations are designed to overcome horizontal fiscal imbalance at the state level. These recommendations relate only to the distribution of the pool; the size of the pool is determined by the Premiers' Conference and is dominated by macroeconomic considerations of the central government. Federal funds are allocated with reference to a comprehensive system that evaluates revenue capacity as well as needs (Rye and Searle 1997; McLean 2004). For Shah (1996, p. 103), "the procedures used for the assessment of both revenue and expenditure need appear to be somewhat crude, imprecise and subjective . . . . [It] could only work if an atmosphere of exceptionally high degree of compromise, cooperation and accommodation prevailed among the governments involved." The resulting transfers are vertical, but they are higher for states with higher needs residuals.[5]

Whereas resource equalization is an established policy in most decentralized or federal countries, the suitability of equalization policies for disparities in needs, costs, or expenditures is a subject of debate, in both theory and practice (Färber and Otter 2003). Among economists the discussion is about the kind of disparities that have to be taken into account and the consequences of the equalization policy in terms of efficiency, incentives, allocative neutrality, and equity. There is no theoretical evidence that equalization of expenditures, needs, or costs can be horizontal. On the contrary, the trend in theory and practice is to view vertical transfers as preferable for equalizing costs and needs and to view horizontal "Robin Hood" solidarity as unsuitable for this purpose (Lotz 1997; Garcia-Milà and McGuire 2004).[6] According to this view, the concepts of high and low needs, the basket of local goods and services to be included in needs, and the standards for the provision of the aided local services cannot be left to subnational governments but need to be determined and controlled by the center.

Although a core theory remains to be further developed on these questions, the general argument can be made that revenue equalization can be horizontal as well as vertical, whereas equalization of expenditures, needs, and costs can only be vertical. In other words, it is conceivable from the allocative and redistributive point of view that high-capacity local governments contribute to redistributing financial resources to low-capacity local governments. There are pros and cons, but acceptance of this kind of financial transfer for reasons of intergovernmental solidarity is broad. In contrast, it is much harder to find good arguments for a horizontal equalization of differences in expenditures, needs, or costs.

Horizontal equalization would mean that beneficiaries of services in a low-cost jurisdiction would accept a tax-price supplement (that is, more expensive public services) in order to subsidize local public services in other, high-cost localities. This would distort the local tax price of public services and result in allocative inefficiency. Other arguments against horizontal equalization include the following:

- There is no rationale for horizontal equalization among municipalities for local public services that are financed through user charges. Pricing these services means that beneficiaries pay for what they receive and not more. Any violation of this rule would disrupt the market-like process and send a false price signal. From the point of view of economic efficiency, it is unrealistic and incorrect to imagine that the beneficiaries of a service who pay fees based on the polluter pays principle or other user charges would support an equalization supplement for the simple reason that the costs of services vary from one jurisdiction to another.[7]
- It would be inequitable to make users in one service district pay a price in excess of the benefits they receive in order to cross-subsidize users in another district who pay less than the costs of the service.
- For local services that are financed through taxes, there is an information problem. Cost compensation necessitates collecting and comparing data about the management of local public services and their various cost functions that allows the exact nature of the costs to be identified. This is not an easy task, because of the large number of local functions, most of which cannot be perfectly mapped.[8] The question is whether differences in costs are due to differences in the quality or level of local public services, X-inefficiencies, or external causes. In case of differences in the level or quality of services, a compromise must be found in order to determine what would be the "adequate" or "standard" level of service. If the causes are X-inefficiencies, new management methods must be imposed (by whom?) to remedy the situation. Only if the differences in costs are the result of external circumstances can financial compensation be justified. In this case, however, the aid should be vertical, because only a higher tier

of government is able to provide funding in a way that is as neutral as possible from an allocative point of view.

Revenue Equalization

Disparities in expenditures, needs, or costs cannot be addressed with an equalization scheme that implies horizontal redistribution from affluent jurisdictions to poorer ones. Accordingly, if the federal government seeks to introduce some kind of horizontal fiscal equalization, the only workable way to do so is to equalize revenues.

Over the past 20 years, revenue equalization has taken such a wide variety of forms that comparing them represents a challenge, as the level of redistribution achieved depends on the equalization formula as well as the effects of the ceiling and floor provisions, the generic solution, and, more fundamentally, the definitions of tax bases used to calculate the entitlements (Smart 2004). Doing so is important, however, because the experience of federations in other countries help policy makers formulate the objectives and develop the tools of horizontal fiscal equalization (Blindenbacher and Watts 2003).

This section presents a way of treating revenue equalization with the help of a graphical tool developed by Dafflon and Vaillancourt (2003). Four issues are addressed: funding an equalization policy, measuring fiscal capacity, designing and calculating the equalization formula, and determining the target level of equalization. The objective is to organize the theoretical arguments in a way that allows the literature to be surveyed around these four issues (figure 13.1).

Per capita public revenues at the disposition of each government unit at the subnational level are shown along the vertical axis before and after horizontal equalization. (Vertical equalization, which is also possible, is treated later in the chapter.) The average level of per capita public revenue is given the index value of 1.00. On the horizontal axis, government units are lined up from poorest to richest, based on a measure of per capita financial/tax capacity, discussed below. A value of 100 represents average capacity. In order to limit the size of the figure, the values of the capacity indicator are set between 30 and 150 points.

Funding Equalization

The first issue concerns the source and importance of tax revenues to be shared and redistributed. Since beneficiary jurisdictions differ in size and population, the redistribution between jurisdictions must take into account

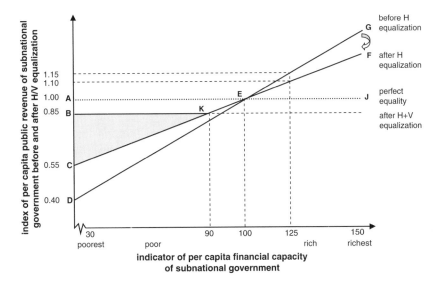

Source: Dafflon and Vaillancourt (2003).
Note: H = horizontal and V = vertical.

FIGURE 13.1 Stylized Representation of Revenue Equalization

the population of each jurisdiction. This is accounted for by using per capita revenue. Along the line AEJ, the beneficiary jurisdiction receives exactly the average amount of public revenue per resident. The basic questions are which revenue (tax) sources are to be shared and according to which decision procedure. Note that the starting point can also refer to the initial assignment of revenue sources to local authorities.[9] In this case, the basic questions are whether block grants or revenue sharing should be added to local own resources if the latter are insufficient, and if yes, in which form. The initial effective level of per capita resources of subnational governments before equalization is represented by the line DEG in figure 13.1. The "poorest" government unit obtains only 40 percent of the per capita national; the "richest" receives funding that corresponds to G, well above the average.

Does the unit by unit initial per capita endowment along DEG need to be corrected because it results in excessively large fiscal disparities? If so, how should the equalization be financed? Several approaches are possible, each with its pros and cons:

■ The amount can be financed out of the general resources of the paying unit(s) and established in their annual budget. This is a very flexible solution, adaptable from one year to another. It has three main drawbacks, however. First, recipient governments are not sure that they will receive a comparable amount (in real value) from one year to another, rendering medium-term planning and policy making very difficult. Second, annual budgetary debates are subject to ad hoc political arrangements, with unstable contours by definition. Third, the annual amount of equalization is at the mercy of the "high-capacity" government units, which will probably attempt to revise their contributions downward.

■ The method of calculating the equalization amount can be explicitly stated in the constitution or in a law in the form of revenue sharing from at least one but preferably several specific tax sources used at the central level (vertical) or the local tier (horizontal). This approach has two main advantages. First, with a specific legal foundation, the political debate on "how much equalization" takes place when the constitution is amended or the law is passed, not on an annual basis when budgets are decided. Second, the approach avoids important variations in the available amounts if the tax sources are sufficiently diversified and chosen in such a way that macroeconomic cycles are partly alleviated. The approach also has two main drawbacks. First, revenue sharing from specific taxes may be subject to the fluctuation of the economy, following ups and downs with perhaps procyclical results. Second, if only one tax source for sharing purposes is used, government units may not collect it as vigorously as if it were their exclusive source of revenue, since collection efforts partly reward other government units through the equalizing transfers.

■ An equalization fund can be established that is fed by the revenues of several tax sources and anchored in the constitution or the law. The fund serves as the source of yearly equalization payments but also contains a "rainy day" element. This type of system has both of the advantages of the second approach. In addition, it can smooth equalization payments by leaving in the funds a part of the contributions in good years, which can be tapped in bad years.

None of these approaches separates vertical and horizontal funding. The first approach is not suitable for horizontal equalization, because it requires annual budgetary negotiation between those local governments that contribute to equalization and the beneficiary local governments. In case of conflict, some form of arbitrage by a higher tier is necessary, a situation that brings verticality into the process.

The second and third approaches can be truly horizontal, but they require the prior interference of a higher government tier in order to include in the constitution or the law the obligation for local governments to participate in some horizontal equalization scheme and the criteria for receiving equalization transfers. Of course, this top-down process need not be imposed on the lower tier. Government units at the lower tier should be involved in the design of the horizontal equalization policy; after all, it is these units that will later support the burden or enjoy the benefits of this policy.[10] If co-participation in the design and decision process is not promoted, the equalization policy becomes a kind of merit good that is implemented top down.

The third approach seems very attractive from the point of view of macroeconomic stability. As a result of the pressure of globalization and tax competition, local governments with high financial capacity can no longer be certain of remaining strong in the future. They could use their budget surpluses to consolidate their own position or to contribute to their own rainy day fund rather than to contribute to horizontal equalization. Theoretically, the equalization system can also serve this purpose. But the two processes do not have the same insurance characteristics: a rainy day fund is analogous to a system of capitalization, whereas a rainy day element within the equalization scheme corresponds to a system of mutual insurance, in which subnational governments exposed to adverse revenue shocks in the short run would see their relative position modified in their favor relative to other subnational governments facing better fiscal conditions (Smart 2004).

Usher (1995) and Buettner (2002), among others, dispute the argument that risk sharing or risk pooling helps external macroeconomic shocks (see von Hagen 2000). The insurance characteristics of the equalization fund would not convince "high-capacity" local governments to make sacrifices in their fiscal positions for the sake of solidarity. This issue is without doubt the principal challenge that horizontal resource equalization will face in the next years.

Measuring Fiscal Capacity

Measuring the fiscal disparities between regions or local governments or setting out a benchmark indicator of their fiscal (tax?) capacities is a crucial problem. Measurement is not easily separable from the objective, and the indicator components often directly influence the calculation of the equalization entitlements. (For the discussion here, the measure is revenue capacity, since the issue is revenue equalization; in other cases, needs would also be taken into account.) The basic concept is thus formulated as follows: jurisdictions with higher-than-average capacity should receive less (pay more), and jurisdictions with lower-than-average capacity should receive more (pay less).

The concept is easier to explain than to implement. An overview of the theoretical literature indicates that there is no easy answer to this technical and politically sensitive question. A variety of measures reflects "best" practice, depending on whether "best" reflects the judgment of public finance economists, macroeconomic analysts, politicians, or the winning or losing jurisdictions. There is general agreement between scholars and politicians, however, that the data series used for measuring capacity should be precise and stable over a range of several years, not susceptible to manipulation, and easily verifiable by all government units and parties involved in the equalization process.

In order to implement equalization programs, policy makers at higher levels of government require accurate measures of the fiscal condition of lower-level units. Such measures are needed to determine whether disparities justify action and to design the appropriate equalizing formula (Ladd 1999b). Three approaches are used to measure the capacity of government units. One is based on macroeconomic figures, such as GNP or national revenue, calculated per government unit and per capita. The other two approaches are derived from the tax system. One is based on the total taxable resources (TTR). The other is based on an RTS for an approximation of taxable capacity. None of these models is exempt from criticism and factual weaknesses. A few country examples illustrate the problems.

Based on taxation, some systems use a single indicator or a single tax (Belgium, for example, uses personal income tax). Others finance these transfers with a large number of taxes (Canada uses 33 different taxes) creating an RTS. Bird and Slack (1990) show that in Canada the RTS is too complicated, too costly to manage, and too open to iterative and endless negotiation on the range of taxes to be included in the calculation of capacity and the weight to be attributed to each type of tax. Barro (1986) and Boothe (1998) also criticize the approach, arguing that it is preferable to use a macroeconomic indicator, such as per capita GDP; per capita personal income (used in some transfer formulas in the United States, including Medicare); or a TTR system derived from gross state product measures (used in one transfer program in the United States). They argue that these methods are simpler than an RTS and less susceptible to distortion, which occurs when provinces reduce their tax bases in the hope of obtaining an increase in equalization benefits. In an RTS the choice of an indicator of taxable capacity can become difficult, as states continuously introduce additional sources of revenues. In Canada, for example, federal taxable income is used as the capacity indicator for the personal income tax—a logical choice, well linked to the measure sought. But personal income is also used, along with other indicators, to measure the tax capacity associated with video lotteries and casinos. In some provinces, these are heavily export oriented; their revenues are thus not linked strongly to personal income in the province in which they are located.

Macro indicators also face measurement issues (Aubut and Vaillancourt 2001). In addition, they serve the objective of redistribution rather than equalization: instead of equalizing the capacity to provide comparable levels of public services at comparable levels of taxation, to use the Canadian definition, they attempt to equalize per capita national income within subnational governments. Switzerland is an interesting case in this respect. The formula of the cantons' financial capacity is a mix of three components: macroeconomic data (per capita national income in the cantons), a sort of RTS à la Suisse (standardized tax revenues from direct taxation in the cantons and theirs communes), and an approximation of regional cost differences of cantonal and local public services (based on population density, surface area cultivable in mountainous regions, and surface area that is economically productive) (Dafflon 2004). The new equalization policy will replace this formula with an RTS indicator.[11] The macroeconomic indicator is being abandoned because the way it is calculated is not reliable. Differences in the cantonal indices depend on whether the calculation is based on GNP or national income. No plausible explanation has been given for these differences from a statistical point of view. The generally accepted conclusion is that each data series mirrors the openness of the cantons' economies and mobility in a completely different manner. An additional conceptual argument is that the measure of the cantons' capacity should reflect only their ability to generate tax revenues and not the state of their economy in a broader sense.

At the local level, TTR- or RTS-like indicators of tax capacity should be preferred, since the smaller the jurisdictions, the more open their economies, making it difficult to obtain significant and relevant macroeconomic indicators. In most cases, such series do not exist at the local level. If they do exist, they are not sufficiently reliable, as most economic parameters are characterized by geographical externalities.

Choosing the appropriate TTR or RTS indicators requires three steps. First, a set of tax sources to be considered is chosen. Second, the tax base for each of the selected tax sources is defined (the need for a common definition depends on whether subnational government units have full sovereignty in their tax legislation and on the degree of harmonization among the various decentralized taxes). Third, the choice of the reference tax rate or tax schedule if capacity is measured through an RTS rather than a TTR.

Economic techniques can be very sophisticated in these matters, but choices are by no means only technical, as the measure of fiscal (tax) conditions of subnational government units determines the extent of solidarity, bringing politics to the forefront.

Equalization Formulas

If equalization is desirable, how is the formula to be devised? Figure 13.1 compares the before and after equalization situations. With no equalization and the possibility of identifying exactly the origin of tax revenues, poor jurisdictions receive less-than-average per capita endowments and rich ones receive higher-than-average amounts (DEG in figure 13.1). Any equalization formula would give more to poor jurisdictions than they would have received based on the origin principle, and rich jurisdictions would receive less (CEF in figure 13.1).

The equalizing performance is represented by the distance between DE and CE for beneficiary jurisdictions and between EG and EF for jurisdictions that support the financial cost of equalization. In the poorest jurisdiction, with a fiscal capacity of 30 index points, equalization increases per capita public revenues from 0.40 (D) to 0.55 (C) of the national average. For a rich subnational government with a capacity of 125 points, equalization reduces per capita public revenues from 1.15 to 1.10 of the national average. Of course, a balanced solution with horizontal equalization requires that benefits (represented by the triangle DEC) and payments (represented by the triangle EGF) coincide. The importance of equalization depends on the equalization formula that gives the slope of CEF after horizontal equalization around point E.

How much high-capacity jurisdictions should contribute and how much low-capacity jurisdictions should be able to claim is not a question that depends only on economic objectives. Policy makers need to choose between equalizing mechanisms that are sophisticated but not easily understood by the public and perhaps less precise formulas that are simpler and more accessible. Simple formulas are of the following type:

$$EQ_i = \left[B^* - \frac{B_i}{P_i} \right] \times t^* \times P_i \times K \qquad (13.1)$$

where EQ_i is the total equalizing transfer that local government i obtains, B is the effective tax base in local government i, B^* is the per capita tax base at a standardized value, P is population (the number of residents in a local region), t^* is the reference tax rate, and K is the coefficient of equalization.

Equation (13.1) compares the amount that jurisdiction i would obtain with the reference tax rate (t^*) applied to its effective per capita tax base (B_i/P_i) and the amount that the same local government i would obtain with the reference tax rate applied to the local governments' average tax base (B^*). Normally, for beneficiary local governments $K < 1$, a local government with a per capita tax base lower than the average would receive only a proportion of the difference; a local government with a per capita tax base greater than the average would contribute only a fraction of its surplus.

Integral compensation ($K = 1$) is a heresy in economic theory and practice. It would mean that each and every local government with an index of financial capacity higher than average would have to abandon its per capita surplus (that is, its public revenue per capita) before equalization on the segment of line EG would be cut back to the average line EJ (at 1.00 on the vertical axis). This would have a disastrous disincentive effect on local taxation. Any local effort to develop a tax base would be annihilated by the equalization system. This is not merely academic rhetoric. In Germany in the 1990s, the Constitutional Court ordered a revision of the compensation scheme through the introduction of a less progressive target after three rich *Lander* complained that the degree of equalization was too high (Zimmermann 1999). For low-capacity local governments, there would be no incentive to adopt measures for economic development and thus increase their per capita tax base, as equalization would automatically make up the difference, pushing up their position from DE to AE in figure 13.1. The challenge is to design an equalization formula that gives sufficient and significant solidarity without providing disincentives. The shift from DEG to CEF represents this attempt.

Equalization Target

Does an equalization policy limit the redistribution formula? In figure 13.1, E represents the neutral position with regard to equalization. With average financial capacity and average per capita tax revenues, a jurisdiction would neither pay nor receive a transfer. E is the relative position of the reference jurisdiction, depending on the basket of taxes selected for equalization and the measure of capacity chosen. But the central point need not be at E. Other equalization targets are also possible, often generating controversies.

Two points should be noted. First, it can be debated whether jurisdictions with a financial capacity slightly below the average should benefit from equalization. On financial, political, and equity grounds, one could argue that only jurisdictions below a certain level of capacity should qualify.

Financial considerations could be one argument: if the target level is set at 90, the higher-level government would need to pay a smaller amount than if it were at 100 (the triangle equivalent to CDE at 100 would be smaller at 90). The political argument is more crucial. Any target level would imply that a boundary is drawn between low-capacity and high-capacity jurisdictions, threatening the nation-state with fragmentation. The question, then, is, how much poorer is too poor?

A second question is illustrated by the triangle BCK. The incidence of the horizontal equalization formula runs along line CE: the poorer a jurisdiction, the more it receives. However, the equalizing payments provided to the poor jurisdictions in the example may be far from sufficient. If they do not suffice, should they be increased? If so, what is the appropriate limit? Figure 13.1 demonstrates a situation in which poor jurisdictions receive equalization transfers that allow their revenue endowment to reach at least 85 percent of the national average, along line BK. But who pays this complementary endowment? Since high-capacity jurisdictions already pay EFG to cover CDE, from what source can the amount equivalent to BCK be financed? In the example, the additional funding comes from the center—that is, equalization is vertical. Fragmentation and equity are no doubt important, but incentives must also be considered. With a complementary endowment such as that depicted in figure 13.1, beneficiary jurisdictions have no incentive to take initiative for their development if they are satisfied with 85 percent of the national average and have no preference for autonomous revenues rather than transfers.

Economists cannot study and propose a good equalization scheme (and later estimate its incidence) without political input. An appropriate scheme cannot be implemented without central and regional politicians determining how much, according to which criteria, to what extent, and for which target to equalize the financial positions of subnational units. Of course, the final result will also depend on the available financial resources. The four issues addressed here are complementary: a moderate equalization formula with significant funding, for example, might produce the same effects as a strongly equalizing formula with more-modest financial means. Beyond what economists say about the efficiency and the incidences of various schemes, these are matters of choice and weight that are in politicians' hands.

Designing Horizontal Equalization

Two main problems arise in designing horizontal revenue equalization. The first is the measure of the local governments' financial capacity indicators.

The second is the insertion of the individual local governments' indicators into a suitable equalization formula. In practice, such an abundance of measures and formulas exist that technical explanations and comparisons of selected schemes require a huge analytical effort (Färber and Otter 2003). Best practice analyses are not relevant, because each system is tailored to the needs and circumstances of the particular state organization under scrutiny and to national diversity. It is nevertheless possible to highlight some similarities and common characteristics.

Indicators of Financial Capacity

Equalizing formulas used in Europe are very similar across countries. Since local governments are small open economies, fiscal capacity is almost exclusively based on tax capacity, and the reference is the RTS. The main difference lies in the list of taxes (and sometimes other revenue sources) that are taken into consideration to assess the tax capacity of each government unit. Based on the philosophy of equation (13.1), the basic idea is to measure local governments' tax potential. If only one local tax existed, the tax potential of individual local governments would correspond to the total tax base of that tax in each local government compared with the average calculated for all local governments.

Several local taxes are usually considered, an approach that makes things a bit more complicated, since tax bases from different tax sources cannot be simply added (Gilbert and Guengant 2001). As a consequence, most systems first calculate, on a per capita basis, one series for each tax source, then rank individual local governments relative to the average value of the series before combining the results of the series in a global indicator. These systems involve the following steps:

1. Select the local taxes to be used to calculate tax capacity. Because of the openness of local economies and the related absence of reliable macroeconomic statistical series, financial capacity indicators can be based on only local taxes or tax bases that are common to all local governments.
2. Calculate the per capita yield of each tax, with reference to a standard tax rate (t^*). In order to obtain a representative result, a standard tax rate t^* is used, rather than the rates of taxation that each individual local government applies. Using t^* measures the potential tax resources of each local government.
3. Determine the number of years to which the calculation applies. For a single local government, the annual yield of local taxes, even at t^*, can be

irregular, depending on which sources of taxation have been assigned to the local tier. Irregular potential resources could induce discontinuity in financial capacity indicators, resulting in variations in the annual amounts received or contributed. This "disturbing" effect adds uncertainty to local governments' budgeting or financial medium-term planning. In general, most equalization policies do not allow annual ups and downs in transfer payments; continuity and predictability in the relative position of individual local governments are sought. One usual way to smooth annual variations is to extend the calculation to a longer period, such as three years.

4. For each tax source, compare the results obtained for each local government to the reference tax yield, normally the average value obtained for all local governments. This result is the tax index of local government i for tax t. This comparison is at the core of the system. It permits the ranking of local governments above or below the average for a particular tax, giving the relative position of each government unit. The average tax yield, which corresponds to the average tax base $B^* \times t^*$, per capita, can be given the reference value of 100 points. There is no need to fix an equalization target for the moment.

5. Calculate the weighted financial capacity indicator for each local government by combining the series for each tax source. The arithmetic is not always straightforward. With several tax sources, the obvious step would be to consider each of them in proportion to the total yield. But this does not necessarily correspond to practice. Tax index series are sometimes given weights that combine the proportion of revenues from each tax source to total tax yield with one or several criteria, such as volatility and risk. The real property tax and the tax on motor vehicles, for example, have a reputation of delivering a reliable yield: real property is immovable and its value normally stable in the medium term, while motor vehicles are indispensable in many countries. In contrast, taxes on mobile factors (such as the corporate profit tax in Switzerland, the tax on business in Spain, and the *taxe professionnelle* in France) involve more risk (delocalization, tax competition, external shock, recession). The alternative view is that these tax yields are returns on investment resulting from local governments' own efforts to enhance their local attractiveness and that they should therefore weigh less in the average calculation, as a reward (or an incentive and mutual insurance) for local policies in a more risky environment.[12]

The calculation of fiscal capacity indicators can be expressed in the following form:

$$T_{ONE_i}^{y1} = B_{ONE_i}^{*y1} \times t_{ONE}^{*} \qquad (13.2)$$

$$IT_{ONE_i} = \frac{\left(\dfrac{T_{ONE_i}}{P_i}\right)^{y1} + \left(\dfrac{T_{ONE_i}}{P_i}\right)^{y2} + (...)^{y3}}{\left(\dfrac{\sum\limits_{j=1}^{N} T_{ONE_j}}{\sum\limits_{j=1}^{N} P_j}\right)^{y1} + \left(\dfrac{\sum\limits_{j=1}^{N} T_{ONE_i}}{\sum\limits_{j=1}^{N} P_j}\right)^{y2} + (...)^{y3}} \times 100 \qquad (13.3)$$

$$FC_i = \left[IT_{ONE_i} \times W_{ONE} \right] + ... + \left[IT_{EIGHT_i} \times W_{EIGHT} \right], \qquad (13.4)$$

where B = the tax base; FC = indicator of financial capacity; IT = index of tax capacity; N = the number of local governments in the region (canton, *Land*, province) in which the horizontal equalization scheme is proposed; P = population (number of residents in a local government); T = tax revenue or tax yield; i = a single local government; ONE, TWO, and so forth = type of local taxation; t = tax rate; $y1$ = reference year 1; and * = a "standardized" value.

Equation (13.2) gives for government i the amount of tax revenue from tax ONE in reference year $y1$. It is the tax revenue that local government i would have obtained had it applied the reference (average) tax rate (t^*) to its tax base. The tax base must be defined in an identical manner and standardized for all local governments considered (it is therefore marked with B^*).

Equation (13.3) is the index of tax capacity for local government i calculated in per capita terms and compared with the average value of all local governments in the territory of reference. IT is calculated as a ratio. The numerator consists of the tax revenue that would have been obtained had locality i applied the corresponding average tax rate to its standardized tax bases, calculated per resident. The denominator consists of the average tax yield per capita for tax ONE, that is, the total tax ONE yield for all local governments divided by the total resident population in N local governments. If the per capita tax yield in locality i equals the average, its IT is 1.00 (100 in figure 13.1). When the per capita tax yield of i is higher than average, IT_i is greater than 100. In equation (13.3) the possibility exists that the index of tax capacity for the various local governments is computed for several years (three in the example). The annual tax yield of certain forms of taxation might be irregular for reasons external to the choice or the management of the individual local governments. Extending the number of reference years is one method of smoothing these irregularities.

The indicator of financial capacity (*FC*) is given in equation (13.4). It follows from equation (13.3) but is adapted to take into account the relative weight of each tax source. The basic consideration is that the yields of the various tax sources do not represent the same proportion in the total amount of the local tax revenues taken into consideration for equalization. Thus any measure or comparison of the local governments' tax potential must consider the structure of local taxation. In equation (13.4) the technique used for that purpose is to calculate the proportion of each tax source in the total tax yield and weigh individual tax indices accordingly. If, for example, the yield of tax ONE for the *N* local governments represents 78 percent of the total tax yield for the reference period (three years in equation 13.3), then W ONE is given a 0.78 value in the equation. Of course, the usual rule that the sum of the weights equals 1 must be respected.

This method offers two advantages. First, since the proportions for each tax are calculated on the basis of the aggregate yield for *N* local governments, it provides a kind of individual insurance for local governments susceptible to abrupt changes in their situation: the change in any local government's series will not be given a weight higher than the average. Second, with the average index value at 100, the system includes any changes in tax yield during the reference period, automatically smoothing irregular yields in individual local governments and integrating the growth rate of the various tax yields in the annual calculation. Therefore, the position of any individual local government is relative not only in terms of its resident population but also in terms of the various rates of growth that affect their own tax sources. Equations (13.3) and (13.4) represent an application of the procedure Boadway and Hayashi (2004) propose for the Canadian Provinces to combine the redistributive function of equalization while allowing it to fulfill a stabilization role.

Equation (13.4) includes eight sources of taxation. France bases its equalization policies on four taxes: the tax on the rental value of residential property, two real estate taxes (on buildings and on land), and the business tax (Gilbert and Guengant 2001). Catalonia, Spain, bases its policies on three taxes: the immovable property tax, the vehicle tax, and the business tax (Castells, Esteller, and Vilalta 2003). Friborg, Switzerland, bases its policies on eight taxes: taxes on personal income, wages at source for foreign workers, personal wealth, business profit, corporate capital, immovable property, motor vehicles, and capital gains (Dafflon and Mischler 2005).

Calculating the financial capacity indicators, like other attempts to establish measures of capacity and rank government units, can never be an exact science. Several technical difficulties are encountered in specific national systems. First, the tax base (B^* in equation 13.2) may not be homogeneous. Even if it can be defined in the same words, local implementation may not yield comparable results. For example, there can be important local differences between the market value and the tax value of immovable properties depending on the date of the last cadastral assessment. Second, only the resident population is used to calculate the relative values that yield IT in equation (13.3). This raises the question of the distinction between the effective domicile and the domicile for tax purpose, as well as the distinction between the resident population and the proportion of the population with a second home. If several population statistics are available, which one should be considered? Third, there is a time lag between the reference years y for calculating T or IT and its use for the horizontal equalization funds.

Possible Equalization Formulas

The crucial problem in equalization is designing an equalizing formula using the indicators of local governments' tax capacity. The choice of a formula is delicate, for two main reasons. The first is technical: formulas that are elegant at first sight may contain technical weaknesses. For example, the ranking of individual local governments may not be smooth along the whole range of capacity indicators, there could be a threshold effect around the mean value of 100 points, or there could be a strong asymmetry because the range of low-capacity local governments runs from the average to zero whereas there is no ceiling for high-capacity local governments.

The second difficulty is political: the formula determines those local governments that will support the burden of equalization and those that will benefit from it. This is not an easy task, and it is eminently a political rather than an economic decision. The usual strategy is to appoint a steering committee with local government representatives and officials or politicians from the higher tier in order to issue a joint proposal that can be accepted by all local governments, contributors, or beneficiaries and that can be effectively managed by the next-higher government tier. Of course, the habitual initial dilemma applies: representatives of contributor local governments try to minimize payments, whereas those from beneficiary local governments seek to maximize them. But there are good reasons, including solidarity and risk pooling, to believe that an acceptable compromise is possible, especially since the status of "have" and "have not" is subject to fluctuation given the uncertainty of the global economy.

The most common formulas for calculating equalizing transfers take the following forms:

$$EQ_i = \frac{P_i \times (FC_i - 100)^\alpha}{\sum\limits_{j=1}^{N-m} P_j \times (FC_j - 100)^\alpha} \times M \times K \qquad (13.5)$$

for contributing local governments , and

$$EQ_i = \frac{P_i \times (100 - FC_i)^\alpha}{\sum\limits_{j=1}^{m} P_j \times (100 - FC_j)^\alpha} \times M \times K \qquad (13.6)$$

for beneficiary local governments.

There are N local governments, of which m have financial capacity indicators lower than average and $(N - m)$ have financial capacity indicators equal to or greater than average. M (money) is the total amount available in the equalization fund. In equation (13.5), local governments with $FC_i > 100$ contribute to equalization in proportion to their population multiplied by the difference between their own financial capacity indicator and the average. That is, the higher their financial capacity, the more they contribute to the equalization fund. The inverse is shown for beneficiary local governments in equation (13.6). K is a coefficient that permits the contributions from high-capacity local governments to low-capacity local governments to be balanced over the reference period. The formula is proportional if α, the power value of the numerator and the denominator, is unity. Increasing the power value reinforces the equalizing effect in the two groups of local governments, those that contribute to and those that benefit from equalization.[13] Within the group of local governments with $FC > 100$, the higher the power value, the more high-capacity local governments will have to contribute to the equalization fund. Among local governments for which $FC < 100$, the lower the local government in the ranking, the more it receives.

Other formulas are possible, such as

$$EQ_i = \frac{P_i \times \left(\dfrac{100}{FC_i}\right)^\alpha}{\sum\limits_{j=1}^{N} P_j \times \left(\dfrac{100}{FC_j}\right)^\alpha} \times M \times K, \qquad (13.7)$$

where the total amount EQ_i received by local government i is proportional to the share of its population P_i within the population of all local governments (ΣP_j, with P weighted by the inverse of financial capacity). In other words, if the financial capacity of a local government is 80, the weight attached to its population P_i is 100/80 = 1.25. Thus for every 100 residents, this local government receives an equalizing amount calculated for 125 residents. Because it has lower-than-average financial capacity, it receives a higher-than-average amount per capita.

A formula used in Switzerland in recent years deserves attention for its remarkable technical characteristics. It takes an exponential form, such as:

$$EQ_i = P_i \times \left[e^{(\beta) \times FC_i} \right] \times M \times K. \tag{13.8}$$

The total amount disposable for equalization (M) is distributed in proportion to the number of residents (P_i) in each local government, weighted by an exponential function comprising the natural log base and, as a variable, the indicator of financial capacity of the concerned local government (FC_i) and an exponent value β that is negative for payment from the equalization fund and positive for contributions to the equalization fund. K is a coefficient similar to that in the two previous formulas that permits contributions to and payments from the equalization fund to be balanced.

Equations (13.5)–(13.8) share common characteristics. Horizontal equalization is based on the residential population of individual local governments and their financial capacity (with an RTS a better term would be *tax capacity*). Statistical data for those series are normally easily available, published, and thus controllable by all actors. M corresponds to the provisional amount contributed by and redistributed to local governments. At the moment of conceptualization, the method does not require that M be fixed; M can be given a hypothetical value, with the actual amount to be paid out subject to political debate. K has the role of balancing the budget over the reference period: with horizontal equalization, experience shows that there are normally fewer contributing municipalities with above-average financial capacity and more below-average beneficiary jurisdictions. Contributions and payments do not always sum to equivalent amounts, so that adjustment is necessary.

A further merit of these formulas, and probably one that explains the recent trend to use them, is that they clearly distinguish between the technical components left to economists and what remains for political debate. Politicians have to determine the power of the function in equations (13.5)–(13.7) and the value of the numerical exponent in equation (13.8), but they cannot manipulate the chosen equation for patronage purpose. The power of the exponent value directly influences the quality of the results and the degree of solidarity between high- and low-capacity jurisdictions. A higher power value in equations (13.5)–(13.7) or a higher positive exponent in equation (13.8) increases the contributions of local governments all the more as their indicator of financial capacity is high and ranks toward the top. Conversely, it increases the transfer received by local governments with the lowest capacity at the bottom ranks.

The Impact of Horizontal Equalization

The measurement of the impact of horizontal equalization raises a number of methodological issues. First, the equalizing performance can be measured in nominal terms (the supplement of financial capacity provided by the equalizing aid valued in money) or in real terms (in terms of purchasing power for local public goods). In the absence of any form of cost or expenditure needs equalization and with possible cost disparities in the production of public goods, the same nominal equalizing grant does not offer the same capacity for financing local services and utilities.

A second question is whether the additional money received by low-capacity local governments should finance additional local services or rather should affect municipal tax rates. Although revenue equalization is essentially unconditional, and therefore leaves it to individual local governments to decide on the use of the transfers, an increasing level of local public services or a diminishing tax effort are not equivalent for measuring the effects of equalization.

A third issue is whether equalization performance should be measured in absolute or relative values. Measuring performance in absolute terms yields information about the equalization effect, whereas measuring performance in relative terms yields information about the equalization incidence, both calculated per resident in most cases. For horizontal equalization, this measure (absolute versus relative) is generally coupled with the gross versus net impact. This is because, unlike vertical equalization, in which the funds are external and paid by the higher-level government, horizontal equalization requires contributions from local governments at the same level. Thus "gross" corresponds to the total amount received, "net" to the amount received minus the contribution paid. In equation (13.5), for example, EQ_i is the gross absolute value paid by local government i. It also implies that without equalization—that is, without $FC_i - 100$—the contribution to the equalization fund would be strictly proportional to the number of residents per local government:

$$contribution_i = \frac{M}{\sum_{j=1}^{N} P_j} \times P_i, \tag{13.9}$$

that is, the average contribution ($M/\Sigma P_j$) multiplied by the population number of local government i. The net absolute value is EQ_i from equation (13.5) minus its contribution from equation (13.9). In per capita terms, the gross relative value is EQ_i/P_i; the net relative value is EQ_i in equation (13.5) minus the contribution$_i$ in equation (13.9) divided by P_i.

A fourth issue is that the equalizing performance can be measured with respect to either the objective fixed by the legislator or the situation that results from the application of the formula. In the first case, the question is to what extent the objective assigned to fiscal equalization has been made explicit and is measurable without ambiguity. Compare, for example, two targets. Under the first, used in Germany, after equalization each jurisdiction should reach a level of at least 85 percent of the average per capita tax yield. Under the second, used in Switzerland, equalization should reduce resource disparities between jurisdictions as much as possible, so that the remaining disparities are politically acceptable. The first policy target is clear and measurable; to what extent the political objective is reached may be subject to economic evaluation. In the second case, the objective cannot be quantified; the question is to what extent fiscal equalization reduces the existing disparities. Comparing the situations before and after equalization is merely a statistical evaluation of the equalizing performance.

A fifth issue deals with the weight given to each jurisdiction in the construction of a synthetic index of equalizing performance. According to a "legalistic" view, all local units are considered equal, regardless of their economic, demographic, social, and geographical situation or status. But other views are possible. Economists consider the relative importance of each subnational or local government. The most straightforward method is proportional to the population size using per capita monetary measures, as in equations (13.5)–(13.8). The contributions of high-capacity local governments and the payments to low-capacity local governments are proportional to the number of their residents (weighted by that part of the formula that specifies their financial capacity). Proportionality should be used consistently throughout the exercise, with regard to both the number of years and the number of different tax types taken into consideration (see equations 13.3 and 13.4). In measuring the financial capacity of local governments, the relative weights of the various tax sources taken into consideration are used.

The traditional method of evaluating equalizing performance is the statistical one defined above. It compares local governments' nominal tax capacities before and after equalization. The comparison is made by means of a synthetic index of the dispersion of tax capacities. One reference example is the Gini index, in which each local government is given the same weight or adjusted by population figures in order to consider the demographic weight of each jurisdiction. Other evaluations are also possible (Dafflon 1995). A related issue is the measurement of the relative contribution of the individual components of the equalizing system to the overall equalization performance. If several tax sources are taken into account, for example, their performance may be examined separately (Gilbert and Guengant 2001, 2003).

Conclusion and Policy Proposals

Due to variations in demographic factors (age, health status, population density), geography (distance from the center, weather, quality of soil), and other factors, regions within most countries do not have uniform tax potential or face uniform production costs of providing public services. To address the problem, both federal and unitary countries use equalization. Both equity and efficiency considerations can be used to justify equalization, with their relative weights differing across countries. All equalization schemes are the result of both economic and political choices.

The following principles should govern the design of an equalization scheme:

- Make the rules explicit and embed them into a strong legal framework, such as a constitutional provision or a general law. Do not review them annually in the course of the budget debate.
- Think things through before introducing an equalization scheme. Simulate not only the current situation but also various scenarios. Use data that are agreed to by all parties and not susceptible to manipulation.
- Use a stable revenue source with a high level of predictability. A set of taxes rather than a single tax and a fund that allows smoothing of ups and downs in transfers are preferable to a simple entry in the annual local governments' budgets, which is more vulnerable to macro fluctuations and political hazard.
- Do not mix equalization transfers and conditional grants. Explicit equalization transfers should be untied, unconditional grants. If equalization is not able to account for all revenue or cost disparities in the provision of a specific public service, cost differentials may be taken into account in setting the level of specific grants.
- Set up an autonomous body in charge of periodically assessing the performance of equalization and advising the government on best practices. Publishing and debating the performance report will allow for a compromise in promoting horizontal solidarity and risk pooling.

1. Because the charter does not specifically consider the division of the state into two or three tiers of government, *local* can also be used in the sense of *subnational* government units—provinces, cantons, and *Länder* at the intermediate tier, municipalities, towns, and communes at the lower tier. For simplicity, this chapter considers only one lower tier of government. Since the concern here is primarily horizontal equalization, this restriction does not change the argument. Multiple tiers need to be considered in assessing vertical equalization, because vertical transfers may flow from the center to the local tier, bypassing the intermediate level. This raises the issue of which tier has the last word on equalization policy. On this question, see the seminal contribution of Boadway and Flatters (1982).

2. In his recent presentation of the first-generation theory of fiscal federalism, Oates (2005, p. 352) considers that the issue is vertical equalization—"equalizing, lump-sum grants from the central government to regional (or local) governments." He makes no reference to horizontal equalization.

3. See Shah (1984, 1996) for a discussion of this distinction in theory and practice. One important difficulty faced in most countries is the scarcity of databases of cost factors (see Färber and Otter 2003 for a discussion of the problem in Europe). Local public accounts are not organized in a way that allows the production functions of the various local public services to be derived. Origins and causes of costs are not easily identifiable; when they are, adequate data do not always exist. The costs of providing primary education, for example, differ across localities. The salaries of teachers are known, but the cost of the teaching material, the technical equipment, and the buildings may not be (amortization and financial costs, for example, are often recorded under a separate budget item). Data may be available on the number of pupils or the number of classes but not both. Cost standards are thus based on fragmented information. The resulting policy measures are strongly disputed at the political level by those who are directly or indirectly concerned by cost equalization in primary education.

4. The measurement of expenditure needs is based on 13 indicators, 9 of which are supposed to be representative criteria for 17 types of expenditures and 4 of which are "politically decided" (Lotz 1997). The number of inhabitants in Danish municipalities is thought to be the correct criteria for the following types of local public expenses: public pensions, employment, town development, environment, libraries, public transport, and administration. The weight given to this criterion is 21 percent. The number of inhabitants ages 7–16 is given the heaviest weight (23 percent).

5. Although formally vertical, such a system may have horizontal effects. The combination of various characteristics of the transfers may lead to situations that cannot be explained directly from the individual characteristics. For instance, the choice of a vertical equalization policy based on closed-end grants will bring about an outcome that is different from what might have been expected. Verticality indicates the formal direction of the transfer flows from a higher government tier to sublevel units (from central to subnational governments or from a subnational government to local governments). The "closed-end" design implies that the disposable resources are not infinite; their amount is fixed by the national constitution or laws and is not negotiable at each annual budgetary round. As a consequence, for any specific local

public task, awarding a targeted cantonal subsidy to one commune will necessarily restrict the amount of funds for the other communes. Local governments must compete with one another for the available resources, which are severely limited by the donor (higher-level) government. With equal access to the granting system, the result of such a mechanism is a revenue transfer from communes enjoying a strong financial position (which receive less) to less affluent communes (which receive more). With a fixed and limited amount of funding, the incidence is horizontal, although the design of the transfer system is vertical and in the command of the higher government tier. A horizontal fiscal equalization scheme would lead to similar results (Dafflon and Tóth 2003).

6. Färber and Otter (2003) analyze equalization systems at the local level in Austria, Flanders (Belgium), Denmark, France, Germany, Italy, Russia, Spain, Fribourg in Switzerland, and the United Kingdom. Cost equalization, if it exists, is nowhere horizontal.

7. The argument, first discussed by Boadway and Flatters (1982), is one of strict equality of treatment of individuals at the local tier of government: individuals pay for what they command and receive in their individual jurisdiction. It may be that a particular service costs more in jurisdiction A than in B, but all users in A and B are treated equally. There is no necessity for a price or fee adjustment between A and B. In fact, any such adjustment would create undesirable side effects.

8. "Perfect mapping" exist when the spatial pattern of the provision of local public goods corresponds exactly to the geographical boundaries of the jurisdictions.

9. Article 9 of the European Charter of Local Self-Government (1985) ("Financial Resources of Local Authorities") states: "1. Local authorities shall be entitled, within national economic policy, to adequate financial resources of their own, of which they may dispose freely within the framework of theirs powers. ... 7. As far as possible, grants to local authorities shall not be earmarked for the financing of specific projects."

10. In Switzerland the cantons and the confederation are always involved in the design of fiscal equalization, but the result is written in the federal constitution and legislation (Dafflon 1995, 2004). The same procedure applies to the cantons: the communes participate in the design stage of equalization policies, but the result, be it a vertical or a horizontal equalization scheme, is written into cantonal law and not in a contract or agreement between local governments, as is the case for intercommunal functions or provision of local public services.

11. The new equalization formula was adopted November 28, 2004, in a federal referendum. Sixty-four percent of the voters and 23 of Switzerland's 26 cantons voted for the new formula. Voters in three cantons (Nidwald, Schwyz, and Zoug) rejected the reform. The practical details of implementation have yet to be worked out; several federal laws will have to be modified, some of which are subject to referendum (requiring a simple majority of voters). The new measures will thus probably not be put into practice before 2008.

12. The theoretical relation between risk-sharing arrangements and equalization belongs to the second-generation theory of fiscal federalism (Oates 2005). One important issue is whether risk sharing should be a federal or a subnational government program if regions differ in terms of incomes or exposure to external shocks. Under such circumstances, Persson and Tabellini (1996) show that vertical

programs tend to oversupply while horizontal programs tend to undersupply insurance. For an overview of the question, see von Hagen (2003) and Oates (2005).

13. There is a technical limit to the value α in the formulas. The maximum value can be computed by an iterative process, with a rule that avoids disincentive effects: no local government should receive an amount of equalization transfers that would allow it to overtake the next local government in the ranking. The basic argument is that if the Nth local government can overtake the local government in the $N - 1$ position through equalization, the Nth local government will have no incentive to improve its position, as the equalization transfer bridges the total gap. The local government in the $N - 1$ position also knows that simply by virtue of equalization, the $N - 2$-positioned local government cannot gain a better position and pass in front. In a sample of 168 communes in the canton of Fribourg, Switzerland, with an indicator of tax capacity based on eight tax sources for the fiscal years 2001 to 2003, the power value in equation (13.5) cannot exceed 2.645 if the "no-overtake" rule is to be observed.

References

Ahmad, E., ed. 1997. *Financing Decentralized Expenditures: An International Comparison of Grants.* Cheltenham, United Kingdom: Edward Elgar.

Ahmad, E., and J. Craig. 1997. "Intergovernmental Transfers." In *Fiscal Federalism in Theory and Practice*, ed. T. Ter-Minassian, 3–107. Washington, DC: International Monetary Fund.

Anderson, J.E., ed. 1994. *Fiscal Equalization for State and Local Government Finance.* Westport, CT: Praeger.

Aubut, J., and F. Vaillancourt. 2001. "Using GDP in Equalization Calculations: Are There Meaningful Measurement Issues?" Revised version of a paper prepared under contract for the Department of Finance, Ottawa, for the August 2001 Charlottetown Conference on Macro Approaches to Equalization.

Bahl, R., J. Martinez-Vazquez, and D.L. Sjoquist. 1992. "Central City-Suburban Fiscal Disparities." *Public Finance Quarterly* 20 (4): 420–32.

Barro, S.M. 1986. "State Fiscal Capacity Measures: A Theoretical Critique." In *Measuring Fiscal Capacity*, ed. H.C. Reeves, 50–86. Cambridge, MA: Lincoln Institute of Land Policy.

Bird, R., and E. Slack 1990. "Equalization: The Representative Tax System Revisited." *Canadian Tax Journal* 38: 913–27.

Blindenbacher, R., and R. Watts. 2003. "Federalism in a Changing World: A Conceptual Framework for the Conference." *In Federalism in a Changing World: Learning from Each Other*, ed. R. Blindenbacher and A. Koller, 7–25. Kingston, Canada: Queen's University Press.

Boadway, R. 1998. "The Economics of Equalization: An Overview." In *Equalization: Its Contribution to Canada's Economic and Fiscal Progress*, ed. R.W. Boadway and P.A. Hobson, 27–82. Policy Forum Series, vol. 31. Kingston, Canada: John Deutsch Institute for the Study of Economic Policy.

———. "The Theory and Practice of Equalization." *CESifo Economic Studies* 50 (1):211–54.

Boadway, R., and F. Flatters. 1982. "Equalization in a Federal State: An Economic Analysis." Paper prepared for the Economic Council of Canada, Supply and Services, Ottawa.

———. 2004. "The Theory and Practice of Equalization." *CESifo Economic Studies* 50 (1): 211–54.

Boadway, R., and M. Hayashi. 2004. "An Evaluation of the Stabilization Properties of Equalization in Canada." *Canadian Public Policy, Analyse de politiques* 30 (1): 91–109.

Boothe, P. 1998. *Finding a Balance: Renewing Canadian Fiscal Federalism.* C.D. Howe Institute, Toronto.

Break, G. 1980. *Financing Government in a Federal System.* Washington, DC: Brookings Institution.

Buettner, T. 2002. "Fiscal Federalism and Interstate Risk Sharing: Empirical Evidence from Germany." *Economics Letters* 74 (2): 195–202.

Castells, A., A. Esteller, and M. Vilalta. 2003. "Tax Capacity Disparities and Fiscal Equalisation: The Case of Spanish Local Governments." In *Reforms of Local Fiscal Equalisation in Europe,* ed. G. Färber and N. Otter, 297–338. Speyerer Forschungsberichte, No. 232, Forschungsinstitut für Öffentliche Verwaltung, Deutsche Hochschule für Verwaltungswissenschaften, Speyer, Germany.

Clark, D. 1969. *Fiscal Need and Revenue Equalization Grants.* Canadian Tax Foundation, Toronto.

Council of Europe. 1985. "European Charter of Local Self-Government." European Treaty Series 122, Strasbourg.

Courchene, T. 1970. "Interprovincial Migration and Economic Adjustment." *Canadian Journal of Economics* 3(4): 550–76.

Dafflon, B. 1995. "Fédéralisme et solidarité: etude de la péréquation en Suisse." *Études et colloques* 15, University of Fribourg, Institute of Federalism, Switzerland.

———. 1998. "Les fusions de communes dans le canton de Fribourg: analyse socio–économique." In *Annuaire des collectivités locales,* 125–66. GRALE and CRNS. Paris: Librairie Technique de la Cour de Cassation.

———. 2004. "Federal-Cantonal Equalization in Switzerland: An Overview of the Reform in Progress." *Public Finance and Management* 4 (4).

Dafflon, B., and P. Mischler. 2005. "Réforme de la péréquation intercommunale dans le canton de Fribourg." White Paper for the Committee on the Reform of the Equalization System between the Communes. Canton of Fribourg, Fribourg, May 21.

Dafflon, B., and K. Tóth. 2003. "Local Fiscal Equalisation in Switzerland: The Case of the Canton Fribourg." In *Reforms of Local Fiscal Equalisation in Europe,* ed. G. Färber and N. Otter, 41–80. Speyerer Forschungsberichte, No. 232, Forschungsinstitut für Öffentliche Verwaltung, Deutsche Hochschule für Verwaltungswissenschaften, Speyer, Germany.

Dafflon, B., and F. Vaillancourt. 2003. "Problems of Equalisation in Federal Systems." In *Federalism in a Changing World: Learning from Each Other,* ed. R. Blindenbacher and A. Koller, 395–411. Kingston, Canada: Queen's University Press.

Else, P. 2003, "Fiscal Equalisation in the United Kingdom: Problems and Prospects." In *Reforms of Local Fiscal Equalisation in Europe,* ed. G. Färber and N. Otter, 225–53. Speyerer Forschungsberichte, No. 232, Forschungsinstitut für Öffentliche Verwaltung, Deutsche Hochschule für Verwaltungswissenschaften, Speyer, Germany.

Färber, G., and N. Otter, eds. 2003. *Reforms of Local Fiscal Equalisation in Europe.* Speyerer Forschungsberichte, No. 232, Forschungsinstitut für Öffentliche Verwaltung, Deutsche Hochschule für Verwaltungswissenschaften, Speyer, Germany.

Fisher, R.C., ed. 1997. *Intergovernmental Fiscal Relations*. Dordrecht, the Netherlands: Kluwer.

Flowerdew, R., B. Francis, and S. Lucas. 1994. "The Standard Spending Assessments as a Measure of Spending Needs in Non-Metropolitan Districts." *Environment and Planning C: Government and Policy* 12 (1):1–13.

Garcia-Milà, T., and T. McGuire. 2004. "Solidarity and Fiscal Decentralization." Paper presented at the National Tax Association's Annual Conference, Chicago, November.

Gilbert, G. 1996. "Le fédéralisme financier: perspectives de microéconomie spatiale." *Revue Économique* 47 (2): 311–63.

Gilbert, G., and A. Guengant. 2001. "Effets redistributifs des dotations de l'État aux communes." GRALE-GIS-CRNS, Commissariat Général du Plan, Paris.

———. 2003. "The Equalising Performance of the Central Government Grants to Local Authorities: The Case of France." In *Reforms of Local Fiscal Equalisation in Europe*, ed. G. Färber and N. Otter, 189–224. Speyerer Forschungsberichte, No. 232, Forschungsinstitut für Öffentliche Verwaltung, Deutsche Hochschule für Verwaltungswissenschaften, Speyer, Germany.

Inman, R.F., and D.L. Rubinfeld. 1996. "Designing Tax Policy in Federalist Economies: An Overview." *Journal of Public Economics* 60 (3): 307–34.

King, D. 1997. "Intergovernmental Fiscal Relations: Concepts and Models." In *Intergovernmental Fiscal Relations*, ed. R.C. Fisher, 19–58. Dordrecht, the Netherlands: Kluwer.

Ladd, H.F. 1994. "Measuring Disparities in the Fiscal Condition of Local Governments." In *Fiscal Equalization for State and Local Government Finance*, ed. J.E. Anderson, 21–53. Westport, CT: Praeger.

———. 1999a. "Fiscal Disparities." In *The Encyclopedia of Taxation and Tax Policy*, ed. J.J. Cordes, R.D. Ebel, and J.G. Gravelle, 123–25. Washington, DC: Urban Institute.

———. 1999b. "Measuring Disparities in the Fiscal Condition of Local Governments." In *The Challenge of Fiscal Disparities for State and Local Governments*, ed. H.F. Ladd, 37–70. Cheltenham, United Kingdom: Edward Elgar.

Lotz, J.R. 1997. "Denmark and Other Scandinavian Countries: Equalization and Grants." In *Financing Decentralized Expenditures: An International Comparison of Grants*, ed. E. Ahmad, 184–212. Cheltenham, United Kingdom: Edward Elgar.

Mau Pedersen, N.J. 2003. "Challenges of the Danish Fiscal Equalisation Scheme: Redistribution and Incentives." In *Reforms of Local Fiscal Equalisation in Europe*, ed. G. Färber and N. Otter, 131–162. Speyerer Forschungsberichte, No. 232, Forschungsinstitut für Öffentliche Verwaltung, Deutsche Hochschule für Verwaltungswissenschaften, Speyer, Germany.

McLean, I. 2004. "Fiscal Federalism in Australia." *Public Administration* 82 (1): 21–38.

Oakland, W.H. 1994, "Recognizing and Correcting for Fiscal Disparities: A Critical Analysis." In *Fiscal Equalization for State and Local Government Finance*, ed. J.E. Anderson, 1–19. Westport, CT: Praeger.

Oates, W.E. 2005. "Toward a Second-Generation Theory of Fiscal Federalism." *International Tax and Public Finance* 12 (4): 349–73.

Persson, T., and G. Tabellini. 1996. "Federal Fiscal Constitutions: Risk Sharing and Redistribution." *Journal of Political Economy* 104 (5): 979–1009.

Petchey, J. 1995. "Resource Rents, Cost Differences and Fiscal Equalization." *Economic Record* 71 (215): 343–53.

Rye, C.R., and B. Searle. 1997. "The Fiscal Transfer System in Australia." In *Financing Decentralized Expenditures: An International Comparison of Grants*, ed. E. Ahmad, 144–183. Cheltenham, United Kingdom: Edward Elgar.

Shah, A. 1984. "Alternative Approaches to the Measurement of Expenditure Needs of Canadian Provinces." Finance Canada Discussion Paper, March.

———. 1996. "A Fiscal Need Approach to Equalization." *Canadian Public Policy, Analyse de politiques* 22 (2): 99–115.

Smart, M. 1998. "Taxation and Dead-Weight Loss in a System of Intergovernmental Transfers." *Canadian Journal of Economics* 31 (1): 189–206.

———. 2004. "Equalization and Stabilization." *Canadian Public Policy, Analyse de politiques* 30 (2):195–208.

Tannenwald, R. 1999. "Fiscal Disparity among the States Revisited." *New England Economic Review* July/August: 3–25.

Ter-Minassian, T., ed. 1997. *Fiscal Federalism in Theory and Practice*. Washington, DC: International Monetary Fund.

Usher, D. 1995. "The Uneasy Case for Equalization Payments." Fraser Institute, Vancouver.

von Hagen, J. 2000. "Fiscal Policy and Intranational Risk-Sharing." In *Intranational Macroeconomics*, ed. G.D. Hess and E. van Wincoop, 272–94. Cambridge: Cambridge University Press.

———. 2003. "Fiscal Federalism and Political Decision Structures." In *Federalism in a Changing World: Learning from Each Other*, ed. R. Blindenbacher and A. Koller, 373–94. Kingston, Canada: Queen's University Press.

Zimmermann, H. 1999. "Experiences with German Fiscal Federalism: How to Preserve the Decentral Content?" In *Fiscal Federalism in the European Union*, ed. A. Fossati and G. Panella, 162–76. London: Routledge.

14

Compensating Local Governments for Differences in Expenditure Needs in a Horizontal Fiscal Equalization Program

ANDREW RESCHOVSKY

In many developed and developing countries, central governments distribute "equalizing" grants to lower-level governments. The grants are usually allocated among states and provinces; in some countries they are also allocated to local governments. Equalizing grants are provided in countries with unitary governments (France); federal systems (Australia, Canada); and mixed systems (South Africa).

The conceptual and theoretical literature delineates several alternative roles for horizontal equalization programs within a system of intergovernmental finance (Buchanan 1950, 1952; Buchanan and Goetz 1972; Flatters, Henderson, and Mieszkowski 1974; Boadway and Flatters 1982; Boadway 2004). In one way or another, all horizontal equalization programs are designed to address the consequences of horizontal fiscal imbalance. In the most general terms, these imbalances exist if governments vary in their ability to raise money to finance the public services for which they are responsible. These differences are often referred to as fiscal disparities.

In many decentralized fiscal systems, subnational governments, at either the provincial or local level, are responsible for providing core public services, such as education, health care, and public safety. One possible goal of an equalization aid program is to ensure that all citizens, regardless of where they live within a country, have access to a minimum amount and quality of either a specific public service, such as primary education or basic health care, or a full array of public services that are the responsibility of subnational governments.

To meet this objective, the donor government could design an equalization grant using a formula that provides each recipient government with a grant equal to the difference between the minimum amount of money needed to provide a basic level of public services for those functions assigned to it and the amount of money that the government could be expected to raise from local sources at a "normal" or "standard" rate of revenue effort. Use of this type of formula ensures that each recipient government has sufficient resources available to provide a basic level of public services as long as each government is required to raise revenue from its own sources at a standardized or required rate.[1] The first term in this formula provides a measure of the expenditure needs of the recipient government; the second term provides a measure of its revenue-raising capacity.

A second possible goal for equalizing grants is to reduce, or even eliminate, fiscal disparities among provincial or local governments. In any decentralized system, some subnational governments face fiscal disadvantages relative to other governments. Governments in the weakest fiscal condition either have relatively low revenue-raising capacity or face relatively high expenditure needs.

One way to characterize the fiscal condition of governments is by comparing the gap between expenditure needs and revenue-raising capacity. This gap is generally referred to as a need-capacity (or fiscal) gap.

Donor governments can reduce fiscal disparities by allocating grants in proportion to the size of need-capacity gaps or by allocating grants only to governments in the weakest fiscal condition (that is, to governments with the largest gaps). This type of grant formula would reduce the fiscal disadvantage of governments in the weakest fiscal health without imposing a minimum tax rate requirement on any recipient government.

A third possible goal of equalization grants, used to justify the use of these grants in a number of federal countries, is based on the principle of horizontal equity.[2] If the residents of different subnational governments agree to tax themselves at the same rates, the grant system should ensure that they have access to the same level of public services. This goal is sometimes referred to as ensuring taxpayer equity (Reschovsky 1994). Progress toward this goal would not only reduce the variation in the average tax price of public services facing residents in different jurisdictions, it should also help reduce fiscally motivated intrajurisdictional migration by both residents and enterprises, thereby enhancing efficiency (Vaillancourt and Bird 2004). As it is nearly inevitable in any decentralized fiscal system that both fiscal capacities and the costs of providing any level or mix of public services differ across subnational jurisdictions, achieving this sort of horizontal equity will require a system of transfers in which the amount of the grant is a positive function of the rate of taxation chosen by each subnational jurisdiction.

This chapter adopts the premise that regardless of which goal a system of horizontally equalizing grants is attempting to reach, expenditure needs should play an important role in the design of grants. All scholars do not accept this premise: some question whether expenditure needs should be incorporated in equalization aid formulas.

A number of countries have established systems of intergovernmental grants designed to reduce fiscal disparities across both provinces and local governments.[3] These grant programs are more common in developed countries than in developing countries. In most countries that use equalizing grants, the source of the grants is the national or central government. One notable exception is the United States, where the federal government provides no unconditional equalizing aid to state or local governments. In the United States, however, state governments provide substantial amounts of equalizing aid to local governments. Nearly all states provide equalizing aid to finance primary and secondary education; some states also fund a wide range of municipal services.[4]

In practice, it is common for grants to be allocated among local governments based on differences in revenue-raising or fiscal capacity. There are fewer examples of grant formulas that explicitly account for differences among provincial and local governments in expenditure needs or need-capacity gaps. Several countries, however, mainly developed ones, do use grant formulas that explicitly account for the expenditure needs of recipient governments.

The rest of this chapter is organized as follows. It begins by defining needs and costs and explaining why costs differ within a country. It then describes three approaches to estimating costs—estimating cost functions, estimating expenditure functions, and relying on expert judgment—before looking at actual costing methodologies used in selected countries. The last section draws conclusions about the kind of methodologies that are likely to work best in developing countries.

Defining Expenditure Needs and Costs

Expenditure needs are a measure of the minimum amount of money necessary for a government to provide the set of public services for which it is responsible. Within any country, expenditure needs can be expected to vary across both provincial and local jurisdictions, for two reasons. The first is that expenditure needs may be higher for some governments than for others because some governments are required to provide a broader range of public services than others. In South Africa and Switzerland, for example, the constitution largely determines the assignment of responsibilities across levels of government. In other countries, such as the United States, the constitution does not explicitly outline the fiscal responsibilities of state and local governments. In many countries, particularly those, such as the United Kingdom, that do not have formal constitutions, the fiscal responsibilities of local governments are specified largely by statute at the national or provincial level.

Increasingly, central governments in OECD countries are imposing public service norms and minimum quality standards on the public goods responsibilities of local governments (Jourmard and Kongsrud 2003). These "mandates" by central governments have a direct impact on the expenditure needs local jurisdictions face.

In many countries, the assignment of public service responsibilities to local governments depends on the size of the jurisdiction. In general, larger local governments are assigned a broader range of public services, with central cities of metropolitan areas often assigned the largest number of functions. In the United States, public safety in rural and suburban jurisdictions is often carried out by higher-level regional governments, while public safety is almost always a municipal government function in larger jurisdictions.

In almost all countries, some public services are the responsibility of local governments. These include sanitation, garbage removal, street repair, street cleaning, fire protection, libraries, and recreation facilities. The assignment of other, generally more costly, functions, such as primary and secondary education, public safety, and public health, vary across countries, with responsibilities for these functions resting with local governments in some countries, with provinces in others, and with the national (or federal) government in still others.

The second, and more important, reason why expenditure needs vary across governments is that the minimum amount of money necessary to meet any given set of service responsibilities or standard for public service provision may differ across local governments for reasons that are outside the control of individual governmental units. That is, the cost of providing a public service may vary across regions.

It is important to make a clear distinction between costs and spending. The level of expenditure in any given provincial or local government on any given public service depends on several factors. High spending levels may reflect the government's desire to provide an especially high level or high quality of service (daily trash collection, for example, or instruction in advanced mathematics in secondary schools). An above-average level of spending may also reflect inefficiencies in the provision of services, due to mismanagement, waste, or corruption. Only that part of the spending necessary to provide a given level of public service that is due to factors over which the local government has no control is included in the cost of providing that service. The methodological challenge is to disentangle data on actual spending into that portion attributable to the costs of the service (sometimes referred to as "cost disabilities"), that portion attributable to local preferences or policies about levels of service provision, and that portion due to inefficiencies.[5]

Why Costs Differ

Before turning to a discussion of actual practice, it is useful to consider why, on conceptual grounds, the costs of providing services may differ across subnational governments. A starting point for any calculation of the costs of public services is a discussion of what level or mix of public services serves as the basis for the calculation. One possibility would be to set this standard at the average level of public services provided by all local or provincial governments.[6] In developing countries, in particular, an appropriate standard for the calculation of expenditure needs and costs would be a level of public service that is considered "basic." Consider the example of basic sanitation. Given spatial differences in population density and other physical characteristics of communities, it is reasonable to define basic sanitation differently in different settings. In rural areas of developing countries, for example, ventilated improved pit latrines might be considered an appropriate means of providing basic sanitation services. In contrast, in cities and other dense urban areas, waterborne sewerage systems are needed to prevent the spread of disease. The provision of basic sanitation services thus requires very different technologies in different places, differences that have potentially important cost implications.[7]

The costs of providing public services are likely to vary across governmental units for four major reasons: differences in the quantity and composition of inputs necessary to produce the public service, differences in factor or input prices, difference in physical characteristics (environmental factors), and differences in the sociodemographic composition of the residents of each government. The inputs needed to produce various public services depend in part on the underlying technology used to produce the service. The labor and equipment needed to provide basic sanitation depend on whether latrines or full-blown sewerage systems are used. A different set of inputs is needed if water is supplied through community standpipes or through in-house plumbing.

For many public services, labor is the most important input. In these cases, the remuneration of labor is the largest component of public spending. The fact that some jurisdictions pay higher wages than others does not automatically mean that high-wage jurisdictions have higher costs than other jurisdictions. In countries in which local governments set the wage rates of local government employees, wages reflect both the preferences of local jurisdictions with respect to the type of employee they wish to hire (which the local government determines) and the characteristics of the labor market (over which the local government has no control). Only the portion of wage costs due to uncontrollable factors should be considered as part of the cost of the public service. The payment of higher wages to attract workers with better qualifications is a choice made by local governments. In contrast, paying higher wages to attract public sector employees to remote areas or to urban areas with high crime rates is part of the cost of service.

The amount and type of resources needed to provide many public goods depend in part on where the public good is produced and delivered. If, for example, the provision of basic roads is defined to mean the availability of a thoroughfare that can be easily used throughout the year, operating costs will include the cost of maintaining the road in passable condition under different weather conditions. A graded dirt road may be adequate in locations with relatively little rain, while a paved surface and regular maintenance will be required in locations subject to frequent torrential rainfalls. Roads in areas subject to frequent freezing and melting will require substantially more maintenance than roads in more-temperate climates.

Another factor that influences the costs of some municipal services is population density. In some cases, higher density can lead to higher costs. Achieving basic fire protection, for example, requires more resources in places where buildings are close together and fires can easily spread. For other local public services, low density may raise costs. For example, providing potable water in a thinly settled, low-density community will require the construction and maintenance of more pipes and pumping stations than in a more densely settled community.

Economies of scale can also have a significant effect on the cost of delivering local government services. For public services characterized by large fixed costs and relatively low operating costs, per capita costs decline dramatically as the scale of operation rises. Water and electricity provision generally enjoy significant scale economies. Empirical evidence from local governments in the United States suggests that many public services provided by local government are subject to U-shaped average costs.[8] This means that larger population size reduces average costs up to the point at which scale economies are exhausted, after which larger population size raises average costs.

The extent to which high costs due to location-specific environmental factors should influence the allocation of grants is controversial. While high-density urban communities might be compensated for the higher costs of delivering some municipal services (due to high density), it is not clear that the same argument should be used to justify providing large grants to small communities located in locations where it is very costly to deliver public services. If, for example, a village is located on the top of a mountain, the costs of supplying water will be very high, because water will need to be pumped up the mountain. If a grant formula fully reflects these extra costs, residents of this village will have no incentive to move away from this inefficient, high-cost location.

The question of what costs or what proportion of costs should be accounted for in grant formulas is obviously a contentious, and highly political, issue. Some countries, notably Japan and Switzerland, provide very large per capita subsidies to guarantee the provision of public services to people who choose to live in very remote, high-cost locations. In Japan the government provides a wide range of services to people living on small islands. In Switzerland the government allocates substantial resources to maintaining public services in small farming villages located high in the Alps.

For some public services, the socioeconomic and demographic composition of the population of a provincial or local government has the potential to influence the costs of providing public services. There is little reason to believe that after controlling for other environmental factors, the costs of providing basic electric services or roads should be affected by the composition of the population. However, the costs of providing other services, such as basic health care, will be affected by the composition of the population. There is ample international evidence that the incidence of health problems is inversely related to income. As a result, the higher the incidence of poverty in a community, the higher the per capita cost of providing basic health care. There is also evidence that demographic factors influence the cost of health care, with costs highest for the elderly and for young children.

The key issue in measuring the costs of public services is identifying which factors are likely to play a role in influencing the costs of services and then determining the quantitative importance of those factors. Examining grant formulas used around the world reveals which factors are used to account for differences in expenditure needs and the weight given to each factor.[9] While an understanding of grant formulas is useful, it does not in itself provide any information about the methodology used to identify which factors influence costs and expenditure needs or to determine the quantitative importance of each factor.

Much has been written about how Australia's Grants Commission determines the expenditure needs of each state. For most other countries, finding a detailed description of the methodology used is difficult. In many countries the cost factors used in grant formulas are the outcome not of careful research but of a largely political process, driven primarily by negotiations over the final distribution of aid.

Approaches to Estimating Costs

Several methodologies can be used to determine the costs of local public services. Where good data on public sector outcomes are available, cost functions can sometimes be estimated directly. Where outcome data are not available, expenditure functions are sometimes used instead. A third approach involves relying on expert judgment to estimate costs.

Estimating a Cost Function

A cost function is a statistical relationship between spending on a given public service, measures of outcomes, and other factors that have an impact on the relationship between spending and the level of public service provision. If it were feasible to estimate cost functions for all government services, it would be relatively easy to calculate an index that would indicate the minimum amount of money each government needed to provide each public service. Summing across all public services for which a government was responsible would provide a good measure of that jurisdiction's expenditure needs.

To provide a picture of how cost functions are estimated, it is useful to start with a public good production function (equation 14.1). This equation allows one to represent the relationship between S_{ij}, public service j provided by local government i; X_{ij}, the vector of inputs needed to produce S_{ij}; and Z_{ij}, a vector of environmental factors that might influence the relationship between inputs and outputs:

$$S_{ij} = g(X_{ij}, Z_{ij}) \,. \tag{14.1}$$

To move from a production function to a cost function, it is necessary to specify a relationship between spending on public good j, E_{ij}, and public good inputs, a vector of input prices P_{ij}, and a vector of unobserved characteristics of the local government that influence public good spending, ε_{ij}. This relationship is represented by equation (14.2):

$$E_{ij} = f(X_{ij}, P_{ij}, \varepsilon_{ij}) \,. \tag{14.2}$$

Solving equation (14.1) for X_{ij} and then plugging X_{ij} into equation (14.2) yields a cost function, in which u_{ij} is a random error term:

$$E_{ij} = h(S_{ij}, P_{ij}, Z_{ij}, \varepsilon_{ij}, u_{ij}). \tag{14.3}$$

The critical methodological question is how one estimates equation (14.3). In addition to local government expenditure data disaggregated by functional category, data on the level of public good outputs, the S_{ij}'s, are needed. Finding measures of public output is often difficult, both conceptually and empirically. For some publicly provided goods and services, especially those that are technically equivalent to private goods, such as the provision of water or electricity or the collection of garbage, physical measures of service delivery are readily available. In many countries data on the number of households supplied with potable water and the number of liters of water consumption are relatively easy to obtain. For other public services, such as police and fire protection, finding a measure of public good output is much more problematic. For example, it is extremely difficult to determine whether low crime rates reflect high-quality police services or the small number of offenders in a community. Communities with a larger number of arrests may not necessarily be safer than communities with lower arrest rates. Measuring the output of schools is fraught with problems. But in a number of countries, results of standardized exams provide one measure of output that has been successfully used to estimate cost functions.

In estimating a cost function, it is important to take account of the fact that public sector output and spending are determined simultaneously. This means that a decision by local government officials to increase local public services will affect spending by the local government, while at the same time, extra local government spending should result in higher levels of public sector output. A standard way to deal with this simultaneity is to use a statistical technique known as two-stage least squares. The public sector output variables are considered endogenous, and a first-stage regression is estimated that attempts to explain variations across local governments in public output using a series of variables that help explain differences in preferences for local public services by local residents, decision makers, or both. Typically, measures of income or tax base in each community are included, as well as other indicators of local preferences, such as the occupations or education levels of local residents.

The measure of input prices, P_{ij}, should include only that portion of the price that is outside the control of local government officials. In countries such as South Africa, where the wages of most local and provincial government employees are set by national wage contract, the variation among subnational governments in input prices is quite limited.

The variation in ε_{ij} in equation (14.3) represents the unobserved factors in each local government that influence the level of spending. One reason why spending may be higher in some jurisdictions than in others is that some local governments operate inefficiently. They may be poorly organized or managed, use inappropriate technology, or employ inadequately trained personnel.

Although measuring inefficiency is very difficult, some recent studies have used complex statistical techniques to identify spending that is high relative to spending in local governments with similar public sector outputs and similar costs. Two such techniques, data envelopment analysis and stochastic frontier analysis, identify the governments operating with the lowest costs and then interpret any extra spending as a measure of local government inefficiency.[10] Street (2003) shows, however, that this kind of efficiency estimate is highly sensitive to the specification of input and outcome variables used to estimate cost functions. He concludes that very little confidence should be placed in the inefficiency estimates, especially when they are applied to individual units, such as school districts or hospitals.

In recent years economists have estimated cost functions for primary and secondary education in the United States, where education is the responsibility of local governments, usually independent school districts (Duncombe and Yinger 2000; Reschovsky and Imazeki 2003; Imazeki and Reschovsky 2005). Financing for schools comes from local property taxes, from grants from state governments, and to a small degree, from the federal government.

Although parameter estimates vary across states, the same cost factors tend to be identified. They include the percentage of students from poor families, the percentage of students with disabilities, the percentage of students with limited proficiency in English, the number of pupils in the district and the square of the number of students (to reflect a U-shaped average cost curve), and a teacher salary index that reflects teacher remuneration rates that are outside the control of the local school district.

Estimating a cost function provides information about the contribution of various characteristics of local governments to the costs of education. To move from an estimated cost function to a measure of expenditure needs for each local government, a cost index must be constructed. The cost index allows all information about costs to be summarized by a single number for each local government. Once policy makers have defined a basic level of service provision, a cost index can be constructed to indicate how much money each local government must spend, relative to a local government with average costs, in order to provide the basic level of service.

The cost index for any individual government is calculated by multiplying each coefficient from the cost function regression by the value of the appropriate cost factors in that community and by the standard or target value of student performance determined by the donor government. The result of this calculation, which can be called the community's hypothetical level of spending, is converted into an index number by dividing it by hypothetical spending in a community with average student and district characteristics. Thus if the average costs of meeting a given performance standard is $5,000, a community with a cost index value of 1.1 would need to spend $5,500 ($5,000 times 1.1) to meet the standard.

Estimating an Expenditure Equation

Because of the heavy data requirements and statistical complexity of estimating cost functions, economists have frequently resorted to estimating reduced-form expenditure equations in an attempt to identify cost factors and determine the expenditure needs of local governments. As in a cost function, the dependent variable in an expenditure equation is per capita expenditure on a particular public service or group of public services. In a typical expenditure equation, however, the independent variables do not include measures of public sector output. Because the specification does not include any public good output measure, simultaneity is not a problem, and the expenditure equation can be estimated using single-equation ordinary least squares.

The standard specification of an expenditure function can be expressed as follows:

$$E_{ij} = k(\mathbf{P}_{ij}, \mathbf{Z}_{ij}, \mathbf{F}_{ij}, u_{ij}), \tag{14.4}$$

where F_{ij} is a vector of variables that explain public good preferences for public service j. As in the previous equations, P_{ij} is a vector of input prices, Z_{ij} is a vector of student and community characteristics, and u_{ij} is a random error term. The F vector will include measures of subnational government resources, such as tax bases and revenue from grants.

One potential problem with using expenditure functions to measure the costs of government services is that it may be difficult to isolate variables that affect costs from variables that indicate differences in public good preferences or demands. As an example, consider the percentage of the population over the age of 65. A heavy concentration of elderly people may increase the costs of providing some services, such as health care. At the same time, to the extent that the elderly have different public good preferences from younger people, the variable may also serve as an indicator of demand. Fortunately, in most cases it is possible to identify variables in an expenditure function as being only or predominantly cost factors or demand factors.

Cost indices can be calculated from an estimated expenditure equation. The first step is to predict what each local government would have spent if it had had average resource and demand variables (the F_{ij}'s) but retained its own values for the cost variables (the P_{ij}'s and Z_{ij}'s). This prediction can be implemented by substituting the average values for the noncost variables and the actual values of the cost variables in the estimated expenditure regression equation. The observed variation in the resulting predicted expenditures will reflect variation in the cost factors alone. The last step involves translating these predicted expenditures into a cost index. This is accomplished by dividing predicted expenditures for each local government by expenditures of the local government with average costs.

Bradbury and others (1984) implement this methodology using data for Massachusetts. During the second half of the 1980s, Massachusetts distributed a portion of its state aid to local governments, using a formula that allocated funds proportionally to need-capacity gaps. The calculation of expenditure needs included a cost index based on the estimation of a reduced-form expenditure function of the type described above.

Another example of the use of this approach comes from Canada, which has long used provincial equalization grants. The Canadian fiscal equalization program is designed to equalize per capita tax burdens; it completely ignores the expenditure side. Shah (1996) criticizes the Canadian system and demonstrates a methodology that could be used to include relative expenditure needs. His approach, which he refers to as a representative expenditure system, estimates reduced-form expenditure equations. He starts by dividing consolidated provincial and local expenditures into eight categories: transportation and communications, social services, health, protective services, postsecondary education, elementary and secondary education, general administrative services, and other expenditures. He then estimates separate regression equations for each spending category based on annual data for each of the 10 Canadian provinces between 1971 and 1981.[11]

As an example of this approach, consider spending on transportation and communications. Shah's expenditure regression equation finds the following cost variables to be statistically significant: paved roads and street per square kilometer of area, the proportion of area that is noncultivatable, annual snowfall, population in metropolitan areas, average weekly private sector wages, and the number of commercial vehicle registrations. Statistically significant noncost factors in his transportation spending regression include federal-provincial transfers, own-source revenues, a time trend, and provincial GDP. Shah uses his regression equation results to calculate "hypothetical" per capita expenditures, using the same procedure described above, namely, substituting actual values for the cost factors and national average values of the noncost factors in each regression equation. Shah then calculates "standardized" per capita expenditures by substituting the average value of all variables in the expenditure regressions. For each category of spending, he then defines expenditure needs as hypothetical expenditures less standardized expenditures.

Reliance on the Judgment of Experts

An alternative to statistical approaches to measuring costs is reliance on expert judgment to identify the minimum costs of providing any given public service. A panel of experts on the production of a particular public service is asked to determine the set of inputs needed to produce the output. This information is then used to determine the minimum spending needed to produce the service in question.

The expert judgment approach has been used in a number of states in the United States to determine the cost of an "adequate" education (Gutherie and Rothstein 1999). It has also played a role in determining cost disabilities in the Australian grant system.

Reliance on expert judgment is essential when data on public sector output are limited, making statistical approaches to estimating costs and spending unfeasible. There are, however, several dangers inherent in this approach. First, the quality and accuracy of any cost estimate depends entirely on the knowledge of the experts. The procedure used to choose the experts is thus very important, especially when there is disagreement among experts concerning the most effective and efficient way to produce a public service.

Second, experts may not be used to answering questions about the least-cost method of providing a service. Engineers' judgments about "best practices" may focus on technical engineering issues and may not consider the fact that an alternate set of inputs may produce an output that is 95 percent as good as the "best" output at a cost that is 25 percent lower. Thus the set of inputs recommended by the expert may be "optimal" in some technical sense but far from optimal from an economic (technical efficiency) perspective.

Expert judgment has been used most frequently to provide estimates of the average cost of delivering a service. This is useful information. But estimation of expenditure needs requires knowledge of how costs differ when environmental (or demographic) characteristics of local governments vary. It is important to know, for example, how the proportion of students from poor families in a school raises the cost of achieving a given level of student academic performance. These questions are very hard to answer, even for experts.

Costing Methodologies in Selected Countries

There appears to be very limited experience in developing countries with the use of intergovernmental grants allocated on the basis of differences in expenditure needs. Most of the examples of costing methodologies thus come from developed countries.

Australia

The best example of a methodological approach to estimating expenditure needs that combines expert judgments with statistical analysis comes from Australia. The Australian grant equalization scheme allocates funds from the national government to the states. The methodology used is of particular interest because it explicitly measures expenditure needs and because the basic grant equalization system has been in operation for several decades. The central goal of the grant system is to provide states with "funding from the Commonwealth such that, if each made the same effort to raise revenue from its own sources and operated at the same level of efficiency, each would have the capacity to provide services at the same standard" (Commonwealth Grants Commission 2002, p. 6).

The Commonwealth Grants Commission is responsible for administering Australia's horizontal fiscal equalization program. To achieve its equalization goal, the commission calculates a "relativity" for each state. The relativity captures the differences in revenue-raising capacity and expenditure need in a single number. The revenue portion of the relativity calculation compares a state's utilization of a revenue source with the population-weighted average utilization for all states. The results are weighted by the relative importance of the revenue source and then summed across all sources (see Rye and Searle 1997).

The central concept in calculating expenditure need is disability. A disability is "an influence, beyond a state's control, that results in it having to spend a different per capita amount than the standard, or raising a different per capita revenue than the standard, if it applies standard policies (including efficiencies) to the provision of a service or the collection of a revenue" (Commonwealth Grants Commission 2002, pp. 27–28). Disabilities are exogenous factors that influence the costs of providing services. The difficulty comes in separating exogenous factors from factors that are within the control of the states. The commission has developed its own technique for this purpose, which it calls the factor assessment method.

The first step in the commission's assessment of expenditure need is to determine which categories of spending should be included in calculating relativities. The second step is determining which disabilities are relevant to each expenditure category. One type of disability is related to demand. Most demand influences stem from differences in the sociodemographic composition of states' populations. Examples include age, sex, income levels, and the percentage of the population that is aboriginal. The second type of disability consists of factors that influence per unit costs, such as the dispersion of the population, economies of scale, and differences in input prices.

The commission has created a set of guidelines to use in determining whether a disability should be applied to any given category of spending (although it admits that selecting the correct disabilities for an expenditure category is often more an art than a science). First, there must be a conceptual basis for the application. If a disability seems counterintuitive, it faces a higher burden of proof before being included in the final calculations. Second, there must be strong empirical evidence that the disability affects the cost of service provision, incomplete evidence backed by strong logic, or a judgment by the commission that the evidence is sufficient.

State disability levels are compared with the national population-weighted average for each expenditure category. The result represents the additional per capita cost each state bears relative to the standard level. These figures are summed across all expenditure categories, and the result is divided by total average per capita spending to yield a measure of each state's relative expenditure needs.

Despite the comprehensiveness and complexity of this methodology, some observers are quite critical of it. Shah (1996) suggests that the Australian approach is

> somewhat crude, imprecise, and subjective. . . . Determinants of expenditure needs are sometimes arrived at using broad judgment rather than any hard quantitative analysis. The procedure involves a detailed analysis of budgetary data and then subjective assessment of relative need, followed by written and oral arguments about principles and methods in adversary proceedings. The process adopted is unnecessarily cumbersome, unduly time-consuming and places too much reliance on broad judgment (p. 103).

Whether Shah's assessment is too harsh is an open question. But the complexity of the Australian system suggests that it would be hard to replicate in other countries, especially developing countries, where local data are often limited.

United Kingdom

Local governments in the United Kingdom receive an annual general-purpose transfer from the central government, known as revenue support grants. These grants are allocated to local authorities on the basis of an estimate of each authority's need-capacity gap. The expenditure need of each local government, known as its standard spending assessment, is calculated each year by the national government's Department of the Environment, Transport and the Regions.

As in Australia, the methodology used to determine standard spending assessments is highly complex. The general approach is to determine spending assessments for seven local government functional spending categories: education, personal social services, police, fire protection, highway maintenance, "all other services," and capital financing. For each category, the spending assessments are determined by using a combination of statistical analysis and professional judgment to determine the magnitude of the "work load" (or alternatively the size of the "client group") receiving services and the effect of underlying characteristics of each local community on the costs of delivering public services.

The approach to measuring the costs of municipal services in the United Kingdom can be illustrated by looking at the standard spending assessment for police. Local government police expenditures are divided into 10 components, and a standard spending assessment is conducted separately for each. For each component, a set of indicators, or characteristics of the local area being served, is identified, using statistical analysis and the judgment of experts on law enforcement. One component of police activities is crime management. Crimes are divided into four categories and a regression model estimated to determine the standard spending assessment for each type of crime. The dependent variable for the "personal crime" regression equation is the average number of personal crime incidents recorded in each jurisdiction in 1990, 1991, and 1992 divided by the "daytime" population in 1991. The independent variables included in the personal crime regression equation are population density, the proportion of households living in rented housing units, and the proportion of the population living in overcrowded conditions.

The next step is to adjust the calculations to reflect an "area cost" factor. The area cost factor is intended to reflect differences in the cost of inputs needed by local governments to provide services. The adjustment primarily reflects differences in labor costs. As local governments must compete in the labor market to hire municipal government employees, the purpose of the labor cost adjustment is to reflect regional wage rates in various professions for employees in both the public and private sectors.[12]

The results of the calculations provide an estimate of the "workload" of each local government, adjusted for input cost differences. As the standard spending assessment measures are based primarily on the characteristics of each community that local government officials are unable to manipulate, in principle these measures provide an appropriate indicator of the needs of each local government. To go from workload to expenditure needs, the regression-determined workloads are multiplied by "control totals," which reflect decisions by the national government on an appropriate level of aggregate local government spending on each function.[13]

Sweden

Fiscal equalization is an important part of Sweden's intergovernmental fiscal system. A basic principle of the Swedish system of local public finance is that all local governments should be able to operate on equivalent economic terms.[14] To implement this principle, the intergovernmental grant system includes both a fiscal capacity and a cost-equalizing component. The system is not structured as a vertical equalization scheme, with a set of grants from the national government. Rather, municipal governments in favorable fiscal conditions send funds to municipalities in weaker fiscal positions.

A system of cost-equalizing aid is generally designed to compensate local governments that face higher costs of providing services for reasons over which they have no control. In such a system, higher spending attributable to preferences for better services or to inefficiencies in service delivery would not be reflected in more aid. This type of system is not used in Sweden, where, as in most other European countries, the distinction between spending and costs is deemed to be of limited importance. Implicitly, actual expenditures are assumed to reflect the true costs of providing a national standard of service.

In Sweden the cost equalization grant going to local government i is defined as the difference between the "standardized cost" in i and the national average cost. Costs are equalized for childcare, individual and family care, care of the elderly, primary and secondary education, streets and roads, water supply, and sanitation.

For each of these public services, standardized costs in each local government are determined by multiplying "demographic costs" by a "volume index" (Chernick 2004). Demographic costs are calculated by taking a weighted average of the number of recipients of each service, where the weights applied to each demographic group reflect actual spending on that service for that demographic group.

The volume index is designed to account for differences in expenditures due to factors other than demographic costs. It is based on an expenditure regression that includes factors reflecting "needs" and factors that reflect difference in preferences. Using childcare as an example, need is measured by the number of full- and part-time working mothers and by a measure of density. Preferences for childcare spending are measured by the income of the jurisdiction (this reflects the fact that in Sweden, high-income families tend to use childcare services more intensively than lower-income families). In the United States regression-based cost indices reflect variations in cost factors while holding preference or demand factors constant. In contrast, in Sweden the volume index reflects variations in both costs and preferences. The difference in approach appears to reflect the fact that in Sweden spending is considered an appropriate measure of the need for the public service.

Japan

Municipal governments and prefectures in Japan receive transfer payments (officially called the local allocation tax) from the national government if their "basic fiscal needs" are larger than their "basic fiscal revenues."[15]

Basic fiscal revenues are a standard measure of local government revenue-raising capacity, calculated by summing the products of local tax bases and a set of standard tax rates set by the national government. Basic fiscal needs are defined as the amount of money needed to provide a standard set of public services at levels prescribed by the central government.

The methodology used to measure basic fiscal needs is similar to that used in Sweden. The central government has defined basic local government services as police, fire, compulsory education (primary and middle school), and the construction and maintenance of parks, local roads, and bridges. The starting point for measuring basic fiscal needs is to measure expenditure needs in a "model local government." In 1989 the model municipal government was assumed to have a population of 100,000 and an area of 160 square kilometers. The next step is to calculate basic fiscal needs for each category of spending in the model community. The calculation involves multiplying a "unit of measurement," such as the population, the number of public school children, or the kilometers of roads, by an appropriate unit cost. As in Sweden, unit costs are based on average levels of spending.

To calculate basic fiscal needs for individual municipalities, the unit cost for each spending category is multiplied by the appropriate unit of measurement and the product is multiplied by a set of "modification coefficients" that allow the basic fiscal needs in the model municipality to be adjusted for institutional, physical, social, and economic characteristics of each municipality. According to Ma (1977), modification coefficients are used to adjust for the impact of economies of scale, population density, cost of living differences, extra costs associated with a particularly cold climate, rapid increases or decreases in population, relatively high debt service ratios, and differences in the composition of the student bodies in each municipality (for example, the proportion of students in high school or in vocational programs).

Decisions about changes in the modification coefficients are made by the staff of the Ministry of Home Affairs, following consultation with local government officials. Local governments reportedly lobby the ministry to include new variables, such as variations in annual snowfall, in the list of modification coefficients (DeWit 2002). To be successful, they need to convince the ministry that adding or changing coefficients would improve the estimate of the basic fiscal needs of local governments.

Little is known about the decision-making process within the ministry, although it does not appear that formal statistical modeling is used to determine the expenditure needs of local governments. Over time, with the addition of new modification coefficients, the formula for allocating municipal grants has become more and more complex. DeWit (2002) suggests that the complexity isolates the process of revising the allocation formula from interference from politicians and other ministries.

Republic of Korea

The Republic of Korea provides its local governments with unconditional revenue through a program known as "ordinary local shared taxes." The basis for the allocation is the difference between each local government's "standardized fiscal needs" and "standardized fiscal revenue."

The purpose of the transfer system is to enable all local governments to supply minimum public services regardless of their fiscal capacity. The government calculates standardized fiscal needs, using a methodology that is similar to that used in Japan to measure "basic fiscal needs." A much more disaggregated system is used to calculate fiscal needs, however. In Korea fiscal needs are calculated separately for 48 functional expenditure categories. The results are then summed to arrive at the total standardized expenditure needs for each local government.[16] Like the Japanese methodology, the Korean methodology adjusts average expenditure needs using a set of adjustment coefficients based on local government characteristics.

France

The central government plays an important role in financing France's 36,500 municipal governments, providing nearly half of total local government revenues. Fiscal transfers from the central government are allocated through a set of independent grant programs, each operating with a different distribution formula.

A central goal of the French system of local government grants is fiscal equalization. The allocation formulas include measures of tax capacity and a few "cost" factors. The choice of these cost factors—population size, number of students, number of public housing units, road mileage, and number of vacation homes—appears to have been quite ad hoc.

In a comprehensive analysis of the French system of local government grants, Gilbert and Guengant (2003) show that both the choice and the weighting of the cost factors in the grant formulas bears little relationship to the factors and weights revealed by an econometric analysis of local government costs. France thus appears to provide a good example of a country in which distributional politics are the major determinant of the measurement of local government "costs."

Hungary

The largest single source of revenue for local governments in Hungary is unconditional normative grants. The formula used to allocate these grants among local governments consists of a large number of elements, most of which reflect a particular function of local government. The actual amounts allocated by each formula element are the product of the target population and a normative per capita spending amount. In 1993, for example, the formula allocated 186,400 forints ($1,958) to each resident of a home for the elderly and 30,850 forints ($324) for each person participating in a daycare program for the elderly or disabled.[17] The formula allocated 27,500 forints ($289) for each kindergarten student, 41,000 forints ($431) for each primary school student, and 62,500 forints ($657) for each secondary school student. Each mentally handicapped primary school student was allocated an additional 70,700 forints ($743). These amounts do not appear to be based on a statistical analysis of costs or spending. Presumably, they reflect judgments by the national government about the relative costs of providing different services to different groups. The relationship between the formula parameters and the actual per person costs of service delivery is not known.

Switzerland

Switzerland is in the process of a major reform of its intergovernmental fiscal system, in particular the fiscal relationships between the national government and the 26 Swiss cantons. The reform proposals, collectively called the "new fiscal equalization," include new fiscal capacity-equalizing grants. It also includes two new grant funds, designed to compensate some cantons for above-average costs over which they have no control. The first of these funds would compensate for geographic factors and low population density; the second would compensate for "sociodemographic burden." The formulas are designed so that spending or taxing behavior of cantonal governments does not affect the distribution of the funds.

Under the reform, the first fund would be allocated to eight cantons that purportedly have exceptionally high costs because of their geographical and topographical characteristics. These characteristics are measured using a "structural index" based on (the inverse of) density, the length of roads per capita, forested area per capita, and the length of rivers and streams per capita. These four factors are combined in an index, with the following weights: 0.5, 0.25, 0.2, and 0.05.

The socioeconomic fund would be distributed to seven cantons with particularly high concentrations of people 65 and older, the poor (those eligible for Swiss social assistance), foreigners, and the unemployed. These groups are combined to make a single index, using weights of 1.5, 2.0, 0.5, and 2.0.

The funds are designed to aid cantons that, because of factors over which they have no control, face higher-than-average costs in delivering the public services for which they are responsible. If the grant formulas are designed correctly, the indices used to allocate the two funds among the cantons should be based on research that demonstrates the relationship between the factors in the index ("cost factors") and the additional costs of providing public services. Thus, for example, given the weight used to construct the sociodemographic index, one would assume that a given percentage of poor people results in four-times-higher costs than the same percentage of foreigners.

The final government report on the new fiscal equalization provides no information on how the indices were constructed or whether their construction was based on empirical studies of the costs of providing public services.[18] One is left with the suspicion that the weights in the indices used in both formulas may have resulted from political compromise over how to distribute grants rather than any research on the relative costs of delivering public services in the cantons.

A simulation of the distribution of money from the socioeconomic fund indicates that the canton of Zurich would be eligible for a grant, while the canton of Bern would not, despite the higher percentage of elderly and poor people in Bern. Bern would not be eligible for a grant primarily because its population includes a lower percentage of foreigners than Zurich.

These results suggest that the weights in the formula are not closely related to cost differences and may well have been determined in an ad hoc manner. Although the overall costs of delivering services are probably lower in Bern than in Zurich, the grant system treats Bern as if its service delivery costs equal the average national costs. Given its high concentrations of elderly people and the poor, this appears unlikely. The formula also treats all foreigners as contributing equally to the extra costs of delivering services. This implies that the move of a middle-class businessman and his family from Germany to Zurich would have the same impact on the costs of delivering public services as the in-migration of a low-income, non-German-speaking family from the former Yugoslavia. This seems highly unlikely.[19]

The Swiss example may parallel the experience in a number of countries that use grant formulas that purport to reflect difference in the costs of service delivery. In many cases, while the cost factors may be appropriate, the weights attached to them appear to have little relationship to actual costs. Reschovsky and Imazeki (2003) show that the weight assigned to poor children in the education grant formula used in Texas is substantially lower than that implied by an educational cost function. They report that state officials indicated that the weights were the result of the political process rather than an analysis of the factors that have an impact on the cost of education.

Lessons for Developing Countries

Horizontal fiscal equalization is pursued in one way or another by many developed and developing nations. Argentina, China, India, and South Africa are among a number of developing countries that have implemented grant programs designed, at least in part, to achieve horizontal fiscal equalization.[20] As discussed earlier in this chapter, the term *horizontal fiscal equalization* encompasses several distinct equalizing goals. These include the guarantee of minimum public service levels to the residents of each province or local jurisdiction, the achievement of horizontal equity by ensuring that residents of different jurisdictions that tax themselves at the same rate will receive equal levels of public service, and the reduction or elimination of fiscal disparities across provinces or local governments. Economists are in general agreement that on theoretical grounds, intergovernmental transfers designed to meet the goals of horizontal equalization should account for both the expenditure needs and the revenue-raising capacity of recipient governments (Vaillancourt and Bird 2004).

Considerably more controversy arises over whether it is feasible to implement formulas that require the measurement of expenditure needs, especially in developing countries, where the required data are generally limited or unavailable. There is no question that the data and resource requirements needed to measure expenditure needs following the Australian model exceed the capacity of any developing country. The question is whether developing countries could use other methodologies for determining expenditure needs, methodologies that are less conceptually pure but also less data intensive.

In a memorandum to the chairman of the South African Financial and Fiscal Commission, Inman argues that because the data needed to construct a conceptually and technically grounded index of provincial government costs were not available, no measure of expenditure needs should be included in any proposed grant formula. Inman fears that unless all the required data are available, any attempt to measure costs will "become an open door to include everyone's favorite measure of provincial 'costliness': urbanization for the urban provinces, ruralness for the rural provinces, percent elderly for the older provinces, percent children for the growing provinces" (1997, p. 3).

Inman raises a legitimate issue; certainly looking around the world one can find examples of politically determined formulas of the kind he describes. At the same time, a number of countries have implemented equalization formulas that include estimates that appear to have been largely immune from political manipulation. In developing countries, where fiscal disparities are attributable primarily to spatial differences in revenue-raising capacities, ignoring differences in costs or expenditure needs makes sense. In countries in which fiscal disparities are due in large part to spatial differences in needs and costs, however, ignoring expenditure needs in grant allocation formulas will substantially reduce the potential effectiveness of policies attempting to achieve horizontal fiscal equalization.

A key principle in developing any measure of expenditure needs to be used in an equalization grant program is that recipient governments must not be able to influence the magnitude of their expenditure needs. If this principle is not respected, recipient governments will have a strong incentive to change their fiscal behavior in ways that will increase their grant allocations.

The review of international experience presented in this chapter clearly indicates that there is no single best methodology for estimating expenditure needs. Many developed countries try to measure the needs and costs of delivering public services by their subnational governments, with varying degrees of success. The methodology chosen in a particular country is influenced in part by the availability of data. Some countries, in particular Australia, measure expenditure needs using a highly data- and resource-intensive methodology. Other countries have developed methodologies with much more limited data requirements. In general, developing countries will need to employ methodologies that are relatively parsimonious in their use of data.

Many countries that have implemented grant schemes that include a measure of expenditure needs have used a methodology that combines limited statistical analysis with the judgments of experts on government finance and public service delivery. A strategy that combines statistical analysis of data with expert opinion may be a realistic approach for many developing countries.

The political acceptance of any allocation mechanism will be enhanced if the methodology used to develop the allocation formula is as straightforward and transparent as possible. In their efforts to achieve as accurate as possible a measure of local government expenditure needs, some developed countries have used methodologies that are highly complex and difficult to understand. In developing countries, both limited data and the absence of institutional capacity place a premium on the use of relatively simple approaches. In fact, there is much to say in favor of the use of simple proxies for expenditure needs or, as Vaillancourt and Bird (2004) suggest, "asymmetric" approaches that provide additional aid to provinces or local governments that are widely recognized as having special needs.

Notes

1. Several state governments in the United States use this type of equalizing formula to fund primary and secondary education. When used to finance education, it is generally referred to as a foundation formula.
2. For a discussion of the equity case for equalization grants, see Yinger (1986).
3. For a discussion of the role of grants in an intergovernmental system, see Boadway and Flatters (1982), Bird and Smart (2002), Bird and Tarasov (2004), and Shah (1996).
4. Sixteen U.S. states provided their municipal governments with unconditional grants for local public services in 2005 (Reschovsky 2004).
5. Most attempts to disentangle public service costs from preferences have occurred in the United States and in Australia, where this conceptual difference is seen as important. In Europe there is less acceptance of the distinction between costs and preferences. Actual spending by municipal governments on public services is more likely to be viewed as a reflection of differences in need. In Sweden, for example, intergovernmental aid formulas designed to allocate funds from the national government on the basis of municipal needs use municipal spending as a measure of municipal needs (Chernick 2004).
6. In nearly all cases, the donor government sets the standard.
7. For a discussion of the application of different definitions of "basic" municipal services in South Africa, see Reschovsky (2003).
8. For a review of the literature on economies of scale, see Duncombe and Yinger (1993).
9. For a recent discussion of the determination of weights related to poverty for use in education grant formulas, see Duncombe and Yinger (2005).
10. For examples of the use of these techniques in measuring the efficiency of U.S. school districts in providing public education, see Deller and Rudnicki (1993); Duncombe, Ruggiero, and Yinger (1996); Gronberg and others (2004); and McCarty and Yaisawarng (1993).
11. A similar approach was used to estimate local government expenditure needs in two U.S. states. See Ladd, Reschovsky, and Yinger (1992) and Green and Reschovsky (1994).
12. For a detailed description of the methodology used to calculate area cost adjustments, see United Kingdom, Department of the Environment, Transport and the Regions (2000).
13. By increasing the control total for one function (for example, police) and decreasing it for another (for example, road maintenance), the government can in effect reallocate

the revenue support grant in favor of local governments with relatively high needs for police and low needs for road maintenance.

14. For a detailed description of the Swedish system of intergovernmental grants, see Chernick (2004).

15. The description of the Japanese transfer system is based in part on Ma (1977).

16. For a detailed description of the Korean intergovernmental fiscal system, see Kim (1997).

17. The description of the Hungarian normative grant program comes from Bird, Wallach, and Pétri (2005).

18. For the final report, see Confederation of Switzerland, Federal Department of Finances (1999).

19. For an assessment of the new fiscal equalization, see Blöchliger and Reschovsky (2003).

20. In many countries, transfer programs that are labeled "equalization programs" are actually intended to achieve goals other than equalization (Vaillancourt and Bird 2004).

References

Bird, Richard M., and Michael Smart. 2002. "Intergovernmental Fiscal Transfers: International Lessons for Developing Countries." *World Development* 30 (6): 899–912.

Bird, Richard M., and Audrey V. Tarasov. 2004. "Closing the Gap: Fiscal Imbalances and Intergovernmental Transfers in Developed Federations." *Environment and Planning C: Government and Policy* 22 (1): 77–102.

Bird, Richard M., Christine I. Wallach, and Gábor Pétri. 2005. "Financing Local Government in Hungary." In *Decentralization of the Socialist State: Intergovernmental Finance in Transition Economies*, ed. Richard M. Bird, Robert D. Ebel, and Christine Wallach, 69–118. Washington, DC: World Bank.

Blöchliger, Hansjörg, and Andrew Reschovsky. 2003. "Reinventing Fiscal Federalism: The Swiss Reforms." *Proceedings of the 95th Annual Conference*, 176–84. Washington, DC: National Tax Association.

Boadway, Robin. 2004. "The Theory and Practice of Equalization." *CESifo Economic Studies* 50 (1): 211–54.

Boadway, Robin, and Frank Flatters. 1982. "Efficiency and Equalization Payments in a Federal System of Government: A Synthesis and Extension of Recent Results." *Canadian Journal of Economics* 15 (4): 613–33.

Bradbury, Katharine L., Helen F. Ladd, Mark Perrault, Andrew Reschovsky, and John Yinger. 1984. "State Aid to Offset Fiscal Disparities Across Communities." *National Tax Journal* 37 (2): 151–70.

Buchanan, James M. 1950. "Federalism and Fiscal Equity." *American Economic Review* 40 (4): 583–99.

———. 1952. "Central Grants and Resource Allocation." *Journal of Political Economy* 60 (3): 208–17.

Buchanan, James M., and Charles J. Goetz. 1972. "Efficiency Limits of Fiscal Mobility: An Assessment of the Tiebout Model." *Journal of Public Economics* 1 (1): 25–43.

Chernick, Howard. 2004. "Fiscal Equalisation between Swedish Municipalities." In *Fiscal Federalism in Unitary States*, ed. Per Molander, 77–100. ZEI Studies in European Economics and Law. Dordrecht, the Netherlands: Kluwer Academic Publishers.

Commonwealth Grants Commission, Government of Australia. 2002. *Information Paper CGC 2002/1: Guidelines for Implementing Horizontal Fiscal Equalization*. September. Canberra: Commonwealth Grants Commission.

Confederation of Switzerland, Federal Department of Finances. 1999. "La nouvelle péréquation financiére entre la confédération et les cantons." Rapport final de l'organisation de projet au Conseil fédéral. Bern.

Deller, Steven C., and Edward Rudnicki. 1993. "Production Efficiency in Elementary Education: The Case of Maine Public Schools." *Economics of Education Review* 12 (1): 45–57.

DeWit, Andrew. 2002. "Dry Rot: The Corruption of General Subsidies in Japan." *Journal of the Asia Pacific Economy* 7 (3): 355–78.

Duncombe, William, and John Yinger. 1993. "An Analysis of Returns to Scale in Public Production, with an Application to Fire Protection." *Journal of Public Economics* 52 (1): 49–72.

———. 2000. "Financing Higher Student Performance Standards: The Case of New York State." *Economics of Education Review* 19 (4): 363–86.

———. 2005. "How Much More Does a Disadvantaged Student Cost?" *Economics of Education Review* 24 (5): 513–32.

Duncombe, William, John Ruggiero, and John Yinger. 1996. "Alternative Approaches to Measuring the Cost of Education." In *Holding School Accountable; Performance-Based Reform in Education*, ed. Helen F. Ladd, 327–56. Washington, DC: Brookings Institution.

Flatters, Frank, Vernon Henderson, and Peter Mieszkowski. 1974. "Public Goods, Efficiency, and Regional Fiscal Equalization." *Journal of Public Economics* 3 (2): 99–112.

Gilbert, Guy, and Alain Guengant. 2003. "The Equalizing Performance of Central Government Grants to Local Government Authorities: The Case of France." *Proceedings of the 95th Annual Conference on Taxation*, 192–202. Washington, DC: National Tax Association.

Green, Richard K., and Andrew Reschovsky. 1994. "Fiscal Assistance to Local Governments." In *Dollars & Sense: Policy Choice and the Wisconsin Budget*, vol. III, ed. Donald Nichols, 91–117. Madison, WI: Robert M. La Follette Institute of Public Affairs, University of Wisconsin-Madison.

Gronberg, Timothy J., Dennis W. Jansen, Lori L. Taylor, and Kevin Booker. 2004. "School Outcomes and School Costs: The Cost Function Approach." Report prepared for the Texas Legislature Joint Committee on Public School Finance, Texas School Finance Project, Austin.

Gutherie, James W., and Richard Rothstein. 1999. "Enabling 'Adequacy' to Achieve Reality: Translating Adequacy into State School Finance Distribution Arrangements." In *Equity and Adequacy in Education Finance: Issues and Perspectives*, ed. Helen F. Ladd, Rosemary Chalk, and Janet S. Hansen, 209–59. Washington, DC: National Academy Press.

Imazeki, Jennifer, and Andrew Reschovsky. 2005. "Assessing the Use of Econometric Analysis in Estimating the Costs of Meeting State Education Accountability Standards: Lessons from Texas." *Peabody Journal of Education* 80 (3): 96–125.

Inman, Robert P. 1997. "Central to Provincial Grants: Formula Design." Memorandum to the Chair of the Financial and Fiscal Commission, Midrand, South Africa.

Jourmard, Isabelle, and Per Marthis Kongsrud. 2003. "Fiscal Relationships across Government Levels." Economics Department Working Paper 375, Organisation for Economic Co-operation and Development, Paris. http://www.olis.oecd.org/olis/2003doc.nsf/linkto/eco-wkp(2003)29.

Kim, Soo Keun. 1997. "Local Autonomy and Fiscal Resources in Korea." In *Financing Decentralized Expenditures: An International Comparison of Grants*, ed. Ehtisham Ahmad, 267–91. Cheltenham, United Kingdom: Edward Elgar.

Ladd, Helen F., Andrew Reschovsky, and John Yinger. 1992. "City Fiscal Condition and State Equalizing Aid: The Case of Minnesota." *Proceedings of the 84th Conference on Taxation of the National Tax Association 1991*, 42–49. Williamsburg, VA: National Tax Association.

Ma, Jun. 1997. "Intergovernmental Fiscal Transfers in Nine Countries: Lesson for Developing Countries." Policy Research Working Paper 1822, World Bank, Washington, DC.

McCarty, Therese A., and Suthathip Yaisawarng. 1993. "Technical Efficiency in New Jersey School Districts." In *The Measurement of Productive Efficiency: Techniques and Applications*, ed. Harold O. Fried, C.A. Knox Lovell, and Shelton S. Schmidt, 271–87. New York: Oxford University Press.

Reschovsky, Andrew. 1994. "Fiscal Equalization and School Finance." *National Tax Journal* 47 (1): 185–98.

———. 2003. "Intergovernmental Transfers: The Equitable Share." In *Restructuring Local Government Finance in Developing Countries: Lessons from South Africa*, ed. Roy Bahl and Paul Smoke, 173–235. Cheltenham, United Kingdom: Edward Elgar.

———. 2004. "The Impact of State Government Fiscal Crises on Local Governments and Schools." *State and Local Government Review* 36 (2): 86–102.

Reschovsky, Andrew, and Jennifer Imazeki. 2003. "Let No Child Be Left Behind: Determining the Cost of Improved Student Performance." *Public Finance Review* 31 (3): 263–90.

Rye, C.R., and B. Searle. 1997. "The Fiscal Transfer System in Australia." In *Financing Decentralized Expenditures: An International Comparison of Grants*, ed. Ehtisham Ahmad, 173–83. Cheltenham, United Kingdom: Edward Elgar.

Shah, Anwar. 1996. "A Fiscal Need Approach to Equalization." *Canadian Public Policy* 22 (2): 99–115.

Street, Andrew. 2003. "How Much Confidence Should We Place in Efficiency Estimates?" *Health Economics* 12 (11): 895–907.

United Kingdom, Department of the Environment, Transport and the Regions. 2000. *Standard Spending Assessments (SSA) Guide to Methodology* 1999–2000. London.

Vaillancourt, François, and Richard M. Bird. 2004. "Expenditure-Based Equalization Transfers." Working Paper 04-10, Georgia State University, Andrew Young School of Policy Studies, International Studies Program, Atlanta.

Yinger, John. 1986. "On Fiscal Disparities across Cities." *Journal of Urban Economics* 19 (3): 316–37.

15

Financing Capital Expenditures through Grants

JEFFREY PETCHEY AND
GARRY MACDONALD

In federal economies and decentralized unitary systems, national governments make grants to subnational governments, such as states or provinces, as well as to local governments, either directly or through the states or provinces; states and provinces, in turn, make grants to local governments. These grants take various forms. They can be unconditional (the recipient government has complete discretion over how the funds are used), conditional (they can be spent only on certain services or only on infrastructure), or matching (requiring a matching contribution from the recipient government). National governments also often implement fiscal equalization schemes between state or provincial regions.

The fiscal federalism literature has much to say about the economic rationale for intergovernmental grants and fiscal equalization schemes. These arguments, summarized in the annex, relate to externalities, optimal fiscal gaps, minimum standards for public services, the efficiency and equity of common internal markets for mobile factors of production, the stability of federal unions, and fiscally induced migration.

The literature makes little reference to capital grants, which can be thought of as a particular type of conditional grant in which the condition is that the grant money be spent on infrastructure rather than recurrent inputs, such as labor or materials. Additional conditions may prescribe that the funds be spent on infrastructure in a particular functional area, such as road, transportation, or health infrastructure. Matching requirements, under which the subnational government must match, at some predetermined rate, the funds received from the center, may also be attached to capital grants.

This chapter begins by providing a rationale for capital grants based on the general arguments for grants. It argues that a case for capital grants can be found in the desire to establish minimum and uniform national standards of service provision, externalities, and fiscally induced internal migration. After setting out these arguments, the chapter discusses the design of capital grant schemes. It stresses the need to ensure that capital grant programs do not establish the potential for strategic behavior by recipient governments, that they take account of the expenditure and tax responses of recipients, and that they make allowance for recurrent expenditures. The third section provides an overview of current practice with regard to capital grants. It shows that capital grants can be formula based or project specific and that they are used mostly in developing countries, in capital-intensive areas such as housing and transport infrastructure. The fourth section presents a formula-based capital grant model developed by the authors for use (principally) in developing countries. The results of simulations are presented based on data for South Africa. The model is a useful instrument that policy makers could use to allocate capital grants to subnational regions to allow the stock of public infrastructure to increase to some uniform minimum standard over some given period of time.

Rationale for Capital Grants

Why do central governments make capital grants to subnational governments to fund capital expenditures? The main reason is their desire to maintain minimum standards. Efficiency arguments can be made for ensuring that services such as education, health, and transportation networks are provided to minimum, and uniform, standards across regions (to ensure efficiency of common internal product and factor markets, for example). Public infrastructure is the major input into the production of these capital-intensive services. Education requires costly buildings, technology, and transportation networks; health care requires hospitals, local medical centers, and high-tech medical equipment. Transportation networks are highly capital intensive, as are public housing programs.

Using capital grants to raise the service-specific per capita capital stock in each region to some nationally agreed upon standard is a de facto way of establishing uniform national standards for the services produced by capital. Ideally, of course, one would like service provision to be uniform and of a minimum standard, but output for most public services cannot be easily measured. In contrast, capital is measurable. If, taking account of interregional differences in capital utilization rates and cost disabilities, capital expenditures can be made uniform across regions and the subnational service-specific per capita capital stock brought up to the national standard (whatever that is), it is likely that service provision will also be uniform and meet some minimum standard (even if that standard is difficult to measure in terms of service output per capita). Ensuring minimum and uniform national standards of capital is thus a proxy for achieving minimum and uniform standards in service provision. This may explain why many capital grants are in highly capital-intensive areas, such as roads, housing, and schools.

A second reason why national governments provide capital grants has to do with the interregional externalities generated by regional infrastructure, which subnational governments may not take into account (see the annex for a discussion of the general externality argument for grants). This is particularly so for highly capital-intensive transportation infrastructure, such as shipping ports, major road networks, airports, and cross-border rail networks. It may also be the case for the less capital-intensive infrastructure used to produce education and health services. Since the output of such services may not be measurable, the center can try to ensure that externalities are taken into account by ensuring that the major input, capital, is provided to the required standards.

A third reason to provide capital grants is that the presence of region-specific fiscal externalities and location-specific economic rents may create differential net fiscal benefits across regions that may cause labor and capital to migrate. As a result, the spatial allocation of mobile factors of production may be inefficient. This leads to an efficiency case for equalization transfers (see Boadway 2004, Petchey and Walsh 1993, and the annex). Differential net fiscal benefits may be reflected in different levels of (per capita) public infrastructure across regions. For example, a natural resource-rich region may provide more funds to public hospitals and schools than a resource-poor region. To the extent that there is some public good component attached to such services, the higher level of provision in the resource-rich region may attract mobile residents from other jurisdictions, driven partly by a wish to benefit from the higher standard of public infrastructure and the services that flow from it. Such migration is inefficient in the sense that it is motivated by a desire to capture the fiscal externalities flowing from public infrastructure in the richer region rather than by economic fundamentals, such as differences in marginal products (wages) across regions. If a national government can use intergovernmental capital grants to establish uniform minimum standards of public infrastructure across regions, it may also reduce inefficient fiscally induced migration.

In developing countries fiscally induced migration can also generate congestion costs in urban areas or regions with larger capital stocks. In South Africa many rural regions have little or no housing, education, and health infrastructure; larger urban areas, such as Cape Town and Johannesburg, have much better infrastructure. There is also evidence of substantial interprovincial labor migration, much of it from poor rural provinces to richer, more urban ones. At least some of this migration is likely to be a response to the presence of better-quality public infrastructure in cities (that is, it is fiscally induced). But migration is also creating externality-type costs at the urban fringes, as shack settlements expand, generating environmental degradation, crime, congestion, and demands on infrastructure. In view of this, one might argue that there is excessive rural-urban migration from a location efficiency point of view and that more public infrastructure should be provided in rural areas in order to slow the rate of migration to more-optimal levels. The goal is not to eliminate mobility but to ensure that the migration that takes place is not fiscally induced.

Various rationales for capital grants can be derived from general theoretical arguments about the need for grants from central to subnational governments. The strongest seems to be the minimum (uniform) standard argument in cases in which the center cannot readily measure or observe outputs but can ensure that inputs, specifically, capital, are provided to a uniform standard across regions. If this is the aim of a capital grants program, it will also reduce any inefficient fiscally induced migration in response to high regional disparities in infrastructure, a potential issue in developing countries. Capital grants motivated by minimum uniform standards will also achieve the equity goal of ensuring that citizens of a federation or decentralized economy have equal access to services regardless of where they live. This may be important for social and political stability in some developing countries and is an important equity goal in its own right.

Are grants the best policy instruments to achieve these goals? Policy instruments other than grants could be used to establish minimum uniform standards in infrastructure and correct for infrastructure-related externalities. For example, minimum national standards could be mandated by central government policy or implemented through cooperative agreements between regions, monitored and enforced by the center.[1] In education, for example, the national government could mandate that class sizes for primary education should be no more than 30 students per classroom. In health it could mandate the number of hospital beds that must be provided per thousand people.

If these mandates are unfunded by the center, financing would be left up to the regions themselves, to be undertaken from their own tax bases, borrowings, or unconditional revenue-sharing grants. The advantage of this approach is that the people who benefit from the expenditure also bear the full burden of the cost. However, this also creates the problem of unfunded mandates, whereby the center sets standards that cannot be funded from local resources. Externalities might be internalized through cooperative arrangements among regions, perhaps monitored and enforced by the center, to ensure nationally efficient levels of investment in national infrastructure.

These options may work best in high-income countries, such as Australia, Canada, and the United States, where subnational governments have full access to capital markets for borrowing, substantial tax bases, and the associated institutional structures and institutional capacity. Even in these countries, however, experience shows that national governments still provide capital grants to regional governments.

Empirical studies document the provision of capital grants by national governments in Australia, Canada, Denmark, Finland, France, Japan, Sweden, the United Kingdom, and the United States. Two types of grant methodologies are used in these countries, project-specific grants and formula-based grants. For project-specific grants, regions submit cost-benefit proposals to the central government, which ranks them in terms of net benefits and allocates funds from a grant pool accordingly. A potential advantage of this approach is that it may enhance efficiency, in the sense that the projects with the highest welfare gains are financed.

In developing countries the approach may be problematic, because lack of institutional capacity at the subnational level may mean that richer regions attract a larger share of the pool of funds available because they have more capacity to submit well-argued proposals.[2] Formulaic approaches allow policy makers to track the impact of grant schemes on subnational capital stocks. Moreover, as noted below, they may be more useful if the aim of the grants is to establish minimum and uniform standards.

Instruments such as mandates and cooperative agreements are much less applicable in developing countries or transition economies, for a number of reasons. First, states or provinces within such economies may have limited tax bases, because of the high degree of centralization of tax powers (due to constitutional or politically imposed constraints). This limits the resources available to subnational governments to meet central mandates or take part in cooperative agreements over standards that are not funded by the center through transfers. Second, subnational governments in such countries often have limited or no access to efficient capital markets. Provincial governments in South Africa, for example, are barred from borrowing and have virtually no tax base, but they are responsible for providing all education and health services.

The case for capital transfers based on minimum national standards thus seems strongest in highly centralized developing countries or transition economies in which subnational governments provide key public services but have limited or no access to capital markets. Even in such cases, capital grants should represent a short-term option, however; in the longer term, such economies should develop more independent subnational governments with full access to capital markets for borrowing. Capital grants should not, therefore, be a long-term substitute for subnational access to efficient capital markets. In the short term, however, this may not be possible or desirable in some countries, and capital grants may be the best feasible option while longer-term reforms are pursued. Once the transition phase is over, general capital grants to subnational governments should not continue to be made, except perhaps if the center wants to provide on-going grants related to infrastructure externalities (for national road and rail networks, for example) or specific services that are important for welfare policy (such as housing support for the very needy), perhaps on a project basis. Interestingly, this is the most important type of capital grant program in developed countries.

Following the transition phase, there may be a case for including the differential regional costs (cost disabilities) of constructing public capital in any equalization program that takes account of expenditure needs. This is currently done to an extent in the Australian equalization model, which estimates expenditure needs based on cost disabilities faced by the states. These cost disabilities are applied to recurrent and capital expenditures undertaken by the states. The recurrent and capital cost disabilities are estimated using an accounting approach rather than an economic methodology. They have been much criticized by economists.

As an alternative, Petchey and others (2000) develop an econometric approach (using state-specific cost functions) to estimate regional capital cost disabilities. Petchey and Levtchenkova (2001) show how the Australian equalization model might be adapted to use capital cost disabilities estimated in this way. They also develop a methodology that equalizes the marginal cost of public capital across states so that when states make capital expenditure decisions, they all face the same opportunity costs at the margin. They also show how such a methodology, which one can think of as a "capital flow" equalization approach (as opposed to approaches that seek to equalize the stock of infrastructure across regions), would influence the pattern of equalization transfers taking place in Australia.

Issues in the Design of Capital Grants

Three issues in the design of capital grants deserve discussion. First, the mechanism used to determine grants should not encourage subnational governments to act strategically in order to influence the size of their grant. The trick here is to ensure that any formula-driven grant model does not include variables that can be influenced by subnational government behavior. The Australian equalization model does not pass this test, as Petchey and Levtchenkova (2004) show. In the equalization model, the expenditure needs of the states, used to determine the distribution of the grant pool, are functions of the collective policies of the states. Hence the state can distort its provision of local public goods in order to influence the standard and hence its future grant.

Second, the reaction of subnational governments to any capital transfer (and other kinds of transfers) must be considered. In the extreme, subnational governments may reduce their own capital spending by one dollar for every dollar of capital grant received. In a less severe response, they are likely to reduce their own spending by some percentage of the grant received and thus free ride on the grant. The center can counteract this in three ways, all of them ineffective to some extent. One is to require that subnational governments match the grant. The second is to mandate that the capital be spent on particular (new) projects that otherwise would not have been funded. The third is to monitor subnational responses and develop a system of carrots and sticks for regions, in order to encourage compliance with the spirit of the transfer program. Whatever mechanism is adopted, these measures cannot ensure that subnational spending responses do not partially offset the intended effects of capital grants, as Martinez-Vazquez (2000) notes. The question of subnational responses to capital grants remains a concern in the use of such transfers.

Third, if capital grants are to be used to achieve a minimum standard of service provision across regions, then given that capital is only one input in the production of such services, thought needs to be given to how the associated recurrent inputs are to be financed. It makes no sense to build a hospital in a poor region, for example, if the local jurisdiction lacks the resources to provide the doctors, nurses, and other staff; material inputs; and on-going maintenance. The design of any capital grant program may thus need to be linked to other funding arrangements that cover the cost of recurrent and other inputs.

Real-World Experience with Capital Grants

The systems of capital transfers used internationally are both highly varied and country specific, making it difficult to generalize about them. This section therefore outlines two capital allocation schemes, using them to highlight some aspects of the two more frequently used capital allocation schemes, those that use an objective formula approach, in which the formula is constructed to achieve specific aims, and those that allocate capital on a project-specific basis.[3]

The first example is the allocation of capital for housing in the United Kingdom. It provides a useful example of a formula-based system and shows how such systems may evolve over time. The second example, from Australia, looks at the allocation of capital to deal with specific projects.

The Formulaic Approach to Capital Grants: Housing in the United Kingdom

The provision of adequate standard affordable housing is a key issue facing the British government. The Office of the Deputy Prime Minister has set a target of delivering adequate-quality social housing and allocated significant capital funding to local authorities to deal with the problem of "nondecent" homes. Since 1987 more than £18 billion of public and private money has been invested in an attempt to raise the quality of social housing, with another £7.5 billion expected to be invested by 2006. The allocation of capital resources to local authorities is formulaic in its approach (though there is a discretionary component), utilizing the generalized needs index to allocate funds across nine regions based on the annual housing capital guidelines.[4] The formula attempts, in a quite sophisticated way, to include weightings based on relative needs or disabilities.

The generalized needs index attempts to assess the relative need of each of the local authority regions for housing capital investment. The index includes three weighted components, each a proxy for capital needs or disabilities in the region. In the 2000/01 allocation, the heaviest weight (55 percent) was attached to the local authority stock condition. This measure is based on the amount of social housing in each regional area. A region with significant social housing would be identified as needing a greater share of funding in order to repair and improve its housing stock. The local authority stock condition also attempts to take into account variations in the average cost of such repairs and improvements, based on the type and age of the housing stock, using information from the 1996 English House Condition Survey. The local authority stock condition identifies six housing types, based on characteristics and age, and then works out an average cost of repairing or improving each type, weighting repair costs at 30 percent and improvement at 70 percent. Thus, for example, a region with a large proportion of pre–1945 dwellings or post–1945 high-rise apartments would be assessed as having greater need than a region with a large proportion of post-1964 low-rise apartments, since older housing and high-rises are deemed to cost more to repair or improve.

The second component of the index (with a weighting of 25 percent in 2000/01) is the new provision indicator, which assesses whether (and to what extent) a region faces an excess demand (or supply) for social housing. This relatively complex indicator combines a number of demand proxies, such as measures of overcrowding, the number of people who would prefer their own accommodation but are forced to share, the number of public and private dwellings that need replacement, and supply proxies, such as vacancy rates and underoccupancy, to produce an indication of a region's expected social housing needs.

The third component of the generalized needs index is the private sector stock condition, which was given a weighting of 20 percent in 2000/01. It is a measure of the cost of the repairs required to bring the region's stock of private sector dwellings up to the desired standard.

In summary, then, the generalized needs index illustrates the application of a disability-weighted, formulaic approach to the allocation of social housing capital across regions in the United Kingdom. As in all such approaches, it is always possible to question the validity of the various proxies for disabilities, consider the inclusion of additional disabilities, and reconsider the weightings assigned to the elements of the index. The 2000 consultation paper "Allocation of Housing Capital Resources 2001/02," did just that, looking at a variety of issues associated with the construction of the index and its use in future capital allocation. Among the issues raised was the possibility of varying the weighting scheme, targeting resources to deprived areas using an index of deprivation, and including in the index components that reflect rural housing needs, special needs groups, and various other special case groups.

The consultation paper also raised the issue of including forward-looking indicators in the index, particularly in the new provision indicator. Doing so clearly makes sense. Formulaic capital allocation schemes often use historical data to calculate the various elements in the index. Such data reflect the best available estimates of the various measures. Capital expenditures also need to be linked to expected future conditions and demand. After all, there is little point building housing in an area if outward migration over the year will alleviate any excess demand pressure. That said, there are obvious difficulties associated with reliably projecting future needs. This issue has recently been taken up in the United Kingdom with the publication of the "Three-Year Revenue and Capital Settlements Consultation Paper" by the Office of the Deputy Prime Minister (2004). In this consultation document, the government proposed implementing a three-year revenue and capital settlement system for local government. The principal argument is that by providing certainty and stability to local authority funding, such a system will ensure greater efficiency in resource usage and facilitate the delivery of higher-quality services across the whole range of local government services, including housing. The document notes that £12 billion a year is spent on capital investment, some of which is allocated on the basis of specific assessment plans from local authorities and some of which is allocated on a formulaic basis (such as funding for housing). The report argues that all capital projects would benefit from the financial stability associated with the three-year planning horizon. Currently, capital allocations are made to the local authorities close to the beginning of the financial year. The report argues that this hinders effective medium-term planning and potentially prevents local authorities from taking advantage of any gains from entering into long-term contracts with suppliers.

The Project-Based Approach to Capital Grants: Roads in Australia

The federal government in Australia provides project-specific capital grants through the Black Spot program of the Department of Transport and Regional Services. The program aims to identify parts of the road transport system that are unsafe and to target national government funding toward improving these roads in order to reduce road accidents and fatalities. This is a good example of the second main type of capital funding allocation model, in which subnational regions (local government authorities) may bid for a share of a pool of central funds, which are allocated based on an evaluation of the projects proposed.

Between 2000 and 2002, the national government committed $40 million a year in real terms to the project. It has extended this commitment to $45 million a year through 2006. While the scheme includes some targeting, with 50 percent of the funding in any state reserved for nonmetropolitan (or rural) areas, the allocation is based on cost-benefit analysis of the projects proposed, with the expectation that a project must achieve a minimum benefit to cost ratio of 2. Each state has a consultative panel to which submissions are sent; it is this panel's job to rank the projects and submit the ranked list to the Department of Transport and Regional Services. The proposals are then forwarded to the relevant minister for consideration using a set of criteria including the eligibility and economic benefit of the projects. To facilitate this system, the Department of Transport and Regional Services has compiled a comprehensive treatment/crash reduction matrix, which provides estimates of the average expected change in a range of crash types that might be expected to result from a range of road modifications. The matrix also estimates costs per casualty of various crash types for both rural and metropolitan regions.

A Capital Grant Simulation Model

A case can be made for capital grants in developing countries or transition economies in which subnational governments have a limited tax base, restricted or no access to efficient capital markets, and limited institutional capacity. Another precondition is that the economy in question have relatively serious deficiencies in public capital, both at the aggregate level and in terms of regional distribution. Many countries in Eastern Europe and Africa meet these conditions. Longer-term reforms in these regions are needed to build institutional capacity at the subnational level, develop capital markets for the provision of long-term loans for subnational governments, improve and strengthen democracy at the local level (to make local decision makers responsive to citizen wishes), and give jurisdictions independent access to tax bases. These reforms may not be feasible, however, and even if they are, they take time to implement. In the meantime, serious issues related to human capital formation, economic growth, and equity of access to public services need to be addressed.

Two formula-based capital grant models have been developed in recent years that are more comprehensive than the models currently used in many countries. These models are particularly applicable in developing countries, but they could also be applied at the supranational level, for example, to allocate capital grants across a regional union of states, such as the European Union, or a continent with a predominance of developing countries, such as Africa.

Three features distinguish these models from existing approaches:

- They measure capital needs of subnational regions on a consistent basis, using a per capita capital stock–based standard.
- The pool of capital grant funds is allocated to regions on the basis of their relative needs.
- Regions with capital backlogs (that is, deficiencies of capital relative to the standard) are identified and allowed to reach the standard over some period of time, while taking account of fiscal and macro-economic constraints.

The first of these models is discussed in detail in Levtchenkova and Petchey (2004). It determines a per capita public capital standard that is to be reached by regions at some time in the future and then tracks a transition path that the regions follow under the grant scheme. If funding is insufficient, some progress toward the target standard is achieved. If funding is adequate, the targets are achieved by the date set. The standard adopted within the model is an international one.

The second model, the details of which are provided in MacDonald, Petchey, and Josie (2005), has a simpler structure. It uses an endogenous within-country standard that is determined in period 1 of the operation of the grant scheme. This model explicitly divides regions into public capital–deficient (backlog) regions and public capital–surplus (nonbacklog) regions. The model shows how the backlog regions can be brought up to a minimum and uniform standard while the nonbacklog regions may also enjoy an increase in their public capital stock per capita.

Both models are conceptually related, although the second is simpler in structure and therefore potentially more applicable in developing countries, since the data requirements are less rigorous.[5] In both cases, the schemes should be used only in the immediate term in developing countries, while longer-term reforms are put into place.

The general aim of the second model is to allocate a pool of capital grant funds in an economy with regions that have disparate amounts of per capita public capital and to do so in a way that brings the poorer regions up to some minimum (uniform) standard while ensuring that per capita capital in the richer regions increases over time. Following an overview of how the model works, it is applied to South Africa to show how these aims can be achieved.

Developing economies such as South Africa have two problems: the overall level of public infrastructure for the provision of major public services is low, and the geographic distribution of public capital is highly uneven. The

TABLE 15.1 Per Capita Capital Stock, by South African Province, 2002

Province	Real capita stock (millions of rand, in 1995 prices)	Population (thousands)	Real capital stock (rand per capita)	Backlog (rand per capita)
Northern Cape	1,742.8	8,88.6	1,961.3	−580.4
Kwa Zulu Natal	17,608.1	9,215.8	1,910.7	−529.8
Mpumalanga	5,404.7	3,157.9	1,711.5	−330.6
North West	6,017.8	3,661.3	1,643.6	−262.7
Western Cape	6,912.0	4,315.6	1,601.6	−220.7
Gauteng	12,831.6	8,109.7	1,582.3	−201.4
Free State	3,085.9	2,860.1	1,078.9	302.0
Limpopo	4,745.2	5,848.2	811.4	569.5
Eastern Cape	4,058.1	7,135.9	568.7	812.2
All provinces	62,407.0	45,170.0	1,380.9	0

Sources: Data on the capital stock by province were supplied by the South African Reserve Bank. Population figures are from Statistics South Africa.
Note: Capital stock includes education, health, transport, welfare, and housing infrastructure.

per capita value of public infrastructure exceeds the national average in six provinces (the Western Cape, the Northern Cape, Kwa Zulu Natal, the North West, Gauteng, and Mpumalanga) and falls below the national average in three others (the Eastern Cape, the Free State, and Limpopo) (table 15.1). If the difference between the national average and the per capita value of public capital in a particular province is defined as that province's "capital backlog," then provinces with a capital surplus will have a negative backlog and those with a capital shortage will have a positive backlog. The model reveals how backlogs can widen and public capital per capita can fall, even in the richer regions, if too small a percentage of GDP is allocated to public capital formation.

Model Description

The model operates over $\tau = 1, \ldots, N$ periods. Suppose that in period 1, a given pool of funds is to be allocated to public capital spending by the national government. The pool can be funded through foreign aid, national tax revenues, or borrowings, or it can be redirected from other national expenditures. Some portion of the pool is to be spent in selected regions to reduce regional disparities (the "backlog component" of the pool), the rest is to be spent across all regions to raise the general level of per capita public capital (the "economic efficiency component" of the pool). The portion of the pool to be allocated to the two components is set within the model as a policy parameter. In this way, the policy maker can choose how quickly regional disparities in the amount of public capital per capita should be reduced relative to general increases across all regions.

The model then determines how to allocate the backlog component of the pool in period 1 across the capital-poor regions. This is done by estimating a minimum per capita standard for public infrastructure (denoted by S) that should be met or exceeded in each region. Various ways of measuring per capita standards can be employed, including a simple national average and a "richest region" standard. Capital deficiencies—positive for regions with backlogs, negative for regions with a capital surplus—can be estimated by applying the per capita standard in each region in period 1. If the richest-region per capita standard is used, all regions except the richest have positive backlogs in period 1. From this information, index numbers (which sum to one) can be created for all the positive backlog regions. These numbers can then be used to determine the share of each backlog region in the backlog component of the grant pool.

The next issue is to determine how the efficiency component of the pool is to be allocated in period 1. There are many possibilities. The one used in the model is a simple equal per capita allocation. This implies that the allocation of the efficiency component is undertaken on the basis of regional population shares. All regions receive a grant from this component of the pool of funds. At the end of period 1, the backlog regions receive their share of the backlog component of the pool as well as their equal per capita share of the efficiency component. The nonbacklog regions receive only their equal per capita share of the efficiency component.

At the commencement of period 2, the backlogs are all re-estimated using the same per capita standard adopted in period 1, taking into account the capital spending undertaken at the end of period 1. The model then makes further allocations to backlog and nonbacklog regions using the same methodology used in period 1. In subsequent periods the same approach is adopted. By some period T, the "convergence period," the per capita capital stocks in the backlog regions converge to the per capita uniform standard set in period 1.

The model assumes the same capital utilization rate across provinces and does not take account of depreciation. Work is continuing on both these issues, as well as on the question of allowing for capital cost disabilities (that is, the notion that a unit of capital provided in one region may not provide the same flow of services as a unit of capital provided in another region because of differences in disabilities, stemming from such factors as different population dispersion and economies of scale in the provision of services).

The model has been applied only to South Africa. It could be used in any decentralized (unitary) country in which the conditions discussed above apply. Where these conditions hold, capital grants can be thought of as national capital spending channeled through notional provincial governments. The spending is undertaken indirectly by the center through conditional grants to the provinces. The model might also be applied at the supranational level, such as the European Union, to allocate capital grants across member countries. It could also be applied to Africa.

Applying the model to a federation with independent subnational governments is more complicated, as regions may have governments that undertake their own (largely independent) spending on public infrastructure. In this case, the center can still allocate conditional grants to the subnational governments, but there is the problem of modeling their response to these grants before the net impact of the central spending on public infrastructure formation can be assessed. This is something that has not yet been taken into account in the model. Therefore, in its current form, the model is more applicable to cases in which subnational governments are spending agents of the center.

Input Database

The input data requirements are as follows. First, some estimate of the capital stock by region is needed at the beginning of the simulation. Providing these data can be problematic for many countries. Even in the United States, Holzt-Eakin (1993) had to estimate these data using capital expenditure weights and the perpetual inventory methodology. In Australia, Petchey and Levtchenkova (2003) used the same approach to generate state and service-specific capital stock estimates for 1960–2002.

For South Africa this approach could not be used, because of insufficient time-series observations for capital expenditures. This is likely to be the case in other developing countries. Approximations of provincial public capital stocks were constructed from aggregate (national) public capital stock estimates, using various simple weighting methodologies (provincial GDP weights, capital expenditure weights) and recent data. The estimates were confirmed by the South African Reserve Bank, which provided estimates of provincial public capital stocks constructed from a database on national public capital stock estimates.[6]

Second, estimates of the provincial populations and their growth rates are needed. These data came from Statistics South Africa. In order to forecast over the simulation horizon, the input database also uses the implied exponential population growth rates for males and females at the required level of disaggregation for the period 1996–2002. These inferred growth rates include provision for interprovincial migration and the apparent underreporting of mortality rates in nonurban regions. Statistics South Africa also attempted to calculate growth rates after incorporating estimates for additional deaths due to HIV/AIDS. These figures were based on estimates of infection rates from prenatal clinic surveys. In the simulations below, the growth rates include the effects of HIV/AIDs. These population growth rates are important, as some estimate or forecast of population growth is required to allow the minimum required grant size in each period of the simulation horizon to be calculated.

Simulations

Two simulations of the capital allocation model were run.[7] In the first, the total pool size is set at a relatively low level, just sufficient to eliminate backlogs but insufficient to ensure that capital stocks per capita keep growing in the nonbacklog provinces. This simulation is designed to show the consequences of underfunding public infrastructure. In the second simulation, the total pool size is set sufficiently large to ensure that per capita capital stocks grow in the nonbacklog regions and that the backlogs in the poorer regions are eliminated within some reasonable period of time.

For the first simulation, the per capita standard in period 1 (2002) is set at R1,381, the level of per capita public capital for all provinces for the five major provincial services (health, education, housing, transportation, and welfare).[8] The portion of the pool allocated to the backlog component is set at 50 percent (in both simulations). With this standard, there are just three backlog provinces: the Eastern Cape, the Free State, and Limpopo. The total backlog for 2002 is R9,989.9 million (in 1995 prices), or about 1.5 percent of South Africa's GDP.[9]

The pool is set large enough to ensure that the aggregate backlogs decline during each period of the simulation and hence that the backlog regions converge to the per capita standard by some period T. However, the size of the pool in this case is too small to ensure that per capita capital stocks in nonbacklog provinces increase as well. The implication is that public capital formation is being underfunded, because insufficient funds are being allocated to the nonbacklog regions to compensate for the additional capital they require just to keep pace with population growth. Nonbacklog regions

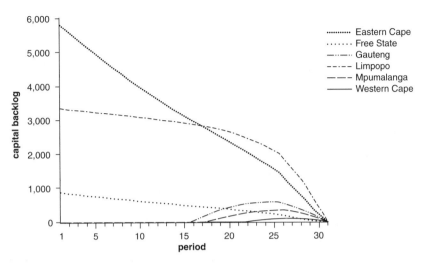

Source: Authors.

FIGURE 15.1 Simulation 1: Backlogs, by South African Province
(*million rand, in 2002 constant prices*)

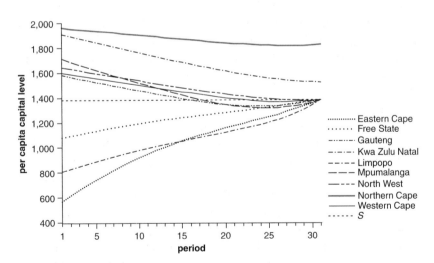

Source: Authors.
Note: The horizontal straight line *S* represents the per capita standard set in period 1.

FIGURE 15.2 Simulation 1: Per Capita Capital Levels, by South African
Province
(*rand, in 2002 constant prices*)

can become backlog regions during the simulation period, particularly if their population growth is high.

It takes 30 years of capital allocations to eliminate the backlogs (figures 15.1 and 15.2). Moreover, because the scheme is underfunded, before the end of the simulation period, seven of the nine provinces develop backlogs.[10] This demonstrates that although the per capita standard is fixed, population growth in the absence of adequate capital funding can lead to backlogs in provinces that initially do not have them. The backlog provinces eventually converge to the per capita standard by the end of the simulation period, but per capita capital stock levels in the (original) nonbacklog provinces decline due to the inadequate size of the pool. As a simple measure of overall convergence, the variance of the per capita capital stocks is calculated at the beginning and end of the simulation. In this case, the variance falls 91 percent.

The total value of the capital spending pool over the 30 periods is R51,516 (in 1995 prices). Using a real interest rate of 5.6 percent, the net present value of the pool in 2002 is R22,867 million, or 3.5 percent of South Africa's 2002 GDP.[11] This is substantially more than the R9,990 million (1.5 percent of GDP) needed in 2002 to eliminate the backlogs immediately. There is thus a benefit from immediately eliminating the backlogs with a once-off initial effort rather than extending the funding over many periods. Of course, delaying funding means that funds can be used for alternative uses. But it also means that the backlog problem becomes larger, because population growth means that more capital is required to meet any per capita standard set in period 1. The simulations indicate that the cost of delay outweighs any benefit.

For the second simulation, the size of the pool is increased to ensure that it is sufficient to eliminate the backlogs and increase per capita capital stocks in the nonbacklog regions.[12] In period 1 the total backlog is still the same as in the previous simulation, so eliminating the backlog in 1 period would still cost about 1.5 percent of GDP in 2002. The larger pool means that backlogs are eliminated much more rapidly (six years). The net present value of the total pool (over six years) is R19,882 million, so although the backlogs are eliminated more quickly, the larger pool size (0.55 − 0.65 percent of GDP) means that the net present value is not much lower than in the first simulation.[13] The net present value still exceeds the cost of immediately eliminating the backlogs.

Figures 15.3 and 15.4 show the evolution of the backlogs and the per capita capital stocks for backlog and nonbacklog regions. While per capita

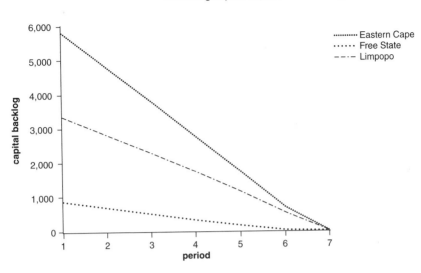

Source: Authors.

FIGURE 15.3 Simulation 2: Backlogs, by South African Province
(*million rand, in 2002 constant prices*)

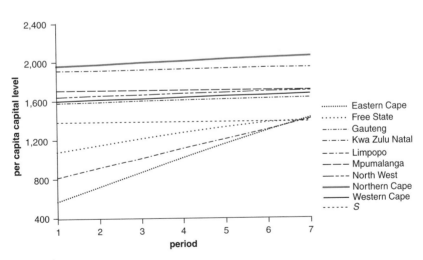

Source: Authors.
Note: The horizontal straight line S represents the per capita standard set in period 1.

FIGURE 15.4 Simulation 2: Per Capita Capital Levels, by South African
Province
(*rand, in 2002 constant prices*)

capital stocks do not converge for all provinces, they do converge overall, and the variance falls 80 percent over the simulation period. Although smaller than in the first simulation, the advantage with the larger pool size is that per capita capital stocks rise in all regions, no further backlogs develop, and the existing backlogs are eliminated in a relatively short period of time. The cost is, of course, that the pool represents a greater burden on GDP on a year-by-year basis. Nevertheless, this appears to be the optimal approach. The previous simulation shows that the problems of underfunding the scheme can lead to backlogs developing and falling standards of per capita capital in nonbacklog regions.

Policy Implications

Like other developing countries and transition economies, South Africa needs to increase its stock of public sector capital in order to provide important services, such as health and education. This capital raises the level of human capital in the workforce and thus increases the potential for economic growth. South Africa also needs to distribute its capital more evenly and to do so on economic grounds.

The model developed here provides a mechanism for allocating funding for capital expenditure across regions in order to eliminate capital backlogs. Simulations with the model make it clear that underfunding such a grant scheme can lead to undesirable consequences, such as declining per capita public capital levels and the development of backlogs in regions that initially do not have them (as population growth outstrips capital formation). This prolongs the period during which backlogs exist and raises the real cost of eliminating them.[14] Adequate funding can ensure rapid elimination of backlogs and raise per capita standards in all regions.

The model allows the minimum level of funding needed to be estimated in order to ensure an outcome in which per capita public capital stocks grow in all regions over time and poorer regions are brought up to some minimum uniform standard. Moreover, while the model does not enforce convergence of per capita standards between backlog and nonbacklog regions or across nonbacklog regions, the simulations for South Africa shows a high degree of convergence in per capita standards. The model also makes a strong case for dealing with the capital backlog problem quickly in South Africa. Doing so will require devoting substantial funding to the project over a short period of time, which will require that the government either attract new foreign aid sources or divert spending from other activities.

Conclusion

National governments in federations or decentralized economies can use capital grants as an effective policy instrument to achieve minimum, uniform standards of provision for major public services, such as transportation infrastructure, health, and education. Such grants may also help internalize interregional infrastructure externalities and reduce fiscally induced, potentially inefficient migration.

This rationale for capital grants is likely to be the strongest in developing countries and transition economies with low levels of public capital per capita (at least by developed economy standards), inequities in the regional distribution of the public capital and (possibly) high levels of fiscally motivated internal migration of labor and private capital, and subnational governments with limited own-source taxes or access to efficient capital markets for infrastructure borrowing. Capital grant programs in such economies should be used only as interim policy measures while longer-term reforms that build institutional capacity and political accountability at the local level, as well as give jurisdictions access to efficient capital markets, are put into place.

This is not to say that capital grants cannot be justified in developed economies not characterized by these conditions. As the case studies show, developed countries use capital grants for public housing and roads. There may be a more limited case for such grants in these economies, however.

Policy makers contemplating using capital grants must decide whether to adopt a formula-based or a project-based approach. In a project-based approach, the central policy maker plays a more passive role, assessing project proposals made by officials from state or provincial governments and then ranking them in terms of net benefit. If the goal is to establish minimum and uniform public service standards, the formula-based model is preferred, as the simulations show. This approach also allows grants to be allocated to each region to correct for regional inequities in the distribution of public capital, something that is more difficult to do with project-based grants. The formula approach, at least as modeled here, also allows the policy maker to simulate various outcomes by adopting different assumptions about the size of the capital spending pool, examine the implications of underfunding public capital formation, analyze what percentage of GDP needs to be put toward public capital formation in order to achieve predetermined standards, and gain some appreciation of how long it will take, given resource constraints, to achieve these standards.

Annex: Economic Rationales for Grants

The literature on fiscal federalism provides several different rationales for grant programs. Each is summarized below.

Fiscal Gap Transfers

The rationale for unconditional transfers to subnational governments derives from arguments about the assignment of tax and spending powers. Efficiency costs are believed to be associated with subnational taxes on mobile factors of production (particularly capital). As a result, the marginal cost of public funds is higher at this level of government than at the national level. In addition, the central government may best be able to raise revenues for the provision of national public goods, including income redistribution and interregional equalization. The implication of this normative perspective is that tax powers should be more centralized than spending powers, resulting in a fiscal gap in which the central government collects more revenue than is required for its own expenditures. Surplus revenue must then be distributed from the center as unconditional transfers, sometimes called revenue-sharing transfers.

Most decentralized economies have substantial fiscal gaps. As a result, substantial revenue-sharing transfers are made to subnational governments. The revenue-sharing process tends to create a divergence between the taxing, spending, and administration authorities of the various levels of governments. Under revenue sharing, the central government finances the program, but the spending and administration of the programs is delegated to the lower levels of government. While it is considered beneficial to link financial and political responsibilities by having the revenue-raising and spending authorities controlled by the same level of government, the social benefits of a revenue-sharing program are likely to outweigh these political efficiencies.

Interregional Externalities

Subnational policies of local or provincial governments can create positive externalities in the form of benefits to people residing outside the government's jurisdiction. To the extent that these externalities are not taken into account by regional governments that care only about their own residents' welfare, provision of local public goods that generate cross-border externalities will be suboptimal from a national perspective (globally inefficient).

Three policy instruments can correct for the inefficiency resulting from interjurisdictional externalities. First, the central government can mandate uniform levels of subnational provision of local public goods. This option is not consistent with a democratic system that values individual sovereignty. Second, regions can cooperate to take account of externalities, with or without central monitoring and enforcement (cooperative federalism). Third, higher-level governments can provide matching grants targeted to programs that generate externalities. Matching grants reduce the relative price of the local public good. If the grant is optimally designed in terms of the matching rate, it encourages the optimal level of provision by the subnational jurisdiction.

Minimum (Uniform) National Standards

National governments may wish to ensure that public services that are important for the creation of human capital, such as health and education, are provided to a minimum national standard across all jurisdictions. The arguments for doing so are efficiency related. First, minimum uniform standards improve the free mobility of capital and labor across regions, increasing the gains from an internal common market (Boadway, Roberts, and Shah 1994a). This applies in particular to major public services such as health, education, and transportation infrastructure. Uniform provision across regions may also reduce any inefficient fiscally induced factor mobility.

Second, education and health are important determinants of human capital formation, which is important for spurring economic growth and raising per capita incomes over time. Since governments are major providers of these public services, they have a role to play in ensuring that such services are provided to increasing standards over time. Regional uniformity of provision of such services is important for maximizing the gains from trade and ensuring the efficiency of internal common factor markets; the level of the standard, and changes in that standard over time, are important for the rate of human capital formation and future economic growth.

Fiscally Induced Migration

Subnational tax and expenditure policies that generate differential net fiscal benefits across regions may lead to fiscally induced factor migration and inefficient mobile factor (capital and labor) location decisions. The principle of equal treatment of equals may also be violated, since individuals who are otherwise identical will be treated differently by the system of local public finance depending on their location. Net fiscal benefits may differ across regions in the presence of location-specific economic rents, fiscal externalities, cost "disabilities" associated with the provision of local services, or differences in income distribution. In such a world, a decentralized equilibrium in which regions choose their tax and expenditure policies competitively is not globally efficient. As Boadway and Flatters (1982) show, there is an optimal equalization transfer that, if implemented by a central government, will ensure that the decentralized outcome is fully efficient.[15] The transfer is not only efficiency enhancing, it also ensures that the principle of equal treatment of equals is satisfied.[16]

Many federations, and decentralized economies, place particular importance on transfers designed to achieve equalization, both across provinces and states and across local governments. The transfers can be administered as self-financing interjurisdictional transfers or arranged directly between regions. They may also be embodied within the revenue-sharing transfers going to regions as a result of fiscal gaps, as in Australia. In such models, the goals of revenue sharing and equalization are achieved in one grant program. But as Petchey and Levtchenkova (2004) show, the interregional transfers that occur in these real-world schemes of equalization do not necessarily replicate the theoretically ideal interregional transfer. This is mainly because they may create incentives for regions to act strategically and because the interregional transfers are based on considerations unrelated to the factors important for efficiency.

Federal Stability

Federations can be viewed as voluntary coalitions of member states that yield certain benefits, such as gains from trade as internal trade becomes free; tax, price, and scale economy benefits in the provision of national public goods; the pooling of risk between heterogeneous member-states; and greater bargaining power with other nations. A federation can also impose costs on particular member-states. One of these stems from the fact that the functions that are centralized will be provided uniformly to all member-states, regardless of possible differences in preferences. This uniformity of provision might lead to a loss of well-being for some states' residents, who are required to consume the same level of a service as residents of other states, whether or not they share the same preferences. Of course, it is possible that the functions centralized in federations will be those for which there is little diversity of preferences.

A federation can yield an excess of benefits over these uniformity (or other) costs (a distributable social surplus), but not all of the parties to a federation will necessarily benefit from or obtain what is perceived to be a fair share of the benefits. Thus in order for a federation to be attractive—that is, for it to make at least one member-state better off while leaving all others at least as well off as they were in autarky—it may have to provide lump-sum transfers (from the distributable surplus) from the "winning" states to the "losing" states.

This is the basis of the compensatory argument for lump-sum transfers of income from states that gain from federation to states that lose. These transfers can be thought of as equalization payments, in the sense that they equalize the net social benefit from federation and are necessary in the interests of obtaining and sustaining federal unity.

In Australia arguments for equalizing grants among the states were many and varied. But the compensatory motive played a significant part in the system of special payments to the less wealthy states in the 1920s and 1930s and in the eventual formalization of these payments in the 1930s through creation of the Commonwealth Grants Commission and the system of equalization that Australia has today (commonly recognized as the most comprehensive system in the world).[17] The principle of "needs" actually adopted by the Commission as the basis for equalization payments to the states may have been, in part, a feasible best way of sustaining some compensatory equalization.

Notes

1. There are, of course, problems with cooperative agreements.
2. This was a concern in the South African context and is a major reason why the Financial and Fiscal Commission there opted for a formula approach in developing capital grant allocation models.
3. See Martinez-Vazquez (2000) for a wider-ranging and more detailed survey of individual country practices for 10 countries.
4. An associate index, the housing needs index, is used to allocate housing capital resources to registered social landlords; it uses two of the three indicators discussed here.
5. The models were developed during a series of projects undertaken for the Financial and Fiscal Commission (FFC), South Africa, some of which were funded under the auspices of AusAid, the Australian government's foreign aid agency. Thanks are due to the staff of the FFC, in particular, Mr. Jaya Josie, for their comments on the modeling process and assistance in constructing the necessary databases. Thanks are also due to the FFC commissioners for their continued commitment to research on capital grant models.
6. The estimates of capital stocks, and the way in which they change over time as a result of implementation of the grant program, do not take account of changes in the quality of public capital. See Hulten (1990) for a discussion.
7. More-detailed results appear in MacDonald, Petchey, and Josie (2005).
8. Ideally, period 1 would be 2006, but the current data set is complete only through 2002.

9. To put this figure into context, between 1995/96 and 2001/02, total public capital expenditure in all provinces averaged less than 1 percent of GDP.

10. The seven provinces with backlogs are the Western Cape, the Eastern Cape, the Free State, Gauteng, Mpumalanga, Limpopo, and the North West. Of these the North West develops a backlog only in the last two periods of the scheme, making it hard to see in the figure.

11. Using data from the International Monetary Fund, Kahn and Farrell (2002) estimate the real interest rate in South Africa in the 1990s to have been about 5.5 percent.

12. Within the model, a series of mathematical constraints allows the policy maker to choose the size of the pool and in so doing choose whether to adequately fund the grant scheme.

13. A discount rate of 5.5 percent is used.

14. Indeed, in some simulations, not presented here, significant underfunding can lead to ever-growing backlogs.

15. Myers (1990) shows that if regions have access to voluntarily interregional transfers, they may make such transfers themselves, without any need for a central authority.

16. See Boadway (2004) for a discussion of the efficiency in migration case for equalization.

17. Particularly important was the need to compensate the smaller primary producing states, such as Western Australia, for the costs imposed on them by the operation of uniform national policies, including the external tariff (which benefited New South Wales and Victoria), centralized wage fixation, and the navigation acts.

References

Boadway, R.W. 2004. "The Theory and Practice of Fiscal Equalization." *CESifo Economic Studies* 50 (1): 211–54.

Boadway, R.W., and F. Flatters. 1982. "Efficiency and Equalization Payments in a Federal System of Government: A Synthesis and Extension of Recent Results." *Canadian Journal of Economics* 15 (4): 613–33.

Boadway, R., and M. Keen. 1996. "Efficiency and the Optimal Direction of Federal-State Transfers." *International Tax and Public Finance* 3 (2): 137–55.

Boadway, R., S. Roberts, and A. Shah. 1994a. "Fiscal Federalism Dimensions of Tax Reform in Developing Countries." Policy Research Working Paper 1385, World Bank, Policy Research Department, Washington, DC.

———. 1994b. "The Reform of Fiscal Systems in Developing and Emerging Market Economies: A Federalism Perspective." Policy Research Working Paper 1259, World Bank, Policy Research Department, Washington, DC.

Financial and Fiscal Commission. 2004. *Financial and Fiscal Commission of South Africa, 2005/06.* Submission to the Division of Revenue, Pretoria.

Holtz-Eakin, D. 1993. "State-Specific Estimates of State and Local Government Capital." *Regional Science and Urban Economics* 23 (2): 185–209.

Hulten, C.R. 1990. "The Measurement of Capital." In *Fifty Years of Economic Measurement: The Jubilee of the Conference on Research in Income and Wealth,* ed. E.R. Berndt and J.E. Triplett, 119–52. Chicago: University of Chicago Press.

Kahn, B., and G.N. Farrell. 2002. "South African Real Interest Rates in Comparative Perspective: Theory and Evidence." South African Reserve Bank Occasional Paper 17, Pretoria.

Levtchenkova, S., and J.D Petchey. 2004. "A Model for Public Infrastructure Equalization in Transitional Economies." Paper presented at the conference "Challenges in the Design of Fiscal Equalization and Intergovernmental Transfers," Georgia State University, Andrew Young School of Policy Studies, Atlanta, GA, October 4–5.

MacDonald, G., J.D. Petchey, and J. Josie. 2005. "Allocating Spending on Public Infrastructure in Developing Economies with Regional Disparities." Curtin University of Technology, School of Economics and Finance, Perth, Western Australia.

Martinez-Vazquez, Jorge. 2000. "An Introduction to International Practices and Best Principles in the Design of Capital Transfers." Georgia State University, Andrew Young School of Policy Studies, Department of Economics, Atlanta, GA.

Myers, G.M. 1990. "Optimality, Free Mobility and the Regional Authority in a Federation." *Journal of Public Economics* 43 (1): 107–21.

Office of the Deputy Prime Minister. 2000. "Allocation of Housing Capital Resources 2001/02." Consultation Paper. London.

———. 2004. "Three-Year Revenue and Capital Settlements." Consultation Paper. London.

Petchey, J.D., and S. Levtchenkova. 2001. "Equalization Grants for the Australian States: Alternative Estimates." Working Paper Series 01.31, Curtin University of Technology, Curtin Business School, School of Economics and Finance, Perth, Western Australia.

———. 2003. "Regional Capital Stock Data for Australia." *Australian Economic Review* 33 (2). 193–97.

———. 2004. "Fiscal Capacity Equalization and Economic Efficiency." Paper presented at the conference "Challenges in the Design of Fiscal Equalization and Intergovernmental Transfers," Georgia State University, Andrew Young School of Policy Studies, Atlanta, GA, October 4–5.

Petchey, J.D., P. Shapiro, G. MacDonald, and P. Koshy. 2000. "Capital Equalisation and the Australian States." *Economic Record* 76 (232): 32–44.

Petchey, J.D., and C. Walsh. 1993. "Conceptual Foundations in Fiscal Equalisation." In *Horizontal Fiscal Equalisation: Efficiency and Equity Issues in Historical, Political and Economic Perspectives,* 56–98. Submission to the South Australian Treasury by the South Australian Centre for Economic Studies, Adelaide, South Australia.

Sturm, Jan-Egbert. 1998. *Public Capital Expenditure in OECD Countries: The Causes and Impact of the Decline in Public Capital Spending.* Cheltenham, United Kingdom: Edward Elgar.

Ter-Minassian, T., ed. 1997. *Fiscal Federalism in Theory and Practice.* Washington, DC: International Monetary Fund.

Zeikate, S. 2002. "Investment Transfers: Survey of Ten Developed Countries." World Bank, World Bank Eastern and Central European Division, Washington, DC.

16

Grants to Large Cities and Metropolitan Areas

ENID SLACK

Intergovernmental transfers provide an important source of revenue for local governments in most countries. Although the public finance rationales for transfers are similar for all types of local governments—vertical fiscal imbalance, horizontal fiscal imbalance, and externalities—the need for transfers will likely be different for different types of local governments. Large cities and metropolitan areas, for example, are different from smaller urban or rural municipalities, because of the size of their population, the high degree of concentration of population, and the presence of a heterogeneous population in terms of social and economic circumstances. In many countries, large cities also serve as regional hubs for people from neighboring communities, who come to shop or use public services that are not available in their own communities.

From a municipal finance perspective, these characteristics of large cities and metropolitan areas are reflected in the magnitude and complexity of the expenditures that local governments in those areas are required to make on municipal services. These characteristics are also reflected in their ability to pay for services: large cities and metropolitan areas generally have greater fiscal capacity than smaller municipalities and rural areas. Large cities and metropolitan areas can thus have greater fiscal autonomy than other urban or rural areas, in terms of both greater responsibility for local services and greater ability to levy their own taxes and collect their own revenues (Bird 1984). Greater fiscal autonomy for large cities and metropolitan areas has implications for the role for intergovernmental transfers in the finances of these cities.

This chapter explores how intergovernmental transfers to large cities and metropolitan areas should differ from those to other areas. The first section of the chapter examines the characteristics of large cities and metropolitan areas, outlines how these characteristics affect expenditures and revenues, and draws implications for designing intergovernmental transfer programs. The second section sets out the standard rationales for transfers and evaluates these rationales in the context of large cities and metropolitan areas. Do these rationales apply to large cities and metropolitan areas in the same way they apply to rural municipalities? Can large cities satisfy these rationales in ways other than through intergovernmental transfers? The third section of the chapter summarizes the results of some empirical studies of intergovernmental transfers to large cities and describes the reliance on transfers by selected large cities around the world. It notes that grants account for different proportions of municipal revenues in different large cities and suggests some of the reasons for these differences. The last section offers some suggestions for the appropriate role for grants to large cities and metropolitan areas. It also identifies information that needs to be collected to gain a better understanding of grants to municipalities of different types and sizes.

Characteristics of Large Cities and Metropolitan Areas and the Implications for Grant Design

In economic theory the major role assigned to local governments is to provide goods and services within a particular geographic area to residents who are willing to pay for them.[1] If the benefits of particular services are confined to local jurisdictions (that is, the actions of one municipality have no effect on other municipalities), efficiency is enhanced, because the mix and level of services can vary according to local preferences. Local officials are in a better position than central government officials to respond to local tastes and preferences.[2] Local governments are generally assigned expenditure responsibilities for a wide range of services, including roads and transit, water and sewerage services, police and fire protection, solid waste collection and disposal, recreation and culture, land use planning, social services, public health, and social housing.

This theory of the role of local governments does not distinguish between large metropolitan areas, medium-size cities, and towns and villages. Yet it is important to make that distinction, because "not all local governments are equal" (Bird 2000, p. 114). There are large and small cities, urbanized and rural municipalities, and rich and poor areas. "A structure that fails to distinguish between major metropolitan areas and small villages makes it difficult to clearly define the functional responsibilities of local government" (Burki, Perry, and Dillinger 1999, p. 24). If all local governments are assigned the same responsibilities, the assignment is likely to reflect what the smallest municipalities can provide. Moreover, the amount of public resources available to different types of local governments is not the same: larger cities and metropolitan areas generally have greater capacity to raise revenues.

Some countries do distinguish among different types of municipalities. One example is the German structure, which gives broader responsibilities to city-states (Berlin, Bremen, and Hamburg) and allows other large municipalities to assume responsibilities of counties. Hamburg, for example, exercises all of the powers of a state government (*Land*) and writes its own constitution. It has exclusive jurisdiction over some policy areas, such as culture and education, and shares jurisdiction with the federal government over others, such as criminal law, health, and welfare. As a city-state, Hamburg also has access to more revenue sources than do other cities. More than 60 percent of its revenue is derived from taxes it shares with the federal government (Petersen 1995). As Hamburg does not differentiate between *Land* and local government matters in the governing of the city, all revenues go into the same government treasury (Petersen 1995).

Expenditure Differences

Governments in large metropolitan areas generally provide more and different services than governments in smaller urban and rural areas. The magnitude and complexity of local government expenditures in large metropolitan areas differ from expenditures in smaller urban or rural areas because of the sheer size of the population in metropolitan areas (generally defined as areas with more than 1 million residents) (Freire 2001), the high degree of concentration of population (large number of people living in close proximity), and the presence of a population that is heterogeneous in terms of social and economic circumstances (Nowlan 1994).

Large cities and metropolitan areas differ not only because of their size but also because they increasingly hold the key to the economic success of the countries in which they are located. Large cities are important generators of employment, wealth, and productivity growth. In the emerging global knowledge-based economy, where innovation is the key to prosperity, firms no longer compete internationally solely on the basis of cost but also on the basis of their ability to develop new products and deliver them in a timely manner (OECD 1996). Most innovation occurs in large cities and metropolitan areas, because the concentration of people and firms increases social and economic interaction and results in greater exchange of ideas among people working in different fields in the same location. People and businesses are attracted to large metropolitan areas because they provide such benefits of close proximity (agglomeration economies) as face to face interaction, the availability of more and better business services, and greater accessibility to a large skilled labor force and transportation and communications networks (Slack, Bourne, and Gertler 2003).

Large cities not only have to ensure access to skilled labor and transportation and communications infrastructure to attract businesses, they also have to provide services that will attract and retain highly trained human capital. Recent studies suggest that "knowledge workers," who seem to be increasingly central to economic success, are attracted by the quality of life that large cities offer (Florida 2002). This means that to be competitive, cities need to provide services such as parks, recreational facilities, and cultural institutions in addition to transportation, water, sewerage, garbage collection and disposal, and police and fire protection. The high concentration of special needs within large metropolitan areas also requires higher expenditures on social services, social housing, and public health. The higher concentration of poverty in large cities necessitates greater expenditures on social services. The higher concentration of people means more specialized police services. Higher densities mean more specialized training and equipment for fire fighters.

Smaller cities may not have a public transit system, because urban densities are not sufficient for a transit system to be economically viable. Cultural facilities (such as opera houses or art galleries) are unlikely to be provided in smaller urban areas, because these facilities require a minimum size to make provision possible. Furthermore, people from outside the metropolitan area make use of the cultural facilities as well as social and medical services but do not directly contribute to the support of those facilities.[3]

Operating expenditures in London, for example, are about 30 percent above the average for all local governments in the United Kingdom (Office of the Deputy Prime Minister 2002). Expenditures are higher on housing (two to three times higher in per capita terms than in the rest of the country) and on health (as a result of both the higher costs of operating in London and the high cost of the five medical schools located there) (Office of the Prime Minister 2003). Other characteristics that differentiate London from other British cities include its ethnic diversity (one in four Londoners is from an ethnic minority); income disparities (although London is a wealthy city, it has the second highest unemployment rate among Britain's regions); and its role as a global city in terms of finance and business services (Office of the Prime Minister 2003).

Expenditures per household in Toronto are about 44 percent higher than in the surrounding region (the Greater Toronto Area), which comprises smaller municipalities and regional governments. Expenditures on social and family services are much higher in Toronto than in the other municipalities because poverty rates in the city are higher than in the surrounding region.[4] Transit expenditures per household are much higher in Toronto, because the city operates an integrated transit system that includes subways, light rail lines, streetcars, and an extensive bus network.[5] Expenditures on policing are higher, reflecting the existence of more specialized units (for example, forensics) and higher crime rates in a large metropolitan area, where there is a large, diverse population and a higher incidence of poverty. Expenditures on culture are higher in Toronto, in part because it can achieve the necessary size required for such facilities to be viable and in part because cultural facilities are used by people coming from outside the city and outside the region. Expenditures per household on fire are somewhat higher, because fire protection is more costly to provide in a large metropolitan area, where population density is much higher and there is a concentration of high-rise office buildings. Smaller urban or rural areas often rely on volunteer fire departments.

Revenue-Raising Differences

In general, the revenue sources that are available to large cities and metro-politan areas should reflect the expenditure responsibilities they are required to undertake: "local authorities' financial resources shall be commensurate with the responsibilities provided for by the constitution and the law" (Euro-pean Charter of Local Self-Government, Article 9, Paragraph 2). In other words, there should be a relationship between the tasks that local govern-ments perform and the financial resources available to them.

According to the benefit model of local government finance, those who pay taxes or user fees to finance local government should be the ones who enjoy the benefits of local expenditures. The efficient provision of goods and services requires local governments to charge directly for services wherever possible (Bird 2001). Charges should be levied on those who receive the benefits from services, where those beneficiaries can be identified. User fees allow residents and businesses to know how much they are paying for the services they are receiving from local governments. Moreover, when proper prices are charged, governments can make more-efficient decisions about how much to produce and residents can make more-efficient decisions about how much to consume. User charges are especially appropriate for services such as water and public transit, the benefits of which are confined largely to users.

A common objection to suggestions to increase reliance on user charge financing is that it would increase regressivity. As many studies have shown, however, almost the opposite is true in large urban areas: those who benefit most from underpricing services are those who make the most use of them, and the poor are not well-represented in this group (Bird and Miller 1989).[6] Another important benefit of more-appropriate pricing of urban services is that it reduces pressure on urban finances indirectly by reducing the apparent need for still more investment in underpriced infrastructure. If a service costs users nothing, they will generally want more of it, but this does not mean that cities should give it to them.

Where user charges cannot be used because the benefits of a particular service are not confined to individual consumers, taxes that are borne by local residents are an appropriate means of finance when the benefit area of the service is largely coterminous with the municipal boundary. Large cities and metropolitan areas are better able to levy taxes than smaller cities and rural municipalities. To the extent that cities rely on property tax revenues, for example, larger, more densely populated cities have a larger per capita tax base than smaller cities or rural areas, where property values are generally lower. Moreover, since commercial and industrial properties are almost always taxed at a higher rate than residential properties (Bird and Slack 2004b), large cities with a high proportion of commercial and industrial properties have greater ability to levy property taxes. Similarly, because of the higher level of economic activity, large cities and metropolitan areas have greater ability to levy income and sales taxes. Sales taxes generate significant revenues for large cities that attract people from neighboring municipalities who come to shop or work there. Indeed, sales taxes are one way to capture the benefits that commuters and visitors enjoy from using services in the municipality.

Where a consolidated one-tier (or two-tier) government covers the entire metropolitan area, the taxable capacity of the local government is larger than for each individual municipality in the region and funding of services is more equitable, because there is a wider tax base for sharing the costs of services that benefit taxpayers across the region. The larger taxable capacity of the consolidated one-tier government also increases its ability to borrow and to recover capital and operating costs from user fees. A consolidated government also provides an opportunity for better service coordination, clearer accountability, more-streamlined decision making, and greater efficiency (Bahl and Linn 1992).

Implications for Grant Design

Large cities and metropolitan areas make greater expenditures and have greater revenue-raising capacity than small cities or rural areas. This means that they can have greater fiscal autonomy than other urban or rural areas—greater responsibility for local services, greater ability to levy their own taxes and collect their own revenues (Bird 1984), and less need to rely on grants from higher levels of government. For these reasons, on a per capita basis, fewer grants to large cities and metropolitan areas should probably be made. As noted below, however, there will still be cases in which some intergovernmental transfers are needed for large cities and metropolitan areas that are providing services such as health and education, the benefits of which spill over municipal boundaries. And, as shown below, many large cities and metropolitan areas around the world still rely on grants for a significant portion of their revenues.

Types of Transfers and Rationales for Their Use

Intergovernmental transfers can take many different forms, depending on the underlying rationale for the transfer. This section describes different types of transfers and the rationales for their use in large cities and metropolitan areas.

Types of Intergovernmental Transfers

Transfers can be unconditional or conditional. Unconditional transfers can be spent on any expenditure function or used to reduce local taxes. No conditions are attached to the use of unconditional funds. In some cases, unconditional transfers are given on a per capita basis. In other cases, the amount of transfer received depends on a formula that may take account of the expenditure needs of the municipality, the size of its tax base, population, or other factors.

Conditional transfers, as the name suggests, have conditions attached to them. These transfers must be spent on specific expenditures, such as roads or parks. Conditional transfers can be lump-sum transfers (also known as block grants), which do not require the municipality to provide matching funds, or they can be matching transfers, which require the recipient to match donor funds. A donor may offer a transfer that covers 80 percent of the cost of road construction. Under this type of transfer, municipalities would have to raise the funds to cover the remaining 20 percent of the cost.

Matching grants can be open ended or closed ended. Open-ended grants have no limits placed on them. This means that whatever the recipient government chooses to spend on the function to which the grant applies, the donor will fund the specified percentage of that amount. Closed-ended grants have upper limits placed on them by the donor. This means that the donor will match funds up to a specified amount.

There are also other ways to place limits on conditional matching grants. For example, the donor can specify the amount of eligible costs. This means that the donor will match funds only for specified, predetermined expenditures.[7] Grants can also be made closed ended by requiring donor approval, either at the political level or by the bureaucracy. This requirement implicitly places a limit on the size of the grant.

Rationales for Intergovernmental Transfers

There are four main rationales for transfers from one level of government to another: vertical fiscal imbalance, horizontal fiscal imbalance, externalities, and political rationales. The type of grant that is appropriate depends on the underlying rationale.

Vertical Fiscal Imbalance

Fiscal imbalance exists when municipalities have inadequate own-source revenues to meet their expenditure responsibilities. Vertical fiscal imbalance refers to the difference between expenditures and own-source revenues at different levels of government. The resulting fiscal gap can be closed by an unconditional transfer that allows the municipality to spend the funds on whatever areas it deems appropriate.

The amount of the transfer allocated for this purpose can be determined in three ways: as a fixed proportion of the revenues of the donor government, on an ad hoc basis, or on the basis of a formula (for example, a percentage of specific local government expenditures or some other characteristics of the local governments such as population) (Bird and Smart 2002). The first option (a fixed proportion of the revenues of the donor government) is known as revenue sharing. Donor governments can allocate a proportion of their total revenue for local governments or a portion of one or more taxes (tax sharing). For example, a provincial or state government may agree to share a percentage of its personal income tax revenues with municipalities. Once the total amount of funds available for grants is determined, funds can be allocated to municipalities on the basis of where they were collected or on the basis of a formula. Tax sharing of some or all of the personal income tax is common in transition economies, such as Hungary, Poland, the Russian Federation, and Ukraine (Bird, Ebel, and Wallich 1995), where revenues are distributed on the basis of geographic origin. This means that taxes are retained by the jurisdiction in which they are collected as opposed to being distributed on the basis of a formula. Revenue sharing on a derivation basis favors richer areas, where revenue collections are the largest. If revenues are distributed on a per capita basis, richer areas give up tax revenues to poorer areas.

The advantage of revenue sharing is that the transfer to municipalities automatically increases as the yield from that revenue source increases. To be a stable source of revenue to municipalities, however, the percentage share going to municipalities has to be maintained over time. This has not been the case in some transition economies. In Bulgaria, for example, the local share of the personal income tax fell from 100 percent in 1991 to 70 percent in 1992 and 50 percent in 1993 (Bird, Ebel, and Wallich 1995). Another disadvantage of revenue sharing is that it does not enhance local autonomy, accountability, or efficiency. Local governments do not set the tax rates or the tax base, and they receive transfer funds regardless of their tax effort.

Intergovernmental transfers that are allocated annually among local governments on an ad hoc basis or through negotiations as part of the central government budgetary process are inherently more centralizing and rarely result in equity, efficiency, or stability (Boex and Martinez-Vazquez 2004). Formula-based allocation mechanisms do not guarantee that grants will be distributed in a way that is fair, efficient, or stable because central governments determine both the variables that are used in the formula and the data underlying them, which can be changed unilaterally.

From the perspective of local governments, transfers are rarely a stable or predictable revenue source. The amount of money local governments receive varies from year to year, in part depending on the fiscal state of donor governments. Lack of predictability makes it difficult for municipalities to plan expenditures. When grants decline, municipalities have to make up the lost revenue by reducing expenditures or increasing local taxes, user fees, or other revenues.

The fiscal gap can be closed in ways other than a transfer to the municipality. Higher-level governments can transfer additional revenue-raising powers to local governments, or they can reduce the expenditure responsibilities that local governments are required to undertake. If higher levels of government "upload" the funding of some services, for example, the expenditure responsibilities at the local level are reduced and so is the local fiscal imbalance. Alternatively, higher levels of government could allow local governments to raise revenues from additional tax sources. Large cities and metropolitan areas could be given access to more revenue sources, leaving intergovernmental transfers to fill the fiscal gap for smaller urban areas. Cities themselves could reduce their expenditures or raise their taxes to address the gap.

Although alternative ways of closing the fiscal gap exist and large metropolitan areas tend to have greater revenues than smaller cities, "few countries permit local governments to levy taxes capable of yielding sufficient revenue to meet expanding local needs" (Bird 2000, p. 114). There may thus still be a need for intergovernmental transfers for large cities and metropolitan areas to address the fiscal gap. Many large cities and metropolitan areas receive a significant portion of their revenues from intergovernmental transfers, as shown below.

Horizontal Fiscal Imbalance

Horizontal fiscal imbalance refers to the difference in resources among governments at the same level. Some municipalities are unable to provide an adequate level of service at reasonable tax rates, whereas other municipalities can. This inability to provide an adequate level of service may occur because the cost of services is higher, the need for services higher, or the tax base smaller.

Tax bases per capita differ across jurisdictions. This means that to collect the same amount of revenue, a jurisdiction with a small per capita tax base will have to levy a higher tax rate than a jurisdiction with a large per capita tax base. The composition of the tax may also affect fiscal capacity. For property taxes, for example, the proportion of taxable assessment that is residential versus commercial and industrial will affect revenue-raising ability.

Expenditures may differ across municipalities because costs may be greater in some municipalities than others or because needs differ across municipalities. This means that more tax revenues are required to provide the same level of service in some jurisdictions than in others. Needs or costs may be greater than average because of geographic location, population density, or other factors. Wages and rents are usually higher in cities with high population density, and the cost per unit to provide services increases with increasing population because of congestion (Fenge and Meier 2001). Needs may be higher for municipalities with a high proportion of low-income households, who require affordable housing and social services.[8]

Measuring need can be difficult and requires considerable data. In the absence of the necessary data, need can be measured by the size of the population (on the assumption that more people means greater need for expenditures) and by using a separate formula for different types of local governments based on size, type, region, and whether it is urban or rural (Shah 2004). This method is used in Colombia and Morocco to measure general expenditure needs. It is also used in the province of New Brunswick (Canada), where municipalities are grouped into six categories according to population size and whether they are urban, suburban, or rural.

Equalization grants, based on expenditure needs and the ability of local governments to levy taxes, can ensure that municipalities with small tax bases and greater costs and needs will be able to levy tax rates that are comparable to other jurisdictions. Generally, the formula calculates the difference between a standardized expenditure and a standardized revenue base. Standardized expenditures are calculated by a standard level of per capita expenditure multiplied by the population of the municipality; standardized revenues are calculated by multiplying a standard tax rate by the tax base of the municipality.

The design of an equalization grant requires a definition of a "standard" or "comparable" level of service. It could be a minimum level, an average level, the level of the highest expenditure municipality, or some standard that reflects an adequate level of service. The problem with any formula that uses standard expenditures is that the "standard" may not adequately recognize differences in needs and costs. Similarly, the standard tax rate could reflect the tax rate of the richest municipality, the average of all municipalities, or some other number.

The amount of equalization will depend on the choice of the standard expenditure and the standard tax rate. The available funds, however, are generally less than the amount required to achieve full equalization. In most countries, budgetary constraints prevent governments from applying full equalization, as Bird and Smart (2002) note. Because they generally equalize up to the "average" rather than the "richest" municipality, municipalities with lower-than-average fiscal capacity remain somewhat disadvantaged.

Large metropolitan areas in most countries should not receive equalization grants, except perhaps in the form of capitation payments for such nationally important but locally provided services as education and health (Bird and Fiszbein 1998). Large metropolitan areas generally have much larger (per capita) tax bases than smaller urban or rural areas because of greater economic activity and higher densities of residential, commercial, and industrial development. Of course, on the expenditure side the costs of services and the need for services may be higher than in other urban areas, but in most countries the cost differences seem unlikely to outweigh the much greater potential tax base. The costs of services in remote areas tend to be even higher than in large metropolitan areas, because of higher transportation costs (greater distances), higher heating costs (climatic conditions), the absence of economies of scale, and other factors (Kitchen and Slack 2001). Furthermore, the use of equalization transfers to large cities will induce migration toward those cities, exacerbating congestion and further increasing the cost of providing services, as Fenge and Meier (2001) argue.

Transfers are not the only way to achieve horizontal fiscal balance. One alternative is to design the governing structure so that it covers the entire metropolitan area. In principle, by combining rich communities and poor communities, equalization can take place, at least within the metropolitan area. Such equity concerns were the main reason why the one-tier governance model was adopted in Cape Town (South Africa) in 2000 (van Ryneveld and Parker 2002). The amalgamation of the City of Toronto is another example of equalization within a metropolitan area. Six municipalities, some rich and some poor, were amalgamated in 1998. The result was a more equitable sharing of the tax base as well as some equalizing of local services so that all residents of the amalgamated city enjoy a similar level of services (Slack 2000).

Another option is regional tax sharing, which involves the sharing of tax revenues without a formal government structure. Minneapolis-Saint Paul (Minnesota) provides an example of this type of arrangement. In the early 1990s, Saint Paul had to raise taxes dramatically and cut services because of increasing social service responsibilities. At the same time, some of the richer suburbs were reducing taxes and maintaining high levels of service. The regionalization of the property tax base made the growing property wealth available to all parts of the region to meet social needs.

Under tax sharing, each city contributes 40 percent of the growth in its commercial and industrial tax base acquired after 1971 to a regional pool. This amounts to about 20 percent of the regional tax base a year. Money is distributed from this pool on the basis of inverse net commercial capacity. This method reduced the tax base disparities on a regional level from 50:1 to 12:1 (Orfield 1997).

Externalities

Grants are also appropriate where services spill over municipal boundaries (as, for example, in the case of regional highways). If the municipality providing the service bases its expenditure decisions only on the benefits captured within its jurisdiction, it may underallocate resources to the service.

One way to provide an incentive to allocate more resources to the service generating the externality is to transfer funds from a higher level of government in the form of a conditional matching grant. The grant should be conditional in that it has to be spent on the service generating the externality. It should be matching to reflect the extent of the externality. For example, if 50 percent of the benefits of highway expenditures spill over existing municipal boundaries, the matching rate should be 50 percent. The rate of grant may decline as expenditures increase, on the grounds that the externalities diminish. Although the notion of a matching rate to reflect spillovers works in theory, in practice it is difficult to measure the magnitude of spillovers for specific services (Bird 2000).

Matching grants for capital projects are particularly important for smaller municipalities, which may not have sufficient revenues and may not be able to access private capital markets easily. For this reason, they therefore require intergovernmental transfers or subsidized loans. Large cities and metropolitan areas have greater borrowing capacity that they can use to fund major infrastructure projects.

The matching rate may differ across jurisdictions, reflecting the fact that externalities are greater in some places than in others (Bird and Smart 2002). In large metropolitan areas, for example, externalities can be internalized within the jurisdiction if the regional boundaries are designed to reflect all users of the service. For services that generate externalities beyond the borders of the metropolitan area (such as education and health), it may still be appropriate to provide a transfer. Transfers from the central government may be justified for municipal functions that contribute to international competitiveness, since the benefits of an internationally competitive metropolitan area extend to the whole country.

Matching grants require that the municipalities contribute a portion of the funds to deliver the service. A uniform matching rate tends to favor richer cities, because they are better able to match funds than poorer cities, unless the grant includes an equalization component. Moreover, a matching grant will stimulate spending only if the municipality has power over expenditures and the ability to increase taxes (Bird, Ebel, and Wallich 1995). In transition economies, where local governments have limited spending discretion and limited taxing authority, matching grants are unlikely to stimulate spending or tax effort.

Conditional grants are fungible in the sense that, even though they come with strings attached, there is no guarantee that the recipient will spend the funds on what the donor government intended. This is particularly true for large cities, which are more likely to already be spending substantial funds in the area specified by the donor government. As the analysis of conditional transfers for health, education, and water projects in Colombia shows, poor municipalities are constrained by national legislation but rich municipalities are able to "reallocate their own-source revenues to undo the effects of conditionality" (Chaparro, Smart, and Zapata 2004).

Of course, in the case of large metropolitan areas, some of these externalities can be internalized within the jurisdiction if boundaries are extended to include all users of the service. Nonetheless, for services that generate externalities beyond the borders of the metropolitan area, transfers may be appropriate.

Political Rationales

In addition to the economic rationales for intergovernmental transfers, there are also political rationales, which are unlikely to be related to fiscal imbalance, externalities, or equalization. Higher-level governments may use conditional, lump-sum grants to encourage local governments to provide at least a minimum standard of service in some areas, such as road safety, ambulance services, and water and wastewater treatment. Intergovernmental transfers are often used to provide incentives for local governments to act as agents of the donor government. In this way, the donor government benefits from local management in providing a service. Conditional grants are sometimes given to acquaint local governments with services they would not have provided on their own, in the expectation that they will eventually take over funding for them and higher-level governments can withdraw (Boadway and Hobson 1993).

Transfers to large metropolitan areas may not be as necessary as they are for smaller urban and rural municipalities. To reduce or eliminate their dependence on intergovernmental transfers, other actions need to be taken. In particular, large cities need own-source revenues that match their expenditure responsibilities, so that they do not face a fiscal gap. This could mean assigning new revenue sources to them. Large cities also need an appropriate governing structure, one that ensures that costs are shared equitably across the metropolitan area and that externalities for most services are internalized. If the rationale for the grant is political, however, these alternatives probably will not work.

Getting Prices Right

Whatever the rationale for intergovernmental transfers, it is important that transfers be designed in a way that does not interfere with the efficient delivery of services. Efficient service delivery requires that those responsible for providing services have a clear mandate, adequate resources, and sufficient flexibility to make decisions and are accountable for the decisions they make (Bird and Vaillancourt 1998).

Municipal governments provide services ranging from those with "private good" characteristics (water, sewerage, garbage collection) to those with "public good" characteristics (parks, street lighting, police protection). Charging wherever possible and getting prices right is important to ensure efficient service delivery. Local governments face no incentive to use proper pricing, however, when grants cover a large proportion of operating and capital costs. Large grants for water treatment plants can reduce a municipality's incentive to use volumetric pricing to reduce the demand for water or to engage in asset management. Transfers should not be designed to discourage municipalities from charging the right price for services. As Bird and Smart (2002, p. 899) note, "the basic task in transfer design is thus to get the prices 'right' in the public sector—right, that is, in the sense of making local governments fully accountable—at least at the margin of decision making—to both their citizens and, where appropriate, to higher levels of government." This rule holds whether grants account for 90 percent of expenditures or 10 percent.

Transfers can distort local decision making. Conditional transfers require municipalities to spend the funds they receive according to guidelines set by the donor government and often require matching funds on the part of the municipality. By lowering the price of some services, a matching transfer encourages municipalities to spend more on those services. In the presence of externalities, this change in behavior may be appropriate. Where there are no externalities, however, or where the amount of the grant exceeds the amount of the externality, the resulting distortion in municipal behavior is inappropriate. As Oates (1999) notes, federal matching transfers in the United States, for example, are generally much larger than can be justified on the basis of externalities.

Transfers can reduce accountability. When two or more levels of government are funding the same service, accountability problems can arise. When users or taxpayers want to complain about a service, they are not sure which level of government is responsible for the problem. When the level of government making the spending decisions (the municipality) is not the same as the level of government that is raising the revenues to pay for them (the provincial, state, or federal government), accountability is blurred. There is no incentive to be efficient when someone else is responsible for funding. Local governments are more likely to carry out their expenditure responsibilities in a responsible manner if they are also raising the revenues to pay for them.

It is important to design the formula in a way that does not discourage municipalities from collecting own-source revenues or finding other ways of balancing their revenues and expenditures, such as through municipal amalgamation or other ways of sharing costs. Bryson, Cornia, and Wheeler (2004) illustrate the potential moral hazard associated with grants from higher levels of government with examples from the Czech Republic and the Slovak Republic. Since the split, property taxes as a percentage of total local government revenues have been much higher in the Slovak Republic (16 percent of revenues) than in the Czech Republic (2 percent of revenues). The authors attribute much of this difference to the much higher grants to municipalities in the Czech Republic (30 percent of local government revenues compared with only 7–17 percent in the Slovak Republic). They caution against central government transfers that merely offset revenues that municipalities could have raised locally.

Grants to Large Cities and Metropolitan Areas

It has been argued to this point that large cities and metropolitan areas are different from small cities and rural municipalities in terms of both their expenditure needs and their ability to raise revenues. This means that they can and should have greater fiscal autonomy than their smaller and rural counterparts and rely less on intergovernmental transfers and more on own-source revenues. Notwithstanding the argument for greater local fiscal autonomy, grant formulas in a number of countries favor large cities and metropolitan areas. Moreover, many local governments in large cities and metropolitan areas rely fairly heavily on intergovernmental transfers.

The first part of this section reviews some empirical studies on how the type and size of a municipality affect the magnitude of intergovernmental transfers. The second part describes intergovernmental transfers in a few selected cities to show that the magnitude and type of grants vary depending on the nature and size of expenditures a city is responsible for, the types of nongrant revenue sources available to it, its fiscal capacity, its location within a regional government structure, and historical and other factors (such as whether it is a capital city).

Empirical Studies of the Incidence of Intergovernmental Transfers

Matching grants are expected to favor large cities and metropolitan areas that are able to match funds; equalization grants are expected to favor poorer, smaller areas with low fiscal capacity. In fact, the incidence of grants is not always as intended or expected. Moreover, few empirical studies of intergovernmental transfers address whether large cities and metropolitan areas receive fewer or more grants than smaller cities and rural municipalities. Some studies analyze how grants vary with expenditure levels and revenue-raising capacity of local governments and with population.

A review of empirical studies on intergovernmental transfers in 12 countries concludes that local expenditure needs, local fiscal capacity, political influence, and population size all play important roles in determining the allocation of grants (Boex and Martinez-Vazquez 2004).[9] The authors concluded that population influenced the allocation of grants with "impressive consistency." In each of the studies they reviewed, local governments with a larger population received significantly fewer per capita grants. The authors point out that many formula-based grants explicitly favor smaller local governments by including an "equal shares" component or lump-sum amount, so that local governments receive the same grant regardless of their population size. The grant that smaller cities receive is thus larger in per capita terms.

Why per capita grants are larger for smaller municipalities is not clear. Boex and Martinez-Vazquez (2004) suggest that it may reflect the fact that donor governments believe that there are economies of scale in the delivery of local services and thus include an equal shares component in the formula. An alternative explanation is that smaller local governments are favored for political reasons.

A study of transfers in Tanzania indicates that urban areas with major expenditure responsibilities receive larger grants, even though they have greater fiscal capacity than rural areas (Boex 2003). Urban local governments in Tanzania likely have a greater need for expenditures, since they serve a broader function as regional hubs. Residents from the surrounding rural area benefit from urban amenities, such as municipal markets, and a significant number of out-of-district students attend urban public schools. Even though urban areas are considerably wealthier than rural areas and collect larger amounts of own-source revenues, the system of transfers in Tanzania has favored urban areas.[10]

An empirical study of state and local transfers in two U.S. states indicates that, other things being equal, per capita grants are negatively related to metropolitan location (represented by a dummy variable) in Georgia (that is, per capita grants are lower in counties with a metropolitan location than in counties without a metropolitan location). The result did not hold in New York State, where the metro dummy was not significant (Bahl and Wallace 2003).[11]

Empirical estimates for 70 major cities in the United States indicate that states provide more grant assistance to cities with greater fiscal need (measured by a standardized needs-capacity gap) (Yinger and Ladd 1989). An earlier study by the same authors suggests, however, that very large cities and cities with relatively poor residents are in much poorer fiscal health than other cities even after state grants (Ladd and Yinger 1989).

A study of the local response to provincial-local transfers in Ontario (Canada) concludes that an increase in population is accompanied by an increase in unconditional grants (Slack 1980). In other words, larger municipalities receive larger unconditional transfers. The study did not differentiate among types of municipalities.

The few studies reviewed here yield inconsistent results in terms of whether larger local governments receive larger per capita grants than smaller local governments. With few exceptions, the studies do not differentiate by type of local government (large city, rural municipality, and so forth). More analysis is needed on a city-by-city basis to draw conclusions about differences in grants to large cities and metropolitan areas. As Bahl and Wallace (2003) note, however, the data necessary to undertake this type of analysis are rarely available in developing countries or transition economies. Even in developed countries, it can be difficult to find comparable information on the revenues and expenditures of individual cities.[12]

Intergovernmental Transfers to Selected Cities

It is difficult to compare grants to large cities with those to smaller cities or rural areas without information on all of the municipalities in each country. For this reason, the information presented below gives only an idea of the types of grants made to specific large cities and their magnitude. Even within the category of large cities, the role of intergovernmental transfers varies. The examples are intended to highlight differences in the dependence on grants because of differences in expenditure responsibilities and differences in own-source revenues. Examples of capital cities highlight why they are a special case.

Differences Based on Expenditure Responsibilities

A city that is required to make a wide variety of expenditures will have a greater need for grants than a city that provides a more limited range of services, other things being equal. Where a city is providing services that spill over the municipal boundary, conditional matching transfers are justified.

Toronto provides an example of a city that delivers a wide range of services, some of which (social assistance, social housing, public health) spill over the municipal boundary. Toronto is the largest city in Canada, with a population of 2.5 million people. In 2003 the city's operating expenditures were almost Can\$7.4 billion (Can\$2,975 per capita).[13] Provincial grants to the city in 2003, largely conditional grants, accounted for 17.6 percent of total revenues. The high proportion of revenues from grants is directly related to Toronto's responsibility to pay part of the costs of social services and public health. The provincial government pays a significant share of these costs in the form of a conditional grant.

Sydney (Australia) provides very few services at the local level. Many services typically considered local are provided by the state (or federal) government. Public order and safety are largely a state responsibility, education is largely a state responsibility with some federal expenditures made as well, health expenditures are shared between the federal and state governments, and social security and welfare expenditures are almost entirely federal. For this reason, state grants represent a fairly small portion of Sydney's total revenues. Total local government expenditures for the Sydney metropolitan area were \$A2.3 billion in 2002, or \$A627 per capita. Transfers accounted for 11.7 percent of revenues. The largest proportion of state grants is for general-purpose intergovernment transactions, followed by road transport and other community development.

A comparison of revenues and expenditures of 10 large and medium-size cities in the United States and one large and one medium-size city in Canada in 2000 found that per capita expenditures were higher in large cities (Slack 2003). Per capita federal transfers tended to be greater for the large cities. Per capita state transfers were generally higher in the large cities as well (with the exception of Atlanta). In the Canadian cities, federal transfers were negligible in both the large city (Toronto) and the medium-size city (London); provincial transfers were roughly comparable in the two cities. This result may suggest that the federal government in the United States plays a greater role in assisting larger cities, where wealth is generated.

In several countries, large cities receive transfers to compensate for the higher costs of producing services or to address spillovers of services into neighboring jurisdictions. In Germany, for example, the fiscal equalization system assumes that city-states have requirements that are in addition to those borne by states. For this reason, the formula for equalization transfers weights the population of city-states at 135 percent of the population of states. In Austria the population of cities with more than 50,000 people is weighted at 233 percent before interregional transfers are calculated (Fenge and Meier 2001). In Australia the high-density population in the Australian National Capital Territory is weighted at 110 percent.

Differences Based on Own-Source Revenues

Reliance on intergovernmental transfers also differs across cities depending on the other sources of revenue available to them. London, England, for example, has few revenue-raising tools at the local level and thus depends heavily on intergovernmental transfers. The Greater London Authority, with a population of 7.4 million, derives its revenues largely from central government grants (63 percent of revenues in 2003/04), followed by user fees (20 percent), property taxes (11 percent), and other miscellaneous revenues (6 percent). The largest portion of the Greater London Authority budget is for transport (54 percent of total expenditures), followed by police (36 percent), fire and emergency planning (5 percent), and economic development (4.5 percent). London's local and regional governments can levy a residential property tax (known as the council tax) and a number of user fees. The nonresidential property tax (nondomestic rate) is set by the central government, with revenues distributed to municipalities as a grant on a per capita basis.

London also receives much higher grants per capita than other parts of the United Kingdom. In 2002/03 grants (including the revenue support grant, business rates, and specific grants) were £1,451 per capita, compared with £992 per capita for local authorities in the rest of the country. Although part of this difference reflects the fact that per capita expenditures are also much higher in London, it also means that "even a city as large and important as London must bid for the resources it needs to Whitehall departments" (London School of Economics and Political Science 2004, p. 64). In general, grants as a percentage of local revenues in the United Kingdom far exceed what can be justified in terms of the presence of externalities or the need to equalize payments to local authorities with relatively high expenditure needs per capita and relatively low resources per capita (Bailey 2005).

Chicago (Illinois) relies less on intergovernmental transfers than London does, but it still relies on federal and state transfers. Chicago spends about $6.3 billion, or about one-third of all government expenditures in the state (Illinois Office of the Comptroller 2003). The city has access to many different types of taxes. It collects locally imposed taxes (property, sales, utility, and other local taxes), which account for 47.4 percent of its revenues, and receives revenues from state taxes (income, sales, motor fuel, and other state taxes), which account for 10.9 percent of its revenues. Fees, charges, and other revenues account for 18.3 percent of revenues. This leaves intergovernmental transfers (mainly federal rather than state grants), which represent 23.4 percent of total revenues. Large cities in the United States receive considerable funding from the federal government. In 2002 local governments in Illinois reported receiving $1.3 billion from the federal government, $1 billion of which went to the city of Chicago.[14]

The Special Case of Capital Cities

Boyd and Fauntroy (2002) look at the governance and financing of 11 national capital cities (Berlin, Bern, Brasília, Canberra, Caracas, London, Mexico City, Ottawa, Paris, Rome, and Washington, D.C.). Since national capital cities are often, but not always, the largest city in the country, this study provides some information on grants to large cities.

Of the 11 cities, 8 are capitals of countries with a federal system (Berlin, Bern, Brasília, Canberra, Caracas, Mexico City, Ottawa, and Washington, D.C.), and 3 are capitals of unitary states (London, Paris, and Rome).[15] Of the eight cities in federal countries, five are located in federal districts or territories apart from state or provincial jurisdictions (Brasília, Canberra, Caracas, Mexico City, and Washington, D.C.); two are both a city and a state (Bern and Berlin); and one (Ottawa) is comparable to other cities within a state or province. The population of the 11 cities ranges from 130,000 to 13 million.

Most national governments provide some financial support to the national capital (table 16.1). The range is from less than 1 percent of the

TABLE 16.1 Transfers to Selected National Capitals

City	Population	Percentage of city budget from central government	Form of transfer and tax powers
Berlin	3.4 million	32 (including payments from states and European Union)	Receives equalization transfers like other states (Berlin is recipient), plus direct payments for culture, infrastructure, and security. City boroughs receive funds from state government.
Bern	130,000	Less than 1 percent from national government, 40 percent from canton	Benefits from revenue sharing from Bern canton; receives small amount from federal government as reimbursement for direct services.
Brasília	2 million	72	Receives large discretionary transfer from federal government.
Canberra	315,000	46	Almost all revenue comes from various federal transfer programs.
Caracas	3.4 million	67 (estimate)	Receives special grants and support.
London	7.4 million	83	Receives general and special grants (for police and transportation).
Mexico City	13 million	39	Receives same aid as state governments but receives more from own revenues than other cities.
Ottawa	1 million	8 (federal only)	Receives payment in lieu of property taxes on federal property; also receives substantial funds from provincial government.
Paris	2.2 million	15	Receives same aid as other local governments plus special payments.
Rome	2.7 million	—	Receives same funding as other cities plus funding from the region.
Washington DC	572,000	10	Receives some special federal payments.

Source: Based on information in Boyd and Fauntroy (2002).
— Not available.

city's annual budget (Bern) to 83 percent (London). Almost all national governments reimburse the capital city for the costs arising from the presence of the national government. These costs include policing, transportation, and cultural activities. Some national governments provide payments in lieu of taxes, but these are really taxes and not grants. In six countries (Australia, Canada, France, Mexico, the United Kingdom, and the United States), the national government restricts the revenue sources of the capital city. In cities such as Berlin, Bern, and Ottawa, which are either city-states or cities within states or provinces, the main intergovernmental transfer comes from the provincial or state government rather than the federal government.

Mexico City receives no special financial assistance from the national government.[16] Brasília and Caracas and (to a limited extent) Canberra and Washington, D.C., receive assistance.[17] Berlin and Ottawa receive a federal grant in lieu of paying property taxes on federal property. Bern receives only reimbursement payments for direct services rendered. In contrast, the three unitary countries—France, Germany, and the United Kingdom—all give their capital cities specific grants for certain purposes.

Summary

There appears to be no pattern in grants to large cities around the world. Some large cities receive a fairly substantial portion of their revenues from grants, others receive only a small proportion of their revenues from grants. Some cities receive unconditional grants, some receive conditional grants, and some receive both. The reliance on grants appears to depend on the nature and magnitude of expenditures large cities are required to make and on the own-source revenues assigned to them. Capital cities are also often treated differently from other cities.

Concluding Comments

In principle, transfers should be less important for large cities and metropolitan areas than for other local governments. Indeed, there seems to be no reason why the wealthiest regions (generally, the large cities and metropolitan areas) should not be able to raise and spend most of their budgets themselves. They may have to depend partly on transfers for financing education and health, however. To reduce their dependence on intergovernmental transfers, large metropolitan areas need an appropriate governing structure, and as a rule they need more and different revenue sources. Cities require a mix of taxes, including both property taxes (for stability) and some form of income or sales tax (for elasticity).

The design of government structure can reduce the need for intergovernmental transfers. A governing structure that encompasses both rich and poor municipalities within the metropolitan area allows for some equalization within the region. Under this arrangement, in principle all municipalities within the region pay comparable taxes and receive comparable services, and fiscal disparities within the region are minimized. Moreover, some externalities are internalized within the regional structure, reducing the need for conditional grants.

Revenues from a mix of taxes would give cities more flexibility to respond to local conditions, such as changes in the economy, demographics, and expenditure needs (Slack 2005). Transfers could then be used only for those expenditures provided at the local level for services that spill over regional boundaries, such as health, education, and social services.

Very little is known about the theory or practice of intergovernmental transfers to cities of different types and sizes. This gap results, at least in part, from the lack of detailed, comparable data on municipal revenues and expenditures. If the necessary data were available, it might be possible to analyze the importance of transfers to municipalities of different types and sizes. Do large cities receive more transfers on a per capita basis than smaller cities and rural municipalities? What types of transfers do they receive? How do they use those transfers? Why do some municipalities receive higher per capita grants than other municipalities? Do higher grants reflect greater expenditure needs or less fiscal capacity, or do they reflect political considerations? More empirical work on intergovernmental transfers for large cities and metropolitan areas, medium-size cities, small cities, and rural municipalities would help answer these questions.

Notes

1. The literature on fiscal federalism assigns three roles to government: stabilization, income redistribution, and resource allocation. Stabilization policy is generally not considered to be an appropriate function of local governments, because they do not have access to monetary policy and because capital and labor flow freely across local jurisdictions. In the case of redistribution, local efforts to address income disparities will likely result in the movement of high-income groups to low-tax areas and low-income groups to high-tax areas. Nevertheless, local governments do engage in redistribution through the act of taxing and spending. See Bird and Slack (1993) for a discussion of the role of local government.

2. This provision of local services does not mean that the municipality has to produce the goods and services itself; the role of local government is to make decisions about which services to provide and how to provide them. Municipalities could, for example, contract out service delivery to another government or to the private sector.

As Osborne and Gaebler (1992) note, local governments need to concentrate more on "steering" (policy making) and less on "rowing" (service delivery).

3. To the extent that the local government can take advantage of economies of scale in service provision, there may be opportunities for lower expenditures per capita for metropolitan services. Economies of scale occur where the per unit cost of producing a service falls as the quantity of the service provided increases. Empirical evidence on the existence of economies of scale is mixed, depending on the service in question and the units of measurement (for example, jurisdiction size or size of the facility) (Hermann and others 1999). There is some evidence that expenditures per capita decline with the quantity provided for "hard" services, such as water, sewerage, and transportation but not for "soft" services, such as police, garbage collection, recreation, or planning (Bird and Slack 1993).

4. The poverty rate in Toronto in 2000 was 22.6 percent, compared with 16.7 percent for the Greater Toronto Area. (Statistics Canada, Census 2001).

5. Expenditures on roads, however, are higher in suburban municipalities, where reliance on automobiles is much greater.

6. Relatively simple pricing systems, such as low initial "life-line" charges for the first block of service use, can deal with any perceived inequity from introducing more-adequate pricing systems.

7. This form of cost sharing can be a problem when the recipient government claims that the donor is not paying its fair share of its costs and the donor claims that the recipient's costs are too high and therefore not eligible for more grant funding.

8. Of course, per capita expenditures could be higher, because of inefficient spending by some municipalities. If inefficiency is the reason for higher expenditures, it will be rewarded by the grant.

9. The 12 countries are Argentina, Australia, Brazil, Indonesia, Israel, Japan, Mexico, Nigeria, the Russian Federation, Tanzania, Uganda, and the United States.

10. The current system of transfers in Tanzania is being replaced.

11. This study also provides an empirical analysis of intergovernmental grants in two provinces in China and one oblast in the Russian Federation. There are no regressions of per capita grants on population or metropolitan location in those analyses, however.

12. In Canada, for example, each province collects comparable revenue and expenditure data for cities within the province, but there are no comparable data for cities countrywide, even though every city files a financial statement.

13. Capital expenditures were Can$904 million in 2003.

14. The U.S. Department of Housing and Urban Development provides federal funds to cities for empowerment zone initiatives, community development block grants, brownfield redevelopment, homeownership, homeless assistance, and other programs. The U.S. Treasury provides tax credits to spur development in low- and moderate-income communities, a low-income housing credit, and other initiatives. The U.S. Department of Justice funds an initiative to fight crime. The U.S. Department of Transportation provides funds for transportation and programs to help low-income people get to work. The U.S. Small Business Administration provides borrowing assistance for small businesses. The U.S. Environmental Protection Agency, through its Better America Bonds program, provides tax credits to support a new financing tool for state and local governments to clean up abandoned industrial sites,

preserve green space, and so forth. The U.S. Department of the Interior provides funds to protect and preserve the environment (Federation of Canadian Municipalities 2001).

15. Bern is the capital of a confederation of cantons.

16. For many years Mexico City received substantial federal financial support for services such as transport (Bird and Slack 2004a).

17. Washington, D.C., cannot levy taxes on the income earned by the two-thirds of its work force that live in the adjacent states of Maryland and Virginia, and it is not allowed to charge tolls on the bridges entering the city. The federal government does not pay taxes on the very large amount of real property it owns in the city, and it does not reimburse the city adequately for the many local services it utilizes (O'Cleireacain and Rivlin 2002).

References

Bahl, Roy, and Johannes Linn. 1992. *Urban Public Finance in Developing Countries.* New York: Oxford University Press.

Bahl, Roy, and Sally Wallace. 2003. "Fiscal Decentralization: The Provincial-Local Dimension." In *Public Finance in Developing and Transitional Countries* (Essays in Honour of Richard Bird), ed. Jorge Martinez-Vazquez and James Alm, 5–34. Cheltenham, United Kingdom: Edward Elgar.

Bailey, Stephen. 2005. "Equalisation of Municipal Input Costs in England: Matters of Principle and Practice." *Environment and Planning C: Government and Policy* 23 (1): 85–100.

Bird, Richard M. 1984. *Intergovernmental Finance in Colombia.* Final Report of the Mission on Intergovernmental Finance. Harvard University Law School, Cambridge, MA.

———. 2000. "Setting the Stage: Municipal and Intergovernmental Finance." In *The Challenge of Urban Government: Policies and Practices*, ed. M. Freire and R. Stren, 113–28. Washington, DC: World Bank Institute.

———. 2001. "User Charges in Local Government Finance." In *The Challenge of Urban Government: Policies and Practices*, ed. M. Freire and R. Stren, 171–82. Washington, DC: World Bank Institute.

Bird, Richard M., Robert D. Ebel, and Christine I. Wallich. 1995. "Fiscal Decentralization: From Command to Market." In *Decentralization of the Socialist State: Intergovernmental Finance in Transition Economies*, ed. Richard M. Bird, Robert D. Ebel, and Christine I. Wallich, 1–67. Washington, DC: World Bank.

Bird, Richard M., and Ariel Fiszbein. 1998. "Colombia: The Central Role of the Central Government in Fiscal Decentralization." In *Fiscal Decentralization in Developing Countries*, ed. Richard M. Bird and François Vaillancourt, 172–205. Cambridge: Cambridge University Press.

Bird, Richard M., and Barbara D. Miller. 1989. "Taxes, Pricing and the Poor." In *Government Policy and the Poor in Developing Countries*, ed. Richard M. Bird and Susan Horton, 49–80. Toronto: University of Toronto Press.

Bird, Richard M., and Enid Slack. 1993. *Urban Public Finance in Canada*, 2nd ed. Toronto: John Wiley and Sons.

————. 2004a. "Fiscal Aspects of Metropolitan Governance." Paper prepared for the Inter-American Development Bank, Washington, DC.

————. 2004b. *International Handbook on Land and Property Taxation.* Cheltenham, United Kingdom: Edward Elgar.

Bird, Richard M., and Michael Smart. 2002. "Intergovernmental Fiscal Transfers: International Lessons for Developing Countries." *World Development* 30 (6): 899–912.

Bird, Richard M., and François Vaillancourt. 1998. "Fiscal Decentralization in Developing Countries: An Overview." In *Fiscal Decentralization in Developing Countries,* ed. Richard M. Bird and François Vaillancourt, 1–48. Cambridge: Cambridge University Press.

Boadway, Robin W., and Paul A.R. Hobson. 1993. *Intergovernmental Fiscal Relations in Canada.* Canadian Tax Paper 96, Canadian Tax Foundation, Toronto.

Boex, Jameson. 2003. "The Incidence of Local Government Allocations in Tanzania." Working Paper 03–11, Georgia State University, Andrew Young School of Policy Studies, International Studies Program, Atlanta, GA.

Boex, Jameson, and Jorge Matinez-Vazquez. 2004. "The Determinants of the Incidence of Intergovernmental Grants: A Survey of International Experience." *Public Finance and Management* 4 (4): 454–79.

Boyd, Eugene, P., and Michael K. Fauntroy. 2002. "Washington, DC and 10 Other National Capitals: Selected Aspects of Governmental Structure." Report prepared as directed in the conference report on the District of Columbia Appropriations Act for Fiscal Year 2002 (H. Rept. 107–321), Washington, DC.

Bryson, Phillip J., Gary C. Cornia, and Gloria E. Wheeler. 2004. "Fiscal Decentralization in the Czech and Slovak Republics: A Comparative Study of Moral Hazard." *Environment and Planning C: Government and Policy* 22 (1): 103–13.

Burki, Shahid Javed, Guillermo E. Perry, and William Dillinger. 1999. *Beyond the Center: Decentralizing the State.* Washington, DC: World Bank.

Chaparro, Juan Canilo, Michael Smart, and Juan Gonzalo Zapata. 2004. "Intergovernmental Transfers and Municipal Finance in Colombia." ITP Paper 0403, University of Toronto, Joseph L. Rotman School of Management, International Tax Program.

Federation of Canadian Municipalities. 2001. "Early Warning: Will Canadian Cities Compete? A Comparative Overview of Municipal Government in Canada, the United States and Europe." Paper prepared for the National Round Table on the Environment and the Economy, Ottawa.

Fenge, Robert, and Volker Meier. 2001. "Why Cities Should Not Be Subsidized." CESifo Working Paper 546, Center for Economic Studies & Ifo Institute for Economic Research, Munich.

Florida, Richard. 2002. *The Rise of the Creative Class.* New York: Basic Books.

Freire, Mila. 2001. "Introduction." In *The Challenge of Urban Government: Policies and Practices,* ed. Mila Freire and Richard Stren, xvii–xli. Washington, DC: World Bank Institute.

Hermann, Zoltán, M. Tamás Horváth, Gábor Péteri, and Gábor Ungvári. 1999. *Allocation of Local Government Functions: Criteria and Conditions. Analysis and Policy Proposals for Hungary.* Fiscal Decentralization Initiative for Central and Eastern Europe, Washington, DC.

Illinois Office of the Comptroller. 2003. *Fiscal Responsibility Report Card 2002.* Springfield.

Kitchen, Harry, and Enid Slack. 2001. "Providing Public Services in Remote Areas." World Bank, Washington, DC.

Ladd, Helen, F., and John Yinger. 1989. *America's Ailing Cities: Fiscal Health and the Design of Urban Policy*. Baltimore, MD: Johns Hopkins University Press.

London School of Economics and Political Science. 2004. *London's Place in the United Kingdom Economy 2004*. London.

Nowlan, David 1994. "Local Taxation as an Instrument of Policy." In *The Changing Canadian Metropolis: A Public Policy Perspective*, vol. 2, ed. Frances Frisken, 799–837. Berkeley, CA: Institute of Governmental Studies Press.

Oates, Wallace E. 1999. "An Essay on Fiscal Federalism." *Journal of Economic Literature* 37 (3): 1120–49.

O'Cleireacain, Carol, and Alice M. Rivlin. 2002. "A Sound Fiscal Footing for the Nation's Capital: A Federal Responsibility." Brookings Institution, Washington, DC.

OECD (Organisation for Economic Co-operation and Development). 1996. "The Knowledge-Based Economy." In *Science, Technology and Industry Outlook*, 229–56. Paris: Organisation for Economic Co-operation and Development.

Office of the Deputy Prime Minister. 2002. "Local Government Finance in England: Key Facts and Trends." *Local Government Financial Statistics, England*, No. 13, London.

Office of the Prime Minister. 2003. "London Analytical Report." Prime Minister's Strategy Unit, London.

Orfield, Myron. 1997. *Metropolitics: A Regional Agenda for Community and Stability*. Washington, DC: Brookings Institution Press and Cambridge, MA.: Lincoln Institute of Land Policy.

Osborne, David, and Ted Gaebler. 1992. *Reinventing Government: How the Entrepreneurial Spirit Is Transforming the Public Sector*. Reading, MA.: Addison-Wesley.

Petersen, Patricia. 1995. "One Man's Meat Is Another Man's Poison: The Disadvantages of Being a City-State in the Federal Republic of Germany." Paper prepared for the American Political Science Association Annual Meeting, Chicago, August.

Shah, Anwar. 2004. "Fiscal Decentralization in Developing and Transition Economies: Progress, Problems, and the Promise." World Bank Policy Research Working Paper 3282, Washington, DC.

Slack, Enid. 1980. "Local Fiscal Response to Intergovernmental Transfers." *Review of Economics and Statistics* 62 (3): 364–70.

———. 2000. "A Preliminary Assessment of the New City of Toronto." *Canadian Journal of Regional Science* 23 (10): 13–29.

———. 2003. "Are Ontario Cities at a Competitive Disadvantage Compared with U.S. Cities? A Comparison of Responsibilities and Revenues in Selected Cities." Report prepared for the Institute for Competitiveness and Prosperity, Toronto, June.

———. 2005. "Easing the Fiscal Constraints: New Revenue Tools in the City of Toronto Act." Paper prepared for the Institute on Municipal Finance and Governance, University of Toronto.

Slack, Enid, Larry Bourne, and Meric Gertler. 2003. "Vibrant Cities and City-Regions: Responding to Emerging Challenges." Paper prepared for the Panel on the Role of Government, Toronto, August.

Statistics Canada. 2001. *Census of Canada 2001*. Ottawa: Statistics Canada.

van Ryneveld, Philip, and Michael Parker. 2002. "Property Tax Reform in Cape Town." In *Property Taxes in South Africa: Challenges in the Post-Apartheid Era*, ed. Michael E. Bell and John H. Bowman, 157–73. Cambridge, MA: Lincoln Institute of Land Policy.

Yinger, John, and Helen F. Ladd. 1989. "The Determinants of State Assistance to Central Cities." *National Tax Journal* 42 (4): 413–28.

17

Grants to Small Urban Governments

HARRY KITCHEN

Small urban governments come in various forms and have a wide range of spending responsibilities. Given this diversity, how should these expenditures be financed? What is the role for local taxation, user fees, and special charges? What is the role for grants from higher levels of government? Does the answer depend on the size of the municipality and the objective of higher-level governments?

This chapter examines these questions. It begins by showing how small urban areas differ from rural areas and large cities/metropolitan areas. It then identifies the major spending responsibilities of urban areas and indicates how they should be financed. The following sections examine the relative importance of grant funding for municipalities in a variety of countries and show how grants should be designed if they are to satisfy criteria for fairness, efficiency, accountability, predictability, and flexibility. The chapter then analyzes whether grants for small urban areas should differ from grants to other types of municipalities. The last section summarizes the chapter's findings.

What Is a Small Urban Area?

Small urban areas take a variety of forms and configurations. Some are contiguous with other small urban areas or with large cities and metropolitan areas. Some are spread throughout the heavily populated parts of countries, surrounded by productive agricultural land that may or may not coexist with commercial and industrial activity. In these settings, the urban area is the hub for much of the economic activity in the area. These small urban areas tend to be more prosperous than rural areas but less prosperous than large cities and metropolitan areas.

Small urban areas are often the norm in mining- and resource-based centers and in sparsely populated areas of a country. They are usually found in remote areas, isolated from other urban areas, neighboring productive agricultural land and significant commercial and industrial activity. Many of these centers are or once were one-company towns. They tend to be located in parts of countries that face harsher climatic conditions than those in more populated and urbanized parts of the country (Kitchen and Slack 2006).

Plant closures have created dying and decaying small urban areas characterized by high unemployment, a declining local tax base, and greater dependence on social service programs. In countries such as the Russian Federation, the problem is exacerbated by the fact that municipal institutions have not formed or have been slow to form because municipal services are or were provided by the major employer. Companies or enterprises often "build and support hospitals, construct and maintain housing, build and run kindergartens and preschools, and make 'voluntary donations' toward financing public transport and to extrabudgetary funds of subnational governments" (Wallich 1994, p. 39), and they provide almost all social expenditures. This practice creates a number of problems. First, company provision of these local public services represents a form of hidden taxation, because the enterprise provides services instead of paying taxes and user fees for these services. Second, the provision of public services in this way does not allow local residents to reveal their preferences. Third, expenditures on public services place a burden on enterprises and put them at a disadvantage in the market economy. (To the extent that these services are considered to be fringe benefits that are necessary to attract labor, however, the first and third points may be less relevant [Wallich 1994].) Fourth, and possibly the most serious problem, is the fact that public service provision disappears when the company terminates its operations.

Governing structures for small urban areas are a mix of single-tier and two-tier systems. In a single-tier system, each municipality is responsible for all services and local governance decisions. Frequently, these municipalities rely on intermunicipal or joint-use agreements or special purpose bodies for sharing some services (such as fire protection and road maintenance) with neighboring jurisdictions. A two-tier municipal governing structure, by comparison, consists of a number of lower-tier municipalities that are included under the umbrella of the upper-tier governing structure. Lower-tier municipalities generally include small cities, towns, villages, and townships. The upper tier is often referred to as a county, region, or district government. In a two-tier system, lower-tier municipalities assume responsibility for specific services; the nature of these services varies considerably across and even within countries. For some services, lower-tier governments rely on intermunicipal agreements. The upper tier is responsible for the remaining services. The upper tier is generally more self-sufficient than the lower-tier government and much less dependent on intermunicipal agreements.

Canada has a mix of single-tier and two-tier local governing systems, with two-tier systems more common. Local governments in Australia and the United Kingdom are predominantly single tier. As part of its municipal reform, the Russian Federation is moving toward a two-tier system of local government. No single governing structure predominates; what works in some countries may not work in others.

What Are the Expenditure Responsibilities of Small Urban Areas?

Small urban areas generally have more responsibilities than rural areas but fewer expenditure responsibilities than large cities and metropolitan areas (Asensio 2006; Bahl and Linn 1992). Large cities and metropolitan areas serve a much larger and more densely concentrated population (Freire 2001), and their local public sector provides a wider range of social and economic services to satisfy a more heterogeneous population (Nowlan 1994). Their local governments generally provide more-sophisticated transportation systems and communication networks as well as better parks, recreational facilities, and cultural institutions (Bird and Slack 2004). In some countries, such as Kenya, large cities are responsible for health and education, while smaller urban centers are not (Kelly 2005). Large urban areas tend to attract low-income people seeking better employment, better educational opportunities, and greater access to a wider range of social services, social housing, and public health (Bird and Slack 2004; Lotz 2006).

Expenditure responsibilities of urban areas vary widely across countries. Much of this variation can be attributed to the types of expenditures assigned to local governments. In Chile, Tanzania, and Uganda, the municipal sector is responsible for education and health (Kelly 2005; S. Letelier 2006). Local spending and its funding in these countries differs from that in countries such as Canada and New Zealand, where education and health are the responsibility of higher levels of government (Kitchen 2002; Dollery 2006). In some countries (Canada, the United Kingdom), police are a local responsibility; in others (France, New Zealand), they are the responsibility of a higher level of government.

Considerable variations in spending patterns are also evident within countries, especially where some have public transit systems and others do not, either because their urban density does not warrant it or because they cannot afford it. Some small urban areas have cultural facilities, public libraries, and recreational programs, while others do not. Small urban areas that function within a single-tier governing structure have a wider range of responsibilities and larger expenditures than small urban areas that function as a lower tier within a two-tier local government structure.

Small urban areas that are vibrant and prosperous have stronger local revenue bases, and they may have stronger expenditure desires than small urban areas in which the revenue base is declining. The expenditure needs of small urban areas that are contiguous to one another or adjacent to larger cities or metropolitan areas may differ from those of isolated urban areas located in sparsely populated areas.

How Should Expenditures Be Financed?

In both developed and developing countries, expenditure responsibilities and access to local tax sources and intergovernmental grants for small urban areas are tightly legislated, regulated, and controlled by higher levels of government. Their spending responsibilities and financing instruments are thus best addressed through the principal-agent model of intergovernmental finance (Bird and Chen 1998; Kitchen 2000). In this model, the higher level of government is the principal and small urban areas (municipalities) are the agents. The principal has the power to change the agents' jurisdictional boundaries, their revenue sources, and their expenditure responsibilities. It can also change the fiscal arrangements it maintains with its agents in order to reconcile its objectives with their objectives. The agents' role is to provide and fund services that benefit local constituents. Consequently, all financing instruments should be addressed on the basis of benefits received. The underlying principle of the benefits received model is straightforward: those who benefit from local public services should pay for them (Duff 2003).

This model can satisfy five important criteria: efficiency, accountability, transparency, fairness, and ease of administration.

■ *Economic or allocative efficiency:* Economic or allocative efficiency is achieved when the tax per unit, charge, or user fee equals the marginal cost of the last unit consumed (that is, price equals marginal cost). Charges applied in this fashion are efficient for funding services for which beneficiaries can be clearly identified and costs derived. Prices or taxes ration output to those willing to pay, and they act as a signal to suppliers (local governments or their delivery agents) that allows them to determine the desired quantity and quality of public output.

■ *Accountability:* Accountability is enhanced when there is a close link between service consumption and the price or tax paid per unit consumed. When taxes and user fees are directly matched to beneficiaries, beneficiaries can determine whether the benefit from the last unit consumed is worth the price or tax paid for its consumption. Taxpayers are then in a position to apply pressure on politicians to improve the efficiency with which services are provided or to stop providing the service.

■ *Transparency:* Transparency is enhanced when citizens have access to information and decision-making forums, so that they are familiar with the way in which local tax rates, charges, and user fees are set. Transparency helps mitigate the risk of corruption by making information available and by ensuring that all public policy decisions are made in an open and transparent manner (IMF 2001).

■ *Fairness:* Fairness is achieved when those who consume public services pay for them. Concerns about the tax burden on low-income individuals should be addressed through income transfers from the provincial or federal government and social assistance programs targeted to people in need. It is far more equitable and efficient to handle income distribution issues through income transfers or targeting than to tamper with charging or taxing mechanisms to accommodate these concerns (Boadway and Kitchen 1999).

■ *Ease of administration:* The easiest financing system to administer is one that is not confusing for taxpayers to understand and requires the least time and effort to administer.

Although the benefits-based model is simple in principle, applying it is sometimes difficult. The ability or capacity to set correct taxes, charges, or user fees depends on the service. For services such as water and sewerage, where specific beneficiaries can be identified, income redistribution is not a goal, spillovers (externalities) are unlikely to exist, and all operating and capital costs can be measured and recorded, setting a fee or charge per liter of water consumed should be relatively easy. For local streets and roads, where it may be difficult to identify specific beneficiaries and local spillovers exist, correctly setting local tax rates to capture local benefits is not so easy, although it can be approximated.

Conditional grants must be spent on specific services or facilities. A matching grant is given only if the municipality agrees to cover a certain percentage of expenditures on a specific service or facility. Matching grants may be open ended or closed ended. Open-ended grants do not specify upper limits on available funds. Closed-ended grants specify upper limits, which may be explicit (by setting dollar limits) or implicit (by requiring higher-level government approval of funded expenditures or by defining eligible costs that are less than total costs) (Bird and Slack 1993). Conditional grants may be used for operating or capital purposes (Bird and Smart 2002).

Conditional grants are appropriate for funding services that generate externalities: benefits from services that spill over into neighboring communities should not be funded from local taxes. They are also appropriate for funding services in which the higher-level government has a direct interest.

Unconditional grants are grants that may be used for any purpose, including the reduction of municipal taxes. The term *unconditional* refers to the use of the grant and not to the conditions of its receipt. Payments or grants-in-lieu of taxes from higher-level governments are unconditional grants. Their receipt depends on the existence of federally and provincially owned properties within a recipient municipality, but the grant may be spent in whatever way the municipality desires. Revenue transfers generated from shared taxes can also be treated as unconditional grants (Asensio 2006). They are used to ensure that minimum service levels are funded without the imposition of excessively high tax rates on local taxpayers.

How Important Are Grants?

The extent to which the municipal sector relies on grant support to meet its expenditure commitments varies across and sometimes within countries (table 17.1).

The wide variance in reliance on grants is due to a number of factors, not the least of which is the spending responsibilities of local governments. In countries in which local governments are responsible for the standard range of local public services plus education and health, grants tend to account for a relatively high percentage of local revenues. In countries in which local governments have relatively few spending responsibilities, grants

TABLE 17.1 Reliance on Grant Support in Selected Countries

Country	Reliance on grant support
Argentina	Conditional and unconditional transfers and tax sharing account for almost 50 percent of local government revenue (Asensio 2006).
Brazil	Grants account for more than 70 percent of municipal revenue (Afonso and Araújo 2006) and are allocated to municipalities on the basis of a formula that includes factors such as population and community size (Bird and Smart 2002).
Canada	Grants account for about 17 percent of all municipal revenues, with about 15 percentage points given as conditional grants and about 2 percentage points given as unconditional grants. Reliance on grants ranges from a low of about 6 percent in British Columbia to a high of about 26 percent in Newfoundland (Kitchen 2004a).
Colombia	Grants account for about 50 percent of all municipal revenues. They are allocated based on a complex formula in which population is assigned a small weight and a local poverty index is assigned a much greater weight. The local poverty index tends to measure urbanization and development. It is based on many factors under the control of local government, including the extent of health and local infrastructure (Chaparro, Smart, and Zapata 2004).
France	About 48 percent of local government revenue comes from central government transfers. All transfers are formula driven and almost totally in the form of block grants with no strings attached. About 3 percent of grant revenue is in the form of specific grants coming directly from a variety of government ministries (Prud'homme 2006).
Japan	Specific-purpose grants account for about 15 percent of all local revenues; unconditional grants have little, if any, relevance. All transfers are automatic and formula driven, with formulas taking into account such factors as population and community size. Nearly all grants are given as block grants with no strings attached (Mochida 2006).
Kazakhstan	Transfers account for about 25 percent of all local revenues. There is considerable variation across oblasts, with the most dependent receiving 71 percent of their revenue from grants (Makhmutova 2006).
Kenya, Tanzania, and Uganda	Local grants from revenue-sharing arrangements provide more than 80 percent of total local government resources in Tanzania and Uganda and about 25 percent in Kenya. In Tanzania about 88 percent of all grant revenue is conditional, in Uganda about 95 percent is conditional, and in Kenya almost the entire grant is in the form of an unconditional block grant (Kelly 2005; Steffensen 2006).

(continued)

TABLE 17.1 Reliance on Grant Support in Selected Countries (*continued*)

Country	Reliance on grant support
Netherlands	Conditional grants account for 37 percent of all municipal spending and are generally used to finance local government expenditures imposed by the central government. Some grants are available to all municipalities, and some are provided only to larger cities. Unconditional grants finance 30 percent of municipal spending and are allocated to municipalities according to a detailed set of more than 40 criteria, set to minimize fiscal disparities and a municipality's ability to influence their share. The same unconditional grant formula applies to all municipalities, although the four largest municipalities seem to be treated more generously. General-purpose grants do not depend on expenditure needs (Allers 2004).
New Zealand	Conditional grants account for 10–11 percent of all local revenues (Dollery 2006). Unconditional grants are almost nonexistent.
Nordic countries	Grants account for 29 percent of total revenue, with the bulk of the grants conditional. Equalization grants are based on both expenditure needs and tax capacity, with richer municipalities contributing to poorer municipalities. The central government plays no role in equalization (Lotz 2006).
South Africa	Grants account for about 11 percent of total operating income. There is considerable variation in the extent to which municipalities depend on grants: smaller poor urban areas and rural municipalities are almost totally dependent on grants, whereas large cities receive relatively little grant support (Heymans 2006).
United Kingdom	General grants account for about 22 percent of local revenue and conditional grants for about 23 percent (King 2006).
United States	No general-purpose federal transfers are provided, and there are no federal programs to equalize the fiscal capacities of subnational governments. Each state transfers revenues to local governments in its own way. Some states provide formula-based allocations, based on a wide variety of formula, for general-purpose or specific-purpose expenditures. Some provide categorical grants, with and without matching requirements (Schroeder 2006).

Source: Author compilation.

are much less important as a source of local revenue. In countries in which the central or national government requires local governments to deliver certain services at minimum standards or to satisfy national criteria or meet national objectives, conditional grants play a more important role as a local revenue source. In countries in which national or provincial/state governments have implemented policies to equalize fiscal capacity of local governments, unconditional grants are an important source of local revenue. In a few countries (France, Japan), grants are automatic and formula driven (Prud'homme 2006; Mochida 2006). In most countries, a mix of formula-based and discretionary grants are provided. In some countries, grant schemes are complicated; in others they are relatively simple and straightforward. In a few countries (Brazil, Chile, South Africa), rural and small poor urban areas are heavily dependent on grants, while cities and metropolitan areas receive relatively little grant support (Heymans 2006; S. Letelier 2006; Afonso and Araújo 2006). In the Nordic countries, equalization grants recognize both expenditure needs and fiscal capacity (Lotz 2006); in many other countries, only fiscal capacity is recognized. Equalization in the Nordic countries is from rich municipalities to poor municipalities and not from the donor government to poor municipalities, as is the practice in most countries. In some countries where expenditures are a component in the transfer scheme, expenditures tend to be based on actual costs rather than needs.

Why Are Grants Provided?

There are two primary rationales for providing grants to local governments, an economic rationale and a political rationale. The economic rationale argues that transfers are justified to correct misallocations of resources that arise from interjurisdictional externalities (spillovers), to close fiscal gaps or remove the vertical imbalance that arises if local authorities' expenditure requirements exceed their ability to raise revenues, and to reduce disparities (horizontal imbalances) among local governments in their ability to provide local services (equalization) (Boadway and Hobson 1993). The political rationale argues that grants provide the donor government with a means to realize particular objectives.

Economic Rationale

Benefits or services provided by municipal governments often extend beyond their jurisdictional boundaries. In such a case, a local government will generally spend too little on the service, because it considers only the value of the benefits to its own residents, not those received by people outside their jurisdiction. One way to encourage the jurisdiction to take account of all benefits is to provide a grant equal to the value of the spillover. For example, if 25 percent of the benefits spill over to people outside the municipality, the grant would have a matching rate of 25 percent.

This situation is best addressed by employing a conditional matching grant. This type of grant differs from an unconditional grant in that it alters the relative price (in terms of the demands on locally raised revenues) of providing municipal services. Conditional matching grants create incentives for municipalities to spend on grant-funded services or facilities rather than on services or facilities that are not funded by grants. The impact of this incentive may depend on whether the grant is open ended or closed ended. An open-ended grant (no upper limit) tends to stimulate local spending more than a closed-ended grant (fixed upper limit). A fixed upper limit for grant support means that the price of undertaking expenditures at the limit is borne entirely by the municipality, because the recipient government is likely to ignore further spillover benefits and will select an expenditure level that is consistent with marginal cost pricing for that municipality alone. That is, a municipality's spending will stop at the point at which the perceived marginal gain to its citizens equals the marginal cost of the expenditures. If, however, the upper limit is not fixed, an incentive exists for additional spending.

This rationale may be more appropriate for some urban areas than for others. It will almost certainly be less applicable to large cities, metropolitan areas, and upper-tier governments in two-tier governing structures, because these units of government are large enough to internalize many of their externalities. The rationale may not be applicable to small urban areas in remote or sparsely populated parts of the country, which are too far away from other areas to produce spillover effects. Externalities are more likely to exist in urban areas that are contiguous (but with independent governing structures) or near one another. Grants may be necessary if the impact of these externalities is to be internalized and taken into consideration in determining service levels.

A serious practical problem with this rationale is the difficulty of obtaining adequate information in a form that is usable. This problem affects governments in both developing and developed countries. How is the degree of externality measured? What is the response to differential matching rates for services that may be partially funded by conditional grants? Are local governments sufficiently constrained by the rules and regulations imposed by higher levels of government so that they have little or no local tax autonomy or flexibility with which to respond to grant incentives? Do local governments, particularly in developing countries, have accounting and budgeting systems that accurately report the costs required for grant purposes?

Whatever the theoretical merits of conditional grants, practical difficulties have led to an array of conditional transfers that are so detailed, complex and unrelated to externalities that their use has led to ineffective local governments in many countries (Bird and Smart 2002).

Grants are also justified in the case of fiscal gaps. A fiscal gap is created when there is a mismatch in the own-source revenues and expenditure responsibilities assigned to local governments (that is, when the expenditure needs of a municipality exceed its ability to raise revenues from local sources). The gap could be filled by transferring additional or new revenue-raising powers to local governments, by transferring some expenditure responsibilities to a higher level of government, or by reducing local expenditures or raising local revenues. But these possibilities are often ignored. Instead, grants from a higher-level government are used to fill the gap.

When such transfers are used, they should take the form of unconditional per capita (or per household) grants, often called "block grants." Block funding is used in many countries for all types of municipalities. It generally avoids the problems created by conditional grants. Furthermore, block grants that are equal in per capita dollars often provide proportionately more revenue for rural and poor small urban areas than they do for large cities, metropolitan areas, and rich small urban areas. This can help equalize the ability of local governments to deliver comparable local service levels (Chaparro, Smart, and Zapata 2004).

In a benefits-based model of municipal finance, one can argue that there is no role for intergovernmental equalization grants to address income distribution objectives. Government to government grants subsidize the cost of municipal services for both rich and poor individuals and households—a consequence that is generally not desired when income redistribution is a goal. In this view, income redistribution objectives should be achieved by providing grants from donor governments to targeted low-income individuals or households, not to municipal governments (Boadway and Kitchen 1999).

Grants to municipal governments distort economic decisions, because they create a wedge between the tax price or user fee paid for municipal services and the cost of providing them. The result of this subsidization may be an overproduction of municipal services. Grants may also discourage local taxpayers (residents and businesses) from leaving decaying or stagnating municipalities or migrating to municipalities where resources might be allocated more efficiently and where there may be better opportunities for employment and education.

Should small urban areas that require equalization grants to survive exist at all (Kitchen and Slack 2006; Slack, Bourne, and Gertler 2003)? Equalization grants may be justified if a municipality is essential to the provision of an important public service, such as national security. In this case, the public good benefit may justify equalization grant assistance to maintain a viable community. If this is not the case, however, policy makers must ask how far a donor government should go in supporting municipalities that are no longer viable.

If national economic efficiency is an important objective, it may be appropriate to encourage people to leave small urban areas that rely largely on equalization grants rather than provide grants that encourage them to stay. That is not to say that people should not remain in communities of this kind if they are willing to pay higher service costs; the point is simply that there may be little economic justification for grant assistance if it is needed to help these communities survive.

Politics, however, frequently leads to a different conclusion. People form emotional attachments to communities; politicians are reluctant to shut communities down and relocate their residents, even if the long-term costs of grant support are high (Kitchen and Slack 2006). As a result, equalization grants are well entrenched in provincial-municipal and territorial-municipal fiscal arrangements in a number of countries.

A major advantage—and indeed, objective—of equalization grants is that they permit municipal governments to provide "comparable" levels of service at "comparable" tax rates. There are at least three reasons why municipal governments may not be able to achieve this outcome in the absence of grants. First, local tax bases differ from one municipality to another. Consequently, a municipality with a small tax base will have to levy a higher tax rate than will a municipality with a large tax base. Second, the costs of providing public services may be higher in one municipality than in another. As a result, the first municipality will require more tax revenue than the second to provide the same level of service. Third, the need for a particular public service may be greater in one municipality than in another, with the result that the first will incur larger expenditures (and require larger revenues) than the second.

The equalization objective is satisfied through the use of unconditional grants. These grants expand local revenues without altering the relative prices of providing the various services. They thus provide no incentive to spend on some services rather than others.

Political Rationale

Donor government's objectives in providing grants may have little to do with the economic rationale. National and subnational governments use conditional grants to control local governments, to fund expenditures and programs mandated by donor governments (Lotz 2006), and to induce municipalities to act, or to reimburse them for acting, as their agents. In this way, the donor government receives the benefit of local management in providing services. Donor governments also use conditional grants to acquaint local governments and their citizens with the benefits of a new service, in the expectation that eventually it will be possible to withdraw the grant and to finance the service locally (McMillan 1995).

Higher-level governments may also wish to promote local government expenditures in certain areas while covering only a portion of total cost. Involvement of this kind may ensure that minimum service standards are met, or it may lead to some form of redistribution that the donor government regards as important even if municipalities do not. Services that higher-level governments may want local governments to provide at some minimum level include road safety, ambulance service, and water and wastewater treatment. In this context, one motive for action by higher-level governments may be concern about spillovers. Preventative health programs, local hospitals, and social services are examples of redistributional services that a higher-level government may wish to encourage. Conditional lump-sum transfers and closed-ended matching grants are the appropriate instruments in this case. Indeed, they have proven to be effective in promoting higher levels of local expenditures in funded municipalities (Gramlich 1977). This result has prompted one analyst to refer to grants of this kind as grants that in effect stretch the central budget (Bird 1993).

Conditional versus Unconditional Grants

Donor governments usually prefer conditional grants, which allow them to control local government spending, while local governments generally prefer unconditional grants, which give them the flexibility to make their own spending decisions. Both donors and recipients tend to prefer one grant over the other for reasons that may have little to do with the objective of the grant program.

The first step in determining whether a grant should be conditional or unconditional is to identify the objectives that the grant is intended to achieve. Once this is done, certain criteria may be used to determine whether the chosen type of grant will achieve the desired goal or objective.

Governments at all levels have an obligation to serve their constituents. To best serve local residents, local services must be the responsibility of the level of government that is best able to recognize and respond to their needs and preferences. Three considerations are relevant to the choice of grant type. First, there must be considerable local autonomy in the selection of services that are provided locally. This is almost never the case for small urban areas. Second, the jurisdictional responsibility for each service must be clear. Third, local politicians must be accountable to the taxpayers for their actions. The greater the local autonomy, jurisdictional clarity, and local accountability, the greater the opportunity for providing sound municipal government.

Different types of grants have different effects on local autonomy. Unconditional grants impinge less on local autonomy than do conditional grants. By allowing local decision makers to select the services on which grant revenue will be spent, unconditional grants have virtually no distortive effects on local priorities—in other words, they are efficient. In contrast, conditional grants can undermine the ability of local governments to respond to local priorities. Matching grants, whether they are open or closed ended, exert more financial leverage on local councils than do lump-sum grants. The degree of distortion and infringement on local autonomy depends on the specificity of the grant and the priority that local government officials assign to the project before the grant is received. In short, the fewer strings attached to a grant, the less it undermines local autonomy.

For each municipal service funded (or partially funded) by grants, there should be a clear assignment of jurisdictional responsibility. The grant formula should be simple enough to be easily understood by legislators and taxpayers. Unconditional grants score well in this regard. Conditional grants blur jurisdictional boundaries. By stating where and how the funds are to be spent, donor governments stake a claim to responsibility in the area to which the grant applies. Moreover, conditional grants are often very complex. Their use may leave smaller municipalities at a disadvantage, since the municipality may not be able to afford the expertise required to cope with auditing and administrative procedures associated with grant programs—or even to understand the programs. This situation is compounded if the grant system includes many conditional grants from different departments or ministries, with varying formulas and criteria for each program. The overall result may be a maze of programs and bureaucracies that waste time and money. Jurisdictional confusion and operational complexities are major drawbacks to the use of conditional grant programs.

It is critical that recipient governments be held accountable for their actions. It may be difficult under an intergovernmental transfer program to see who has jurisdictional responsibility in all program areas. As a result, taxpayers may not be sure where their tax dollars are going, whom they should turn to when they want information or assistance, or whom they should hold accountable for the program. Conditional grants in particular may make it difficult for taxpayers to express their preferences. If a grant is earmarked for a particular service, it is important to stipulate who is responsible for providing the service and who is accountable for implementing it. Unconditional grants do not seriously impede local governments' accountability for their actions.

Unconditional and conditional grants are designed to cope with very distinct and often opposing situations. Donor governments, however, frequently claim a particular objective and then use the wrong instrument to achieve it. For example, higher-level governments often justify conditional grants on the grounds that they help financially pressed local governments. In fact, unconditional grants are more appropriate for this purpose; the more appropriate use for conditional grants is the funding of spillover benefits.

Does Community Size Affect Grant Size?

Comparable cross-country data on grant funding to small urban areas versus large cities/metropolitan or rural areas are not available. Most countries use a "one size fits all" approach to structuring grant formulas and allocation schemes. Conditional grants are often the most important and are provided as long as certain conditions are met (the money must be spent on specific projects or for specific functions or services). The conditionality does not depend on the size of municipality but on the type and level of spending on the funded service. A municipality that spends proportionately more on the funded service receives proportionately more in grants.

Unconditional grants are often based on population, a poverty index, or both. They are not based on the size category of the municipality. Formula-driven equalization grants based on fiscal capacity or fiscal capacity and expenditure needs generally do not recognize community size (exceptions include Austria, Brazil, and Japan, which include community size as a component in the allocation formula).

For the provincial-municipal equalization grant program in the province of New Brunswick (Canada), each of the 103 incorporated municipalities is assigned to one of seven groups. Each group includes municipalities with similar characteristics. Measures of similarity include population size, location (remote versus more populated part of the province), spending responsibilities, and tax base. Groups include large cities, rural areas, small urban areas with a wide range of spending responsibilities, small urban areas with a narrow range of spending responsibilities, and so forth. Equalization is restricted to municipalities within each group, although the formula is identical for every group and is based on a measure of both fiscal capacity and expenditure need. There is no equalization across groups. The province gives each group a sum of money, which varies from group to group and from year to year. There is no precise allocation scheme for apportioning the grant pool to different groups. Instead, apportionment is determined by the province following discussions with municipal associations. A similar municipal equalization program (sometimes called the "silo approach") is used in some states in Germany (Kitchen 2002).

How Should Grants Be Designed?

The strongest economic rationale for conditional grants is their potential usefulness in funding the portion of benefits from local services that spill over into other jurisdictions. In practice, however, the value of the spillover is difficult, if not impossible, to measure. Indeed, donor governments generally issue conditional grants not because they are concerned about spillovers but because they wish to fulfill a particular political objective. The principles that govern the design of conditional grants differ from those governing unconditional grants.

Conditional Grants

By their nature, conditional grants are designed to provide incentives for municipalities to spend funds in specific ways or on specific projects. Conditional grants that are designed to cover the cost of externalities can be allocatively efficient (that is, neutral in their impact on municipal spending decisions). If, as is more likely, they are provided to partially support expenditure programs or projects desired by donor governments, they may be allocatively inefficient, since they will distort the spending decisions of recipient governments.

Unconditional Grants

Unconditional grants should provide equity, efficiency, predictability, flexibility, and accountability. Formula-based grants are preferred over ad hoc and discretionary grants, because they increase the likelihood of satisfying these criteria.

- *Equity:* Vertical equity is achieved when a municipality's revenue-raising capabilities are consistent with its expenditure responsibilities and needs.

A municipality whose revenue base is not large enough to meet its expenditure needs will require a grant to meet those needs. Horizontal equity exists when two municipalities with the same expenditure needs but different tax bases are able to provide a comparable level of service at comparable tax rates. The municipality with the smaller tax base or the greater need will require a grant if it is to provide services comparable to those in other municipalities.

■ *Economic efficiency:* Economic efficiency is achieved if a grant does not affect the expenditure patterns of a recipient government or if it affects spending in a way that corrects for existing distortions in expenditure practices. A grant is not efficient if a municipality can affect the size of the grant it receives by manipulating its expenditures.

■ *Predictability and flexibility:* Predictability is important because municipalities need to be able to budget and plan for the future. At the same time, grants should be flexible enough to allow municipalities to respond to changing economic circumstances.

■ *Accountability:* Accountability implies that local residents should be able to hold local government responsible for the way in which grant funds are spent. If unconditional grants enhance accountability at the local level, they may diminish it at the level of the donor government, since in passing on funds without conditions, the donor government also passes on much of the responsibility for using funds equitably and efficiently.

■ *Ease of administration:* A grant should be easy and inexpensive to administer.

In general, it is not possible to achieve all of these principles at the same time; satisfying one principle may mean sacrificing another. For this reason, it may be necessary to emphasize some criteria more than others. Most observers deem equity and economic efficiency to be the most important criteria.

Grant programs should encourage municipalities to practice fiscal restraint, reduce costs, and achieve efficiency in service delivery. Grants should not provide incentives for municipalities to spend more than they need to meet their expenditure needs. Grants should not reward inefficiency at the local level.

In designing an unconditional or equalization grant, it is necessary to decide what level of service will provide the basis for equalization across municipalities. It could be a minimum level of service, the average level, the level of the municipality with the highest expenditure, or an "adequate" level of service, however, defined. The choice of service level will determine the degree of equalization and the amount of the grant. Only equalization to the level of the municipality with the highest expenditure provides full equalization; this alternative is the most costly one for the granting government. Equalization to a minimum level provides the least equalization; it is the least costly to the donor government. Equalization to the average level is the most widely used alternative. It implies, however, that the original inequality between below-average and above-average municipalities remains, though it will be reduced.

There are three general types of unconditional transfers: per capita grants, fiscal capacity equalization grants, and expenditure/fiscal capacity equalization grants. A per capita grant provides the same amount of revenue per capita to each municipality. The larger the municipality's population, the larger its total grant. Per capita grants are generally used to close a fiscal gap or reduce a vertical fiscal imbalance. They are block grants designed without an equalization component, although they may have an equalizing effect on the ability of local governments to deliver comparable levels of service.

Per capita grants are neutral (allocatively efficient) in their effect on expenditures, because they do not distort the relative prices of providing local services. They are predictable to the extent that population is predictable, but they are not necessarily flexible. A municipality that loses population but still has the same expenditure requirements, for example, will see its grant diminish. Per capita grants are easy to understand and simple to administer. Like all unconditional grants, they lack accountability for donor governments because the donor has no control over how the money is spent.

In summary, per capita grants are relatively easy to administer but deficient in other important ways. Because they are based on population, per capita grants do not reflect expenditure needs. Furthermore, grants of this kind do not take account of a municipality's ability to raise revenues from its own sources.

Fiscal capacity grants are designed to help municipalities whose tax base per capita is less than some "standard." This standard may be defined as the average tax base per capita, the tax base per capita in the municipality with the highest tax base per capita, or some other measure. The most commonly used measure is the average tax base per capita. Of course, the composition of the local tax base may vary. In countries with a property tax, the base could include some measure of property value or property size. In countries without a local property tax, the tax base could include some other economic or income-based measure.

A fiscal capacity grant is equal to the difference between the revenues that would be collected if the standard tax rate were applied to the standard tax base and the revenues obtained by applying the standard tax rate to the actual tax base. If a municipality's tax base per capita is less than the standard for the group, the municipality receives a grant; otherwise, it does not.

The formula for a fiscal capacity grant is

$$GR^i = t^*[(B/P)^* - (B/P)^i]P^i,$$

where GR^i is the grant to municipality i, t^* is the standard tax rate, $(B/P)^*$ is the standard tax base per capita, $(B/P)^i$ is the tax base per capita in municipality i, and P^i is the population in municipality i.

This type of grant is generally preferred to a per capita grant, since the calculation of the grant includes a measure of fiscal capacity. It does not, however, include a measure of expenditure needs. A fiscal capacity grant is neutral, since municipalities cannot affect the amount of the grant by altering their expenditure or tax decisions. The grant amount is predictable to the extent that the tax base is predictable; it is flexible in the sense that it provides increased assistance if the tax base per capita falls relative to the standard. Because the tax base is uniform, the grant is fairly simple to administer. It is as accountable as the per capita grant.

Fiscal capacity grants are designed to provide assistance to municipalities whose per capita tax bases are less than the standard. The following example illustrates the impact of this type of grant. Assume that the standard, or average, tax base per capita is $1,000 and that the standard tax rate is 20 percent. If the tax base in municipality A is $800 per capita, the municipality will receive a grant per capita that equals .2(1,000 – 800), or $40. If the tax base per capita of a municipality exceeds the average (or standard), the municipality will not receive any grant revenue. Since this grant does not recognize expenditure needs, the grant is often deemed inferior to one that considers expenditure needs.

Many observers regard grants that are based on fiscal capacity alone as inferior to grants that are based on expenditures as well (Bird and Smart 2002). Grants that take account of expenditures ensure that every municipality can provide at least a standard level of service by levying a standard tax rate. In the absence of the grant, some municipalities will fall short of this goal, not only because their fiscal capacity is lower than that of other municipalities but also because their needs and costs are greater. One way to measure need is to include some measure of municipal expenditure in the grant formula.

The problem with any grant formula based on standard expenditures is that the standard may not adequately recognize differences in needs and costs across municipalities. Nevertheless, a formula that captures the needs and costs that most municipalities face is almost certainly better than one that does not attempt to capture needs and costs at all.

The general formula for capturing both expenditures and fiscal capacity is the following:

$$GR^i = [(E/P)^* - t^*(B/P)^i]P^i,$$

where $(E/P)^*$ represents standard expenditures per capita.

A grant of this type permits each municipality to provide a standard level of expenditures at a standard tax rate. It is more equitable than a fiscal capacity grant, since it takes into account the cost of services provided (as measured by expenditures). Expenditure/fiscal capacity grants do not reward inefficiency, and they do not help municipalities meet needs or costs that exceed the standard needs or costs. The grant amounts are predictable to the extent that the tax base and expenditures per capita are predictable. These grants are flexible, in that the amount of the grant will change as the municipality's fiscal position changes. Finally, although the formula for this type of grant is not as simple as the formula for a per capita grant, the grant is relatively simple to administer.

One could easily vary the formula given here to take into account different measures of the expenditure variable. Possible measures include standard expenditure per capita as measured by the average expenditure per capita for all services, standard expenditure per capita only if it exceeds actual expenditure, standard expenditure per capita weighted by a factor that captures the conditions or circumstances (such as population density) that lead to higher costs, standard expenditure per capita as measured by average expenditure per capita for municipalities grouped by similar characteristics (large urban versus small urban versus rural or even small urban of a particular type versus small urban of another type), and standard nondiscretionary expenditures per capita.

Using standard expenditures as measured by average expenditures for all municipalities ensures that every municipality, regardless of the size of its tax base, can make the average per capita expenditure without having to levy a tax rate that is higher than the average tax rate. The grant will cover expenditures only up to the average amount. The municipality will have to fund any additional expenditure from locally generated revenues. If a municipality currently spends less than the average amount, using average expenditures in the formula means that it may receive more than its expenditure needs.

Since the use of average expenditure ensures that each municipality has sufficient resources to meet the average level of expenditures, it does not reward inefficiency. At the same time, however, it does assist municipalities with greater-than-average needs or costs. This general grant formula is generally recommended on equity and efficiency grounds.

To address the situation in which actual expenditures are less than the average expenditure, one could modify the formula by using actual expenditures per capita $(E/P)^i$ rather than average expenditure per capita $(E/P)^*$ for municipalities spending less than the average. The problem with this solution, however, is that it creates an incentive for municipalities that are currently spending less than the average to spend more. In any case, it complicates the formula, and it does not recognize the factors that cause differences in expenditures across municipalities.

One way to address these differences is to incorporate a weighting factor into the formula to account for specific characteristics of a municipality that affect its expenditure needs or costs. For example, if lower density leads to higher costs, then a measure of density would provide additional grants to low-density municipalities.

With a weighting factor, the grant formula becomes

$$GR^i = [(E/P)^* w^i - t^*(B/P)^i]P^i,$$

where w^i is the weighting factor in municipality i.

Differences across municipalities can also be addressed by grouping them according to characteristics that reflect similarities. For grant purposes, municipalities could be grouped according to size, location, spending responsibilities, expenditure needs, tax base, or other measures.

Calculating grants on this basis assumes that all municipalities within a group have similar needs and costs. If a municipality spends more than the standard (average) for the group, the grant will not compensate it. To the extent that expenditures above the standard reflect inefficiency, they should not be rewarded. If, however, the additional expenditures reflect other uncompensated differences within the group, an increase in the grant is justified.

Organizing municipalities into groups is the best way to compare them in terms of costs and needs for the purpose of calculating grants. Once the groups are determined, it should be fairly simple to administer the grant. Since the group approach treats similar municipalities in a similar fashion, it is fair; since it does not allow a municipality's expenditures to affect the size of the grant, it is efficient.

The expenditure/fiscal capacity formula could also use actual expenditures instead of standard expenditures. This approach would ensure that each municipality could provide its current level of expenditures by levying an average tax rate. Substituting actual expenditures for standard (average) expenditures, the formula becomes

$$GR^i = [(E/P)^i - t^*(B/P)^i]P^i,$$

where $(E/P)^i$ represents actual expenditures per capita.

The advantage of using actual expenditures is that the formula for each municipality will reflect that municipality's needs and costs. This approach assumes that actual expenditures reflect what municipalities need to spend. The disadvantage of using actual expenditures is that it discourages both local revenue-raising effort and local expenditure restraint, since the largest transfers are given to municipalities with the highest expenditures and lowest taxes. Furthermore, to the extent that differences in actual expenditures across municipalities reflect municipal inefficiency, the formula may perpetuate that inefficiency.

Instead of calculating grants on the basis of actual expenditures, one could use expenditures on nondiscretionary services. The case for equalization is far weaker for discretionary spending than it is for nondiscretionary spending. Discretionary spending refers to expenditures, such as those for recreation, culture, and libraries, over which municipalities have a reasonable amount of control; services that could be provided by the private, or volunteer, sector; or services that are less essential than other municipal services. Although essential services vary from country to country, they generally include police protection, fire protection, water and sewerage services, and transportation. The grant calculation should exclude spending on services that ought to be funded by user fees. This includes water and sanitary sewerage, public transit, and recreation. Debt service charges should also be excluded, because they may have been incurred to fund capital projects such as recreational facilities and administration buildings—expenditures over which the municipality had considerable discretion. Debt service charges for water and sewerage should be funded from user fees.

One problem with isolating specific expenditures for inclusion in the grant formula is that municipal accounting practices may differ. Some municipalities may allocate a portion of general government expenditures to some or all of these specific expenditure functions, while others may not. Municipalities face an incentive to alter accounting or recording practices to include as many expenditures as possible in categories on which the grant is determined. If this method of calculating grants is used, it is important to ensure that all municipalities follow similar accounting practices (Kitchen 2003).

Should Grants to Small Urban Areas Differ from Grants to Other Municipalities?

Small urban areas differ from large cities/metropolitan areas and rural areas. They also differ among themselves, both within and across countries. These areas differ in terms of the level and range of public spending, the prosperity and vibrancy of the local economy, the geographic location of municipalities (remote versus populated area), and the governing structure, to name the most obvious differences.

Like large cities/metropolitan areas and rural areas, small urban areas fund their expenditures from a combination of local taxes, user fees, charges, permits, licenses, and grants. International experience suggests that the most responsible and accountable local governments are those that raise their own revenues and set their own tax rates and user charges (Bird 2001; Kitchen 2004b). Unless local governments can alter tax rates and user fees, they will not be as accountable and autonomous as they could be. Moreover, the ability to set local tax rates gives them the flexibility to change these rates in response to local circumstances. Large cities and metropolitan areas have the greatest likelihood of generating sufficient funds to meet their expenditure needs. Some prosperous and relatively rich small urban areas may also be able to operate in this manner, as might some small urban areas in two-tier local governing structures. For many small urban areas, however, greater reliance on grants will be the norm if these municipalities are to be fiscally viable. This is particularly true for small urban areas that are poor and remote.

Conditional grants with a matching provision should be provided to all types of local governments for services that generate spillovers or for services in which the donor government has a direct interest. Unconditional grants should be provided to close the fiscal gap (or reduce vertical imbalance) and to provide some equalization (to reduce horizontal imbalance).

For small urban areas, a per capita or block grant could address the vertical fiscal imbalance issue. Some of the horizontal imbalance could be removed through an equalization grant that includes a measure of expenditure need and a measure of fiscal capacity. Furthermore, all municipalities within a country should be grouped according to similarities, with the equalization grant formula applied to all municipalities within each group.

Small urban areas could be grouped in a number of ways. These could include grouping small urban areas with similar spending responsibilities in a group, small urban areas with a similar local tax base in a group, small urban areas in remote areas in a group, small urban areas near large cities and metropolitan areas in a group, and so on. Since there are no uniform international standards that can be used to establish the groups, the choice should depend on country-specific circumstances, including the availability of data that permit the measurement of both tax capacity and expenditure needs.

Once the groups are determined, any remaining differences in characteristics across municipalities within each group could be dealt with by applying a weighting factor to average expenditures. Since the case for equalization is weaker for nondiscretionary spending than for discretionary spending, further refinements to the equalization formula could include nondiscretionary spending rather than total spending for each group. For this to work, however, all municipalities would have to operate with uniform and detailed budgeting and accounting systems and adopt a common practice for financing services from local taxes versus user fees and charges—a difficult and potentially daunting task for local governments in most countries.

Summary

Small urban areas take on a variety of forms and configurations. Some are rich, some are poor; some are in isolated and remote areas, some are in heavily populated areas; some operate within a two-tier local governance structure, others operate as a single tier. Differences such as these translate into differences in expenditure needs and in the fiscal capacity of the local revenue base. Some municipalities are able to meet their expenditure commitments from their local revenue base, while others need assistance, in the form of grants.

Regardless of why grants are given, they should be equitable and neutral (economically efficient) in their impact. Grant programs should recognize and respond to fiscal pressures faced by municipalities while encouraging municipalities to exercise fiscal restraint, reduce costs, and deliver services efficiently. Grants should not provide incentives for municipalities to spend more than is required to meet their expenditure needs, and they should not reward inefficiency at the local level.

Grants fall into two general categories. In principle, conditional grants are justified to correct the misallocation of resources that arise from interjurisdictional externalities (spillovers). In practice, however, conditional grants are seldom provided for this purpose. Instead, donor governments use them to satisfy various political objectives.

Unconditional grants are justified to close a municipality's fiscal gap and reduce disparities in the ability of municipal governments to provide local services (equalization). Some countries use unconditional grants that are simple, while others apply more-complicated grant formulas. Some provide per capita grants, while others allocate grants to municipalities with inadequate or insufficient fiscal capacity. Still others take into consideration expenditure needs and the municipality's ability to raise its own revenues. The formula for an unconditional grant should include both a measure of expenditure need and a measure of fiscal capacity. A formula that does so is equitable, because it allows each municipality to provide an average level of service at an average rate of tax. The formula is also neutral, since it does not provide an incentive to increase the grant by increasing expenditures. The formula yields predictable amounts of grant revenue and is flexible, because it responds to changes in expenditure needs and tax base. This type of grant is fairly straightforward and relatively simple to administer. In terms of accountability, a grant of this kind is as satisfactory as any of the other unconditional grants.

To apply the expenditure/fiscal capacity formula, a country must establish measures of expenditure needs and fiscal capacity. In countries with a functioning property tax system, the standard measure of fiscal capacity is property values. In countries without a fully functional property tax system, fiscal capacity can be measured by some other economic factor, such as the income tax base. It could even include an index that measures differences in such characteristics as welfare or social housing needs across municipalities. Doing so, however, would require additional socioeconomic and financial information.

Measuring expenditures is somewhat more complicated, since expenditures vary across municipalities, for a variety of reasons. An appropriate expenditure measure recognizes differences in costs and needs but not differences attributed to inefficient spending. It groups similar municipalities together, so that a standard (average) measure of expenditure can be used to reflect the costs and needs of each municipality in the group. Any remaining differences in characteristics across municipalities can be dealt with by applying a weighting factor to standard expenditures.

References

Afonso, José Roberto R., and Erika Amorim Araújo. 2006. "Local Government Organization and Finance: Brazil." In *Local Governance in Developing Countries*, ed. Anwar Shah. Washington, DC: World Bank Institute.

Allers, Maarten. 2004. "Improving the Fiscal Health of Large Cities: Lessons from Other Countries. Cities, Regions, Data Sources: The Netherlands." University of Groningen, Netherlands.

Asensio, Miguel A. 2006. "Local Government Organization and Finance: Argentina." In *Local Governance in Developing Countries*, ed. Anwar Shah. Washington, DC: World Bank Institute.

Bahl, Roy, and J. Linn. 1992. *Urban Public Finance in Developing Countries*. Washington, DC: World Bank and Oxford University Press.

Bird, Richard M. 1993. "Threading the Fiscal Labyrinth: Some Issues in Fiscal Federalism." *National Tax Journal* 46 (2): 207–27.

———. 2001. "Subnational Revenues: Realities and Prospects." World Bank Institute, Washington, DC.

Bird, Richard M., and Duan-jie Chen. 1998. "Federal Finance and Fiscal Federalism: The Two Worlds of Canadian Public Finance." *Canadian Public Administration* 1 (1): 50–74.

Bird, Richard M., and Enid Slack. 1993. *Urban Public Finance in Canada*. 2nd ed. Toronto: John Wiley and Sons.

———. 2004. "Fiscal Aspects of Metropolitan Governance." International Tax Program Paper 0401, University of Toronto, Joseph L. Rotman School of Management.

Bird, Richard M., and Michael Smart. 2002. "Intergovernmental Fiscal Transfers: International Lessons for Developing Countries." *World Development* 30 (6): 899–912.

Boadway, Robin W., and Paul A.R. Hobson. 1993. *Intergovernmental Fiscal Relations in Canada*. Toronto: Canadian Tax Foundation.

Boadway, Robin W., and Harry Kitchen. 1999. *Canadian Tax Policy*. 3rd ed. Toronto: Canadian Tax Foundation.

Chaparro, Juan Camilo, Michael Smart, and Juan Gonzalo Zapata. 2004. "Intergovernmental Transfers and Municipal Finance in Colombia." International Tax Program Paper 0403, University of Toronto, Joseph L. Rotman School of Management.

Dollery, Brian. 2006. "Local Government Organization and Finance: New Zealand." In *Local Governance in Industrial Countries*, ed. Anwar Shah. Washington, DC: World Bank Institute.

Duff, David G. 2003. "Benefit Taxes and User Fees in Theory and Practice." Research Paper 45 for the Panel on the Role of Government in Ontario. http://www.law-lib.utoronto.ca/investing/index.htm.

Freire, Mila. 2001. "Introduction." In *The Challenge of Urban Government: Policies and Practices*, ed. Mila Freire and Richard Stren, xvii–xli. Washington, DC: World Bank.

Gramlich, Edward M. 1977. "Intergovernmental Grants: A Review of the Empirical Literature." In *The Political Economy of Fiscal Federalism*, ed. W.E. Oates, 219–39. Lexington, MA: Lexington Books.

Heymans, Chris. 2006. "Local Government Organization and Finance: South Africa." In *Local Governance in Developing Countries*, ed. Anwar Shah. Washington, DC: World Bank Institute.

IMF (International Monetary Fund). 2001. "Code of Good Practices on Fiscal Transparency." Washington, DC.

Kelly, Roy. 2005. "Local Government Organization and Finance in East Africa." World Bank, Washington, DC.

King, David. 2006. "Local Government Organization and Finance: United Kingdom." In *Local Governance in Industrial Countries*, ed. Anwar Shah. Washington, DC: World Bank Institute.

Kitchen, Harry. 2000. "Municipal Finance in a New Fiscal Environment." *Commentary* 147, C.D. Howe Institute, Toronto.

———. 2002. *Municipal Revenue and Expenditure Issues in Canada*. Toronto: Canadian Tax Foundation.

─────. 2003. "Municipalities: Status and Responsibilities, Budgeting and Accounting." In *Analysis of Revenues and Expenses of Local Budgets,* ed. N. Glavatskaya, 146–72. Moscow: Institute for the Economy in Transition.

─────. 2004a. *Financing City Services: A Prescription for the Future.* Halifax, Canada: Atlantic Institute for Market Studies.

─────. 2004b. "Local Taxation in Selected Countries: A Comparative Examination." Paper prepared for the Consortium for Economic Policy Research and Advice (CEPRA), Association of Universities and Colleges of Canada, Ottawa.

Kitchen, Harry, and Enid Slack. 2006. "Providing Public Services in Remote Areas." In *Perspectives on Fiscal Federalism,* ed. Richard M. Bird and François, Vaillancourt, 123–39. Washington, DC: World Bank.

Lotz, Jørgen. 2006. "Local Government Organization and Finance: Nordic Countries." In *Local Governance in Industrial Countries,* ed. Anwar Shah. Washington, DC: World Bank Institute.

Makhmutova, Meruert. 2006. "Local Government Organization and Finance: Kazakhstan." In *Local Governance in Developing Countries,* ed. Anwar Shah. Washington, DC: World Bank Institute.

McMillan, Melville L. 1995. "A Local Perspective on Fiscal Federal: Practices, Experiences and Lessons from Developed Countries." World Bank, Washington, DC.

Mochida, Nobuki. 2006. "Local Government Organization and Finance: Japan." In *Local Governance in Industrial Countries,* ed. Anwar Shah. Washington, DC: World Bank Institute.

Nowlan, David. 1994. "Local Taxation as an Instrument of Policy." In *The Changing Canadian Metropolis: A Public Policy Perspective,* vol. 2, ed. Francis Frisken, 74–91. Berkeley, CA: Institute of Governmental Studies Press.

Prud'homme, Rémy. 2006. "Local Government Organization and Finance: France." In *Local Governance in Industrial Countries,* ed. Anwar Shah. Washington, DC: World Bank Institute.

S. Letelier, Leonardo. 2006. "Local Government Organization and Finance: Chile." In *Local Governance in Developing Countries,* ed. Anwar Shah. Washington, DC: World Bank Institute.

Schroeder, Larry. 2006. "Local Government Organization and Finance: United States." In *Local Governance in Industrial Countries,* ed. Anwar Shah. Washington, DC: World Bank Institute.

Slack, Enid, Larry S. Bourne, and Meric S. Gertler. 2003. "Small, Rural, and Remote Communities: The Anatomy of Risk." Research Paper 18, Panel on the Role of Government in Ontario. http://www.law-lib.utoronto.ca/investing/index.htm.

Steffensen, Jesper. 2006. "Local Government Organization and Finance: Uganda." In *Local Governance in Developing Countries,* ed. Anwar Shah. Washington, DC: World Bank Institute.

Wallich, Christine I. 1994. "Intergovernmental Fiscal Relations: Setting the Stage." In *Russia and the Challenge of Fiscal Federalism,* ed. Christine I. Wallich, 254–76. Washington, DC: World Bank.

18

Intergovernmental Transfers and Rural Local Governments

MELVILLE L. MCMILLAN

This chapter provides insight into intergovernmental transfers to rural local governments by examining local governments in three geographically, culturally, economically, and historically diverse countries: India, Latvia, and Canada (the province of Alberta). The three settings provide interesting contrasts and illustrate important features that are common to many countries. The analysis begins with a profile of rural local government in each country. Then an integrating overview focuses on transfers, and the chapter ends with conclusions.

Country Profiles

India

About 75 percent of India's population lives in rural areas. There are three tiers of rural local government bodies: the district (*zilla panchayat*), the block (*taluk panchayat*), and the village (*gram panchayat*) level. As of 1994 India had 474 *zilla panchayats*, 5,906 *taluk panchayats*, and 227,698 *gram panchayats*, with median populations of 1.4 million people in the *zilla panchayats*, 114,000 in the *taluk panchayats*, and 2,700 in the *gram panchayats* (Rao and Singh 2005).

The various local bodies have a long history in India, but it was not until 1993 that they received constitutional recognition. The 73rd Amendment to India's constitution defines 29 functional responsibilities for rural local governments, considerably expanding the potential role of substate bodies and allowing the states the option to assign other responsibilities to them. But the amendment made most of those responsibilities concurrent with state governments, mandated direct elections for the councils at each level (including special provisions for representation of women and of various castes and tribe-based groups), and required the establishment of state finance commissions to make recommendations on the devolution of the financial resources necessary to enable local authorities to accomplish their assigned functions and to periodically review the functional assignment and their funding.

The constitutional amendment appears not to have accomplished as much as its advocates intended. To satisfy the amendment, the states largely redefined state agencies that were delivering services at the substate level as local governments, assigned them their existing programs and staff (still state employees), and provided the other resources required for their oper-ation through specific-purpose grants. This approach greatly constrained rural local governments. Only the *gram panchayats* have any taxing power, and even that is limited. The *zilla* and *taluk panchayats* rely entirely on specific-purpose transfers. These transfers define their programs, which can-not be modified to better reflect local priorities. The *gram panchayats* have only slightly more discretion.

Expenditures by local governments in India in 1997/98 amounted to 2.2 percent of GDP; about one-quarter of the required funds came from own sources (revenue collection). Urban government accounted for 36 percent of local expenditures but more than 90 percent of the revenue collected by local bodies. Rural local bodies spent the equivalent of 1.4 percent of GDP (10 percent of state-level expenditures), but only 3 percent of that was financed from own revenues. Among rural local bodies, only the *gram pan-chayats* collected a significant amount of revenue, and that represented only about 10 percent of their expenditures. The *zilla* and *taluk panchayats*, which accounted for more than 70 percent of rural local body expenditures, had no significant revenues of their own.[1]

A survey of a representative sample of local authorities in Karnataka, a pioneer in decentralization to local bodies (along with Kerala, West Bengal, and a few other states), provides further insight into finance patterns across rural bodies. Expenditures by Karnataka's rural bodies represent about 6.5 percent of regional GDP (the equivalent of 20 percent of state expenditure).

Expenditure *by gram panchayats*, however, at only 0.4 percent of GDP, is of the same magnitude as that for all India. Spending by the *zilla* and *taluk panchayats* accounts for almost 95 percent of expenditures by local rural bodies, while the *gram panchayats* account for only 5.5 percent. In Karnataka, however, revenue collection by the *gram panchayats* finances almost one-quarter of their outlays. These revenues represent 99 percent of all revenue collections by rural local bodies.[2]

Overall, rural local bodies play a small role in consolidated state-local finances. Among the three tiers, the *zilla* and *taluk panchayats* dominate expenditures but have essentially no own revenue, relying instead on transfers from higher-level governments. Only the *gram panchayats* generate a measurable amount of revenue, and that is small relative to their expenditures.

To assess transfers, it is necessary to identify the responsibilities of the recipient governments and the purpose and distribution of the transfers. Figures for 12 grant/expenditure categories show the per capita amount transferred to each of the three levels of rural local bodies in Karnataka in 2000/01 (table 18.1). Given the strictly tied nature of the funding and the lack of other revenues, these categories are taken to closely reflect the expenditure allocation.[3] Education, sports, and culture account for almost half of all grants to and outlays by rural bodies. Other than health and public health, no other category represents as much as 10 percent of transfers/outlays. The *taluk panchayats* receive more than 80 percent of funds for education, sports, and culture. Funding for education, for which they are primarily responsible, accounts for more than 70 percent of their total funds. Housing (6.7 percent of total funds) and social security/welfare (6.3 percent) are the next largest areas of *taluk panchayats* funding.

Funds to *zilla panchayats* are more dispersed across categories. Education, sports, and culture is the largest category, at about 20 percent of funding. Among rural bodies, the *zilla panchayats* are primarily responsible for public works (99 percent of all rural funds), water and sanitation (90 percent), and health and public health (73 percent). Each of these categories accounts for 13–17 percent of *zilla panchayat* funds.

The *gram panchayats* have limited funds and responsibilities. Transfers for rural development (which likely include some public works) represent two-thirds of *gram panchayat* funding. Rural employment (through poverty alleviation employment programs) accounts for almost all of the rest. Both programs are shared with the *zilla panchayats* and to a lesser extent, with the *taluk panchayats*. (For more details, see Rao, Nath, and Vani 2004.)

TABLE 18.1 Functional Division of Transfers to Rural Local
Government in Karnataka, India, 2000/01
(*rupees per capita*)

Expenditure category	Zilla panchayat[a]	Taluk panchayat[a]	Gram panchayat[a]	Total[b]
Education, sports, and	119.06	518.69	0	637.76
culture	(18.70)	(81.30)		(48.37)
Health and public	92.40	34.19	0	126.60
health	(73.00)	(27.00)		(9.60)
Water and sanitation	67.10	4.94	2.92	74.97
	(89.50)	(6.60)	(3.90)	(5.69)
Social security and	38.33	45.54	0	83.88
welfare	(45.70)	(54.30)		(6.36)
Housing	8.57	48.46	0	57.03
	(15.00)	(85.00)		(4.33)
Rural development	42.87	26.59	46.18	115.64
	(37.10)	(23.00)	(39.90)	(8.77)
Rural employment	20.33	2.75	21.58	44.66
	(45.50)	(6.10)	(48.30)	(3.39)
Agriculture and	44.89	33.57	0	78.47
irrigation	(57.20)	(42.80)		(5.95)
Power	0.20	2.08	0	2.28
	(8.80)	(91.20)		(0.17)
Industry	11.67	0.19	0	11.87
	(98.30)	(1.70)		(0.90)
Public works, roads,	78.40	0.78	0	79.18
and bridges	(99.00)	(1.00)		(6.00)
Other	6.29	0	0	6.29
	(100.00)			(0.48)
Total (US$1 = 46.3 rupees)	530.13	717.80	70.68	1,318.61
	(40.20)	(54.40)	(5.40)	(100.00)

Source: Rao, Nath, and Vani 2004.
a. Figures in parentheses are percentage distributions of expenditure in category across three levels of rural local bodies.
b. Figures in parentheses are percentage of total spending by rural local bodies.

Own-source revenues of *gram panchayats* in Karnataka equal 16.2
rupees per capita, or 22 percent of total revenues. These revenues come
primarily from property taxes (on nonagricultural land) (48.6 percent),
rents (11.5 percent), license fees (11.4 percent), water charges (7.4 percent),
and other sources (21.1 percent). Own-source revenues are modest at best,
but there appears to be little enthusiasm, and perhaps only limited ability, to
generate additional own-source revenue.

State finance commissions afforded an opportunity to define the new tier of local government and to see that it was appropriately financed. But to date, these commissions have demonstrated limited success. In its first report, for example, Karnataka's commission recommended that 36 percent of the state's own revenues be directed to local governments. The commission recommended that 31 percent of these funds be distributed among rural bodies, with 40 percent going to the *zilla panchayats*, 35 percent to the *taluk panchayats*, and 25 percent to the *gram panchayats*. These recommendations were not followed. Instead, the tasks and staff of the existing state agencies responsible for local services were assigned to the *zilla* and *taluk panchayats*, which received transfers from the state to meet salary and other expenses. In Karnataka as elsewhere, this widely followed approach to devolution to the new local bodies has stymied their development as autonomous and effective authorities.

Difficulties arose for a variety of reasons. The transfer of existing programs, staff, and funding tied the hands of local bodies. The *zilla* and *taluk panchayats* rely entirely on state and central government grants, almost all of which are designated for specific purposes. The fact that few resources are fungible means that local bodies have little if any ability to modify programs to better reflect local interests or pursue additional or alternative activities. The transition also led to a complex array of grant schemes or programs: by 2001/02 about 600 transfer schemes applied to rural local governments in Karnataka. Only eight applied to the *gram panchayats*. The complexity and large number of schemes suggests a high degree of state direction and limited scope for local decision making.

Another problem with the transfer programs is the lack of a systematic distribution of funds among local bodies at each *panchayat* level. For example, the state finance commission in Karnataka recommended that distributions take into consideration population, area, and backwardness—that is, that they reflect fiscal need and capacity. Despite their recommendation, the distribution of funds does not appear to take these considerations into account. Indeed, more funds appear to go to *gram panchayats* in better-off *zilla panchayats* than to those in fiscally disadvantaged areas. There is no understandable formula for distributing funds; programs lack transparency and local bodies lack any mechanism by which to monitor or audit their distribution to determine whether they are fair and reasonable. In addition, the allocation criteria do not reflect program objectives. Transfers are not understood, and they are variable and uncertain. The fact that payments due to the electricity authority are deducted from transfers to the *gram panchayats* further obscures the grant system.

While easing the transition, a major impediment to the development of an effective tier of local authorities is the fact that that staff transferred to the new rural local bodies continue to be state employees. Salaries are paid by the state (accounting for 58 percent of transfers in Karnataka), and careers are determined by state rather than local authorities. Hence loyalties are at best divided, and accountability to local bodies is limited.

Education has been the focus of some attention. Contributors to the volume by Dethier (2000), such as Rajaraman (2000), highlight the serious problem of teacher absenteeism and the inability of parents and their local representatives to control it. This very fundamental deficiency with a major service illustrates the magnitude of the problem. Lack of local control extends to maintenance of school buildings and provision of other school resources.

A major problem is that the elected bodies at the local level are weak. Even at the level of the *gram panchayat*, where most of the strengthening of the representative system might have been expected (and was certainly hoped for), local councils have limited authority and influence. Despite the electoral reform and some revitalization of the *gram sabha* (village assembly), the *gram panchayats* have not emerged as effective local governments. A significant part of the problem may be attributed to the fact that they lack control even over local matters important to residents because of failures in the assignment of responsibilities, resources, and (perhaps) revenue-generating authority. In large part, they are too small to matter. In the decision-making structure, political voice has not replaced hierarchy.

The *zilla* and *taluk panchayat* levels face an even more difficult situation. All levels suffer from lack of transparency and accountability to local voters and their representatives. Public sector workers are often not accountable to those with good information or who have an important stake in an issue. The lack of accountability to those served and their representatives can be expected to contribute to the capture of programs by unintended beneficiaries (Rajaraman 2000). Along with other institutional factors, it may also contribute to difficulties in getting local bodies or beneficiaries to accept responsibility for maintaining infrastructure (Bardhan 2000). There is some evidence that local schooling and health services perform better where local government is stronger (Mahal, Srivastava, and Sanan 2000).

Rural local governments in India have made limited progress in transforming themselves into effective local governments. Their lack of significant progress was largely preordained by the way in which power was devolved. As Rao, Nath, and Vani (2004) note, that method "robbed the system of the very essence of decentralization" (p. 126) and made "the entire fiscal decentralization process a hostage to the transfer system" (p. 173).

Latvia

After independence, Latvia's public sector was transformed by a dramatic decentralization that placed significant responsibilities and financial resources in the hands of a multiplicity of local governments.[4] As of early 2004, there were 536 local governments: 7 major (republican) cities, 56 towns, 453 rural municipalities (*pagasts*), and 20 amalgamated town and rural municipalities *(novads)*. There were also 26 regional districts *(rajons)*.[5] The seven major cities serve as both local governments and regional districts.

About 70 percent of Latvia's 2.5 million people live in urban areas, with 32 percent living in the capital, Riga. Towns average about 6,300 people. Rural municipalities average about 1,700 people.[6] The large number of small municipalities and the limitations on their ability to provide municipal services is a concern that is being addressed.

Latvian law identifies 17 permanent functions for municipalities. Major functions include providing kindergarten, primary, and secondary education; social assistance; housing; utilities; roads and streets; and waste collection and disposal. Municipalities may also be assigned temporary responsibilities and take on some functions voluntarily.

Especially after centralization of the health care system to the national level in 1998, the regional districts have few responsibilities (primarily public transportation, civil defense, and voluntary tasks, which usually involve assisting their local governments). Regional districts are governed by councils made up of the chairs of their municipalities. While they are financed almost entirely by transfers, they determine the allocation of their budgets. Regional district spending represents about 2.6 percent of total public spending. The figure represents about 18 percent of the spending of subnational authorities outside of large cities (that is, spending in regional districts, towns, and rural municipalities). Because of their relatively minor role, little attention is paid here to regional districts.

The responsibilities of the municipal governments are best appreciated by looking at Latvia's expenditure budgets (table 18.2). Outlays for education dominate local government spending, representing half of local budgets. General services account for 13.1 percent of spending and housing (including community amenities such as street lighting and sanitation)

TABLE 18.2 Local Government Spending in Latvia, 1999

Function	Percentage of budget	Percentage of consolidated government expenditure
Education	49.7	65.2
General	13.1	37.6
Housing and community amenities	11.5	79.0
Social security and welfare	8.0	1.0
Recreation and culture	5.8	43.1
Transportation and communication	4.1	18.5
Public order and safety	1.8	6.3
Health	1.2	2.4
Other	12.0	23.4
Total	**100.0**	**20.5**
Million lats (US$1 = 0.58 lats)	310.2	20.5
Percentage of GDP	8.0	n.a.
Regional districts		
Billion lats (US$1 = 0.58 lats)	39.4	2.6
Percentage of GDP	1.0	n.a.

Source: OECD 2000.
Note: Local government includes cities, towns, and rural municipalities. n.a. = not applicable. Figures for regional districts are shown separately in the table.

11.5 percent. The magnitude of housing partly reflects the carryover from the collective housing of the Soviet era.

After 1997, when health funding was centralized, the share of subnational budgets assigned to health dropped from almost one-quarter to about 1 percent, while that going to education increased. More-recent (but incomplete) data indicate that the expenditure patterns shown in table 18.2 continue.

On the revenue side, taxes account for about 60 percent of revenue, nontax revenue for 20 percent, and grants for 20 percent (table 18.3). Although taxes dominate local revenues, there are no purely municipal taxes. The central government defines the tax bases and rates, leaving the municipalities no room for discretion (with an exception noted below). The personal income tax, which accounts for almost half of local governments' revenues, is a state tax that is shared with local governments. The local government in which the taxpayer maintains a residence receives 71.6 percent of this tax. The real property tax base, assessments, and rates are set by the state. Property was taxed at 1.5 percent of assessed value until 2002, when

TABLE 18.3 Local Government Revenues in Latvia, 1999

Revenue source	Percentage of revenue	Percentage of consolidated government revenue
Tax	60.7	17.1
Personal income	46.9	—
Property	11.8	—
Goods and services	1.0	—
Nontax revenue	19.8	31.7
Enterprise surpluses and property income	0.1	—
Fees, sales, and fines	7.7	—
Other	12.0	—
Grants	19.5	76.1
Specific purpose	17.4	—
General purpose	1.6	—
Total revenue	**100.0**	**22.6**
Million lats	365.1	22.6
Percentage of GDP	9.4	n.a.
Regional districts		
Nontax revenue	26.9	11.8
Grants	73.1	23.9
Total	**100.0**	**1.9**
Million lats	30.5	1.9
Percentage of GDP	0.8	n.a.

Source: OECD 2000.
Note: Local government includes cities, towns, and rural municipalities. — = not available, n.a. = not applicable. Figures for regional districts are shown separately in the table.

the rate was reduced to 1.0 percent. Residential property not used for commercial purposes began to be taxed in 2004. Municipal governments have the authority to grant tax benefits (relief) for certain types of property. Those benefits may be for 25, 50, 75, or 90 percent of the property tax. The real property tax is collected directly by local governments. Other taxes account for only minor shares of municipal revenues.

Municipalities have access to various forms of nontax revenue, including revenue from fees, sales, fines, and other sources, such as duties or licenses. Local governments determine these charges themselves. Net returns from leasing municipal property and from operating municipal enterprises are essentially nil.

Grants represent about 20 percent of revenues. While there is an equalization system that provides unconditional grants to some governments (discussed below), almost all the transfers to local governments are specific-purpose transfers, for education, culture, planning, and local public investment programs.

Total local revenue amounted to 365.1 million lats in 1999 (9.4 percent of GDP and 22.6 percent of consolidated government revenue). The regional districts had revenues of 30.5 billion lats (0.8 percent of GDP), bringing the sub-national total to about 10 percent of GDP, a level that has been relatively constant over the years despite some changes in expenditure responsibilities. Regional governments receive no tax revenues, obtaining almost three-quarters of their funds from transfers and the remainder from nontax sources.

Local and regional expenditures and revenues do not exactly match. For local governments, revenues exceed expenditures by almost 55 million lats. This can be explained largely by the fact that reported expenditures are current expenditures rather than total expenditures.[7] Earmarked (specific purpose) grants became a larger share of local revenues in 2002.

Before 1997 local governments had the authority to borrow in the capital markets, subject to some supervision and controls. Supervision and controls have been tightened substantially since then, and local borrowing is now controlled by the Ministry of Finance. Limited local government borrowing has been approved since 1996.

While general-purpose grants are small overall, the equalization fund providing them is an important source of revenue for towns and rural municipalities, which, on average, obtain about 25 percent of their funds from those transfers. The equalization fund is primarily an intermunicipal redistribution device. In 1999 about 80 percent of the funds for equalization came from contributions by "rich" municipalities. The other 20 percent came from the central government.

Equalization operates as follows. Based on forecasts, the revenue of each local government (revenue capacity) is determined. A notional measure of expenditure need is then determined for each local government. Revenue capacities and notional expenditures are summed across all local governments, with the difference determining the relative contributions of local and state government to the fund. The larger the gap (that is, the greater the difference between notional expenditures and revenues), the larger is the state share. There can be considerable negotiation about these calculations, and fiscal circumstances can change the state share contributed.

Once the notional expenditure is determined, that sum is allocated between cities (45 percent) and towns, rural municipalities, and *rajons* (regional districts) (55 percent), based on earlier expenditure patterns. These amounts are then allocated among their respective units according to an index of relative need based on six criteria: population, number of children 0–6, number of children 7–18, number of people above working age, number of children in children's homes, and number of elderly in homes. The criteria are weighted to reflect responsibilities and expenditures. Local governments contribute to the fund if their forecast tax revenues (excluding nontax revenues) exceed their notional expenditures by more than 10 percent, contributing 45 percent of the surplus, up to a maximum of 35 percent of revenues.

Relatively few municipalities contribute. Cities are the main contributors (five of seven contributing entities in 1999), with Riga and Ventspils making the largest per capita contributions. Most rural municipalities do not contribute; among those that do, the per capita amount is typically small. The *rajons*, which have no tax revenues, contribute nothing.

Distributions from the fund depend on the difference between forecast revenues and notional expenditures. The *rajons* receive 100 percent of the difference. Cities with projected revenues of less than 95 percent of notional expenditures receive payments to bring them up to the 95 percent level. Towns and rural municipalities with forecast revenue of less than 90 percent of notional expenditure receive a transfer sufficient to bring them to the 90 percent level. Cities with revenue of 95–110 percent and towns and rural municipalities with revenue of 90–110 percent of their notional expenditures neither contribute nor receive payments. No city received a payment from the fund. While full information for other types of municipalities is unavailable, the data indicate that almost all rural municipalities received a payment. The average per capita payment to rural municipalities and towns was 26.2 lats. Combined with the average 79.6 lats of own resources, this yielded total resources of 105.8 lats per capita before specific-purpose grants. This amount is roughly equivalent to the 104.9 lat average available to the cities. Per capita local resources range from 85 to 163 lats—a significant range but smaller than the range in tax revenues of 32–208.[8]

One reason for the considerable fiscal disparity among local governments and for the importance of equalization is the small size of many of Latvia's municipalities. Such small municipalities are unusual, especially in a small and relatively densely populated country. Even allowing for intermunicipal cooperation, the small size impedes service delivery and cost effectiveness. The issue is of special concern in the case of rural municipalities with fewer than 1,700 people.

Territorial reform has been on the agenda since the mid-1990s, and there has been some modest reduction in numbers over time. In 1998 the state government pressed the issue with legislation creating a Council for Administrative-Territorial Reform to investigate and recommend changes that were to have been implemented in 2004. Various options were proposed and discussed. At the regional level, it appears that five planning regions may evolve in place of the 26 regional districts. At the municipal level, there have been five proposals, suggesting 33–109 *novads* (amalgamations of rural municipalities and towns). None of these options has met general acceptance. Twenty *novads* have formed voluntarily. The 2004 Union of Local and Regional Government report does not indicate what action, if any, is being taken in the case of the *novads*. However, as of early 2006, 26 *novads* and 26 *rajons* still existed.

Responsibilities for social assistance complicate local government, contributing to the need for territorial reform and to demands for (as well as limitations of) equalization. Local governments are responsible for providing aid to the poor. While local delivery has some advantages, local finance is not recommended. Latvia's central government offers guidelines, but it provides no financial assistance. The level of assistance is generally low and the distribution uneven. Few poor households receive aid, but those that do receive significant sums, although the amount is highly variable. There is also considerable regional variation. In about half the regions, aid per poor person is less than half the national average, while in the other half it is 1.5–7 times the average (World Bank 2000). Social assistance competes unsuccessfully with the other demands on local governments, and the priority given to it and its implementation is uneven. While equalization helps, poverty is not an explicit criterion for determining need, so there is little if any equalization for social assistance expenditures. In addition, equalization funds are unconditional; social assistance must thus compete, probably on a somewhat uneven playing field, with other uses for its share.

Larger local governments will help reduce disparities in fiscal capacities, but they will not solve the problem. To resolve the issue, the central government will need to play a more active role in financing social assistance—by providing conditional grants, for example, or assuming responsibility for service provision.

Decentralization after independence saw significant responsibilities and resources assigned to a multiplicity of local governments. About 85 percent of local governments are rural and have small populations. In addition to providing local infrastructure and amenities, subnational authorities (local governments and regional districts) were responsible for a number of social services, including schooling, social assistance, and health care. Local governments often found it difficult to deal with this breadth of responsibilities. Responsibility for health services was subsequently assumed by the central government. That reform left regional governments with minor responsibilities and left municipalities with schooling as their major expenditure. Responsibility for providing social assistance for the poor still remains at the local level. Although such assistance does not consume a large share of local budgets, service is uneven across poor individuals and local jurisdictions. This is an area ripe for greater central participation.

Latvia's municipalities control limited sources of revenues. The source over which they have clear control is nontax revenue (fees, charges, licenses, and returns from municipal property and enterprises). These sources of revenue provided about 20 percent of revenues in 1999. Although their importance has grown rapidly, there may be some scope for expanding this area.

Other revenues are essentially state-determined transfers—shared taxes or grants. It is sometime said that there is no municipal tax in Latvia. The personal income tax is a central tax, 71.6 percent of which goes to the taxpayer's local government. This source of income represents half of local government revenues. Taxes on real property have the potential to grow in importance, but to date their contribution to municipal budgets has not changed much. Taxes on real property are also centrally determined, but local governments have the option of providing varying degrees of tax relief on certain categories of property. These concessions give local governments some control over this revenue source. The tax system affords local governments little capacity to adjust tax revenues in a way that ensures that local services better reflect local priorities or to relate changes in local services to local taxes; there is a very limited linkage between benefits and tax cost, especially for marginal changes.

Grants account for 20 percent of local government revenues. Most transfers from the central government are designated for specific purposes. Unconditional transfers, while small overall, are especially important for small and rural local governments. Fiscal capacity and resources are spread very unevenly among local governments, and most rural municipalities are fiscally disadvantaged. Under the "Robin Hood" equalization system, rural municipalities typically benefit, with the bulk of equalization funding coming from an intermunicipal transfer from rich (largely large urban) municipalities to poor (largely small rural) municipalities. On average, equalization transfers contribute the equivalent of about one-third of own revenues to the rural municipal budgets. These transfers go a long way toward reducing fiscal disparities among local governments and, in particular, benefiting rural authorities and their residents.[9]

Canada (Alberta)

Local governments in Canada have no constitutional standing but are the responsibility of the provinces. Conditions therefore differ from province to province. For this reason, and because national data on local government finances do not distinguish between rural and urban local governments, examination of a single province makes sense.

Local government in Canada consists primarily of municipal government (villages, towns, cities, and, in rural areas, counties and municipal districts) and local school authorities.[10] This discussion focuses on municipal governments, because over the past 25 years most Canadian provinces have assumed responsibility for school finance. In Alberta, for example, locally elected school authorities (effectively) no longer have taxing powers and simply administer funds allocated to them by the provincial government. The lack of ability to tax throws into question their standing as a local government as opposed to an agent of the province.

Alberta had a population of 2.96 million in 2001. The province has 14 cities, the largest of which are Calgary, with a population of 876,519, and Edmonton, with a population 648,284; both cities have metropolitan regions of more than 1 million people. Other cities in Alberta have populations of 11,000–76,000. Alberta also has 110 towns (municipalities with populations of 1,000–10,000, with an average population of 3,520) and 103 villages (municipalities with populations of 300–1,000, with an average population of 395) (2001 official population list).[11] Alberta has 64 rural municipalities (municipal districts or counties), with an average population of 6,429.

Rural municipalities in Canada do not overlap the towns, villages, or cities encompassed by their boundaries. Rural and urban municipalities in Alberta are distinct, physically separate, and responsible for providing similar services to their residents. In addition, there are a number of specialized municipalities, bringing the total number to 359, with an average population of 8,054. Another 60,000 people in the province live in *metis* settlements and Indian reserves.

Alberta is 80 percent urban and 20 percent rural.[12] In rural areas, agriculture accounts for 15–20 percent of employment; the natural resource sector (oil and gas and, in some cases, forestry) for about 7 percent; and secondary industry (construction and manufacturing) for about 15 percent.

Even in rural areas, however, the service sector (about evenly divided among consumer, production, and government services) dominates, accounting for about 60 percent of employment. Agriculture and the resource sector are more important in rural municipal districts, since primary industries represent less than 6 percent of employment in urban areas. Farms are typically family operated, cover large areas, and use substantial capital inputs. Farm families normally reside on their farms and so are scattered across rural districts, along with some nonfarm rural residents. There is considerable physical and social mobility in Alberta and in Canada. People living on farms and in rural areas are well educated and earn good incomes. In Alberta and in Canada, the incomes of rural residents are about 80 percent of those for residents of major urban areas (Statistics Canada 2004).

The responsibilities of municipal governments are outlined in legislation. Typical services provided include roads, streets, sidewalks, and street lighting; public transit; police, fire and emergency, and ambulance services; drainage, water supply, and distribution; sanitary sewer services and sewerage treatment; garbage collection and waste disposal; parks and playgrounds; recreation and cultural facilities and programs; cemeteries; regulation of commercial operations; animal and weed control; visitor information; and local and social services. These services correspond to those of municipalities in most provinces. Significant omissions from the list of municipal responsibilities are schooling, hospitals and medical care, and social assistance for the poor.

The level and allocation of expenditures provides insight into the magnitude and relative importance of municipal activities in Alberta (table 18.4). Municipal expenditures average $1,729 per capita in Alberta, slightly above the Canadian average of $1,545.[13] At 3.3 percent of GDP, municipal expenditures in Alberta are somewhat below the Canadian average of 4.3 percent. The reason why is that the province is a major energy producer. While Alberta is consistently a high-income province, volatile oil and gas prices cause incomes and GDP to fluctuate considerably.

The dominant expenditure areas are transportation, the environment (water, sewerage, and solid waste), protection (police, fire, and ambulance), and recreation, which together account for 80 percent of total outlays. This pattern is typical of municipal expenditures in other provinces, with the exception of Ontario, which is unique in Canada in imposing relatively large social service responsibilities on its municipalities.

Per capita expenditures of rural municipalities (municipal districts and counties) are roughly equal to the provincial average. This is not the case for all classes of municipalities. Per capita spending by large cities ($1,884) and

TABLE 18.4 Municipal Government Expenditure in Alberta, Canada, 2001
(percent, except where otherwise indicated)

Function	Rural municipalities	All municipalities
Transportation	59.0	32.4
Environment	12.5	19.9
General government	11.2	11.5
Protection services	5.8	16.9
Planning and development	5.4	5.1
Recreation and culture	4.7	12.2
Public health and welfare	1.0	1.9
Other	0.4	0.1
Total	**100.0**	**100.0**
Canadian dollars per capita (US$1 = Can$1.55)	1,772	1,729
Percentage of GDP	n.a.	3.3

Source: Alberta Municipal Financial Information System.
Note: The Canadian dollar exchange rate has fluctuated widely in recent years. At this time, it was unusually low. In early 2006, it was relatively high, at US$1 = Can$1.16.

rural municipalities ($1,772) is relatively high, while spending by smaller urban centers tends to be below average (towns, for example, spend just $1,497 per capita). Outlays for transportation (roads) dominate rural municipal expenditures (59 percent of the total), while urban areas spend about half that (including public transit). Expenditures in the other major categories are relatively and absolutely smaller in rural areas than in urban centers. These areas have less need for publicly supplied environmental services (water, sewerage, and garbage disposal). Protection accounts for less than 6 percent of outlays in rural areas, in large part because areas with populations of less than 2,500 are not required to fund policing, which is provided by the province. Recreation and cultural spending is also lower, as rural residents typically use (and sometimes contribute to) recreation services in neighboring urban centers.

Municipalities in Alberta, as in the rest of Canada, rely heavily on revenues they raise themselves from their own sources (taxes, charges, fees). Own revenues represented 86.3 percent of total revenues in 2001, with the remaining 13.7 percent provided by intergovernmental transfers (table 18.5). The property tax is the major source of tax revenue, generating about 36 percent of the revenue of municipalities in Alberta. A somewhat broader measure, property and related taxes, accounts for 44.4 percent in Alberta and 52.2 percent across all Canadian municipalities (McMillan 2006).

TABLE 18.5 Municipal Government Revenue, Alberta, Canada, 2001
(percent, except where otherwise indicated)

Source	Rural municipalities	All municipalities
Own-source revenue		
Net property taxes	57.1	35.8
Sales and user charges	5.9	23.8
Return on investments	4.2	4.7
Licenses, permits, and fines	1.2	3.3
Local improvement taxes	0.3	0.8
Development levies	0.3	3.1
Business taxes	0.0	4.4
Other	8.3	10.3
Total	77.3	86.3
Transfers		
Provincial	22.0	13.2
Federal	0.7	0.5
Total revenue per capita (Can$)	1,847	1,713

Source: Alberta Municipal Financial Information System.

Business taxes, another form of tax revenue, are collected only by major cities. Revenue from sales and user charges (primarily from water and sewerage services and from recreation facilities and services) provide almost one-quarter of total revenues, as is characteristic of other Canadian municipalities.

Rural municipalities rely more heavily on property taxes, which account for 57.1 percent of their revenues. Sales and user charges generate only 5.9 percent. Own-source revenues in rural municipalities provide 77.3 percent of total revenue, with transfers accounting for the remaining 22.7 percent.

Residential and other land and improvements (nonfarm, nonresidential real property) are the source of 75 percent of municipal property taxes in Alberta and of more than 95 percent in urban municipalities (table 18.6). Farm property provides only 9.2 percent of property taxes in rural municipalities—less than residential property, which provides 17.6 percent. Linear property (oil and gas wells, pipelines, and electricity and telecommunication facilities) provides almost half of total property tax revenue in Alberta's rural municipalities. The extensive facilities of the energy industry in rural areas make it the major contributor to this source of property taxes.

Intergovernmental transfers to municipal governments come almost entirely from the provincial government: federal transfers to Canadian

TABLE 18.6 Sources of Property Tax Revenue, Alberta, Canada, 2001
(*percent*)

Type of property	Rural muncipalities[a]	Urban municipalities[b]	All municipalities
Residential	17.6	56.1	43.5
Farmland	9.2	0.1	4.7
Other land and improvements[c]	12.6	39.6	31.4
Machinery and equipment	12.3	0.8	4.8
Linear	48.0	3.3	15.5
Railroads	0.3	..	0.1

Source: Alberta Municipal Financial Information System.
a. Municipal districts and counties.
b. Cities, towns, and villages.
c. Excludes machinery and equipment.
.. Negligible.

municipalities represented just 0.4 percent of revenues in 2001. Federal transfers are becoming somewhat more important with new federal initiatives, but they represented only about 2 percent of revenues in 2005 (McMillan 2006).

Transfers to municipalities in Alberta, as in most provinces, are primarily specific-purpose grants. General-purpose grants represented only 0.9 percent of the 13.2 percent of revenues coming from provincial transfers in 2001. While some provinces have sophisticated equalization programs that provide a significant portion of provincial transfers, Alberta's unconditional grants are the modest outdated remnants of an earlier scheme. Transfers to rural municipalities provided 22.7 percent of revenues. More than 70 percent of those transfers were directed to transportation, and 14 percent went to environmental programs. In Alberta about 40 percent of transfers to municipalities went to transportation and 31 percent to recreational programs in 2001. (This distribution was probably distorted by an exceptionally large recreation grant to the City of Calgary.) While about 60 percent of transfers to all municipalities support capital outlays as opposed to operating costs, 85 percent of transfers to rural municipalities are for operations and road grants. These grants are based on the characteristics of the road system; capital grants depend on where construction is taking place.

Provincial transfers to municipalities fell sharply in Alberta (and other provinces) in the 1990s, when the provincial and federal governments were reducing and eliminating deficits. Grants to municipalities fell from about 20 percent of revenues at the beginning of the 1990s to 13 percent in 2001. Now flush with oil and natural gas revenues, Alberta has announced a five-year infrastructure grant program that will increase provincial transfers by about 75 percent. This money is to be allocated on a per capita basis. The percentage of municipal funds provided by grants in Alberta will thus go from about 20 percent to about 13 percent and back to 20 percent within 15 years.

Revenues exceeded expenditures in rural municipalities in 2001. For municipalities in total, revenues essentially matched expenditures. This does not mean that the municipalities do not run deficits or have debt; many municipalities borrow to finance some of their capital spending. Per capita debt is a modest $108 for rural municipalities. It is considerably higher for towns and cities, where it averages about $730 per capita (largely for utility finance). Borrowing is (essentially) allowed only to support capital expenditures; it is regulated by the provincial government to ensure that borrowers are able to repay the funds. A provincial authority also borrows on behalf of municipalities and then on-lends to them. Such regulation and provincial-level borrowing agencies exist in other provinces as well.

Municipal governments in Alberta are responsible for property-related services (roads and streets, water and sewerage, drainage, waste management, parks, fire protection, property development and zoning) and services that are local in the sense that they benefit people living in the municipality (recreation, police and emergency services, business regulation, public health). For rural municipalities, roads are the major service provided. These services provide local benefits and can also be delivered efficiently at the local level.

Municipal government is not responsible for social services. These services normally involve a significant amount of redistribution and inter-jurisdictional spillovers. Local governments are therefore not well suited to finance them. The province provides comprehensive health coverage and assistance to the poor. Schooling has become a provincial responsibility in all but two provinces, although Alberta relies on elected local school boards (without tax powers) to manage its delivery.

Given the local benefits generated by municipal services, heavy reliance on local finances is reasonable. For numerous services (such as water), user charges are effective in constraining demand and getting beneficiaries to pay. For local governments, the property tax works well for financing services providing local but not individually identifiable direct benefits (such as roadways). A variety of licenses, fees, and other revenue sources can be used to distribute the fiscal burden.

In general, given the high reliance on local own revenues to fund municipal services that provide predominately local benefits, the municipal financing system in Alberta affords a good benefit-cost linkage, so that local residents can readily assess the merits of expenditure proposals. Rural municipalities, however, may be benefiting substantially from taxes on linear property that likely exceed the costs of the associated services. Tax exporting appears to be a possibility.

Transfers are relatively modest, but they are more important for rural than urban municipalities. Some transfers are indirect. For example, rural (and small urban) municipalities do not need to contribute toward policing costs. The abrupt cutoff for the small urban municipalities (recently moved to those with populations of less than 5,000) is arbitrary and unfair. Conventional cash transfers are almost entirely specific-purpose transfers. It is difficult to see a connection between the importance of transfers and spillovers. A grant system relying more heavily on formula-based unconditional funding might be an improvement.

Municipalities in Alberta have experienced huge fluctuations in their provincial grants. This has contributed to discussions about more-reliable transfer finance and alternative sources of own revenue. It is unlikely that this will lead to novel (for Alberta and Canada) results. However, some assistance might result from the provincial government abandoning its property tax, which contributes to the provincial funding of schools (about two-thirds the level of municipal property taxes), and leaving the property tax solely to municipal governments. With schooling now entirely a provincial funding responsibility, conventional provincial taxes (on income and consumption, for example) are more suitable than relying on a carryover of the local school property tax.

Overview and Reflections

Striking differences are apparent in local governments and local public finances across countries. These differences are particularly great across rural local governments (table 18.7, see p. 532). Intergovernmental transfers represent almost 100 percent of rural municipal government revenues in India but only about 13 percent in Alberta, Canada. Funds generated from own resources—that is, revenue sources over which local governments have control in terms of levying taxes and setting rates—range from 3 percent (India) of all revenues to 77 percent (Alberta). In Latvia strictly own-source revenues are relatively modest, accounting for less than 25 percent of all revenues (about 10 percent in rural and small urban areas). Shared taxes, at more than 60 percent of total revenue, are important contributors to municipal revenues there. Across all three case examples, rural local governments generate less own revenue and rely more heavily on grants than their urban counterparts or local governments on average.

Responsibilities have a major influence on finances. Core municipal responsibilities are a basic set of functions assigned to local governments almost everywhere. They include providing purely local amenities, such as transportation, water and sewerage services, drainage, solid waste collection and disposal, parks, recreational and cultural facilities, business regulation, and planning and zoning. These are services that make a local environment functional and pleasant.

Major differences are apparent in responsibilities for social services, especially schooling and health care. In India and Latvia, schooling accounts for about half of local government budgets. Local governments are responsible for both primary and secondary schooling, although the level and coverage differs. Municipal governments are not responsible for schooling in Alberta. This distinction is somewhat artificial, however, as schools are funded by the provinces but managed by locally elected school boards that are independent of municipal governments. Lacking (their former) taxing powers, school boards can no longer be considered true local governments. Such a distinction is not made in the other cases examined here. Hence for comparability, the organization of schooling in Alberta needs to be noted.[14] To some extent and to varying degrees, provincial and local authorities have always shared responsibilities for financing and delivering schooling in the province. Somewhat parallel to the provincialization of school finance in Alberta is the central government's assumption of responsibility for health insurance from regional governments in Latvia.

Local governments in Alberta differ from those in India and Latvia in another way. Rural municipalities in Alberta are distinctly rural, in that they do not include villages and towns.[15] In contrast, Indian villages and towns are explicitly part of the rural local authorities. In Latvia the data do not distinguish between small municipalities that are rural and those that are urban. However, a number of combined rural and urban municipalities—*novads*—now exist. Differences in the rural-urban balance of municipalities results in varying expenditure patterns. This variation is most obvious in and a striking feature of Alberta's rural municipalities, where transportation services (that is, roads) dominate expenditures, at almost 60 percent of their budgets.

Responsibilities affect the fiscal magnitude of local governments in the economy and in the public sector. Municipal government accounts

TABLE 18.7 Summary Information on Rural Local Governments in India, Latvia, and Canada (Alberta)

Item	India	Latvia	Canada (Alberta)
Constitutional recognition	Yes (1993)	No	No
Local government expenditures as			
Percentage of GDP	2.2 local, 1.4 rural	8–9	3.30[a]
Percentage of consolidated government	14.2 local, 9.0 rural	23	a
Population, rural (percent)	75	30 (50 in rajons)	20
Size of local government	Zilla panchayats: 1.4 million; Taluk panchayats: 114,000; Gram panchayats: 2,700	1,700 rural; 4,700 local	6,400 rural; 8,000 local
Responsibilities	29 listed	17 permanent	Broadly defined but provincially constrained
Core municipal	Yes	Yes	Yes (roads 60% of rural expenditures versus 33% of local expenditures)
School	Yes	Yes	No (provincial)
Health	Some	No	No (provincial)
Notable other	—	Social assistance	—

Revenue sources (percent)			
Own	25 local, 3 rural	20	86 local, 77 rural
Shared	—	60[b]	14 local, 23 rural
Transfers	75 local, 97 rural	20 local, 25+ rural	
Types of own revenue (percent)			
Property taxes	Yes (not agricultural land)	Very limited	36 local, 57 rural
Charges and fees	Yes	Yes	25 local, 6 rural
Intergovernmental transfers			
Unconditional		1.6% of local revenue, 25% of rural revenue[c]	0.9% of local revenue
Specific purpose	600 grants	17% of local revenue	13% local, 22% rural
School	50% of grants	—	[d]
Health	10% of grants	—	—
Notable other	—	—	Transportation: 40% local, 70% rural
Borrowing	Yes, state controlled	Tightly controlled, very little borrowing	Yes, provincial authority to monitor and assist municipal borrowing

Notes: Information is typically for local governments. Where a distinction is possible, local government information is designated local and that for rural local governments as rural.

a. Canadian average is 4.3 percent of GDP and 11.1 percent of consolidated government. If school districts are included, the Alberta percentage is 5.8 percent of GDP and the Canadian figures are 7.3 percent of GDP and 19 percent of consolidated government.

b. Personal income taxes and property taxes.

c. Equalization is mostly intermunicipal and benefits mostly local governments in rural areas.

d. Province allocates funds to local school boards to operate schools.

for 4.3 percent of GDP in Canada and 11.1 percent of consolidated government expenditures. If school spending is added, these percentages rise to 7.3 and 19 percent.[16] Including schooling, expenditures by local authorities in Canada (about 7–9 percent of GDP and 19–23 percent of consolidated government) are similar to those in Latvia. In contrast, despite similar designated responsibilities, local governments in India spend only about 2.2 percent of GDP. In Karnataka, however, local spending is a relatively high 6.5 percent of state GDP.

Responsibilities also affect funding patterns. In Alberta, where municipal governments have only core responsibilities, property tax and user charges generate 86 percent of municipal revenue. In rural municipalities, where roads represent the main responsibility, property taxes raise 57 percent of local revenue (what transfers are available are directed mostly to supporting transportation services). In India and Latvia, property taxes are not an important source of revenue, especially in rural areas; pure own-source revenue makes only modest contributions to the budgets.

The property tax is not well suited to financing social programs such as schooling. This is a reason for the move to entirely provincial funding of schooling in Alberta and in most Canadian provinces. Other countries have found other solutions. In India grants designated for schooling represent at least half of local revenues; schooling is fully funded by specific-purpose transfers. Grants dedicated to local health care are also important in India.

In Latvia social programs are funded by a 71.6 percent share of the personal income tax. Latvia's local governments have no control over the amount of shared revenues. They must, however, rely on the own revenues they control and for which they answer directly to local voters for further funds. Latvia has a quite transparent local financing system that benefits small and rural municipalities. While income taxes are shared with the originating municipality, Latvia's significant equalization system substantially reduces fiscal disparities among municipalities, shifting funds from larger and rich urban areas to poor and generally smaller urban and rural municipalities.

In Alberta and India, fair allocations depend on the system of specific-purpose grants. School finance in Alberta is formula and per student based, and the process is transparent. Although largely objective, formula based, and open, the multiplicity of specific grants to municipalities in Alberta is probably less transparent. Allocations in India are obscure, and local communities have little control or influence over the use of funds.

Local fiscal systems emerged from diverse backgrounds. In India, systems designed (especially) for rural authorities have recently developed from highly centralized administrative structures that appear reluctant to devolve, let alone decentralize. Very little spending by rural authorities is at the village level, where there are (albeit possibly weak) elected bodies. The large size (and importance) of the two upper-tier rural local authorities in India contrasts with the small sizes in Latvia and Alberta, where decision making is decentralized to the local level.

Latvia's multiplicity of very small (especially rural) local governments is a vestige of the administrative structure of the Soviet era. The system is in the process of being reorganized into larger, more functional units.[17]

In contrast to (rural) local governments in India and Latvia, those in Alberta have not experienced recent upheaval. In fact, they have evolved gradually over the province's 100-year history, with increasing provincial and reduced local authority. The provincialization of school finances a decade ago is the most recent step along that path. The fairly narrow and very local responsibilities of municipal government allow for a high degree of local fiscal independence, which functions well even for jurisdictions with small populations.

Conclusion

The role of transfers in local government finance depends very much on the assignment of responsibilities and the assignment of revenue sources. The services that local governments typically provide can be allocated to two broad categories: core municipal services and social programs. Core services tend to be related to property, while social programs are oriented directly to people. User charges and certain taxes (particularly the property tax) are efficient and fair for a very broad range of core services, and they can often be relied on to provide the bulk of required funding. Such revenue sources are directed to making the beneficiary pay, a policy that has merit on both efficiency and equity grounds. Transfers related to core services are largely for efficiency improvement (correcting for spillovers, for example), but they are also often used to provide general financial assistance and to implement some equalization.

Revenue sources suited to funding core services are not well suited for financing social programs. Some social programs, however, particularly education, benefit from community scrutiny and can operate efficiently at a relatively small scale. Hence it is not unusual for schooling to be a responsibility of local government or, if responsibility is at the provincial or national level, to operate with significant local citizen input and direction. If education is a local responsibility, social programs are normally supported by large specific-purpose transfers from higher-level governments or local governments receive shares of taxes normally imposed by the higher-level authorities (such as consumption taxes and income taxes) and levied by them. Because shared revenues are typically outside the control of local governments, even when they share part of the revenue, shared taxes have a strong parallel to transfers, although there are normally fewer or weaker explicit conditions attached to the funds. Small size and rural locations may impose fiscal disadvantages on the cost or the revenue side of local government budgets. Evidence from rural (and small) municipalities in India, Latvia, and Alberta, Canada, suggest that decision makers recognize such factors and so structure municipal finance programs so that those municipalities need to demand less from their own resources.

Notes

The author thanks the many colleagues who offered suggestions and materials for consideration, particularly Jameson Boex and M. Govinda Rao.

1. The data for this estimate come from Rao and Singh (2005).
2. The data for this estimate come from Rao, Nath, and Vani (2004).
3. Because the *gram panchayats* have some own revenue, their expenditures are about 30 percent greater than the transfers reported in table 18.1.
4. For information on local government in Latvia, see Maurina and Priede (2003), OECD (2000), Martinez-Vazquez and Boex (n.d.), Union of Local and Regional Governments of Latvia (2004), Vanags and Vilka (2001), and World Bank (2000).
5. These figures come from the Union of Local and Regional Governments of Latvia (2004). The divisions into subnational authorities primarily reflected administrative units under the Soviet system.
6. One-hundred eighty municipalities (34 percent) have populations of less than 1,000, 384 (72 percent) have populations of less than 2,000, and 489 (91 percent) have populations of less than 5,000 (Union of Local and Regional Governments of Latvia 2004).
7. The source (OECD 2000) refers to a total basic budget and to special budget revenues. The basic budget revenues of the subnational units reported there correspond closely to the combined municipal and regional district revenues in table 18.3.
8. These figures are individual municipality values aggregated to the regional level. The ranges across individual municipalities would be larger.
9. Despite these positives, much about the equalization program is still debated. See, for example, Martinez-Vazquez and Boex (n.d.).
10. In addition, a variety of special purpose local authorities can be found.
11. The official population list and other information about Alberta municipalities can be found at the Web site of Alberta Municipal Affairs, www.municipalaffairs. gov.ab.ca.

12. The rural municipalities, which account for about 14 percent of the population, do not conform exactly to this urban-rural distinction.
13. Dollar figures are in Canadian dollars.
14. For comparison, school board expenditures in Alberta represent about 45 percent of combined school and municipal expenditures.
15. This is unlike school districts outside Alberta's major urban areas, which include towns and villages with the surrounding rural areas. Alberta has 359 municipalities but only about 60 school districts.
16. Due to the cyclical impact of resource revenues, the 3.3 percent of GDP in Alberta is somewhat below the Canadian average, despite an above average level of per capita expenditure. National figures for Canada enable comparisons to be made with consolidated government expenditures that are more representative of municipal governments in Canada.
17. The use of regional authorities is mixed in Canada. In India and Latvia, where regional authorities are ubiquitous, they emerged from a highly centralized form of government.

References

Bardhan, Pranab. 2000. "Local Governance and Delivery of Public Goods." In *Governance, Decentralization and Reform in China, India and Russia*, ed. Jean-Jacques Dethier, 179–88. Boston: Kluwer Academic Publishers.

Dethier, Jean-Jacques. 2000. *Governance, Decentralization and Reform in China, India and Russia*. Boston: Kluwer Academic Publishers.

Mahal, Ajay, Vivek Srivastava, and Deepak Sanan. 2000. "Decentralization and Public Sector Delivery of Health and Education Services in India." In *Governance, Decentralization and Reform in China, India and Russia*, ed. Jean-Jacques Dethier, 235–69. Boston: Kluwer Academic Publishers.

Martinez-Vazquez, Jorge, and Jameson Boex. n.d. "A Review of Latvia's Equalization Fund." In *The Design of Equalization Grants: Theory and Applications*, ed. Jorge Martinez-Vazquez and Jameson Boex, 65–88. Country Case Study. Washington, DC: World Bank Institute.

Maurina, J., and M. Priede. 2003. "Implications of Territorial Reforms on Different Aspects of Life of Local Governments of Jelgava District." www.uwe.ac.uk/bbs/sglg/maur.doc.

McMillan, Melville L. 2006. "Local Government Organization and Finance: Canada." In *Local Governance in Industrial Countries*, ed. Anwar Shah. Washington, DC: World Bank Institute.

OECD (Organisation of Economic Co-operation and Development). 2000. "Fiscal Design across Levels of Government: Year 2000 Surveys, Country Report: Latvia." Directorate for Financial, Fiscal and Enterprise Affairs, FDI2000/220301/2, Paris.

Rajaraman, Indira. 2000. "Fiscal Features of Local Goverance in India." In *Governance, Decentralization and Reform in China, India and Russia*, ed. Jean-Jacques Dethier, 189–227. Boston: Kluwer Academic Publishers.

Rao, M. Govinda. 2003. "Challenges to Fiscal Decentralization in Developing and Transitional Economies: An Asian Perspective." In *Public Finance in Developing and*

Transitional Counties: Essays in Honor of Richard Bird, ed. Jorge Martinez-Vazquez and James Alm. Cheltenham, United Kingdom: Edward Elgar.

Rao, M. Govinda, and Nirvikar Singh. 2005. *The Political Economy of Federalism in India*. New Delhi: Oxford University Press.

Rao, M. Govinda, H.K. Amar Nath, and B.P. Vani. 2004. "Rural Fiscal Decentralization in Karnataka State." In *Fiscal Decentralization to Rural Local Governments in India*. New Delhi: Oxford University Press.

Statistics Canada. 2004. "The Rural-Urban Income Gap within Provinces: An Update to 2000." *Rural and Small Town Canada Analysis Bulletin* 5 (7): 1–20.

Union of Local and Regional Governments of Latvia. 2004. "Local and Regional Governments in Latvia." www.lps.lv.

Vanags, Edvins, and Inga Vilka. 2001. "Local Government Reform in the Baltic Countries. www.uni-stuttgart.de/soz/avps/rlg/papers/.

World Bank. 2000. *The Republic of Latvia Poverty Assessment*. Vol. 1. Report 20707-LV, Poverty Reduction and Management Unit, Washington, DC.

Index

Boxes, figures, notes, and tables are indicated by *b, f, n,* and *t,* respectively.

accountability, 55–56, 133, 203–4, 321, 487
  achieving through performance-
    oriented transfers, 9, 11–15
  Brazil, 155
  and common pool problem, 150
  and conditional vs. unconditional
    grants, 495–97
  and design of unconditional
    grants, 499
  of governments to citizens, 229–30
  and guidelines for designing fiscal
    transfers, 15–17
  impact of grants on, 10*t*1.1
  impact of revenue decentralization
    on, 58
  and overlapping responsibilities,
    166
  political, 41, 96, 157
  for pricing of services, 467
  problems of, 468
  regional, 73, 136
  and revenue sharing, 333
  rural local governments, 516
  subnational governments, 149–50,
    168*n*3
  United States, 160, 161
accounting, 96, 103–4
actual expenditures per capita, 503–4
ad hoc grants, 42
adjustment coefficients, 416
administration of grants, 487, 499

adverse selection, 83
adverse shocks, 140
AFCD. *see* Aid to Families with
  Dependent Children (AFCD),
  United States
Afonso, J. R. R., 491
agency costs, 305–6, 310
agenda setting, 177, 227–28, 254*n*1
agents of the citizenry, 316*n*2
agglomeration costs, 90–91
agglomeration economies, 456
aggregate demands, 125, 138
aggregate resources, 346
aggregate shocks, 125
aggregate tax revenues, 331–32
agricultural income, 325, 336–37*n*2
Ahmad, E., 368–69
Aid to Families with Dependent Children
  (AFCD), United States, 241–43*t*8.1,
  247–50, 255*nn*7–12
Aizenman, J., 140
Alberta, Canada, 524–30, 531,
  532–33*t*18.7, 536*nn*11–13
Alesina, A., 186–87
allocation of products, 56
allocation of resources, 19, 75, 98–99,
  325, 476*n*1
allocation of transfers, 460–61
allocative efficiency, 487
Araújo, E. A., 491
area cost factor, 413

539

Argentina, 489t17.1
 convertibility law, 195–96
 intergovernmental relations, 183
 per capita transfers, 209
 soft budget constraints, 153–54
 transfer formula, 216
Ariff, M., 347
Asdrubali, P, 109, 118, 129n2
Asensio, M. A., 485, 488
asking-for-more-trouble transfers, 18b1.1
asymmetric federalism, 187
asymmetric generalized equalization
 schemes, 79
asymmetric shocks, 108
 adjustments to, 115–16
 Europe, 116
 and fiscal insurance studies, 118–21,
 129n11
 and fiscal transfers, 113
 market-based insurance studies, 117–18
 and regional insurance, 113–14
 and soft budget constraints, 143
 and vertical fiscal imbalances, 143–44
Athanasoulis, S., 118, 120
Atkeson, A., 109, 117, 118
Aubut, J., 22, 377
Austin-Smith, D., 184
Australia, 329, 370, 472
 accuracy of predictions of new
 institutional economics, 310–16
 and capital cost disabilities, 431
 capital stock data, 439–40, 449n6
 Commonwealth Grants Commission,
 300–301, 404, 410–11, 449
 costing methodologies, 410–12
 equalization schemes in, 70, 93,
 355–56, 449, 450n17
 features of, 34t1.5, 36
 and fiscal needs, 24, 30–31, 342–43
 interregional, 78, 80
 expenditure needs, 25
 secondary education expenditures,
 314t10.4
 soft budget constraints, 159–60
 and specific-purpose grants, 92, 429,
 434–35
 and vertical grants, 209

Austria, 472
autonomy, local, 9
average expenditure per capita, 503–4
average producer costs per person, 88

backlog regions, 436–38, 440–44, 445,
 450nn8–13, 450n14
Bahl, R., 280, 370, 485
Baicker, K., 234, 241t8.1, 248, 249–50,
 255n8, 255nn11–12
Bailey, S. J., 177, 226
bailouts, 174, 253
 Brazil, 155
 Canada, 161
 costs of denying, 142–43
 and Goodspeed's model, 141
 Hungary, 158–59
 and second generation theories of
 transfers, 230
 and soft budget problems, 190–92
 Sweden, 152–53
 and "too-big-to-fail" theory, 139
 Ukraine, 156
 United States, 160, 161
Baker, M., 207, 242t8.1, 250
banking sector, Argentina, 153–54
bankruptcy law, Hungary, 158–59
Barati, I., 2
Bardhan, P., 516
Baretti, C., 115, 191, 212, 229, 238t8.1,
 245, 349
Barro, S. M., 346–47, 351, 376
basic fiscal revenues, 414–16
Bayoumi, T, 114, 117, 118, 120, 121
Becker, E., 235
Becker, G. S., 183
Beierl, O., 276, 285
Belgium, 282
 administrative proceedings, 283
 dispute resolution, 281
 legal framework study conclusions,
 284
 procedures of establishment and
 modification of transfers, 276
 system of government, 263, 289n2
benefit model of local government
 finance, 457–58, 486–88, 493

benefit spillovers. *see* spillover of benefits
Bergstrom, P., 238*t*8.1, 245
Bezdek, R., 250
Bird, R. M., 165, 173, 176, 192, 209, 259
  accountability of local governments, 505
  and budget constraints, 464
  characteristics of large cities, 453–55
  conditional grants, 488, 493
  on consumption tax, 326
  and efficiency, 399
  expenditure vs. fiscal capacity grants, 501
  on externalities, 465
  on fiscal federalism, 476*n*1, 495
  and horizontal equalization, 419, 421, 422*n*20
  matching grants, 466
  principal-agent model, 486
  on RTS, 376
  on service delivery, 458, 467
  on small urban areas, 485
  study on transfers, 284–85
  on taxation, 324, 325, 329, 330, 333, 458, 462
  and transfer design, 467
  on types of grants, 464
  on unconditional transfers, 279
  vertical fiscal imbalances, 461
Blindenbacher, R., 372
block grants, 2, 73, 493, 505
  AFDC, 248
  for alcohol and drug abuse programs, 234
  and expenditure needs, 369
  incentive effects of, 206–8
  TANF, 247, 248, 250, 255*n*8
  tax sharing as substitute for, 335
  vs. matching grants, 205–6
Boadway, Robin, 15, 22, 173, 175, 340
  and conditional grants, 466
  on decentralization, 260–61
  economic rationale for grants, 491
  and efficiency issues, 180, 367, 427
  and equalization costs, 369
  on equalization systems, 23, 24, 215, 384, 448

"Grants in a Federal Economy", 55–74
  and horizontal transfers, 211, 397
  and migration incentives, 219–20
  and minimum national standards, 447
  on resource allocation, 325
  revenue generation, 344
  and risk sharing, 107, 108, 109
  on targeting grants, 493
  on vertical equity, 342
  and vertical fiscal imbalances, 17, 143–44
Bobson, P., 173
Boex, J., 193, 293, 299, 309, 461, 469
Bolton, P., 187
Boothe, P., 346, 352, 353, 376
Borcherding, T. E., 226
borrowing, 141, 142
  Argentina, 153–54
  Australia, 159–60
  borrowing capacity, 286, 465
  Canada, 161, 529
  Germany, 147–50
  Hungary, 157–59
  incentives for, 148–49
  rural local governments, 520, 533*t*18.7
  Sweden, 152–53
  Ukraine, 156
  United States, 160
Bosnia and Herzegovina, 76, 105*n*1
bottom-up approach to
  intergovernmental grants, 177–78, 181
Bourne, Larry, 456
Bourne, L. S., 494
Bradbury, Katharine L., 408
Bradford, D., 176, 226
Brainard, W., 236
Braun, D., 267, 282
Brazil, 167, 489*t*17.1
  consumption tax base, 326
  need factors in health care grants, 38*t*1.6
  setting minimum standards for grants, 40
  and soft budget problems, 155–56, 192
Brennan, G., 133
Breton, A., 321
Brock, R., 184, 185, 188

Brosio, G., 277, 280
Bryson, P. J., 468
Buchanan, J., 133, 397
Bucovetsky, S., 108, 206, 214, 231
budget constraints, 110, 135, 232–33, 249
budgets, 94
  balanced-budget constraint, 232
  budget-maximizing hypothesis,
      227–28, 254n1
  and bureaucracy, 98–99
  and discretionary transfers, 165–66
  extra-budgetary funds, 333
  and flypaper effect, 177
  Germany, 148
  Latvia, 517–18, 536n7
  output-oriented budgeting, 101–3
  of regional governments, 134
  South Africa, 287
  and timing of disbursements of grants,
      251
Büettner, T., 115, 122, 148, 215, 375
Bulgaria, 330, 461
bureaucracies
  budgeting process, 98–99
  and fiscal discipline, 97–98
  and flypaper effect, 177
  and functional agencies, 99–100
Burgess, R., 331–32
Burki, S. J., 455
Byoumi, T., 109

Cai, H., 229
Canada, 218, 252, 369, 370
  accuracy of predictions of new
      institutional economics, 310–16
  base tax-back system, 349, 350
  data collection, 471, 477n13
  education financing, 41
  equalization system, 70, 121, 354–55,
      384
    definition, complexity, and
        transparency of, 350–52
    features of, 34t1.5
    horizontal equalization, 107–8
  expenditures, 471, 477n13, 485–86
    estimating an expenditure equation,
        408–9

  measures of expenditure needs, 24,
      25, 28t1.4
  theory-based representative
      expenditure system, 27, 29
  fiscal arrangements committee,
      296–98
  governing structure, 485
  law and political economy in, 260–62
  migration in, 366–67
  output-based transfers, 37, 38
  regional insurance, 121–22
  reliance on grant support, 489t17.1
  RTS, 376
  rural local governments in, 524–30,
      536nn11–13
  soft budget constraints, 161–62
  taxation, 346–48, 353
    consumption tax base, 326
    tax rates, 215, 349
  and vertical grants, 209
Canada Assistance Plan (CAP), 247–48,
      250
canonical system, 213
capacity equalization, 88, 212–15, 216, 417
capital cities, intergovernmental grants
      to, 473–75, 478nn15–17
capital-deficient regions, 436, 437–38
capital grants, 42–43, 465
  conclusions concerning, 445
  economic rationales for, 446–47
  formulaic approach to, 429, 432–34,
      449n4
  input databases, 439–40, 449n6
  issues in design of, 431–32
  project-based approach to, 429,
      434–35
  rationales for, 426–31, 445
  simulation models, 435–44, 449nn5–6,
      450nn8–14
capitalization, 20
capital markets, 109–10, 129n2, 435
  and regional risk sharing, 114
  United States, 117, 118, 160
capital-surplus regions, 436, 437–38
capitation payments, 464
Caplan, A., 197n10
Card, D., 221n3

case studies of legal architecture of
transfers
  common findings, 287–88
  conclusions concerning, 284–87, 290n16
  conditional and unconditional
    transfers, 278–80, 289n15
  dispute resolution and adjudication,
    280–83
  legal basis of transfer systems, 265–75
  procedures for establishing and
    modifying transfers, 275–78,
    289n13
  systems of government in countries,
    263–65, 289n2
  see also empirical studies
cash accounting, 103
cash assistance programs, 248, 255n7
Castells, A., 384
central governments
  and allocation formulas, 416–17
  Australia, 159–60
  consequences of failures of, 194t6.1
  costs of denying bailouts, 142–43
  and designing fiscal arrangements, 44,
    46–48
  and equalization schemes, 164–65
  Hungary, 158–59
  and intergovernmental transfers, 137
    allocation of transfers, 185–86, 197n8
    discretionary transfers, 165–66
    equitable share formula for,
      45–46b1.3
  Italy, 150–51
  mandating minimum national
    standards, 429
  and market discipline, 163–64
  and overlapping responsibilities, 166
  and political economy, 140–41
  revenue sharing systems, 328–30
  Sweden, 152–53
  tax powers, 134
  and tax sharing, 333
  Ukraine, 156–57
  and vertical fiscal imbalance, 163
centralization
  political, 188–89, 197n9
  of taxing powers, 324–25

Chaparro, J., 208, 466, 493
Chen, D., 486
Chernick, H., 207, 232, 234, 248, 255n7,
  421n5
Chicago, Illinois, 473
Chile, 80, 209
China, 35–36, 188, 193, 332–33
Choudhry, Sujit, 259–92
citizen's preferences, link to public
  policies, 260
city-state structure, 455
Clark, D., 370
claws back, 92, 105n5
closed-ended grants, 7–9, 237, 250, 253,
  254n2
  and budget constraints, 232–33
  for large cities and metropolitan areas,
    460
  and local priorities, 42
  United States, 237
  upper limits of, 488
  vs. open-ended grants, 492
closeness proxy, 179
coalitions, 305
  bargaining strength of, 227–28,
    254n1
  coalition parties, 182
Colombia, 208, 209, 221n2, 463, 466,
  489t17.1
command-and-control, 18b1.1
commissions, 274–75, 299–300,
  303, 304
  and holdup problems, 193
  role in fiscal systems, 47
  see also specific countries
commitment, problems with, 189–94,
  197n10
common agency model, 184, 185
common pool problem, 138, 140, 142,
  181–83, 196n4
  and accountability, 150
  Argentina, 154
  and decision making, 191
  as externality, 144
  Germany, 149
  Ukraine, 157
  United States, 161

Commonwealth Grants Commission,
    Australia, 78, 80, 355, 357, 404,
    410–11, 449
communism, 188
competition, 133
    fiscal, 229–30
    intergovernmental, 321
    interjurisdictional, 228, 231
    interregional, 176, 196n2
    for mobile tax bases, 134
    negative impact of, 229
    political, 158, 176–81, 196n4
    promotion of, 173
    and revenue sharing, 323–24
    and tax-base sharing, 328
    see also political competition
compliance, 234
conciliation, 282
concurrent tax powers, and revenue
    sharing, 323–24
conditional grants, 5–9, 56, 91, 288, 425,
    426
    and accountability, 12
    Belgium, 278
    criticism of, 261
    design of, 498
    economic rationale for providing,
        492–93
    for education, 13–14
    endogeneity of, 232, 235
    and externalities, 465–66
    and financing systems, 488
    fungibility of, 466
    Germany, 278–79
    India, 278, 279–80, 289n14
    to large cities and metropolitan areas,
        460
    nonmatching, 4–5
    output based, 39
    for public services, 62–63, 466
    to small urban areas, 505, 506
    South Africa, 278, 280, 287, 289n15
    specific-purpose closed-ended
        matching grants, 243–44t8.1,
        250–52
    United States, 161
    vs. unconditional grants, 495–97

Connolly, S., 177, 226
constitutional law, 266–67
    Argentina, 154
    Belgium, 278
    Brazil, 155–56
    Germany, 147, 148, 267–71, 276–79,
        281, 285
    India, 271–73, 286, 289nn10–11
    judicial review and adjudication of
        transfers, 283
    limits of, 288
    Nigeria, 299
    and revenue sharing, 323
    South Africa, 273–75, 277–78, 280,
        281, 289n13, 289n15
    Sweden, 152
    tax sharing, 329, 331, 334
    Ukraine, 156–57
constitutions
    Belgium, 263, 267
    and equalization schemes, 77,
        78–79, 80
    and federal-regional fiscal relations,
        65–67
    India, 512
    and provision of public services, 62
    as stage of decision making, 194–95,
        195t6.2, 196
consumption, 319, 351–52
consumption smoothing, 109–12, 118,
    129nn2–3, 129n5
consumption tax base, 325–27,
    337nn3–4
contingent entitlements, 87
contract-based management, 9
contractual arrangements, 94–96, 193
    and coordination of interagency
        decisions through microtransfers,
        96–104, 105n7
    and output-oriented budgeting, 102
convertibility law, 195–96
cooperative agreements, 429, 449n1
cooperative outcomes, 140
core support groups, 179
Cornes, R., 197n10
Cornia, G. C., 468
corporate taxes, 325

cost indices, 407, 408, 414
costs, 88, 143, 464
    agency, 305–6
    agglomeration, 90–91
    approaches to
        Australia, 410–12
        France, 416–17
        Hungary, 417
        Japan, 414–16
        Republic of Korea, 416
        Sweden, 413–14
        Switzerland, 417–19
        United Kingdom, 412–13,
            421–22n13
    of borrowing, 153–54, 160, 161
    cost-benefit proposals, 429, 435, 530
    cost disabilities, 401, 430–31
    differences in, 368–69, 391n3
    for education, 391n3
    equalization of, 35, 371, 413–14
    estimating cost functions, 404–7
    estimating expenditure equation,
        407–9, 421n11
    of expenditure needs, 400–401
    of microtransfers, 103–4
    of public services, 401–4, 421nn5–6
    reliance on expert judgments to
        measure, 409–10
    transactions, 183, 197n6, 305–6
    see also expenditure needs
cost-sharing programs, 5–9, 460, 468,
    477n7
    see also matching grants
Courant, P. N., 227
Courchene, T. J., 121, 129n10, 346, 356,
    366–67
Craig, J., 368–69
Craig, S., 228, 237, 239–40t8.1, 243t8.1,
    246, 248
credit markets, Brazil, 155
credit ratings, 168n3
cultural facilities, 456
currency, and regional risk sharing,
    112–13, 129n9
Currie, D. B., 279
customs duties, 331, 332
Czech Republic, 468

Dafflon, Bernard, 108, 361–424
Dahlberg, M., 138, 152, 191, 238t8.1, 245
Dahlby, B., 115, 215, 221n4, 347
data collection, 470, 477n12
    and economic rationale for grants, 492
    population impact on size of grants,
        497–98
Deacon, R. T., 226
debt service, 504
decentralization, 173
    Boadway's views of, 260–61
    Brazil, 155
    disincentives from tax sharing in
        decentralized tax administrations,
        332–33
    and equalization transfers, 19, 228–31
    fiscal, 136, 141–42, 176, 320
    India, 512
    Latvia, 522–23
    link to efficiency, 133
    and local fiscal disparities, 363–66
    and market discipline, 163–64
    and market-preserving federalism,
        188–89
    overview, 55–56
    and soft budget problems, 141–42, 191
    and spillovers, 134
    of taxation, 17, 73, 204–5
decentralized leadership model, 197n10
decision making
    arguments for, 260
    autonomy in, 208
    and common pool problem, 191
    decentralized, 44, 204
    determining expenditure needs, 415–16
    and moral hazard problem, 231
    stages of, 194–95, 195t6.2, 196
    by two levels of government, 46–47
defaults, United States, 160
deficits
    deficit grants, 19
    Hungary, 158
    India, 286
    and intergovernmental transfers, 149
    South Africa, 287
    United States, 195
Delors, J., 108

DelRossi, A. F., 182
demand, income elasticity of, 233–34
demand shocks, 124
demographic factors
  and costs of public services, 403–4
  and expenditure needs, 23
  and net fiscal benefits, 341
Denmark, 35, 369, 391–92*n*4
design of fiscal transfer schemes, 390,
    498–504
  bridging vertical fiscal gaps, 17–19
  capital grants, 431–32
  and characteristics of large cities and
    metropolitan areas, 454–55,
    476–77*nn*1–2
  concerns in, 31–33
  and definition of standard, 463–64
  designing equalization formulas,
    86–92
  features used to assess legal aspects of
    transfers, 261–62
  and fiscal equalization transfers,
    19–36
  formulas for, 398
  interpersonal equalization across
    jurisdictions, 82–86
  interregional equalization within the
    public sector, 78–82
  legal instruments of, 265–75
  measuring expenditure needs, 23–29
  measuring fiscal capacity, 20–23
  overview, 15–17, 78
  principles and practices in, 48–51
  responsibility for in selected countries,
    295*t*10.1
  see also equalization transfer systems
Dethier, J., 516
Dewatripont, M., 190
DeWit, A., 415, 416
Dillinger, W., 191, 455
disabilities, 411–12, 430–31
disaggregated targeting, 286
discretionary spending, 504
discretionary transfers, 151, 165–66
disentanglement of functions, 94
disincentives for tax sharing, 331
disparities, 476*n*1, 521–22

dispute resolution, 73
  ad hoc political negotiations, 282
  administrative proceedings, 283
  case studies, 280–83
  constitutional principles, 281–82
  judicial review and adjudication, 283
  mediation and conciliation, 282
distortionary taxes, 221*n*4
distributional costs, 143
distributive equity, 65
district power equalization grants, 21*b*1.2
Dixit, A. K., 178, 179–81, 184, 196*n*3,
    197*n*7
Dollery, B., 486
Duff, D. G., 486
Duncombe, W., 240*t*8.1, 246

Ebel, R. D., 324, 325, 329, 330, 333, 461,
    466
econometrics
  to estimate cost disabilities, 430–31
  issues arising in estimating public
    good expenditure model, 232–33
economic efficiency, 487
economics
  and interregional equalization systems,
    78–82
  in large cities and metropolitan areas,
    455–57, 477*nn*3–5
  and rationale for providing grants,
    491–94
economic union, 64–65, 66
economies of scale, 403, 469, 477*n*3
education, 42, 234
  application of results-based chain to,
    11, 11*f*1.5
  conditional grants for, 13–14
  cost factors, 391*n*3
    reliance on expert judgments on
    costs of, 409–10
  equalization formulas, 421*n*1
  estimating cost function of, 406–7
  expenditures for in Australia,
    314*t*10.4
  India, 513, 514*t*18.1, 516
    reliance on expert judgments on costs
    of, 409–10

rural local governments, 531,
    537nn14–15
school financing, 20, 21b1.2, 41, 221n3
and setting of minimum standards for
    grants, 40
and Title I grants, 235–36, 247, 255n5
United States, 235–36, 239–41t8.1,
    245–47, 252, 255n3, 255n5
efficiency issues, 219, 362, 366–68, 399
and capital grants, 427–28, 429
and contributions to central
    governments, 184–85
and decentralization, 133
and design of unconditional grants, 499
efficiency-enhancing transfers, 94, 95,
    98–99, 103, 448
and equalization, 340–41
in federations, 65
and functional-agency approach to
    public administration, 98–99
impact of microtransfers on, 101
intragovernment, 93–98, 106n8
and policy outcomes, 203
and political economy, 180–81
and revenue sharing, 323–24
efficient government hypothesis, 228
effort. see fiscal effort
eligibility equalization schemes, 79, 82
eligibility restrictions, 255n12
Else, P., 369
empirical studies
    general-purpose nonmatching grants,
        237, 245, 254n2
    of intergovernmental transfers
        impact of (1973–2005), 238–44t8.1
    to large cities and metropolitan
        areas, 469–71, 492nn9–12
    measuring of impact of transfers on
        local fiscal behavior, 231–36
    on regional insurance, 119t4.1, 121–23
    United States
        fiscal insurance against asymmetric
            shocks, 118–21, 129n11
        market-based insurance against
            asymmetric shocks, 117–18
    see also case studies of legal
        architecture of transfers

endogeneity of grant variables, 232, 235,
    237, 254, 255n13
enforcement, 73, 195, 229
Enikolopov, R., 188
environmental factors, and costs of
    public services, 403
equalization needs, 368–72, 391–92nn3–8
equalization transfer systems, 213, 216,
    352–53, 361, 391n10, 494
    alternative "nonmacro" base, 353–54
    approaches to, 77–82
    Australia, 30–31, 159–60, 312f10.3,
        355–56
    base tax-back, 349, 350
    Canada, 121, 354–55
    comparative practices of, 30–31, 33–36
    and consumption smoothing, 109–12
    definition, complexity, and
        transparency of, 350–52
    features of in selected countries, 34t1.5
    federal-regional, 68–72
    and fiscal capacity, 20–23
    formulas for, 343–46, 378–79
    Germany, 147–50, 268–71
    goals of, 398–99
    incentive problems, 348–49
    institutional arrangements for, 304–6,
        316nn2–3
    interpersonal equalization across
        jurisdictions, 82–86
    interregional within public sector,
        78–82
    macro bases as measures of fiscal
        capacity, 346–54
    measuring expenditure needs, 23–29
    and moral hazard problem, 231
    objectives of, 211
    and other types of transfers, 341–43
    overview, 19–20
    political expediency of, 77–78
    principles for, 92–93
    rate tax–back, 348, 349
    and regional stabilization, 112–13,
        129nn8–9
    reliance on grant support, 489–90t17.1
    and risk sharing, 107–9
    self-financing, 31

South Africa, 356–57
  theory of, 340–45, 358n1
  and vertical fiscal gaps, 59–61
  see also design of fiscal transfer
    schemes; horizontal equalization
    systems; *specific type of grant*
equitable shares program, 280
equity issues, 33, 57, 180, 362, 368
  and design of unconditional grants,
    498–99
  distributive, 65
  fiscal, 194
  impact of microtransfers on, 101
  interjurisdictional, 33, 76–78, 105n1
  and one-tier governments, 464
Eskelund, G., 135, 162, 165, 167, 189
Esteller, A., 215, 384
Europe, asymmetric shocks, 116
European Charter of Local Self-
    Government, 2, 362, 364, 391n1,
    392n9
European Commission, 108, 118, 119
European Monetary Union, 108
European Union, features of regional
    policies of, 81–82, 105n2
exchange rates, 112–13
executive federalism committees, 47
expenditure function, 407–8
expenditure needs, 93
  ad hoc determination of, 24–25
  and allocation of grants, 469, 470
  and capital grants, 430
  costs of, 400–401
  defining of, 400–401
  formulas to measure, 419
  lessons for developing countries,
    419–21, 422n20
  measures of, 23–29, 420, 463
  see also costs
expenditures, 2, 4, 8, 64, 70, 463
  Argentina, 154
  asymmetric response to, 236
  Australia, 25, 30–31, 70, 314t10.4
  as basis of transfers, 471–72, 477n13
  Canada, 24–25, 28t1.4, 457, 477nn4–5
  categories of, 28t1.4
  and decentralization, 204–5

decentralizing expenditures vs.
    decentralizing revenues, 58–59
  as determinant of demand for public
    goods, 231–36
  differences in large cities and
    metropolitan areas, 455–57,
    477nn3–5
  discretionary, 236
  endogeneity issues, 235, 251
  and equalization schemes, 70, 164–65,
    368–72
  estimating an equation for, 407–9,
    421n11
  expenditure/fiscal capacity grants,
    501–4, 507
  financing of in small urban areas,
    486–88
  Germany, 148–49, 285
  Hungary, 157–59
  imbalance between tax sources and,
    342–43
  impact of grants on, 10t1.1
    1973–2005, 238–44t8.1
    specific-purpose nonmatching
      grants, 239–41t8.1, 245–47,
      255nn3–6
    specific-purpose open-ended
      matching grants, 241–43t8.1,
      247–50
  India, 279–80, 512–13
  and local fiscal policies, 364
  measurement of, 391n4, 507
  per capita, 472, 477n3, 477n8, 503–4
  and private income accounts, 233
  and reliance on grant support, 488,
    489–90t17.1
  representative expenditures system, 25
  and revenue sharing, 321–23, 336n1
  rural local governments
    Canada (Alberta), 525–26, 529,
      532t18.7, 534, 537n13
    India, 532t18.7
    Latvia, 517–18, 520–21, 532t18.7
  for secondary education, 314t10.4
  short-run and long-run impact of
    grants on, 235–36
  small urban areas, 485–86

South Africa, 275
and specific-purpose closed-ended
matching grants, 243–44*t*8.1,
250–52
theory-based representative system,
27, 29, 30
Ukraine, 156–57
United Kingdom, 456–57
experts
to estimate costs of public services,
409–10
on law enforcement, 413
used in Australia, 410
explicit equalization standards, 36
externalities, 214, 427, 488
created by competition, 229–30, 231
creation of, 192, 197*n*10
and economic rationale for grants, 492
forms of, 144
horizontal, 197*n*10
interregional, 446–47
in large cities and metropolitan areas,
465–66
negative, 138, 229–30
region-specific, 427–28

fairness factors, and financing systems, 487
Farber, G., 369, 370, 391*n*3, 392*n*6
Fatas, A., 109, 120, 129*n*11
federal finance, vs. fiscal federalism, 186
federal fiscal systems
design of in Canada, 296–98
federal-provincial, 47, 151
and regional insurance, 120–21
United States, 118–21, 129*n*11
federal governments
Brazil, 155–56
and designing fiscal arrangements, 44,
46–48
federal-regional fiscal relations, 65–74
as first mover, 72, 74*n*2
and grants
federal-regional conditional grants,
72–74
to large cities, 473, 477–78*n*14
size of equalization grants, 71
structure of, 142

and intragovernment relations, 96
and provision of public services, 62
federalism
asymmetric, 187
fiscal. *see* fiscal federalism
laboratory federalism, 97, 105*n*7
and local fiscal disparities, 363–66
market-preserving, 188–89, 197*n*9
views of, 94, 95
federal loyalty principle, 281
federal-provincial fiscal systems, 47, 161,
296–98
federal-regional fiscal relations
constitutional context for, 65–67
intergovernmental fiscal relations,
67–74
federations
efficiency in, 65
and federal stability, 448–49, 450*n*17
imbalance between tax sources and
expenditures, 342
and provision of public services, 62
Feldstein, M. S., 210
Fenge, R., 464, 472
Figuieres, C., 215, 229–30
Filimon, R., 3, 177, 227, 241*t*8.1, 246
financial capacity, measuring of, 389
Financial Planning Council, Germany,
298–99
financial sector
Argentina, 153–54
Canada, 161
Hungary, 158
Ukraine, 156, 157
fire alarm oversight, 305, 308, 309*t*10.2,
316*n*3
first-generation theories of impact of
transfers, 226–28, 253, 254*n*1,
391*n*2
Fiscal and Financial Commission, South
Africa, 303, 316
fiscal arrangements committees, Canada,
296–98
fiscal benefits, 59–61
fiscal capacity, 19–20, 60
correcting for differences in, 71–72
empirical estimates of, 217

expenditure/fiscal capacity grants,
501–4
Germany, 285
and grants
allocation of, 469, 470, 500
design of, 500–501
equalization grants, 32, 68–72, 285
horizontal grants, 216–17
matching grants, 7
impact of composition of tax on, 462
Latvia, 522
macro bases as measures of, 346–54
measures of, 20–23, 351–52, 375–78
Sweden, 413–14
and transfer programs, 35–36
fiscal competition, and second-generation
theories of transfers, 229–30
fiscal discipline, 143
enforcement of, 195
and hierarchical mechanisms, 167
role of vertical fiscal imbalances in,
162–63
through microeconomic incentives,
97–98
Ukraine, 157
fiscal disparities, 361, 420
and devising equalization formulas,
378–79
elimination of, 398–99
and equalization targets, 379–80
Latvia, 521–22, 534
local governments, 363–66
and needs equalization, 368–72,
391–92nn3–8
and revenue equalization, 372–80,
392nn9–10
and secessions, 19
sources of, 364–66
fiscal effort, 216, 217–19, 234, 247
fiscal equalization transfers *see* design of
fiscal transfers; equalization transfer
systems; intergovernmental transfers;
objectives of fiscal transfers
fiscal equity, 194
fiscal federalism, 319, 391n2, 392–93n12
Belgium, 284
conflicting objectives of, 55–56

Germany, 268–71
India, 279, 286–87, 289n14
law and political economy of, 260–62
rationales for grant programs, 446–47
roles of government, 476n1
vs. federal finance, 186
fiscal gaps, 461–62
and economic rationales for grants,
446, 493
and equalization transfers, 448
role of grants in closing of, 57–59
see also vertical fiscal imbalances
fiscal illusion hypothesis, 227
fiscal imbalances, 460–62
Indonesia, 187
South Africa, 287
fiscal indiscipline, 145
Argentina, 153–54
Brazil, 155–56
Hungary, 159
Sweden, 152–53
fiscal institutionalization, Argentina, 154
fiscal needs, 26t1.3, 370
fiscal relations, 67–74
constitutional context for, 65–67
design of, 220–21
institutional arrangements for, 44,
46–48
intergovernmental, 67–74
role of vertical fiscal imbalances in,
162–63
Fisher, R., 240t8.1
Fitts, M. A., 182, 197n5
Flatters, F. R., 211, 219, 367, 397, 448
flexibility issues, and design of
unconditional grants, 499
Florida, R., 456
Flowerdew, R., 369
flypaper effect, 3, 176–77, 196n2
and asymmetric response to
expenditures, 236
different findings on, 252
of general-purpose transfers, 225–26
impact of coalitions on, 228
impact of education grants, 246
model specification issues, 233–34
and public service grants, 207–8

and soft budget constraint, 247
sources of, 237, 245
and timing of use of grants, 251
formulas, 192, 215, 429, 445, 491
for allocation of grants, 76, 159–60,
209, 416–21, 461
for capital grants, 42–43, 432–34,
435–36
and costs of public services, 403, 404
for distribution of funds, 216, 217
for equalization, 215–16, 343–45,
378–79, 385–88, 393n13, 398,
421n1
designing of, 86–92
equitable share formula for transfers,
44, 45–46b1.3
for expenditure/fiscal capacity grants,
501–4, 507
for expenditures, 158
for fiscal capacity grants, 501–2
foundation formula, 421n1
general-purpose transfers, 4
macro formulas, 345–46
to measure expenditure needs, 419
politically determined, 420
population based, 216
for revenue-sharing arrangements,
333–36, 337nn5–6
tax devolution, 335–36
for transfers in India, 272–73
for unconditional grants, 280, 459–60
foundation grants, 21b1.2
France, 416–17, 489t17.1, 491
Francis, B., 369
Fraser, J. M., 301
fraternal programs, 33–36
free-market economy, Hungary, 157–59
free trade, 129n2
Freire, M., 455, 485
Frenkel, J., 108
functional agencies, 99–101
FUNDEF funds, 40
fungibility hypothesis, 7, 8, 234,
251–52, 466

Gaebler, T., 476–77n2
Galper, H., 235, 239t8.1

game theory model, 228
Gamkhar, Shama, 225–58, 234, 235, 236,
238t8.1
study of impact of grants, 242–43t8.1,
245, 250, 251, 255n3, 255n13
gap-filling transfers, 272
Garciá–Milà, T., 141–42, 370
GDP. see gross domestic product (GDP)
Gendron, P., 326
generalized equalization schemes, 78, 79,
91
generalized needs index, 432–34, 449n4
general-purpose grants, 2–4, 9, 209, 220
and fly-paper effect, 225–26
to local governments, 43–44
New Zealand, 101–2
general-purpose nonmatching grants,
237, 238–39t8.1, 245, 252–53, 254n2
geographical factors
as basis for revenue distribution, 461
and costs, 417–18
Gérard, M., 266
German Democratic Republic, 289n6
Germany, 85, 191, 212, 245
accuracy of predictions of new
institutional economics, 310–16
ad hoc political negotiations, 282
dispute resolution, 281
equalization system, 77
features of, 33, 34t1.5, 35
formulas for, 379
horizontal equalization, 107–8
Financial Planning Council, 298–99
judicial review and adjudication of
transfers, 283
legal architecture of, 267–71, 284–85,
289nn6–7
living conditions, 78, 80
mediation and conciliation, 282
procedures of establishment and
modification of transfers, 276–77
soft budget constraints, 147–50, 168n3
system of government, 263–64
tax sharing arrangements, 328–29
types of municipalities, 455
Gertler, M. S., 456, 494
Gilbert, G., 365t13.1, 381, 384, 390, 416

Gillen, David, 3
GNP. *see* gross national product (GNP)
Goetz, C. J., 397
Goldfeld, S., 236
Goldstein, M., 108
Gomez-Lobo, A., 39, 40
Gonzalez, P., 39
Goodhart, C. E. A., 109, 112, 121
goods and services, 464, 493
　Argentina, 153–54
　Australia, 159–60
　Brazil, 155
　and capitation payments, 464
　charges for, 458–59, 477n6
　costs of, 464
　cross-border movement of, 72
　estimating a cost function for, 404–7
　Germany, 147
　Italy, 150
　levels of, 447, 462–63, 494
　local public goods, 86–92
　minimum standards of, 426–29, 429,
　　431–32, 447, 466
　preferences or demands for, 260–61, 408
　provision of, 340, 454, 464, 476–77n2
　responsibilities for, 166, 400–401
　Sweden, 152
　United States, 161
　see also consumption tax base; public
　　services; service delivery
goods and services tax (GST),
　315f10.4a–4b, 326, 327
Goodspeed, T. J., 138, 141–42, 148, 190–91
Gordon, N., 39, 234, 235, 239t8.1, 246,
　255nn4–5
governance, 9
　and accountability, 12–13
　centralized, 133–34
　decentralized, 133
　and guidelines for designing fiscal
　　transfers, 15–17
government systems, 101, 464
　Belgium, 263
　Germany, 263–64
　India, 264, 512–13
　rural local governments, 512–13
　single-tier system, 484

　South Africa, 264–65
　two-tier municipal structure, 484–85
Gramlich, E. M., 3, 234, 236, 495
　econometric issues, 232
　impact of grants, 226, 227
　study of impact of grants, 239t8.1
　subsidy program, 8
grants
　conceptual impacts of, 10t1.1
　first-generation theories of impact of,
　　226–28, 254n1
　taxonomy of, 10t1.1, 204–5
　see also equalization transfer systems;
　　specific type of grant
grants-in-aid, India, 272, 279
Green, R. K., 421n11
Grewal, B. S., 334
gross domestic product (GDP), 376
　and budget controls, 106n8
　state GDP, 20–21
Grossman, G. M., 184, 197n7
Grossman, P. J., 179, 184, 185, 188, 234
　study of impact of grants, 239t8.1,
　　243t8.1, 245
gross national product (GNP), 346–48, 351
gross state products, 120
Guengant, A., 381, 384, 390, 416

Haggard, S., 196
Hamilton, B., 228, 233
Hamilton, J., 228
Hammond, G. W., 109, 112
hard budget constraints, 143, 153–54
harmonization
　of policies, 63–64, 66
　of regional expenditures, 73
　of taxes, 342
harmonized sales tax (HST), 326
Hayashi, M., 215, 384
health care sector
　Canadian Health Transfers, 37, 39
　and equalization of risk structures,
　　82–84
　Italy, 150
　need factors used in grant financing,
　　37, 38t1.6
Hellerberg, M., 182

Helpman, E., 184, 197n7
Henderson, V., 397
Hermann, Z., 477n3
Hermanutz, D., 346, 352
Hernandez, Antonio, 296
Hettich, W., 180
Heymans, C., 491
hierarchical mechanisms, 166–67, 174, 194
    Australia, 159
    Brazil, 155–56
    Canada, 161–62
highways and roads, 207, 251–52,
        255n13, 465
    Canada, 457, 477n5
    maintenance grants, 40
    and project-specific grants, 429, 434–35
Hindriks, J., 215, 229–30
Hines, J. R., 177, 207, 226
Hobson, P., 344, 466, 491
Hochreiter, E., 129n8
holdup problems, 192–93
Holzt-Eakin, D., 439
horizontal equalization systems, 107–8,
        112, 216, 392n2, 419–20, 422n20
    arguments against, 371–72
    Australia, 410–11
    formulas for, 378–79, 385–88, 393n13
    Germany, 268
    impact of, 388–90
    and indicators of financial capacity,
        381–85, 392–93n12
    and need-capacity gaps, 368–72
    overview, 361–62, 380
    principles to govern design of, 390
    and revenues, 372–80, 392nn9–10
    see also equalization transfer systems
horizontal equity, 19, 33, 60–61
    Canada, 261
    and equalization, 348
    principle of, 340
horizontal externalities, 197n10
horizontal imbalances, 271, 328, 334,
        397–98, 462–65, 477n8
horizontal inequity, 60–61
horizontal transfers
    description of, 211–16, 221nn3–4
    and fiscal capacity, 216–17

fiscal effort, 216, 217–19
Germany, 268–71
    and migration incentives, 219–20
    and regional insurance, 121–22
Horn, M. J., 305, 306
housing, 429, 432–34, 449n4, 463
housing needs index, 449n4
HST. see harmonized sales tax (HST)
Huber, B., 115, 191, 212, 229, 238t8.1,
        245, 349
Hueglin, T., 297
Hulten, C. R., 449n6
human capital, 447
Hungary, 157–59, 417
Huther, J., 13

Ihori, T., 230
Imazeki, J., 419
incentives, 41, 152, 203, 218
    for bailouts, 139
    of block grants, 206–8
    for changing tax rates, 349
    complementarity of, 115
    for complexity of transfers, 308–9
    concluding comments concerning,
        220–21
    creation of, 14–15
    for excessive borrowing, 148–49
    and management paradigm, 12–13
    microeconomic, 97–98
    migration, 219–20
    provided by RTS approach, 348–49
    for providing services and facilities, 492
    rate tax-back, 348–49
    for revenue raising, 211–12
    and risk avoidance, 114–16, 129n10
    for services provision, 37
    and tax revenues, 229–30
    for tax sharing, 331–32
    and transfer systems, 134–35, 466
    and unfunded mandates, 85
    see also horizontal transfers; vertical
        transfers
income
    effects of transfers on, 6–7, 10t1.1
    elasticities of, 233–34, 249–50,
        255nn10–11

and federal matching grants, 234
and tax sharing, 335
income disparities, 476*n*1
income risk, 110–12
independent agency model, 295*t*10.1
Australia, 300–301
India, 302–3
South Africa, 303
transaction costs and outcomes,
311*t*10.3
Uganda, 304
independent grant commissions,
295*t*10.1, 300–304, 307–8, 309*t*10.2,
310–16, 311*t*10.3
India, 42, 288
consumption tax base, 326–27
dispute resolution, 281
finance commissions, 302–3
legal architecture of transfers, 271–73,
285–87, 289*nn*10–11, 290*n*16
procedures of establishment and
modification of transfers, 277
profile of rural local governments in,
511–36*n*3, 531, 532–33*t*18.7
shareable and nonshareable taxes, 331,
332*f*11.2
system of government, 264
tax rates, 336*n*1
tax sharing, 331
Indonesia, 36, 187
and capital grants, 42
general-purpose transfers, 209
and minimum standards for grants, 40
Regional Autonomy Advisory Board,
299
industrial products tax, 326
inefficiency factors, 406, 447, 477*n*8
information
acquiring and processing of, 9, 11
transmission of, 183–84
infrastructure
Canada, 457, 477*n*5
impact on expenditures, 235
as major input in capital-intensive
services, 426–28
project-specific grants, 429, 434–35
and regional stabilization, 42–43

Ingram, J. C., 112
Inman, R. P., 137, 142–43, 167, 183
on coalitions, 197*n*5, 228
and cost methodologies, 419–20
and fiscal disparities, 365*t*13.1
and hardening of local budgets, 195
normative theory of transfers, 174
and pork barrel politics, 181–82, 196*n*4
and soft budget problems, 191
study of impact of grants, 239–40*t*8.1,
243*t*8.1
innovation, sources of, 456
input-based conditionality, 4
inputs
and costs of public services, 402
flexibility in, 13
input databases and capital grants,
439–40, 449*n*6
institutional arrangements for transfers,
44, 46–48
assessment of, 308–10
central/national government agency
model, 294, 295*t*10.1
grants commissions, 295*t*10.1,
300–304, 307–8, 309*t*10.2
independent agency model, 295*t*10.1,
300–304, 307–8, 309*t*10.2
intergovernmental forum model,
295*t*10.1, 296–300, 306–7, 308,
309*t*10.2, 316*n*4
national legislature model, 295*t*10.1,
296
and new institutional economics
framework
comparison of alternate
arrangements using, 306–10
evaluating equalizing transfers
using, 304–6, 316*nn*2–3
and outcomes of equalization
programs, 310–16
overview, 293–94, 316*n*1
institutional capacity, 429, 435, 449*n*2
institutional economics approach, 9
institutional reform, 194–96, 196
instruments
of intergovernmental transfers, 2–9
of interregional transfers, 80*t*3.1

insurance
  empirical studies, 118–21, 129*n*11
  and moral hazard problem, 114–16,
    129*n*10, 231
  mutual insurance vs. self-insurance,
    113–14
  and regional risk sharing, 110–11
integration, political, 186–87
interagency grants, 92–93
interagency relations, and microtransfers,
  96–104, 105*n*7
intergovernmental committees, 47–48
intergovernmental forum model for
  transfers, 295*t*10.1, 296–300, 306–7,
  308, 310–16, 316*n*4
intergovernmental relations, 185–89,
  197*nn*8–9
  Argentina, 183
  and the holdup problem, 193
  and soft budget problems, 190
intergovernmental transfers, 95, 137, 149,
  173–74
  Argentina, 153–54
  conclusions about impact of, 252–54
  dispute resolution and adjudication,
    280–83
  empirical studies of, 469–71,
    492*nn*9–12
  on impact of (1973–2005),
    238–44*t*8.1
  measuring impact of on local fiscal
    behavior, 231–36
  Germany, 147–50
  Hungary, 157–59
  Italy, 150–51
  to large cities and metropolitan areas,
    471–75, 477–78*nn*13–17
  measure of impact on fiscal behavior,
    231–36
  and political competition, 177–80,
    196*n*3
  procedures for establishing and
    modifying of, 275–78, 289*n*13
  Sweden, 152–53
  theoretical hypotheses of impact in
    local government behavior,
    226–31, 253, 254*n*1

types of, 459–60, 492*n*7
Ukraine, 156–57
see also equalization transfer systems;
  large cities and metropolitan
  areas; legal framework of
  transfers; *names of countries*; rural
  local governments; small urban
  areas; *specific transfer system*
interjurisdictional competition, 228, 231
interjurisdictional equalization, 82–86
interjurisdictional equity, 33, 76–78, 105*n*1
intermunicipal equalization, 79
internal economic union, 64–65, 66
internal migration, 80
interpersonal equity, 33
interregional equalization, 78–82
interregional externalities, 427, 446–47
interstate sale of goods tax, 326, 327
intragovernment efficiency, 93–98, 106*n*8
inverse net commercial capacity, 465
invoice sightseeing, 326, 337*n*4
Italianer, A., 108, 121, 122
Italy, 150–51
Itaya, J., 230

Jacobsen, K., 234
Japan, 414–16, 489*t*17.1, 491
Johansson, E., 179
Jones, J. D., 250
Jones, M., 154, 183, 185, 188, 191
Joshi, V., 332
Josie, J., 436
judiciary, and dispute resolution, 283

Kazakhstan, 489*t*17.1
Keen, M., 180
Kelly, R., 485–86
Kenen, P. B., 109, 112
Kenya, 489*t*17.1
Khemani, S., 286
King, D., 365*t*13.1
Kitchen, Harry, 483–509
Knight, B., 207–8, 232, 237, 243*t*8.1, 250,
  251, 255*n*13
knowledge workers, 456
Kommers, D. P., 269, 270
Kontopoulos, Y., 182

Republic of Korea, 210, 416
Kornai, J., 136, 137, 189, 230
Köthenbürger, M., 214–15

labor
    allocation of, 220
    and costs of public services, 402
    migration of, 366–67
laboratory federalism, 97, 105n7
labor markets, 113, 129n9
Ladd, H. F., 364, 369–70, 376, 421n11, 477
large cities and metropolitan areas
    characteristics of, 454–55,
        476–77nn1–2
    conclusions concerning transfers to,
        475–76
    expenditure differences in, 455–57,
        477nn3–5
    infrastructure of, 428
    intergovernmental grants to, 471–75,
        477–78nn13–17
    revenue-raising differences, 457–59,
        477n6
    types of transfers and rationales for
        use, 459–60, 492n7
    see also municipal governments; small
        urban areas
Larsen, C., 270, 276
Latvia, rural local governments in, 517–24,
    531, 532–33t18.7, 534, 536nn5–8
legal framework of transfer systems,
    287–88
    Belgium, 266–67
    condition and unconditional transfers,
        278–80, 289n15
    dispute resolution and adjudication,
        280–83
    Germany, 267–71, 289nn6–7
    India, 271–73, 289nn10–11
    legal basis overview, 265–66
    lessons drawn from case studies,
        284–87, 290n16
    overview, 259–60
    and political economy of fiscal
        federalism, 260–62
    procedures to establish and modify
        transfers, 275–78, 289n13

South Africa, 273–75
    see also constitutional law
legislation
    Belgium, 266–67, 276, 284
    Canada, 525
    Germany, 267–71
    limits of, 288
    national legislature model for
        transfers, 296
    and social benefits, 84
    South Africa, 273–75, 277–78, 289n13,
        303
legislative powers
    and common pool problem, 182–83,
        197n5
    and federal-regional fiscal relations,
        66–67
    and national standards of public
        services, 62–63
    and pork barrel politics, 182–83, 197n5
Leite-Monteiro, M., 187
Lescure, R., 121, 122
Levaggi, R., 240t8.1, 247
leverage ratios, 86
Levtchenkova, S., 431, 436, 439, 448
Lexcure, R., 108
Lichtblau, K., 115, 191, 212, 229
    and equalization, 349
    study of impact of grants, 238t8.1, 245
Linn, J., 385
Little, I.M.D., 332
Litvack, J., 135, 162, 165, 167, 189
living conditions
    Germany, 267, 268
    uniformity of, 77, 78, 80
lobbying activities, 174, 183–85
local authority stock condition, 432
local governments, 42, 182, 204, 324,
    362, 399
    Brazil, 155–56
    and budget-maximizing hypothesis,
        227–28, 254n1
    Canada, 161–62
    capacity equalization, 212–15
    collection of taxes set by central
        governments, 212–13
    costing methodologies, 414–17

education costs, 407
equalization formulas for, 378–79,
    385–88, 393*n*13
equalization targets, 379–80
externalities issues, 446–47, 465–66
fiscal disparities, 363–66
horizontal fiscal imbalances, 462–65,
    477*n*8
impact of horizontal equalization on,
    388–90
India, 516–17
and indicators of financial capacity,
    381–85, 392–93*n*12
Italy, 150–51
Latvia, 517–24, 536*nn*5–8
and needs equalization, 368–72,
    391–92*nn*3–8
public services, 204, 400, 401–2,
    467–68
revenues
    differences between revenues and
        expenditures, 457–59, 477*n*6
    and revenue equalization, 372–80,
        392*nn*9–10
    revenue sharing systems, 211–12,
        328–30
role of, 454, 476*nn*1–2
and soft budget constraints, 150–51
and spending assessments, 412–13,
    421–22*n*13
Sweden, 152–53
tax rates, 212–14
transfers
    characteristics of and implications
        of grant design for, 454–55,
        476–77*nn*1–2
    conditional vs. unconditional
        grants, 495–97
    cost equalizing grants, 414
    equitable share formula for,
        45–46*b*1.3
    expenditures as basis of, 471–72
    grants to contrasted with grants to
        small urban areas, 505–7
    impact on behavior of, 231–36
    incentive effects of vertical transfers,
        206–8

political rationales for transfers to
    large cities and metropolitan
    areas, 466–67
reliance on grant support, 488–91
short-run vs. long-run impact of
    grants on, 235–36
state-province transfers, 43–44
theoretical hypotheses of impact on,
    226–31, 254*n*1
United States, 160–61
and vertical fiscal imbalances, 460–62
see also rural local governments
location-specific economic rents, 427–28
Lockwood, B., 108
London, England, 456–57, 472–73
Londregan, L., 178, 179–81, 184, 196*n*3
Lotz, J., 370, 495
Lucas, S., 369
lump-sum compensation, 181
lump-sum grants, 205–6
    and effort restrictions, 234
    as equalization transfers, 449
    impact of, 246–47, 255*n*3
    for large cities and metropolitan areas,
        460
    and local spending, 176

Ma, J., 193, 197*n*9, 333, 415
MacDonald, Garry, 425–51
MacDougall Report, 108, 118, 119, 121
machine politics, 179
macroeconomics
    Brazil, 155–56
    indicators for measuring fiscal
        capacity, 20–23
    and regional risk sharing, 112–13
    of regional risk sharing and
        stabilization, 123–25
macroeconomic stability
    and infrastructure deficiencies, 42–45
    and intragovernment efficiency, 97–98,
        106*n*8
    and revenue equalization, 375
macro formulas, 71, 345–46
see also formulas
Mahal, A., 516
Makipaa, A., 122

Malaysia, 42, 347–48, 349, 354
managers and management, 11–13, 99
Marchand, M., 206
marginal utility, 111
market adjustment mechanisms, 112–13, 129*nn*8–9
market discipline, Hungary, 157
market mechanisms, 115, 163–64
Martinez-Vazquez, J., 193, 293, 299, 309, 370, 449*n*3
and allocation of grants, 469
and capital grants, 431
on transfers to local governments, 461
Maskin, E., 137, 190
Massachusetts, 408
Masson, P. R., 114, 120, 121
matching grants, 5–9, 425, 426
and interregional externalities, 447
for large cities and metropolitan areas, 460
for local tax rates, 215
vs. block grants, 205–6
see also closed-ended grants; conditional grants; open-ended grants
Mathews, R., 334
Mau Pedersen, N. J., 369
McGuire, M. C., 180, 234, 244*t*8.1, 251–52
McGuire, T. G., 234
McGuire, T. J., 141–42, 370
McLean, I., 370
McMillan, Melville L., 3, 495, 511–38
mediation, 282
Meier, V., 464, 472
Mélitz, J., 120, 122
merchandise circulation tax, 326
Mexico, 212
Mexico City, Mexico, 475, 477*8n*16
microtransfers, 94–95
and contractual arrangements, 96
costing and pricing of, 103–4
and design of interagency relations, 96–104, 105*n*7
impact on efficiency and equity, 101
Mieszkowski, P., 397
migration, 116, 399
and Canada, 366–67
fiscally induced, 428, 447–48, 450*n*15

grants and migration incentives, 219–20
and interregional equalization, 79–80
of labor, 366–67
prevention of, 493
and quality of infrastructure, 427–28
toward large cities, 464
Migue, J., 115
Miller, B. D., 458
minimum standards, 37–41, 447
mandated by central governments, 429
of public infrastructure, 428
as rationale for capital grants, 426–29
of service, 431–32, 466
see also national standards
Minneapolis-Saint Paul, Minnesota, 464
Mischler, P., 384
mission creep, 307
mobility of populations, 219–20, 366–67
Mochida, N., 491
models
benefit model of local government finance, 457–58, 486–88, 493
of capital grants, 435–44, 449*nn*5–6, 450*nn*8–14
of central/national government agency transfers, 294, 295*t*10.1
costs of denying bailouts, 142–43
of incentives for borrowing and spending decisions under fiscal decentralization, 141–42
intergovernmental forum model for transfers, 295*t*10.1, 296–300
median voter model of public good demand, 231–32
national legislature model for transfers, 295*t*10.1, 296
one-tier government model, 464
of political competition, 178–79
of political economy, 116–17, 140–41, 174
of regional stabilization and regional risk sharing, 126–28, 129*nn*14–15
of soft budget problems, 140–41, 190–91
symmetric response model, 251
"too-big-to-fail" theory, 139–40

of tradeoff between risk sharing and fiscal discipline, 143
of vertical fiscal imbalances, 143–44
modification coefficients, 415
Moffitt, R., 207, 232–33, 243*t*8.1, 248, 249, 250, 255*nn*9–10
monitoring, of performance, 11–12
moral hazard, 228
  and insurance, 114–16, 129*n*10, 231
  and personalized local public services, 87–88
  and political economy effects, 116–17
  and social benefits, 84, 85
moral suasion, 63, 67, 73
Mork, E., 238*t*8.1, 245
Morocco, 209
mortality rates, 440
Motala, Z., 275
Motinola, G., 189
Mundell, R., 109, 112, 115, 129*n*9
municipal governments, 148, 208, 467
  Argentina, 154
  grants to
    conditional vs. unconditional, 495–97
    contrasted with grants to small urban areas, 505–7
    expenditure/fiscal capacity grants, 501–4
    impact of, 245
    population size link to grant size, 497–98
    unconditional grants for, 421*n*4
  and horizontal equalization, 371, 392*n*7
  intermunicipal equalization, 79
  Japan, 415
  Latvia, 517–19, 521–23
  rural local governments, 524–30, 536–37*nn*11–13
  South Africa, 280
  Sweden, 152–53
  see also large cities and metropolitan areas
Murphy, K. M., 185
Murray, C., 316
Myers, G. M., 219–20, 450*n*15
Myles, G. D., 215, 229–30

Nash bargain, 116
Nash equilibrium, 220
Nath, H.K.A., 517
national capital cities, 473–75, 478*nn*15–17
National Finance Commission, Pakistan, 299–300
national governments, national-state expenditures, Canada, 27–29
national standards, 72
  of public services, 62–63
  for services, 427
  United States, 161
  see also minimum standards
national vertical equity, and tax-transfer system, 63
need-capacity gaps, 368–72, 370, 470
  definition, 398
  and expenditure equation, 408
  United Kingdom, 412
need factors, 361
  for aided service, 212
  as basis of revenue sharing, 335
  and equalization, 216
  measures of, 210–11, 463
negative externalities, 138, 229–30
negative integration, 64, 66
net equalization systems, 61
net fiscal benefits, 59–61
  creation of, 427–28
  differences in, 341, 347, 353–54
  equalization of, 340–41
  and fiscally induced migration, 447–48, 450*n*15
  from public budgets, 82
  and tax sources, 347
Netherlands, 490*t*17.1
Neumann, R., 353
new fiscal equalization, 417
new institutional economics
  accuracy of predictions of, 310–16
  assessment of institutional arrangements used, 308–10
  comparing alternate institutional arrangements using, 306–10
  for evaluating equalizing transfers, 304–6, 316*nn*2–3
new provision indicators, 433, 434

New Zealand, 97, 99, 101–3, 106n8,
490t17.1
Nigeria, 299
Niskanen, W. A., 98
nominal exchange rates, 113
nonbacklog regions, 436, 437–38,
440–44, 450nn8–13
noncooperative games, 321, 336n1
noncooperative outcomes, 140
nonmatching assistance, 2–3
nonmatching transfers, 4–5
nonprofit institutions, 104
Nordic countries, 185, 490t17.1, 491
normative theory of intergovernmental
transfers, 158, 173, 174–75, 196n1
norm of deference, 182, 183
North, D., 304
Norway, 185
notional bases, 350
Nowlan, D., 485

Oakland, W. H., 365t13.1
Oates, W. E., 3, 176, 236, 319, 468
decentralizing decision making, 60, 204
and fiscal equalization, 20
fiscal illusion hypothesis, 227
impact of grants, 228, 229, 230, 231,
238t8.1, 242t8.1, 245, 255n3
and risk sharing, 107, 392–93n12
and spillovers, 206
on veil hypothesis, 226
Oates decentralization theorem, 60, 204
objectives of fiscal transfers
achievement of, 61–65
bridging vertical fiscal gaps, 17–19
compensating for benefit spillovers,
41–42
and fiscal equalization transfers, 19–36
influencing local priorities, 42
setting national minimum standards,
37–41
Obstfeld, M., 109, 115–16, 122, 129n2,
129n8
Olson, J., 236
Olson, M., 180, 197n6
open-ended grants, 488
and conflict of priorities, 42

effect of, 6–7, 9, 10t1.1
for large cities and metropolitan areas,
460
vs. closed-ended grants, 492
operating grants, 40
opportunistic behaviors, 9, 11
optimal equalization transfers, 448
optimal fiscal gaps, 144
optimum currency areas theory, 112–13,
129n9
ordinary local shared taxes, 416
Orfield, M., 465
Organisation for Economic Co-operation
and Development, 145–46
Osborne, D., 476–77n2
Otter, G., 369, 370, 391n3, 392n6
outcomes, 12
Pareto-efficient, 180, 197n10, 319
redistributive, 229–30
and soft budget constraint, 140
and transactions costs, 309t10.2,
311t10.3
output-based transfers, 4, 9, 11–12, 99
Canada, 37, 38
features of, 13, 14t1.2
and results-based accountability, 13–15
output-oriented budgeting, 101–3
outputs, 88, 124, 404–5
oversight, 67
by federal government, 73
fire alarm oversight, 305, 308,
309t10.2, 316n3
Ownings, S., 184, 185, 188

Pakistan, 42, 299–300, 335
Papke, L. E., 240t8.1, 246
Pareto-efficient outcomes, 180, 197n10,
319
Pareto improvement, 219
Parker, M., 464
partisan links, 188, 191
passing-the-buck transfers, 18b1.1
paternal programs, 33–36
Payne, A. A., 207, 221n3, 242t8.1, 248, 250
Peloquin, D., 316n3
per capita capital stock, South Africa,
437t15.1

per capita expenditures, 472, 477*n*3,
477*n*8, 525–26
per capita fiscal capacity, 35
per capita grants, 209, 469, 493
design of, 500
United Kingdom, 472–73
United States, 469, 470, 472, 477*n*11
per capita public capital, 436
simulations of capital grants, 440–44,
450*nn*8–13
South Africa, 436–37
per capita tax bases, 462, 464, 501
per capita utility, 220
percentage equalization grant, 21*b*1.2
perceptions of fiscal transfers, 17, 18*b*1.1
perfect mapping, 371–72, 392*n*8
performance-oriented transfers, 9,
11–15, 99
Peri, G., 109, 115–16, 122, 129*n*2, 129*n*8
peripheralized federation, 188
Perotti, R., 182, 186–87
Perrin, Benjamin, 259–92
Perry, G., 191, 455
Persson, Torsten, 111, 115, 116, 117, 184,
392–93*n*12
Pestieau, P., 206
Petchey, Jeffrey, 369, 435–51
Petersen, P., 455
Petter, A., 261
Pettersson-Lidbom, P., 152
Philippine Islands, vertical grants, 208–9
Pigouvian subsidy, 206
Pisani-Ferry, J., 108, 121, 122
Pisauro, G., 138, 162
police expenditures, United Kingdom,
412–13
policies and policy making, 196, 229, 362
Belgium, 267
for capital grants, 444, 445, 450*n*15
and cross-border transactions, 64
determinants of, 188, 259
and efficiency and equity issues, 180,
366–68
and federal-regional conditional
grants, 72–74
and fiscal condition measurements, 376
and flypaper effect, 177

harmonization of, 63–64, 66
and interregional equalization
instruments, 80*t*3.1
and political contributions, 184–85
and preferences of citizens, 204
and principles of transfer systems, 48–51
principles to govern design of
equalization systems, 390
results-oriented regional policy, 81
setting minimum uniform standards,
428–29
see also efficiency issues; equity issues
political capital, 179, 184
political centralization, and market-
preserving federalism, 188–89, 197*n*9
political competition, 158, 176–81,
196*nn*3–4
political economy
and fiscal disparities, 364
models, 116–17, 140–41, 174
and regional insurance, 116–17
political entrepreneurship, 180–81
political institutions
Brazil, 155–56
Canada, 161
Hungary, 158
Ukraine, 157
political integration, 186–87
political parties, and federalism, 188
political separation, 186–87
politics, 96, 188, 196
absence of leadership in, 193–94
ad hoc political negotiations, 282
and allocation of grants, 469
and bureaucracy, 98–99
contributions to obtain favorable
policies, 184–85
distributive, 178, 179, 183, 417
and equalization schemes, 77–78, 380,
494
formulas for, 358–88, 393*n*13, 420
and the flypaper effect, 176–77, 196*n*2
motives of governments, 176–81
political bargaining, 306, 314*n*4
political rationales for transfers to
large cities and metropolitan
areas, 466–67

and rationale for providing grants,
494–95
rural local governments, 516
polluter pays principle, 371
population
and allocation of grants, 208–9, 469
as basis of revenue sharing, 335
Canada (Alberta), 524, 536nn11–12
and capital stock input database,
439–40
and costing methodologies, 418–19
and equalization schemes, 89–91, 472
in large cities and metropolitan areas,
455, 457
Latvia, 517
mobility of, 366–67
and per capita grants, 469
and public services, 402–4, 463
and regional representation, 179–80
rural local governments, 543t18.7
and size of grant, 497–98
tax-sharing arrangements, 217
and vertical grants, 209
see also migration
pork barrel politics, 178, 181–82, 188,
191, 196n4
pork barrel transfers, 18b1.1, 286
Porto, A., 180, 209
positive integration, 66
positive-sum games, 185
Poterba, J., 195
poverty
and allocation of grants, 209, 470
Canada, 457, 477n4
and costs of public services, 403–4
as demand determinant, 234
Latvia, 522
poverty ratio, 337n6
poverty reduction, 81
predictability issues, and design of
unconditional grants, 499
prices
distortions of, 100
elasticities of, 182–83, 248–50,
255nn10–11
flexibility of, 112–13, 129nn8–9
input prices, 406

of public services, 458, 467–68, 477n6,
492
and revenue sharing, 335
stability of, 124
principal-agent relationship, 84–85, 95,
98, 228, 486
prisoners' dilemma, 184, 197n7
private income accounts, 233–34
private sector stock condition, 433
production functions, 404–5
productivity shocks, 124
profits, 325, 348
project-specific grants, 429, 434–35, 445
property taxes, 228
prospective voting, 178, 196n4
protectionism, 188
provincial governments, 33, 333, 342,
347, 349
and alternative "nonmacro" base,
353–54
Argentina, 153–54
base tax-back system, 349, 350
Canada, 24–25, 27, 28t1.4, 161–62
and costs of public services, 401–2
and equalization schemes, 343, 345,
350–52, 356–57
federal-provincial fiscal arrangements
in Canada, 296–98
grants
capital grants, 430
expenditures as basis for, 471
per capita transfers, 209
population size link to size of, 497–98
provincial-local transfers, 470
reliance on grant support, 491
state-province transfers to local
governments, 43–44
using GNP to calculate transfers,
3436–48
Hungary, 159
and level of public services, 27t1.4,
225–26
per capita capital stock, 437t15.1
and policies for interregional
externalities, 446–47
provincial-state expenditures, 25, 27,
28t1.4

provision of goods and services, 340
role in fiscal transfers, 277–78
and setting minimum standards, 39
South Africa, 280, 287, 437t15.1
weighting of factors for expenditures
   in, 24–25, 28t1.4
Prud'homme, R., 491
public administration, functional-agency
   approach to, 09–101
public choice theory, 173, 194
public debt, 140, 230
public good production function, 404–5
public goods
   econometric issues in estimating
      expenditure model for, 232–33
   and equalization schemes, 86–92
   expenditures as determinants of, 231–36
   level of, 139
   see also goods and services
public health services, 82–86
public housing, 99, 106n9
public management framework, 9
public policies. see policies and policy
   making
public-private partnerships, 94
public safety, 400
public sector
   and functional agencies, 99–100
   interregional equalization within, 78–82
   and microtransfers, 103–4
public services, 23, 101, 492, 504, 529
   assignment of responsibilities for,
      400–401
   Canada, 25
   and conditional vs. unconditional
      grants, 495–97
   costs of, 401–4, 421nn5–6, 494
   and equalization grants, 68–72
   and estimating a cost function, 404–7
   and estimating an expenditure
      equation for, 407–9, 421n11
   expert judgment on costs of, 409–10
   and flypaper effect, 207–8, 233–34
   and interregional equalization, 79–80
   levels of, 227, 499–500
   measurement of fiscal needs by
      category of, 26t1.3

norms and minimum quality
   standards of, 400
personalized local services, 86–89
property-related, 529
provision of
   by companies or enterprises, 484
   at comparable levels, 59–60
   standards for, 37, 62–63, 401, 421n6,
      447
rural local governments, 531
standards of, 37, 62–63, 401, 421n6, 447
unconditional grants for, 421n4
in unitary systems, 69–70
see also goods and services; service
   delivery
public spending, 3
purchase agreements, New Zealand, 102
Purfield, C., 287

Qian, Y., 189, 197n9
quality of life, 456
Qureshi, Z., 209

Rajaraman, I., 516
Ramaphosa, Cyril, 275
Rao, M. Govinda
   on decentralization, 517
   fiscal imbalances, 319–38
   grants in India, 272, 286–87
redistribution of transfers, 57, 83, 218,
   476n1
   and fiscal insurance against asymmetric
      shocks, 118–21, 129n11
   intermunicipal, 520
   interregional, 211
   policies for, 180–81, 195
   and regional insurance, 121
   and revenue equalization, 372, 375
   and tax-transfer system, 63
redistributive outcomes, 229–30
reforms, 207
   grant program in Colombia, 208
   institutional, 193–96
Regional Autonomy Advisory Board,
   Indonesia, 299
regional governments, 134, 136, 137, 166
   conditional grants to, 72–74

and discretionary transfers, 165–66
equalization schemes, 164–65
interregional equalization within
public sector, 78–82
European Union, 81–82, 105n2
federal-regional fiscal relations, 65–74
harmonization of expenditure
programs, 73–74
and hierarchical mechanisms, 167
Hungary, 157–59
Italy, 150–51
and legislative powers, 66–67
and market discipline, 163–64
policies of, 79–82
and risk avoidance, 114–16, 129n10
role of vertical fiscal imbalances in,
162–63
and soft budget constraints, 150–51
solidarity among, 76–77
spending and borrowing forms, 141–42
Sweden, 152–53
see also regional risk sharing; soft
budget constraints
regional-local services, 37–41
regional representation, 179–80
regional risk sharing, 107
conclusions concerning, 125–26
and consumption smoothing, 109–12,
129nn2–3, 129n5
macroeconomics of, 123–25
mutual insurance vs. self-insurance,
113–14
overview, 109
and regional stabilization, 112–13,
126–28, 129nn8–9, 129nn14–15
regulatory bodies, 100
rent-seeking activities, 180, 183–85,
196nn4, 197nn5–8
representative expenditure system, 408
representative tax system (RTS), 44, 213,
339
advantages of, 352–53
arguments for replacing, 348–49
criticisms of, 350–52
failings of approach, 345–46
and federal-regional equalization
grants, 68–69

and measurement of fiscal condition,
376–78
and measuring fiscal capacity, 20–23
use in Australia, 355–56
use in Canada, 354–55
Usher's views of, 347–48
Reschovsky, Andrew, 397–424
residence, and fiscal inequity, 19–20
resource allocation, 19, 75, 98–99, 180,
325, 476n1
resource rents, 342–43
resource-requirements gap, 370
resources
and costs of public services, 402
and equalization, 351–52, 362
and fiscal transfers, 35
measures of aggregate resources, 346
results-oriented regional policies, 81
retail sales tax, 326
retrospective voting, 178, 196n4
revenue capacity, as equalization
standard, 93
revenue equalization
and equalization formulas, 378–79
and equalization targets, 379–80
funding equalization systems, 372–75,
392n10
and measuring of fiscal capacity,
375–78
overview, 372
revenue-generating capacity, 287
Revenue Mobilization, Allocation and
Fiscal Commission, Nigeria, 299
revenue pooling, 212
revenue raising, 347
Australia, 160
capacity for, 68–71, 213
and equalization schemes, 164–65
Japan, 415
and relativity calculations, 411
revenues, 115, 342
Argentina, 154
assignment of, 363–66
Brazil, 155
compared to expenditures in large
cities and metropolitan areas,
457–59, 477n6

and decentralization, 56, 204–5
  decentralizing revenues vs.
    decentralizing expenditures,
    58–59
and funding equalization, 372–75
Germany, 267–68
from grants, 471–72
Hungary, 158–59
India, 272, 289n11, 512–13
measurement of, 352–53
rural local governments
  Canada (Alberta), 526, 530,
    533t18.7
  India, 530, 533t18.7
  Latvia, 518–21, 523, 533t18.7, 536n7
sources of, 461–62, 472–73, 476
South Africa, 273–74
subnational governments in Germany,
  147–50
Ukraine, 156–57
used as basis of transfer calculation,
  35–36
revenue-sharing arrangements, 189, 208,
  446, 448, 461
  conclusions concerning, 336
  concurrency, competition, and
    efficiency of, 323–24
  in different countries, 328–30
  disincentives in decentralized tax
    administrations, 332–33
  federal system of, 213
  formulas for, 333–36, 337nn5–6
  India, 286, 290n16
  as instrument of transfers, 321–23,
    336n1
  in multilevel fiscal systems, 328–33
  sharing tax base of direct taxes,
    324–25, 336–37n2
  sharing the consumption tax base,
    325–27, 337nn3–4
  South Africa, 287
  from specific taxes or aggregate central
    revenues, 331–32
  types of, 322–23
Ribar, D. C., 241–42t8.1, 248, 249
Riker, W., 188
risk-avoidance strategies, 114–16, 129n10

risk management, and soft budget
  constraints, 138
risk pooling, 116
risk-sharing mechanisms, 392–93n12
  impact of political economy on, 116–17
  international, 129n3
  and moral hazard, 114–16, 129n10
  overview, 107–9
  regional governments, 109–14
  and soft budget constraint, 143
risk structures, and provision of public
  health services, 82–84
roads. *see* highways and roads
Roberts, S., 13, 340, 447
Robin Hood programs, 33–36, 370, 523
Rodden, J., 135, 145–49, 162, 165,
  166–67, 189, 192
Rodriguez, E., 209
Roemer, J. E., 177, 207
Roland, G., 137, 187, 197n9
Romania, 329
Romer, T., 3, 177, 207, 227, 241t8.1, 246
Rosen, H. S., 3
Rosenthal, H., 3, 177, 207, 227, 241t8.1,
  246
Rothstein, R., 409
RTS. *see* representative tax system (RTS)
Rubinfeld, D. L., 183, 227, 365t13.1
rules of transfers, 143
rural areas, infrastructure of, 428
rural local governments
  Canada (Alberta), 524–30,
    536nn11–13
  conclusions concerning, 535–36
  India, 511–17, 536n3
  Latvia, 517–24, 536nn5–8
  overview and reflections on, 530–35,
    537nn14–17
  summary information on, 532–33t18.7
  see also local governments
Russia, 188
Russian Federation, 193, 484, 485
Rye, C. R., 370, 411

Sachs, J., 108, 118–19, 120
Sala-i-Martin, X., 108, 118–19, 120
sales tax, 326, 337n3, 458

Sanan, D., 516
Sanguinetti, P., 143, 154, 180, 183, 185
    link between poverty and transfers, 209
    and soft budget problems, 191
Sastry, M. L., 271, 272, 279
Sato, Motohiro, 173–201, 187
Searle, B., 293, 299, 309, 370, 411
secession, threat of, 187
second-generation theories on impact of
    transfers, 228–31, 253, 392–93n12
service delivery, 12, 89, 96
    Canada, 529
    and capital grants, 426–28
    costing methodologies for
        Australia, 411–12
        France, 416–17
        Hungary, 417
        Republic of Korea, 416
        Sweden, 413–14
        Switzerland, 417–19
        United Kingdom, 412–13,
            421–22n13
    and externalities, 465–66
    and fiscal capacity, 216–17
    functional agency approach to, 100–101
    in large cities, 454, 476–77n2
    link to output-based transfers, 11
    pricing of, 467–68
    reliance on expert judgment for costs
        of, 410
    South Africa, 45–46b1.3
    see also goods and services; public
        services
Shah, Anwar, 320, 340, 356, 369, 447, 463
    and expenditure equation, 408–9
    and fiscal disparities, 365t13.1
    on general-purpose transfers, 209
    guide to fiscal transfers, 1–53
    impact of transfers, 225–58, 244t8.1,
        251, 252
    institutional arrangements for
        transfers, 293–317
    and need-capacity gap, 370, 392n3
    on revenue sharing, 335
    use of Stone-Geary utility function, 235
    views of equalization schemes, 285,
        286, 287

Shankar, R., 19
Shen, C., 46
Shleifer, A., 185, 188, 192–93
Shroder, M., 242t8.1, 248
silo approach to equalization, 498
Silva, E., 197n10
Silvestre, J., 177, 207
Sim, S., 234, 251
simulations, capital grants models,
    440–44, 450nn8–13
Singh, N., 272, 286–87, 336n1
single-tier governing structure, 484
Sjoquist, D. L., 370
Slack, Enid, 376, 476, 476n1
    on conditional grants, 488
    grants to large cities and metropolitan
        areas, 452–81
    justification for grants, 494
    on small urban areas, 484, 485
S. Letelier, L., 485–86, 491
Slovak Republic, 468
small urban areas
    description of, 483–85, 506
    design of fiscal transfer schemes,
        498–504
    expenditures of, 485–86
    financing of expenditures, 486–88
    grants to contrasted with grants to
        other municipalities, 505–7
    importance of grants to, 488–91
    population size impact on grant size,
        497–98
    rationales for providing grants, 491–97
    see also large cities and metropolitan
        areas
Smart, Michael, 165, 173, 176, 346, 461,
    464
    and budget constraints, 464
    on conditional grants, 466, 488, 493
    on economic activities, 367
    expenditure vs. fiscal capacity grants,
        501
    on externalities, 465
    incentive effects of grants, 203–23
    and revenue equalization, 372, 375
    study of impact of grants, 242t8.1,
        248, 250

and transfer design, 467
on unconditional grants, 493
Smith, S., 109, 112, 121
Smoke, P., 288
Snoddon, T., 115
social assistance, Latvia, 522
social citizenship, 60, 65
social harmony, 77
social housing, 432–33
socialist economy, 189–90
social services, 463, 464, 529, 531–33, 534
social space, 84
sociodemographic index, 417–18
socioeconomic funds, 417–19
socioeconomics, and public
    expenditures, 233
soft budget constraints, 166, 189–92,
    197*n*10, 228, 247
    Argentina, 153–54
    Australia, 159–60
    Brazil, 155–56
    Canada, 161–62
    causes of, 74*n*2
    conclusions from literature, 162–67
    conditions necessary for, 137
    country-level evidence overview, 145–47
    credibility and reputation effects,
        142–43
    and discretionary transfers in, 165–66
    future research of, 144–45
    Germany, 147–50, 168*n*3
    hierarchical mechanisms, 166–67
    Hungary, 157–59
    implications of, 137–38
    Italy, 150–51
    and market mechanisms, 163–64
    overview of, 136–37
    political economy models of, 140–41
    role of equalization schemes in, 164–65
    rules vs. discretion, 143
    and second-generation theories of
        transfers, 230–31
    summary of findings in literature,
        167–68
    Sweden, 152–53
    theoretical literature overview, 138–39
    "too-big-to-fail" theory, 139–40

Ukraine, 155–57
United States, 160–61
    and varying degrees of
        decentralization, 141–42
    and vertical fiscal imbalance, 143–44,
        162–63
Sole, A., 215
solidarity, 375
    among regional governments, 76–77
    and risk sharing, 108
Sørensen, B., 109, 118, 129*n*2
Sorensen, R. J., 182, 184, 185
South Africa, 282, 283, 288, 406, 428
    capital stock data, 439–40, 449*n*6
    dispute resolution, 281–82
    equalization schemes, 356–57
    and expenditure needs, 24–25, 31, 400
    Fiscal and Financial Commission, 303,
        316
    grants
        capital grants model description,
            437–39
        equitable share formula for
            transfers, 44, 45–46*b*1.3
        formula-based, 449*n*2
        judicial review and adjudication of
            transfers, 283
        legal architecture of transfers in,
            273–75
        need factors in health care grants,
            38*t*1.6
        policy implications for capital
            grants, 444, 445, 450*n*15
        procedures of establishment and
            modification of transfers,
            277–78, 289*n*13
        reliance on grant support, 490*t*17.1
        simulations of capital grants
            models, 440–44, 450*nn*8–13
    legal framework study conclusions, 287
    mediation and conciliation, 282
    per capita public capital, 436–37
    system of government, 264–65
Spahn, Paul Bernd, 267, 285
    equity and efficiency of transfers,
        75–106
    specific equalization systems, 79–80, 81, 82

specific-purpose closed-ended matching
grants, studies of impact of,
243–44t8.1, 250–52
specific-purpose nonmatching grants,
impact of, 239–41t8.1, 245–47, 253,
255nn3–6
specific-purpose open-ended matching
grants, studies of impact of,
241–43t8.1, 247–50, 253
specific-purpose transfers, 4–9, 91–92,
93, 105n4, 220
Australia, 159
and budgets, 98
impact of efficiency and equity on, 101
India, 512
rural local governments, 533t18.7, 534
United States, 237
spending, 182, 342
Argentina, 154
Canada, 525–26
constitutional basis for power of, 267
and estimating cost function, 406
and form of fiscal decentralization,
141–42
German powers of, 270
Latvia, 518t18.2
and levels of public services, 401
powers of in South Africa, 275
on public services, 207
Sweden, 152–53
variations in patterns of, 486
spending power, 67
spillover of benefits, 5, 134, 192, 495
and bailouts, 190–91
compensating for, 41–42
and economic rational for grants,
491–92
in federations, 206
and financial crises, 143
interjurisdictional, 209–10
measures of, 465
and open-ended matching grants, 7
and transfers to large cities, 472
Spolaore, E., 187
Srivastava, V., 516
stabilization, 112–13, 120, 129nn8–9
and infrastructure deficiencies, 42–43

and macroeconomics of regional risk
sharing, 123–25
model of and risk sharing, 126–28,
129nn14–15
national, 125
policies for, 476n1
standards
definition of, 463–64
of equalization, 92–93
see also minimum standards; national
standards
state governments, 491
and aid to local governments, 399
Australia, 25, 30–31, 159–60
Brazil, 155–56
and fiscal equalization programs,
31–33
impact of grants on, 246–47
labor and capital incomes, 117–18
national-state expenditures, 27, 29
setting of taxes collected by local
governments, 212–13
state-province to local government
transfers, 43–44
United States, 160–61
state gross domestic product (GDP),
20–21
state-independent transfers, 16–17
state-local expenditures, Australia, 25,
30–31
state-local revenues, 32–33
Statistics South Africa, 439–40
Stern, N., 331–32
Stine, W. F., 236, 255n3
Stone-Geary utility function, 235
Street, A., 406
structural equalization transfers, 105n3
structural grants, Belgium, 267
structural index, 417–18
structure-induced equilibrium, 182
subnational governments, 2, 229
accountability of, 149–50, 168n3
and capital grants, 430, 431–32
and equalization transfers, 36,
343–45
and fiscal decentralization, 55–56
Italy, 150–51

rationale for unconditional transfers
to, 446
and revenue sharing, 321–23, 336n1
subsidy programs, 100, 101
conditional nonmatching transfers, 4–5
effects of, 6–7
and expenditures, 8
and matching transfers, 5–6
Pigouvian subsidy, 206
rates, 210
substitution effect of transfers, 6, 10t1.1
supplementary grants, Germany, 269–70,
278, 279
supply and demand elasticities, 124
supply shocks, 115
Sury, M. M., 272
Sweden, 191
costing methodologies, 413–14
impact of grants on, 245
and soft budget problems, 152–53
swing voter theory, 179
Switzerland, 369, 377, 387, 392nn10–11,
393n13
costing methodologies, 417–19
and expenditure needs, 400
features of fiscal equalization transfers,
34t1.5, 35
Sydney, Australia, 471
symmetric response model, 251
Szalai, A., 2

Tabellini, G., 111, 115, 116, 117, 184,
392–93n12
take-up rate for welfare payments, 87
TANF. see Temporary Assistance to Needy
Families (TANF), United States
Tannenwald, R., 370
Tanzania, 470, 477n10, 489t17.1
Tarasov, A. V., 259, 279, 284
taxation, 230, 325, 336, 486
ability to bear burden of, 20–22
and achieving national vertical equity,
63
Belgium, 266–67
Canada, 345–54, 346–48, 353, 376
and consumption smoothing, 110–12
decentralization of, 17, 73, 204–5

distortionary taxes, 221n4
and efficiency issues, 180
and efficient government hypothesis,
228
and financial capacity, 381–85, 388–90,
392–93n12
and fiscal competition, 229–30
and fiscal gaps, 446, 462
and fiscal transfers, 31–33, 35
Germany, 267–68, 289n7
goods and services tax, 315f10.4
imbalance between tax sources and
expenditures, 342–43
impact of grants on, 253–54
India, 272, 289n11, 336n1
in large cities and metropolitan areas,
458
and microtransfers, 103–4
municipal business taxes, 215
and national capital cities, 473–75
and net fiscal benefits, 341
nonshareable taxes, 331, 332f11.2
policies of
harmonizing policies, 63–64
redistributive tax policies, 134
regional policies, 115
tax transfer policies, 229
and possible equalization formulas,
385–88, 393n13
and provision of local goods, 90–91
rates set by central government and
collected by local governments,
212–13
and revenue decentralization, 59
and revenue sharing, 321–23, 331–32,
336n1
rural local governments, 518–19, 523,
526–27, 529–30, 533t18.7
shared and shareable taxes, 331,
332–33, 332f11.2, 461, 464, 530
tax disharmony, 321–22, 334
taxing powers, 320–21, 324, 326–27
tax transfer policies, 229
total taxable resources, 376
welfare implications of tax assignment,
321, 322f11.1
see also revenues; revenue-sharing

tax bases, 213–15
  alteration of, 350
  and calculation of equalization
    transfers, 345–54
  and capital grants, 435
  competition for, 134
  difference in, 494
  distribution of, 349
  and equalization grants, 71
  mobility of, 320
  per capita, 462, 501
  regionalization of, 464–65
  and tax rates, 217
tax-base sharing, 17
  analysis of, 323–27, 336–37nn2–4
  conclusions on, 328
tax capacity, 89
  indicators of, 387, 393n13
  of local governments, 385–86
tax credits, 477–78n14
tax-price supplements, 371
tax rates, 212–14
  Canada, 215, 349
  and equalization grants, 463
  and fiscal capacity, 217
  and fiscal effort, 217–18
  India, 336n1
  of local governments, 212–14
  and spending levels, 3
  Sweden, 152
  and vertical grants, 210
tax-rental arrangements, 333–34
tax tourism, 326, 337n4
Temporary Assistance to Needy Families
  (TANF), United States, 247, 248,
  250, 255n8
Thaler, R. H., 177, 207, 226
Tiebout, C., 133–34, 204, 260
Tiebout model, 60
Title I grants, United States, 235–36, 247,
  255n5
Tommasi, M., 143, 154, 183, 185, 188
  on revenue sharing, 330
  and soft budget problems, 191
"too-big-to-fail" theory, 139–40, 166
"too sensitive to fail" theory, 166
top-down approach to
  intergovernmental grants, 177–78

topographical characteristics, and costs,
  417–18
Toronto, Canada, 457, 464, 471, 477nn4–5
total taxable resources (TTR), 376–78
Toth, K., 391–92n5
traditional transfers, features of, 13,
  14t1.2
transaction costs, 183, 197n6, 305–6
  and institutional arrangements, 310
  and new institutional economics, 310
  and outcomes, 309t10.2, 311t10.3
transfers. *see specific type of transfer*
transit systems, 456, 486
transparency, 350–52, 487
Treisman, D., 188, 192–93, 229
Tremblay, J., 143–44
TTR. *see* total taxable resources (TTR)

Uganda, 304, 489t17.1
Ukraine, soft budget constraints, 155–57
unconditional grants, 76, 425, 426
  Australia, 159
  design of, 498–504
  and equalization programs, 32
  Germany, 278–79
  in large cities and metropolitan areas,
    459–60
  per capita, 493, 494
  and population size, 470
  rationale for, 446
  to rural local governments, 533t18.7
  to small urban areas, 506
  South Africa, 278, 280, 289n15
unemployment rates, 115–16
unfunded mandates, 84–86, 87, 429
unhappy constituents, 305, 308, 309t10.2,
  316n3
Unified Health System, Brazil, 40–41
unitary systems
  capitals of, 473–75
  and citizens' preferences for good and
    services, 260–61
  equalization schemes, 79–80, 81, 82,
    340
  and horizontal inequity, 60
  intragovernment efficiency and
    macroeconomic stability, 97
  levels of public services, 69–70

United Kingdom
  costing methodologies, 412–13,
    421–22n13
  expenditures, 456–57
  and fiscal responsibilities of local
    governments, 400
  formula-based grants, 429, 432–34,
    449n4
  governing system, 485
  housing, 432–34, 449n4
  per capita grants, 472–73
  reliance on grant support, 490t17.1
  and vertical expenditures, 369
United States
  asymmetric shocks
    fiscal insurance studies, 118–21
    market-based insurance studies,
      117–18, 129n11
  capital stock data, 439–40, 449n6
  estimating cost function of education
    in, 406–7
  financing of schools, 20, 21b1.2
  grants
    closed-ended matching transfers,
      237, 254n2
    education grants, 234, 239–41t8.1,
      245–47, 252, 255nn3–6
    endogeneity of grant variables, 237
    impact of, 245
    to large cities, 473, 477–78n14
    per capita, 469, 470, 472, 477n11
    reliance on grant support, 490t17.1
    Title I, 235–36, 247, 255n5
    welfare grants, 247–50, 255nn9–12
  and rent-seeking activities, 185
  soft budget constrains, 160–61
  and states' fiscal deficits, 195
  tax credits, 477–78n14
unity of nations, 187
universalism, 182
urban areas, expenditure responsibilities,
  485–86
user fees, 371, 458–59, 527, 529
Usher, D., 347–48, 352–53, 375

Vaillancourt, F., 22, 369, 399, 467
  and equalization mechanisms, 108,
    422n20

  and fiscal disparities, 365t13.1
  and horizontal equalization, 419, 421
  and macro measurement issues, 377
  and revenue equalization, 372, 373f13.1
value added tax (VAT), 212
  Australia, 329
  Belgium, 266
  Brazil, 326
  Canada, 326
  China, 333
  Germany, 267–68, 329
  India, 327
  and microtransfers, 104
Van der Stichele, G., 266, 267, 284–85
Vani, B. P., 517
van Ryneveld, P, 464
van Wincoop, E., 118, 120
Vegas, E., 39
veil hypothesis, 226
Velasco, A., 182
Verdonck, M., 266, 267, 284
vertical allocation, 363
vertical equalization, 112, 361, 370,
  391n1, 391–92n5
vertical equity, 33, 63, 342
vertical fiscal gaps, 56–59
  creation of, 230
  and decentralization, 204–5
  as objective of fiscal transfers, 17, 19
  size of, 72, 74n2
  Ukraine, 157
vertical fiscal imbalances, 17, 134,
  135–36, 146, 323
  Argentina, 153–54, 154
  Belgium, 284
  and block grants, 505
  and equalization, 342–43
  Germany, 147–49, 284–85
  and hierarchical mechanisms, 167
  Hungary, 157, 159
  in large cities and metropolitan areas,
    460–62
  role of, 162–63
  and soft budget constraints, 143–44
  and tax sharing, 334–35
  Ukraine, 157
  United States, 161
vertical rebalancing, 87

vertical transfers
cross-country evidence, 208–11
Germany, 285
incrementality of, 206–8, 221n2
matching vs. block grants, 205–6
overview, 205
Vigneault, Marianne, 133–71
Vilalta, M., 384
Vishny, R. W., 185
Vithal, R., 271, 272, 279
volume index, 414
von Hagen, Jurgen, 166, 191, 375
and common pool problem, 138, 182
stabilization by sharing risk, 107–32
voters and voting
and flypaper effect, 176–77, 196n2
swing voter theory, 179
voter behavior, 178–79
voting equilibrium, 116–17

wages
flexibility of, 112–13, 129nnn8–9
South Africa, 406
wage shocks, 124
Wallich, C. I., 324, 325, 329, 330, 333
company support for services, 484
on matching grants, 466
on revenue sharing, 461
Walsh, C., 427
Warren, L. S., 215
Warren, N., 115
Washington, D. C., 475, 478n17
water and sewer service, 40
Watts, R., 372
Webb, S. B., 191, 196
Wehner, J., 303

Weingast, B. R., 189
welfare, 234, 255n3
Canada, 247–48, 250
impact of grants on, 10tt1.1
and implications of tax assignment,
321, 322f11.1
personalized local public services, 86–89
and unfunded mandates, 84–86
United States, 247–50
Wheeler, G. E., 468
Wildasin, D. E., 134–35, 139, 148, 166
on matching grants, 206, 215
and soft budget problem, 190–91
Wilhelm, M. O., 241–42t8.1, 248, 249
Williamson, J., 196
Wilson, Leonard S., 339–59, 347, 354
Wilson, N., 221n4
Winckler, G., 129n8
Winer, S. L., 180
Wittman, D. A., 180
Wong, C., 333
World Bank, 41, 287, 333
Wyckoff, P. G., 177
Wyplosz, C., 108, 109, 112

Yinger, J., 240t8.1, 246, 421n11, 470
Yosha, O., 109, 118, 129n2
Young, A., 197n9

Zambia, 210
Zampelli, E. M., 235, 244t8.1, 251, 252
Zanola, R., 240t8.1, 247
Zapata, J. G., 208, 466, 493
zero-sum games, 185
Zhuravskaya, E., 188, 193
Zumer, F., 120, 121, 122